Scott Foresman - Addison Wesley

MATH

AUTHORS

Randall I. Charles

Dinah Chancellor   Lalie Harcourt   Debbie Moore   Jane F. Schielack
John Van de Walle   Ricki Wortzman

Linda Bailey • Carne S. Barnett • Diane J. Briars • Dwight A. Cooley • Warren D. Crown
Martin L. Johnson • Steven J. Leinwand • Pearl Ling • Shauna Lund
Freddie Lee Renfro • Mary Thompson

Scott Foresman

Editorial Offices: Glenview, Illinois • Parsippany, New Jersey • New York, New York
Sales Offices: Parsippany, New Jersey • Duluth, Georgia • Glenview, Illinois
Carrollton, Texas • Ontario, California

Cover artist: Robert Silvers was taking photographs and playing with computers by the time he was ten. Eventually he melded his interests in computer programming and photography to produce a program that divides images into a grid and matches them with images from a database. The results are mosaics such as the one on this cover.

ISBN 0-328-02179-2

Printed in the United States of America.

4 5 6 7 8 9 10 VO64 11 10 09 08 07 06 05 04 03 02

CHAPTER 1

Numbers to 12 and Graphing

Theme: Off to School 1

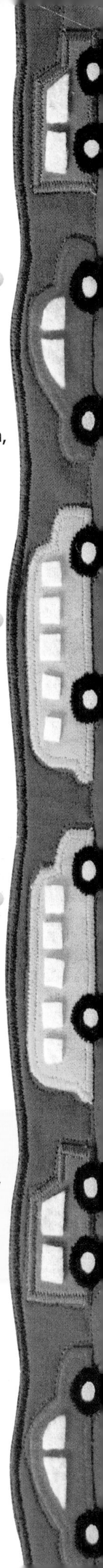

CHAPTER 2

Addition and Subtraction Readiness

Theme: Fun and Games 49

Problem Solving
Make a Table,
Critical Thinking,
Visual Thinking

Connections
Math at Home, Mental Math,
Journal, Logical Reasoning,
Patterns

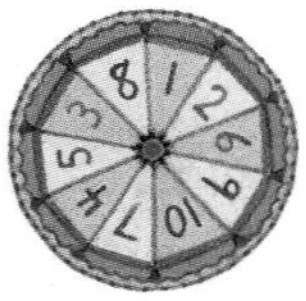

Problem Solving
Draw a Picture,
Patterns, Critical Thinking,
Estimation

Connections
Mental Math,
Algebra Readiness,
Write About It,
Reading for Math, Journal,
Tell a Math Story, Patterns

Connections
Math in Your World,
Math and Language Arts,
Math at Home

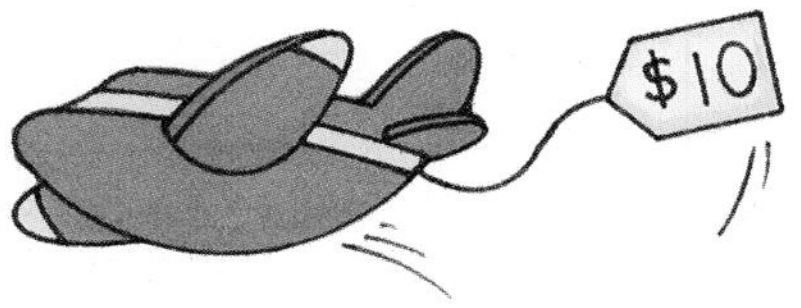

CHAPTER 3

Addition and Subtraction Concepts

Theme: Coming and Going 89

CHAPTER 4

Facts and Strategies to 12

Theme: Boxes, Bags, and Baskets 131

CHAPTER 5

Geometry and Fractions

Theme: Food for Thought 173

Problem Solving
Make a Table, Patterns, Critical Thinking, Visual Thinking

Connections
Math at Home, Write About It, Reading for Math

Problem Solving
Use Data from a Picture, Visual Thinking, Estimation, Critical Thinking

Connections
Tell a Math Story, Mental Math

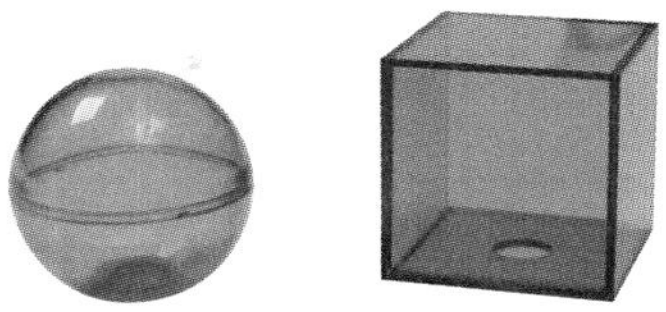

Connections
Math in Your World, Math and Art, Math at Home

CHAPTER 6

More Fact Strategies

Theme: Creeping Critters 217

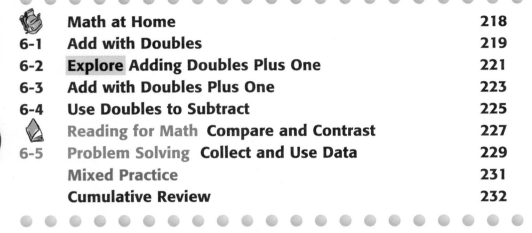

CHAPTER 7

Numbers to 60 and Counting Patterns

Theme: Collections 255

CHAPTER 8

Place Value

Theme: Sports 293

Problem Solving
Use Objects, Critical Thinking, Visual Thinking, Estimation

Connections
Math at Home, Journal, Tell a Math Story

Problem Solving
Collect and Use Data, Visual Thinking, Critical Thinking, Patterns

Connections
Mental Math, Reading for Math, Write About It, Patterns, Geometry

Connections
Math in Your World, Math and Physical Education, Math at Home

CHAPTER 9

Money

Theme: To Market, To Market 331

Problem Solving
Use Data from a Picture, Patterns, Critical Thinking

Connections
Math at Home, Mental Math, Write About It, Journal

Problem Solving
Make a List, Critical Thinking

Connections
Reading for Math, Journal, Patterns

Connections
Math in Your World, Math and Social Studies, Math at Home

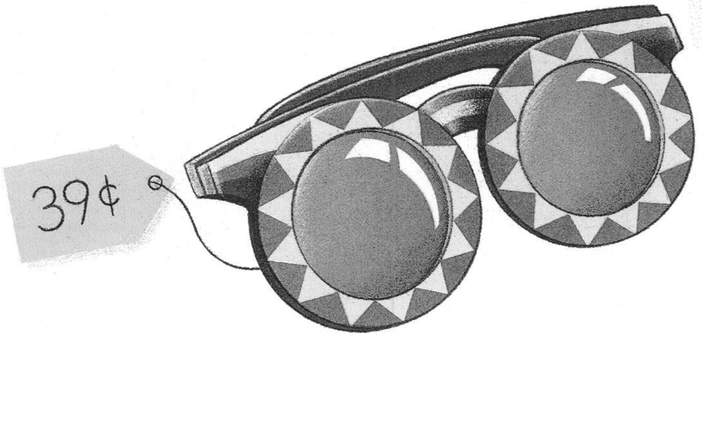

CHAPTER

10

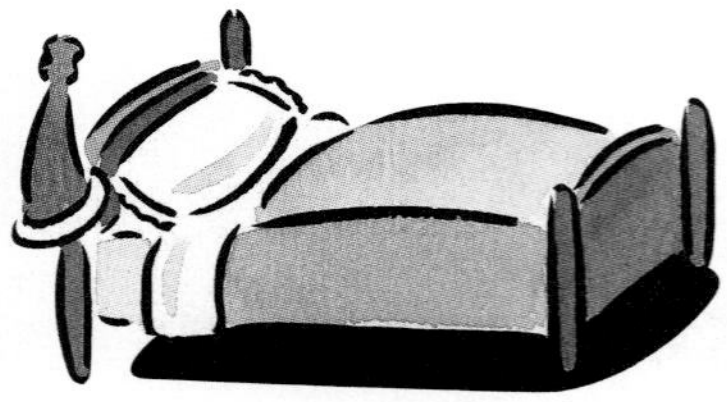

Telling Time

Theme: Timekeepers 365

Problem Solving
Logical Reasoning,
Visual Thinking,
Critical Thinking

Connections
Math at Home,
Write About It, Journal

Problem Solving
Too Much Information,
Critical Thinking, Patterns,
Visual Thinking

Connections
Tell a Math Story,
Reading for Math, Journal

Connections
Math in Your World,
Math and Social Studies,
Math at Home

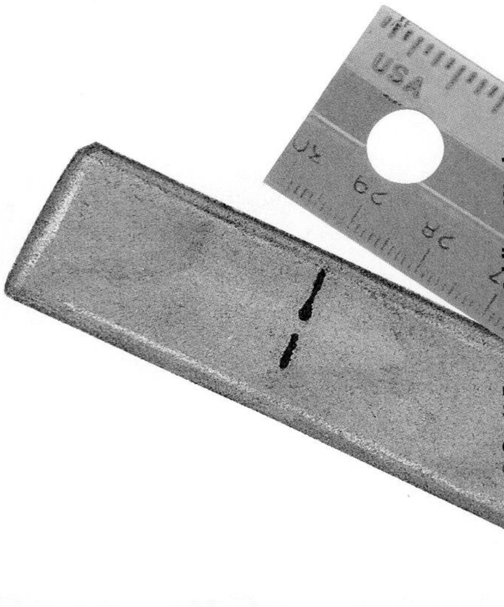

CHAPTER

11

Measurement

Theme: In the Garden 403

CHAPTER 12

Facts and Strategies to 18

Theme: Animals All Around 447

Problem Solving
Choose a Strategy, Visual Thinking

Connections
Math at Home, Mental Math, Tell a Math Story

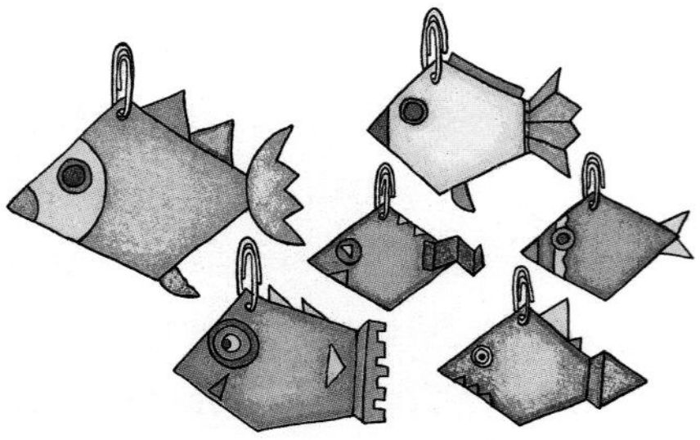

Problem Solving
Choose an Operation, Patterns, Critical Thinking

Connections
Write About It, Tell a Math Story, Reading for Math, Algebra Readiness, Money

Connections
Math in Your World, Math and Social Studies, Math at Home

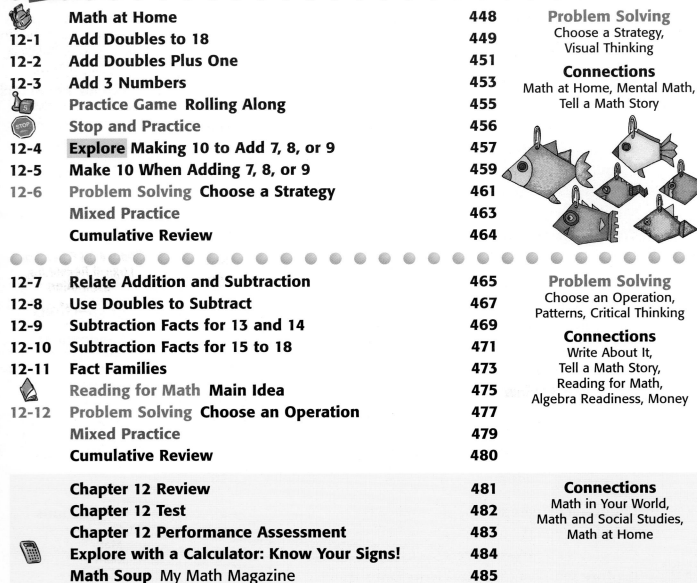

CHAPTER 13

Two-Digit Addition and Subtraction

Theme: Here Comes Summer! 489

MATHmatazz
Tree House
Welcome

CHAPTER

1

Numbers to 12 and Graphing

Notes for Home: Your child counted the objects and people in the groups shown in the picture.
Home Activity: Ask your child to find a group at home and count how many.

Math at Home

Dear Family,
Our class is starting Chapter 1. We will learn about numbers to 12 and graphing. We can count groups at home and make graphs. We can have fun doing the activities below.

Peas on a Plate

Frozen peas are great to count because when you are finished, you can eat them! Count a group of peas from 1 to 12 on a plate and ask your child to show and count another group with more. Then have your child do it again for a group with fewer.

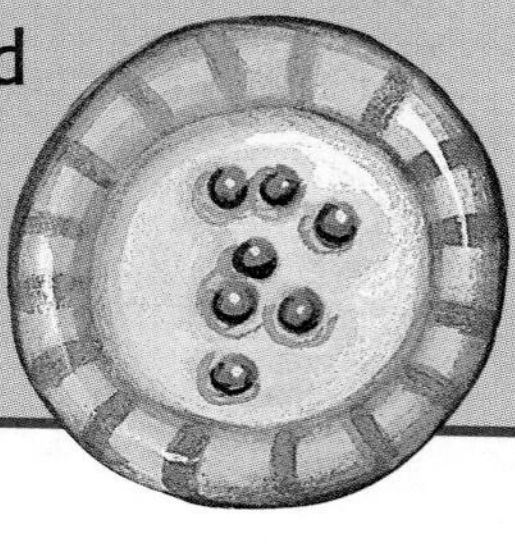

"Eggs-actly" Twelve

The twelve sections of an egg carton are great for teaching counting and numbers. Use small objects such as dried beans, paper clips, or buttons, and have your child count aloud as he or she makes groups from 1 to 12 in each section.

Community Connection

When taking a walk, have your child find and count objects in groups of 1 through 12, for example, 5 leaves on a branch or 4 swing seats.

Visit our Web site. www.parent.mathsurf.com

Name

Numbers 1, 2, 3

Learn

1 one

2 two

3 three

Check

1 Draw.

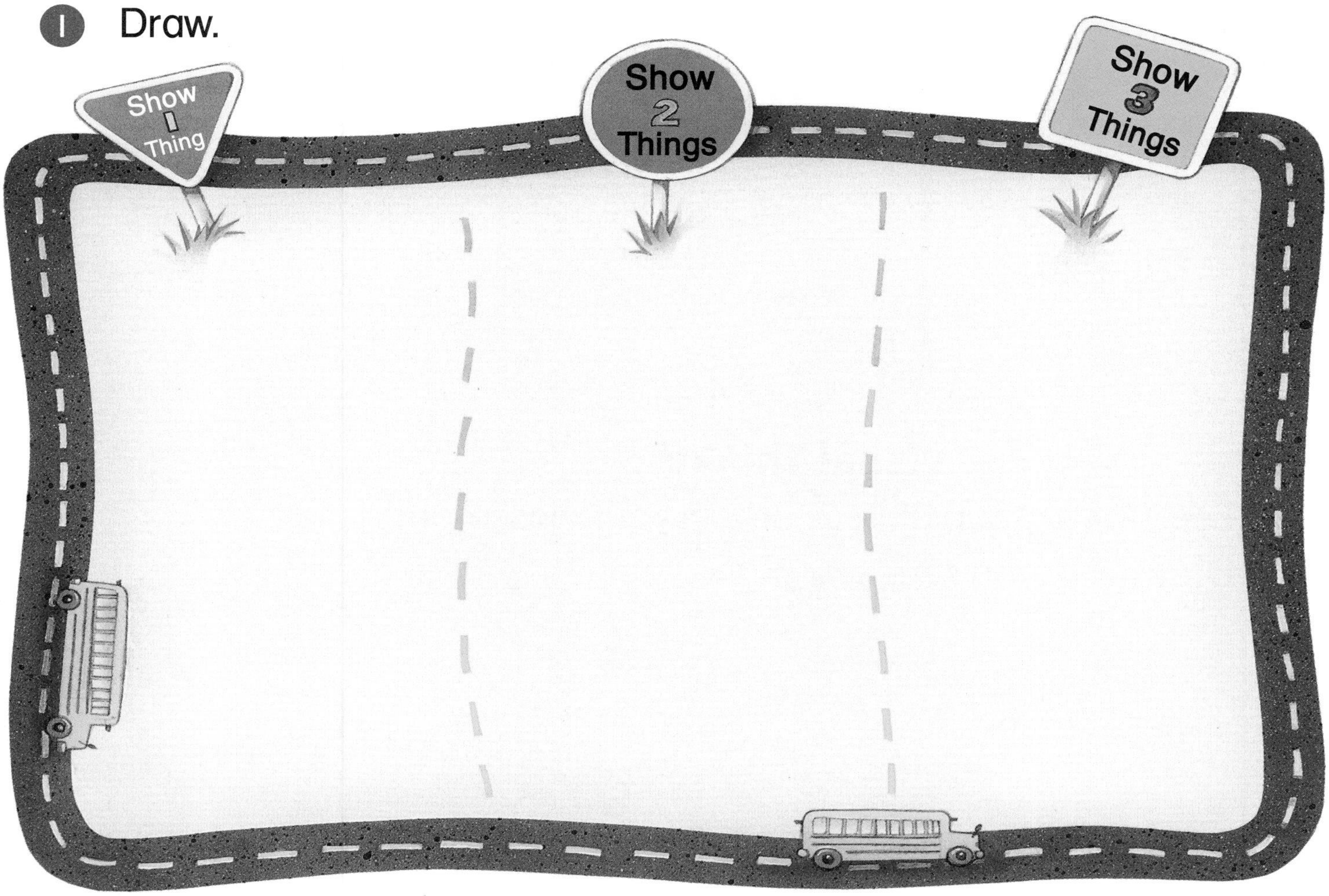

Talk About It What did you find?
How many did you find?

Notes for Home: Your child counted and made groups of 1, 2, and 3. *Home Activity:* Ask your child to put together groups of 1, 2, and 3 objects that are found around your home.

Write 1, 2, and 3.

2 | | | | ● ● ● ● ● ●

3 2 2 2 ● ● ● ● ●

4 3 3 3 ● ● ● ● ●

Write how many.

5

- - - - - - - -

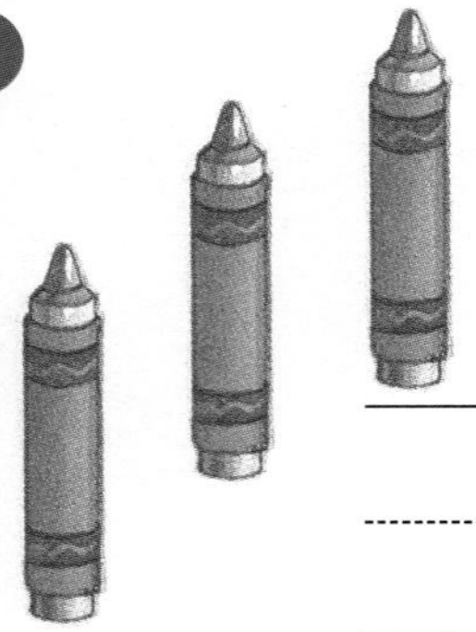

6

- - - - - - - -

7

- - - - - - - -

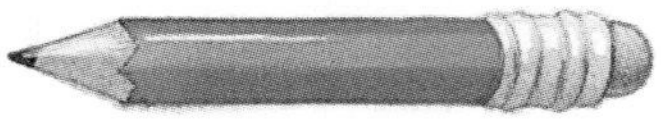

Problem Solving Visual Thinking

8 Look for a group of 1, 2, or 3 in your classroom.
Draw what you see.

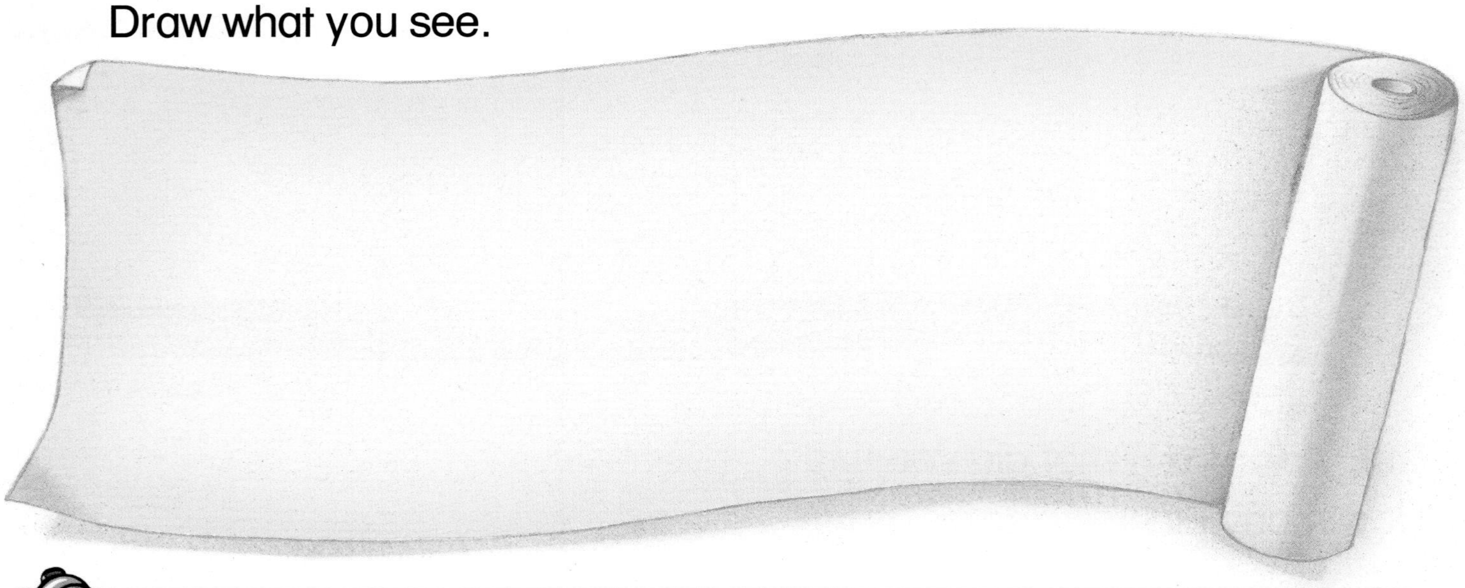

 Notes for Home: Your child wrote the numbers 1, 2, 3. *Home Activity:* Ask your child to find a group of 1, 2, or 3 objects at home and write the number for how many.

Name

Numbers 4, 5, 6

Learn

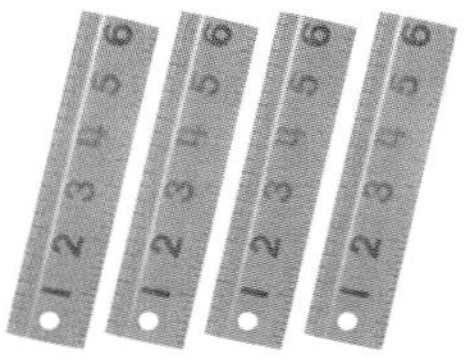

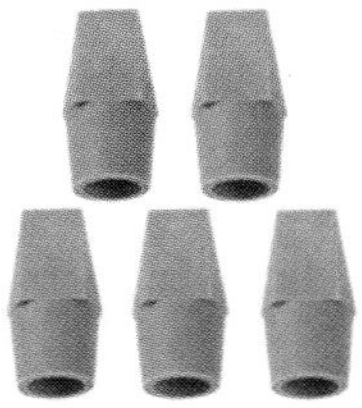

4 four ____ 5 five ____ 6 six ____

Check

1 Draw 4 ▲. Write how many.

2 Draw 5 ■. Write how many.

3 Draw 6 ●. Write how many.

Talk About It Name four things you like in your lunch.

Notes for Home: Your child counted and drew objects in groups of 4, 5, and 6.
Home Activity: Ask your child to count the groups of objects at the top of the page.

Practice

Write 4, 5, and 6.

❹ 4 4 4

❺ 5 5 5

❻ 6 6 6

Write how many.

❼  ______

❽ 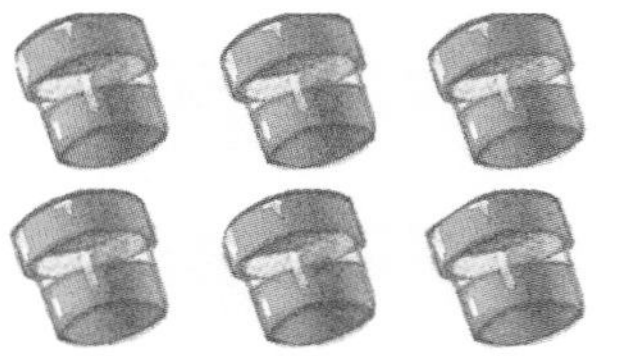 ______

❾ 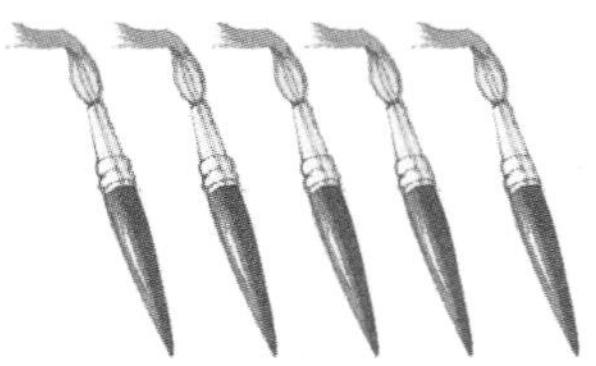 ______

PRACTICE

Mental Math

Write the next number.

❿ 1, 2, 3

⓫ 3, 4, ______

⓬ 2, 3, ______

⓭ 4, 5, ______

Notes for Home: Your child wrote the numbers 4, 5, and 6. *Home Activity:* Ask your child to practice writing the numbers 1 through 6 on a sheet of paper.

Name

Numbers 7, 8, 9

Learn

7 seven

8 eight

9 nine

Check

1. Circle 7 .
2. Circle 8 .
3. Circle 9 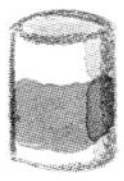.

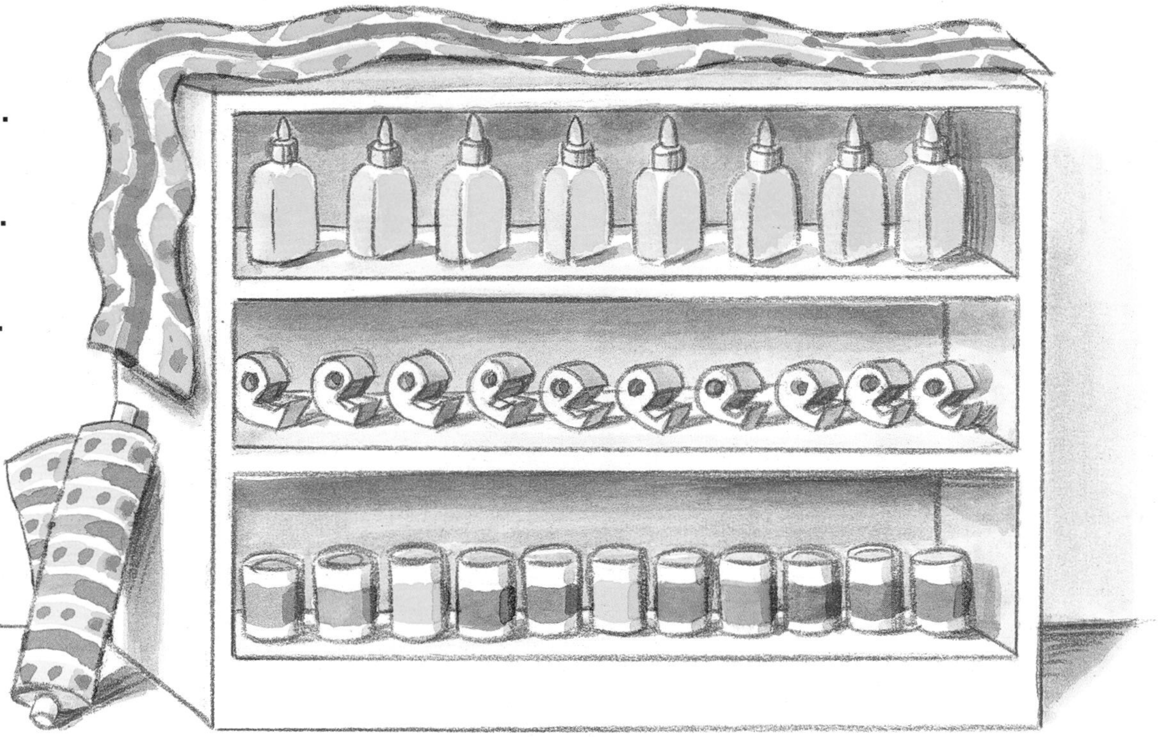

Talk About It Did you circle more  or more ?

Did you circle fewer  or fewer ?

Notes for Home: Your child counted 7, 8, and 9 objects. *Home Activity:* Arrange objects in groups of 1 through 9, and have your child count and tell how many.

Practice

PRACTICE

Write 7, 8, and 9.

4 7

5 8

6 9

Write how many.

7

7

8

9
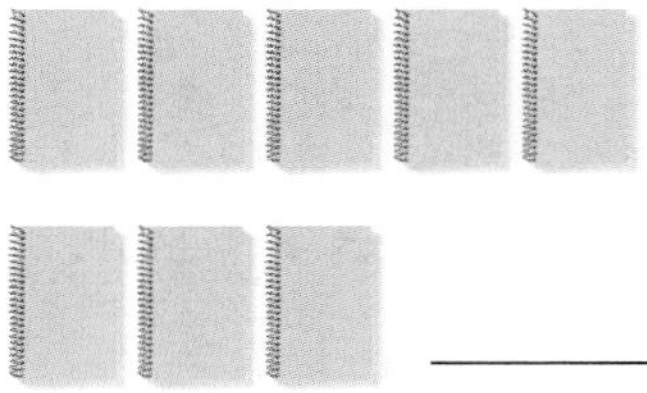

10

11
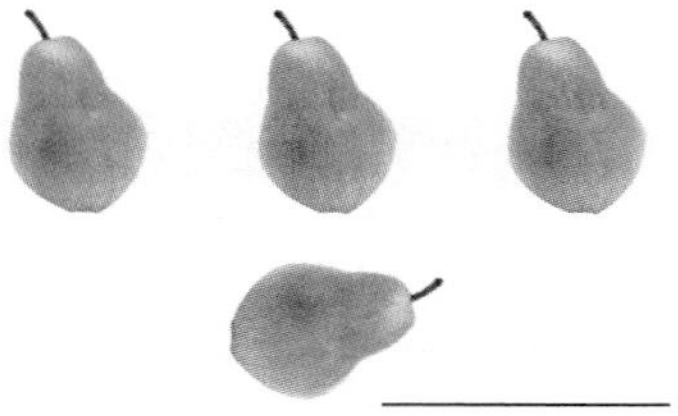

12
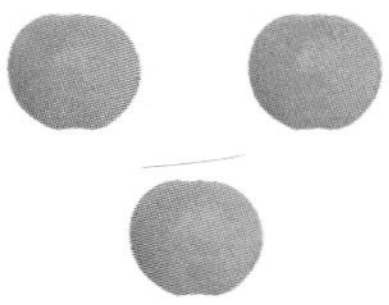

Journal

13 Draw 7 things.

14 Draw 8 things.

15 Draw 9 things.

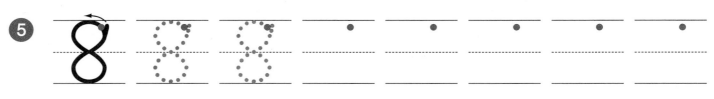

Notes for Home: Your child wrote the numbers 7, 8, and 9. *Home Activity:* Show your child a group of 7 objects and ask him or her to guess how many and then count to check. Repeat using 8 and 9 objects.

Name ______________________________

Zero

Learn

4 four

0 zero

I have no cookies. Zero! None! Nada!

Check

How many?
Write the number.

1
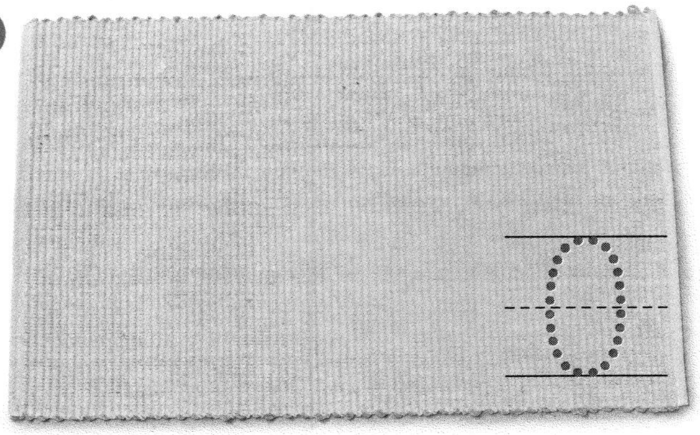

2
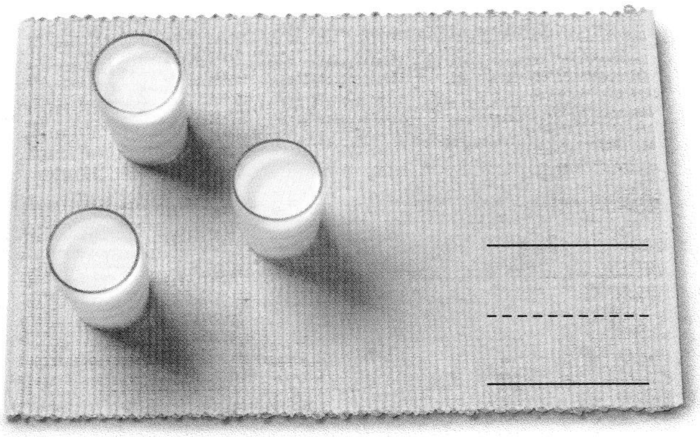

3
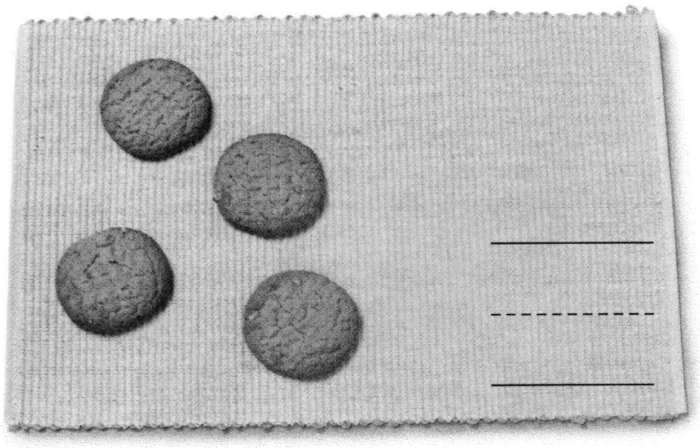

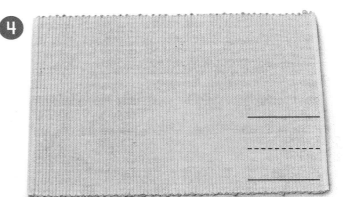

4

Talk About It When would you like to have 0 of something?

Notes for Home: Your child learned that 0 means none. *Home Activity:* Ask your child to use objects around your home to count and show the numbers 0 through 9.

Practice

Write 0.

5 0

Write how many.

6

7

8

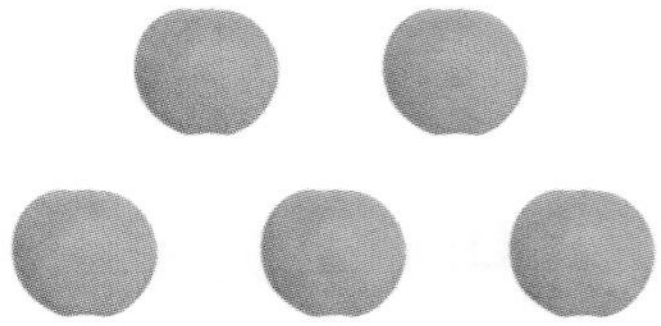

9

10

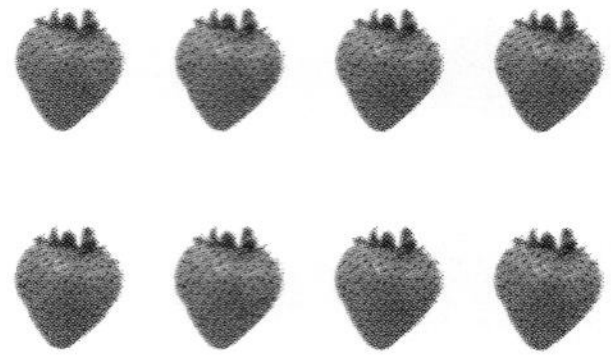

11

PRACTICE

Tell a Math Story

12 Use numbers to tell a story about what you see.

Notes for Home: Your child wrote the number 0. *Home Activity:* Ask your child to tell you the math story he or she made up for the picture on this page.

Name

Numbers to 10

Learn

10 ten 10

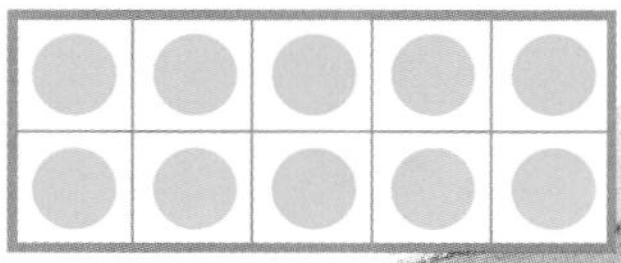

Check

Write the number or draw the picture.

1. 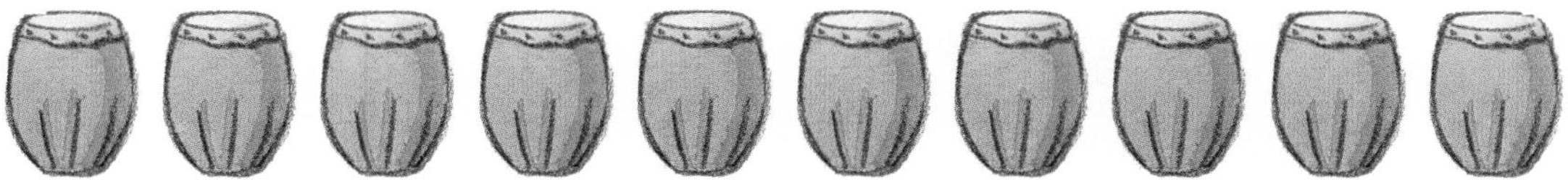 10

2.  ______

3. 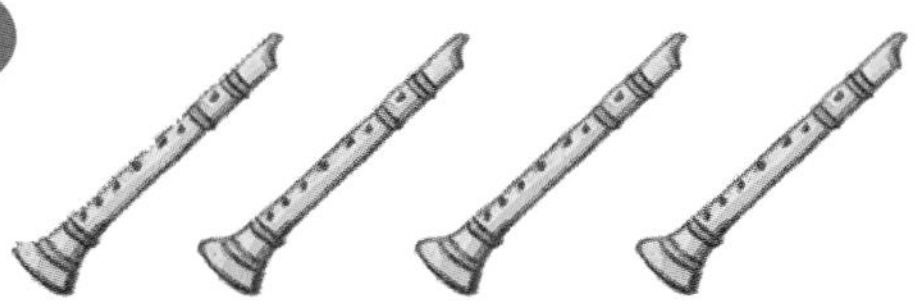 ______

4.  6

Talk About It Where can you find a group of ten?

Notes for Home: Your child counted to 10. *Home Activity:* Ask your child to find and count 10 of something at home.

Practice

Write 10.

5 10

How many? Write the number or draw the picture.

6 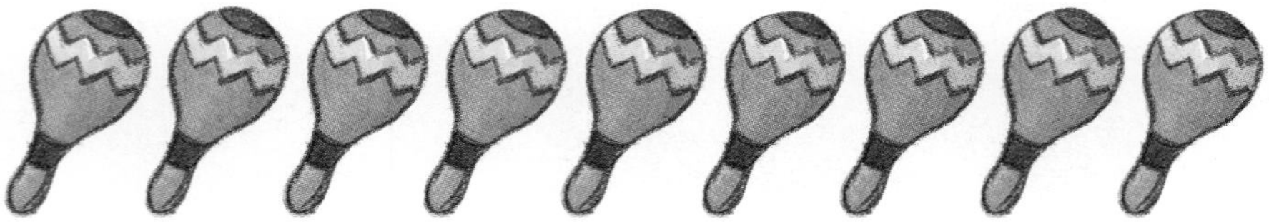

9

7 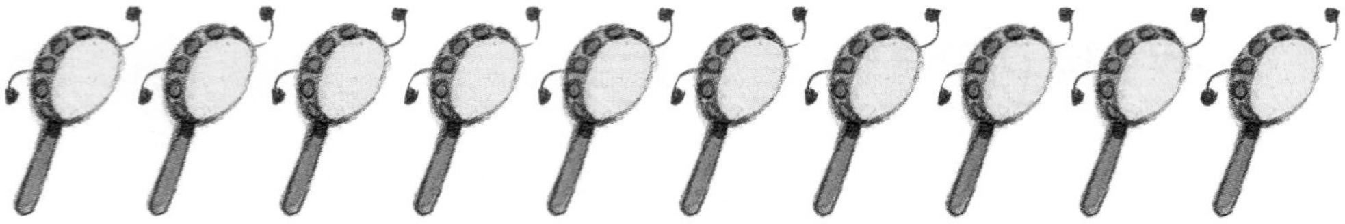

8 

5

9 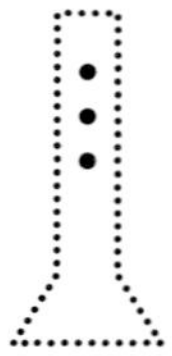

10

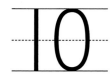

PRACTICE

Problem Solving Visual Thinking

10 Circle the picture that shows 10.

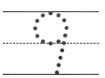

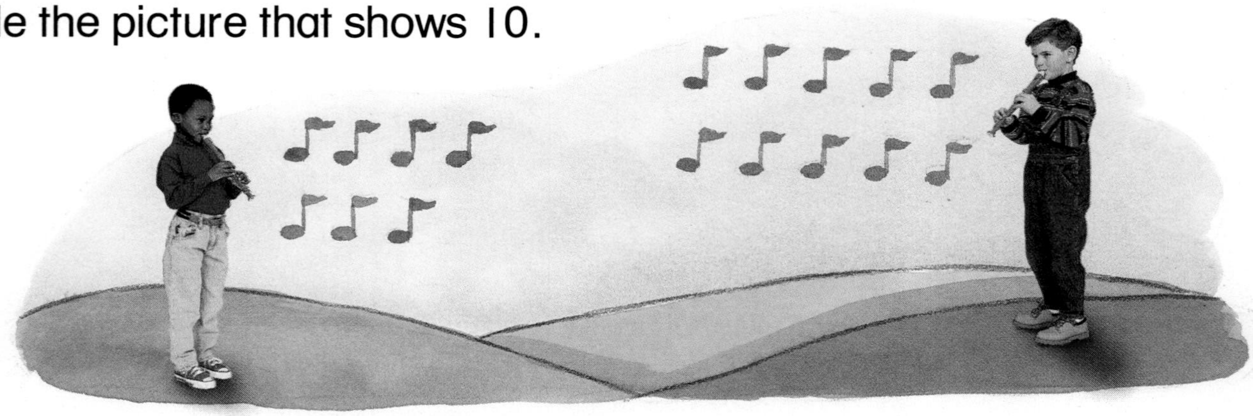

Notes for Home: Your child wrote the number 10 and counted and drew up to 10 objects. *Home Activity:* Ask your child to find 1 to 10 objects, then count the objects and write the number.

For additional practice, see Skills Practice Bank, page 525, Set 1.

Name ___________________________

Reading for Math

Use Picture Clues

Look at the picture. Write the number.

1. Ann and Alex rode their bikes to school.
   They put the bikes in the bike rack.
   Now there are ? bikes in the bike rack.
   Circle each bike.

How many bikes are in the bike rack? 5

2. The children like to look at the turtles.
   Elena put a new turtle in the tank today.
   Now there are ? turtles.
   Circle each turtle.

How many turtles are in the tank? _____

Talk About It How do you know how many turtles there are?

Notes for Home: Your child used pictures as clues to answer questions. *Home Activity:* Read the stories aloud with your child. Ask your child to draw three more turtles in the tank. Ask, "Now how many turtles are there?"

Look at the picture. Write the number.

3 Sayat has markers to use at school.
She has ? markers.
Circle each marker.

How many markers are on her desk? _____

4 The children like to sing and play.
Ms. Welte gave drums to ? children.

How many children have drums? _____

Journal

5 Write the numbers and the words for 1 through 10.

Notes for Home: Your child practiced using pictures as clues to answer questions.
Home Activity: Ask your child to tell you how many children are not playing drums in the last story.

Name

Problem Solving: Use Data from a Picture

Learn

PROBLEM SOLVING GUIDE

Understand • Plan • Solve • Look Back

Check

Look at the picture.

1. Write how many .

5

2. Write how many 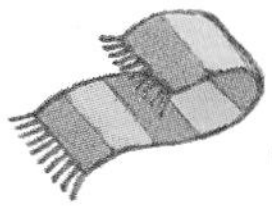.

3. Draw a 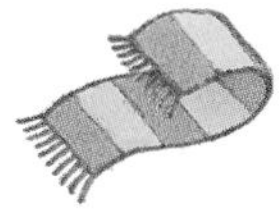 for each child.

4. How many did you draw?

Talk About It What did you do to find how many?

Notes for Home: Your child counted the items in the pictures to gather data. *Home Activity:* Ask your child to look around the room and count similar objects.

PROBLEM SOLVING

Practice

Look at the picture.

5 Write how many  .

4

6 Write how many  .

7 Draw a  for each child.

8 How many did you draw?

Critical Thinking

9 Draw a child on each swing. How many children are in the picture now?

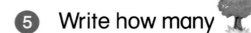

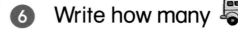

Notes for Home: Your child solved problems using pictures. *Home Activity:* Ask your child to count the other objects on the page such as children, buses, swings, and birds.

Name

Mixed Practice

Lessons 1–6

Concepts and Skills

Write how many.

1. 

2. 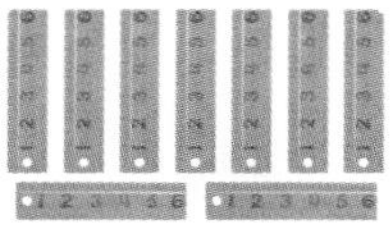

3. 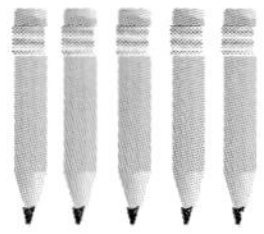

4. 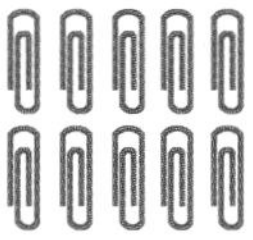

5.

6. 

Problem Solving

Look at the picture.

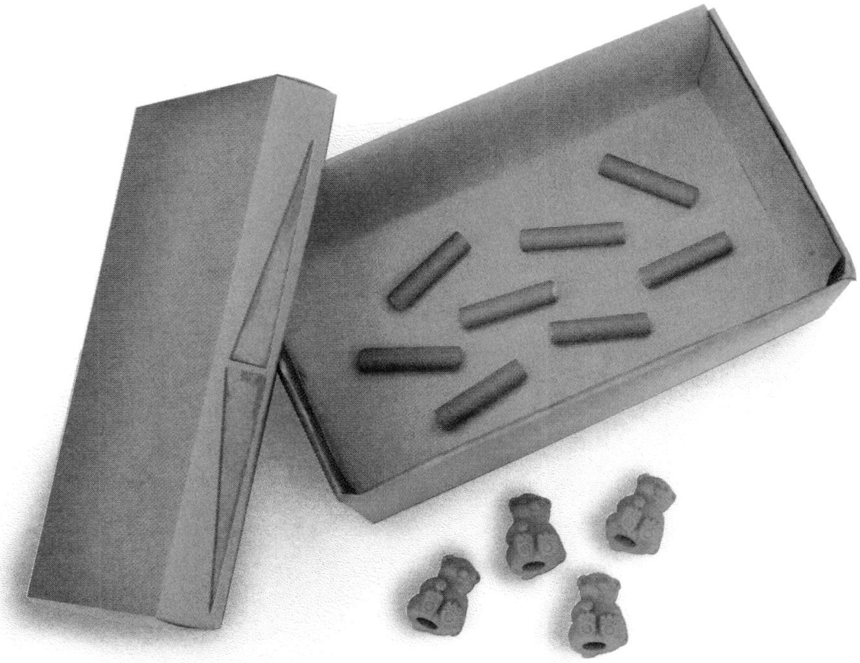

7. Write how many  .

8. Write how many  .

Journal

9. Write the numbers and draw pictures to show from 0 to 10.

Notes for Home: Your child practiced counting and identifying groups for 0 through 10.
Home Activity: Ask your child to count objects at home and write the numbers.

Name ______________________________

Cumulative Review

Chapter 1

Concepts and Skills

1 Circle the ones that are the same size.

2 Circle the ones that are the same shape.

Test Prep

Fill in ○ for the correct answer.

3 How many  ?

3 ○ 4 ○ 5 ○ 6 ○

4 How many  ?

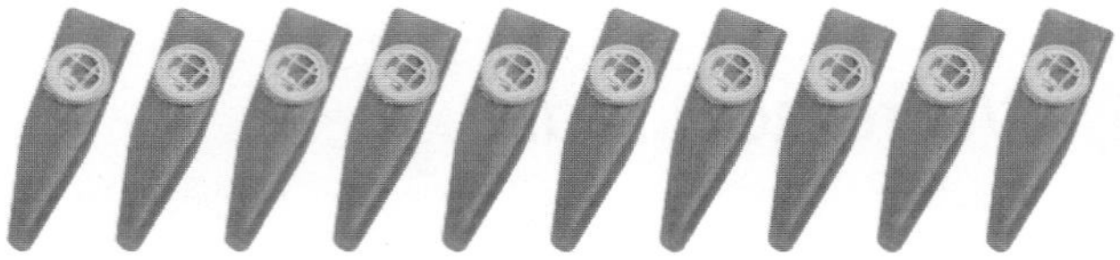

7 ○ 8 ○ 9 ○ 10 ○

5 How many  ?

1 ○ 2 ○ 3 ○ 4 ○

6 How many  ?

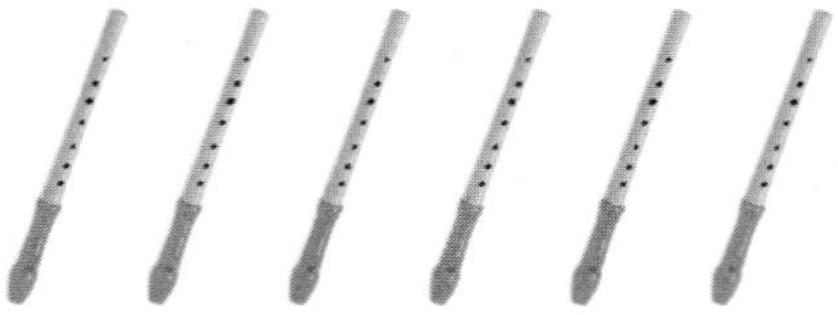

6 ○ 7 ○ 8 ○ 9 ○

Notes for Home: Your child reviewed sorting by size and shape, and counting from 1 to 10 objects.
Home Activity: Ask your child to explain how to find the correct answers in Test Prep.

Name

Explore More and Fewer

Explore

Count the cubes.

Write how many. ____

I have 5 Snap Cubes. Do you have more or fewer?

Choose some cubes.
Draw your cubes.
Write how many.

Circle your answer.

1	____	more than 5 fewer than 5
2	____	more than 5 fewer than 5
3	____	more than 5 fewer than 5

Share

How do you know if you have more or fewer?

Notes for Home: Your child counted Snap Cubes and told whether the group had more or fewer than 5. *Home Activity:* Ask your child to show you more or fewer than 5 pennies or paper clips.

EXPLORE

Connect

Write how many.

Circle the group that has more.

4

5 7

5

6

7

Write how many.

Circle the group that has fewer.

8
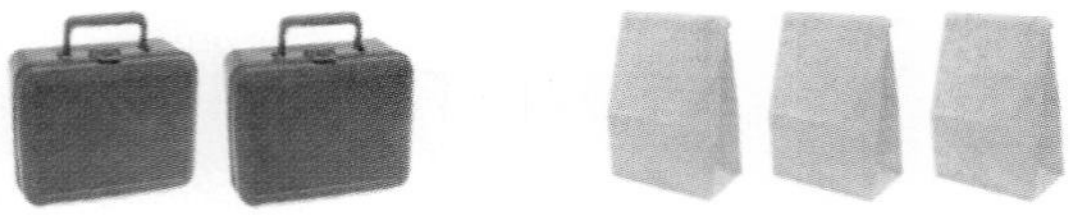

9

EXPLORE

Problem Solving Critical Thinking

10 Are there more children or  ?
How do you know?

Notes for Home: Your child practiced telling which group had more and which group had fewer.
Home Activity: Arrange two unequal groups of objects, each with 10 or fewer objects. Ask your child to tell which group has more.

Name

Order Numbers to 10

Learn

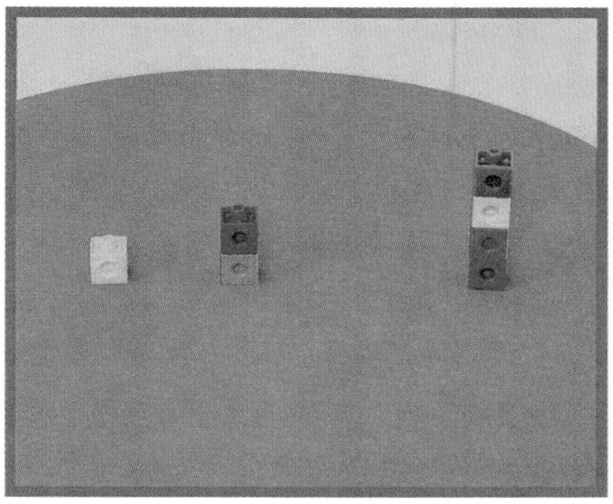
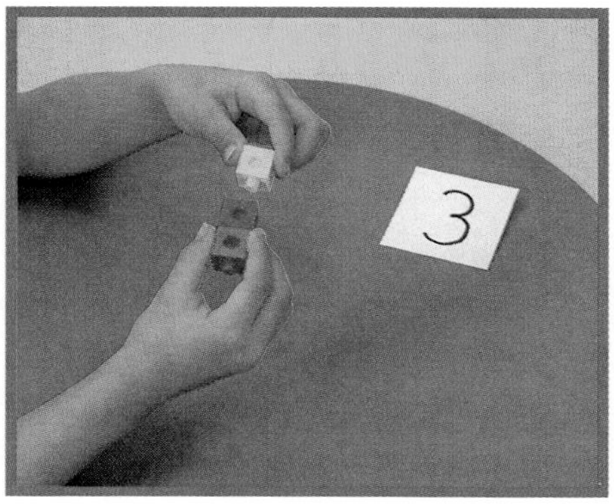

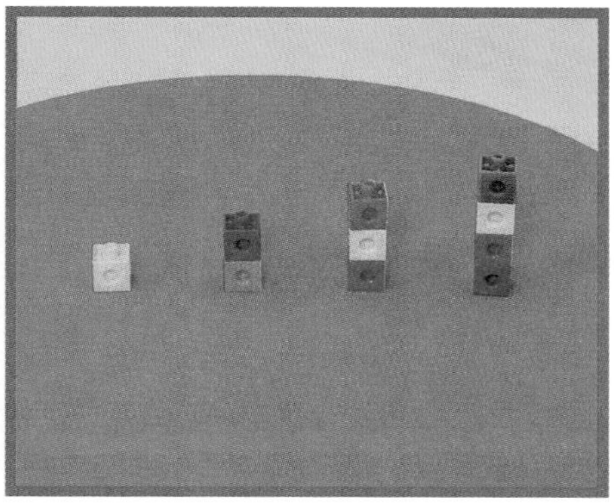

Check

Draw the missing towers. Write how many.

1

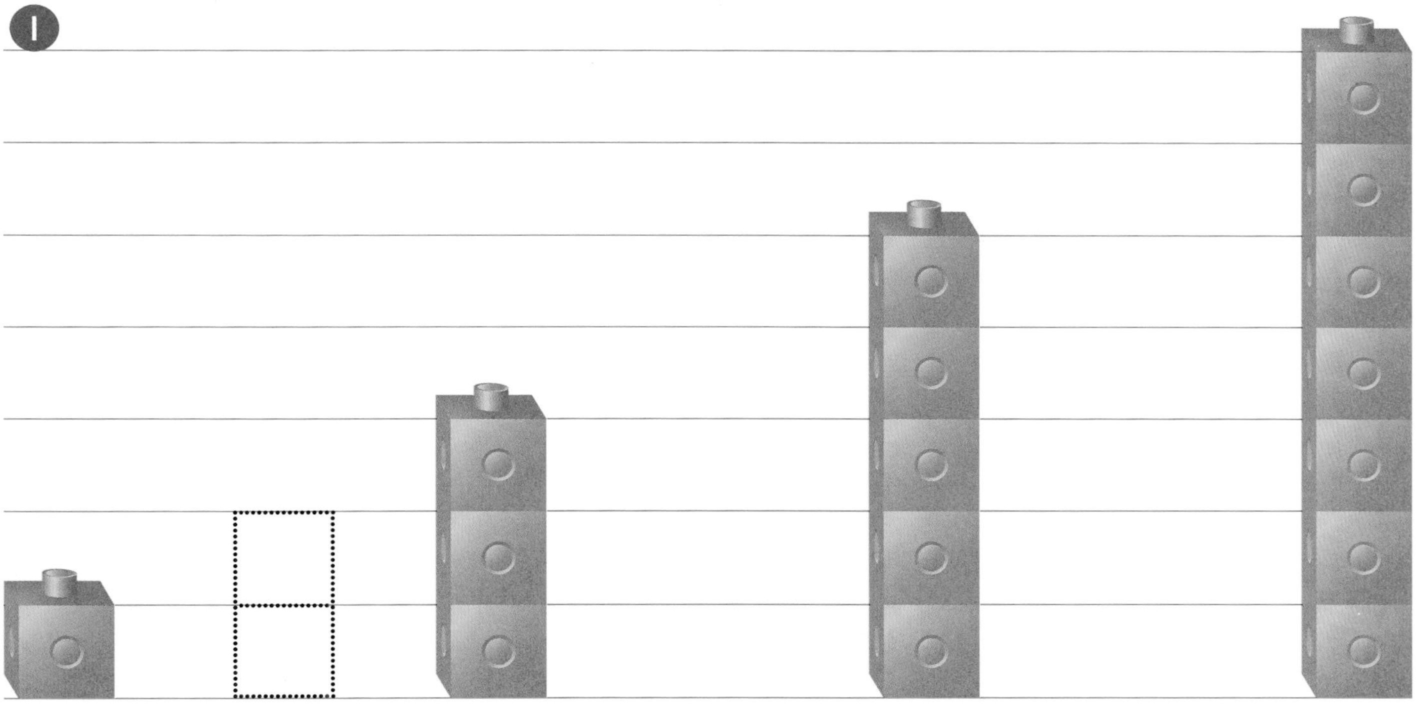

1 2 ___ 4 ___ 6 ___

Talk About It What numbers come before 3?

Notes for Home: Your child learned to order numbers. *Home Activity:* Say aloud a sequence of three numbers and ask your child to say the number that comes next.

Draw the missing towers. Write how many.

❷

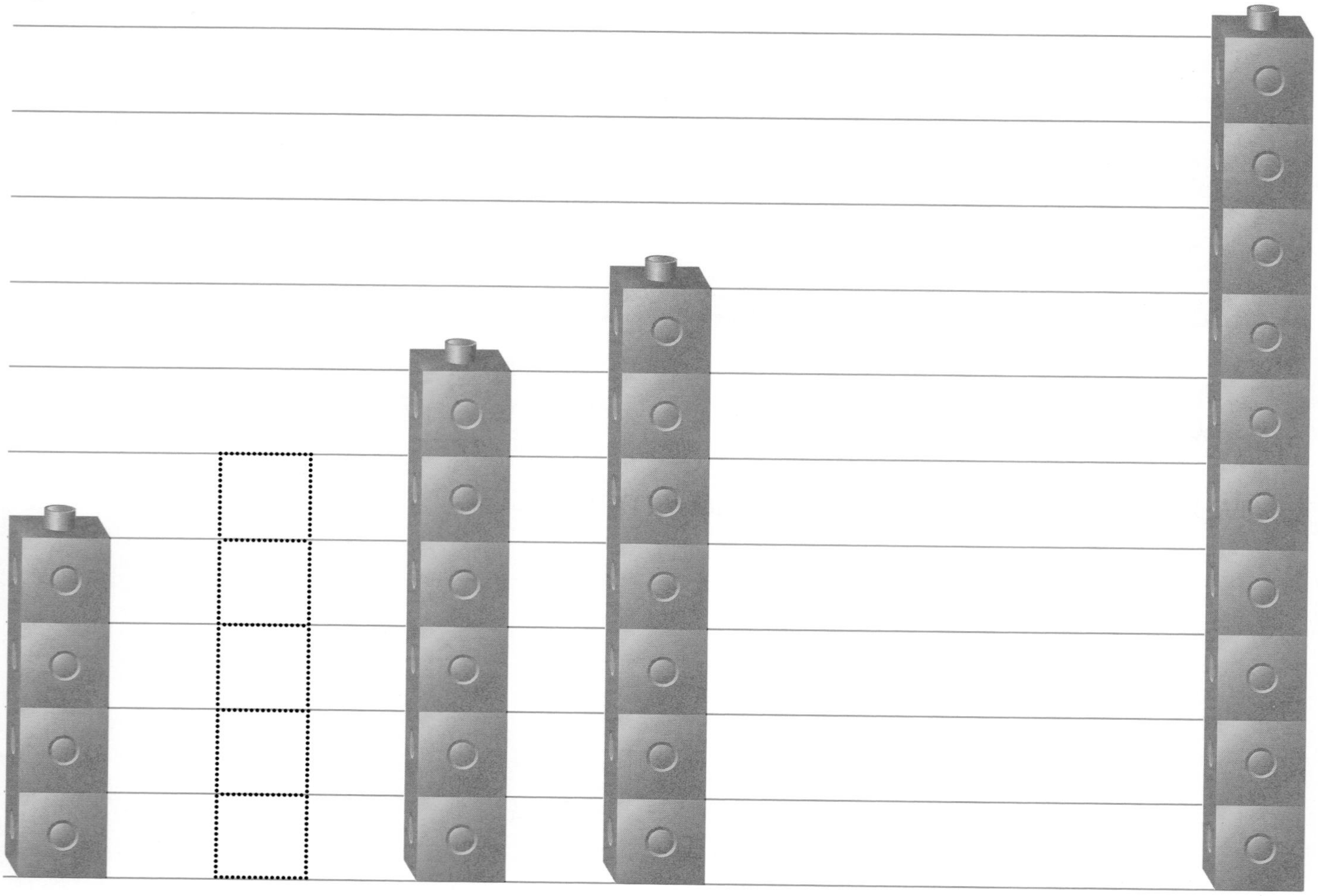

4 ___ 5 ___ ___ ___ 8 ___ 9 ___ ___

Problem Solving Critical Thinking

❸ Van made these 3 towers.
Use  to make Van's towers.
Put the towers in order.
Make the missing towers.

Notes for Home: Your child practiced ordering numbers from 1 through 10. *Home Activity:* Write a sequence of three numbers and ask your child to write the number that comes next.

Name

Understand 11 and 12

Learn

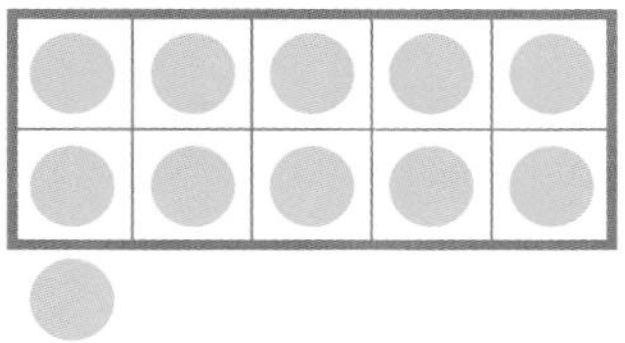

This shows 10 and 1.
10 and 1 is 11.

11 eleven

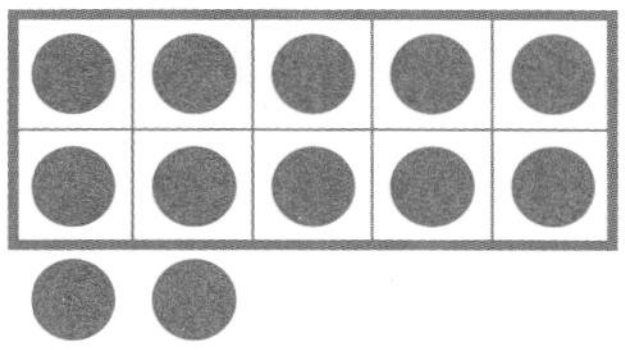

This shows 10 and 2.
10 and 2 is 12.

12 twelve

This holds 10 counters.
I think I have too many.
Get it? Two too many!

Check

Circle the number.

1 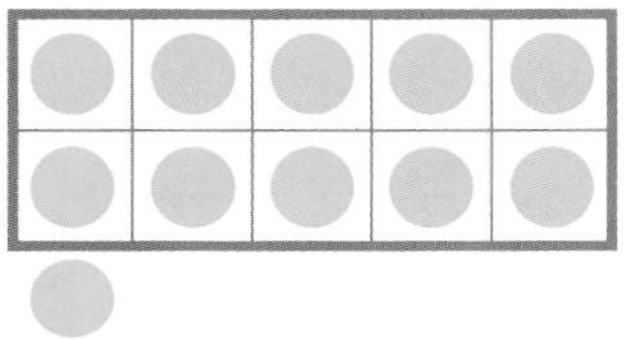

10 11 12

2 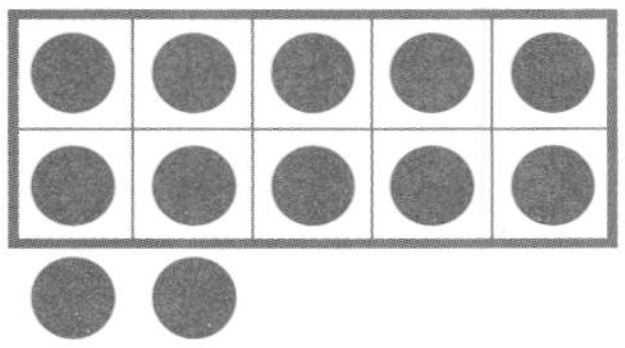

10 11 12

3 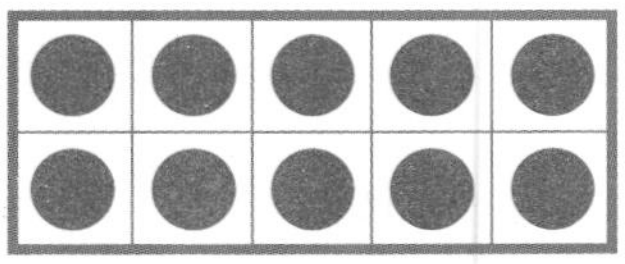

10 11 12

Talk About It How does a 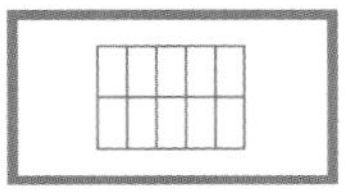 help you know a number is 12 without counting?

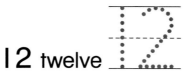

Notes for Home: Your child learned that 11 is 1 more than 10 and that 12 is 2 more than 10.
Home Activity: Arrange 10 like objects in 2 rows of 5. Ask your child how many. Then add 1 or 2 more objects next to the 10. Ask your child to tell how many.

Practice

Write how many.

4 

12

5 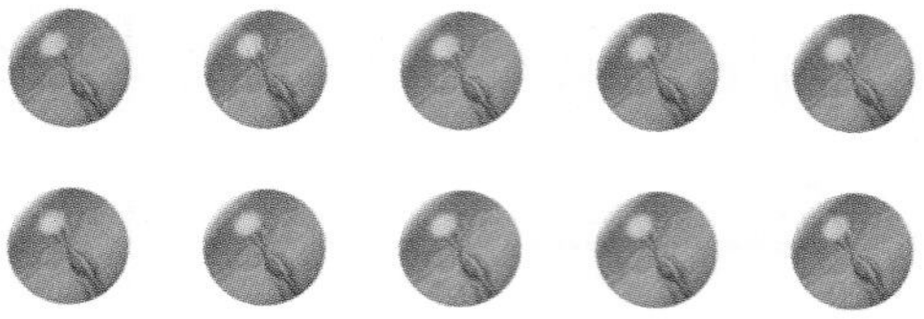

____

6 

____

7 

____

8 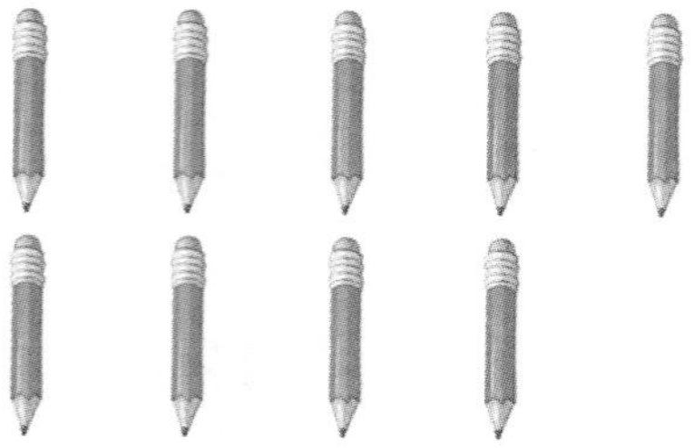

____

9 

____

PRACTICE

Problem Solving

10 Solve.

Ana has . Niko has .

How many in all? ____

Notes for Home: Your child counted from 1 to 12. *Home Activity:* Ask your child to make a group of 11 or 12 objects such as pennies or buttons.

For additional practice, see Skills Practice Bank, page 525, Set 2.

Name ______________________________

Practice Game

Crayon Count

Players 2

What You Need

2 dot cubes

12 crayons for each player

I have 5.
You have 2. I get a crayon for my box.

How to Play

1. Each player rolls 2 dot cubes and counts the dots.
2. The player with more dots puts one crayon in his or her box below.
3. The first player with 12 crayons wins.

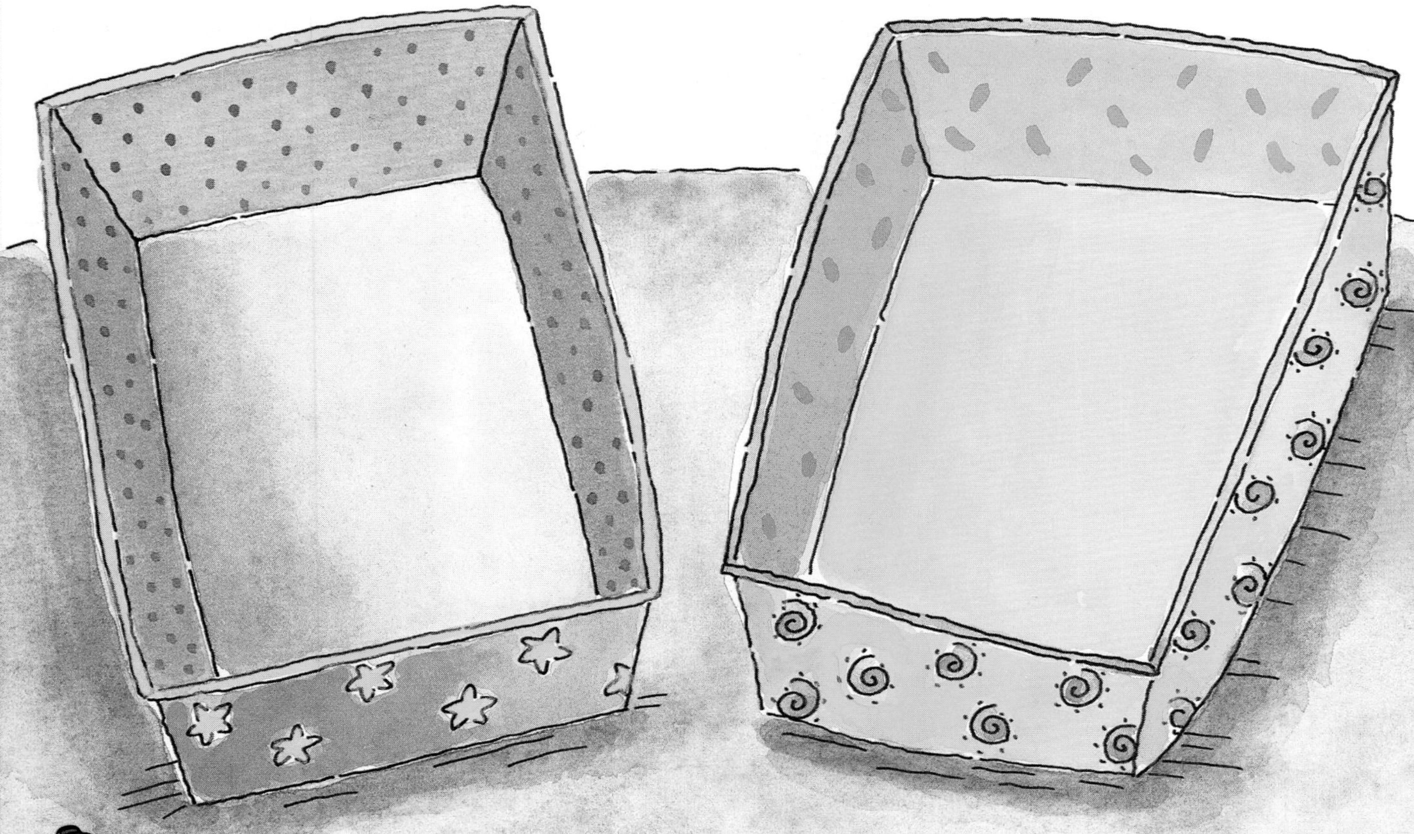

PRACTICE

Notes for Home: Your child played a game that involved counting to 12. *Home Activity:* Play the game with your child. Objects such as pennies might be used in place of crayons. A deck of cards can replace dot cubes by using the numbered cards ace (1) through six. Turn over two cards each turn.

Name ____________________

STOP and Practice

Write how many.

1

____

2

____

3

____

4
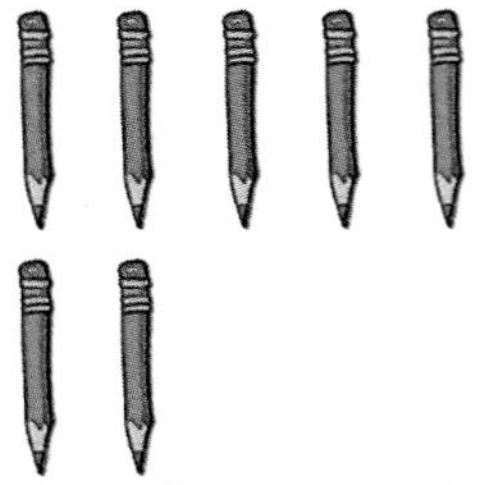
____

5

____

6

____

7
____

8

____

Number Fun!

9 Connect the dots in order.
Color the picture.
What do you see?

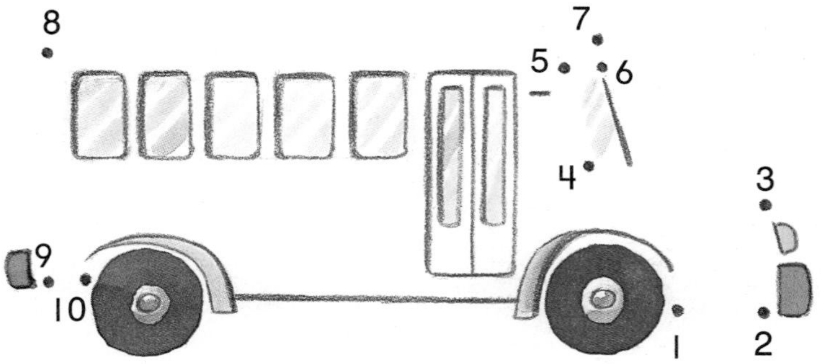

Notes for Home: Your child practiced counting and writing 0 through 10. *Home Activity:* Ask your child to point to two of the groups in Problems 1 through 8 and tell you which has more and which has fewer. Repeat with two other groups.

PRACTICE

Name

Problem Solving: Look for a Pattern

Learn

PROBLEM SOLVING GUIDE

Understand • Plan • Solve • Look Back

Check

Circle what comes next.

1

2

3

Talk About It How are the patterns the same? How are the patterns different?

Notes for Home: Your child discovered and then continued a pattern to solve a problem.
Home Activity: Ask your child to arrange spoons and forks in a pattern.

PROBLEM SOLVING

Practice

Complete each pattern. Color what comes next.

4 

5 

Complete the pattern. Draw what comes next.

6 

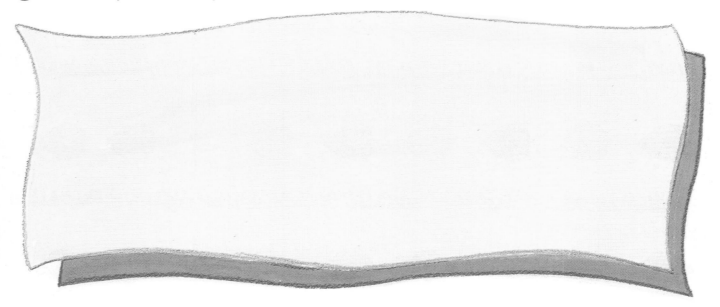

Write your own pattern.

7 Make your own pattern. Draw it 3 times.

Journal

8 Find and draw 3 patterns you see in your classroom.

Notes for Home: Your child completed a pattern and made his or her own pattern. *Home Activity:* Ask your child to say the patterns on this page aloud, and then tell how the pattern would continue.

Name

Mixed Practice

Lessons 7–10

Concepts and Skills

1 Write how many.
Circle the group that has fewer.

_____ _____

2 Write how many.

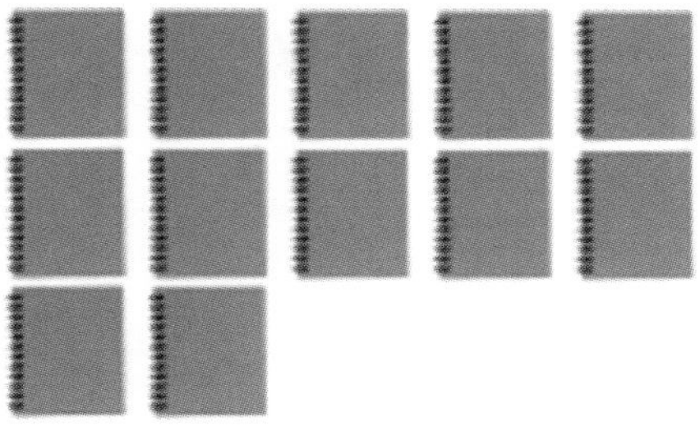

_____

3 Draw the missing towers. Write how many are in each.

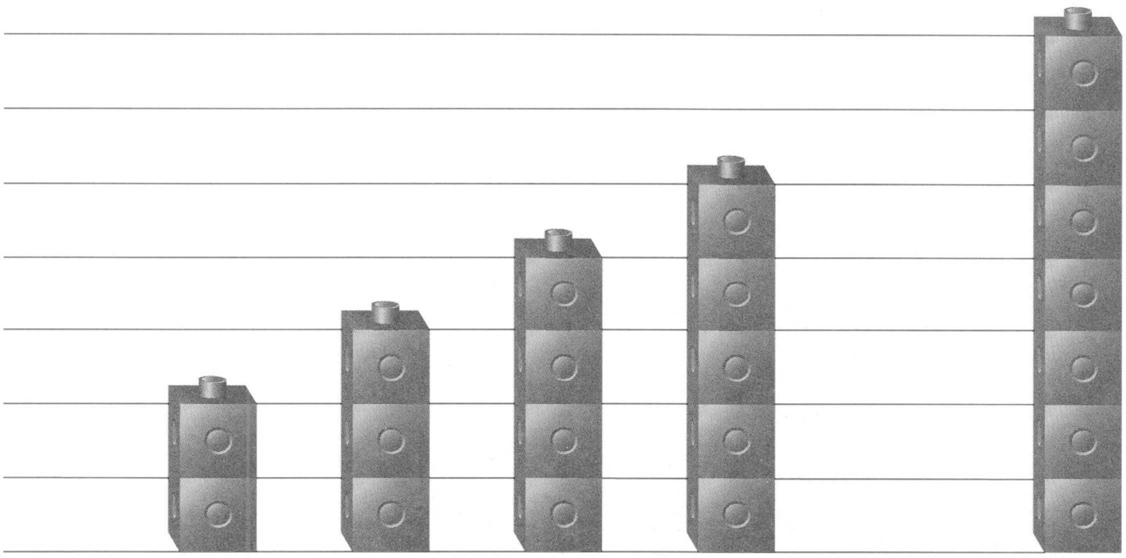

_____ _____ _____ _____ _____ _____ _____

Problem Solving

4 Draw what comes next in the pattern.

Journal

5 Draw a pattern. Use colors and shapes in your pattern.

Notes for Home: Your child reviewed ordering numbers and looking for patterns.
Home Activity: Ask your child to draw and explain a pattern.

Name ______________________

Cumulative Review
Chapter 1

Concepts and Skills

1. Draw 5 pencils.
   Write how many. ____

2. Write how many keys.

____

3. Write the missing numbers.

0		2		4

4. Write the missing numbers.

6		8	9	

Test Prep

Fill in the ○ for the correct answer.
What comes next in the pattern?

5. 

○ ○

6. 

○ ○

Notes for Home: Your child reviewed counting and ordering numbers from 1 to 12 and continued a pattern. *Home Activity:* Ask your child to tell what comes next in each pattern.

Name ______________________________

Explore Sorting and Classifying

Explore

Color and cut out your shapes.
Sort them into 2 groups.
Sort again in a different way.

Share

What's your rule? Tell how you sorted your shapes.

Notes for Home: Your child sorted shapes into groups. *Home Activity:* Ask your child to describe some of the ways to sort the shapes.

EXPLORE

Connect

Circle the shape that goes with the group.

All these shapes are yellow. I circled the yellow one.

1

2

3

4

Problem Solving Visual Thinking

5 Count the shapes above. Write how many.

_____ _____ _____ _____

Notes for Home: Your child sorted shapes by color and size. *Home Activity:* Ask your child to explain how he or she knew which shape belonged in the group.

Create a Graph

Kurt and I sorted these. We have more crayons than pencils.

Check ●

Work with a partner.

Sort , , and to make a graph.
Use your graph to answer.

1 How many ? _____ **2** How many ? _____

3 How many ? _____

Which has more? Circle to answer.

4 **5** **6**

Talk About It How else can you sort , , and ?
Use the graph.

 Notes for Home: Your child made a graph with objects and counted and compared amounts.
Home Activity: Look at the graph on this page with your child and ask if there are fewer pencils
or markers.

Practice

Use the graph. Which has more? Circle the answer.

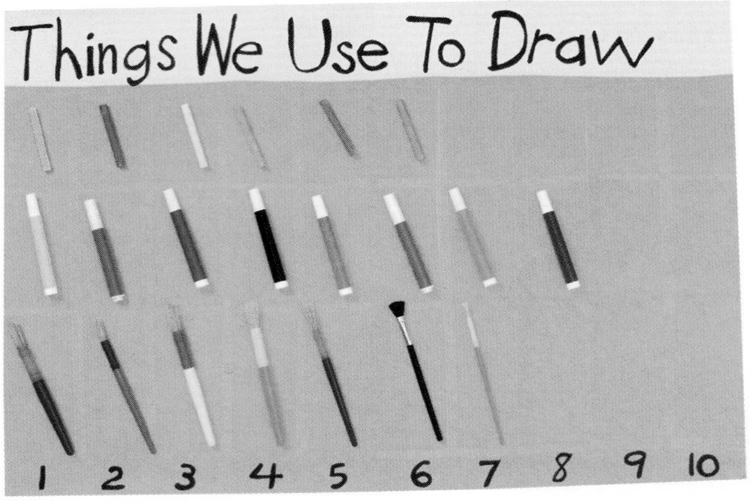

7 

8 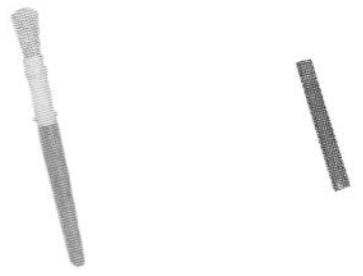

9 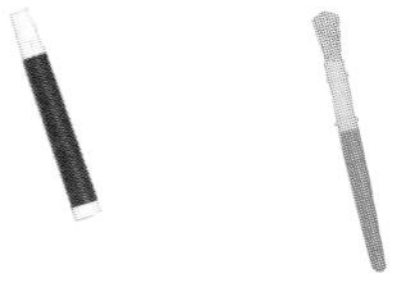

Use the graph. Which has fewer? Circle the answer.

10 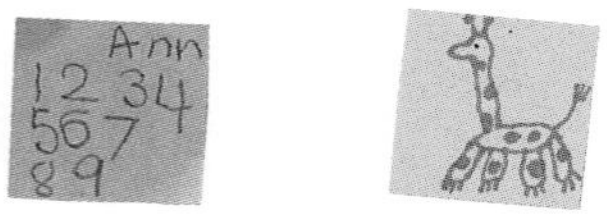

11 

12 Add a paper to one row. Tell how many are in that row now.

Write About It

13 What 3 things would you graph? Why?

____

____

Notes for Home: Your child used graphs to tell if there were more or fewer. *Home Activity:* Ask your child to make a graph with objects such as toys. Then ask your child questions about more and fewer.

Name ______________________________

Create a Pictograph

Learn

Check

Look at the graph above. Make a pictograph.
Color one picture for each piece of fruit shown.

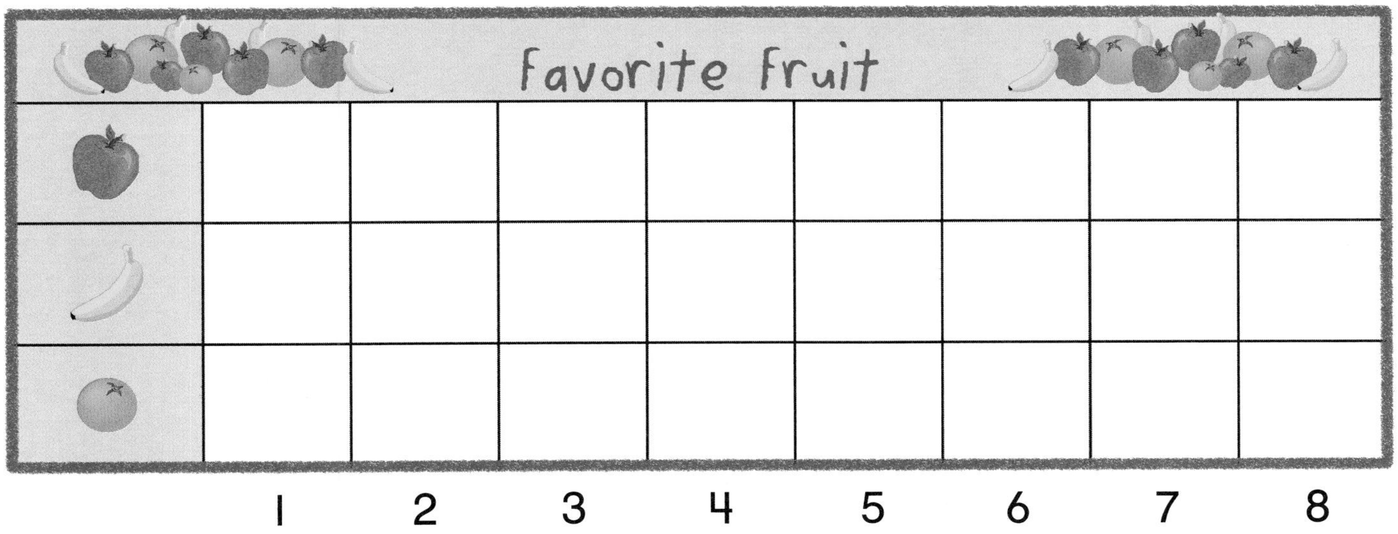

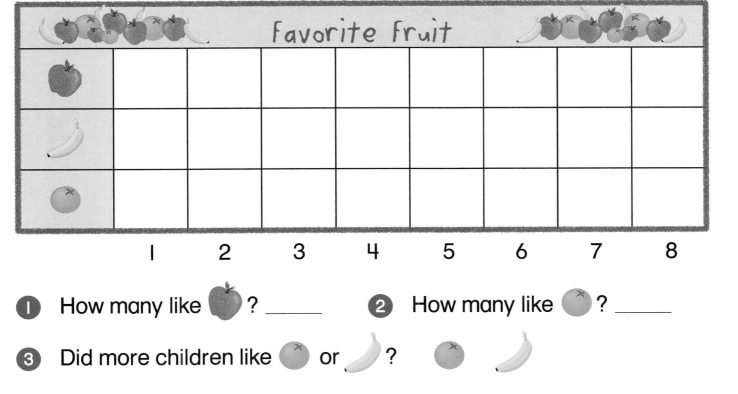

1. How many like  ? ______
2. How many like  ? ______
3. Did more children like  or  ?  

Talk About It How are pictographs like graphs with real things? How are they not alike?

Notes for Home: Your child made a pictograph. *Home Activity:* Ask your child to tell what the pictograph shows.

Practice

Color the graph to show how many of each.

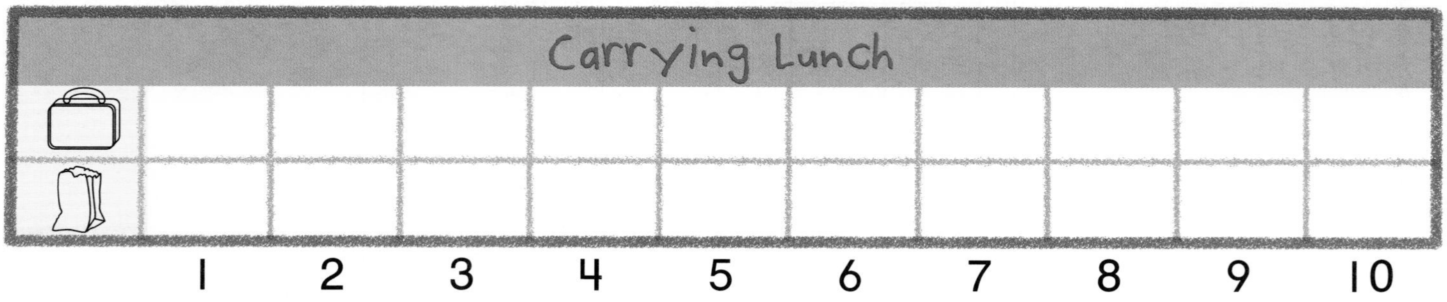

4 How many  ? _____

5 How many  ? _____

Sort another way.

Count the  and  that have 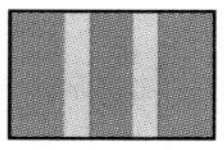.

Count the  and  that are 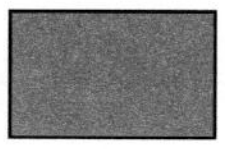.

Color the graph to show how many of each.

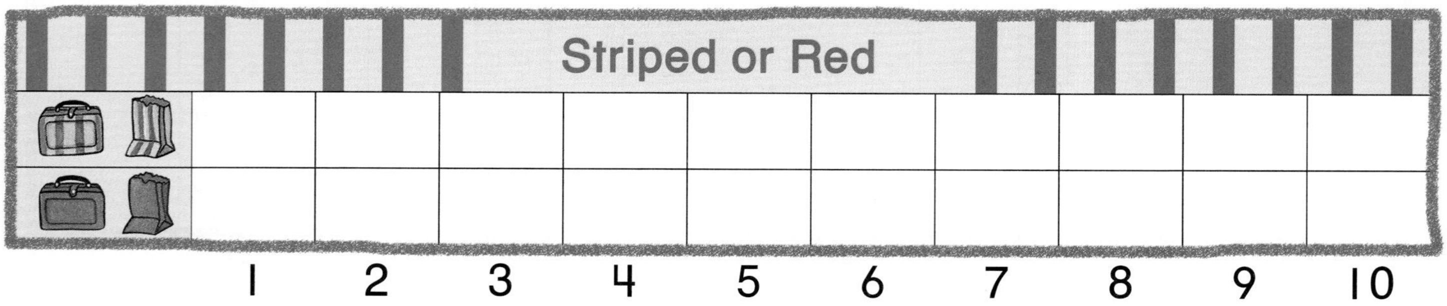

6 How many more 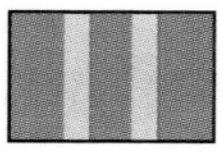 than  ? _____

Problem Solving Critical Thinking

7 How does the graph show you more or fewer  ?
Do you have to count them?

Notes for Home: Your child created and used a pictograph. *Home Activity:* Ask your child to tell you how these two graphs are different.

PRACTICE

Name

Problem Solving: Make a Bar Graph

Learn

PROBLEM SOLVING GUIDE

Understand • Plan • Solve • Look Back

Keller School has lunch choice day.
Room 9 made these choices.

Hamburger
Taco
Pizza

Yum! I can color my choice on the bar graph.

Add a dot for your choice.
Which lunch did Room 9 choose most?

Check

1. Complete the bar graph.
   Color one box for each choice.

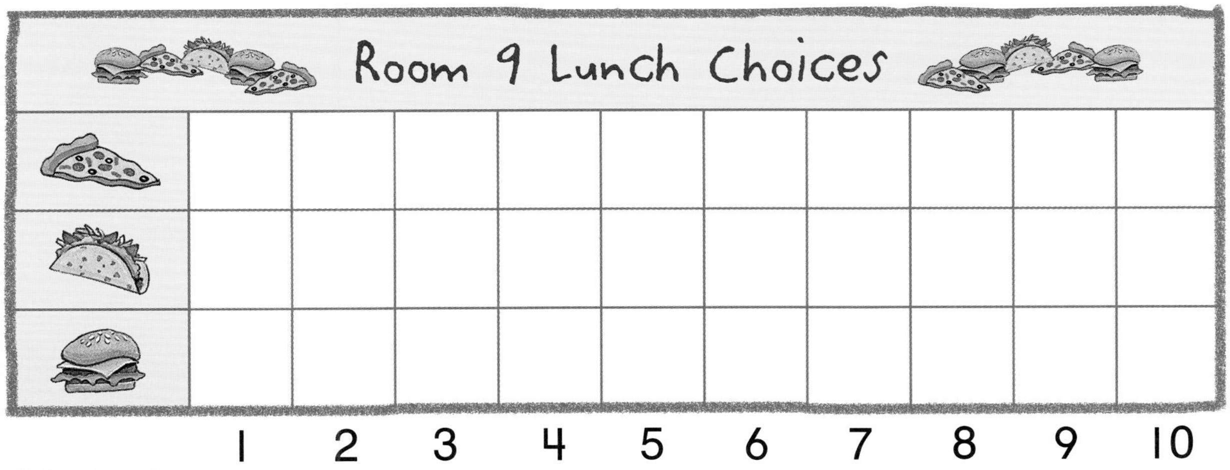

Circle the answer.

2. Fewer children chose 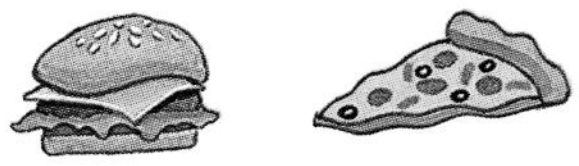 .

3. Which lunch did they pick most? 

Talk About It How does the bar graph show the lunch they picked most?

Notes for Home: Your child completed a bar graph to solve a problem. *Home Activity:* You may want to talk about your lunch choice. Then ask your child to color a box in the graph to show your choice.

Practice

4 Make a bar graph.
Color a box for each lunch.

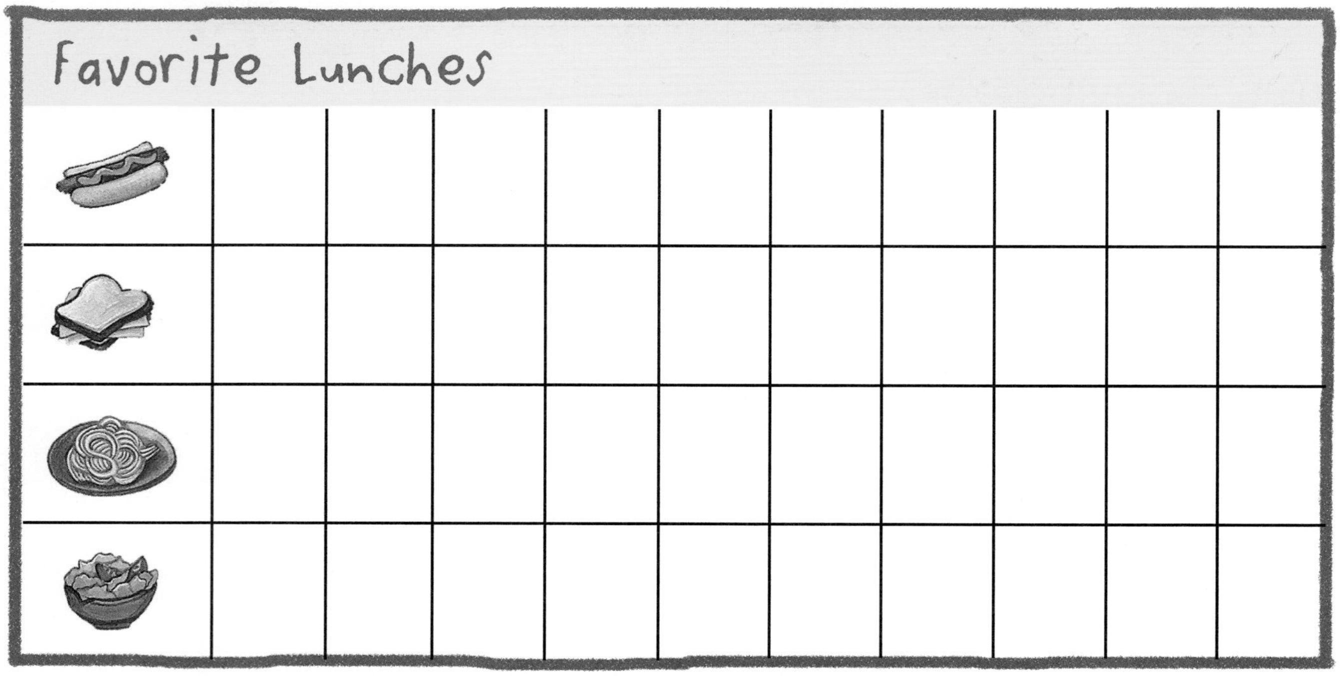

Write the number.

5 How many more 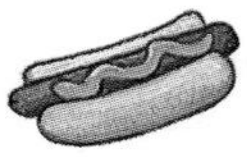 than  ? _____ more

6 How many fewer  than  ? _____ fewer

7 How many more 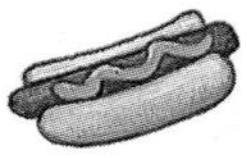 than  ? _____ more

Tell a Math Story

8 Tell a friend a math story about the graph.

Notes for Home: Your child made a bar graph and told a math story using the information on the graph. *Home Activity:* Ask your child to explain what the graph shows.

For additional practice, see Skills Practice Bank, page 525, Set 3.

Name ______________________________

Mixed Practice

Lessons 11–14

Concepts and Skills

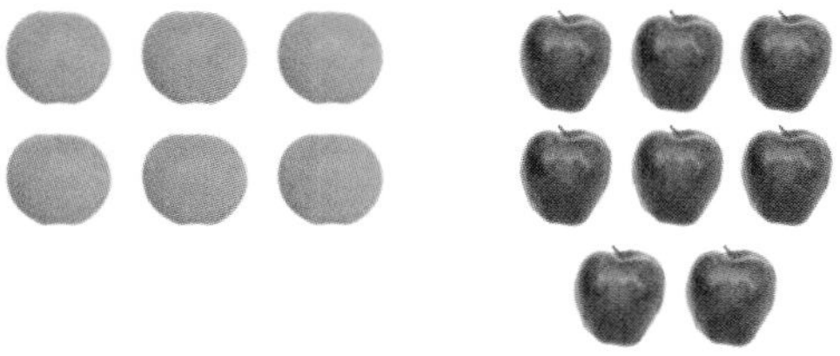

1 Make a pictograph.

Draw each [orange] and [apple].

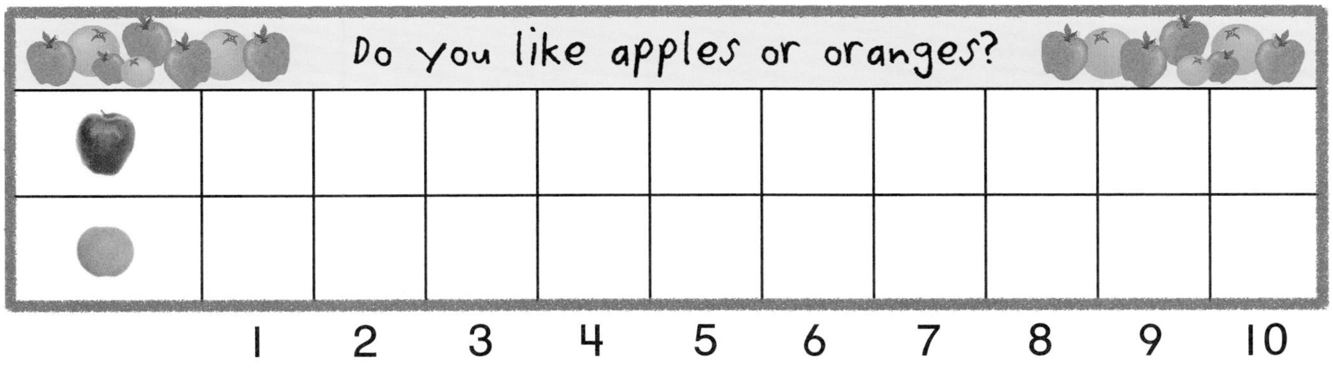

2 Are there more [apple] or [orange]?

Problem Solving

Use the graph.

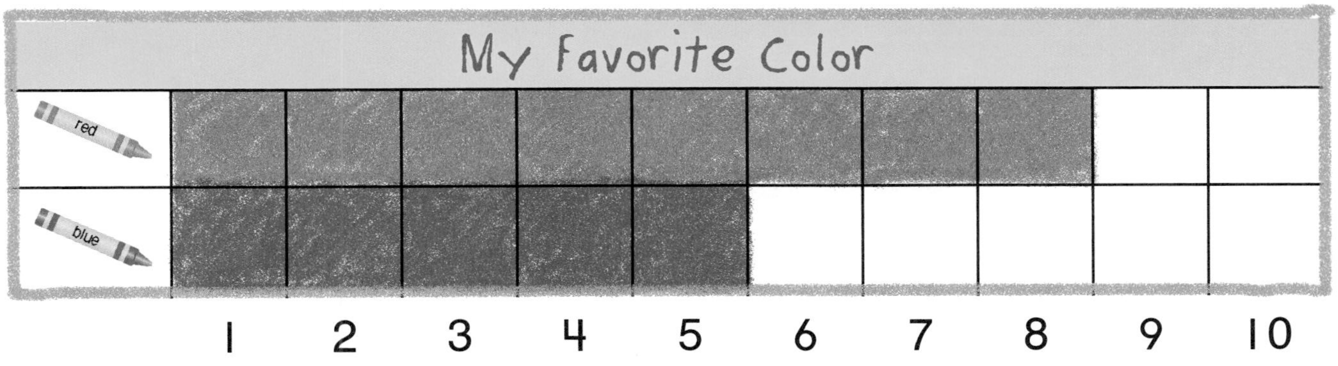

3 How many [red]? ______

4 How many more [red] than [blue]? ______ more

Journal

5 Ask a question about the graph. Tell the answer.

Notes for Home: Your child practiced using graphs to answer questions. *Home Activity:* Ask your child to make a real object graph of objects such as their toys.

MIXED PRACTICE

Name ______________________________

Cumulative Review
Chapter 1

Concepts and Skills

Circle what comes next.

1  

2  

Problem Solving

Use the graph. Circle the answer.

3 More children come in a 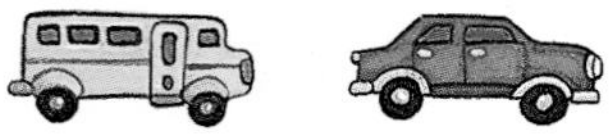.

4 Fewer children come on a .

Test Prep

Fill in the ○ for the correct answer.
What goes with the group?

5 

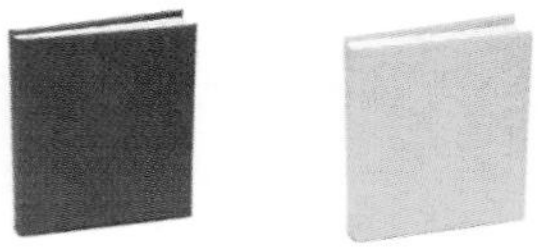

○ ○

6 

○ ○

Notes for Home: Your child reviewed concepts taught in Chapter 1. *Home Activity:* Ask your child to tell you which object belongs to each group in Test Prep. Have them tell you why it belongs.

Name ______________________________

Chapter 1 Review

Vocabulary

Write how many.

Circle the group that has more.

1 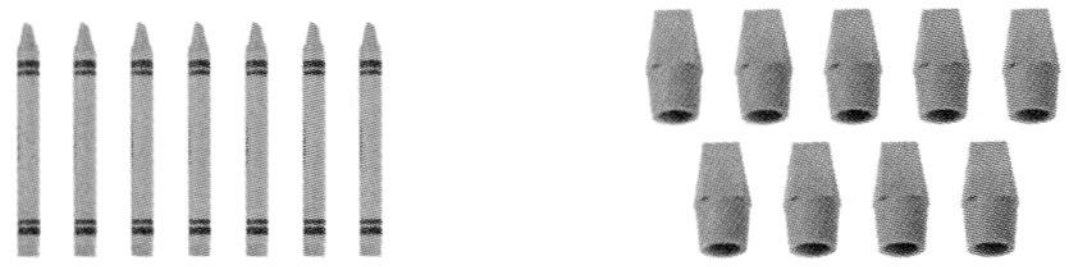

_____ _____

Write how many.

Circle the group that has fewer.

2 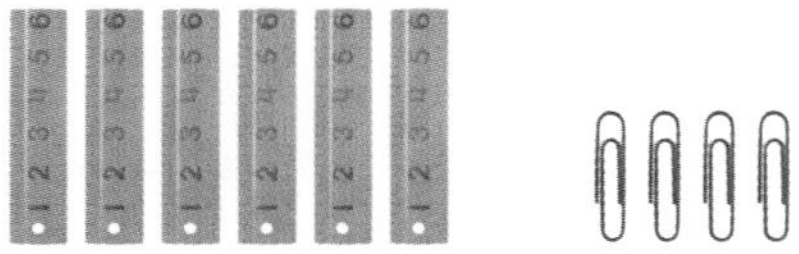

_____ _____

Concepts and Skills

Write the number.

3 

0 _____ 2 3 _____

4 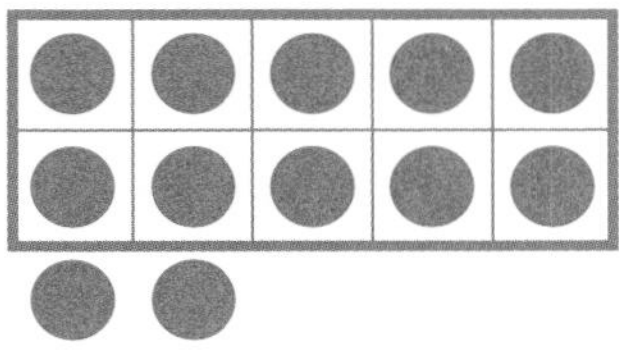

_____

Circle the shape that goes with the group.

5 

Problem Solving

6 Use the graph. Circle the answer. There are more  .

1 2 3 4 5 6

Notes for Home: Your child reviewed the vocabulary, concepts, skills, and problem solving skills taught in Chapter 1. *Home Activity:* Ask your child to sort some objects you have at home and tell why the objects were sorted that way.

CHAPTER REVIEW

Name

Chapter 1 Test

Write how many.

1 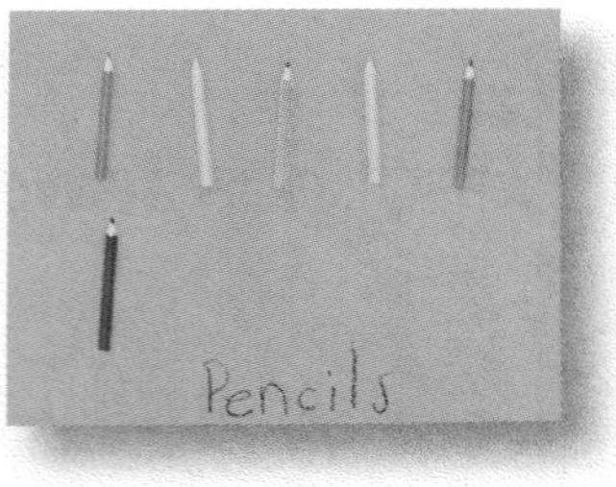

______

2 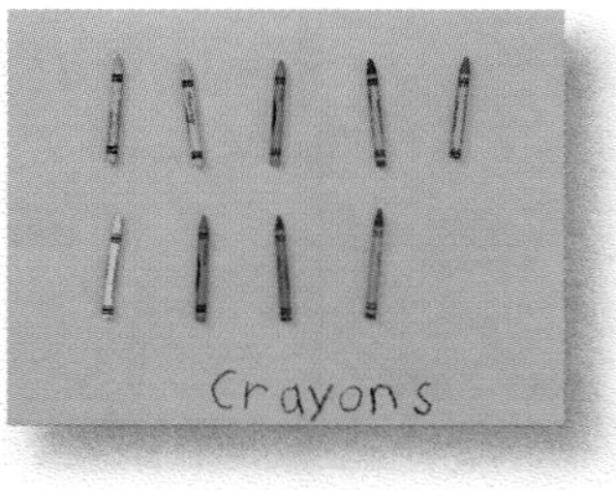

______

3 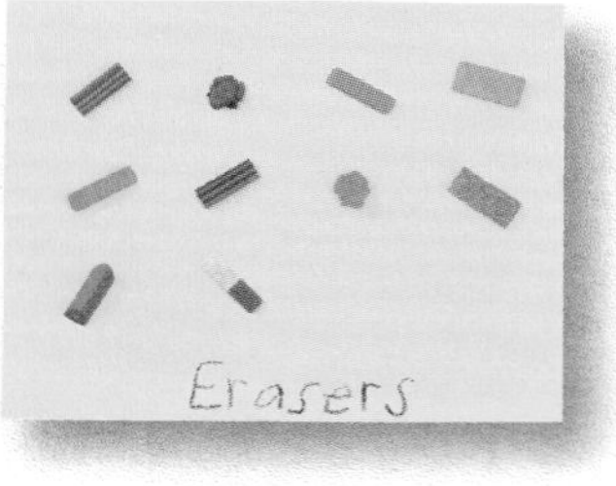

______

4 Complete the graph. Use the pictures above.

Tim and Judy's Supplies												

	1	2	3	4	5	6	7	8	9	10	11	12

Use the graph. Circle the answer.

5 There are fewer  .

6 How many paint brushes? **0** **3** **9**

7 Write the numbers

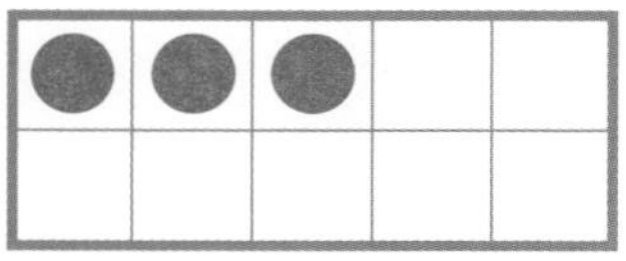 ______

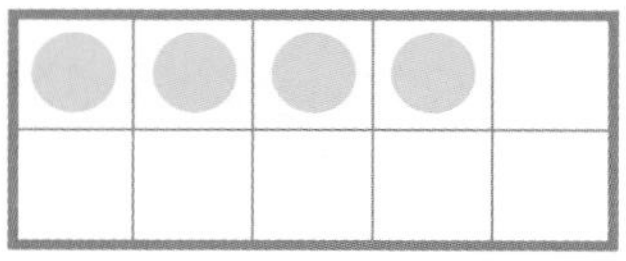 ______

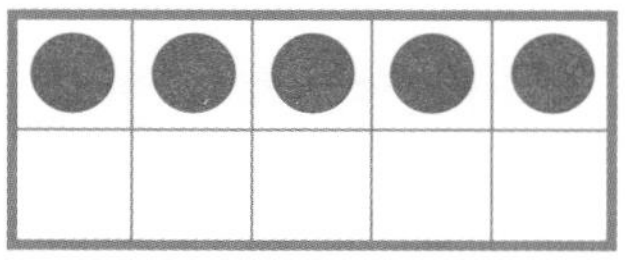 ______

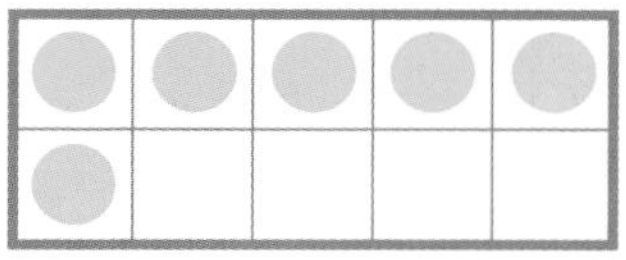 ______

8 Complete the pattern. Draw what comes next.

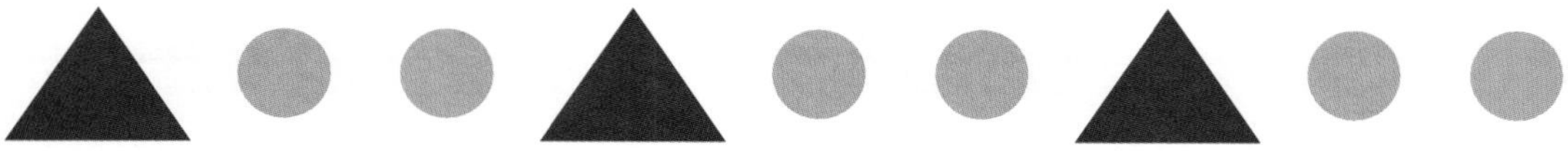

Notes for Home: Your child completed a test on all the skills in Chapter 1. *Home Activity:* Ask your child to explain one of the problems.

Name ____________________

Performance Assessment

Chapter 1

Show What You Know

Write how many.

1.  ____

2. children ____

3.  ____

4.  ____

Ask 10 friends. Make a graph.

How Do We Go Home?

	1	2	3	4	5	6	7	8	9	10

Problem Solving Critical Thinking

5. Which group has fewer?
What else can the graph tell you?

Notes for Home: Your child used information to make a graph. *Home Activity:* Ask your child to tell you a math story about the picture on this page using the words *more* and *fewer.*

Name ______________________

Explore with a CALCULATOR

Get to Know Your Calculator

Keys You Will Use [ON/C]

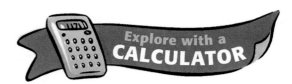

Use your calculator to show numbers.

Press [ON/C] [3]. Write the number.

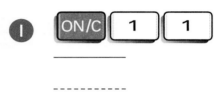

3

Use your calculator to show other numbers.

Write the numbers you see.

1. [ON/C] [1] [1] ______
2. [ON/C] [8] ______
3. [ON/C] [6] ______
4. [ON/C] [9] ______
5. [ON/C] [7] ______

Draw the keys you press to show each number.

6. 11. [ON/C] [1] [1]
7. 12. [ON/C] [ ] [ ]
8. 10. [ON/C] [ ] [ ]

Tech Talk Your calculator shows 13.
What keys did you press? [ON/C] [ ] [ ]

Visit our Web site. www.parent.mathsurf.com

The Name Game

Make a graph like this one for your family's names.

Who has the longest name in your family?
Who has the shortest?
Whose name has the most letters?
Whose name has the fewest letters?

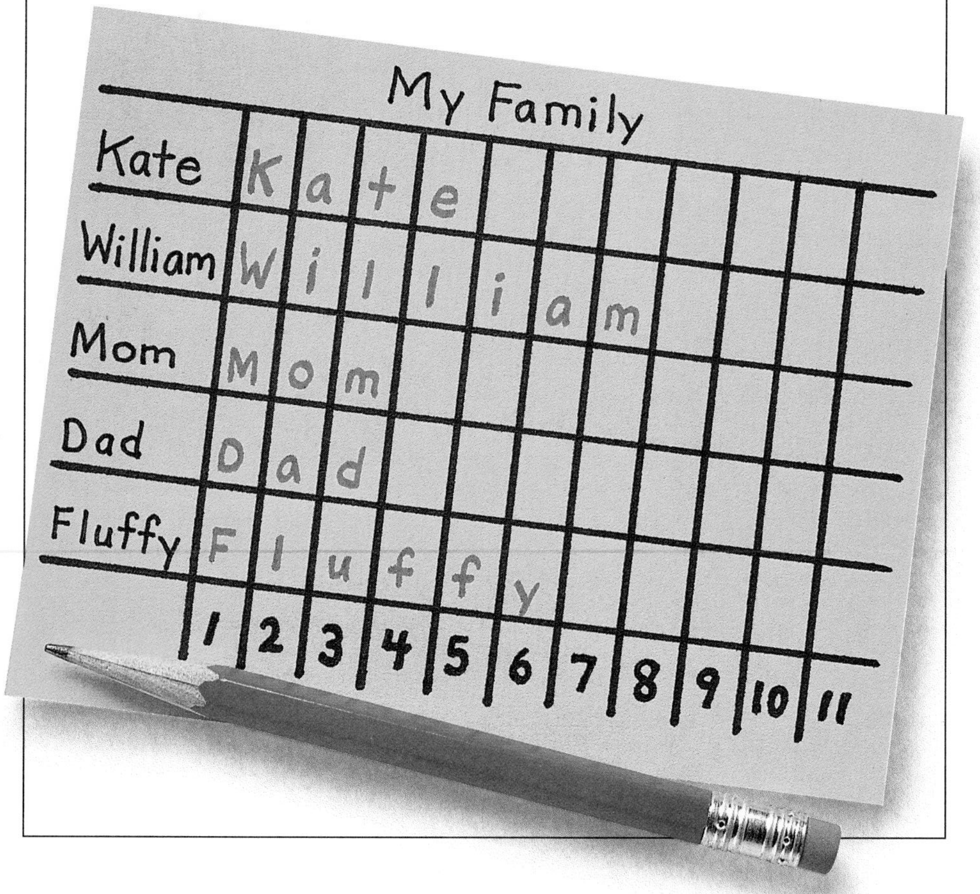
My Family
Kate K a t e
William W i l l i a m
Mom M o m
Dad D a d
Fluffy F l u f f y
1 2 3 4 5 6 7 8 9 10 11

Fold down

MathSoup

Scott Foresman - Addison Wesley My Math Magazine No. 1

Off to School!

Count the children in each group. Which group has more?

School Is Out!

What You Need

game marker for each player
2 coins

How to Play

1 Start your markers on the school.
2 Decide who will go first.
3 Toss the two coins.

Two heads means move one space.

Two tails means move two spaces.

One head, one tail means move three spaces.

4 Do what the space tells you to do.
5 The first player to reach home wins.

School
You lost your hat. Go back 1 space.
You're home!

How do bees get to school?
They take the buzz.

Which Way Warren?

Connect the dots from 1 to 12 to help Wendy and Warren get to school safely.

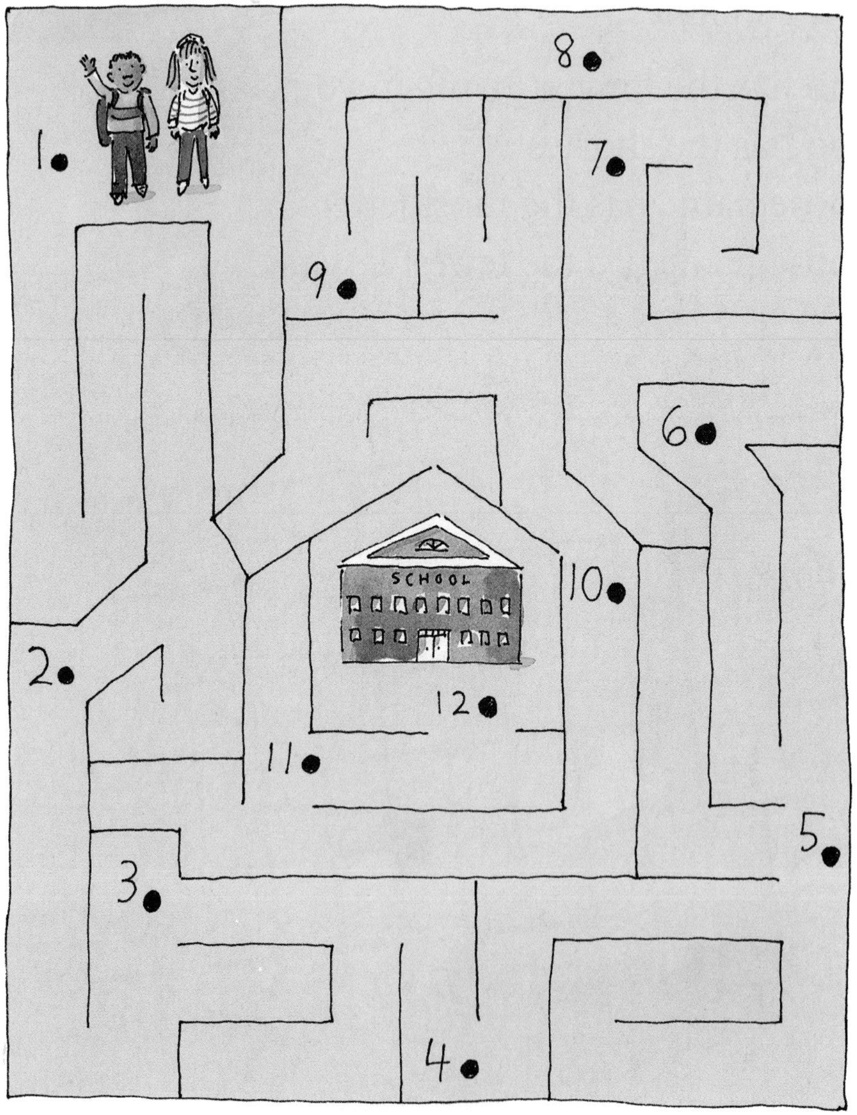

Notes for Home: Your child counted 1, 2, or 3 to move along a game board. *Home Activity:* You might wish to play the game with your child.

Lines and Signs

Each safety sign has its own shape. Use the numbers to connect the dots to show the shapes.

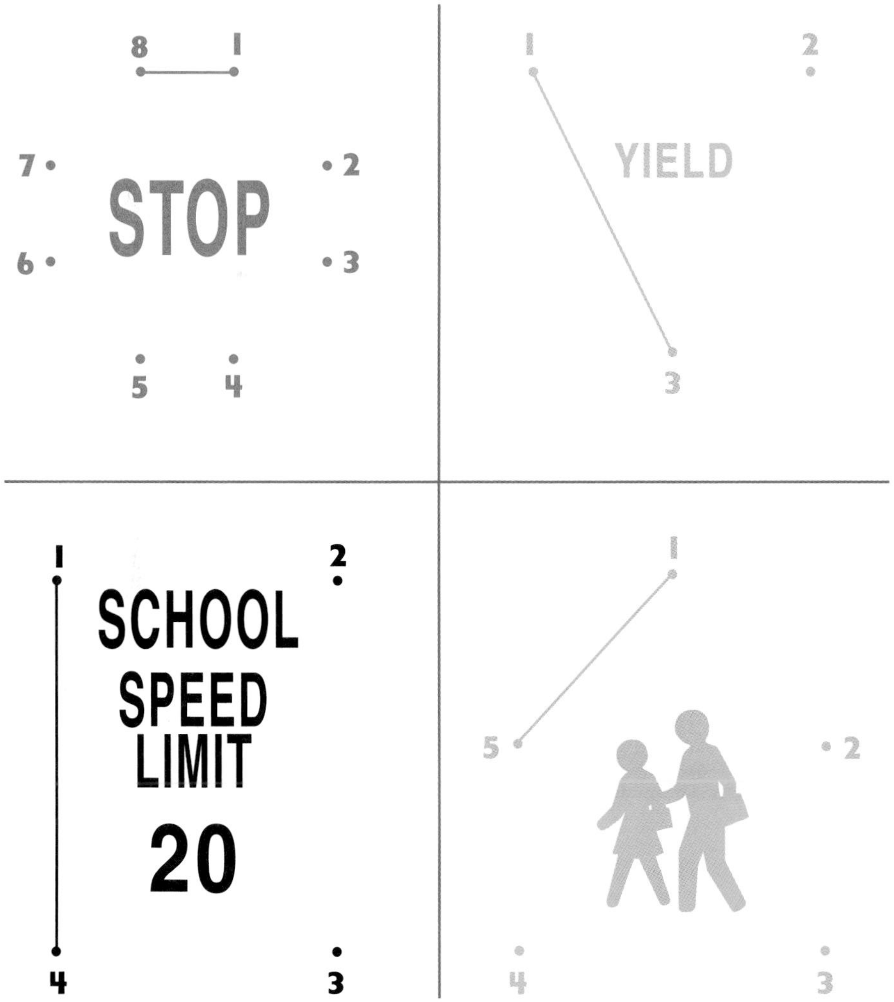

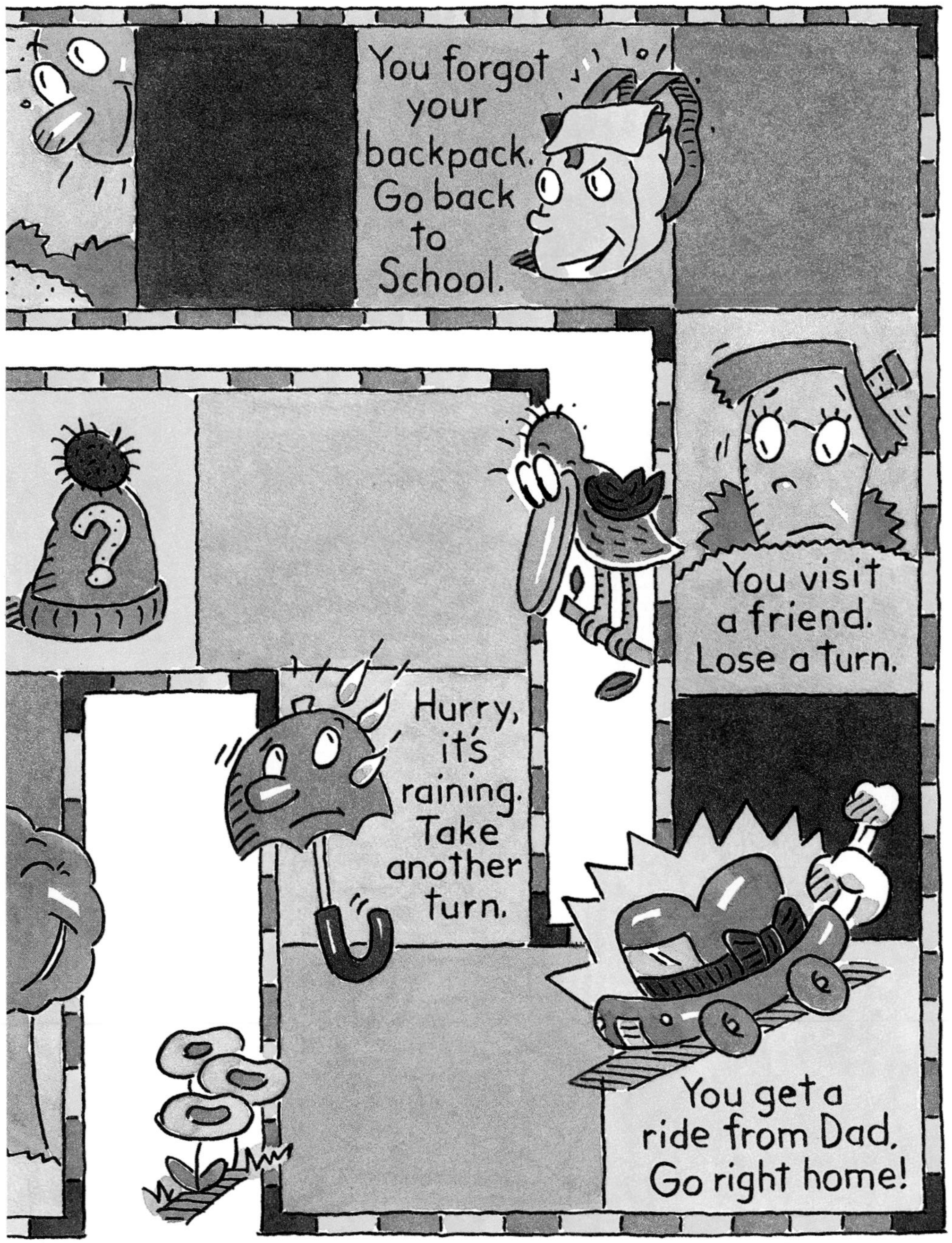

Notes for Home: Your child ordered numbers from 1 to 12 to complete safety signs. *Home Activity:* Have your child name the numbers that come just before 10 (9); 7 (6); and the numbers that come before 4 (1, 2, 3).

Something's Fishy

These fish are in the wrong school!
Find and circle all 12 hidden fish.

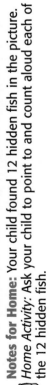

Notes for Home: Your child found 12 hidden fish in the picture.
Home Activity: Ask your child to point to and count aloud each of the 12 hidden fish.

CHAPTER

2 Addition and Subtraction Readiness

Fun and Games

Notes for Home: Your child looked for ways that numbers are used in a game.
Home Activity: Play the game with your child.

Math at Home

Dear Family,
Our class is starting Chapter 2. We will learn about ways to help us get ready to add and subtract. Here are some activities we can do together to help me learn.

Heads or Tails?
Show your child a group of 6 pennies, all showing heads. Turn over 2 or 3 to show tails. Have your child tell you how many pennies show heads, how many show tails, and how many in all.

Button Count
Use objects such as beads or buttons. Show between 6 and 9 objects. Ask your child to guess how many more make 10. Then use objects to check the guess.

Community Connection

At a local park or playground, find games or sports that use numbers. Talk with your child about the different ways numbers are used for fun.

Visit our Web site. **www.parent.mathsurf.com**

Name

Explore Ways to Make 4 and 5

Explore

Use 1 or 2 colors of . Find ways to make 4.
Show what you make.

1

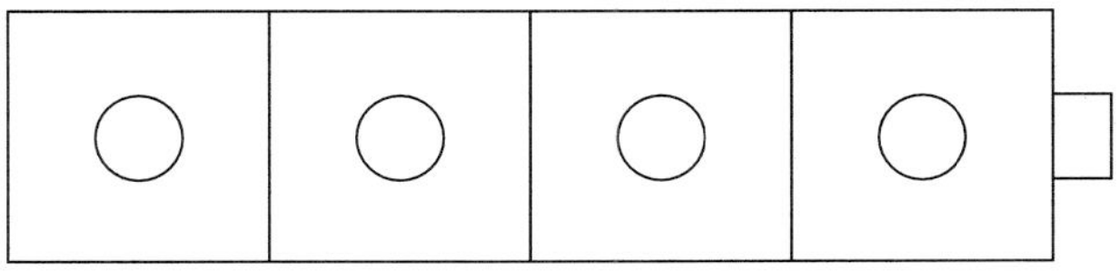

2

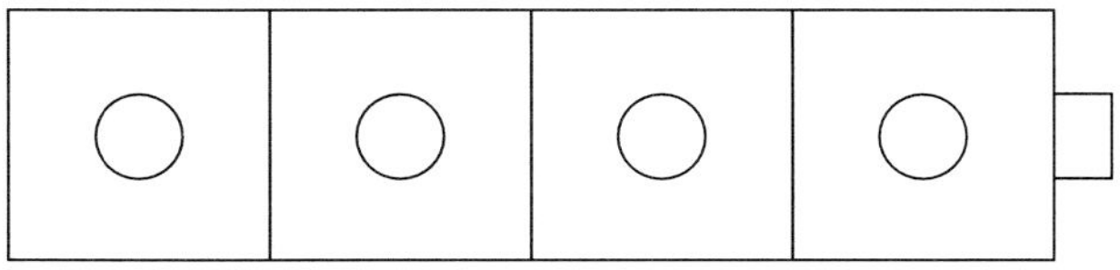

3

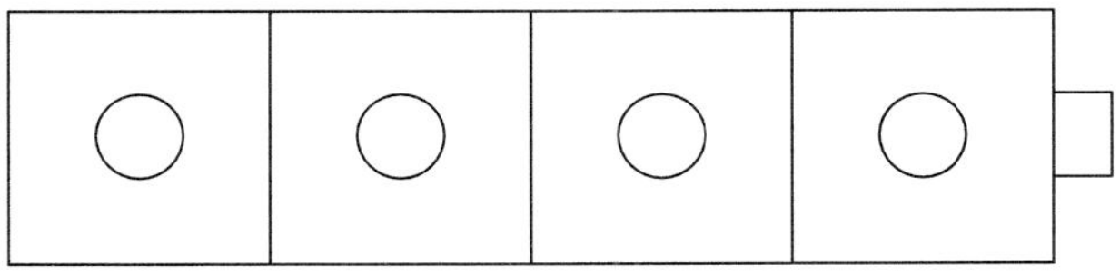

4

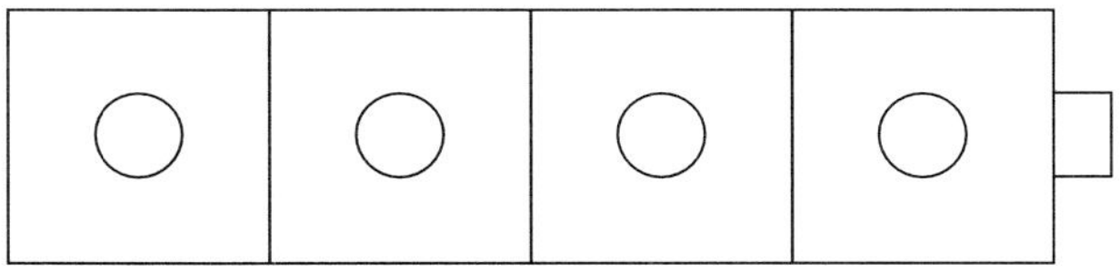

5

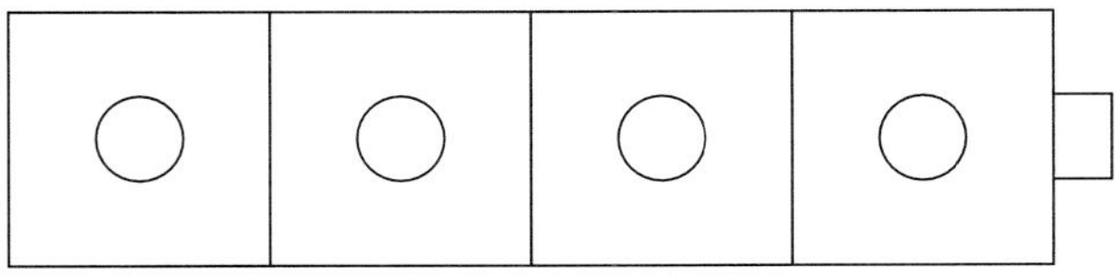

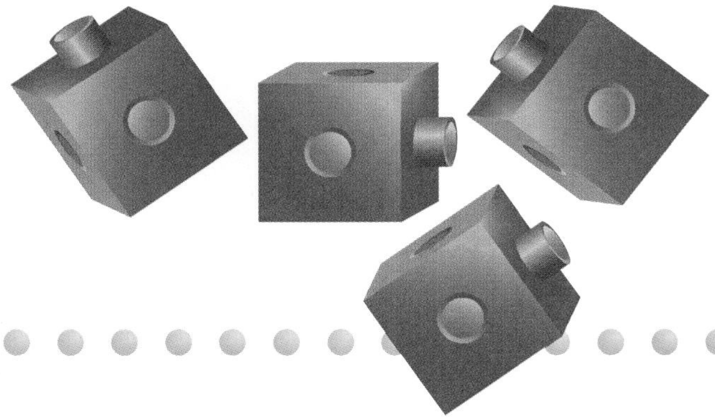

Share

Tell about the ways you made 4.

Notes for Home: Your child used Snap Cubes to find different ways to make 4.
Home Activity: Ask your child to tell you one way to make 4.

Connect

Use 1 or 2 colors of [cube]. Show ways to make 5.
Write the numbers.

6

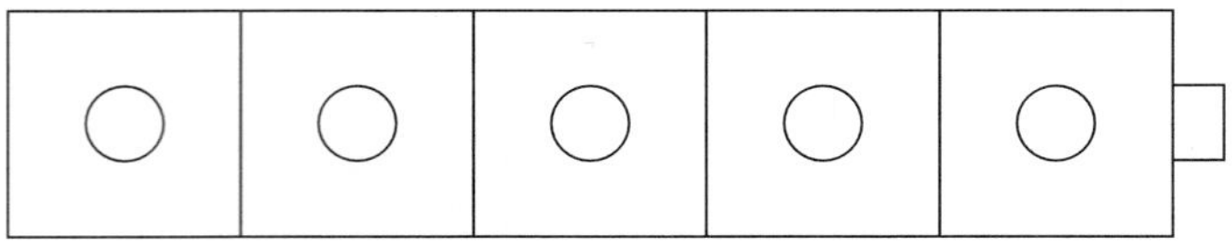

4 and 1 is 5.

7

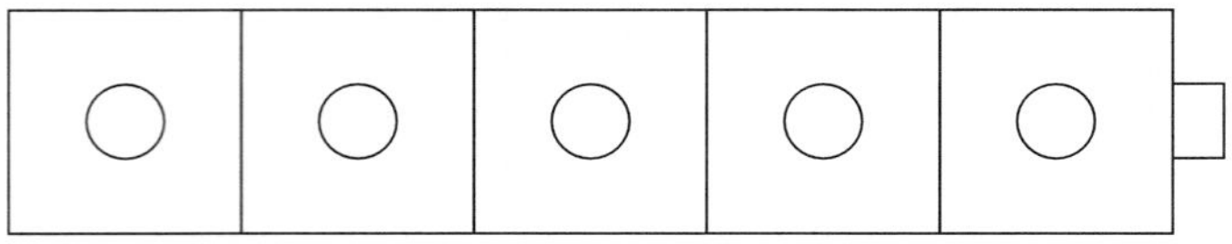

5 is _____ and _____.

8

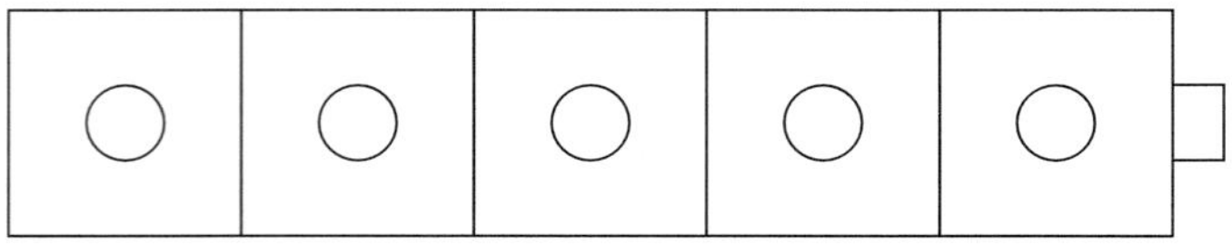

_____ and _____ is _____.

9

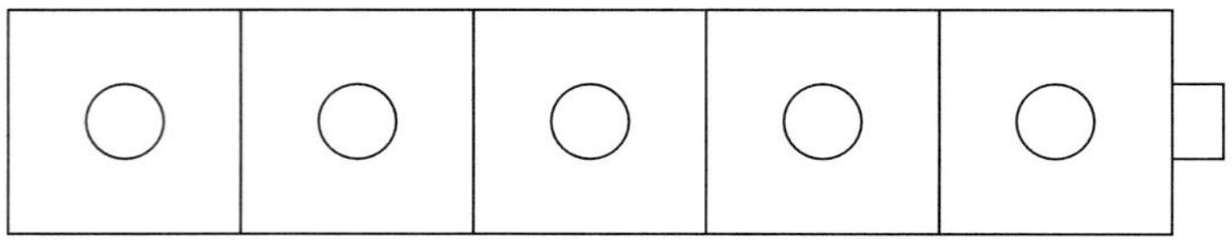

_____ is _____ and _____.

10

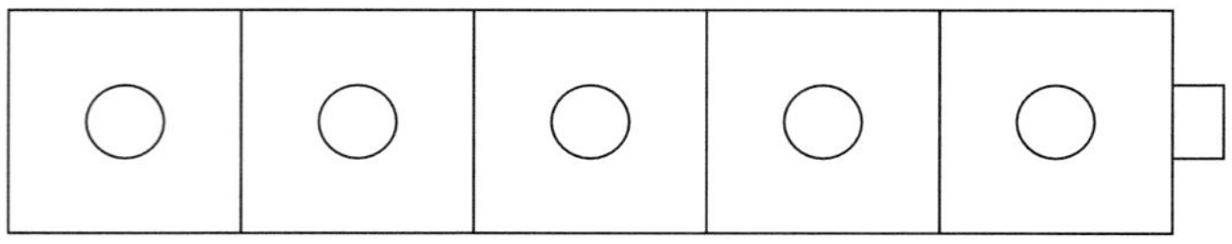

_____ and _____ is _____.

11

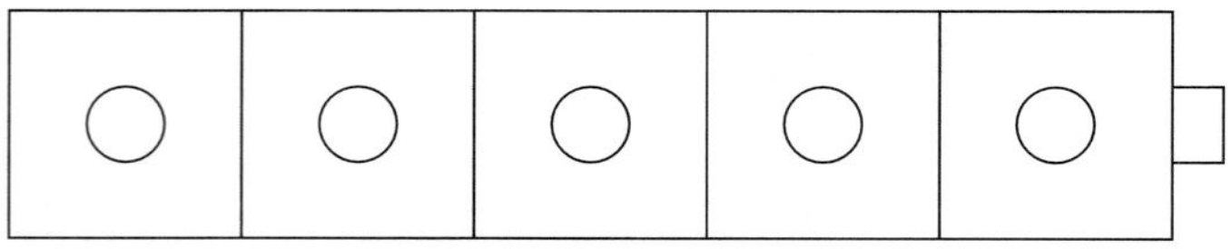

_____ is _____ and _____.

Problem Solving Critical Thinking

12 How can you use [cube] to show that 2 and 3 is the same as 3 and 2?

Notes for Home: Your child used Snap Cubes to find ways to make 5. *Home Activity:* Ask your child to use two kinds of objects such as pennies and buttons to show a way to make 5.

EXPLORE

Name

Ways to Make 6 and 7

Learn

4 and 2 is one way to make 6.

Check

Use 1 or 2 colors of [cube].
Show ways to make 6. Write the numbers.

1.

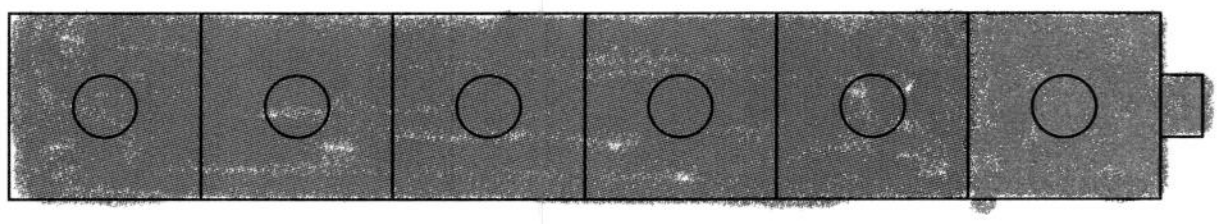

5 and 1 is 6.

2.

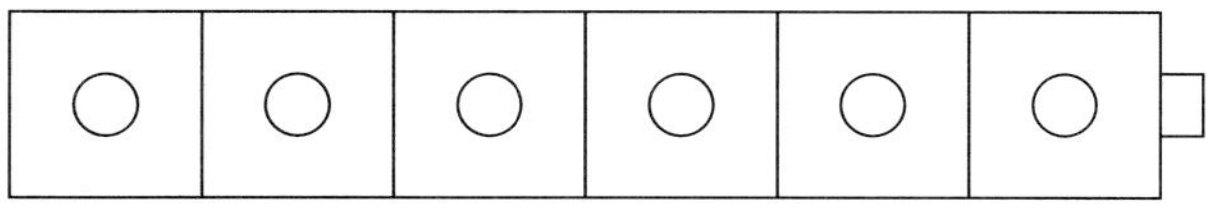

6 is ____ and ____.

3.

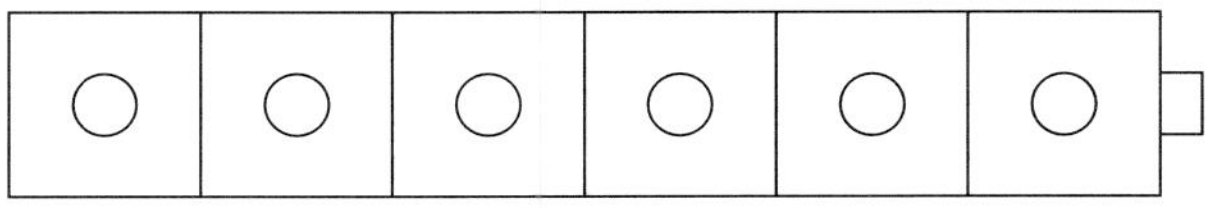

____ and ____ is ____.

4.

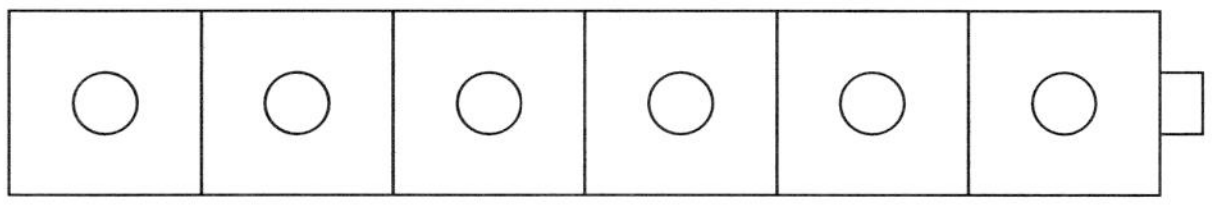

____ is ____ and ____.

5.

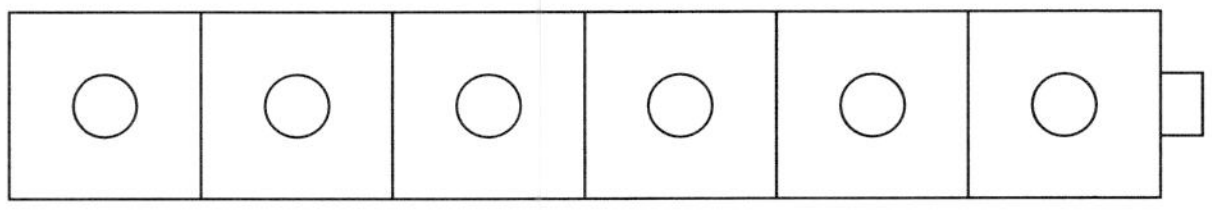

____ and ____ is ____.

6.

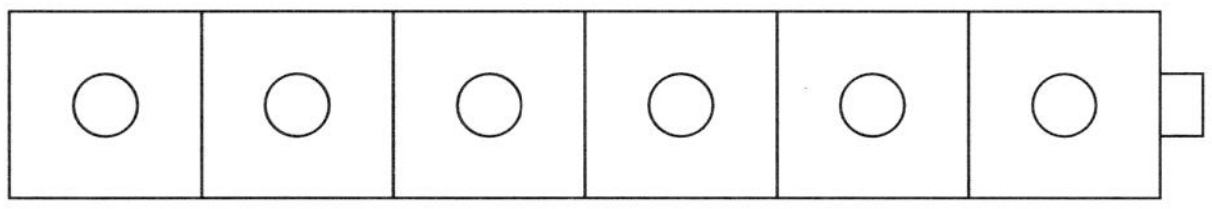

____ is ____ and ____.

Talk About It How could you make 7 with 2 colors of [cube]?

Notes for Home: Your child used Snap Cubes to find different ways to make 6. *Home Activity:* Ask your child to tell you about one way to make 6.

Practice

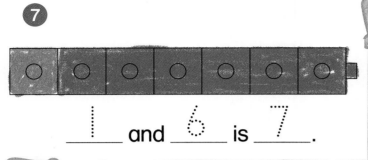

Use 1 or 2 colors of [cube].
Show ways to make 7. Write the numbers.

7. 1 and 6 is 7.

8. ____ is ____ and ____.

9. ____ is ____ and ____.

10. ____ and ____ is ____.

11. ____ and ____ is ____.

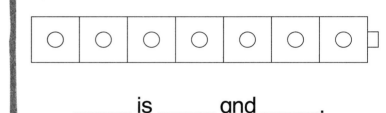

12. ____ is ____ and ____.

PRACTICE

Mental Math

Solve.

13. You have 4.
Circle the card you need to make 7.

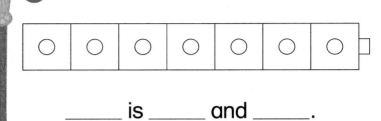

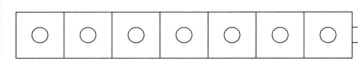

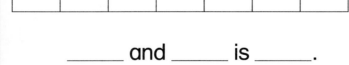

Notes for Home: Your child used Snap Cubes to find different ways to make 7. *Home Activity:* Ask your child to use two kinds of objects, such as paper clips and buttons, to show ways to make 7.

Name

Ways to Make 8 and 9

Learn

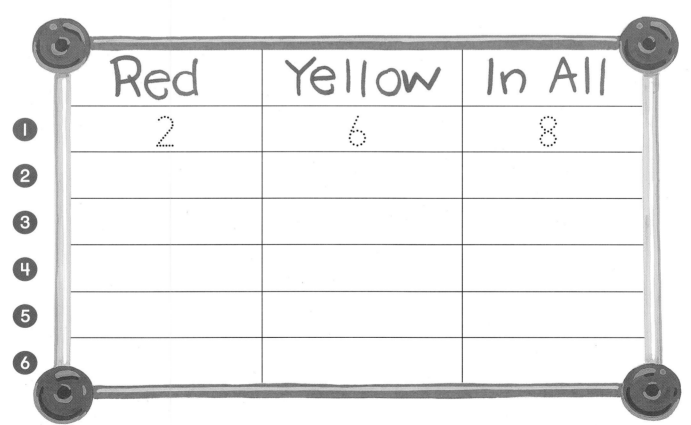

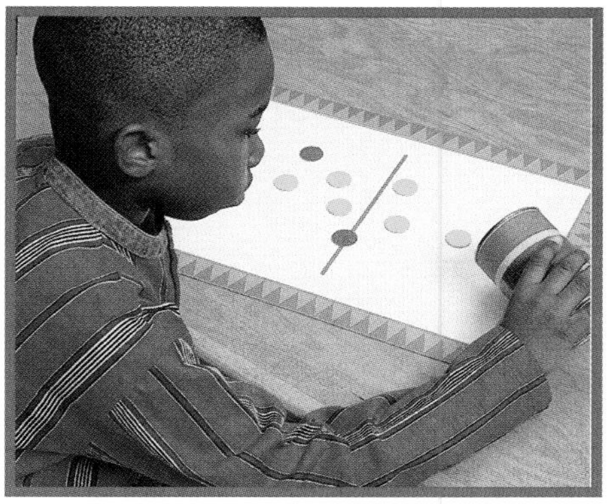

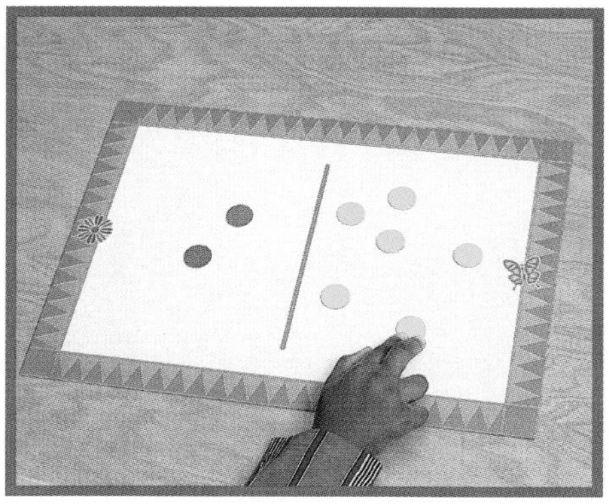

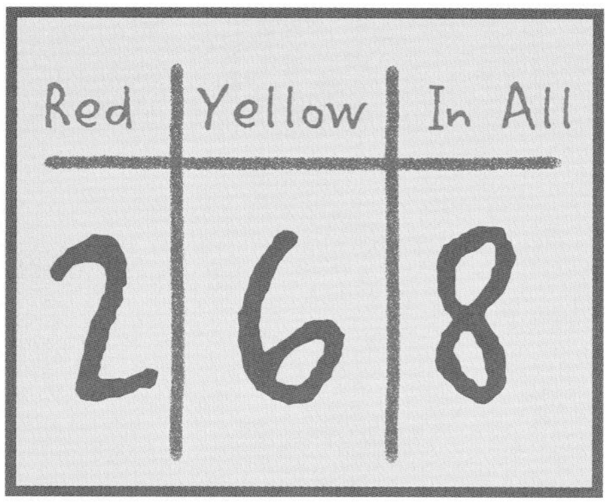

Spill 8 .

Show red and yellow on your .

Use the table to record.

Check

Spill and show ways to make 8. Record the ways.

	Red	Yellow	In All
1	2	6	8
2			
3			
4			
5			
6			

Talk About It What are other ways to make 8?

Notes for Home: Your child used two-color counters to find different ways to make 8.
Home Activity: Ask your child to tell you some ways to make 8.

Practice

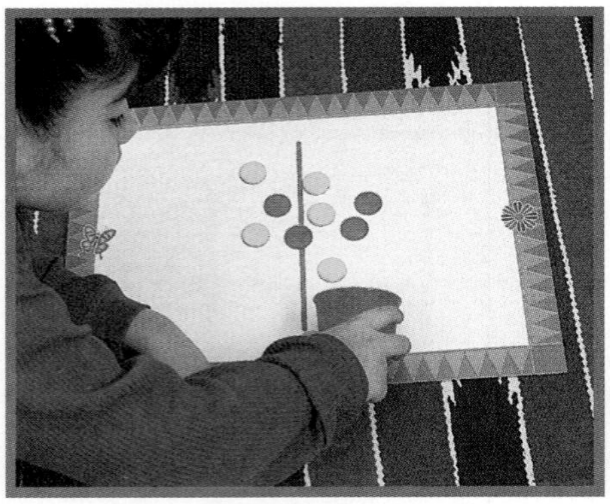

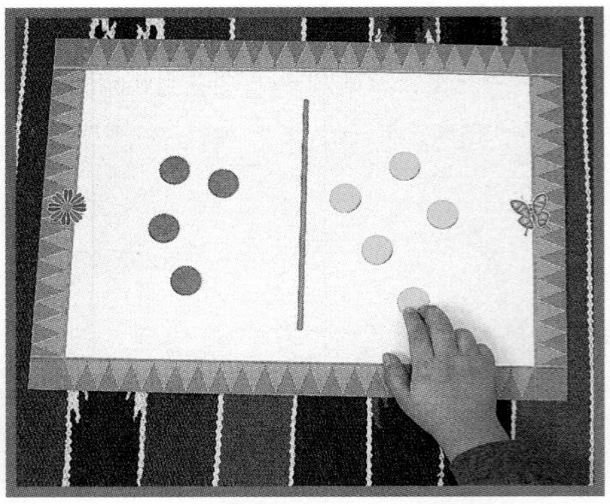

Spill 9 ⬤⬤.

Show red and yellow on your ▯.

Use the table to record.

Spill ⬤⬤ and show ways to make 9. Record the ways.

	Red	Yellow	In All
7	4	5	9
8			
9			
10			

PRACTICE

Problem Solving Visual Thinking

11 Match the groups with the same number.

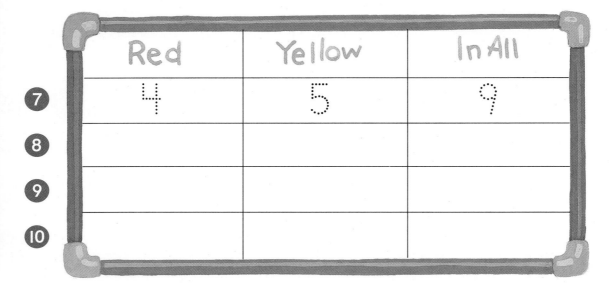

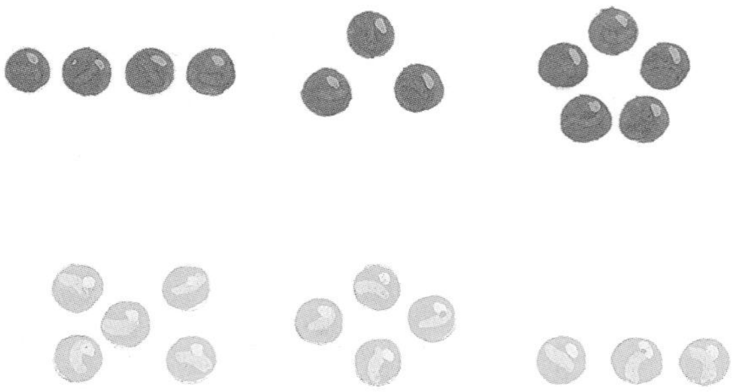

Notes for Home: Your child used two-color counters to find different ways to make 9. *Home Activity:* Ask your child to use two kinds of objects such as dried beans and buttons to show two more ways to make 9.

For additional practice, see Skills Practice Bank, page 526, Set 1.

Name

Ways to Make 10

Learn

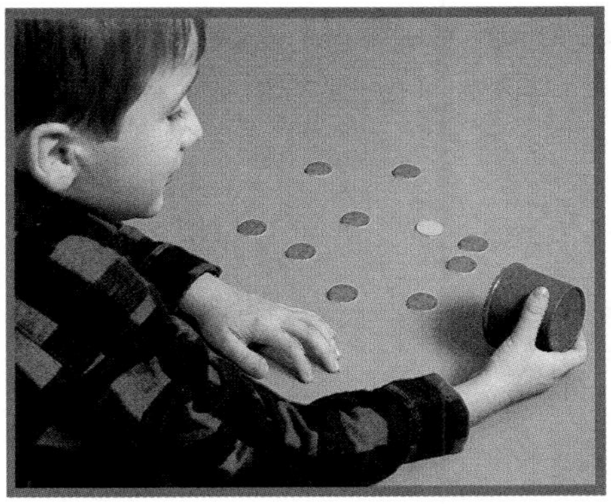

Spill 10 .

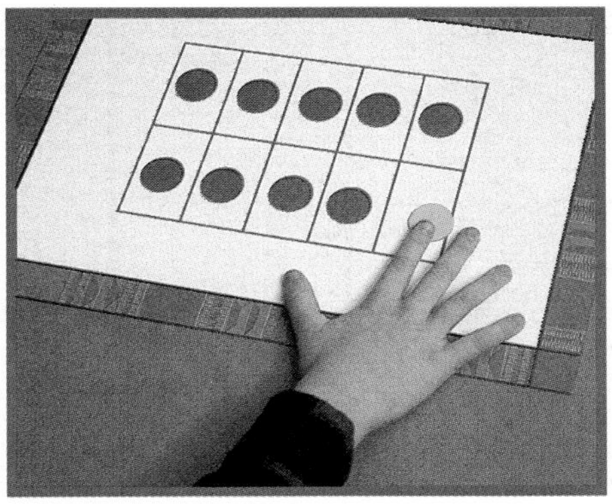

Show red and yellow on your .

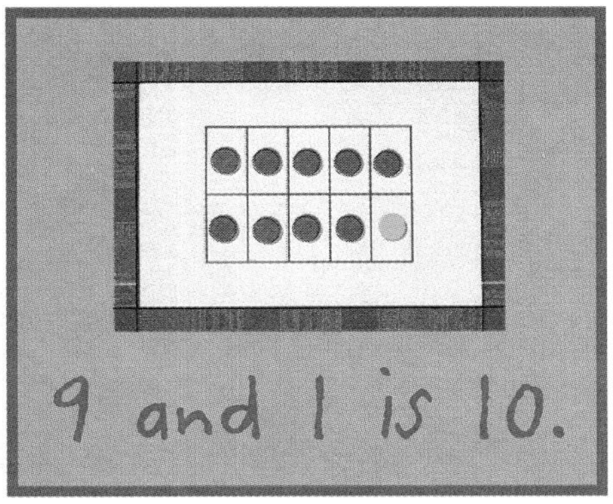

Color to record.

Check

Spill and show ways to make 10. Record the ways.

1 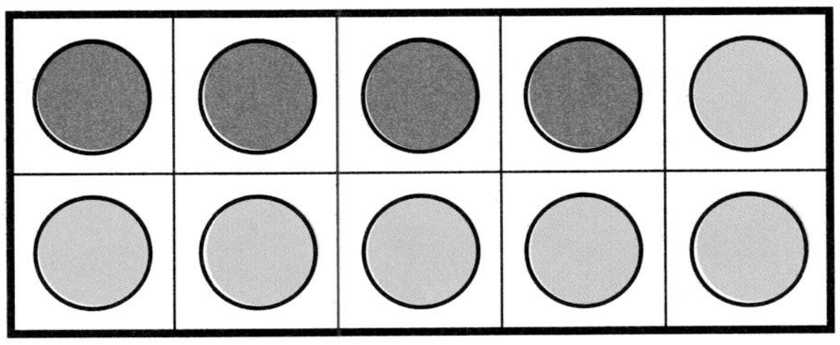

4 and 6 is 10.

2 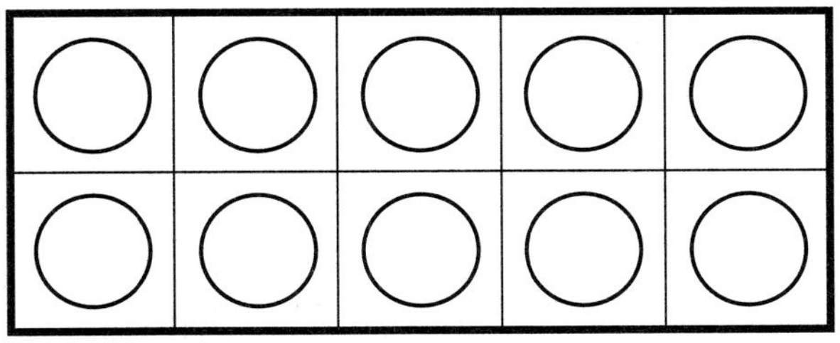

_____ and _____ is _____.

Talk About It Are there more ways to make 10? How could you find out?

Notes for Home: Your child used two-color counters and a ten-frame to find different ways to make 10. *Home Activity:* Ask your child to tell you how a ten-frame helps you see ways to make 10.

Practice

Spill and show ways to make 10. Record the ways.

3
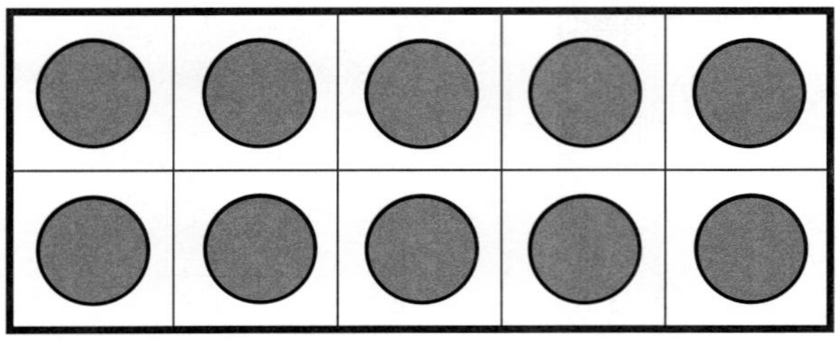

10 and 0 is 10.

4
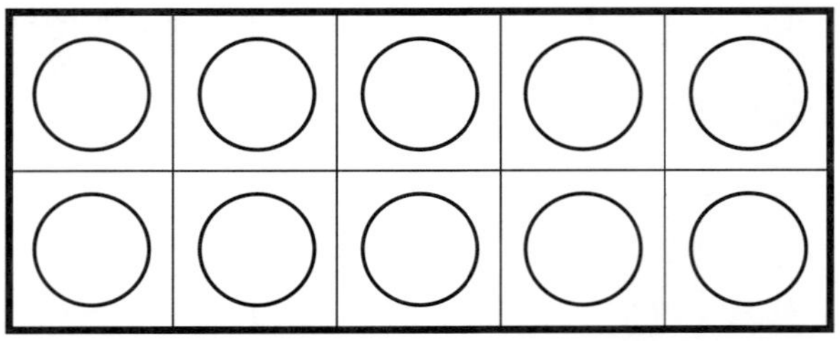

_____ and _____ is _____.

5
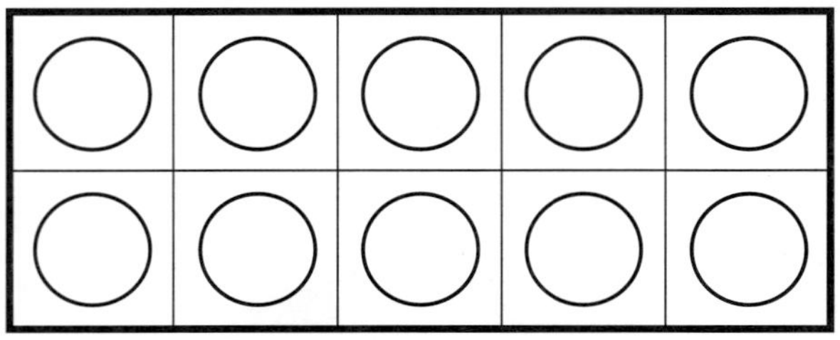

_____ and _____ is _____.

6
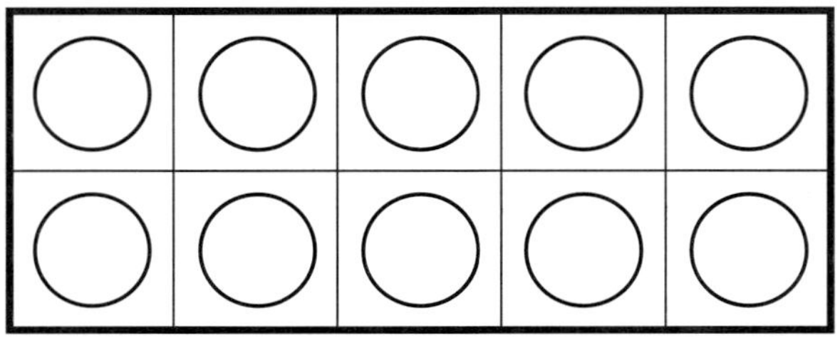

_____ and _____ is _____.

7
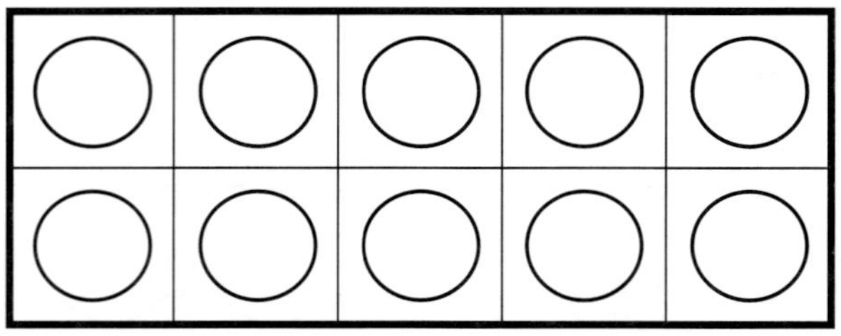

_____ and _____ is _____

8
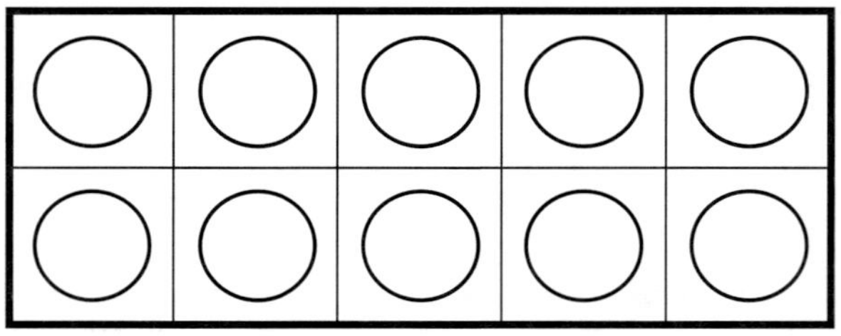

_____ and _____ is _____.

Journal

9 How are these the same?
How are these different?

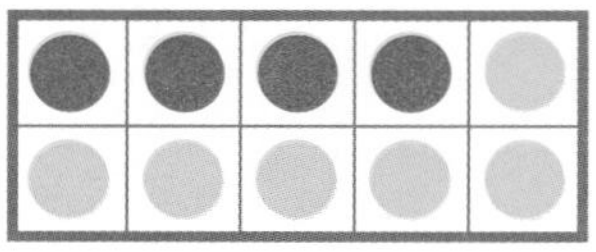

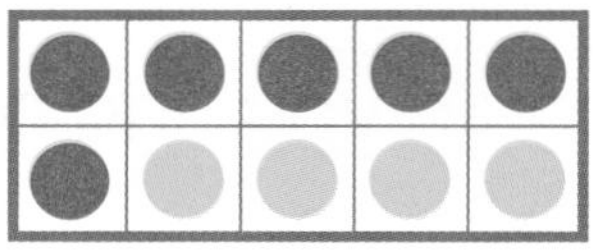

Notes for Home: Your child continued to look for ways to make 10. *Home Activity:* Ask your child to tell you some of the ways he or she found to make 10.

PRACTICE

Name ______________________________

Practice Game

Make the Number

Players 2

What You Need

pencil and paper clip

2 sets of dot cards 0–10

How to Play

1. Mix up the number cards. Put them facedown.
2. Take turns using the pencil and paper clip to spin.
3. Turn over two cards.
4. If the dots on the cards make the spinner number, keep the cards.
5. If not, turn the cards facedown again.
6. Play until all cards are taken.
7. The player with the most cards wins.

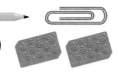

3 and 2 make 5. You can take the number cards.

Notes for Home: Your child practiced making numbers to 10. *Home Activity:* Play the game with your child by using 20 index cards or paper squares with one number from 0 to 10 written on each card.

Name ____________________

STOP and Practice

Look at the ▢▢. Write the numbers.

❶

_____ and _____ is _____.

❷

_____ and _____ is _____.

❸

_____ and _____ is _____.

❹

_____ and _____ is _____.

❺

_____ and _____ is _____.

❻

_____ and _____ is _____.

Logical Reasoning

❼ Matt has 8 ▢▢.

He has 2 more ▢ than ▢.

How many of each does he have?

_____ ▢ _____ ▢

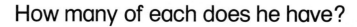

Notes for Home: Your child wrote a number sentence for each Snap Cube picture.
Home Activity: Ask your child to explain how he or she solved the Snap Cube riddle.

PRACTICE

Name

Problem Solving: Make a Table

Learn

PROBLEM SOLVING GUIDE

Understand • Plan • Solve • Look Back

How many ways can you put

5 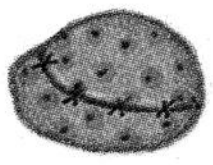 into a □ and a ○?

Make a table to find out.

There are _____ ways.

□	○	In All
0	5	5
1	4	5

Check

1 How many ways can you put

6 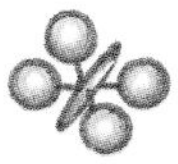 into 2 ?

There are _____ ways.

		In All
0	6	6
1	5	6

Talk About It Look for patterns.
Tell about any pattern you see.

Notes for Home: Your child used the strategy Make a Table to help solve problems.
Home Activity: Ask your child to use objects and show you how many ways there are to make 4.

PROBLEM SOLVING

Practice

2 How many ways can you hold 9  in 2  ?

		In All
0	9	9
1	8	9

3 How many ways can you put 10  into 2  ?

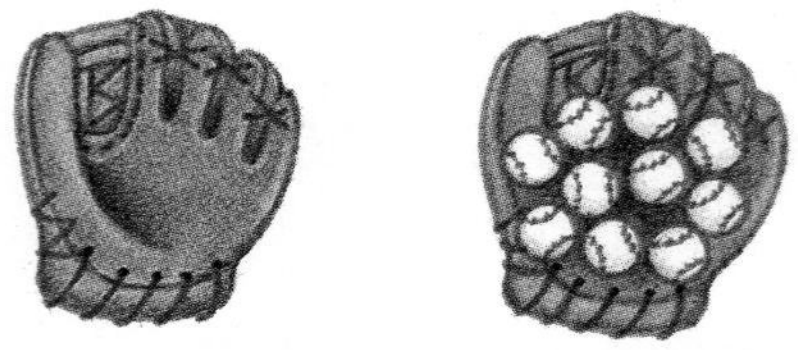

		In All
0	10	10

Problem Solving Critical Thinking

4 How many ways are there to make 7?

5 How many ways are there to make 8? How do you know?

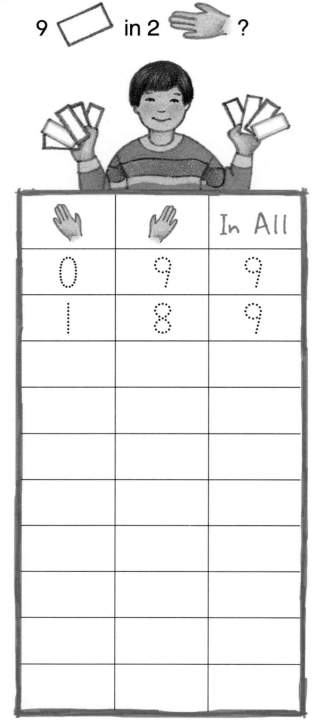

Notes for Home: Your child made tables to find all the ways to make 9 and 10. *Home Activity:* Ask your child how many ways 7 objects can be placed on 2 dishes. Help your child record the ways in a table like those on this page.

For additional practice, see Skills Practice Bank, page 526, Set 2.

Name

Mixed Practice

Lessons 1–5

Concepts and Skills

Use 1 or 2 colors to make 5 and 6.

Color. Write the numbers.

1 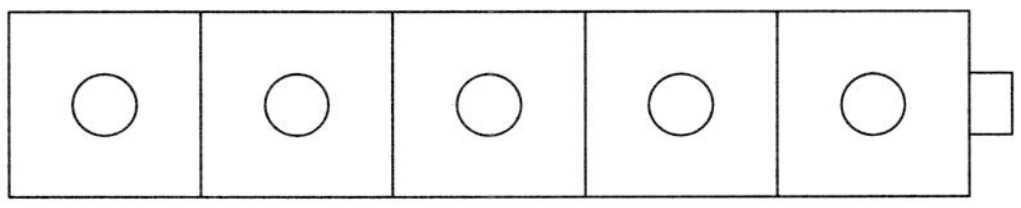

_____ and _____ is _____.

2 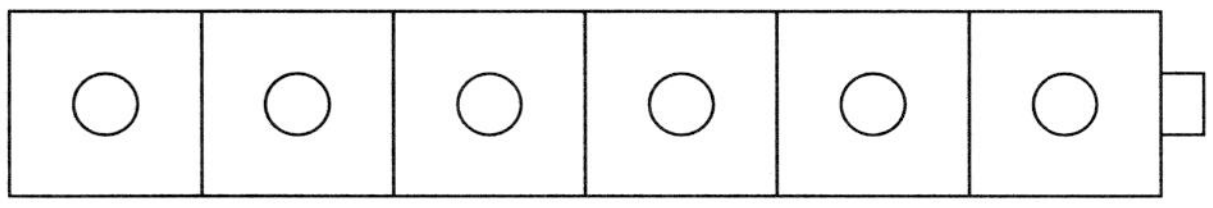

_____ and _____ is _____.

Write the numbers.

3 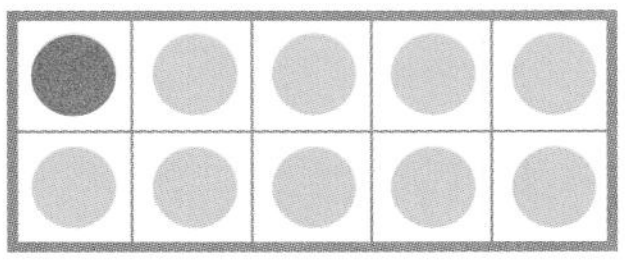

_____ and _____ is _____.

4 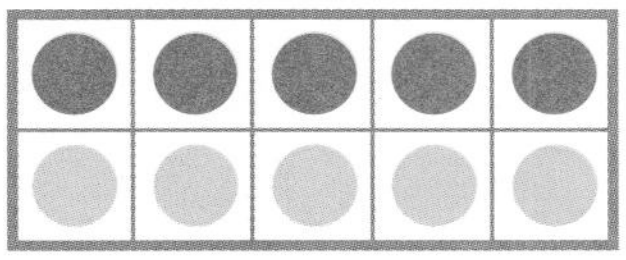

_____ and _____ is _____.

Problem Solving

5 How many ways can you put

3  on 2 ?

_____ ways

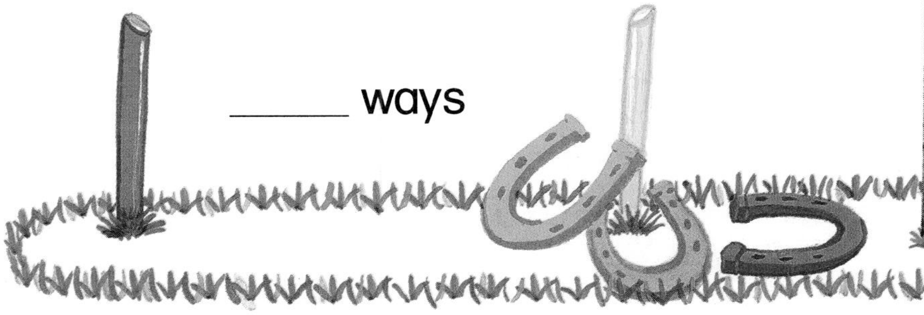

		In All

Journal

6 Write a math story for 6 and 2 is 8.

Notes for Home: Your child practiced finding ways to make numbers through 10.
Home Activity: Ask your child to tell or draw a story about 2 groups of toys.

MIXED PRACTICE

Name ______________________________

Cumulative Review

Chapter 1–2

Concepts and Skills

Write how many.

1  ______

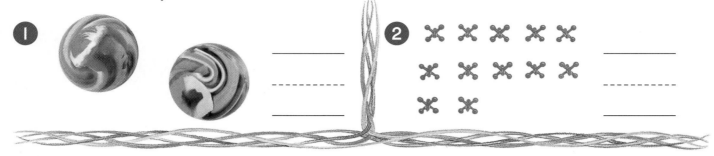

2  ______

Use the graph. Write the number.

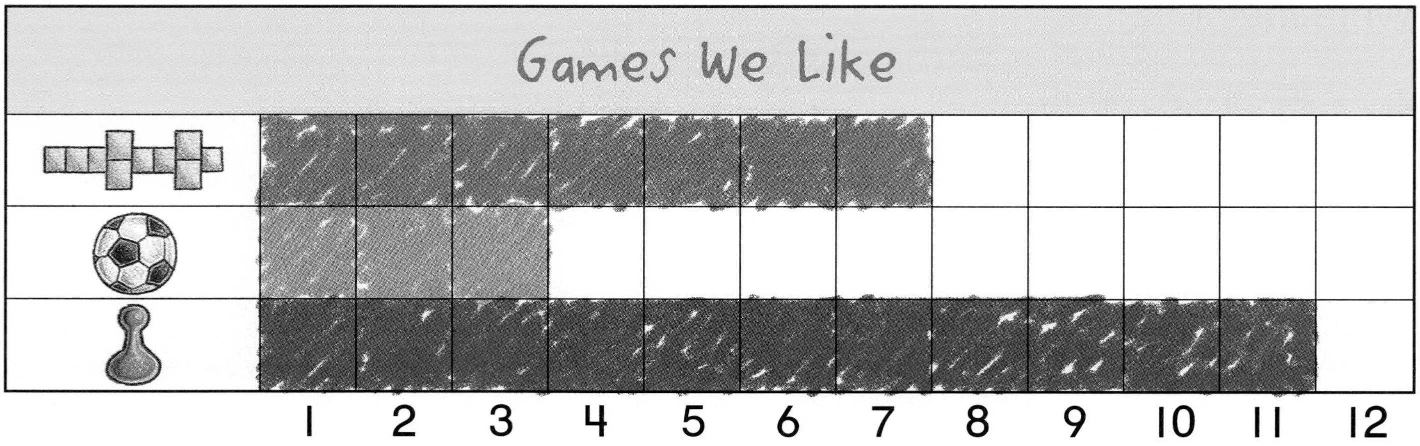

3 How many more like  than 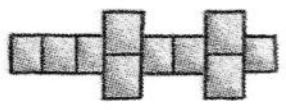? ______

4 How many fewer like  than ? ______

Test Prep

Fill in the ○ for the correct answer.

5 What comes next?

8	6	7	5
○	○	○	○

Notes for Home: Your child reviewed counting to 12 and reading a graph. *Home Activity:* Make a graph of your family's favorite sports or games.

Name ______________________________

More and Fewer

Learn

My train has 1 fewer.

My train has 1 more.

Check

Use . Write how many.

1.  5

   Make a train with 1 fewer.

   Write how many now. 4

2.  ______

   Make a train with 2 fewer.

   Write how many now. ______

3.  ______

   Make a train with 1 more.

   Write how many now. ______

4.  ______

   Make a train with 2 more.

   Write how many now. ______

Write how many.

5.  ______

6.  ______

7. How many more are in the blue train than in the red train? ______

Talk About It

Pick a number. What is 1 more? What is 1 less?

Notes for Home: Your child showed 1 or 2 more or fewer than a given amount. *Home Activity:* Show your child 7 objects and ask for a number that is 1 more and a number that is 1 fewer.

Practice

Use a cube. Write how many.

8 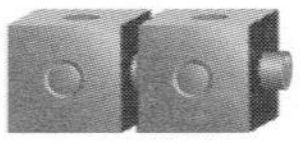 2

Make a train with 2 more.

Write how many now. 4

9  ____

Make a train with 2 fewer.

Write how many now. ____

10  ____

Make a train with 1 fewer.

Write how many now. ____

11  ____

Make a train with 1 more.

Write how many now. ____

12 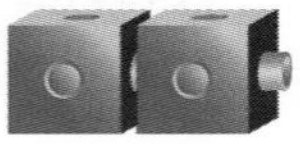 ____

Make a train with 2 fewer.

Write how many now. ____

13  ____

Make a train with 1 more.

Write how many now. ____

PRACTICE

Write how many.

14  ____

15  ____

16 How many more are in the green train than in the orange train? ____

Mental Math

17 Circle the number that is 2 less than 5.

Notes for Home: Your child practiced showing 1 or 2 more or fewer than a given amount. *Home Activity:* Ask your child to tell you the number that is 2 less than 10, and the number that is 2 more than 10.

Name

Odd and Even Numbers

Learn

even
odd
Even numbers make pairs. Odd numbers have one left over.

Check

Make pairs. Draw what you make.
Circle odd or even.

1. Use 4 counters.

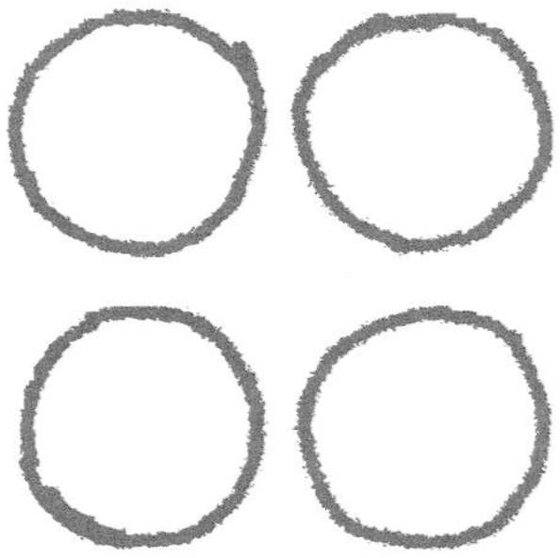

odd
even

2. Use 5 counters.

odd
even

Talk About It How do you know a number is even?

Notes for Home: Your child made pairs of counters to find out if a number is odd or even. *Home Activity:* Show your child 1 to 12 objects. Ask your child to pair the objects, then tell if the amount is odd or even.

Practice

PRACTICE

Make pairs. Draw what you make.
Circle odd or even.

3. Use 6 .

odd

even

4. Use 7 .

odd

even

Write your own number.

5. Use . How many did you use? _____

odd

even

Problem Solving Patterns

6. Color even numbers blue. Color odd numbers red.

1	2	3	4	5	6	7	8	9	10

7. What color did you color the number 8? ______________________

8. What pattern do you see? ______________________

Notes for Home: Your child used objects to decide whether a number is odd or even.
Home Activity: Ask your child to show groups of 2, 4, 6, and 8 objects and tell why each of these numbers is even.

Name ______________________________

Ways to Make 11 and 12

Learn

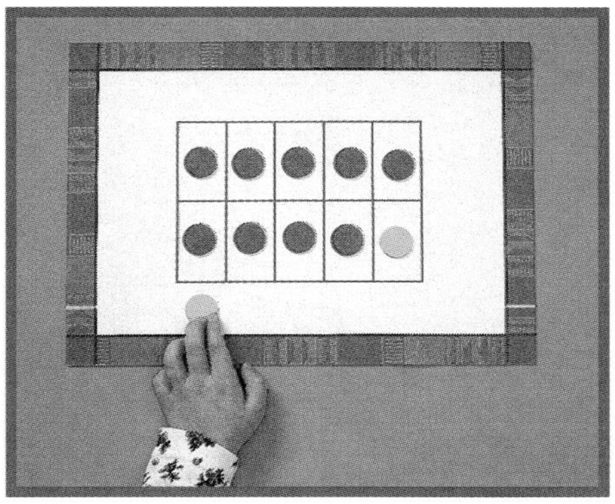

Spill 11 counters. Show on the ten-frame. Write the numbers.

Check

Use counters and ten-frame.
Spill and show ways to make 11. Record the ways.

1. 1 and 10 is 11.
2. ____ and ____ is ____.
3. ____ and ____ is ____.
4. ____ and ____ is ____.
5. ____ and ____ is ____.
6. ____ and ____ is ____.

Talk About It How does the ten-frame help you see 11 quickly?

Notes for Home: Your child used two-color counters and a ten-frame to find ways to make 11.
Home Activity: Use 11 pennies and have your child show you some ways to make 11.

Practice

Use counters and ten-frame.

Spill and show ways to make 12.

Record the ways.

7. 3 and 9 is 12.

8. ____ and ____ is ____.

9. ____ and ____ is ____.

10. ____ and ____ is ____.

11. ____ and ____ is ____.

12. ____ and ____ is ____.

13. ____ and ____ is ____.

14. ____ and ____ is ____.

15. ____ and ____ is ____.

16. ____ and ____ is ____.

Problem Solving Critical Thinking

17. Show 12 with 3 colors.

Use blue, yellow, red to record.

Write the numbers.

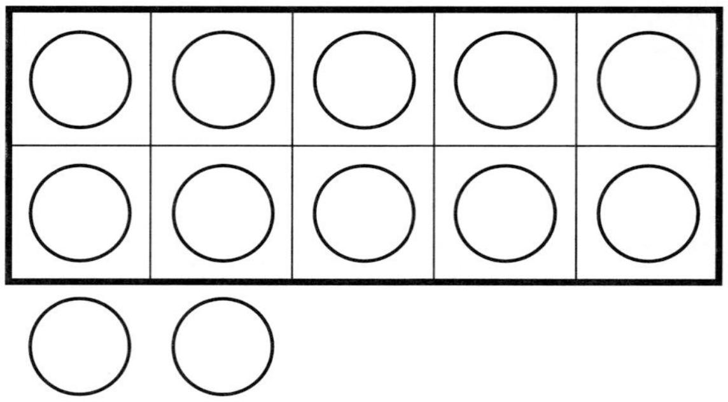

____ and ____ and ____ is ____.

Notes for Home: Your child used two-color counters and a ten-frame to find ways to make 12.
Home Activity: Ask your child to tell you about one way to make 12.

Name ______________________________

Find Missing Parts Through 7

Learn

7 in all.

Move 4.

How many were hidden?

There are 3 under the tub!

Check

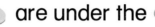

Use . How many  are under the  ?

1 5 in all

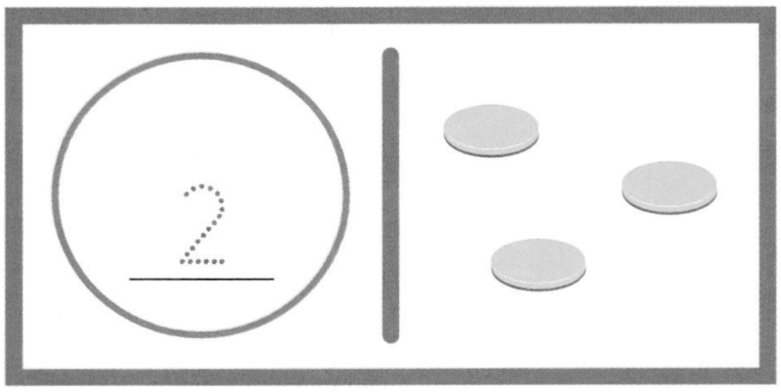

2 7 in all

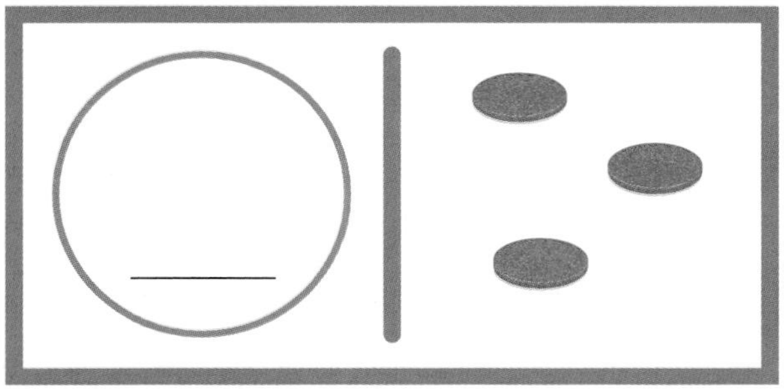

3 2 in all

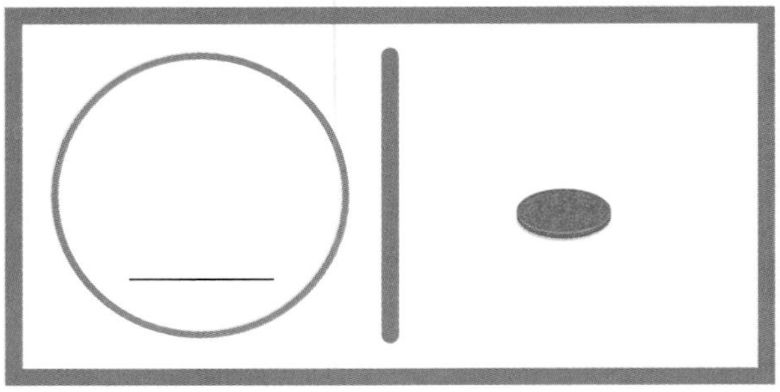

4 6 in all

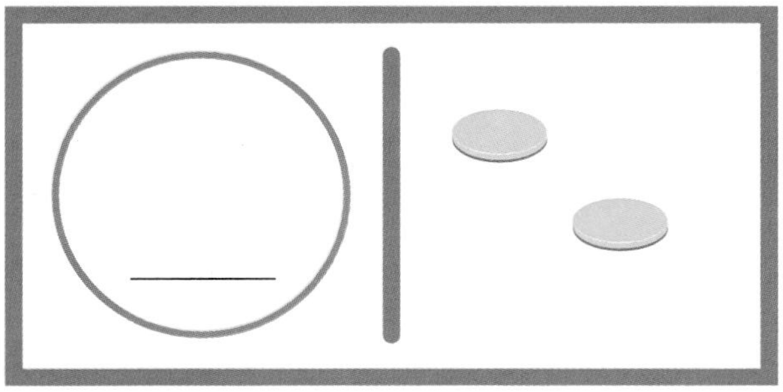

Talk About It How do you know how many  are hidden?

Notes for Home: Your child found how many counters were hidden. *Home Activity:* Secretly place 6 pennies in your hand, then remove 4 and show them to your child. Tell your child you have 6 pennies in all and ask how many are still hidden.

Practice

How many  are under the ?

5 6 in all

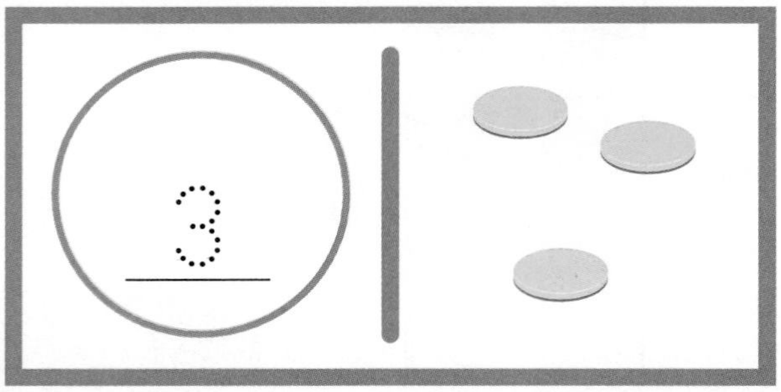

6 3 in all

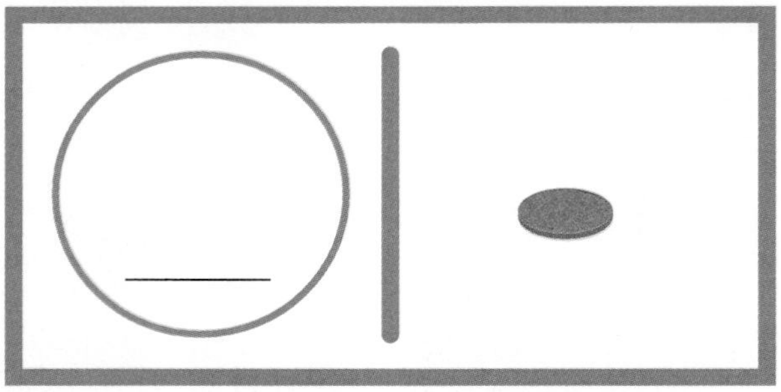

7 7 in all

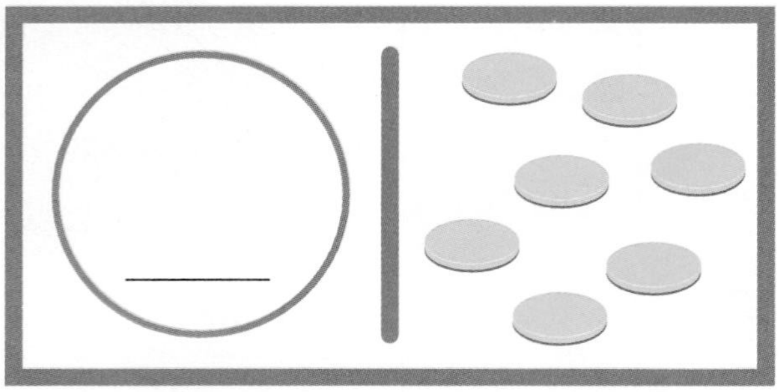

8 6 in all

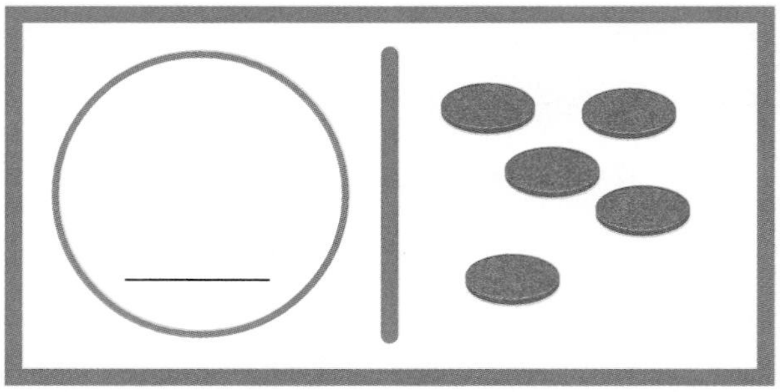

9 5 in all

10 7 in all

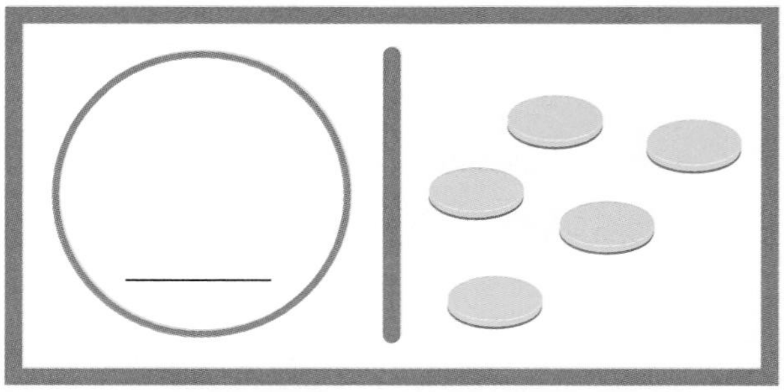

PRACTICE

Problem Solving Estimation

11 Work with a friend. Put some things in a .
Have your friend estimate how many.
Count them. Take turns.

Notes for Home: Your child practiced finding how many counters were hidden.
Home Activity: Take turns making up number stories about missing parts.

Name

Find Missing Parts Through 10

Learn

8 in all.

Move 4.

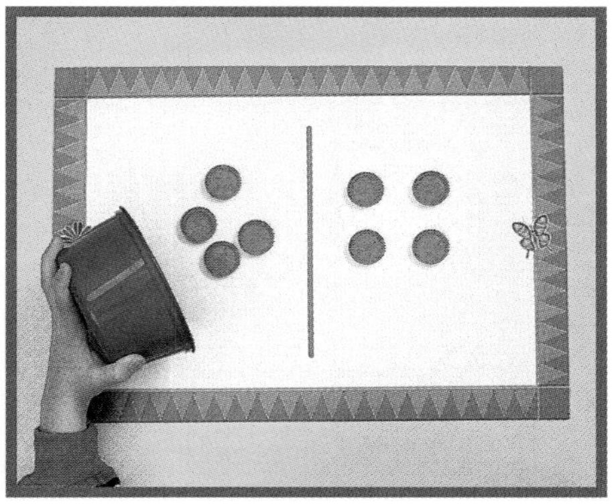

How many were hidden?

There are 4 under the tub!

Check

Use . How many are under the ?

1 8 in all

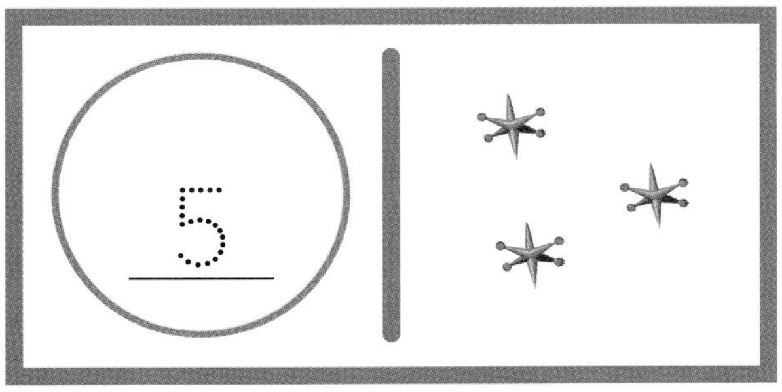
5

2 9 in all

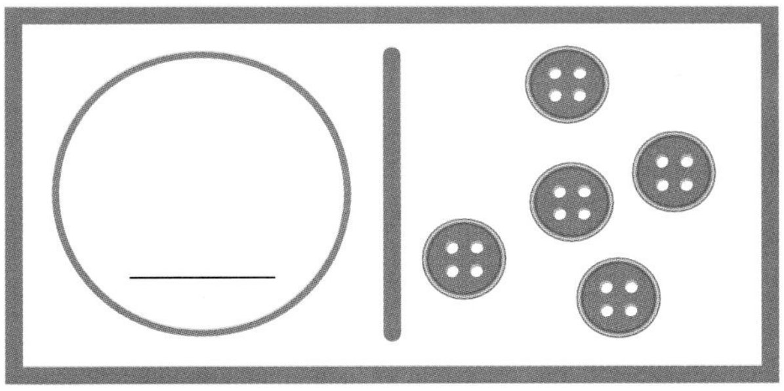

3 10 in all

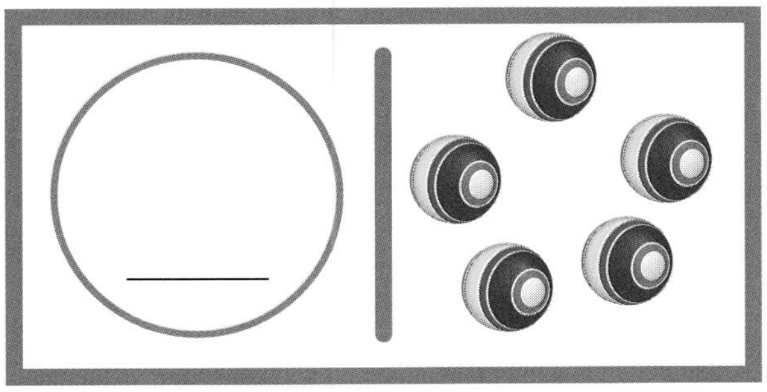

4 10 in all

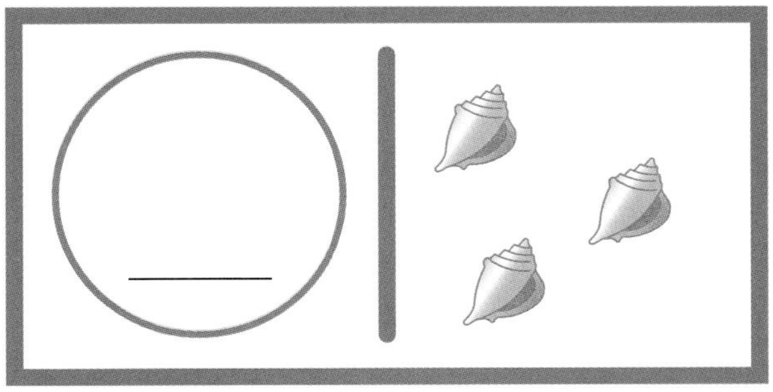

Talk About It How did you find how many are hidden?

Notes for Home: Your child found missing parts for numbers through 10. *Home Activity:* Hold up some fingers and ask your child how many fingers are still down.

Practice

How many things are under the ?

5 4 in all

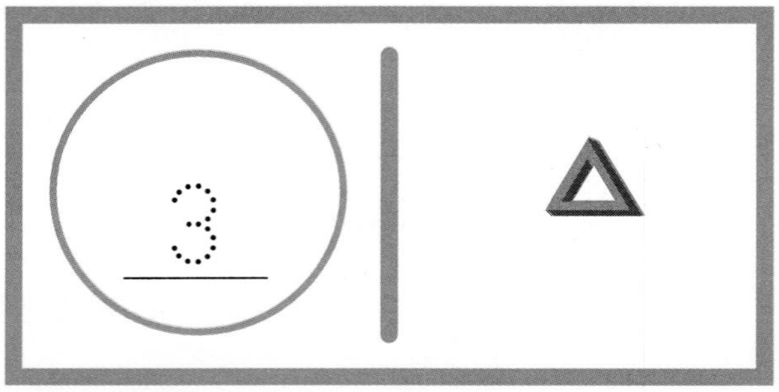

6 9 in all

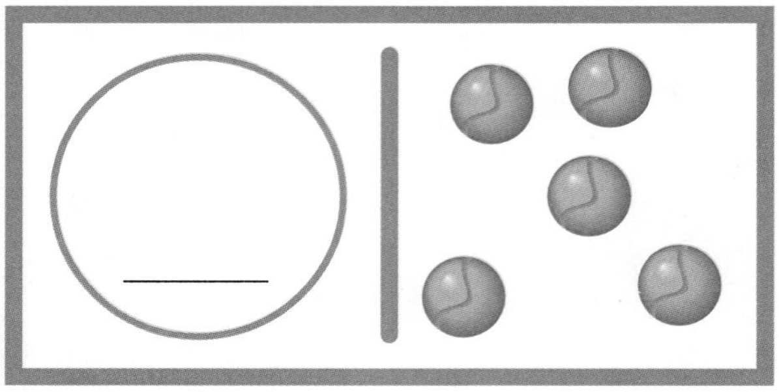

7 5 in all

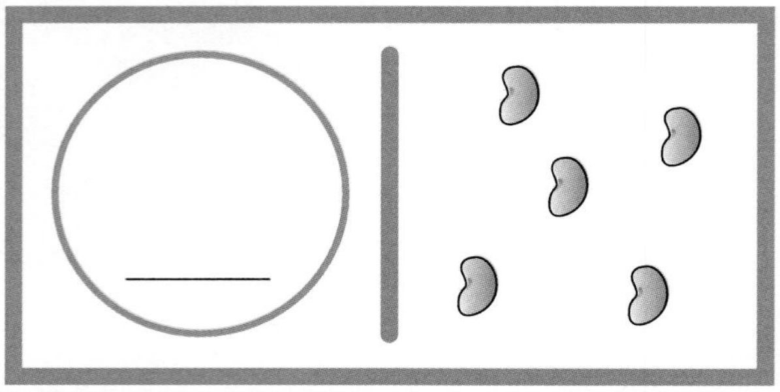

8 10 in all

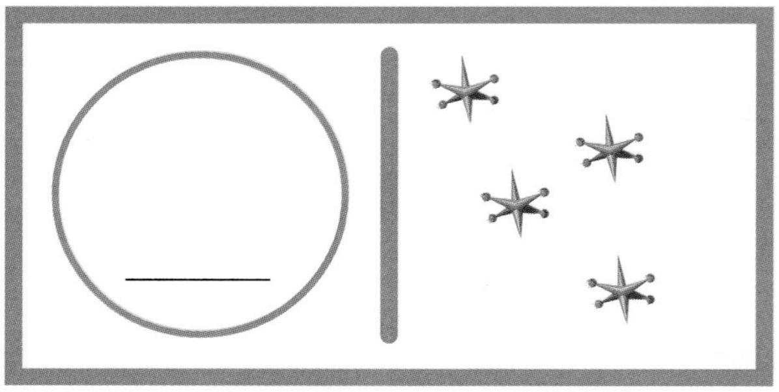

9 8 in all

10 10 in all

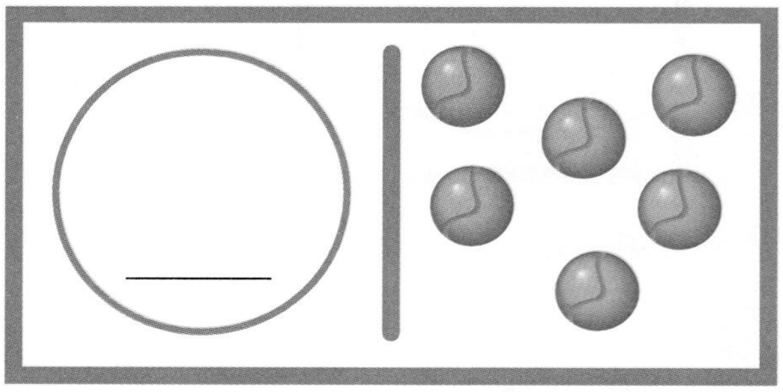

Write About It

11 Make up your own.
Have a friend solve it.

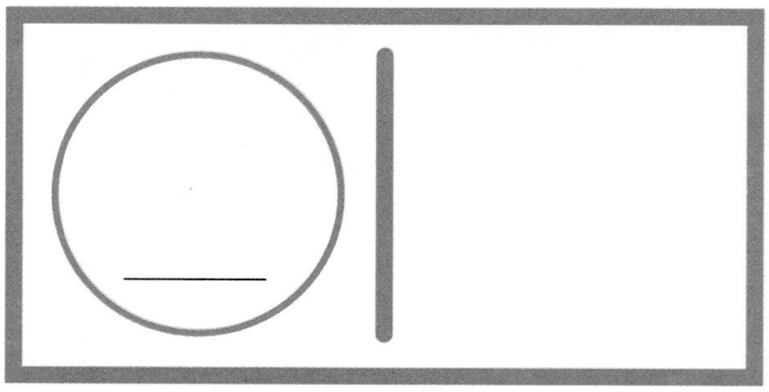

_____ in all

Notes for Home: Your child practiced finding the hidden counters. *Home Activity:* Have your child place 10 objects such as buttons under a container. Remove some and show them to your child. Then ask your child to tell how many buttons are still hidden under the container.

For additional practice, see Skills Practice Bank, page 526, Set 3.

Name ______________________

Reading for Math

Picture the Details

Nate went to the park. Nate had 3 red balloons.
Keesha went to the park too.
Nate gave Keesha a balloon.
Draw a picture that shows the story.

Circle the picture that answers the questions best.

1. What does Nate have at the end of the story?

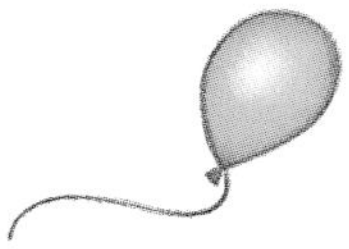

2. What does Keesha have?

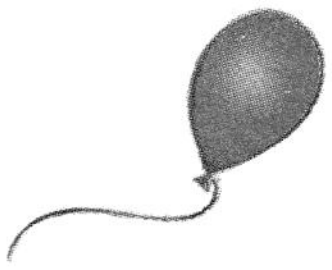
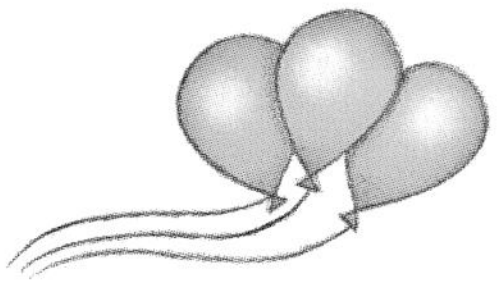

Talk About It Compare your picture with a friend's picture. How are your pictures the same? How are they different?

Notes for Home: Your child listened to a story and used pictures to answer questions about it. *Home Activity:* Read a story to your child and ask him or her to draw a picture that shows something that happens in the story.

Lamar and Eric like to play soccer.
Lamar has two soccer balls.
Eric has one yellow dog.
The dog plays with one ball.
The boys play with the other ball.
Draw a picture that shows the story.

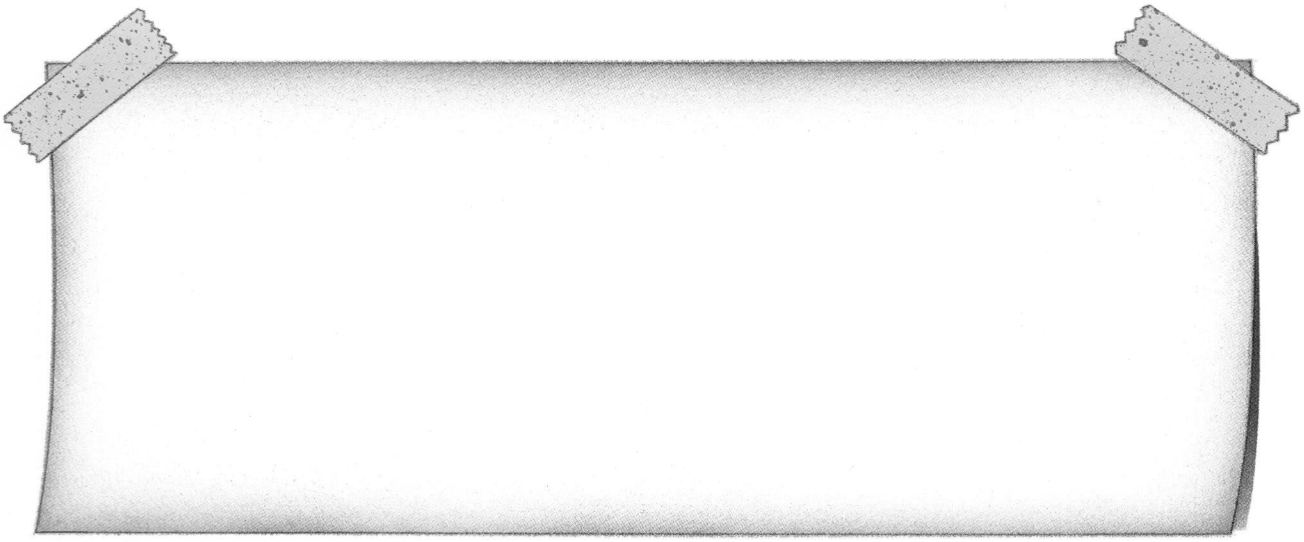

Circle the picture that answers the question the best.

3 What do Eric and Lamar like to play?

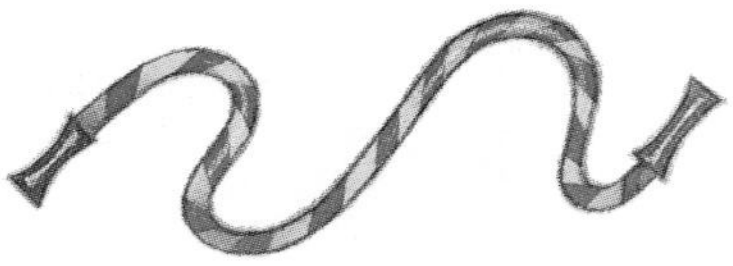  

4 How many soccer balls does Lamar have?

Journal

5 What game do you like to play?
Write a math story about your game.

Notes for Home: Your child pictured the details as he or she listened to a story and answered questions. *Home Activity:* Read a short story to your child and talk about what happens.

Name

Problem Solving: Draw a Picture

Learn

PROBLEM SOLVING GUIDE

Understand • Plan • Solve • Look Back

3 and 3 is 6.

Check

Draw a picture to show the problem. Write how many in all.

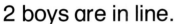

1. 4 boys are on the  .
   2 boys are in line.
   How many boys in all?

   4 and 2 is __6__.

2. Jane has 5  .

   Lin has 3  .

   How many  in all?

   5 and 3 is ____.

Talk About It Tell a math story about one of your pictures.

Notes for Home: Your child solved problems using the strategy Draw a Picture.
Home Activity: Ask your child to tell a story about one picture and tell how many in all.

Practice

Draw a picture to show the problem.
Write how many there are.

3. 3 children jumped rope.
   4 children played ball.
   How many children in all?

   3 and 4 is 7.

4. A boy had 3  .
   A girl had 1  .
   How many  in all?

   3 and 1 is _____.

5. 2 boys had red  .
   2 boys had blue  .
   How many boys in all?

   2 and 2 is _____.

Tell a Math Story

6. Draw a picture of something you like to do. Tell a math story about your picture.

Notes for Home: Your child used the strategy Draw a Picture to solve more problems.
Home Activity: Find pictures of children playing games in magazines or photo albums. Ask your child to tell a number story for each picture.

Name

Mixed Practice

Lessons 6–11

Concepts and Skills

1. Use .

Write how many. | Make a train with: | Write how many now.

_____ | I fewer | _____

Write the numbers.

2. 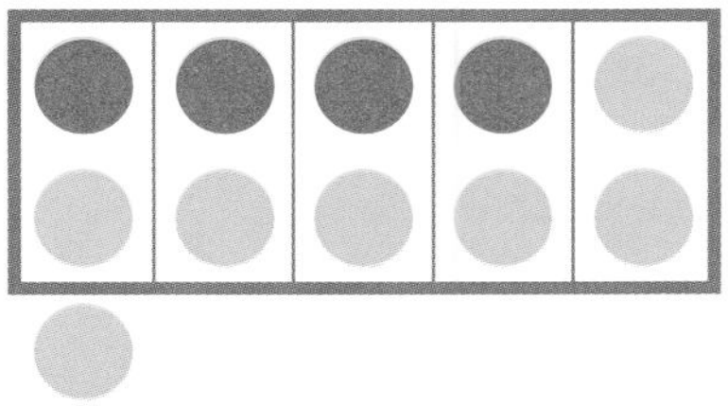

_____ and _____ is _____.

How many are under the ?

3. 6 in all

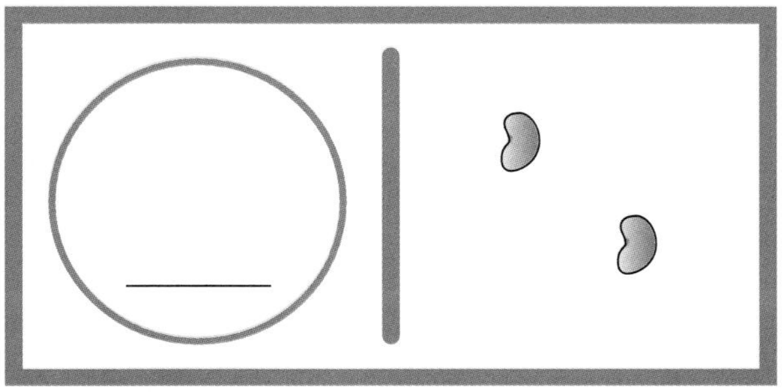

Problem Solving

4. Draw a picture to show the problem.

I girl played.
2 more girls came.
How many girls in all?

I and 2 is _____.

Journal

5. Draw a picture to show 4 and 5 is 9.

Notes for Home: Your child practiced writing number sentences, finding missing numbers, and drawing pictures to solve problems. *Home Activity:* Ask your child to tell you a story about the number sentence 3 and 8 is 11.

MIXED PRACTICE

Name ______________________________

Cumulative Review

Chapters 1–2

Concepts and Skills

Circle the one that belongs.

1 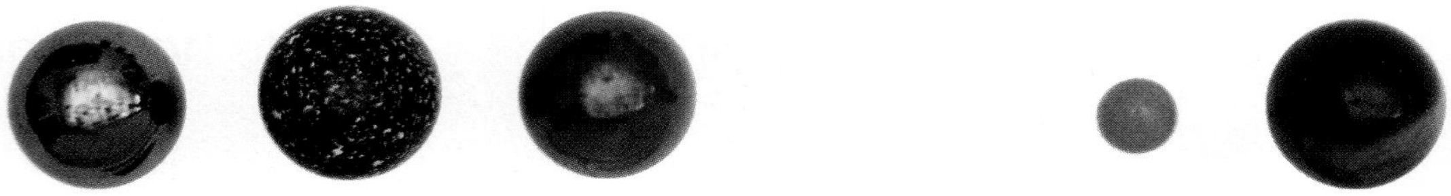

2 Draw the missing tower.
Write how many in each tower.

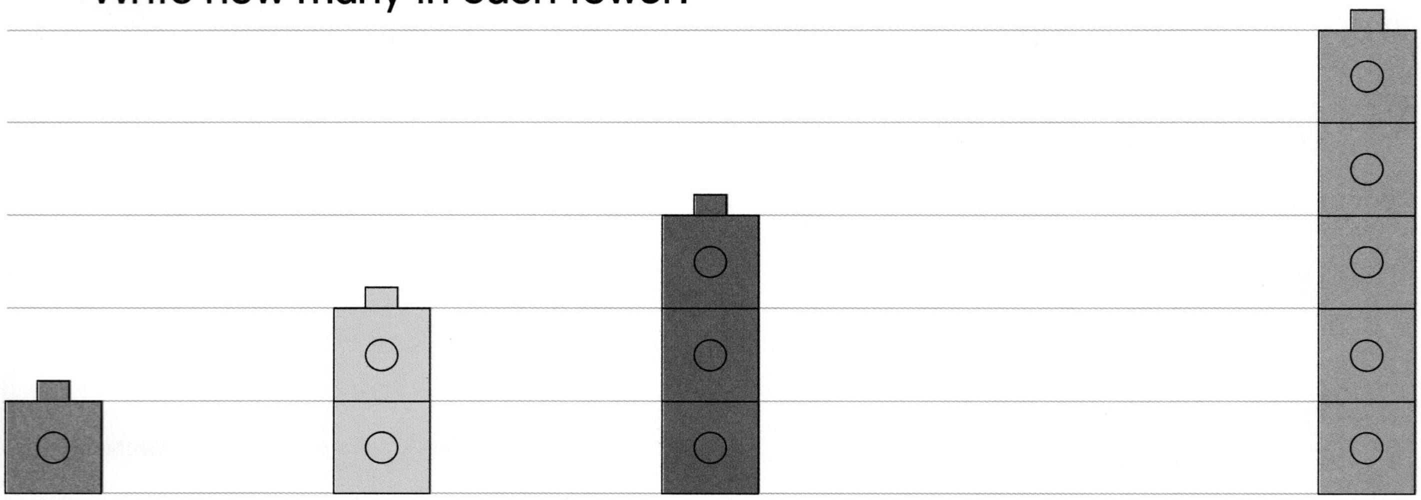

______ ______ ______ ______ ______

Test Prep

Fill in the ○ for the correct answer.

3 Use the graph.

How many ?

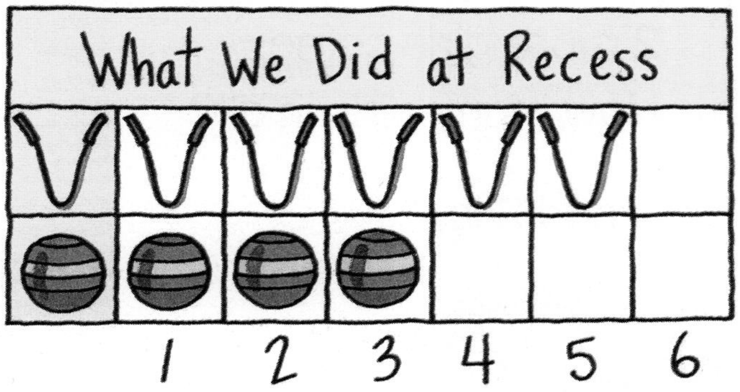

3	4	5	6
○	○	○	○

Notes for Home: Your child reviewed counting to 12 and reading a graph. *Home Activity:* Make up a What Belongs? game like Exercise 1 using coins or buttons.

Name ______________________________

Chapter 2 Review

Vocabulary

1 Make a train with 2 more.
Write how many. ____

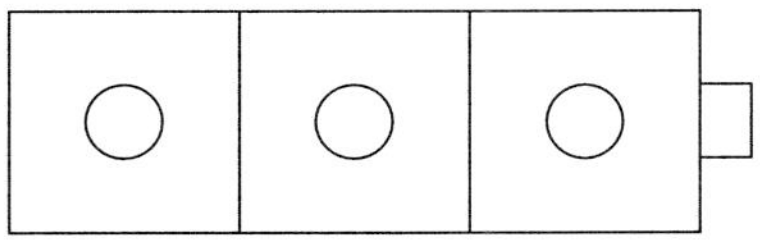

2 Circle odd or even.

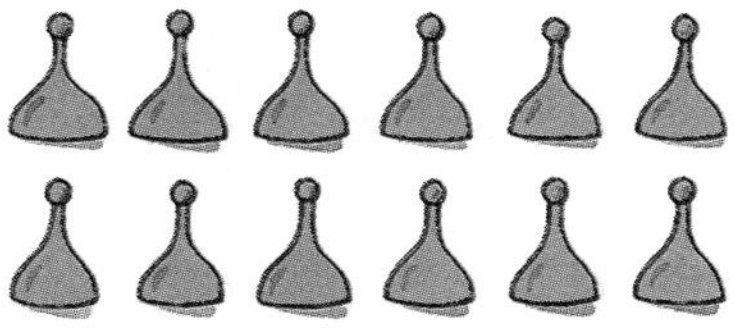

odd

even

Concepts and Skills

3 Write the numbers.

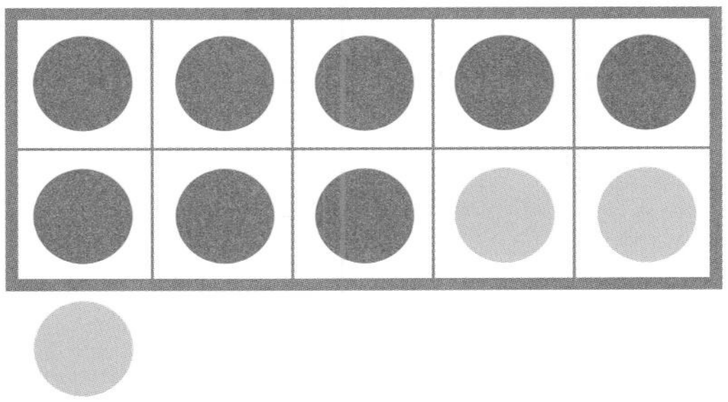

____ and ____ is ____.

4 How many under the ?

8 in all

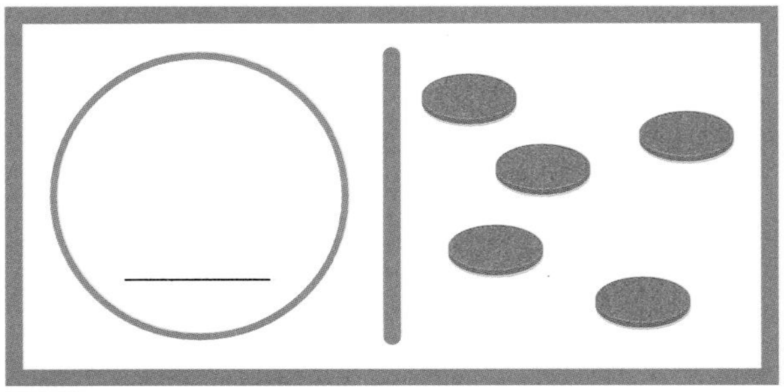

Problem Solving

5 How many ways can you put 3 into 2 ?

____ ways

Notes for Home: Your child reviewed the concepts taught in Chapter 2. *Home Activity:* Have your child use heads and tails of pennies to tell you a story for Exercise 4.

Name

Chapter 2 Test

1 Draw a picture to show the problem.

A girl had 2 cars. A boy had 3.

How many cars in all?

2 and 3 is ____

2 How many ways can you put 3 eggs into 2 baskets?

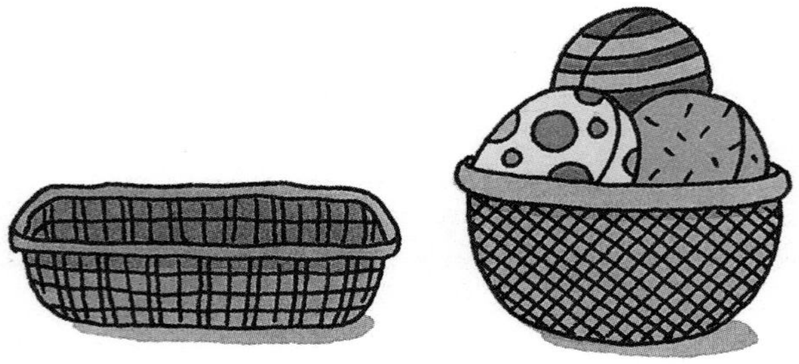

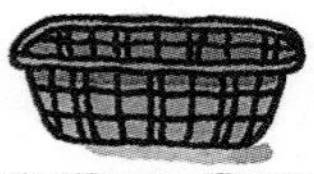	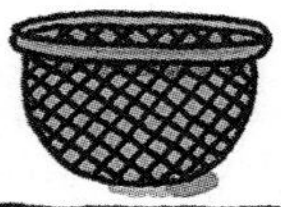	In All

There are ____ ways.

3 How many are under the bowl?

9 in all

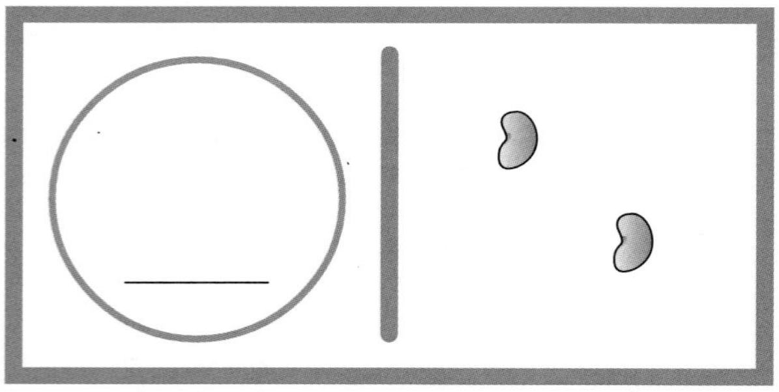

4 Make a train with 1 more. Write how many.

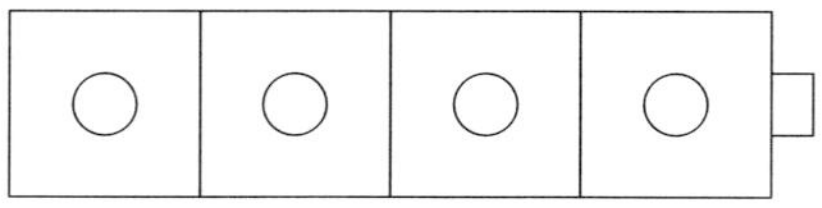 ____

5 Circle odd or even.

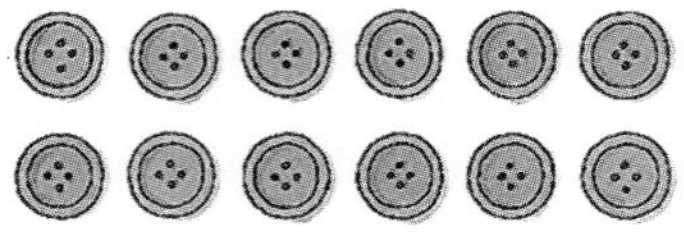

odd

even

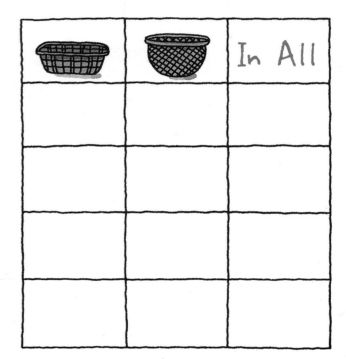

Notes for Home: Your child was assessed on Chapter 2 concepts, skills, and problem solving. *Home Activity:* Ask your child to count and combine groups of objects at home such as toys, blocks, or books.

Name ____

Performance Assessment

Chapter 2

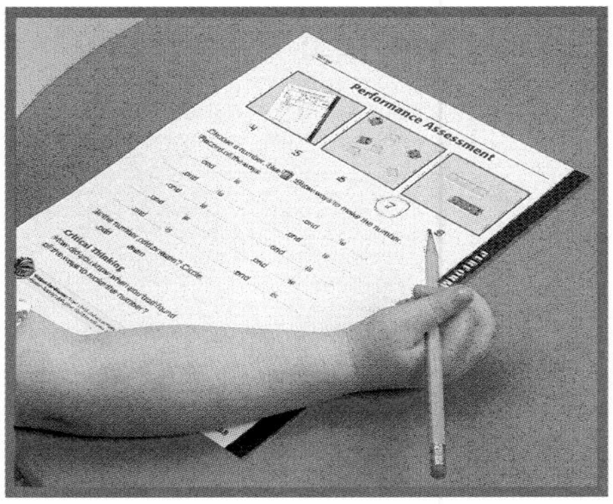

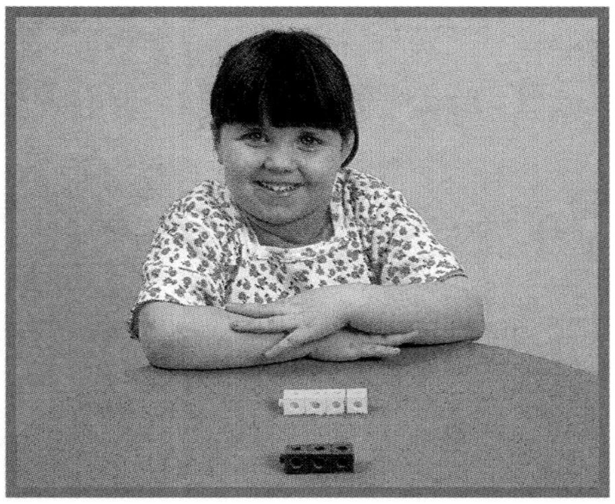

4 5 6 7 8

Choose a number.

Use cubes. Show ways to make the number.
Record all the ways.

1. _____ and _____ is _____.
2. _____ and _____ is _____.
3. _____ and _____ is _____.
4. _____ and _____ is _____.
5. _____ and _____ is _____.
6. _____ and _____ is _____.
7. _____ and _____ is _____.
8. _____ and _____ is _____.
9. _____ and _____ is _____.
10. _____ and _____ is _____.
11. Is the number odd or even? Circle.

odd **even**

Problem Solving Critical Thinking

12. How did you know when you had found all the ways to make the number?

Notes for Home: Your child did an activity to assess understanding of Chapter 2 skills and concepts. *Home Activity:* Ask your child to tell you about the number shown above.

Name ______________________________

Explore the World Wide Web

Computer Skills You Will Need [Use a mouse.]

You can use the Internet to find information. You can find information about these things and much more!

yourself	animals
other children	places

Make a list of 3 things you would like to find out about.

1. ______________________________
2. ______________________________
3. ______________________________

Go to [www.mathsurf.com/1]. **Click** on Chapter 2.

Click the [Forward] and [Backward] to see more.
Did you find some information you wanted?
Write about it.

____

____

Tech Talk What happens when you click [Forward]?

What happens when you click [Backward]?

Visit our Web site. www.parent.mathsurf.com

Name Your Game

Ask your family and friends what games they like to play. Draw a picture or write the name of the game at the bottom of the graph. Each person who likes that game can color in a box on the graph.

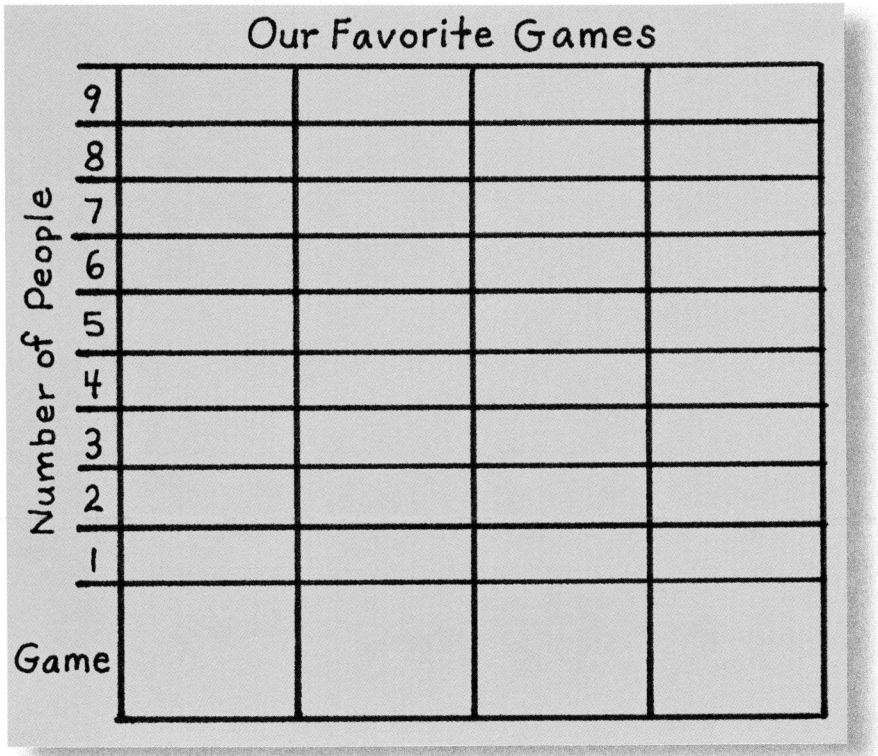

Fold down

MathSoup

Scott Foresman - Addison Wesley My Math Magazine No. 2

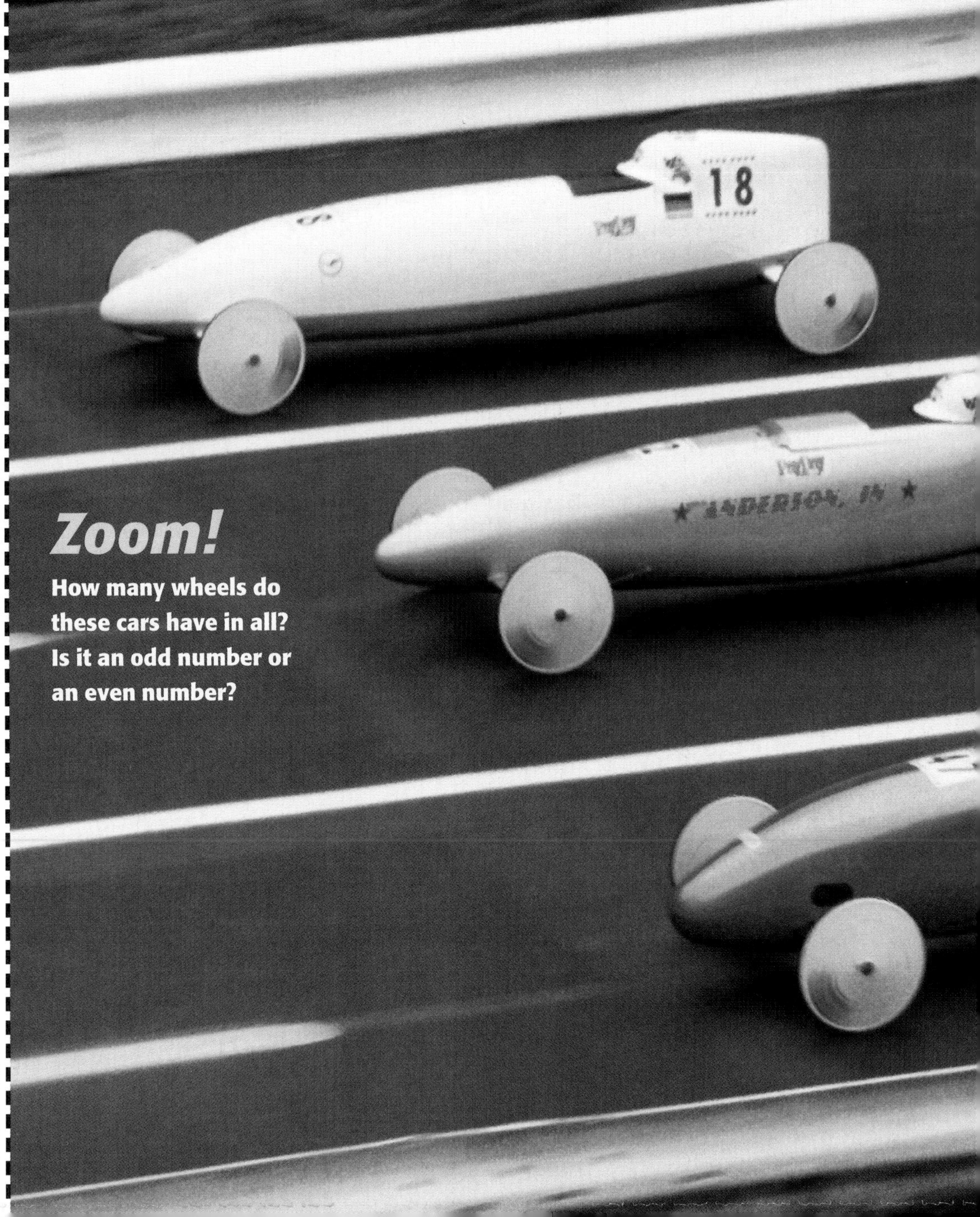

Zoom!

How many wheels do these cars have in all? Is it an odd number or an even number?

Soap Box Search

Help the drivers get ready for the big race!

1 Find Cheryl's jacket.

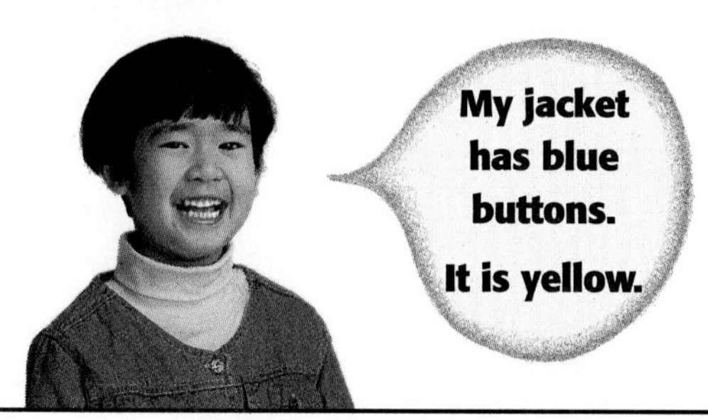
My jacket has blue buttons.
It is yellow.

2 Find Amir's helmet.

My helmet has a number more than 5.
The number is odd.
My helmet is green.

7
2
5
3

3 Find Shannon's race car.

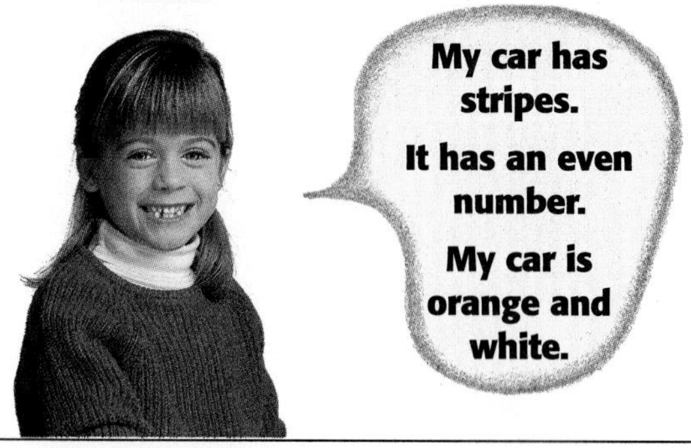
My car has stripes.
It has an even number.
My car is orange and white.

11
3
6
7

Notes for Home: Your child solved puzzles using logic.
Home Activity: Ask your child to explain how to solve each puzzle.

This One is Fun!

Write the numbers to finish the rhymes.
Use the picture for help.

1 All the children like to skate.

5 and 3 is always ______ .

2 The hoop is up above the door.

9 is the same as ______ and ______ .

3 Swimming in the pool is fun.

6 is the same as ______ and ______ .

Notes for Home: Your child completed poems by using rhyming numbers. *Home Activity*: Ask your child to show you the words that rhyme in each poem.

Pairs of Fun

Circle the two groups that are the same.

1

2

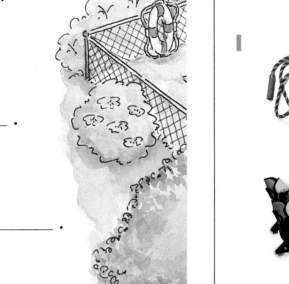

Lay Down Tracks

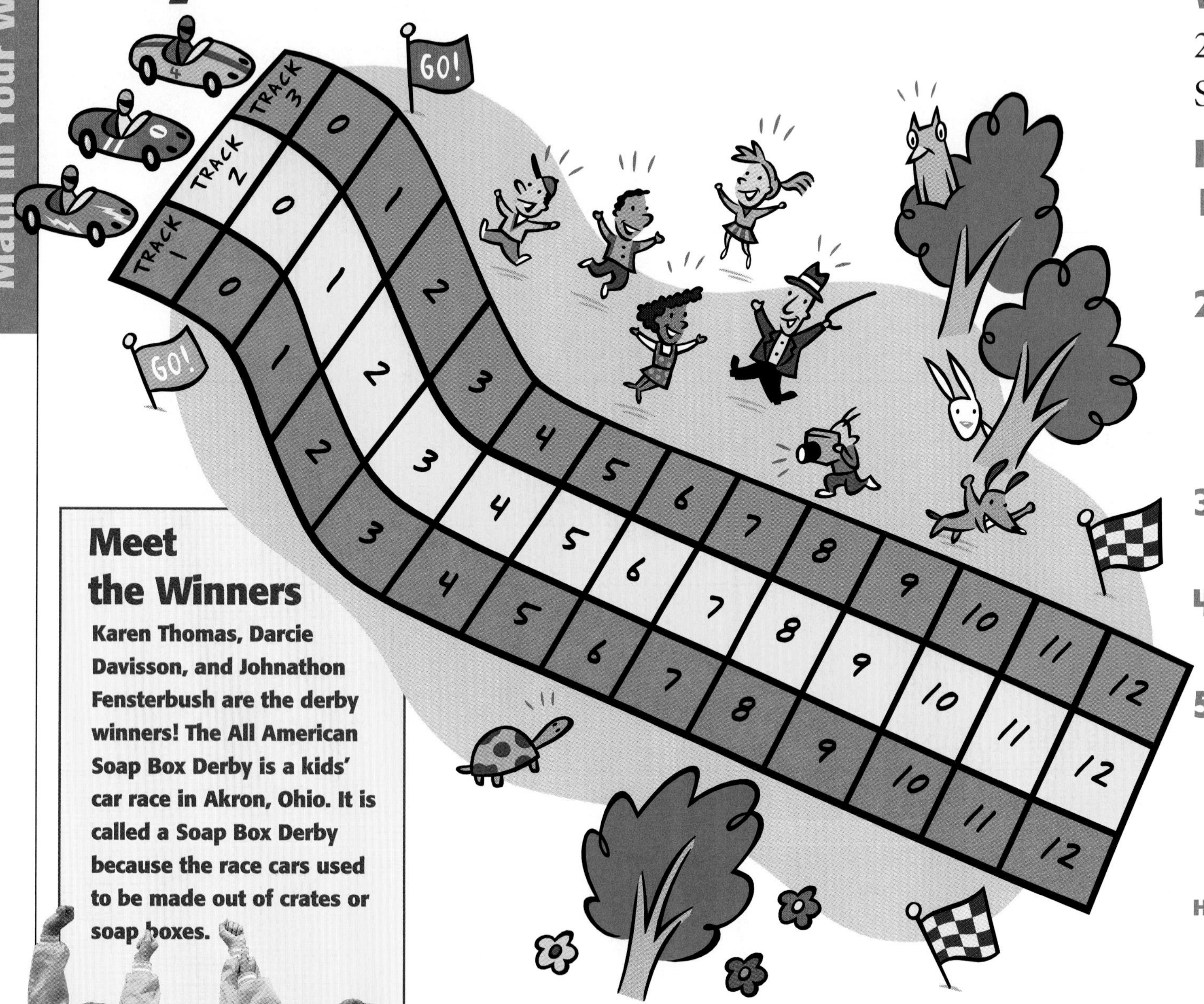

Players 2 or 3

What You Need

2 dot cubes

Small game markers

How to Play

1 Take turns rolling the cubes. Count the dots.

2 Put game markers on the number you rolled or any two numbers that show a way to make the number.

3 If a number is covered, you cannot use it again.

4 If you cannot find a way to make the number, you are out.

5 When all players are out, count one point for each square that is not covered. Player with the lowest score wins.

Hint: Try to cover the big numbers first.

Meet the Winners

Karen Thomas, Darcie Davisson, and Johnathon Fensterbush are the derby winners! The All American Soap Box Derby is a kids' car race in Akron, Ohio. It is called a Soap Box Derby because the race cars used to be made out of crates or soap boxes.

Notes for Home: Your child played a game using different ways to make numbers. *Home Activity:* Play the game with your child.

CHAPTER

3 Addition and Subtraction Concepts

Coming and Going

Tell math stories about coming and going.

Notes for Home: Your child discussed the movement in the picture as groups of people and objects joining or separating. *Home Activity:* Ask your child to tell you a math story about some part of the picture.

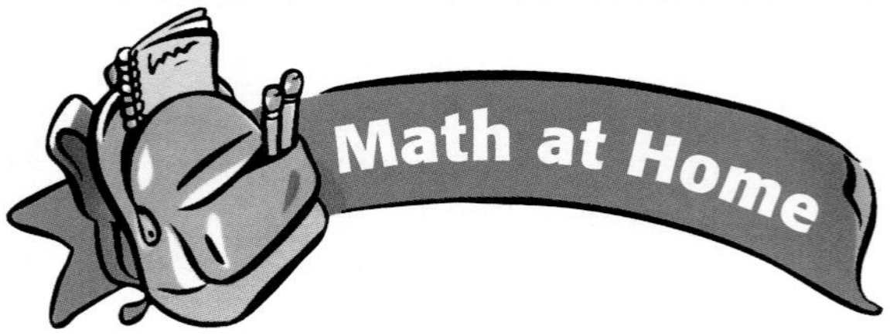

Dear Family,
Our class is starting Chapter 3. We will learn more about adding and subtracting. We will add numbers with sums (totals) to 12. We will subtract from numbers up to 12. Here are some activities we can do together.

Number Detective
Play an addition and subtraction game with household objects such as pasta, buttons, or pennies. Separate 12 objects into two groups and ask your child to tell how many there are all together. Then take away one group and ask your child to tell how many are left.

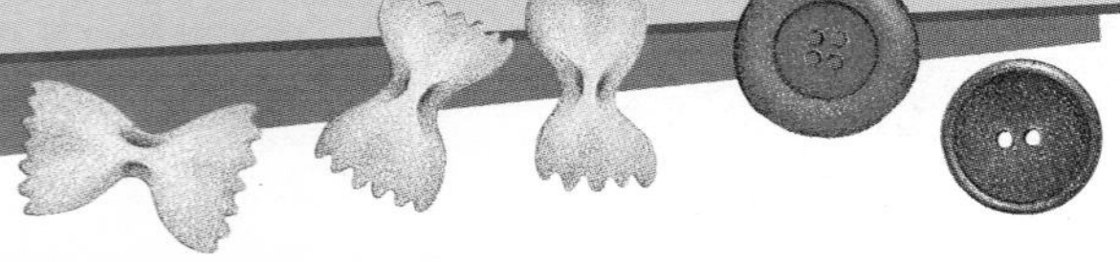

Numbers for Lunch
Make up simple addition and subtraction stories at mealtime. For instance, I had 5 crackers. I ate 2. How many do I have left?

Community Connection

When you take your child to the grocery store, look for ways to show addition and subtraction. For example: We put 6 bananas in the cart. Now we put in 2 oranges. How many pieces of fruit in all?

Visit our Web site. www.parent.mathsurf.com

Name

Explore Addition

Explore

Use  to show children.
Make up math stories about coming to school.

Share

Tell your math story.

Notes for Home: Your child explored addition by using counters to tell math stories.
Home Activity: Ask your child to tell you a math story using buttons or beans as counters.

Connect

Solve each problem.
You can use  .

1. There are 2  .
   7 more  come.
   How many in all?
   2 and 7 is 9.

2. 3  are in the lot.
   5 more  come.
   How many in all?
   _____ and _____ is _____.

3. There are 7  .
   There are 4  .
   How many in all?
   _____ and _____ is _____.

4. There are 6 boys and 4 girls.
   How many children in all?
   _____ and _____ is _____.

EXPLORE

Problem Solving Visual Thinking

5. Tell a math story about the picture.

Notes for Home: Today your child solved addition problems. *Home Activity:* Ask your child to tell you how to solve Exercise 2.

Name _____

Learn •

part		part		in all
2	and	5	is	7.
2	plus	5	equals	7.
2	+	5	=	7

2 + 5 = 7
is called a
number sentence.
I can write it as
7 = 2 + 5, too!

Check •

You can use and ☐. Make two parts.
Write the number sentence.

1 $\underline{3} + \underline{5} = \underline{8}$

2 $\underline{} + \underline{} = \underline{}$

3 $\underline{} + \underline{} = \underline{}$

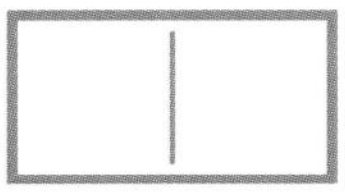

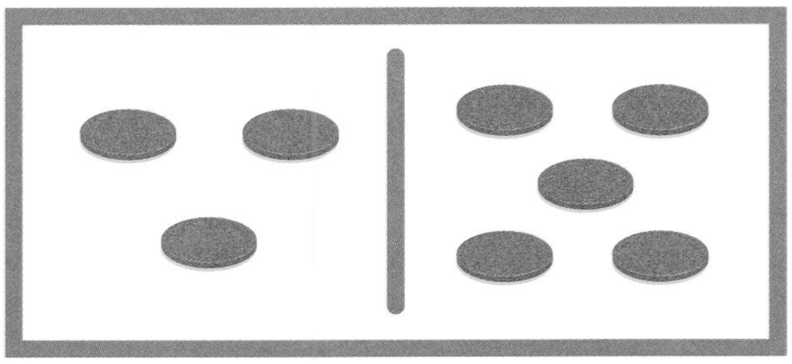

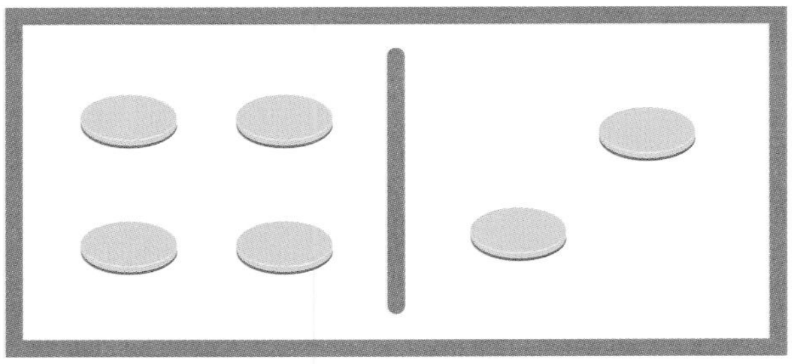

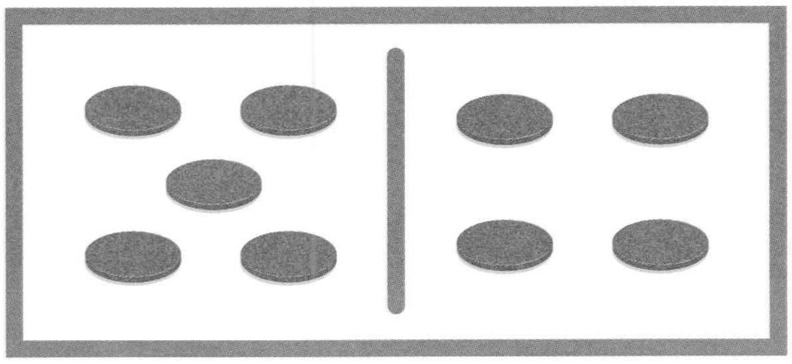

Talk About It Tell another way to make 9.

Write a number sentence.

Notes from Home: Your child learned about the plus sign (+) and the equal sign (=).
Home Activity: Ask your child to tell what each sign means.

Practice

You can use [counters] and [part-part mat]. Show the parts.
Write the number sentence.

4
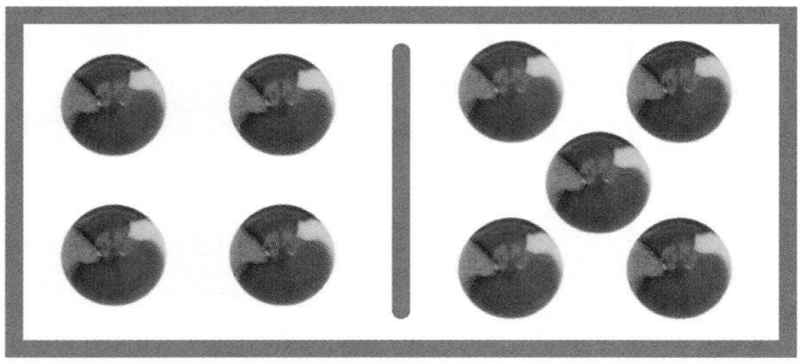

4 + 5 = 9

5
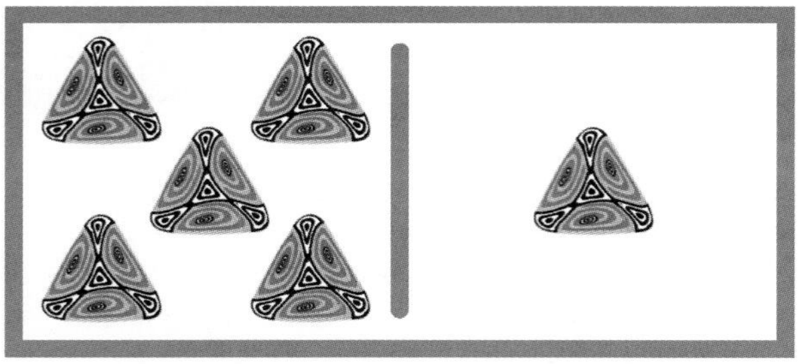

____ + ____ = ____

6
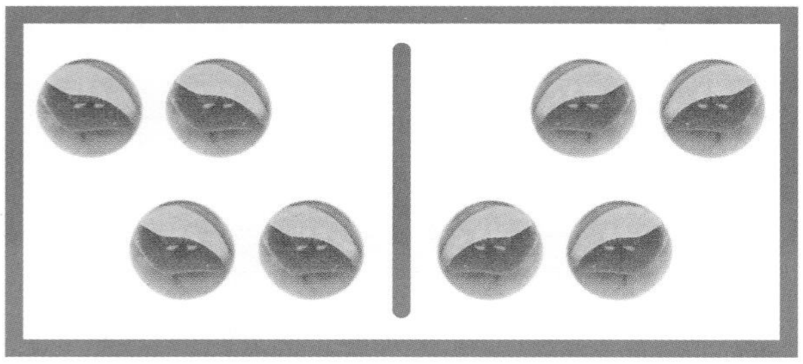

____ + ____ = ____

7

____ + ____ = ____

8
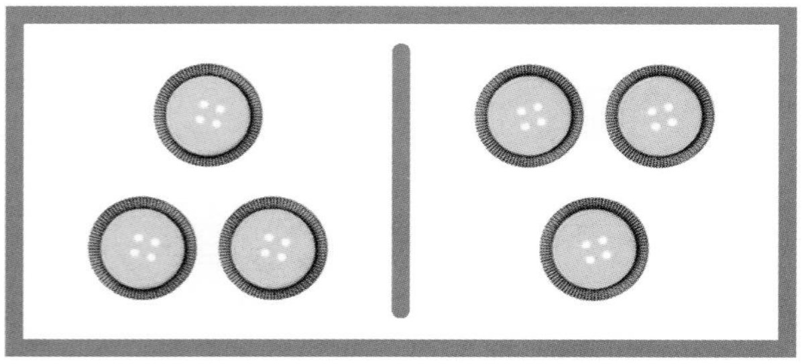

____ + ____ = ____

PRACTICE

Tell a Math Story

9 Tell a math story to a friend. Your friend can show it with [counters].

Notes for Home: Your child used counters and wrote number sentences to show addition.
Home Activity: Ask your child to tell you a math story for one of the exercises.

Name

Problem Solving: Use Addition

Learn

PROBLEM SOLVING GUIDE

Understand • Plan • Solve • Look Back

There are

3 and

4 .

How many in all?

Read.

Show.

3 + 4 = 7

7 in all

Write.

Check

Use to show the story.

Write a number sentence. Write how many in all.

1. There are
3 and 2 .
How many in all?

3 + 2 = 5

5 in all

2. There are 7 .
4 more come.
How many now?

___ + ___ = ___

___

3. There are
4 and 6 .
How many in all?

___ + ___ = ___

___ in all

Talk About It Tell a math story. Say the number sentence.

Notes for Home: Your child read math stories and wrote the number sentences to answer the questions. *Home Activity:* Ask your child to read one of the exercises and tell how to solve it.

PROBLEM SOLVING

Practice

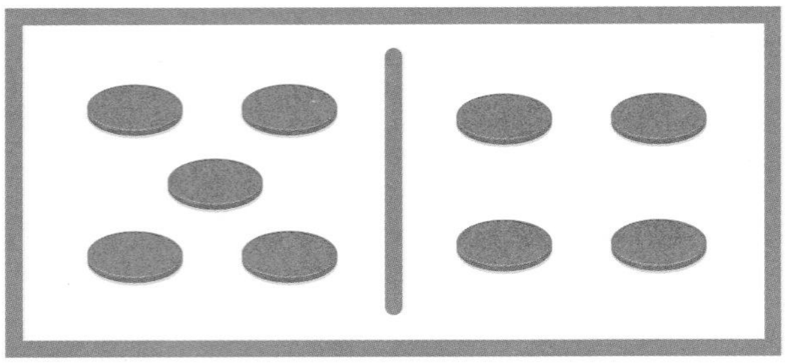

Use  to show the story.
Write a number sentence.
Write how many in all.

4. There are 5 .
   4 more  come.
   How many now?

   5 + 4 = 9

   9 

5. There are 4 
   and 2 .
   How many in all?

   ___ + ___ = ___

   ___ in all

6. There are 4 
   and 4 .
   How many in all?

   ___ + ___ = ___

   ___ in all

7. There are 2 .
   7 more  come.
   How many now?

   ___ + ___ = ___

   ___ 

Critical Thinking

8. Write a number sentence to go with the picture.

   ___ + ___ = ___

   ___ in all

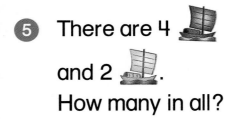

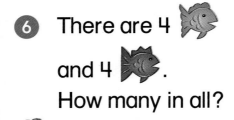

Notes for Home: Your child wrote number sentences to solve problems. *Home Activity:* Tell your child a math story with a sum up to 12, and ask your child to write a number sentence for the story.

Name ____________________

Addition Sentences to 12

Learn

3

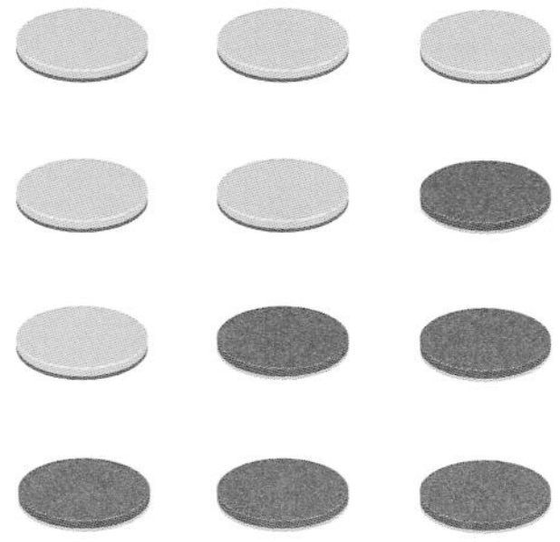

3 + 0 = 3

2 + 1 = 3

1 + 2 = 3

0 + 3 = 3

You can make 3 in many ways.

Check

Use counters. Show some ways to make each number.
Write the number sentences.

1 8

3 + 5 = 8

___ + ___ = ___

___ + ___ = ___

2 6

___ + ___ = ___

___ + ___ = ___

___ + ___ = ___

3 5

___ + ___ = ___

___ + ___ = ___

___ + ___ = ___

4 10

___ + ___ = ___

___ + ___ = ___

___ + ___ = ___

Talk About It Share your sentences for 6 with a friend.
Can you find more than 3 ways to make 6?

Notes for Home: Your child used counters to find different number sentences for the same number.
Home Activity: Ask your child for a way to make 5 (3+2).

Practice

Use .

Show some ways to make each number.

Write the number sentences.

5. **7**

2 + 5 = 7

___ + ___ = ___

___ + ___ = ___

6. **12**

___ + ___ = ___

___ + ___ = ___

___ + ___ = ___

7. **11**

___ + ___ = ___

___ + ___ = ___

___ + ___ = ___

8. **9**

___ + ___ = ___

___ + ___ = ___

___ + ___ = ___

PRACTICE

Problem Solving Visual Thinking

9. Draw boxes to make 4.
Complete the number sentences.

Notes for Home: Your child used counters to continue writing addition sentences. *Home Activity:* Ask your child to use objects such as buttons to show more ways to make 12, for example, 7 + 5, 6 + 6, 9 + 3, and 8 + 4.

Name ______________________________

Add in Vertical Form

Learn

Here are 2 ways to show addition.

2 + 4 = 6 (sum)

$$\begin{array}{r} 2 \\ +\ 4 \\ \hline 6 \end{array}$$ (sum)

I get it!
The sum is the
same both ways!

Check

Write the sum.

1

2 + 3 = 5

$$\begin{array}{r} 2 \\ +\ 3 \\ \hline 5 \end{array}$$

2

2 + 2 = ____

$$\begin{array}{r} 2 \\ +\ 2 \\ \hline \end{array}$$

3

3 + 3 = ____

$$\begin{array}{r} 3 \\ +\ 3 \\ \hline \end{array}$$

4

4 + 1 = ____

$$\begin{array}{r} 4 \\ +\ 1 \\ \hline \end{array}$$

5

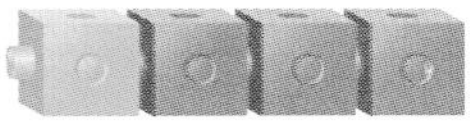

1 + 3 = ____

$$\begin{array}{r} 1 \\ +\ 3 \\ \hline \end{array}$$

6

2 + 1 = ____

$$\begin{array}{r} 2 \\ +\ 1 \\ \hline \end{array}$$

Talk About It Why is the sum the same both ways?

Notes for Home: Your child learned that addition can be shown both horizontally and vertically. *Home Activity*: Ask your child to make up more addition problems and show them both ways.

Write the sums.
You can use .

7

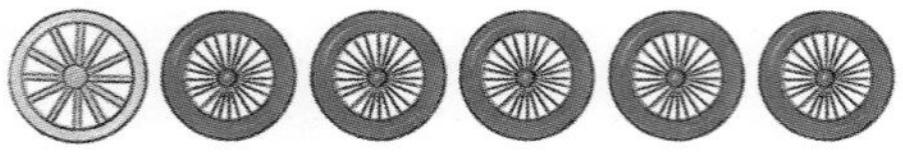

$1 + 5 = \underline{6}$

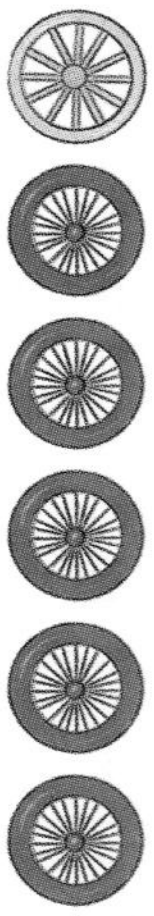

$\begin{array}{r} 1 \\ + 5 \\ \hline \end{array}$

8 $3 + 6 = \underline{}$ $\qquad \begin{array}{r} 3 \\ + 6 \\ \hline \end{array}$

9 $8 + 2 = \underline{}$ $\qquad \begin{array}{r} 8 \\ + 2 \\ \hline \end{array}$

10 $4 + 7 = \underline{}$ $\qquad \begin{array}{r} 4 \\ + 7 \\ \hline \end{array}$

11 $9 + 0 = \underline{}$ $\qquad \begin{array}{r} 9 \\ + 0 \\ \hline \end{array}$

12
$\begin{array}{r} 1 \\ + 9 \\ \hline \end{array}$
$\begin{array}{r} 3 \\ + 5 \\ \hline \end{array}$
$\begin{array}{r} 1 \\ + 4 \\ \hline \end{array}$
$\begin{array}{r} 2 \\ + 6 \\ \hline \end{array}$
$\begin{array}{r} 8 \\ + 1 \\ \hline \end{array}$
$\begin{array}{r} 4 \\ + 6 \\ \hline \end{array}$
$\begin{array}{r} 2 \\ + 3 \\ \hline \end{array}$

Problem Solving

Solve each problem.

13 There are 6 🛷.

5 more 🛷 come.

How many now?

$\begin{array}{r} \square \\ + \square \\ \hline \square \end{array}$

14 There are 2 🚲

and 5 🚲.

How many in all?

$\begin{array}{r} \square \\ + \square \\ \hline \square \end{array}$

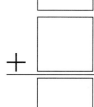

 Notes for Home: Your child solved addition problems that were shown both horizontally and vertically. *Home Activity:* Point to any problem on this page and ask your child to tell you how to find the sum.

For additional practice, see Skills Practice Bank, page 527, Set 1.

Name ______________________________

Reading for Math

Sequencing

A math story has a beginning, a middle and an end.
Read a math story.

There are 6 .

3 more  come.
How many are there now?

1 Draw pictures to show what happens in the beginning, middle, and end.

Beginning

There are 6 .

Middle

3 more  come.

End

How many are there now?

Talk About It Tell a math story to your partner. How does your story begin? What happens in the middle? How does it end?

Notes for Home: Your child sequenced events in a math story to help solve a problem.
Home Activity: Ask your child to tell about the beginning, the middle , and the end of the math story.

Read the math story.

8  go up.

4  go up with them.

How many go up in all?

❷ Draw pictures to show the math story.

Beginning

Middle

End

Notes for Home: Your child sequenced events in a math story to help solve a problem.
Home Activity: Ask your child to tell you a new math story. Talk about what happens in the beginning, middle, and end.

Name

Problem Solving: Draw a Picture

Learn

PROBLEM SOLVING GUIDE

Understand • Plan • Solve • Look Back

Luz and Tom drew pictures
to show the math story.
They wrote a number sentence
for the story.

There are 6 cars.

5 more cars come.

How many are there now?

6 + 5 = 11 cars

Check

Draw a picture to show the story.
Write a number sentence.

1. There are 6 trucks.

   4 more trucks come.

   How many are there now?

   ____ + ____ = ____ trucks

Talk About It What did you draw? Why?

Notes for Home: Your child solved addition problems using the strategy "Draw a Picture."
Home Activity: Ask your child to talk about the number of objects he or she drew for the problem.

Practice

Draw a picture to show the story.
Write a number sentence.

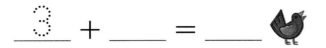

2. 3  fly.

   5 more  fly with them.
   How many fly in all?

   3 + ____ = ____ 

3. There are 2 .

   3 more  come.
   How many are there now?

   ____ + ____ = ____ 

 **Write your own** numbers.

4. ____  are in a tree.

   ____  are on the ground.
   How many are there?

   ____ ◯ ____ = ____ 

Journal 

5. How does drawing a picture help solve a problem?

Notes for Home: Your child solved addition problems by drawing pictures. *Home Activity*: Ask your child to tell you how drawing a picture can help solve a problem.

PROBLEM SOLVING

Name

Mixed Practice

Lessons 1–6

Concepts and Skills

Write a number sentence.

1. 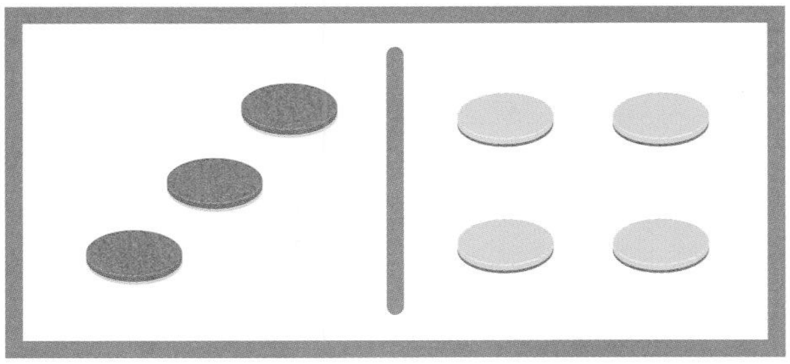

____ + ____ = ____

2. 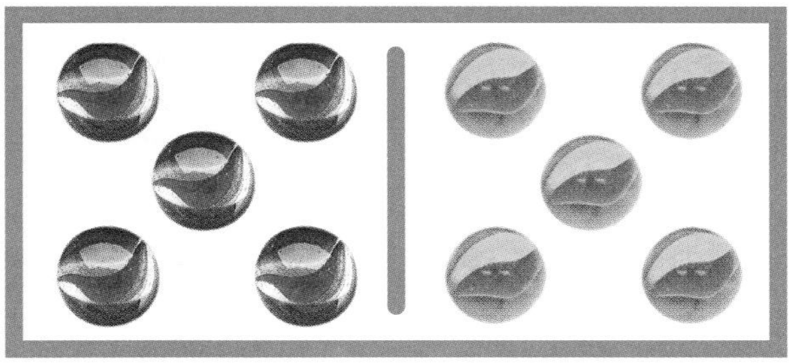

____ + ____ = ____

Write the sum. You can use .

3.

7	8	2	4	0	3	2
+ 3	+ 4	+ 6	+ 1	+ 7	+ 3	+ 4

Problem Solving

Use or draw a picture.

Write a number sentence.

4. 4 play.

2 more come.

How many are there now? ____ + ____ = ____

Journal

5. Draw a picture to show a math story.

Write the number sentence.

Notes for Home: Your child practiced addition for sums through 12. *Home Activity:* Ask your child to tell you how to add vertically.

Name ______________________________

Cumulative Review

Chapters 1–3

Concepts and Skills

How many  are under the  ?

1 10 in all

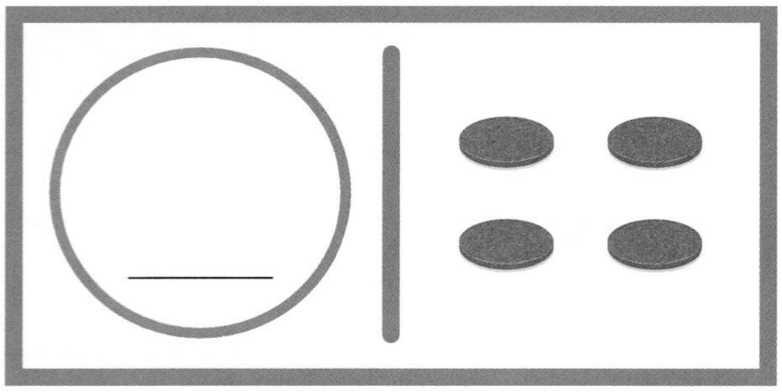

2 8 in all

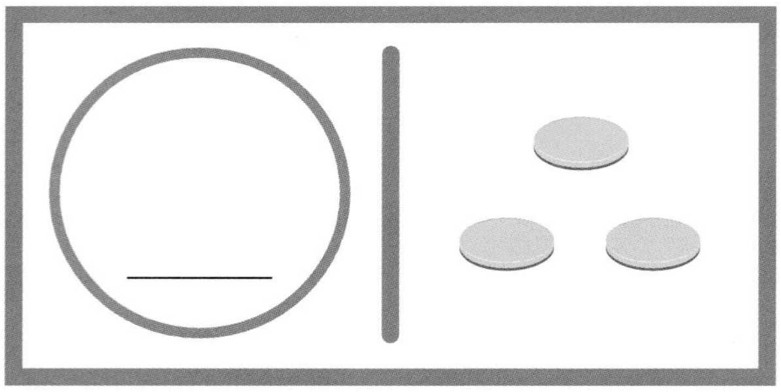

Look at the pattern.
Draw the next two shapes.

3 

4 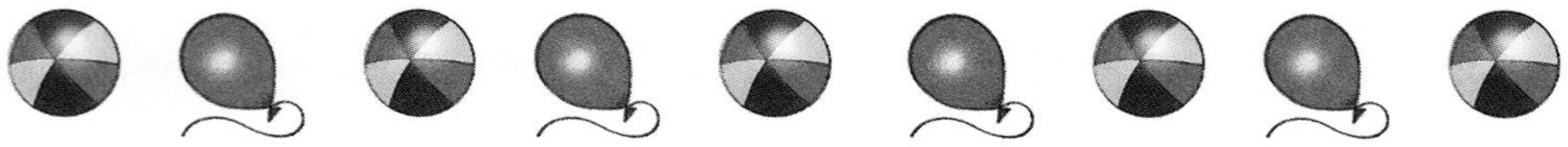

Test Prep

Fill in the ○ for the correct answer.

5 There are 6  .

3  land.
How many are there now?

3 ○ 5 ○ 6 ○ 9 ○

6 Tim sees 2  .

He sees 4  .
How many does Tim see?

2 ○ 4 ○ 6 ○ 7 ○

Notes for Home: Your child reviewed finding missing parts of a number, patterns, and addition problem.
Home Activity: Ask your child to tell how he or she chose the correct answers in Test Prep.

Name

Explore Subtraction

Explore

Use  to show children.
Tell math stories about going home.

Share

Tell your math story.

Notes for Home: Your child explored subtraction by using counters to tell math stories.
Home Activity: Ask your child to tell you a math story using small objects such as coins and the picture on this page.

Connect

Solve each problem.

You can use  .

1. 9  are at school.
   5  drive away.
   How many are left at school?
   4 are left.

2. 6  are at school.
   3  drive away.
   How many are left at school?
   _____ are left.

3. 9 children are in the van.
   2 children get out.
   How many are left
   in the van?
   _____ are left.

4. 7 children ride the bus.
   5 children get off.
   How many are left
   on the bus?
   _____ are left.

Problem Solving Patterns

5. Draw  to complete the pattern.

Notes for Home: Your child solved subtraction problems. *Home Activity:* Ask your child to use pennies or other small objects to show you how he or she solved one of the exercises.

EXPLORE

Name

Show Subtraction

Learn

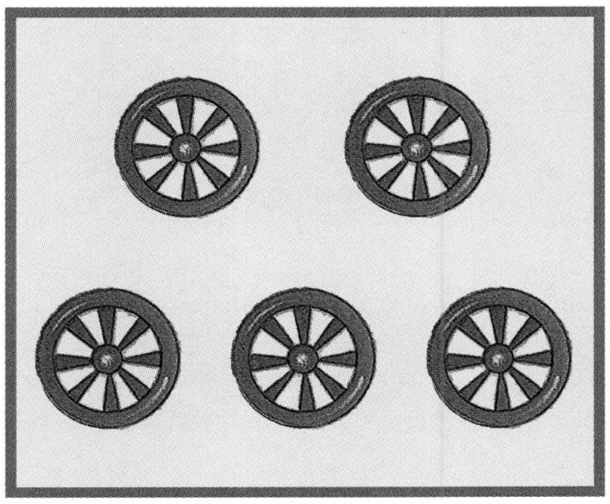

Show how many.

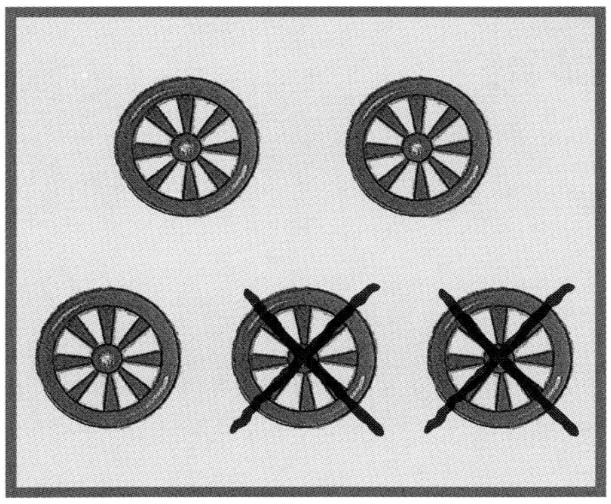

Cross out to subtract.

5 − 2 = 3

Write the number sentence.

Check

Cross out. Subtract.

1

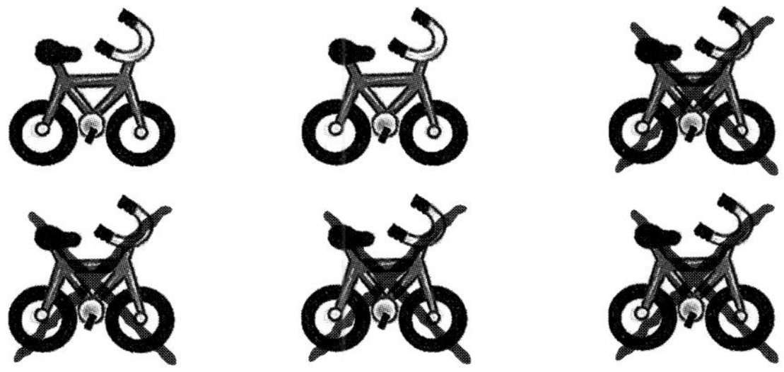

6 − 4 = 2

2

11 − 4 = ____

3

10 − 7 = ____

4

9 − 3 = ____

Talk About It Tell how crossing out helps you to subtract.

Notes for Home: Your child crossed out objects in a picture to show how many were left and then wrote the number using the minus sign. *Home Activity:* Ask your child to tell about one of the exercises.

Practice

Cross out. Subtract.

5 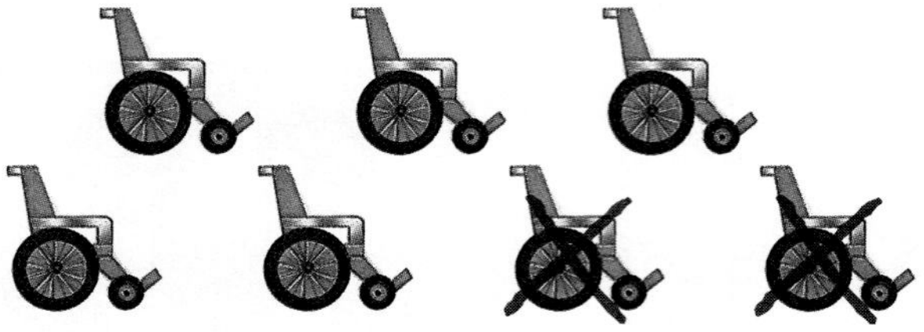

7 − 2 = 5

6 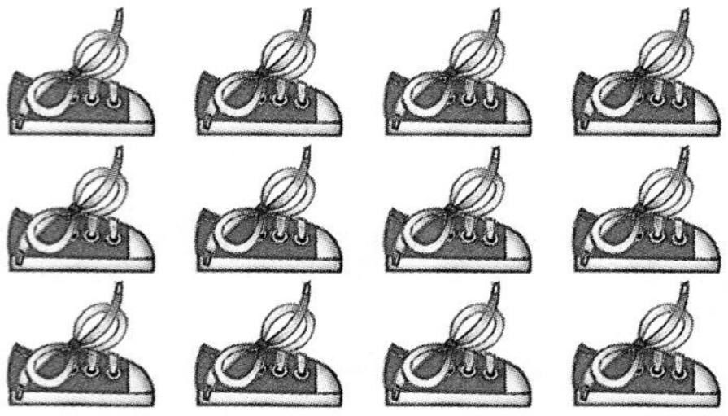

12 − 5 = ____

Subtract.

7. 9 − 1 = ____ 6 − 2 = ____ 8 − 1 = ____
8. 3 − 2 = ____ 5 − 1 = ____ 9 − 2 = ____
9. 6 − 5 = ____ 4 − 1 = ____ 11 − 2 = ____

PRACTICE

Mental Math

10. Use the clues.
Write each number.

My number is 2 more than 4.
My number is 1 less than 10.

My number is ____.

My number is ____.

Notes for Home: Your child practiced subtraction by crossing out objects in a picture and then writing how many were left. *Home Activity:* Do the Mental Math activity with your child. Use different numbers.

Name ______________________________

Problem Solving: Use Subtraction

Learn

PROBLEM SOLVING GUIDE

Understand • Plan • Solve • Look Back

How many in all? How many go away? How many now?

4 – 1 = 3

Check

Use . Show the story.
Write the number sentence.

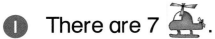

1 There are 7 .
4  take off.
How many now?

7 – 4 = 3

2 There are 6 .
2  fly away.
How many now?

___ – ___ = ___

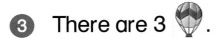

3 There are 3 .
2  go up.
How many are left?

___ – ___ = ___

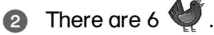

4 There are 9 .
4  pop.
How many are left?

___ – ___ = ___

Talk About It Is 4 – 3 = 1 the same as 4 – 1 = 3? Explain.

Notes for Home: Your child solved problems using subtraction. *Home Activity:* Ask your child how to solve the problems on this page.

Use .

Show the story. Write the number sentence.

5 There are 9 .

3 blow away.

How many are left?

9 — 3 = 6
___ ___ ___

_____ are left.

6 There are 11 .

6 fly away.

How many now?

_____ _____ _____

_____ .

7 There are 8 .

4 take off.

How many now?

_____ _____ _____

_____ 🎈

8 There are 10 ✒ .

3 ✒ take off.

How many are left?

_____ _____ _____

_____ are left.

Tell a Math Story

9 Tell a math story about the picture.
Write the number sentence.

_____ _____ _____

 Notes for Home: Your child read math stories and wrote number sentences to answer the questions.
Home Activity: Ask your child to tell a math story for 6 − 3.

Name

Subtract in Vertical Form

Learn

Here are two ways to show subtraction.

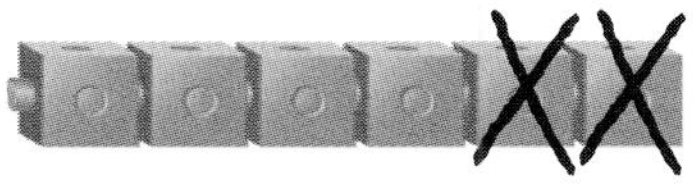

$6 - 2 =$ 4

difference

The answer is the same both ways.

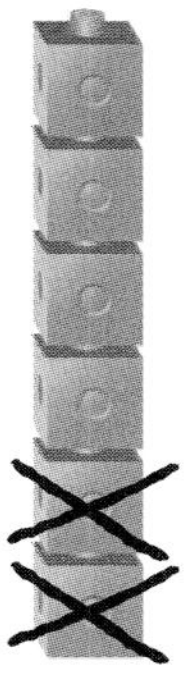

$$\begin{array}{r} 6 \\ -\ 2 \\ \hline 4 \end{array}$$

difference

Check

Use cubes to subtract.

1.

$5 - 1 =$ 4

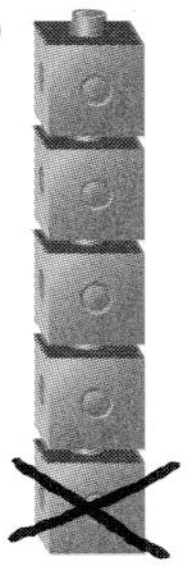

$$\begin{array}{r} 5 \\ -\ 1 \\ \hline 4 \end{array}$$

2.

$3 - 2 =$ ____

$$\begin{array}{r} 3 \\ -\ 2 \\ \hline 1 \end{array}$$

3.

$4 - 3 =$ ____

$$\begin{array}{r} 4 \\ -\ 3 \\ \hline \end{array}$$

4.

$4 - 1 =$ ____

$$\begin{array}{r} 4 \\ -\ 1 \\ \hline \end{array}$$

5.

$6 - 4 =$ ____

$$\begin{array}{r} 6 \\ -\ 4 \\ \hline \end{array}$$

6.

$5 - 4 =$ ____

$$\begin{array}{r} 5 \\ -\ 4 \\ \hline \end{array}$$

Talk About It Why is the answer the same both ways?

Notes for Home Your child learned that subtraction can be shown both horizontally and vertically.
Home Activity: Ask your child to make up more subtraction problems and show them both ways.

Practice

You can use cubes to subtract.

7

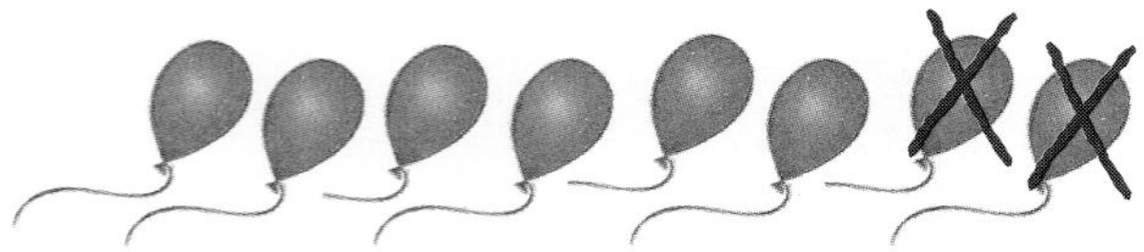

8 − 2 = 6

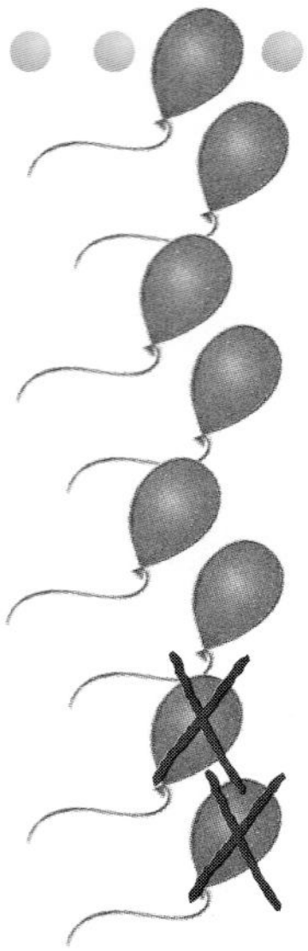

$$\begin{array}{r} 8 \\ -\ 2 \\ \hline 6 \end{array}$$

8 12 − 3 = ____ $\begin{array}{r} 12 \\ -\ 3 \\ \hline \end{array}$

9 9 − 9 = ____ $\begin{array}{r} 9 \\ -\ 9 \\ \hline \end{array}$

10 10 − 5 = ____ $\begin{array}{r} 10 \\ -\ 5 \\ \hline \end{array}$

11 7 − 1 = ____ $\begin{array}{r} 7 \\ -\ 1 \\ \hline \end{array}$

12 $\begin{array}{r} 9 \\ -\ 7 \\ \hline \end{array}$ $\begin{array}{r} 6 \\ -\ 1 \\ \hline \end{array}$ $\begin{array}{r} 9 \\ -\ 1 \\ \hline \end{array}$ $\begin{array}{r} 7 \\ -\ 2 \\ \hline \end{array}$ $\begin{array}{r} 11 \\ -\ 7 \\ \hline \end{array}$ $\begin{array}{r} 8 \\ -\ 7 \\ \hline \end{array}$

PRACTICE

Problem Solving

Solve the problem.

13 There were 7 hot air balloons.
Now there are 4.
How many flew away?

____ flew away.

14 Martha had 10 balloons.
Now she has 3.
How many popped?

____ popped.

Notes for Home: Your child practiced both horizontal and vertical subtraction. *Home Activity:* Point to any problem and ask your child to tell you how to find the answer.

For additional practice, see Skills Practice Bank, page 527, Set 2.

Name ________________________________

Practice Game

Twelve Toss

Players 2

What You Need

2 dot cubes

16 two-color counters

How to Play

1. Take turns tossing the cubes.
2. Add or subtract.
3. Say a number sentence.
4. Put a counter on the answer.
5. The first player with 4 in a row wins.

I have 4 and 5.
Should I add to get 9
or subtract to get 1?

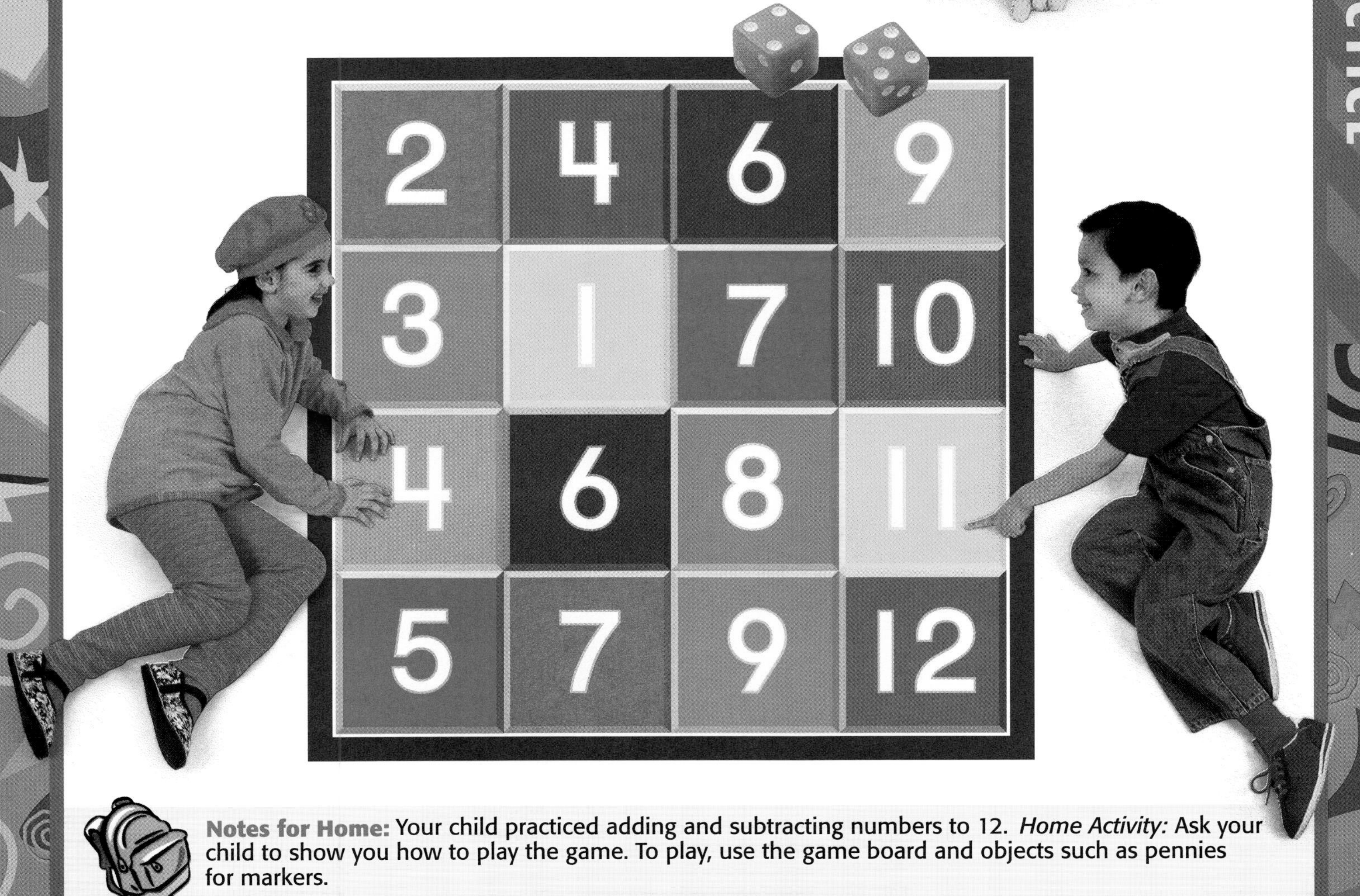
2 4 6 9
3 1 7 10
4 6 8 11
5 7 9 12

PRACTICE

Notes for Home: Your child practiced adding and subtracting numbers to 12. *Home Activity:* Ask your child to show you how to play the game. To play, use the game board and objects such as pennies for markers.

Name ______________________

STOP and Practice

Add. You can use .

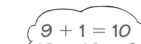

1

1	3	1	2	1	4	3
+ 5	+ 4	+ 7	+ 3	+ 3	+ 5	+ 5

2 $3 + 3 =$ ____ $1 + 3 =$ ____ $2 + 7 =$ ____

Subtract. You can use .

3

5	11	8	4	9	7	6
− 4	− 3	− 6	− 1	− 4	− 3	− 3

4 $7 - 1 =$ ____ $10 - 6 =$ ____ $12 - 3 =$ ____

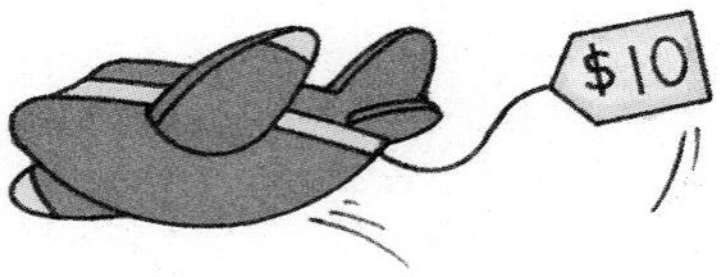

5 Finish this poem.
Try to make it rhyme.

I had 9 dollars.
My grandma gave me 1.
I spent 10 dollars.

Now I have __________ .

Notes for Home: Your child demonstrated his or her knowledge of addition and subtraction to 12. *Home Activity:* Have your child use objects such as pennies to show an addition and a subtraction problem.

PRACTICE

Name _____

Relate Addition and Subtraction

Learn

"I can use the train to add."

"I can use the train to subtract."

"$2 + 5 = 7$ helps me know that $7 - 5 = 2$."

$2 + 5 = 7$ $7 - 5 = 2$

Check

Use . Make a train.
Complete the number sentences.

1

$4 + 2 = \underline{6}$

$6 - 2 = \underline{4}$

2

$3 + 2 = \underline{\hspace{1cm}}$

$5 - \underline{\hspace{1cm}} = \underline{\hspace{1cm}}$

3

$\underline{\hspace{1cm}} + \underline{\hspace{1cm}} = \underline{\hspace{1cm}}$

$8 - \underline{\hspace{1cm}} = \underline{\hspace{1cm}}$

Talk About It How can $3 + 2 = 5$ help you solve $5 - 2$?

Notes for Home: Your child learned how addition and subtraction are related. *Home Activity:* Ask your child to use pennies to make up more related addition and subtraction problems.

Practice

You can use cubes.

Complete the number sentences.

4 

5 + 4 = 9

9 − 4 = 5

5 

___ + ___ = ___

6 − ___ = ___

6 

___ + ___ = ___

10 − ___ = ___

7 

___ + ___ = ___

8 − ___ = ___

PRACTICE

Problem Solving Critical Thinking

8 How many ways can you subtract from 3?

3 − ___ = ___ 3 − ___ = ___

3 − ___ = ___ 3 − ___ = ___

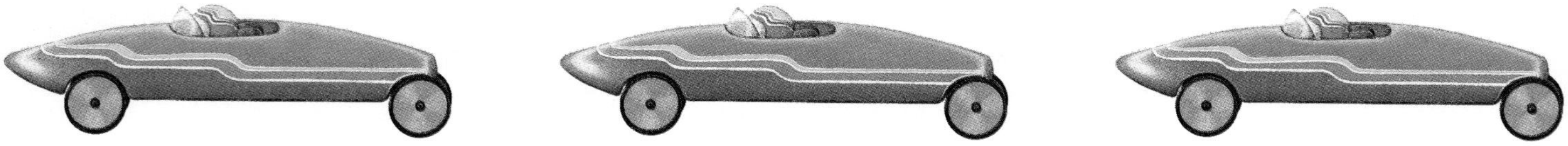

Notes for Home: Your child practiced writing related addition and subtraction sentences. *Home Activity:* Show your child 8 pennies arranged in groups of 3 heads and 5 tails. Ask your child to write an addition and subtraction sentence about the pennies.

Name

Problem Solving: Choose an Operation

Learn

PROBLEM SOLVING GUIDE

Understand • Plan • Solve • Look Back

You can add or subtract to solve a problem.

2 children jump rope.
1 more child comes.
How many jump rope now?

add **subtract**

2 + 1 = 3

Check

Use  to show the story.
Circle add or subtract. Write the number sentence.

1. There are 4 .
3  hop away.
How many are left?

add **subtract**

____ ◯ ____ = ____

2. 7  march together.
2 more march with them.
How many march in all?

add **subtract**

____ ◯ ____ = ____

Talk About It Tell a math story about the toys coming and going.

Notes for Home: Your child read math stories, decided whether to add or subtract, and then solved the problems. *Home Activity:* Ask your child to tell an addition story and a subtraction story about favorite toys.

Practice

Use counters to show the story.
Circle add or subtract. Write the number sentence.

3. There are 6 fish. — **add** **subtract** (circled)

   2 fish swim away.
   How many are there now?

   6 − 2 = 4

4. There are 3 ladybugs. — **add** **subtract**

   3 more ladybugs walk by.
   How many in all?

   ____ ◯ ____ = ____

5. 2 ducks are in the box. — **add** **subtract**

   5 more ducks come.
   Now how many are in the box?

   ____ ◯ ____ = ____

6. 8 turtles play. — **add** **subtract**

   3 turtles crawl away.
   How many play now?

   ____ ◯ ____ = ____

Journal

7. Think about things you have that come and go.
   Write an addition story.
   Write a subtraction story.

Notes for Home: Your child read math stories, chose and wrote the addition or subtraction sign, and then solved the problems. *Home Activity:* Ask your child to tell an addition and subtraction story about things that come and go.

For additional practice, see Skills Practice Bank, page 527, Set 3.

Name

Mixed Practice

Lessons 7–12

Concepts and Skills

Subtract.

You can use .

1

6	7	9	8	10	9	5
− 4	− 1	− 5	− 7	− 9	− 2	− 3

2 Write the number sentences.

___ + ___ = ___

9 − ___ = ___

Problem Solving

Write the number sentence.

3 There are 8 .

1 more  comes.

How many are there now?

___ ◯ ___ = ___

4 There are 5 .

3  pull away.

How many are left?

___ ◯ ___ = ___

Journal

5 Write a math story about 6 children.

Write a number sentence for your story.

Notes for Home: Your child practiced subtraction concepts and relating addition and subtraction. *Home Activity:* Ask your child to write a math story about your family, using related addition and subtraction facts.

Name ______________________________

Cumulative Review

Chapters 1–3

Concepts and Skills

Use 2 colors.

Color to show 2 ways to make the number.

Write the numbers.

1 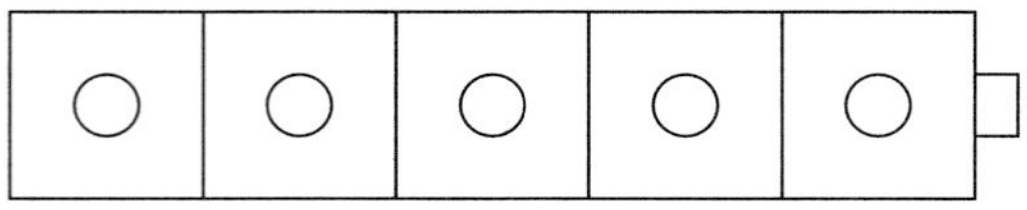 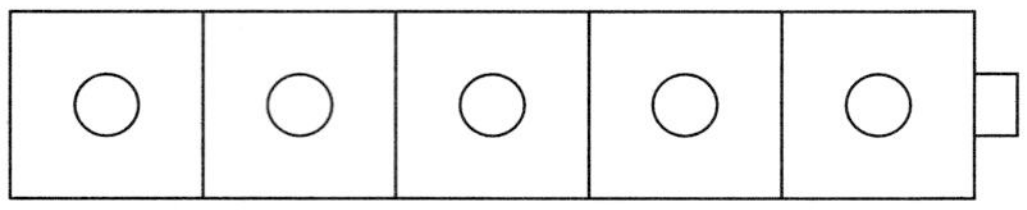

_____ and _____ is 5.   _____ and _____ is 5.

Draw a picture to match the number sentence.

Write how many in all.

2 

$4 + 1 = $ _____.

Test Prep

Fill in the ○ for the correct answer. Choose the number sentence.

3 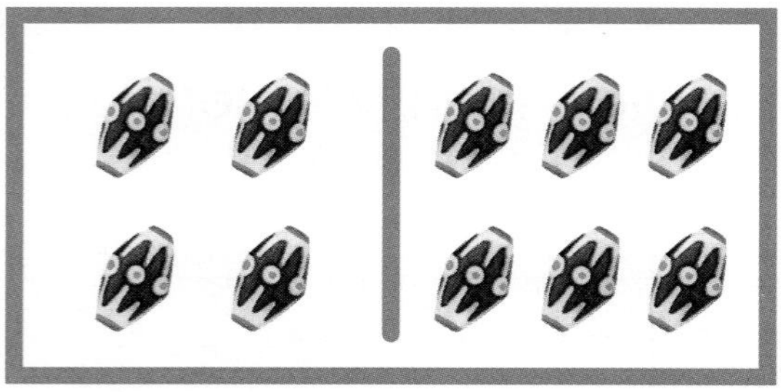

- ○ $3 + 6 = 9$
- ○ $4 + 6 = 10$
- ○ $3 + 4 = 7$
- ○ $6 - 4 = 2$

4 There are 9 

and 1  comes.

How many in all?

- ○ $9 + 1 = 10$
- ○ $7 + 2 = 9$
- ○ $9 - 1 = 8$
- ○ $5 - 4 = 1$

Notes for Home: Your child reviewed finding combinations for numbers and drawing a picture to solve a problem. *Home Activity:* Ask your child to solve a problem similar to one in Test Prep.

Chapter 3 Review

Vocabulary

1 Write a number sentence. ____ + ____ = ____

2 Write the sum.

$8 + 2 =$ ____

3 Write the difference.

$6 - 1 =$ ____

Concepts and Skills

Use . Write the answer.

4

$4 + 4 =$ ____

Add.

5
$$9 \quad\quad 7 \quad\quad 7$$
$$+2 \quad\quad +1 \quad\quad +4$$

Cross out 🧊🧊.
Write the answer.

6

$9 - 6 =$ ____

Subtract.

7
$$9 \quad\quad 5 \quad\quad 6$$
$$-1 \quad\quad -5 \quad\quad -1$$

Problem Solving

Read the math story.
Write the number sentence.

8 There were 5 .
2 ran away. How many are left?

____ ◯ ____ = ____

Notes for Home: Your child reviewed the concepts taught in Chapter 3. *Home Activity:* Ask your child to make up math stories using addition and subtraction.

Chapter 3 Test

1 Complete the
number sentences.

___ + ___ = ___

5 − ___ = ___

2 Subtract.

6 − 3 = ___

3 Add. Use .

$$\begin{array}{r} 6 \\ +\,3 \\ \hline \end{array} \qquad \begin{array}{r} 7 \\ +\,5 \\ \hline \end{array} \qquad \begin{array}{r} 2 \\ +\,8 \\ \hline \end{array}$$

4 Subtract. Use ⬤ ⬤ .

$$\begin{array}{r} 10 \\ -\,3 \\ \hline \end{array} \qquad \begin{array}{r} 8 \\ -\,5 \\ \hline \end{array} \qquad \begin{array}{r} 4 \\ -\,2 \\ \hline \end{array}$$

5 Read the math story. Use ⬤ ⬤ .
Write the number sentence.

5 children play tag.
3 more children come.
How many are there now?

___ ◯ ___ = ___

6 Draw a picture.
Write the number sentence.

There are 7 .

2 🐟 swim away.
How many are there now?

___ ◯ ___ = ___

Notes for Home: Your child was assessed on addition and subtraction. *Home Activity:* Ask your child
to tell a math story for objects at home.

Name ____________________

Performance Assessment

Chapter 3

$2 + 4 = 6 \quad 6 - 2 = 4$

Use counters and a workmat to add and subtract.
Write number sentences with 6.

1 ___ + ___ = 6
___ + ___ = 6
___ + ___ = 6
___ + ___ = 6
___ + ___ = 6
___ + ___ = 6
___ + ___ = 6

2 6 − ___ = ___
6 − ___ = ___
6 − ___ = ___
6 − ___ = ___
6 − ___ = ___
6 − ___ = ___
6 − ___ = ___

Problem Solving Critical Thinking

Choose a number
sentence you wrote.
Draw a picture about it.

Notes for Home: Your child showed knowledge of addition and subtraction. *Home Activity:* Ask your child to make two groups using objects such as forks and spoons, then write number sentences about the groups.

Name ______________________________

Explore with a CALCULATOR

Does This Add Up?

Keys You Will Use [ON/C] [+] [−] [=]

You can use your calculator to count by one.

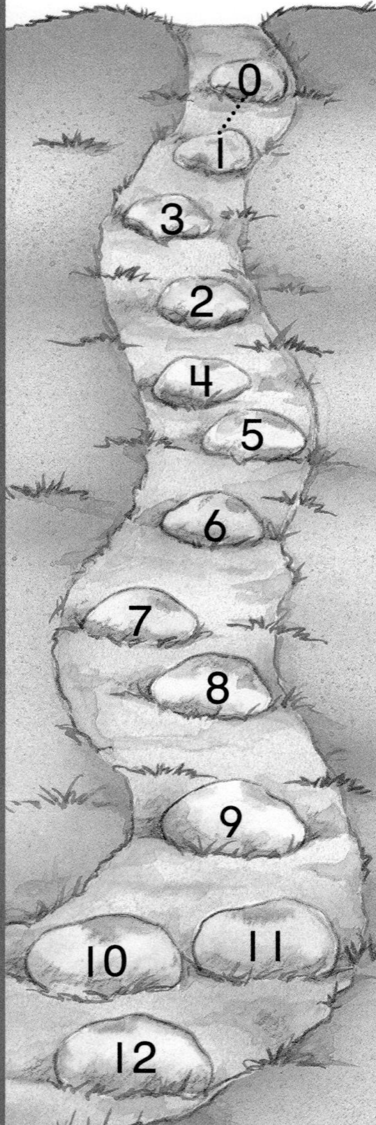

1. Press [+] [1] [=].
2. Draw a line from 0 to the number shown in the display.
3. Press [=] again.
   Draw a line to the next number.
4. Continue pressing [=].
   Draw the path down the hill.
5. Now climb back up the hill.
   You should see [12.].
6. Press [−] [1] [=].
   Draw a line to the number shown in the display.
7. Continue pressing [=].
   Draw the path up the hill.

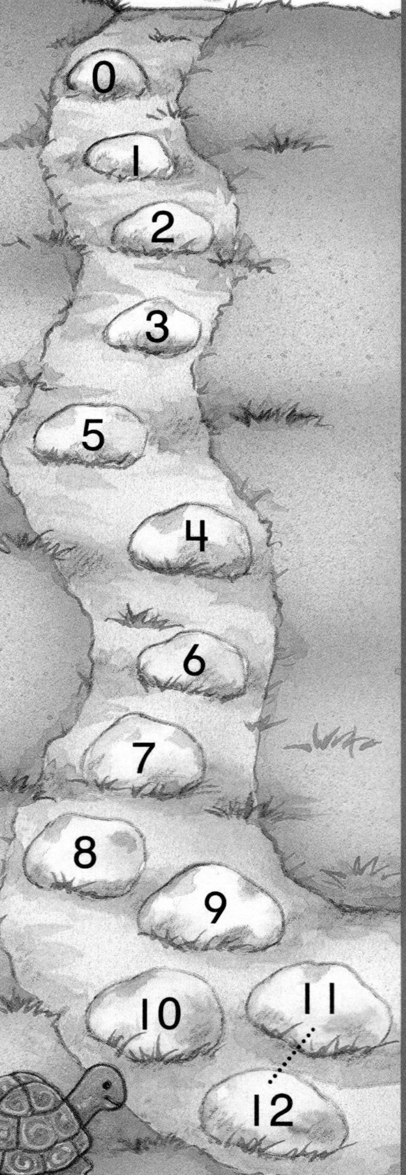

Tech Talk What happens each time you press [=]?

Visit our Web site. www.parent.mathsurf.com

The Whole Story

1 Look around your house.
2 Find things that have pieces.
3 Draw a picture of what you find.
4 Ask someone at home to help you.

Match It Up!

Match a picture to a number sentence.

$3 + 5 = 8$

$6 + 4 = 10$

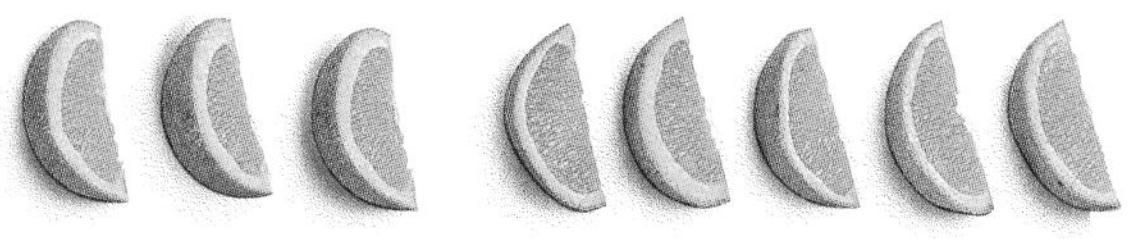

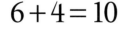

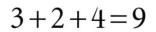

$3 + 2 + 4 = 9$

Draw your own pictures and number sentences. Share them with a family member.

Fold down

MathSoup

Scott Foresman - Addison Wesley My Math Magazine No. 3

Meet a Math Creature!

Here is a silly creature. Add buttons so there are more buttons than toes.

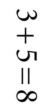

Math in Your World

Dotty Dominoes

Bag It!

Make a target like this one. Toss two bean bags on the target. Add your scores.

1 What is the greatest score you can get? ______

2 What is the lowest score you can get? ______

3 Find 2 ways you can get a score of 9.

____

4 Make another target. Make 5 easier to get.

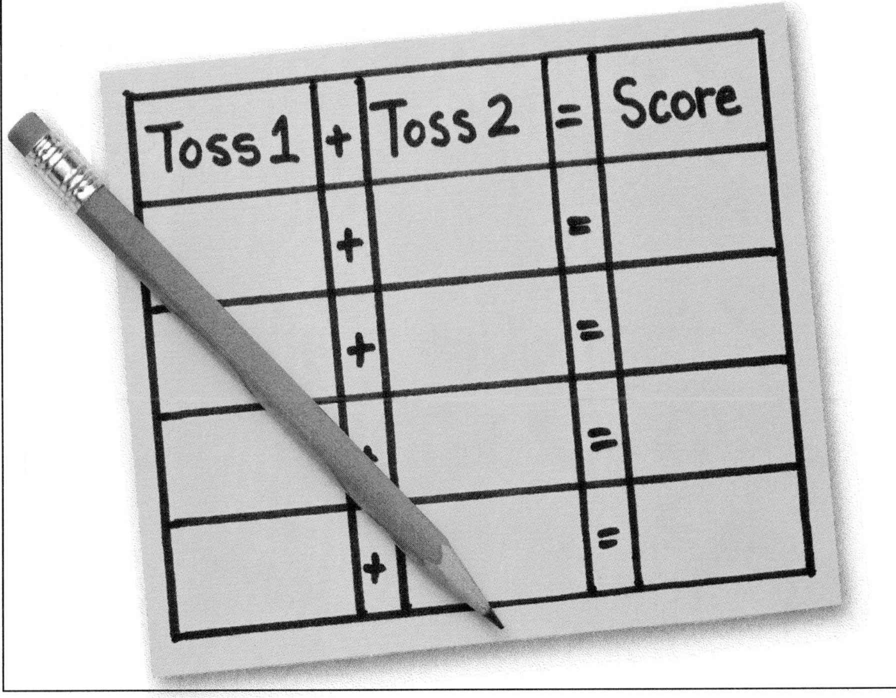

Notes for Home: Your child played a bean bag game to practice addition. *Home Activity:* Make a target using other numbers. Ask your child to explain the rules, then play together.

Dominoes is a game that comes from China. Try playing one of these games with a friend.

Row Row Row of Dots

1 Put the dominoes face down in rows.
2 Pick one. Add the number of dots.
3 Pick another. Add the number of dots.
4 If the sums match, keep the pair. If not, turn them back over.
5 Play until all matches have been made.
6 The player with more dominoes wins.

Peek-a-Dot

1 Take turns with a friend.
2 Choose a domino. Tell the sum.
3 Cover one side.
4 The other player tells how many dots are hidden. That player keeps the domino if he or she is right.
5 The player with more dominoes wins.

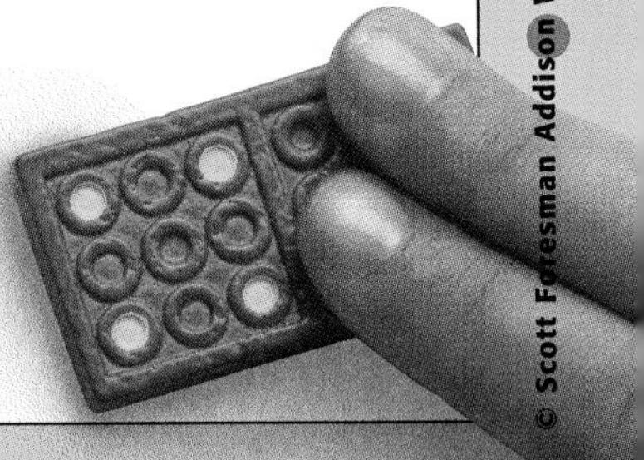

Notes for Home: Your child used dominoes to play addition games. Each domino has two parts with 0 through 6 dots on each part. *Home Activity:* Help your child draw a domino, then tell how many dots in all.

Creature Count

1 How many?

_____ (dark spot) _____ (white spot) _____ (feather)

_____ (antenna) _____ (eye) _____ (boot)

2 How many (dark spot) and (eye) in all? _____

3 How many (eye) and (feather) in all? _____

4 How many more (boot) than (eye)? _____

5 How many more (feather) than (antenna)? _____

How does a creature count to 11?
Answer: On his fingers!

Notes for Home: Your child practiced addition and subtraction. *Home Activity:* Draw a silly creature. The drawing should have countable parts. Point to two different parts and ask your child to tell how many in all.

CHAPTER

4

Facts and Strategies to 12

Boxes, Bags, and Baskets
Let's show 2 groups that make 12 in all.

Notes for Home: Your child made groups of objects to practice addition.
Home Activity: Ask your child to use objects such as pennies to make two groups that total 12.

Math at Home

Dear Family,
Our class is beginning Chapter 4. We will learn ways to help us add and subtract numbers up to 12. Ask me to tell you about addition and subtraction as I learn more about them.

The Count On Clothesline

Write numbers from 0 to 12 on index cards. Then, using clothespins or paper clips, hang the number cards in order on a string. Point to a number and have your child count on 1, 2, or 3. For example, point to 6 and ask your child to count on 1 and say 7.

Count Back to Subtract

Put 10 objects such as buttons or pennies in a row. Ask your child to count back as he or she removes 1 or 2 objects to find how many are left. For 10 – 2, have your child push away 2 while counting backwards from 10.

Community Connection

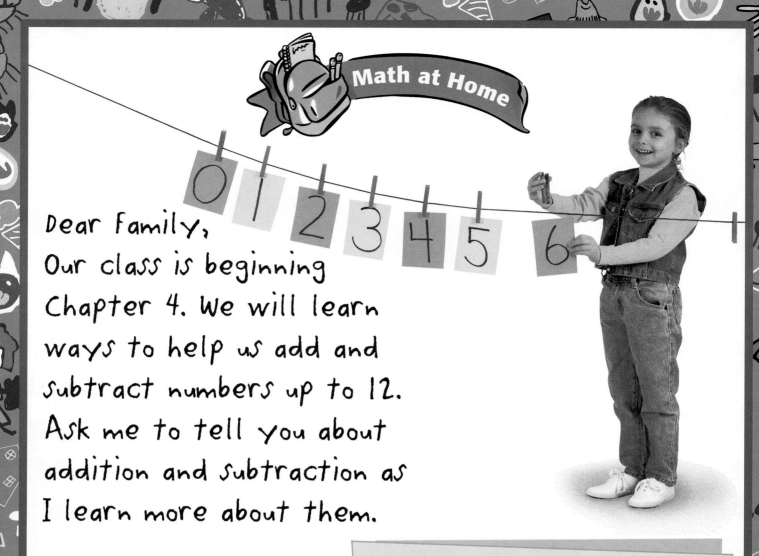

When in a multi-storied building, use the stairs with your child to the next floor. Count the stairs going up 1, 2, 3, 4, . . . , and count the stairs backward 12, 11, 10, 9, . . . going down.

Visit our Web site. www.parent.mathsurf.com

Name ________________

Count On 1 or 2

Learn

I say 5. Then I count on one more and say 6.
I say 5 and count 6, 7.

$5 + 1 =$ 6 $\qquad$ $5 + 2 =$ 7

Check

Count on to add.

1. 

$7 + 1 =$ 8

2. 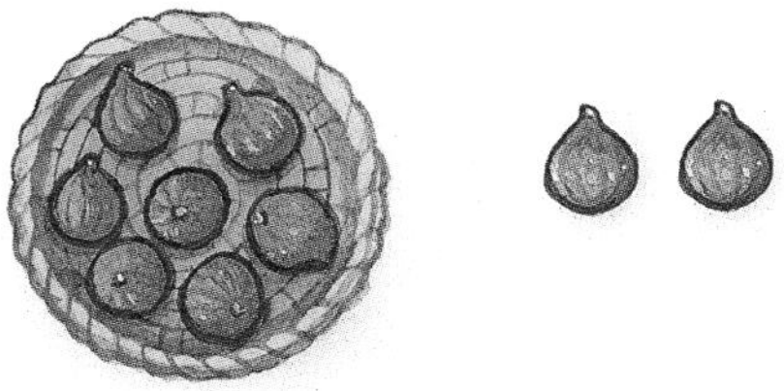

$7 + 2 =$ ____

3. 

$$\begin{array}{r} 6 \\ +\ 1 \\ \hline \end{array}$$

$6 + 1 =$ ____

4. 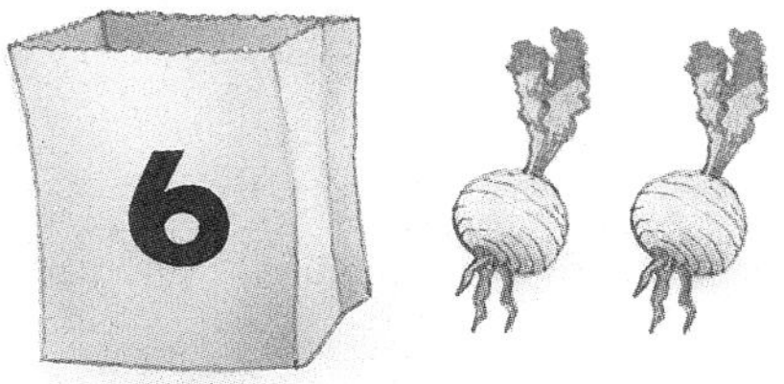

$$\begin{array}{r} 6 \\ +\ 2 \\ \hline \end{array}$$

$6 + 2 =$ ____

Talk About It Tell how you add on 1 more or 2 more.

Notes for Home: Your child counted on to add 1 or 2 to a number. *Home Activity:* Ask your child to tell you how to find 3 + 1.

Practice

Count on to add.

5 

$$\begin{array}{r} 8 \\ +\ 1 \\ \hline 9 \end{array}$$

$8 + 1 = $ 9

6 

$$\begin{array}{r} 8 \\ +\ 2 \\ \hline \end{array}$$

$8 + 2 = $ ____

7 $5 + 1 = $ ____ $2 + 2 = $ ____ $3 + 2 = $ ____

8 $9 + 2 = $ ____ $9 + 1 = $ ____ $1 + 1 = $ ____

9

$\begin{array}{r} 6 \\ +\ 1 \\ \hline \end{array}$	$\begin{array}{r} 6 \\ +\ 2 \\ \hline \end{array}$	$\begin{array}{r} 4 \\ +\ 1 \\ \hline \end{array}$	$\begin{array}{r} 4 \\ +\ 2 \\ \hline \end{array}$	$\begin{array}{r} 7 \\ +\ 1 \\ \hline \end{array}$	$\begin{array}{r} 7 \\ +\ 2 \\ \hline \end{array}$

10

$\begin{array}{r} 9 \\ +\ 1 \\ \hline \end{array}$	$\begin{array}{r} 3 \\ +\ 2 \\ \hline \end{array}$	$\begin{array}{r} 5 \\ +\ 2 \\ \hline \end{array}$	$\begin{array}{r} 2 \\ +\ 1 \\ \hline \end{array}$	$\begin{array}{r} 3 \\ +\ 1 \\ \hline \end{array}$	$\begin{array}{r} 8 \\ +\ 2 \\ \hline \end{array}$

PRACTICE

Problem Solving **Patterns**

11 What pattern do you see?
Complete the pattern.

____

Notes for Home: Your child practiced adding 1 or 2 to a number. *Home Activity:* Say a number from 2 to 9. Ask your child to repeat the number and count on 1, then repeat and count on 2 more.

Name ______

Explore Turnaround Facts

Explore

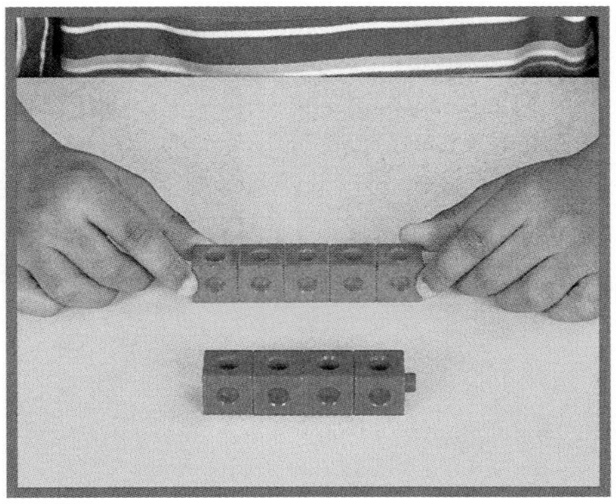

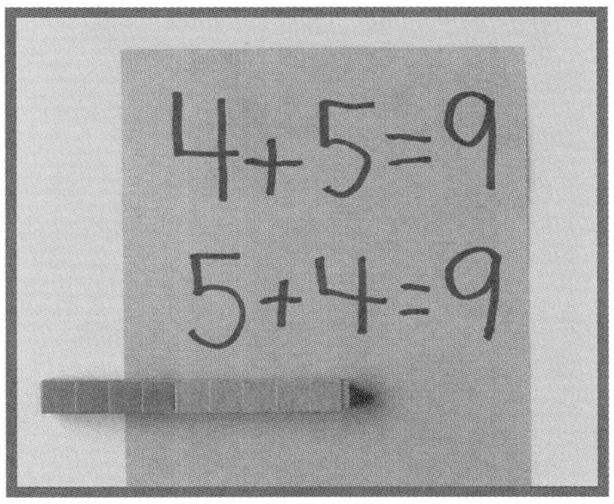

Work with a partner.
Use 2 colors of .

Make trains.

Put the trains together.
Write 2 addition sentences.

Use 2 colors of 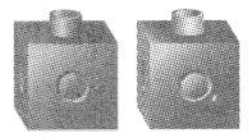 to make a train.
Color to show your train. Write 2 addition sentences.

1

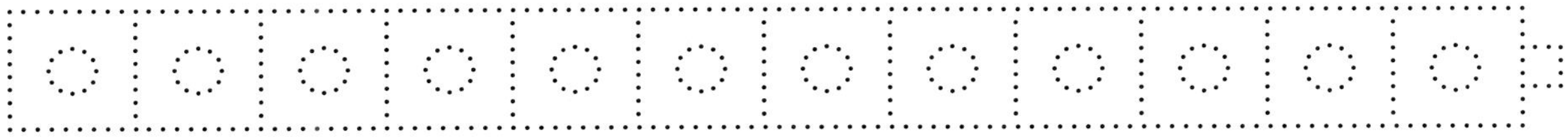

_____ + _____ = _____   _____ + _____ = _____

2

_____ + _____ = _____   _____ + _____ = _____

Share

If you know 6 + 3 = 9, what other fact do you know?

Notes for Home: Your child learned that facts like 3 + 5 and 5 + 3 always have the same sum. These are called turnaround facts. *Home Activity:* Ask your child to tell you the turnaround facts for 3 + 2 = 5 (2 + 3 = 5), and 4 + 1 = 5 (1 + 4 = 5).

EXPLORE

Connect

I write 4 + 1 = 5 for this train.
When I turn the train around, I can write 1 + 4 = 5.

4 + 1 = 5　　　　1 + 4 = 5

3 Make a 7 train. Write 2 turnaround facts.

___ + ___ = ___　　　　___ + ___ = ___

4 Make a 9 train. Write 2 turnaround facts.

___ + ___ = ___　　　　___ + ___ = ___

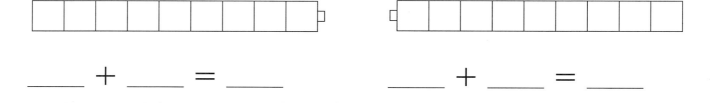

Problem Solving Visual Thinking

5 Tell how the bags are alike and different.

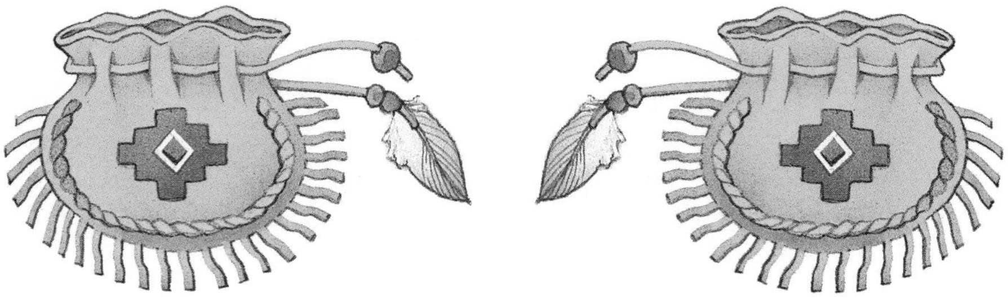

Notes for Home: Your child continued learning about addition facts. *Home Activity:* Ask your child to make two groups using objects such as beans or buttons, and then tell you two addition facts about the groups, for example a group of 4 and a group of 2: 4 + 2 = 6; 2 + 4 = 6.

EXPLORE

Name ______________________________

Count On from Any Number

Learn

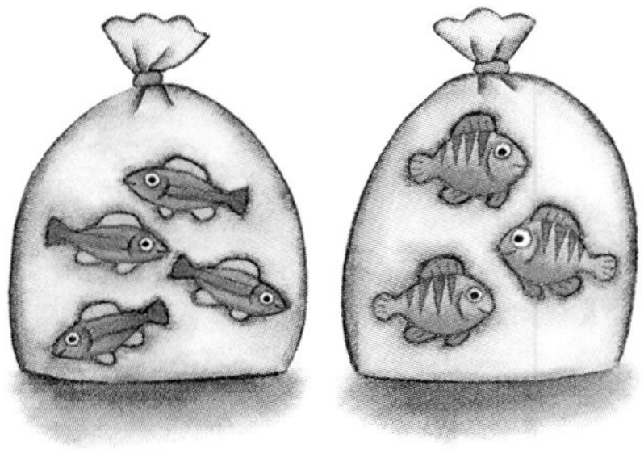

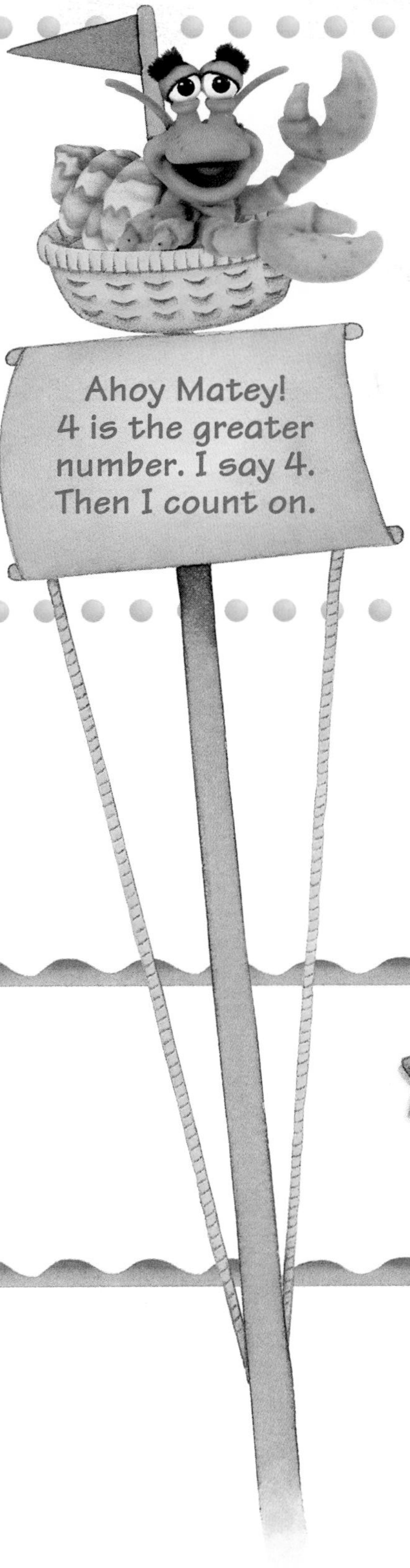

$4 + 3 =$ 7 $\qquad$ $3 + 4 =$ 7

Check

Count on to add.

1.  $7 + 1 =$ 8 $\qquad$  $1 + 7 =$ ____

2. 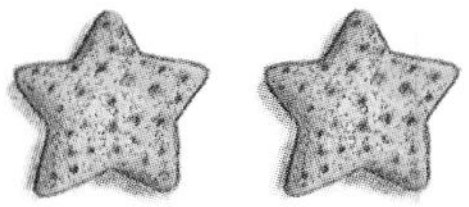 $6 + 2 =$ ____ $\qquad$ 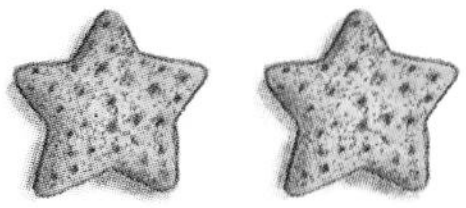 $2 + 6 =$ ____

3. 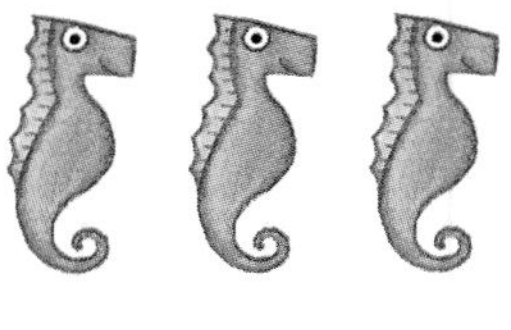 $5 + 3 =$ ____ $\qquad$ $\begin{array}{r} 3 \\ +\ 5 \\ \hline \end{array}$ 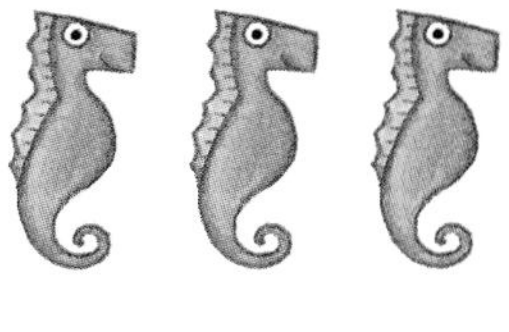

Talk About It Why do you start with the greater number?

Notes for Home: Your child chose the greater number and then counted on to add 1, 2, or 3.
Home Activity: Say a number from 3 to 9 and ask your child to add 1, 2, or 3.

Practice

Think of the greater number.
Count on to add.

4 $7 + 2 = \underline{9}$

$$\begin{array}{r} 2 \\ +\,7 \\ \hline 9 \end{array}$$

5 $3 + 8 = \_\_\_$ $3 + 9 = \_\_\_$ $1 + 8 = \_\_\_$

$8 + 3 = \_\_\_$ $9 + 3 = \_\_\_$ $8 + 1 = \_\_\_$

6 $\begin{array}{r} 5 \\ +\,1 \\ \hline \end{array}$ $\begin{array}{r} 1 \\ +\,5 \\ \hline \end{array}$ $\begin{array}{r} 2 \\ +\,4 \\ \hline \end{array}$ $\begin{array}{r} 4 \\ +\,2 \\ \hline \end{array}$ $\begin{array}{r} 6 \\ +\,3 \\ \hline \end{array}$ $\begin{array}{r} 3 \\ +\,6 \\ \hline \end{array}$

7 $\begin{array}{r} 7 \\ +\,1 \\ \hline \end{array}$ $\begin{array}{r} 1 \\ +\,7 \\ \hline \end{array}$ $\begin{array}{r} 5 \\ +\,3 \\ \hline \end{array}$ $\begin{array}{r} 3 \\ +\,5 \\ \hline \end{array}$ $\begin{array}{r} 8 \\ +\,2 \\ \hline \end{array}$ $\begin{array}{r} 2 \\ +\,8 \\ \hline \end{array}$

PRACTICE

Tell a Math Story

8 Look at the picture.
Think of a math story.
Tell it to a friend.

Notes for Home: Your child practiced adding 1, 2, or 3 to the greater number. *Home Activity:* Say 8 and ask your child to add 1, then add 2, and then add 3.

For additional practice, see Skills Practice Bank, page 528, Set 1.

Use a Number Line to Count On

Learn •

I start with 5 cubes and count on 3 more.

5, ... 6, 7, 8. There are 8 cubes in all.

$$5 + 3 = \underline{8}$$

Check •

Use with the number line. Write the sum.

1 $8 + 1 = \underline{9}$ $5 + 2 = \underline{}$ $3 + 6 = \underline{}$

2 $1 + 4 = \underline{}$ $1 + 5 = \underline{}$ $3 + 5 = \underline{}$

3 $2 + 6 = \underline{}$ $2 + 1 = \underline{}$ $3 + 2 = \underline{}$

4

7	6	1	4	1	2	3
+1	+3	+8	+3	+6	+7	+3

Talk About It Tell how you find a sum using a number line.

Notes for Home: Your child used a number line to add 1, 2, or 3 to a number.
Home Activity: Ask your child to show how the number line can be used to add 5 + 2.

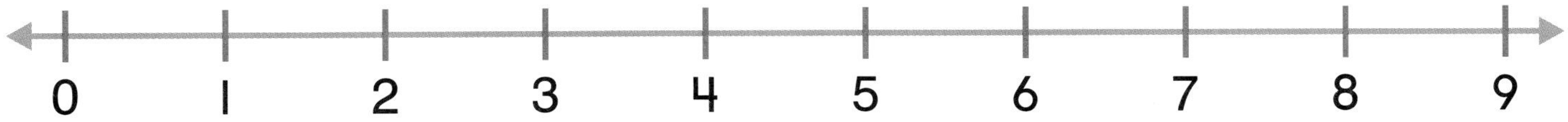

Practice

You can use the number line. Write the sum.

5. $6 + 1 =$ 7 $\qquad 5 + 3 =$ ___ $\qquad 2 + 1 =$ ___

6. $1 + 7 =$ ___ $\qquad 3 + 3 =$ ___ $\qquad 3 + 2 =$ ___

7. $8 + 1 =$ ___ $\qquad 3 + 4 =$ ___ $\qquad 4 + 2 =$ ___

8. $2 + 2 =$ ___ $\qquad 8 + 1 =$ ___ $\qquad 5 + 2 =$ ___

9. $\begin{array}{r} 3 \\ +\ 1 \\ \hline \end{array} \quad \begin{array}{r} 5 \\ +\ 1 \\ \hline \end{array} \quad \begin{array}{r} 6 \\ +\ 3 \\ \hline \end{array} \quad \begin{array}{r} 4 \\ +\ 2 \\ \hline \end{array} \quad \begin{array}{r} 1 \\ +\ 1 \\ \hline \end{array} \quad \begin{array}{r} 6 \\ +\ 2 \\ \hline \end{array}$

10. $\begin{array}{r} 3 \\ +\ 6 \\ \hline \end{array} \quad \begin{array}{r} 1 \\ +\ 2 \\ \hline \end{array} \quad \begin{array}{r} 3 \\ +\ 4 \\ \hline \end{array} \quad \begin{array}{r} 3 \\ +\ 3 \\ \hline \end{array} \quad \begin{array}{r} 1 \\ +\ 4 \\ \hline \end{array} \quad \begin{array}{r} 7 \\ +\ 2 \\ \hline \end{array}$

Write your own number sentences.

11. ___ $+ 2 =$ ___ $\qquad$ ___ $+ 3 =$ ___

Mental Math

12. What number is 2 more than 9? How can the number line help?

Notes for Home: Your child used a number line to add numbers. *Home Activity:* Ask your child to tell you how to use the number line to add 1, 2, and 3 to 9.

PRACTICE

Name ______________________________

Add Zero

Learn

How many in each part? How many in all?

$4 + 1 =$ 5

$4 + 0 =$ 4

Check

Add.

1. 

   $0 + 5 =$ 5

2. 

   $0 + 0 =$ ____

3. 

   $6 + 2 =$ ____

4. 

   $$\begin{array}{r} 7 \\ +\ 0 \\ \hline \end{array}$$

Talk About It Add 0 to a number. What is the sum?

Notes for Home: Your child learned to add zero to a number. *Home Activity:* Hold up 3 fingers on one hand and make a fist with the other hand to show zero. Ask your child to tell an addition fact about your fingers (3 + 0 = 3).

Practice

Add.

5 

$4 + 0 = \underline{4}$

6 

$\begin{array}{r} 3 \\ +\ 0 \\ \hline \end{array}$

7 $4 + 3 = \_\_\_$ $2 + 0 = \_\_\_$ $0 + 7 = \_\_\_$

8 $5 + 1 = \_\_\_$ $0 + 0 = \_\_\_$ $3 + 9 = \_\_\_$

9 $\begin{array}{r} 0 \\ +\ 6 \\ \hline \end{array}$ $\begin{array}{r} 5 \\ +\ 0 \\ \hline \end{array}$ $\begin{array}{r} 3 \\ +\ 6 \\ \hline \end{array}$ $\begin{array}{r} 8 \\ +\ 0 \\ \hline \end{array}$ $\begin{array}{r} 3 \\ +\ 7 \\ \hline \end{array}$ $\begin{array}{r} 5 \\ +\ 2 \\ \hline \end{array}$

10 $\begin{array}{r} 3 \\ +\ 8 \\ \hline \end{array}$ $\begin{array}{r} 1 \\ +\ 7 \\ \hline \end{array}$ $\begin{array}{r} 0 \\ +\ 1 \\ \hline \end{array}$ $\begin{array}{r} 3 \\ +\ 5 \\ \hline \end{array}$ $\begin{array}{r} 6 \\ +\ 2 \\ \hline \end{array}$ $\begin{array}{r} 9 \\ +\ 0 \\ \hline \end{array}$

PRACTICE

Think what you know about adding 0.

Problem Solving Critical Thinking

11 Try this super fact. $100 + 0 = \_\_\_$

Write your own super fact. $\_\_\_ + 0 = \_\_\_$

Notes for Home: Your child practiced adding zero. *Home Activity:* Ask your child to tell a math story that includes adding zero.

Name ______________________________

Add with 5

Learn

There is a row of 5 for each number.

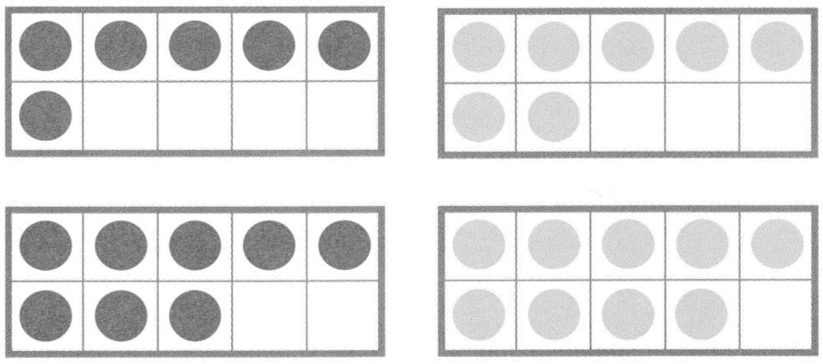

"When one part is 5, I can think of my ten-frame to find how many in all."

Check

Draw more counters. Write the sum.

1. 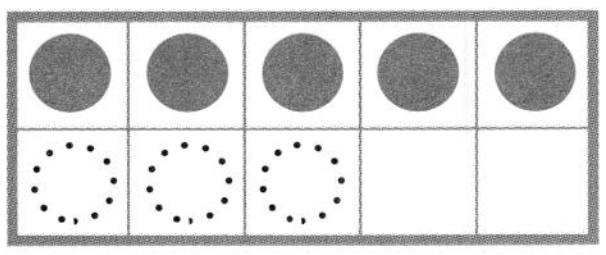

$$\begin{array}{r} 5 \\ +\ 3 \\ \hline \end{array}$$

5 + 3 = 8

2. 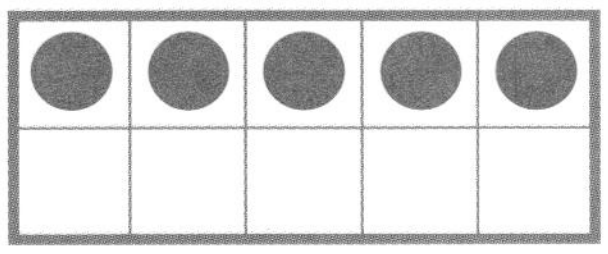

$$\begin{array}{r} 5 \\ +\ 1 \\ \hline \end{array}$$

5 + 1 = ____

3. 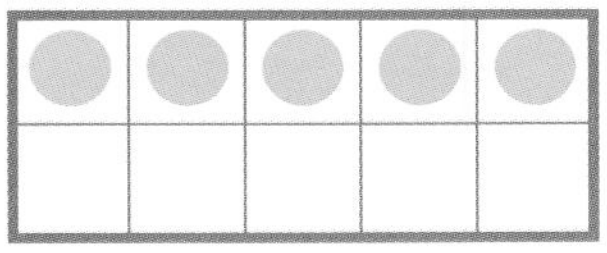

$$\begin{array}{r} 5 \\ +\ 5 \\ \hline \end{array}$$

5 + 5 = ____

4. 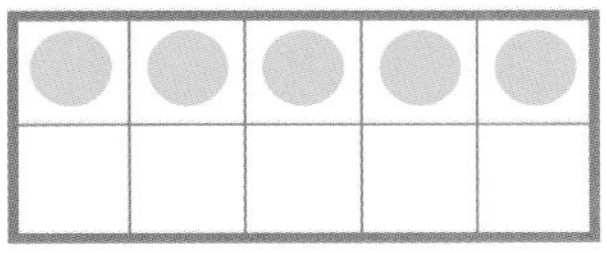

$$\begin{array}{r} 5 \\ +\ 0 \\ \hline \end{array}$$

5 + 0 = ____

5. 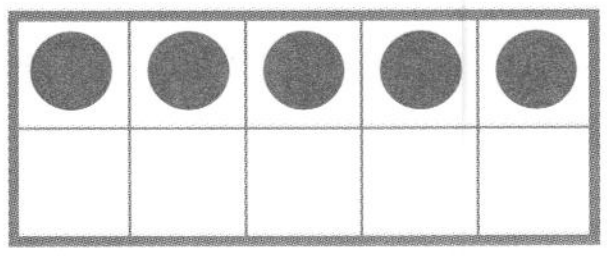

$$\begin{array}{r} 5 \\ +\ 4 \\ \hline \end{array}$$

5 + 4 = ____

6. 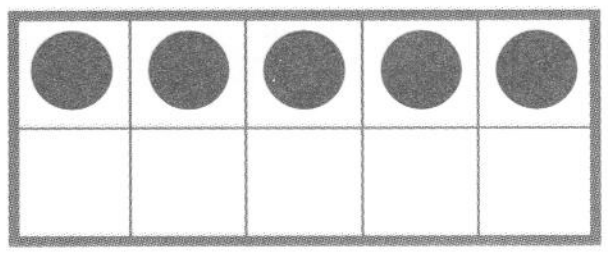

$$\begin{array}{r} 5 \\ +\ 2 \\ \hline \end{array}$$

5 + 2 = ____

Talk About It What pattern do you see in the Learn?

Notes for Home: Your child added 5 to numbers. *Home Activity:* Hold up five fingers on one hand and 1, 2, or 3 fingers on the other hand. Ask your child to tell you the number sentence.

Practice

Add.

7. $2 + 5 = 7$ $4 + 5 =$ ___ $5 + 3 =$ ___

8. $\begin{array}{r} 6 \\ +5 \\ \hline \end{array}$ $\begin{array}{r} 5 \\ +0 \\ \hline \end{array}$ $\begin{array}{r} 7 \\ +5 \\ \hline \end{array}$ $\begin{array}{r} 4 \\ +5 \\ \hline \end{array}$ $\begin{array}{r} 1 \\ +5 \\ \hline \end{array}$ $\begin{array}{r} 5 \\ +5 \\ \hline \end{array}$ $\begin{array}{r} 5 \\ +2 \\ \hline \end{array}$

Mixed Practice Add.

9. $\begin{array}{r} 4 \\ +2 \\ \hline \end{array}$ $\begin{array}{r} 9 \\ +3 \\ \hline \end{array}$ $\begin{array}{r} 0 \\ +8 \\ \hline \end{array}$ $\begin{array}{r} 7 \\ +2 \\ \hline \end{array}$ $\begin{array}{r} 4 \\ +5 \\ \hline \end{array}$ $\begin{array}{r} 4 \\ +3 \\ \hline \end{array}$ $\begin{array}{r} 8 \\ +2 \\ \hline \end{array}$

10. $\begin{array}{r} 5 \\ +3 \\ \hline \end{array}$ $\begin{array}{r} 0 \\ +0 \\ \hline \end{array}$ $\begin{array}{r} 3 \\ +7 \\ \hline \end{array}$ $\begin{array}{r} 6 \\ +0 \\ \hline \end{array}$ $\begin{array}{r} 5 \\ +7 \\ \hline \end{array}$ $\begin{array}{r} 1 \\ +6 \\ \hline \end{array}$ $\begin{array}{r} 2 \\ +7 \\ \hline \end{array}$

PRACTICE

Problem Solving Critical Thinking

11. Circle what you can buy with  and .

Notes for Home: Your child practiced adding 5, 0, and 1, 2, or 3. *Home Activity:* Point to one or two facts on this page and ask your child to show it using small objects such as buttons or beans.

Name ________________________________

Problem Solving: Make a List

Learn

PROBLEM SOLVING GUIDE
Understand • Plan • Solve • Look Back

Pat wants **exactly** 8 cards.

This is a list of the choices using 2 packs of cards.

1 pack of 3 cards and 1 pack of 5 cards
1 pack of 6 cards and 1 pack of 2 cards
2 packs of 4 cards

Check

1. Aldo wants exactly 7 cards.
   Make Aldo's list.

1 pack of __4__ cards and 1 pack of __3__ cards

1 pack of _____ cards and 1 pack of _____ cards

1 pack of _____ cards

Talk About It What is one way to get 12 cards using 2 packs?

Notes for Home: Your child solved problems by making a list of possible choices. *Home Activity:* Ask your child to use the picture on this page to list the ways to get 6 cards.

Choose 2 boxes. Make a list.

2 You want exactly 10 toys.

1 box of __2__ toys and 1 box of _____ toys

1 box of _____ toys and 1 box of _____ toys

1 box of _____ toys and 1 box of _____ toys

2 boxes of _____ toys

3 Your friend wants exactly 11 toys.

1 box of _____ toys and 1 box of _____ toys

1 box of _____ toys and 1 box of _____ toys

1 box of _____ toys and 1 box of _____ toys

Critical Thinking

4 Add the numbers in squares.
Add the numbers in circles.
Add the numbers in triangles.
What do you find?

□ + □ = _____

○ + ○ = _____

△ + △ = _____

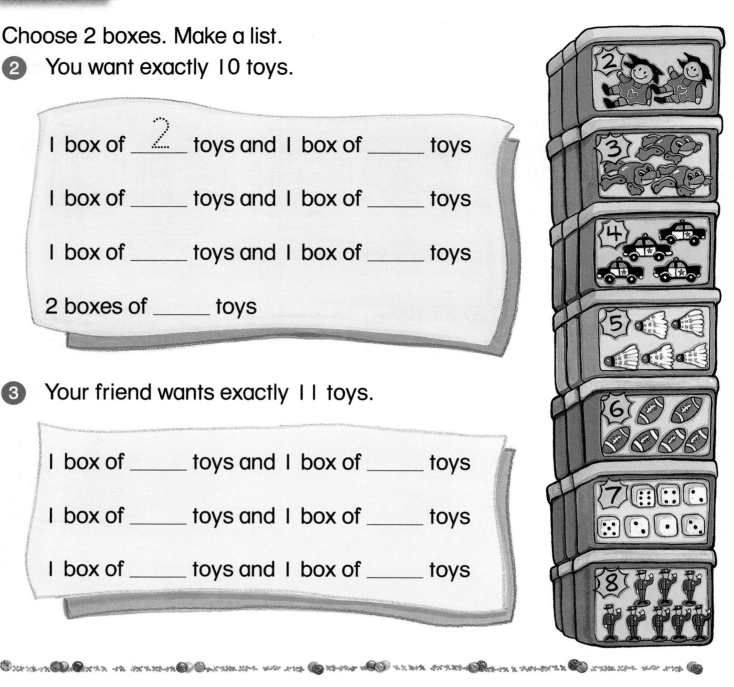

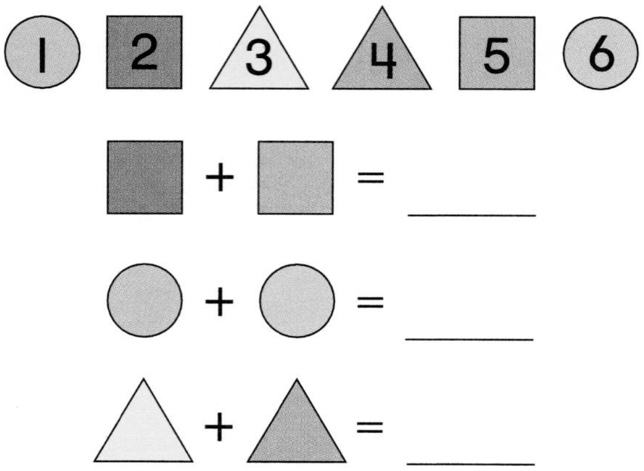

Notes for Home: Your child solved problems by choosing numbers to add to get a given sum.
Home Activity: Ask your child to list 3 ways to get 12 toys.

Name

Mixed Practice

Lessons 1–7

Concepts and Skills

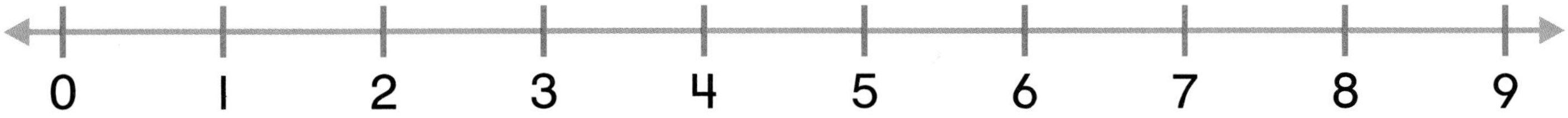

Count on to add. You can use the number line.

1

7	3	4	6	1	7	3
+ 1	+ 6	+ 3	+ 2	+ 8	+ 2	+ 5

Add.

2 $9 + 3 =$ ____ $5 + 6 =$ ____ $0 + 4 =$ ____

3

6	2	1	9	5	4	5
+ 2	+ 6	+ 9	+ 1	+ 4	+ 5	+ 5

Problem Solving

4 Kay wants exactly 5 hats. Make a list.

1 sack of ____ hats and 1 sack of ____ hats

1 sack of ____ hats

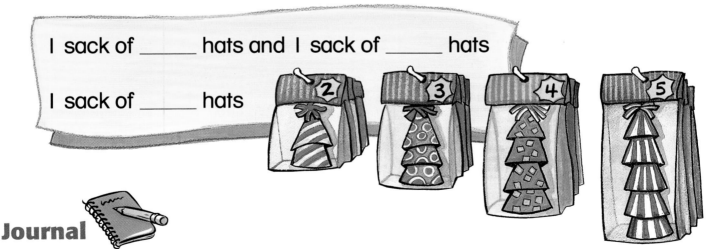

Journal

5 Draw pictures to show ways to make 7.

Notes for Home: Your child practiced addition facts to 12. *Home Activity:* Ask your child to draw pictures of two groups that make 6.

For additional practice, see Basic Facts Review, page 540, Set 1.

Name ______________________________

Cumulative Review

Chapters 1–4

Concepts and Skills

Write the missing numbers.

1. 1 2 3 ____ ____ 6 7 ____ ____ 10

2. 10 ____ 8 ____ ____ 5 4 3 ____ ____

Write the number sentence.

3. 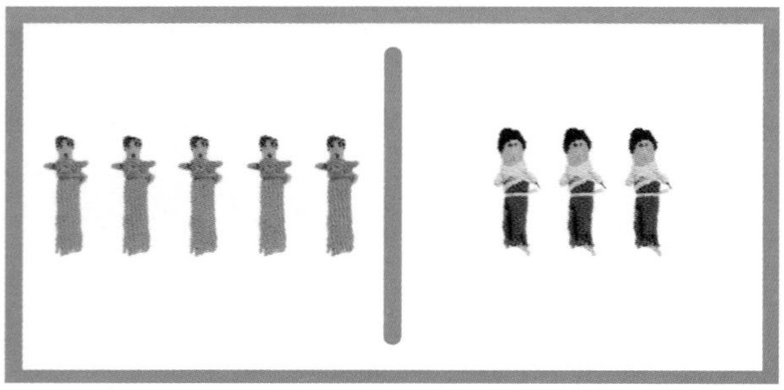

____ + ____ = ____

4. 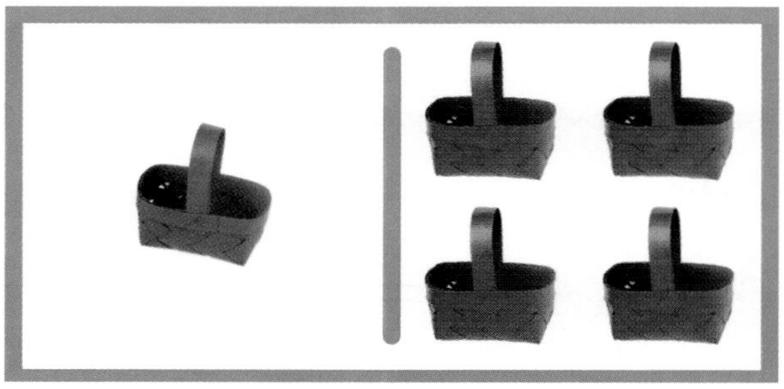

____ + ____ = ____

Test Prep

Fill in the ○ for the correct answer.

Solve. You can use  .

5. 

$10 - 4 =$ ____

5 ○ 6 ○ 7 ○ 8 ○

6. 9  float.
6 swim away.
How many are left?

9 ○ 6 ○ 3 ○ 1 ○

Notes for Home: Your child reviewed ordering numbers, addition, and subtraction.
Home Activity: Have your child write the numbers 1 to 10 on index cards, shuffle the cards, and lay out the cards in order.

Name _____

Use a Number Line to Count Back

I start with 6 cubes
and count back 2 cubes.
There are 4 cubes left.

$$6 - 2 = \underline{4}$$

Check

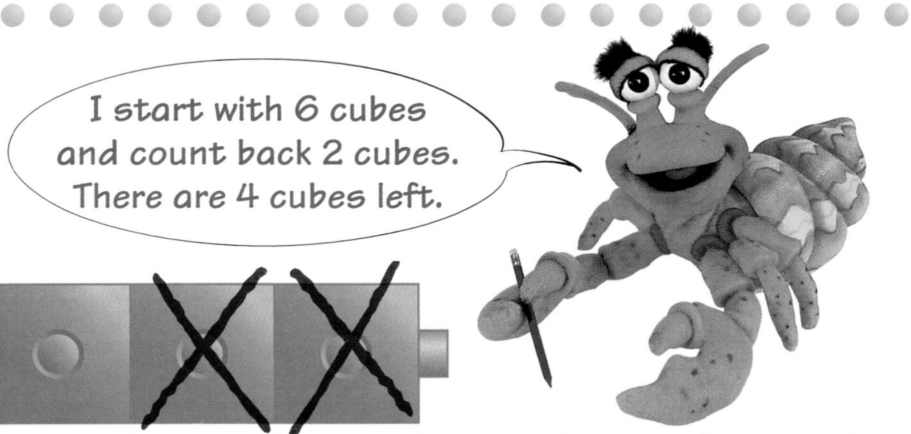

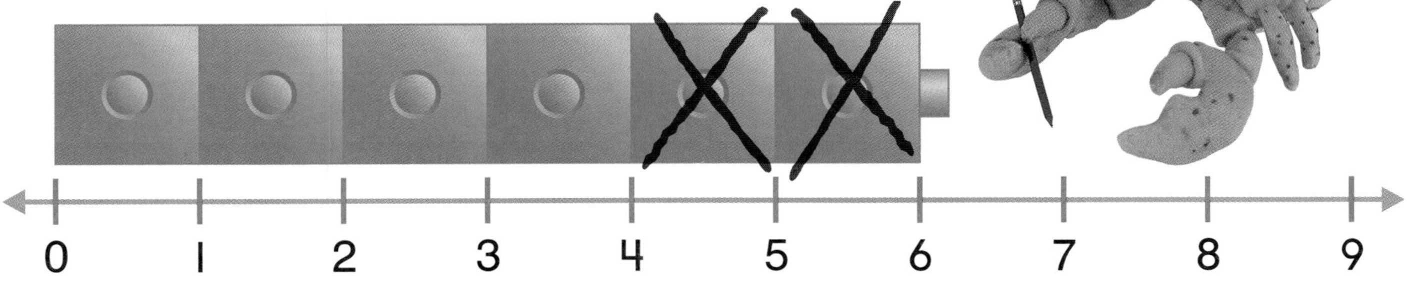

Use with the number line. Write the difference.

1 $2 - 1 = \underline{1}$ $9 - 2 = \underline{}$ $5 - 3 = \underline{}$

2 $2 - 2 = \underline{}$ $4 - 3 = \underline{}$ $7 - 1 = \underline{}$

3 $9 - 1 = \underline{}$ $8 - 2 = \underline{}$ $9 - 3 = \underline{}$

4

5	6	7	6	4	8	5
-2	-1	-2	-3	-2	-1	-1

Talk About It Tell how you subtract using a number line.

Notes for Home: Your child used a number line to subtract 1 or 2. *Home Activity:* Ask your child to show you how to solve $9 - 2$.

Practice

0 1 2 3 4 5 6 7 8 9

You can use the number line.
Write the difference.

5 $6 - 2 = \underline{4}$ $3 - 1 = \_\_\_$ $8 - 1 = \_\_\_$

6 $5 - 2 = \_\_\_$ $4 - 2 = \_\_\_$ $3 - 2 = \_\_\_$

7

1	9	4	5	2	8
− 1	− 2	− 1	− 1	− 2	− 2

8

2	6	6	9	7	7
− 1	− 2	− 1	− 1	− 1	− 2

Write your own number sentences.

9 $\_\_\_ - 2 = \_\_\_$

10 $\_\_\_ - 2 = \_\_\_$

11 $\_\_\_ - 1 = \_\_\_$

12 $\_\_\_ - 1 = \_\_\_$

Mental Math

13 Choose any number.
Count back 2.
Write the answer.

$11 - 2 = \_\_\_$

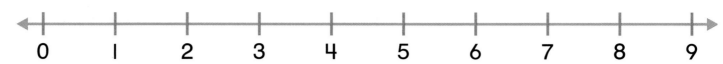

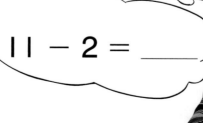

Notes for Home: Children practiced subtracting by counting back. *Home Activity:* Ask your child to draw a number line and then use it to solve 9 − 3.

PRACTICE

Name

Count Back 1 or 2

Learn

I say 6. Then I count back 1 and say 5.
I say 6, then 5, 4.

6 − 1 = 5   6 − 2 = 4

Check

Count back to subtract.

1. 

9 − 1 = 8

2. 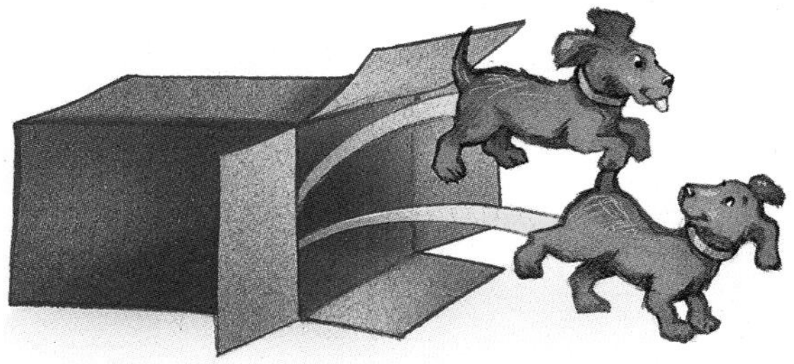

5 − 2 = ____

3. 

$\begin{array}{r} 8 \\ -\ 2 \\ \hline \end{array}$

8 − 2 = ____

4. 

$\begin{array}{r} 10 \\ -\ 1 \\ \hline \end{array}$

10 − 1 = ____

Talk About It How do you find 7 − 2?

Notes for Home: Your child counted back to subtract 1 or 2 from a number. *Home Activity:* Ask your child to tell you how to find 5 − 1.

Practice

Count back to subtract.

5

$$\begin{array}{r} 8 \\ -\ 2 \\ \hline \end{array}$$

8 − 2 = 6

6

$$\begin{array}{r} 8 \\ -\ 1 \\ \hline \end{array}$$

8 − 1 = ____

7 3 − 2 = ____ 5 − 1 = ____ 7 − 1 = ____

8 2 − 1 = ____ 7 − 2 = ____ 6 − 1 = ____

9
$$\begin{array}{r} 3 \\ -\ 1 \\ \hline \end{array} \quad \begin{array}{r} 5 \\ -\ 2 \\ \hline \end{array} \quad \begin{array}{r} 8 \\ -\ 1 \\ \hline \end{array} \quad \begin{array}{r} 9 \\ -\ 2 \\ \hline \end{array} \quad \begin{array}{r} 10 \\ -\ 2 \\ \hline \end{array} \quad \begin{array}{r} 3 \\ -\ 2 \\ \hline \end{array} \quad \begin{array}{r} 5 \\ -\ 1 \\ \hline \end{array}$$

10
$$\begin{array}{r} 10 \\ -\ 1 \\ \hline \end{array} \quad \begin{array}{r} 4 \\ -\ 2 \\ \hline \end{array} \quad \begin{array}{r} 11 \\ -\ 2 \\ \hline \end{array} \quad \begin{array}{r} 7 \\ -\ 2 \\ \hline \end{array} \quad \begin{array}{r} 4 \\ -\ 1 \\ \hline \end{array} \quad \begin{array}{r} 6 \\ -\ 2 \\ \hline \end{array} \quad \begin{array}{r} 9 \\ -\ 1 \\ \hline \end{array}$$

PRACTICE

Problem Solving

Solve.

11 There are 10  in a . 2 jump out.

How many are left? ____

12 There are 6  on a . 1 jumps off.

How many are left? ____

Notes for Home: Your child practiced counting back 1 or 2 to subtract. *Home Activity:* Say a number from 2 to 9. Then ask your child to count back 1 and then 2 from the number you named.

Name ______________________________

Practice Game

Count Down

Players 2

What You Need

workmat 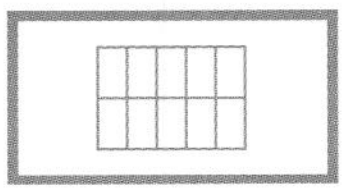

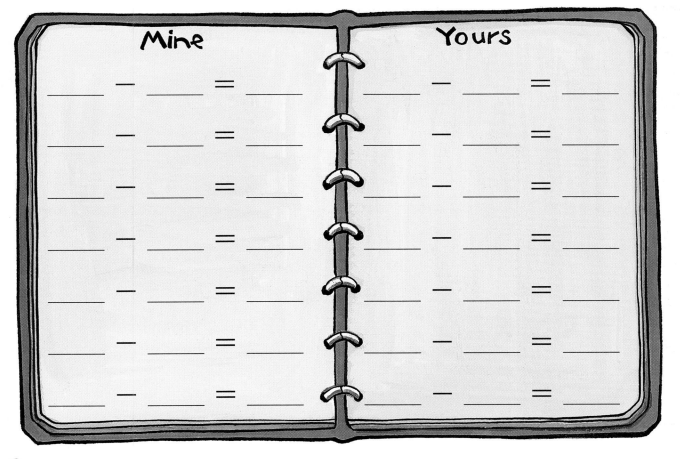

10 counters

How to Play

1. Put the counters on the workmat.
2. Take turns removing 1 or 2 counters.
3. Write a number sentence that tells about your turn.
4. The player who takes away the last counter wins.

Mine	Yours
___ − ___ = ___	___ − ___ = ___
___ − ___ = ___	___ − ___ = ___
___ − ___ = ___	___ − ___ = ___
___ − ___ = ___	___ − ___ = ___
___ − ___ = ___	___ − ___ = ___
___ − ___ = ___	___ − ___ = ___
___ − ___ = ___	___ − ___ = ___

Notes for Home: Your child played a game to practice subtracting 1 or 2. *Home Activity:* Ask your child to show you how to play the game. To play, draw a workmat like the one shown on this page and use objects such as pennies or beans for counters.

PRACTICE

Name ____________________

STOP and Practice

0 1 2 3 4 5 6 7 8 9

You can use the number line.

Add.

1

5	3	6	4	5	7	6
+ 2	+ 1	+ 2	+ 3	+ 0	+ 2	+ 3

2 $3 + 5 =$ ____ $4 + 2 =$ ____ $1 + 7 =$ ____

3 $0 + 0 =$ ____ $3 + 3 =$ ____ $2 + 3 =$ ____

Subtract.

4

6	9	8	3	4	7	9
− 1	− 1	− 2	− 1	− 1	− 2	− 2

5 $8 - 1 =$ ____ $8 - 1 =$ ____ $6 - 2 =$ ____

Solve each problem.

6 There are 6 .
2 more come.

____ in all

7 There are 7 .
2 crawl away.

____ left

Notes for Home: Your child practiced adding and subtracting. *Home Activity:* Ask your child to circle all the problems on this page that subtract 1. Then help them write three more problems that subtract 1.

PRACTICE

Name ______________________________

Subtract All and Subtract Zero

Learn

No one ate any carrots.
How many are left?

5 − 0 = 5

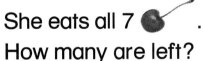

A bunny ate all 5 carrots.
How many are left?

5 − 5 = 0

Check

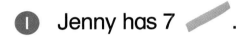

Use counters to show the story. Write the difference.

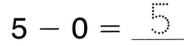

1. Jenny has 7 carrots.
   She eats 0 carrots.
   How many are left?
   7 − 0 = 7

2. Jenny has 7 cherries.
   She eats all 7 cherries.
   How many are left?
   7 − 7 = ____

3. Kenji has 6 plums.
   He eats all 6 plums.
   How many are left?
   $\begin{array}{r} 6 \\ -\ 6 \\ \hline \end{array}$
   6 − 6 = ____

4. Kenji has 6 peppers.
   He eats 0 peppers.
   How many are left?
   $\begin{array}{r} 6 \\ -\ 0 \\ \hline \end{array}$
   6 − 0 = ____

Talk About It Circle the problems that subtract 0.
What pattern do you see?

Notes for Home: Your child subtracted all and 0 from a number. *Home Activity:* Ask your child to tell you what happens when all the objects are subtracted from a group, and when 0 objects are subtracted from a group.

Practice

Solve.

5 There are 12 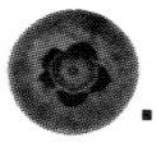.
All are eaten.
How many are left?

$$\begin{array}{r} 12 \\ -\ 12 \\ \hline \end{array}$$

12 − 12 = 0

6 There are 9 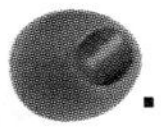.
No one ate any.
How many are left?

$$\begin{array}{r} 9 \\ -\ 0 \\ \hline \end{array}$$

9 − 0 = ____

Subtract.

7 5 − 5 = ____ 5 − 0 = ____ 10 − 10 = ____

8

8	8	3	2	11	4	6
− 0	− 8	− 3	− 2	− 0	− 0	− 6

Mixed Practice Subtract.

9 10 − 2 = ____ 6 − 6 = ____ 9 − 1 = ____

10

11	3	8	7	4	11	7
− 2	− 0	− 1	− 1	− 2	− 11	− 0

Problem Solving Critical Thinking

11 Try this super fact. 50 − 0 = ____

 **Write your own** super fact. ____ − 0 = ____

Notes for Home: Your child practiced subtraction. *Home Activity:* Ask your child to use counters such as buttons or beans to show 9 − 9 and 9 − 0.

PRACTICE

For additional practice, see Skills Practice Bank, page 528, Set 2.

Name _____

Subtract with 5

Learn

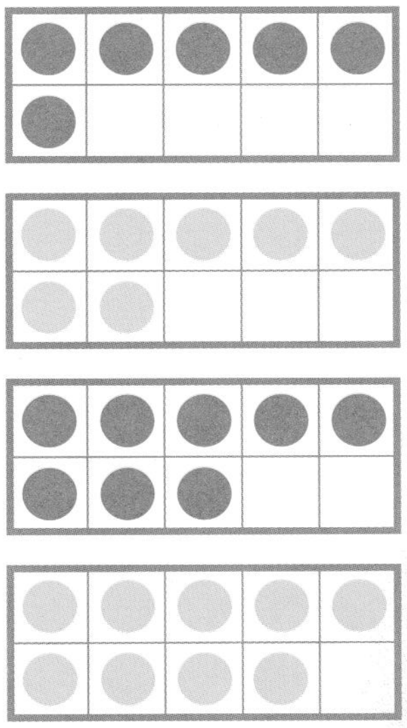

One part is 5.

To subtract 5, we can cover the top row and count how many are left.

Check

Use the ▭. Cover 5 ⬭ ⬭ .
Write the difference.

1

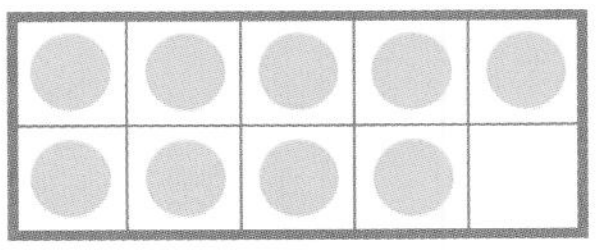

$$9$$
$$- 5$$

$$9 - 5 = \underline{4}$$

2

$$10$$
$$- 5$$

$$10 - 5 = \underline{}$$

3

$$8$$
$$- 5$$

$$8 - 5 = \underline{}$$

4

$$6$$
$$- 5$$

$$6 - 5 = \underline{}$$

Talk About It How do you use the ▭ to subtract 5?

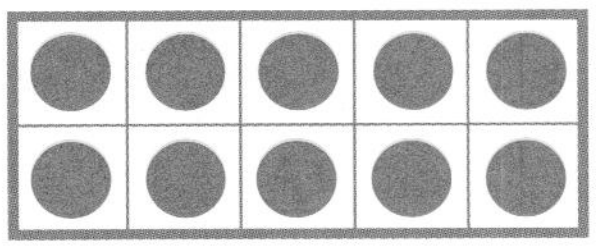

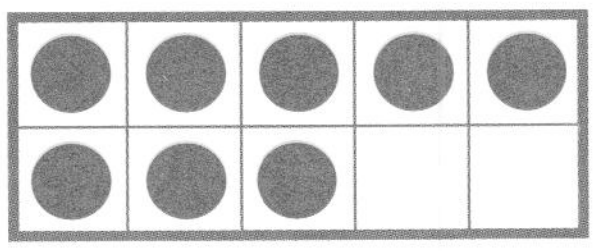

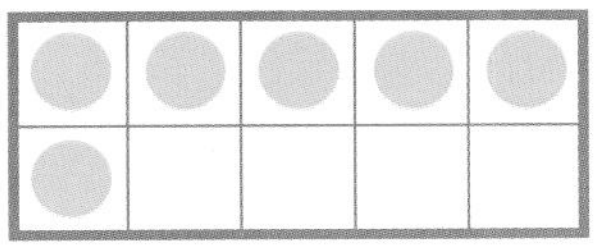

Notes for Home: Your child subtracted 5 from a number. *Home Activity:* Ask your child to tell you a math story for $10 - 5 = 5$.

Subtract.

5 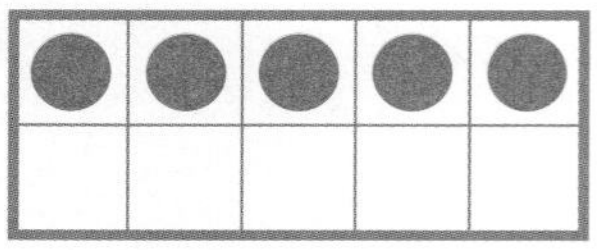

$\begin{array}{r} 5 \\ -\ 5 \\ \hline \end{array}$

$5 - 5 =$ 0

6 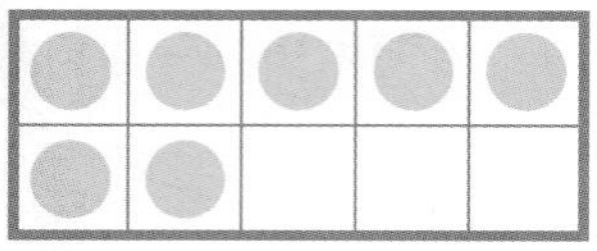

$\begin{array}{r} 7 \\ -\ 5 \\ \hline \end{array}$

$7 - 5 =$ ____

7 $10 - 5 =$ ____ $6 - 5 =$ ____ $5 - 5 =$ ____

8 $\begin{array}{r} 10 \\ -\ 5 \\ \hline \end{array}$ $\begin{array}{r} 6 \\ -\ 5 \\ \hline \end{array}$ $\begin{array}{r} 7 \\ -\ 5 \\ \hline \end{array}$ $\begin{array}{r} 11 \\ -\ 5 \\ \hline \end{array}$ $\begin{array}{r} 12 \\ -\ 5 \\ \hline \end{array}$ $\begin{array}{r} 9 \\ -\ 5 \\ \hline \end{array}$ $\begin{array}{r} 8 \\ -\ 5 \\ \hline \end{array}$

Mixed Practice Subtract.

9 $\begin{array}{r} 8 \\ -\ 2 \\ \hline \end{array}$ $\begin{array}{r} 9 \\ -\ 0 \\ \hline \end{array}$ $\begin{array}{r} 6 \\ -\ 2 \\ \hline \end{array}$ $\begin{array}{r} 9 \\ -\ 1 \\ \hline \end{array}$ $\begin{array}{r} 7 \\ -\ 7 \\ \hline \end{array}$ $\begin{array}{r} 3 \\ -\ 1 \\ \hline \end{array}$ $\begin{array}{r} 6 \\ -\ 1 \\ \hline \end{array}$

10 $\begin{array}{r} 4 \\ -\ 0 \\ \hline \end{array}$ $\begin{array}{r} 7 \\ -\ 1 \\ \hline \end{array}$ $\begin{array}{r} 5 \\ -\ 2 \\ \hline \end{array}$ $\begin{array}{r} 8 \\ -\ 5 \\ \hline \end{array}$ $\begin{array}{r} 6 \\ -\ 6 \\ \hline \end{array}$ $\begin{array}{r} 7 \\ -\ 2 \\ \hline \end{array}$ $\begin{array}{r} 9 \\ -\ 2 \\ \hline \end{array}$

Problem Solving

11 There are 8  in all.

How many 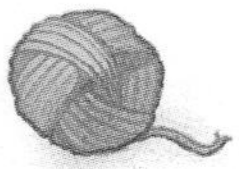 are in the basket?

____ 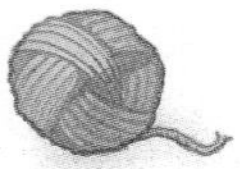

Notes for Home: Your child practiced subtracting with 5, counting back 1 or 2, and subtracting zero. *Home Activity:* Point to one or two facts on the page and ask your child to show it using small objects such as buttons or beans.

Name ______________________________

Reading for Math

Details and Facts

Jack and Linda were helping Dad carry grocery bags. Jack looked in the car. There were 5 bags in the trunk.

"I can carry these 3 bags," Jack said. "Can you get the rest, Linda?"

"OK," Linda answered. "I will get them."

1. What were Jack and Linda doing? ______________________________

____

2. Where were the grocery bags? ______________________________

____

3. How many bags were there? ______

4. How many bags can Jack carry? ______

Talk About It How many grocery bags will Linda carry? How do you know?

Notes for Home: Your child answered questions that focused on the details of a math story. *Home Activity:* Take turns telling math stories about the things you do around the house. Discuss the details of the stories you make up.

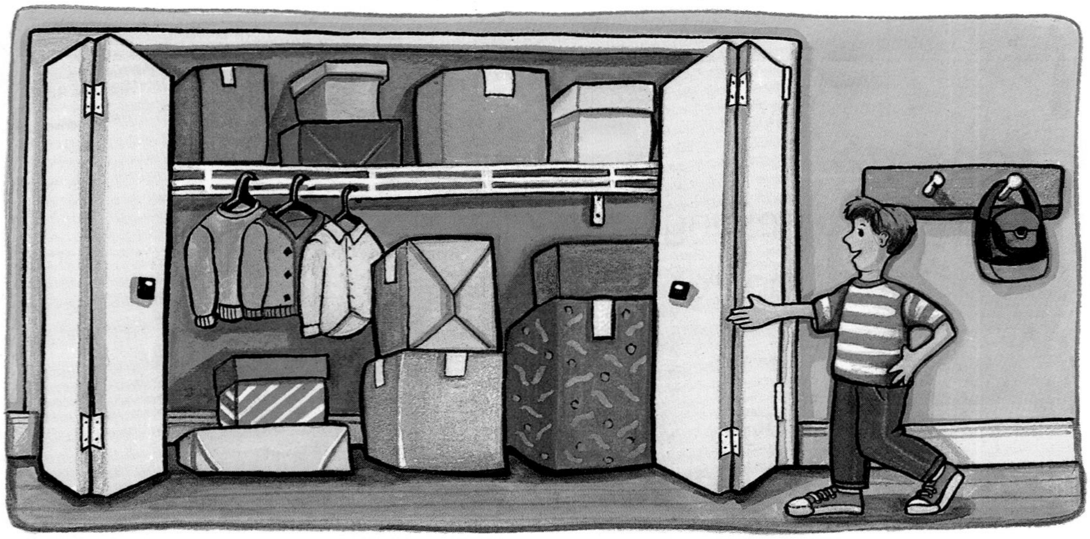

"So many boxes!" said Bryson. "I cleaned my bedroom. I put my things in boxes. I put the boxes in the closet. Now I have 5 boxes on the top shelf and 6 boxes on the floor."

5. What did Bryson do? ______________________________

____

6. Where did he put the boxes? ______________________________

____

7. How many boxes are on the top shelf? _____

8. How many boxes are on the floor? _____

9. How many boxes all together? _____

Journal

10. Write your own math story about things you keep in boxes. Don't forget the details!

Notes for Home: Your child prepared for a Problem Solving lesson about writing number sentences. *Home Activity:* Read a favorite story with your child. Talk about important details in the story.

Name

Problem Solving: Write a Number Sentence

Learn

PROBLEM SOLVING GUIDE
Understand • Plan • Solve • Look Back

Rita has 8 .

She eats 3.

How many are left?

$8 - 3 = 5$

Check

Use 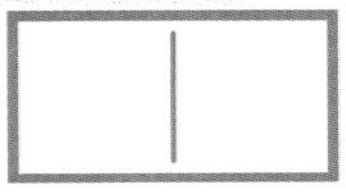 and .
Show the story.
Write a number sentence.

1. Marta buys 6 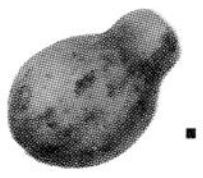.

   Jon buys 3 .

   How many  do they have?

   ____

2. Lin fills a 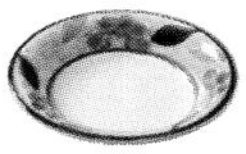 with 12 apples.
   Her friends take 5 apples.
   How many apples are still in the 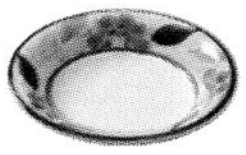?

   ____

Talk About It How do you know when to add?
How do you know when to subtract?

Notes for Home: Your child decided whether to add or subtract, and then wrote a number sentence to solve a problem. *Home Activity:* Ask your child to make up a math story for the number sentence 4 + 2 = 6.

Practice

You can use  and 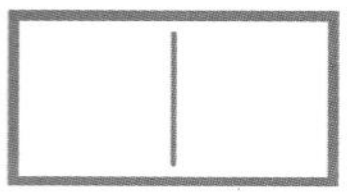 to show the story.
Write a number sentence.

3. 8  are in a box.

The children use all 8 .
How many are left?

8 − 8 = 0

4. 6 children put their  on the table.

5 more children put their  on the table.

How many are on the table?

____

5. Ray has 4 .

Anna has 4 .

How many in all?

____

6. Sal has 6 .
He eats 2.
How many are left?

____

Write About It

7. Here is the number sentence. 7 − 7 = 0

You write the story. ________________________________

____

____

____

Notes for Home: Your child wrote number sentences to solve problems. *Home Activity:* Tell a simple story problem such as "There are 6 children playing. 2 go home. How many are left?" Have your child write a number sentence for the story.

For additional practice, see Skills Practice Bank, page 528, Set 3.

Name

Mixed Practice

Lessons 8–12

Concepts and Skills

0 1 2 3 4 5 6 7 8 9

Count back to subtract.

1	10	7	9	11	6	8	5
	− 1	− 2	− 1	− 2	− 1	− 2	− 1

Subtract.

2	7	7	5	5	9	9	3
	− 7	− 0	− 0	− 5	− 9	− 0	− 0

Problem Solving

You can use 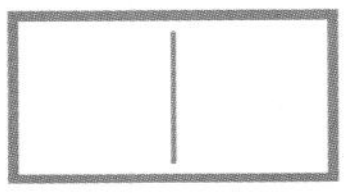 and  to show the story.
Write the number sentence.

3 There are 9 .

Tom brings 3 more.
How many are there?

____

4 There are 6  in a pack.

Ken eats 1 .
How many are left?

____

Journal

5 Draw a number line from 0 to 12. Write a math story and a number sentence. You can use your number line to help.

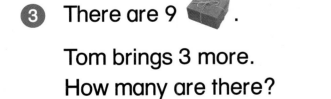

Notes for Home: Your child practiced subtraction and problem solving. *Home Activity:* Use a picture book to make up subtraction stories with your child.

For additional practice, see Basic Facts Review, page 540, Set 2.

Name ____________________

Cumulative Review

Chapters 1–4

Concepts and Skills

Add.

1. $\begin{array}{r}2\\+\ 4\\\hline\end{array}$ $\begin{array}{r}2\\+\ 6\\\hline\end{array}$ $\begin{array}{r}5\\+\ 6\\\hline\end{array}$ $\begin{array}{r}4\\+\ 3\\\hline\end{array}$ $\begin{array}{r}6\\+\ 5\\\hline\end{array}$ $\begin{array}{r}9\\+\ 1\\\hline\end{array}$ $\begin{array}{r}3\\+\ 5\\\hline\end{array}$

Problem Solving

Use the graph. Write the number.

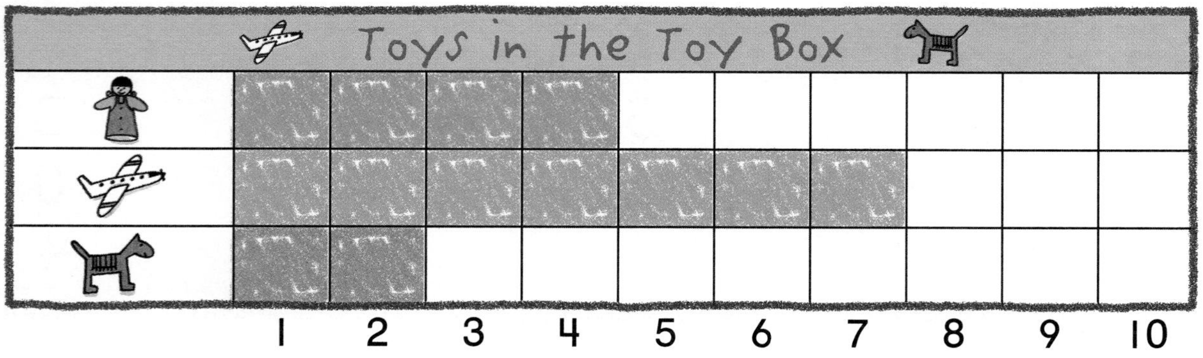

2. How many more  than  ? ______ more

3. How many fewer  than  ? ______ fewer

Test Prep

Fill in the ○ for the correct answer.

You can use the number line to count on.

4. $3 + 8 =$ ______

○ 9 ○ 10 ○ 11 ○ 12

5. $5 + 2 =$ ______

○ 8 ○ 7 ○ 6 ○ 4

Notes for Home: Your child reviewed using a graph and addition. *Home Activity:* Ask your child to read the graph on this page and tell you if there are more planes or more dolls in the toy box (planes).

Name ______________________________

Chapter 4 Review

Stay Sharp

CHAPTER REVIEW

Vocabulary

1 Write 2 turnaround facts.

____ + ____ = ____

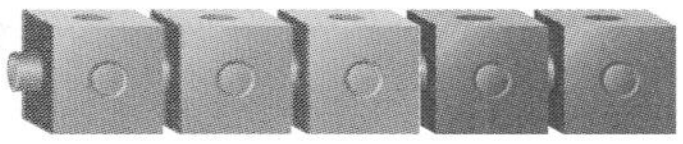

____ + ____ = ____

Count on to add.

2 $4 + 2 =$ ____

Count back to subtract.

3 $6 - 1 =$ ____

Concepts and Skills

Add.

4

7	5	0	6	3	8	4
+ 0	+ 6	+ 2	+ 2	+ 5	+ 1	+ 3

Subtract.

5

10	6	9	9	5	11	7
− 5	− 0	− 9	− 2	− 1	− 2	− 2

Problem Solving

Write a number sentence.

6 Ahmad has 3 .

He has 2 .

How many pets in all?

____

7 There are 10 .

2 fly away.

How many are left?

____

Notes for Home: Your child reviewed vocabulary, addition and subtraction, and writing number sentences. *Home Activity:* Have your child use objects such as pennies or paper clips to show you how to solve some of the problems on this page.

Name ______________________________

Chapter 4 Test

Add.

❶ 7 + 3 = ____ 9 + 1 = ____ 2 + 5 = ____

❷

1	5	6	3	2	8	4
+ 5	+ 1	+ 3	+ 6	+ 8	+ 2	+ 3

❸

0	6	5	8	7	4	2
+ 4	+ 5	+ 2	+ 0	+ 5	+ 5	+ 8

Subtract.

❹ 9 − 2 = ____ 6 − 1 = ____ 8 − 2 = ____

❺

5	9	7	11	6	4	3
− 0	− 5	− 2	− 5	− 0	− 2	− 1

❻

12	4	7	6	8	4	6
− 5	− 4	− 5	− 6	− 5	− 1	− 2

Problem Solving

Write a number sentence.

❼ Bill has 4 .
He gives 2 away.
How many are left? ______________________

Notes for Home: Your child was assessed on adding, subtracting, and writing number sentences. *Home Activity:* Ask your child to circle all the problems on this page that subtract 5 and use their hands to show each problem.

Name ____________________

Performance Assessment

Chapter 4

Take 2 cards.

Write a number sentence.

Write the turnaround fact.

Use number cards from 0 to 6.

Write the number sentence. Write the turnaround fact.

1. ____ + ____ = ____ ____ + ____ = ____

2. ____ + ____ = ____ ____ + ____ = ____

3. ____ + ____ = ____ ____ + ____ = ____

Use number cards from 0 to 6. Take one card.
Complete each number sentence.

4. 10 − ____ = ____

5. 12 − ____ = ____

6. 9 − ____ = ____

7. 8 − ____ = ____

Problem Solving Critical Thinking

8. How can you get 0 left when you subtract?

Notes for Home: Your child did an activity that assessed addition and subtraction through 12.
Home Activity: Ask your child to solve basic facts such as 5 + 4 = 9, 9 − 4 = 5.

Name ______________________________

Explore with a CALCULATOR

What Toy Is in the Box?

Keys You Will Use ON/C + =

Use your calculator to add 1, 2, or 3.

Then color the number you add.

	Press	Press + and =.	Calculator shows
1	7	1 2 3	10.
2	4	1 2 3	5.
3	3	1 2 3	6.
4	6	1 2 3	8.
5	5	1 2 3	7.

Tech Talk What keys do you press to subtract? ON/C ☐ ☐

Visit our Web site. www.parent.mathsurf.com

A Nutty Trick

Amaze your friends and family.
Say that you know how many peanuts are in the bag.

Here's How

1. Secretly put 12 peanuts in a paper bag.
2. Have someone take out a handful.
3. Ask, "How many did you take out?" Subtract that number from 12.

   12 – _____ = _____

4. Now you can tell how many peanuts are in the bag.

   Do it again with a different number of peanuts.

Fold down

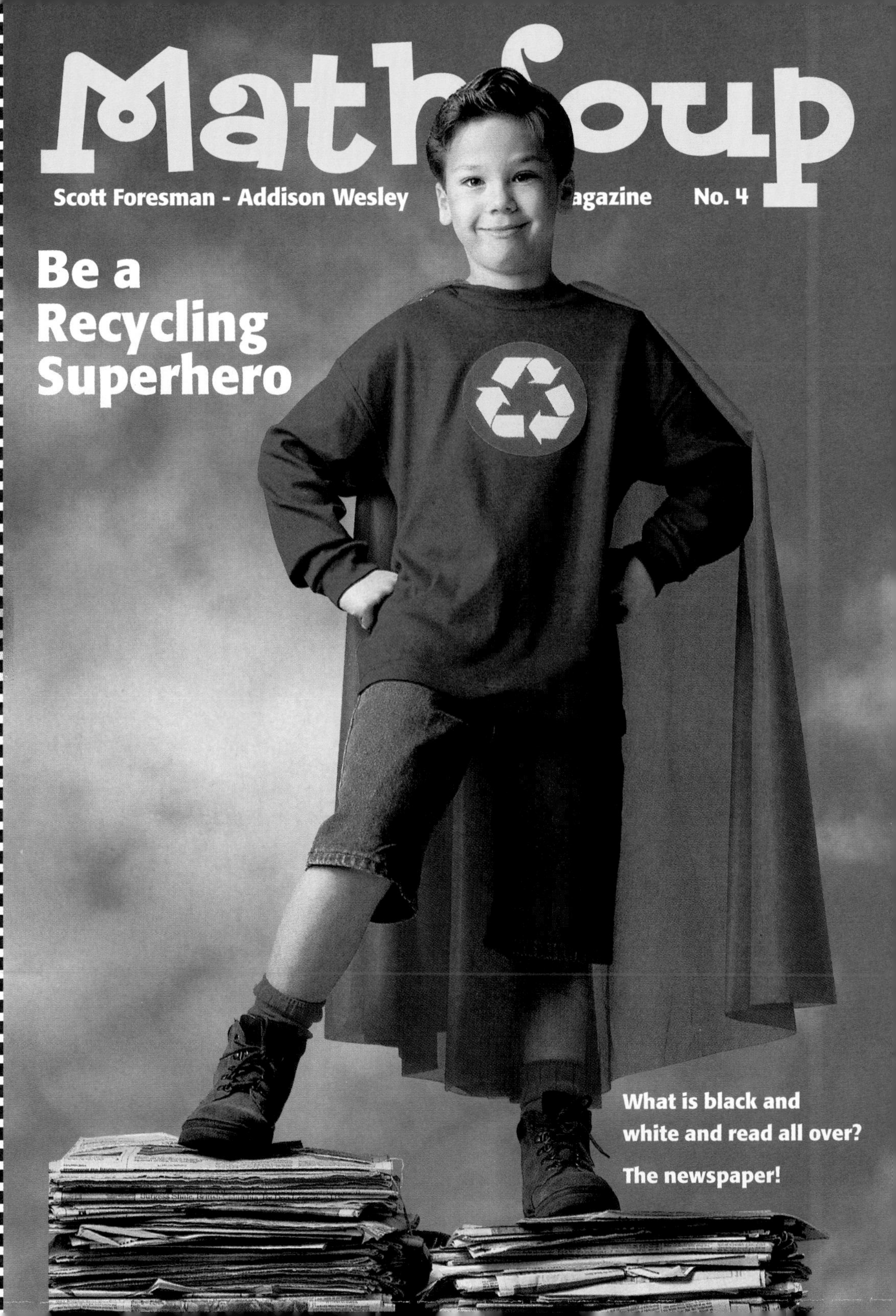

MathSoup
Scott Foresman - Addison Wesley
agazine No. 4
Be a Recycling Superhero
What is black and white and read all over?
The newspaper!

All Wrapped Up

Hannah forgot which box is Fred's present.
Use the clues to help Hannah solve the puzzle.

Plastic Wear

Would you wear a plastic bottle or two? These two children are! The bottles are made into a fiber which is woven into a cloth and then made into hats.

Notes for Home: Your child used clues to compare objects.
Home Activity: Show your child two or three different things and ask how are they alike and how are they different.

Track Your Trash

How much trash do you throw out? Would you believe 1,500 pounds every year? That's equal to the weight of one, big cow.

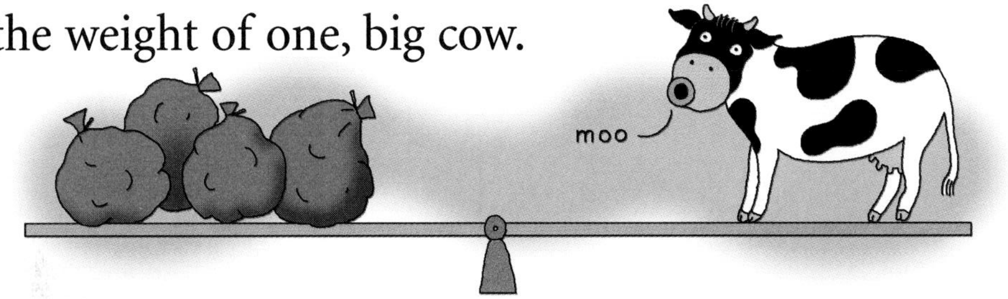

What's in your recycle box?

Make a graph.
Color one box for each thing you recycled.
If you recycled three cans, color three boxes.

We Recycle

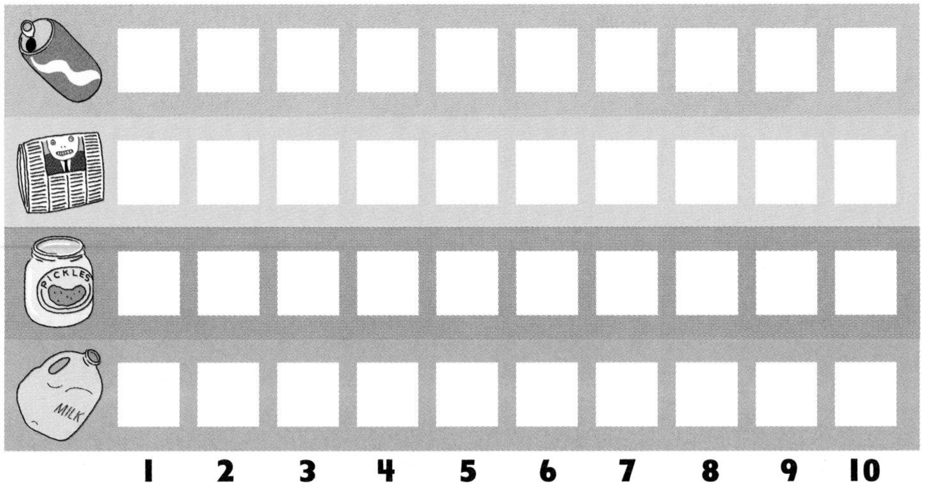

Clues:
Fred's present has

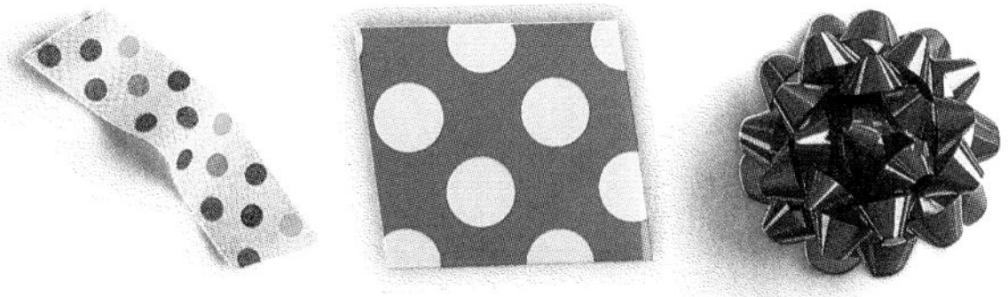

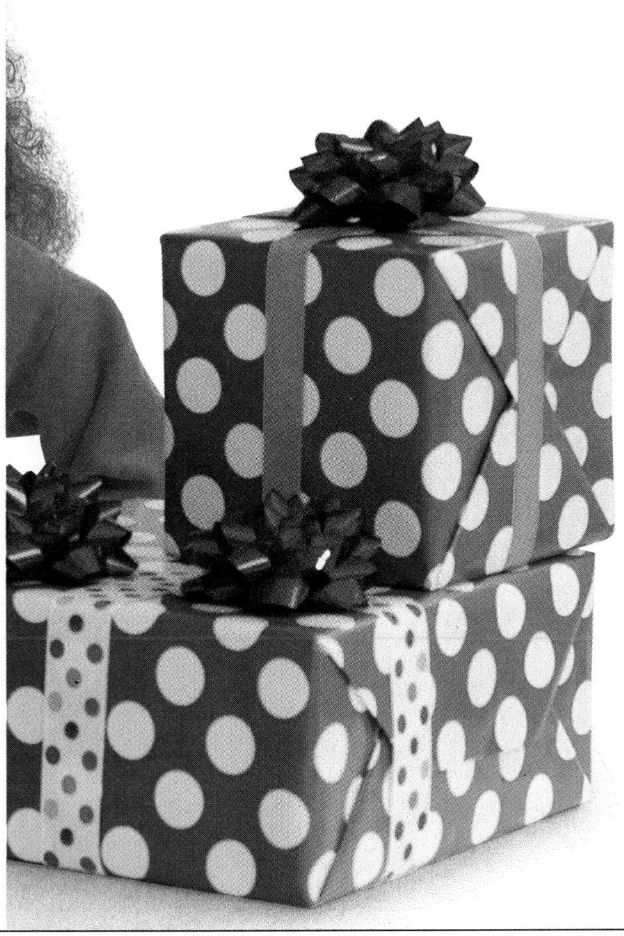

Make your own puzzle.
Color the boxes.
What clues will you use?

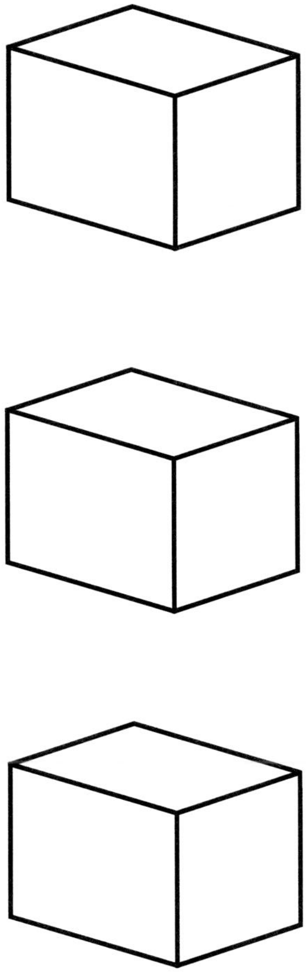

Notes for Home: Your child learned that a graph can be used to keep track of recyclable items. *Home Activity:* Encourage your child to make a weekly home recycling graph.

Gone Fishin'

Did you ever fish in a bag?

What You Need

A ruler or a stick for a "fishing pole".

Paper fish, each with a number from 1 through 9.

A big paper bag, a small magnet, string, and a paper clip.

How to Play

1 Tie the magnet to the string.

2 Tie the string to your "fishing pole."

3 Put a paper clip on each paper fish.

4 Put the fish into the bag.

Now, go fishing with a couple of friends!

5 Each player tries to catch two fish. Add the numbers.

6 The player with the greater sum wins.

7 Put the fish back in the bag. Play again!

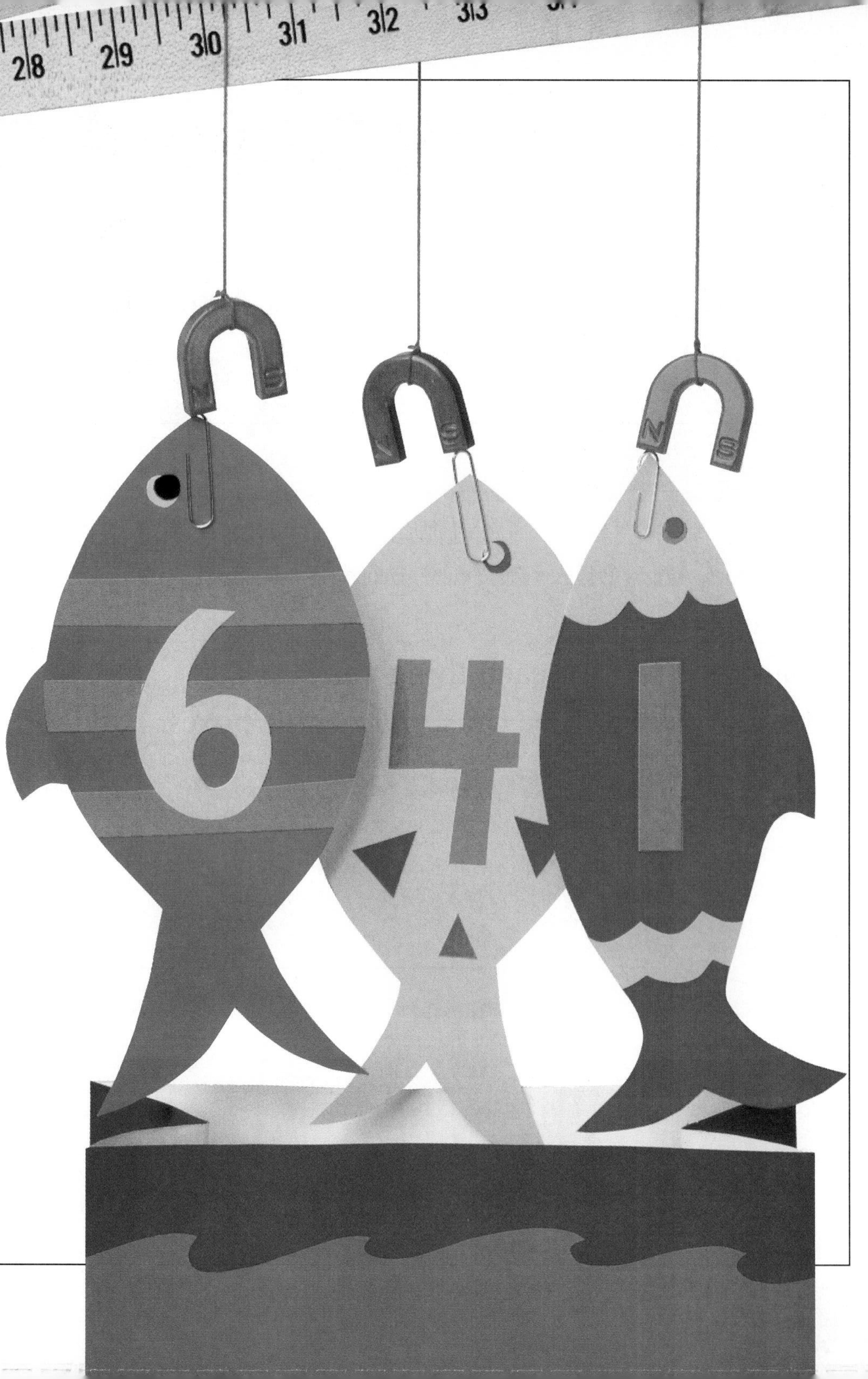

Notes for Home: Your child discovered that a paper bag can be used for an addition game. *Home Activity:* Encourage your child to make up a game using bags or boxes.

CHAPTER

5 Geometry and Fractions

Food for Thought

Notes for Home: Your child discussed the shapes and solids in the picture. *Home Activity:* Play "I Spy" with shapes. For example, "I spy something that is a rectangle." Give more clues if they are needed: "The rectangle is taller than a person."

Math at Home

Our class is starting Chapter 5. We will learn about geometry and fractions. We can describe shapes at home and talk about things we cut into equal parts. Here are some other activities we can do at home.

Guess the Box

Gather a few small boxes and cans that are different sizes and shapes. Take turns describing the shape of one container. The other person tries to figure out which can or box is being described.

Sandwich Shapes

Make sandwiches and cut them in half (or thirds or fourths) before serving. What different shapes can you make?

Community Connection

When you take your child to the grocery store, look at some of the boxes and describe their shapes. Can you find boxes that have square faces, rectangular faces, or circular faces?

Visit our Web site. **www.parent.mathsurf.com**

Name

Explore Solids

Explore

Sort your solids into 2 groups.
Draw or write to show
how you sorted. Sort 2 ways.

1

2

Share

How did you sort?

Notes for Home: Your child sorted three-dimensional objects, such as blocks, into groups.
Home Activity: Ask your child to describe ways to sort the objects.

EXPLORE

Connect

sphere cylinder cone

These are round and curved. They roll.

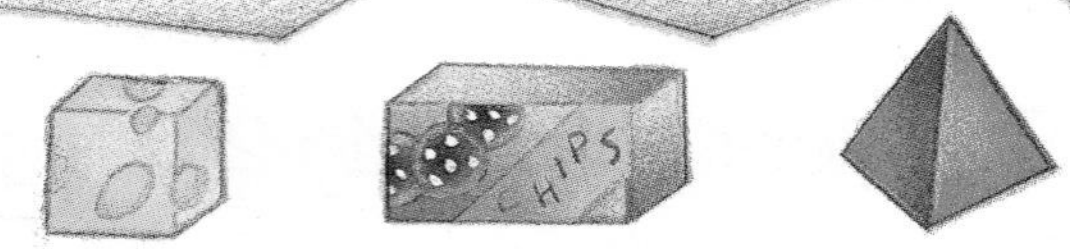

cube rectangular prism pyramid

These can stack and slide.

Draw a solid that belongs.

Draw a solid that does not belong.

	Belongs	Does not belong
3 		
4 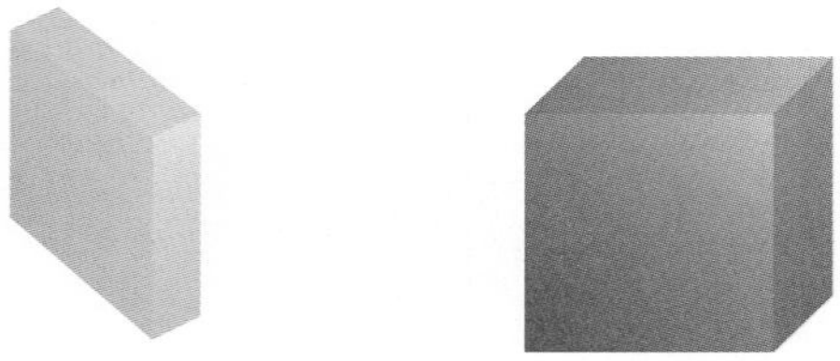		

Problem Solving Patterns

Circle the solid that comes next.

5 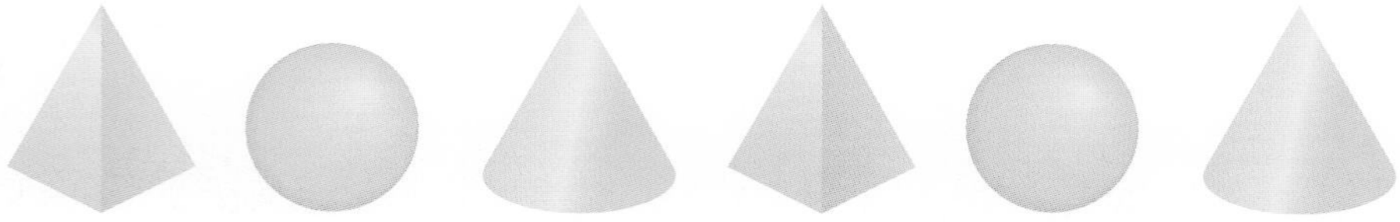 

6 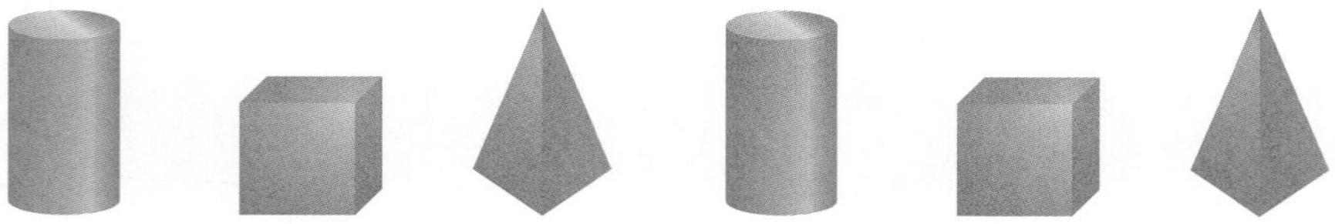 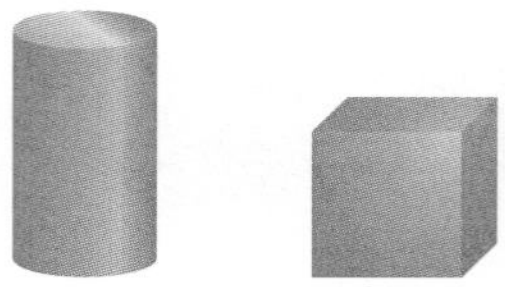

EXPLORE

Notes for Home: Your child described similarities and differences between solid shapes. *Home Activity:* Use blocks, boxes, cans, and other containers to play What's my rule? Choose 3 that are the same in some way, and ask your child to tell you how they are alike. Take turns.

Name _____

Learn

When I draw around the face of this cylinder I get a circle.

Faces of Solids

rectangles [_____] [__]

square

circle ◯

triangle △

Check

1 Draw to make a circle.

Draw or write to show what solid you used.

2 Draw to make a square.

Talk About It How did you decide which solid to use?

Notes for Home: Your child traced around sides of three-dimensional solids to make a circle or square. *Home Activity:* Give your child a three-dimensional solid such as a box or can to trace. Ask your child to tell what the shape will be before he or she does the tracing.

Practice

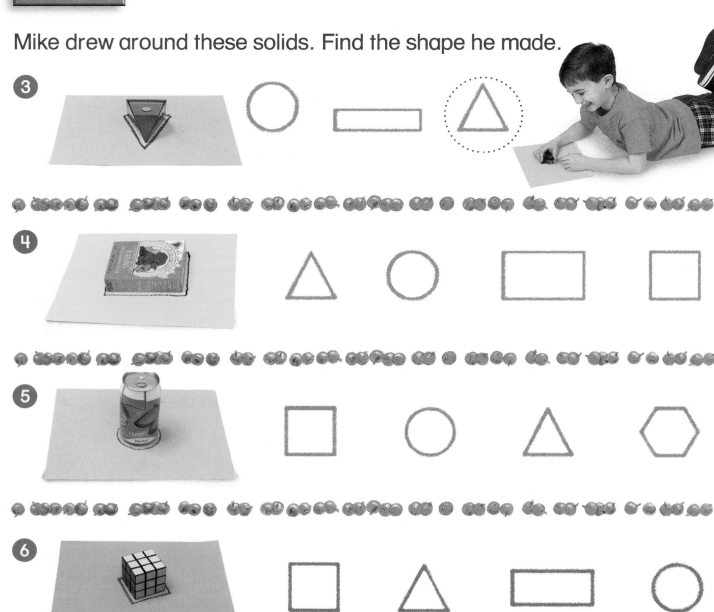

Mike drew around these solids. Find the shape he made.

3  

4  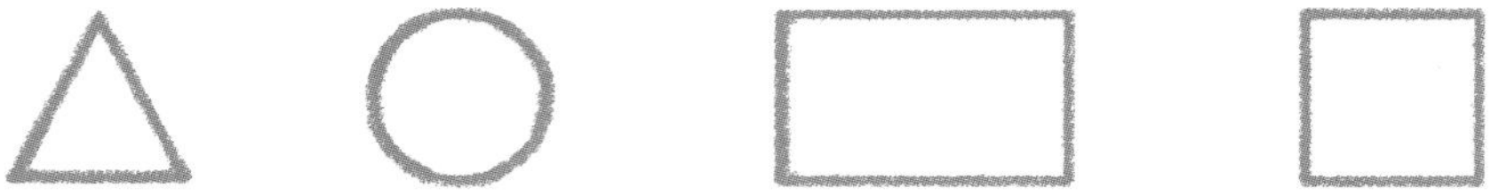

5  

6  

Problem Solving Critical Thinking

7 Find objects like these in your classroom.
How are they alike and different?

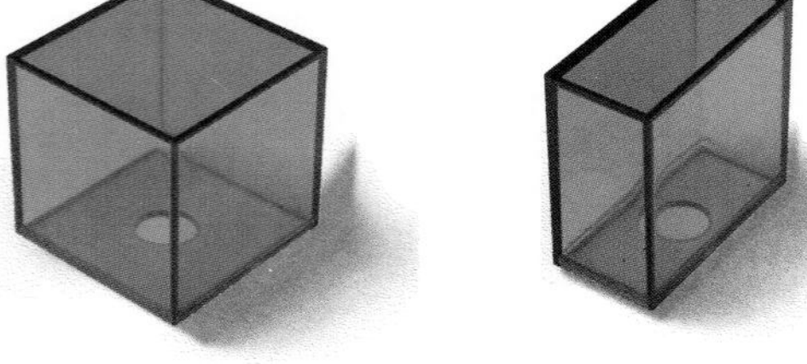

____

____

Notes for Home: Your child predicted which shape would result from tracing around the solid shown. *Home Activity:* Show your child one face (side) of a box. Ask what shape you would make if you traced around that face (side).

Name

Explore Shapes

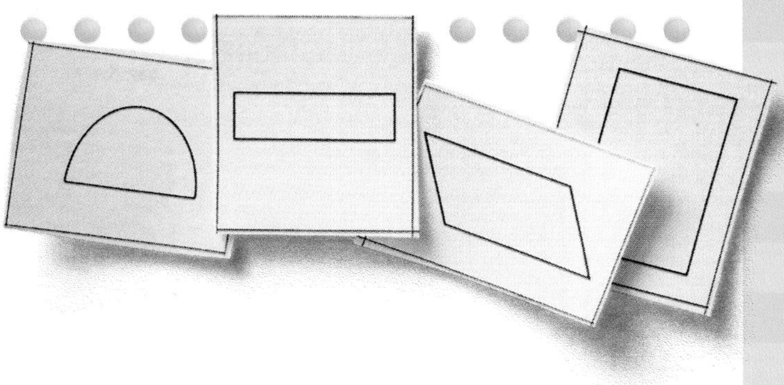

Explore

Sort your shapes into 2 groups.
Draw or write to show how you sorted.
Sort 3 times.

1

2

3

Share

How did you sort the shapes?

Notes for Home: Your child sorted pictures of shapes into groups, then recorded the ways he or she sorted. *Home Activity:* Ask your child to tell you about one way he or she sorted.

Connect

rectangles | triangle | circle

square

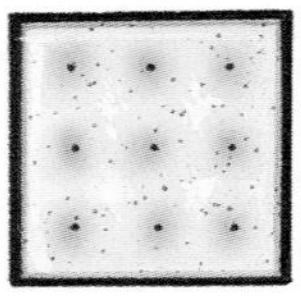

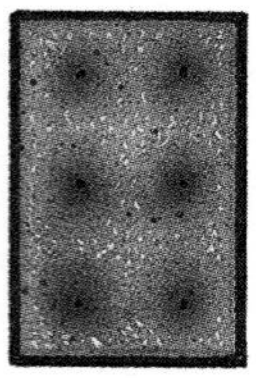

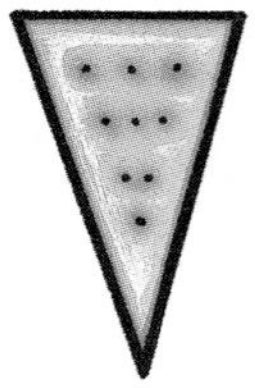

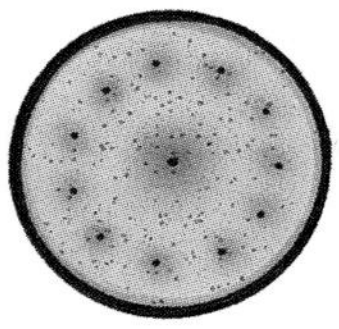

4 sides
4 corners

4 sides
4 corners

3 sides
3 corners

0 flat sides
0 corners

Draw a shape that belongs.
Draw a shape that does not belong.

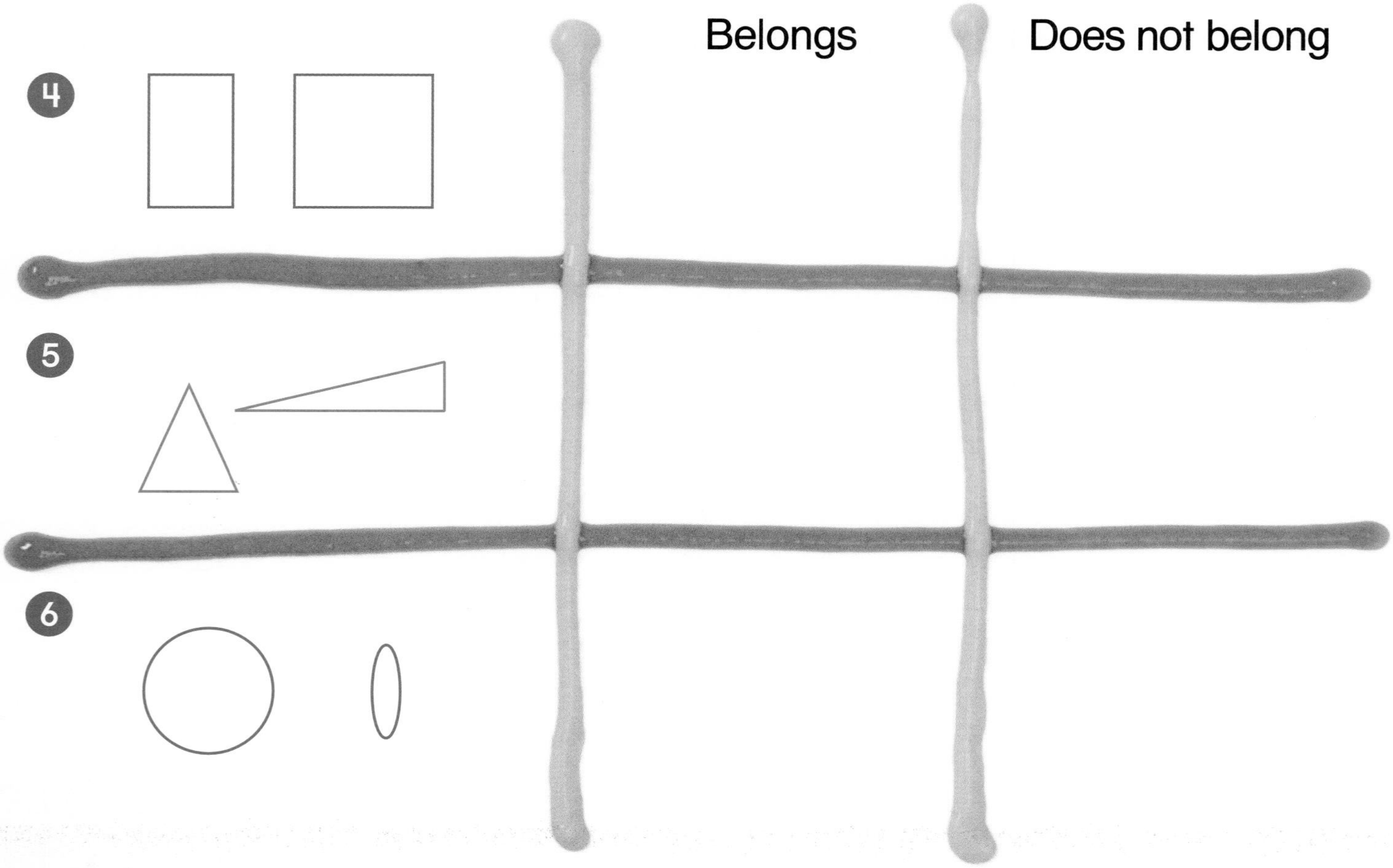

EXPLORE

Problem Solving Critical Thinking

7 If a shape has 5 sides, how many corners will it have? How many corners does a shape with 6 sides have? How do you know?

Notes for Home: Your child compared shapes to find similarities and differences. *Home Activity:* Look for tile floors. See how many different shapes of tiles you can find. Collect the shapes by making a rubbing, tracing, or drawing of the shapes.

Name

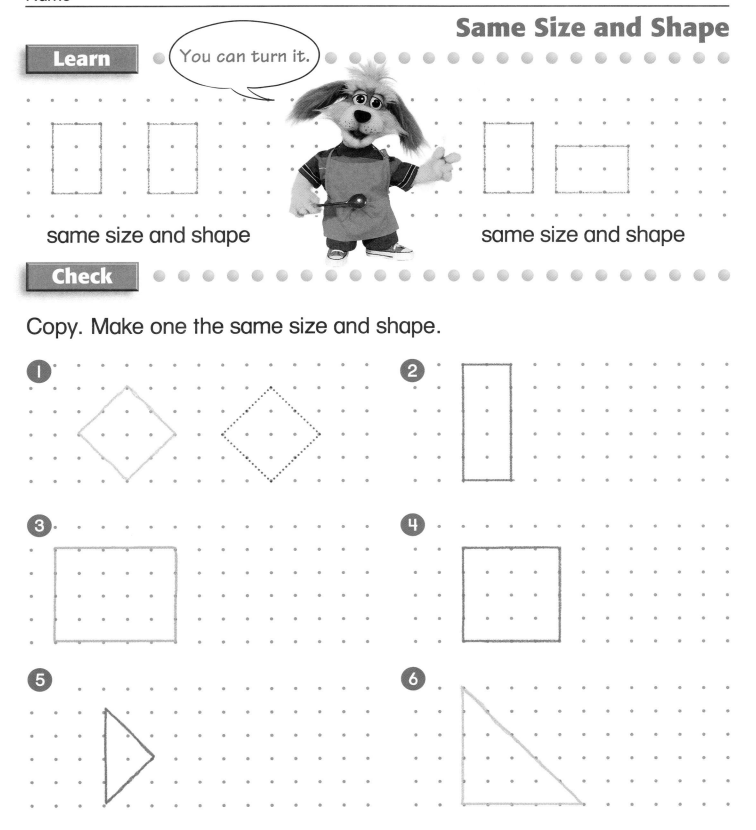

Same Size and Shape

Learn

same size and shape

same size and shape

Check

Copy. Make one the same size and shape.

1

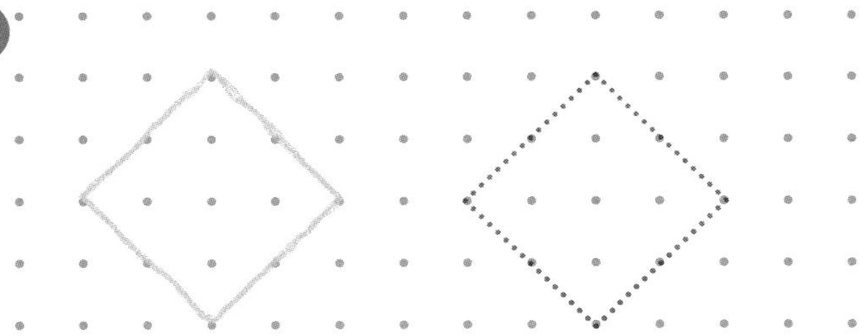

2

3

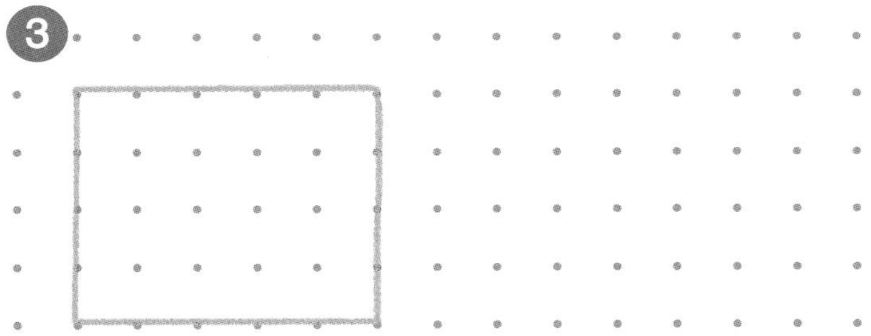

4

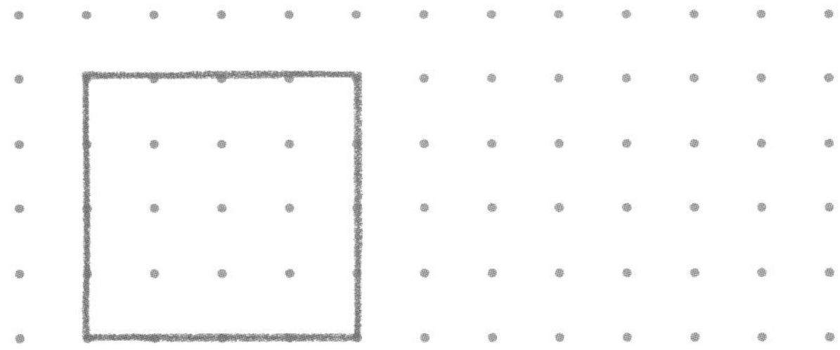

5

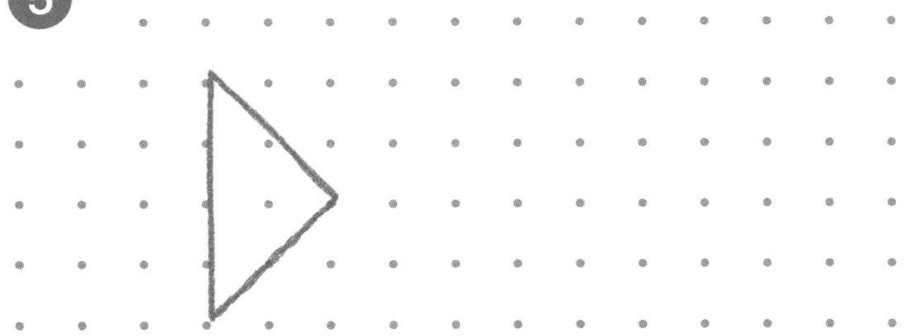

6

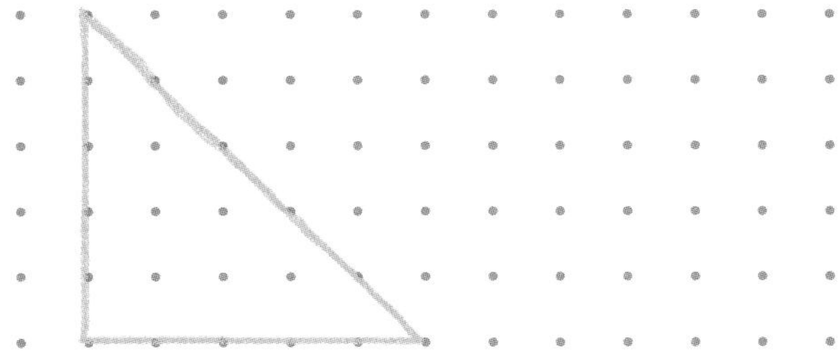

Talk About It How did you know the figures were the same size and shape?

Notes for Home: Your child made shapes exactly the same size and shape as the examples given. *Home Activity:* Draw dot grids like the ones on this page, but just 5 dots across by 5 dots down. See how many different triangles you and your child can make.

Practice

PRACTICE

Circle the ones that are the same size and shape.

7
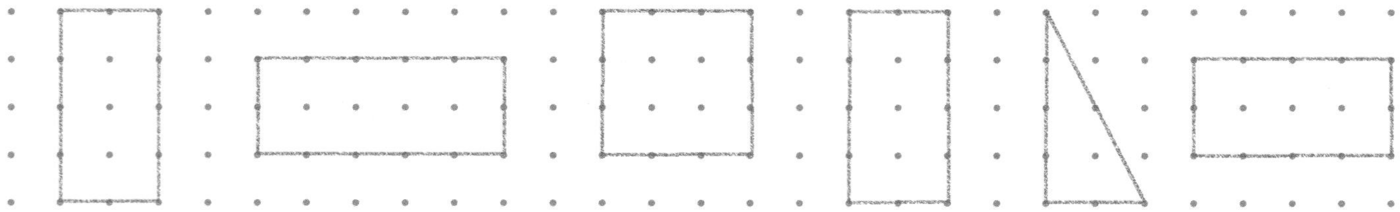

8
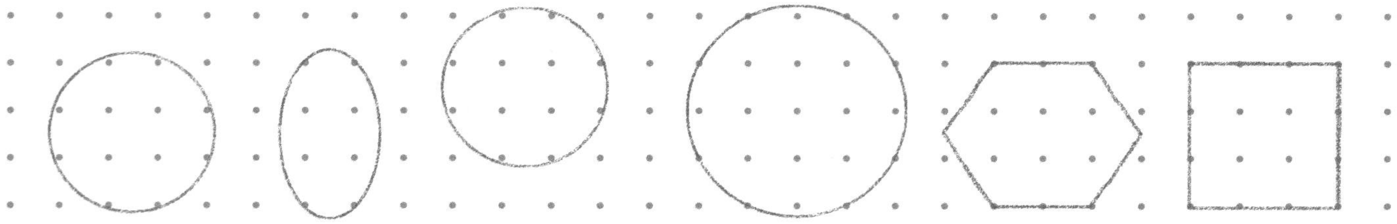

9
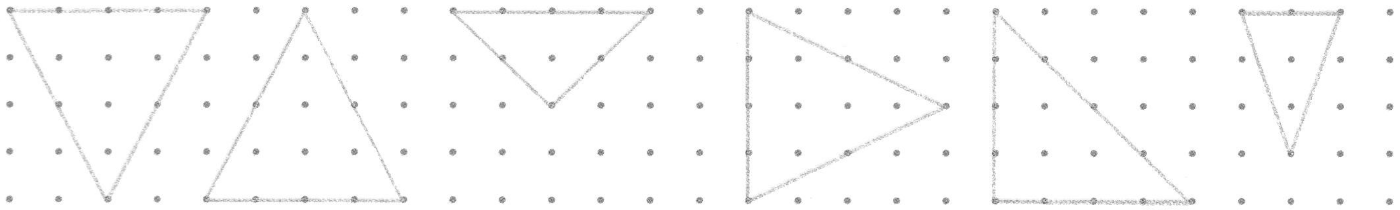

10
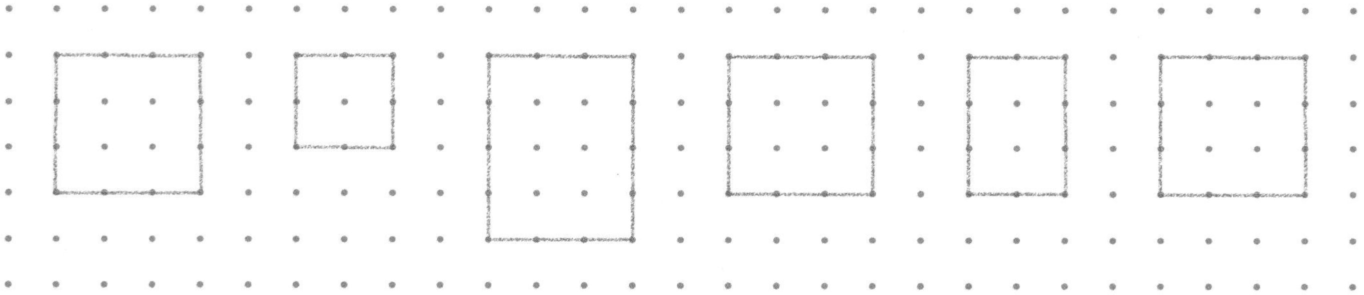

Write About It

11 Draw a shape. Have a friend draw one that is the same size and shape.

Notes for Home: Your child matched figures of the same size and shape. *Home Activity:* Draw dots in a grid like the exercises on this page. Make grids with 5 dots across and 5 dots down. See how many different 4-sided shapes you and your child can draw on the grids.

For additional practice, see Skills Practice Bank, page 529, Set 1.

Name ______________________________

Symmetry

Learn

Fold. Draw. Cut. Open.

Both parts match when I fold on this line.

Check

Draw the fold line.

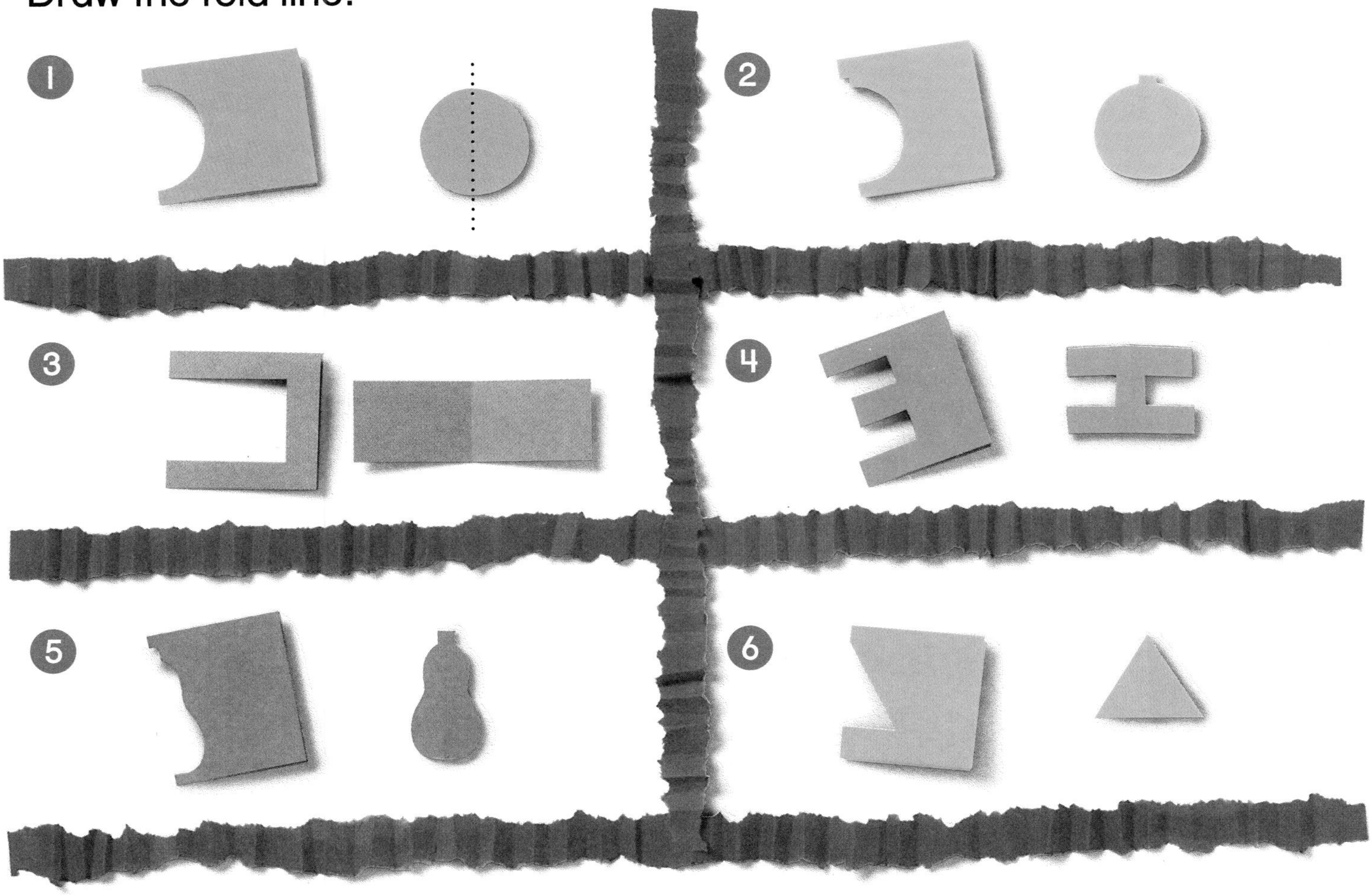

Talk About It What happens when you fold this rectangle on the line?

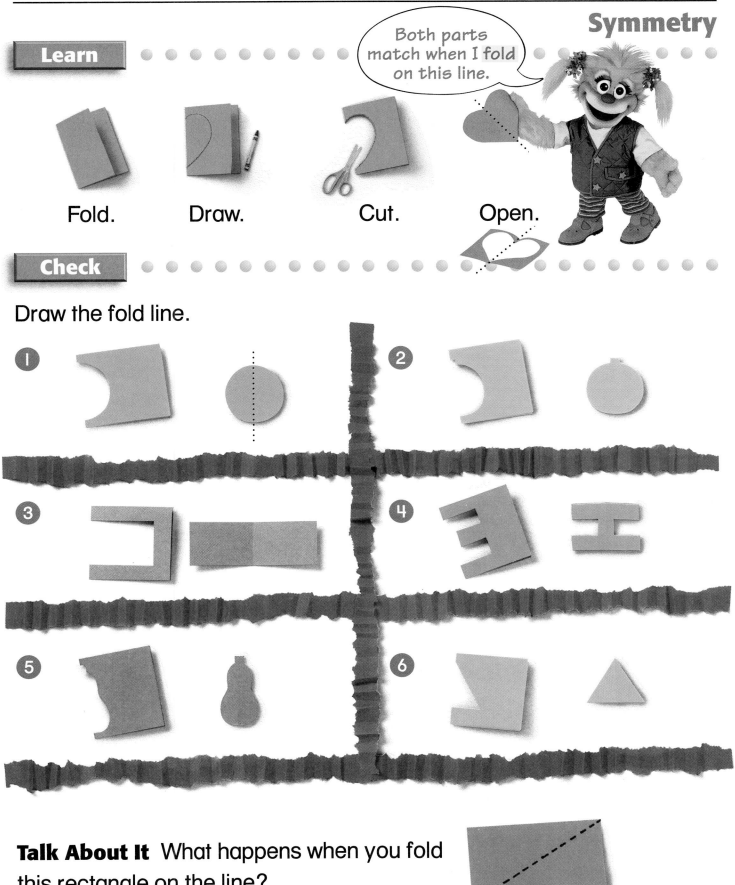

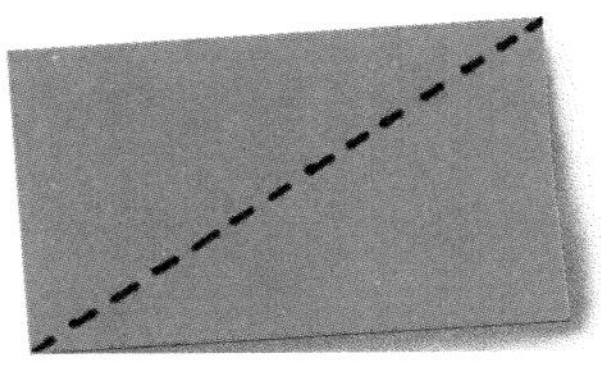

Notes for Home: Your child found lines of symmetry. *Home Activity:* Cut out doilies or snowflakes by folding paper different ways and cutting shapes from the folded edges.

Practice

Circle the shapes if the parts match when you fold on the line.

7 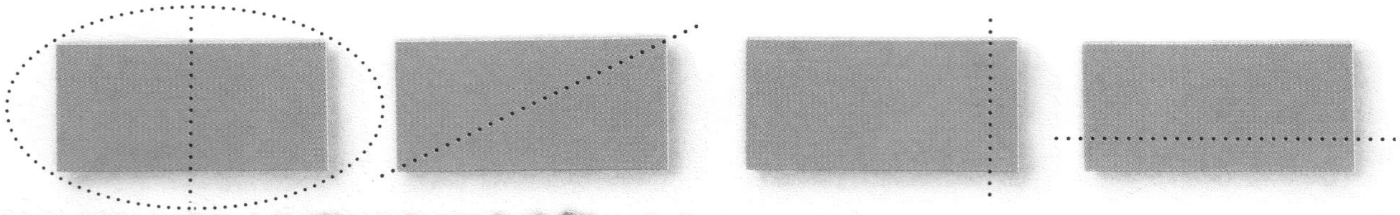

8 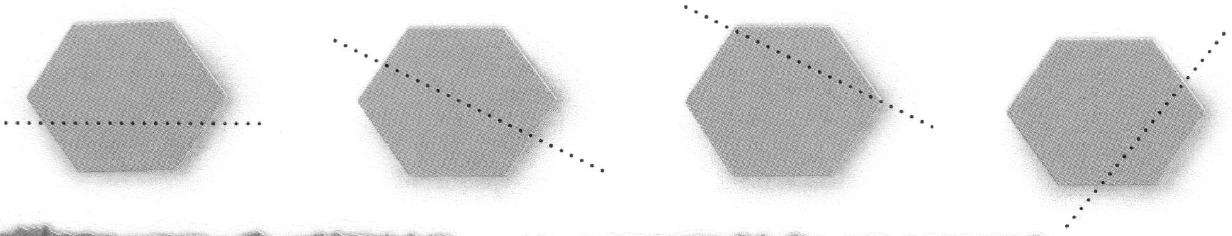

9 

10 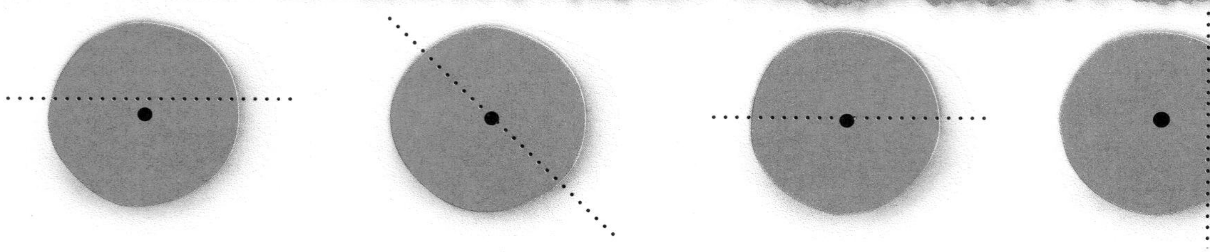

Problem Solving Visual Thinking

11 Draw to make two parts that match.

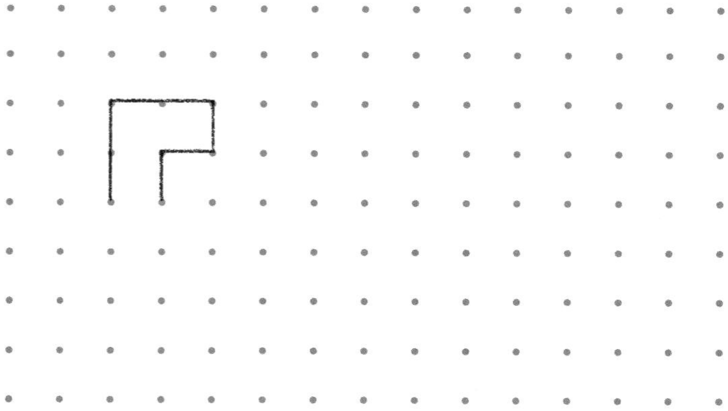

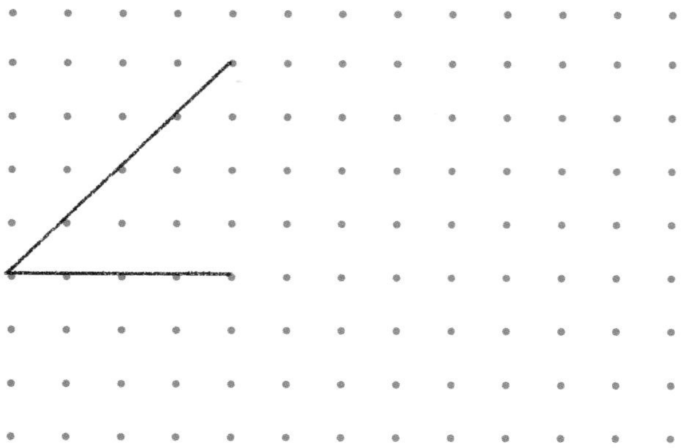

Notes for Home: Your child identified lines of symmetry. *Home Activity:* Find objects at home and in your neighborhood that are symmetrical, such as windows, tables, lamp posts, or leaves. Keep a list of the things you find together.

Name ______________________________

Reading for Math

Read a Table

Snacks We Ate This Week

	Monday	Tuesday	Wednesday	Thursday	Friday
	2	3	5	0	4
	2	1	3	1	4
	1	0	1	2	0
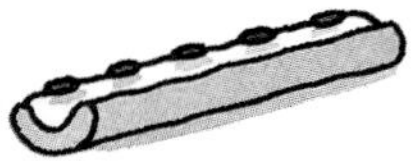	4	2	6	3	1

You can use .
Read across the rows.

1. How many  did we eat this week? _____

2. How many  did we eat? _____

Read down the columns.

3. How many snacks did we eat on Thursday? _____

4. How many snacks did we eat on Monday? _____

5. How many 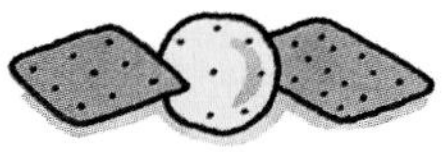 did we eat on Wednesday? _____

Talk About It What else can you tell about the snacks we ate?

Notes for Home: Your child learned how to read a table. *Home Activity:* Look for charts and tables in newspapers and magazines. Talk about the information they show.

Nida's Slice	4	3	1
Darnell's Slice	0	5	2
Make Your Own			

Read across the rows.

6. How many  did Darnell's slice have? _____

7. How many 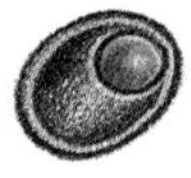 did Nida's slice have? _____

Read down the columns.

8. How many  were on the slices? _____

9. Who had more  Nida or Darnell? __________

Journal 

10. Choose the things you like on a pizza.
Fill in the table. Write about your pizza.

Notes for Home: Your child read a table to answer questions. *Home Activity:* Make a table of your own. What kind of information could you show?

Name

Problem Solving: Make a Table

Learn

PROBLEM SOLVING GUIDE

Understand • Plan • Solve • Look Back

Shapes I Used		
1st	1	0
2nd	0	2

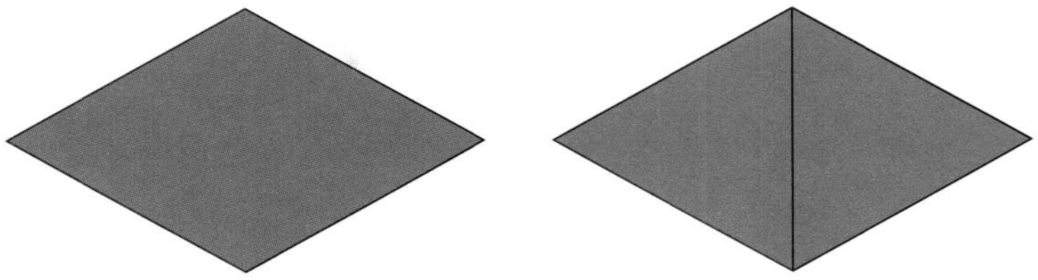

Check

I found 2 ways to make this shape.

1. Use pattern blocks.
How many ways
can you make a ?
Record the blocks you used.

Ways to Make

Shapes I Used			
1st way	1	0	0
2nd way	0		
3rd way	0		

There are _____ ways to make the .

Talk About It Did you use the or the ?
Why or why not?

Notes for Home: Your child used pattern blocks to investigate ways to put shapes together to form other shapes. *Home Activity:* Make some paper squares. Cut some in half to make triangles or rectangles. See what patterns you can make using your squares, triangles, and rectangles.

2 Use pattern blocks. How many ways can

you make a ? Record the blocks you used.

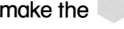

Ways to Make ⬡				
Shapes I Used	⬡	▽	◆	▲
1st way	1	0	0	0
2nd way	0			
3rd way	0			
4th way	0			
5th way	0			
6th way	0			
7th way	0			
8th way	0			

I found _____ ways to make the ⬡ .

Patterns

3 Draw what comes next.

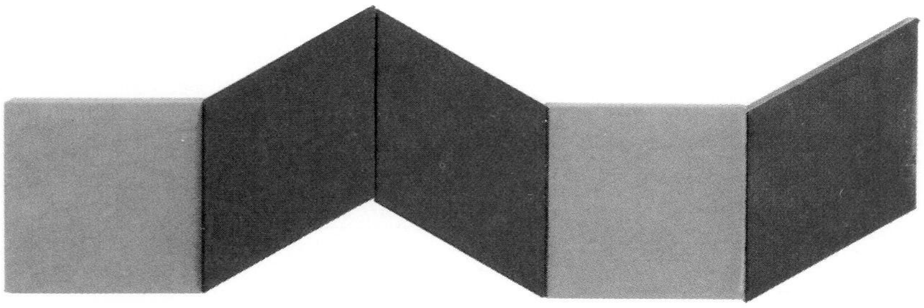

Make some patterns of your own.

Notes for Home: Your child used pattern blocks to find many different ways to make a hexagon and recorded all the ways in a table. *Home Activity:* Choose a shape. Make a picture in which everything is made from just one shape.

Name

Mixed Practice

Lessons 1–6

Concepts and Skills

1. Circle the solids that can roll.

2. Draw one the same size and shape.

3. Circle the shape if both parts match when you fold on the line.

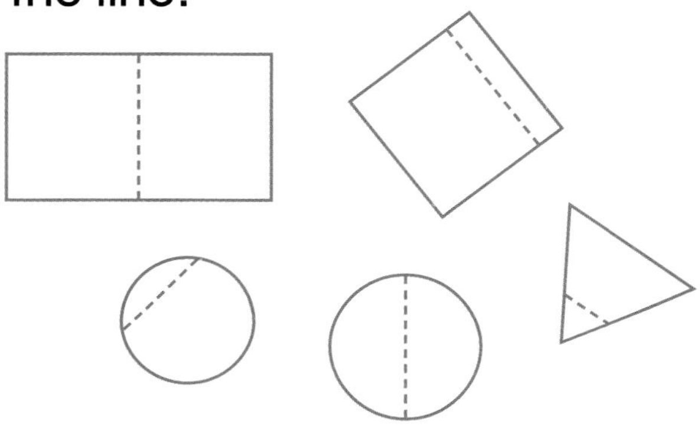

Problem Solving

4. How many of each shape are there? Record the numbers in the table.

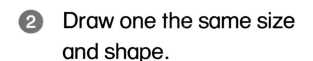

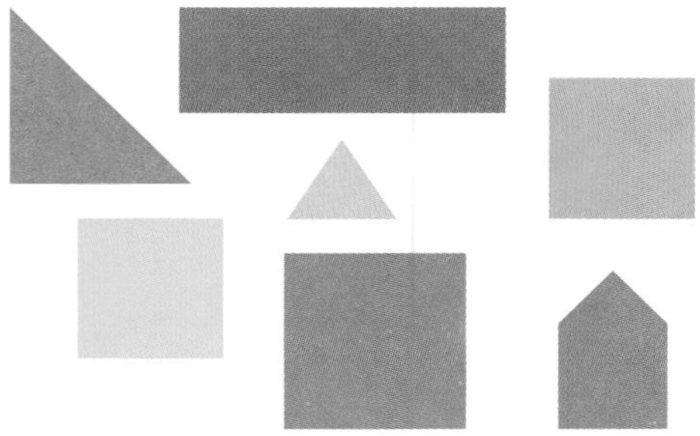

	3 sides	4 sides	5 sides
Number of Shapes			

Journal

5. Find an object in the classroom. Write about the shape of the object.

Notes for Home: Your child practiced identifying shapes. *Home Activity:* Ask your child to find boxes at home and talk about the faces of each.

Name ______________________________

Cumulative Review

Chapters 1–5

Concepts and Skills

Add.

1. $1 + 7 =$ ____ $7 + 1 =$ ____
2. $9 + 2 =$ ____ $2 + 9 =$ ____
3. $6 + 3 =$ ____ $3 + 6 =$ ____

Subtract.

4.

8	10	6	9	5	7	2
− 2	− 1	− 0	− 9	− 1	− 2	− 0

Problem Solving

5. Draw a picture to match the number sentence.
Write how many in all.

$4 + 7 =$ ____

$11 - 7 =$ ____

Test Prep

Fill in the ○ for the correct answer.
Add or subtract.

6. $4 + 0$
○ 0
○ 4
○ 5
○ 10

7. $5 - 5$
○ 0
○ 1
○ 5
○ 10

8. $6 - 5$
○ 11
○ 2
○ 1
○ 9

Notes for Home: Your child reviewed the concepts taught in Chapters 1–5. *Home Activity*: Ask your child what 8 − 0 equals and explain why.

Name

Explore Fair Shares

Explore

Use a paper rectangle for each sandwich.

Use a paper circle for each apple.

Use [cube] for the glasses of juice.

Use [counters] for the cookies.

1. Give each child a fair share of the lunch.

Share

How can you tell that the children got fair shares?

Notes for Home: Your child is beginning to learn about fractions by making fair shares.
Home Activity: Help your child make fair shares with a snack or food at dinner.

Connect

Use paper rectangles for sandwiches.
Use paper circles for apples.
Use  for glasses of milk. Use  for cookies.

Make fair shares for each group. Show your work below.

2 

3 

4 

EXPLORE

Problem Solving Critical Thinking

Solve.

5 Kris and Mia want to share some pizza. There are 4 slices of pizza. How can they make fair shares?

Notes for Home: Your child practiced making fair shares. *Home Activity:* Use 12 small objects, such as paper clips, to see how many different ways you can find to make fair shares.

For additional practice, see Skills Practice Bank, page 529, Set 2.

Name

Halves

Learn

Remember,
fair shares
have equal parts.

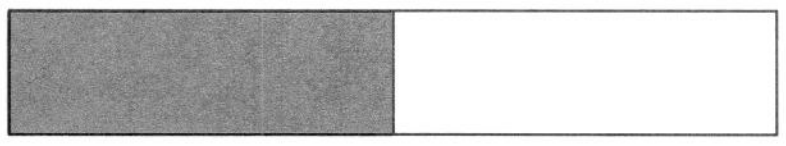

1 out of 2 equal parts is red.

One half is red.

$\frac{1}{2}$ is red.

2 equal parts are halves.

Check

Circle the shapes that show one half.

1 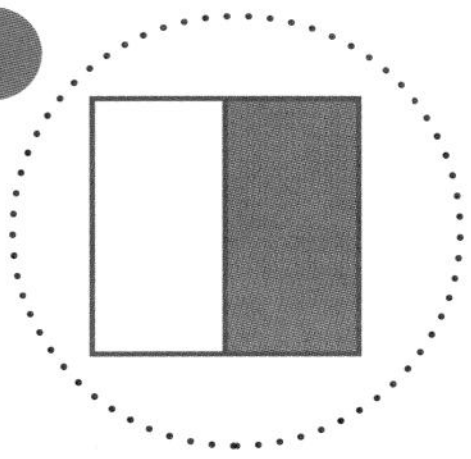

2 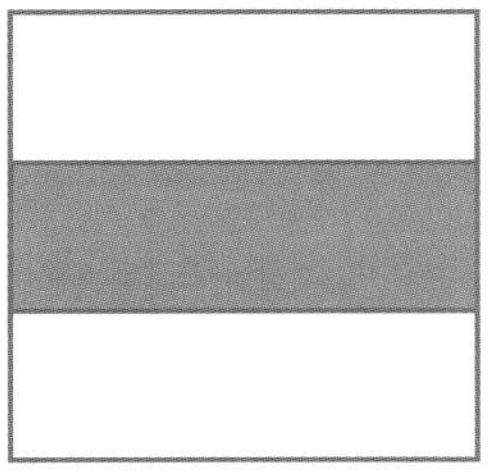

3 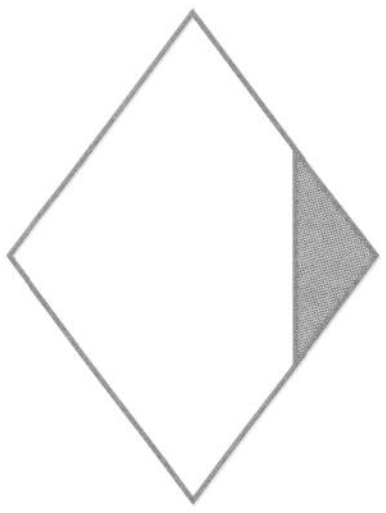

4 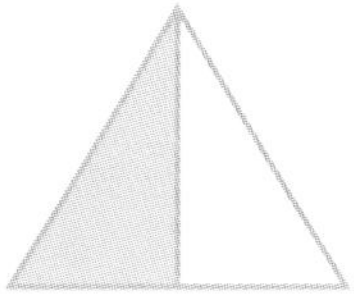

5 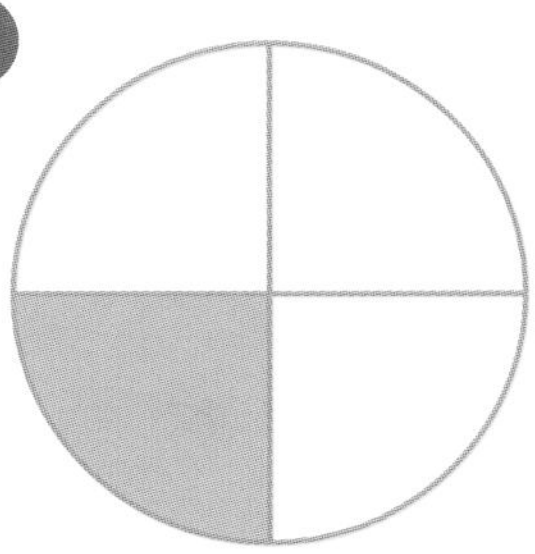

6 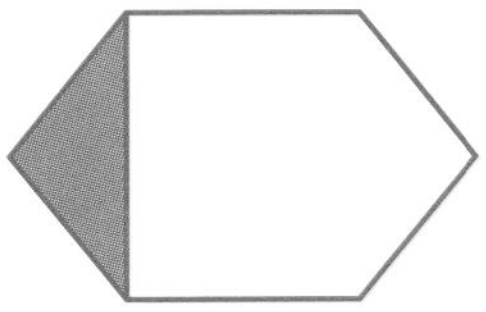

7 

8 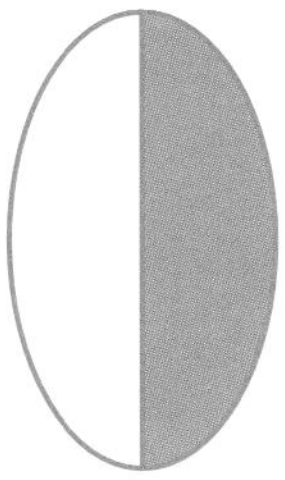

Talk About It These do not show one half.
Tell how you know.

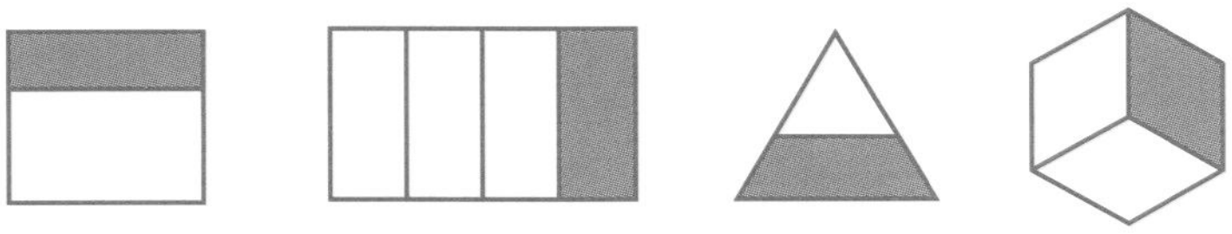

Notes for Home: Your child identified halves. *Home Activity:* Find things at home that have two equal parts.

Practice

Color to show one half.

9 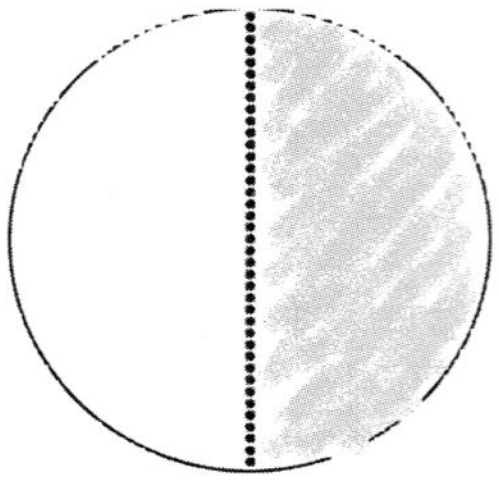

10 

11 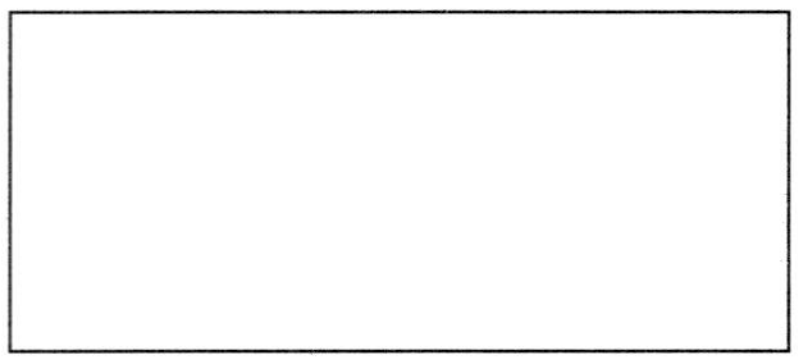

12 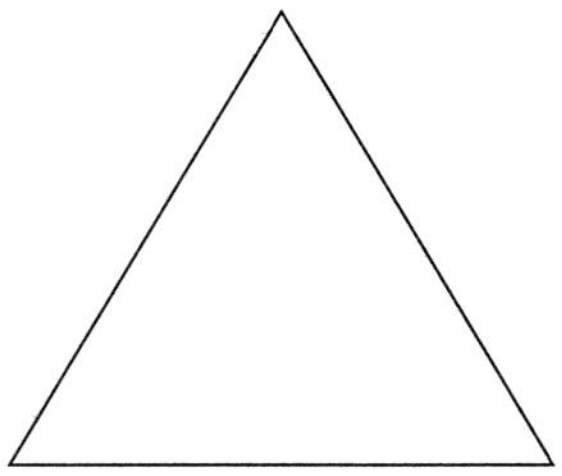

13 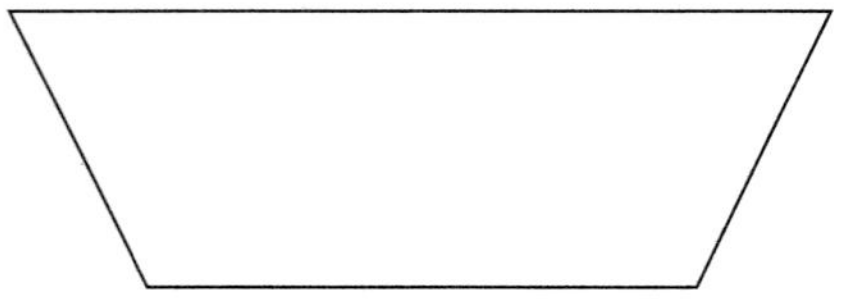

14 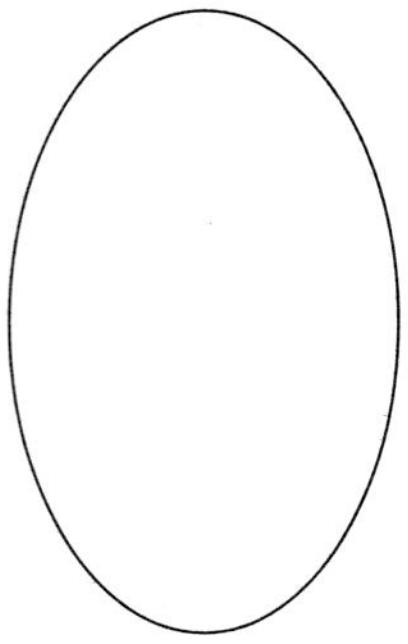

15 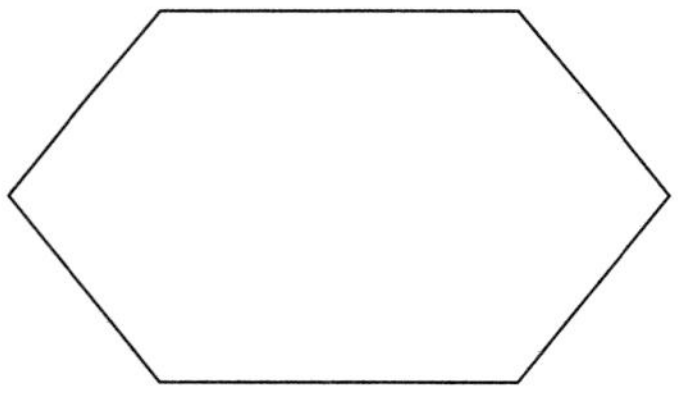

16 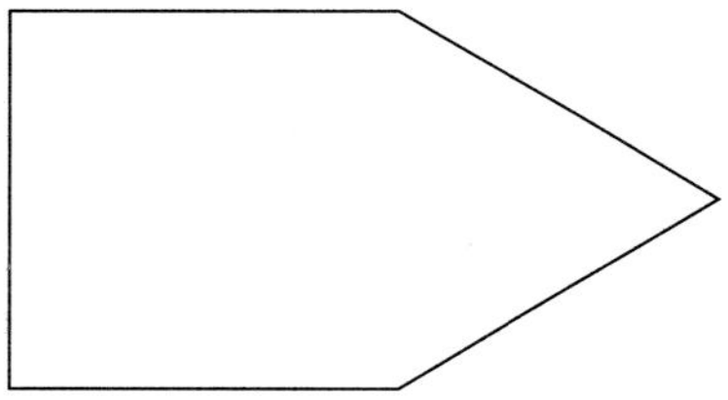

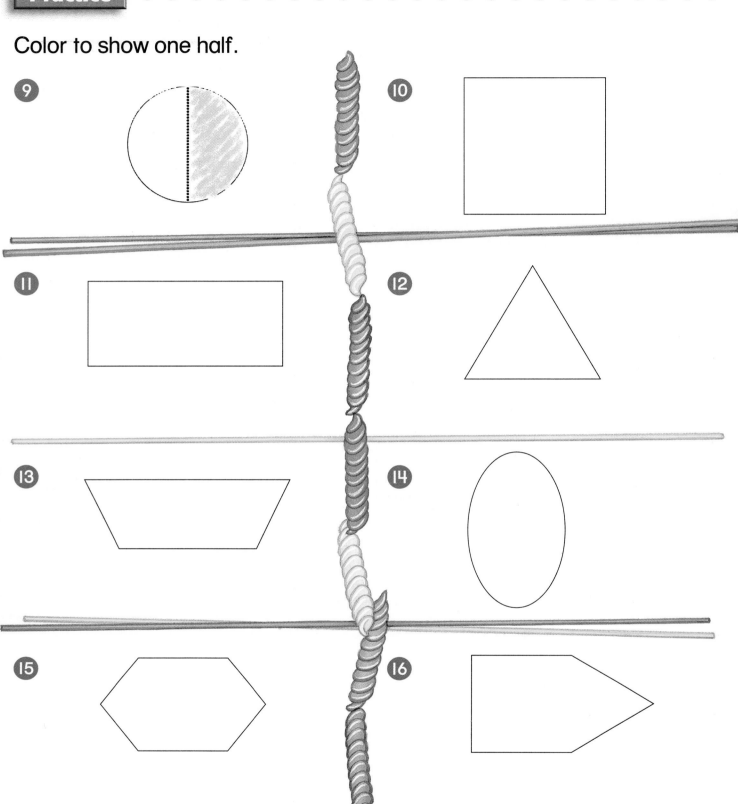

PRACTICE

Tell a Math Story

17 Tell a story about a time when you had one half of something.

Notes for Home: Your child showed halves of whole shapes. *Home Activity:* Think of some things that can not be cut in half. How could two people share them fairly?

Name ___________________

Fourths

Learn

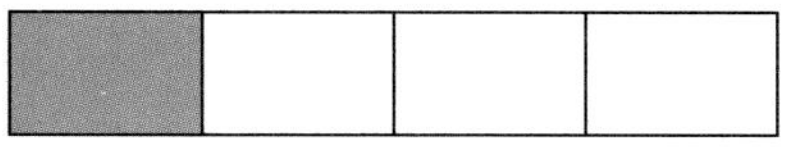

1 out of 4 equal parts is blue.

One fourth is blue.

$\frac{1}{4}$ is blue.

4 equal parts are fourths.

Check

Circle the shapes that show one fourth.

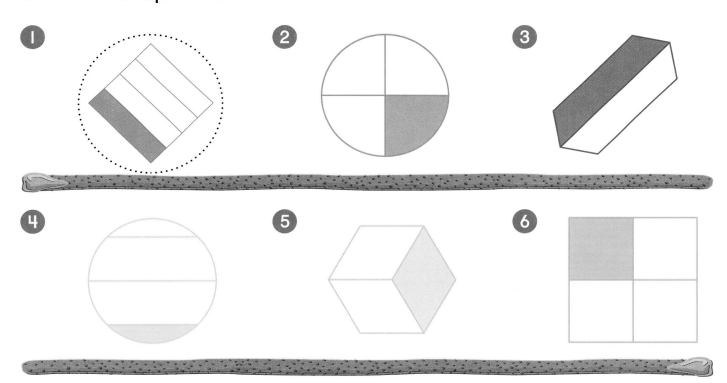

1. 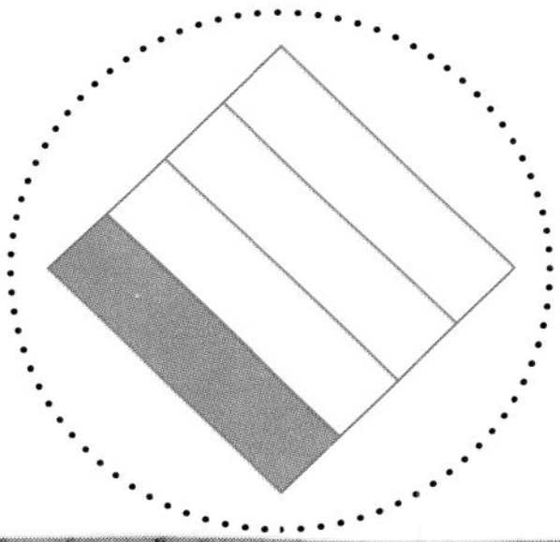

2. 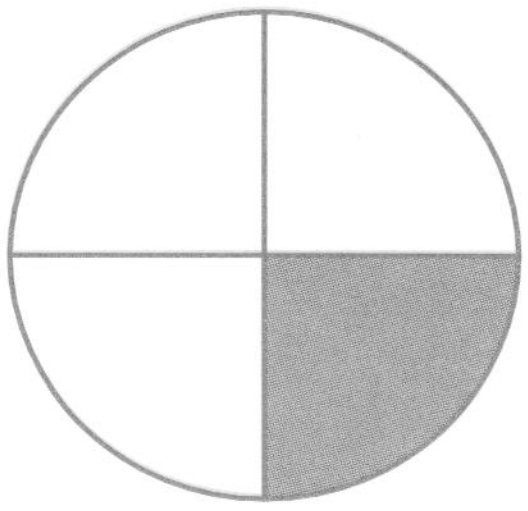

3. 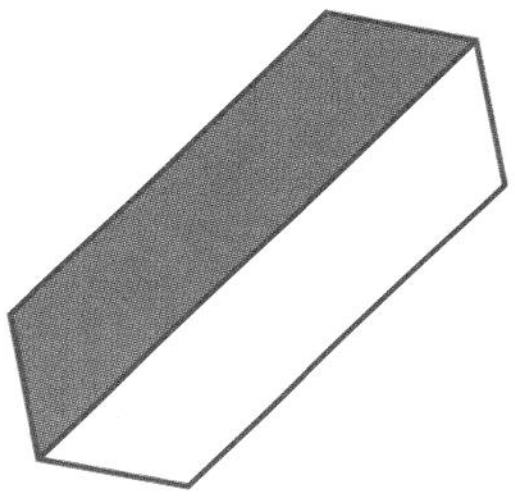

4. 

5. 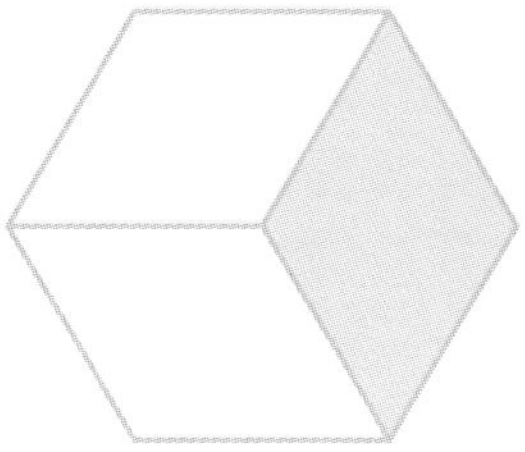

6. 

Talk About It These do not show one fourth. Tell how you know.

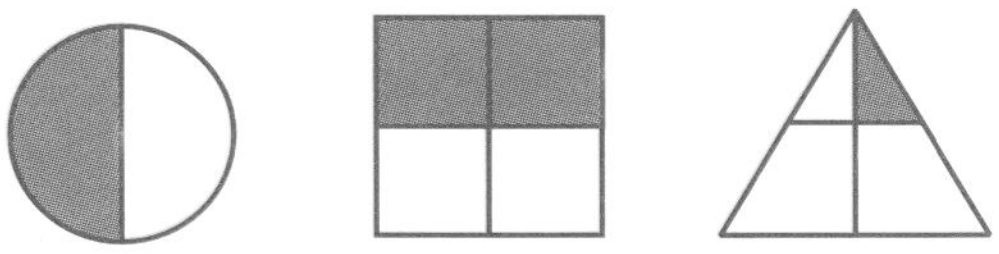

Notes for Home Your child identified shapes that show fourths. *Home Activity:* Find things at home that have four equal parts.

Practice

Color to show one fourth.

7
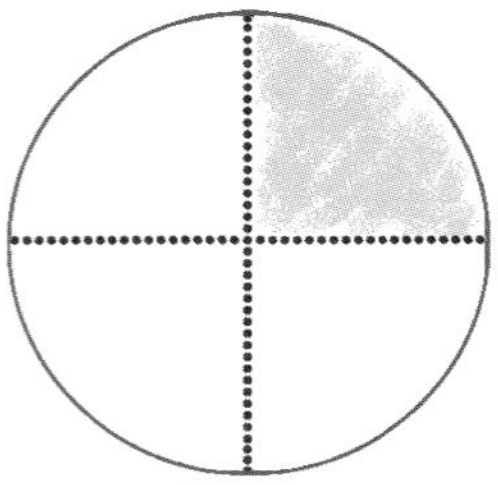

8

9
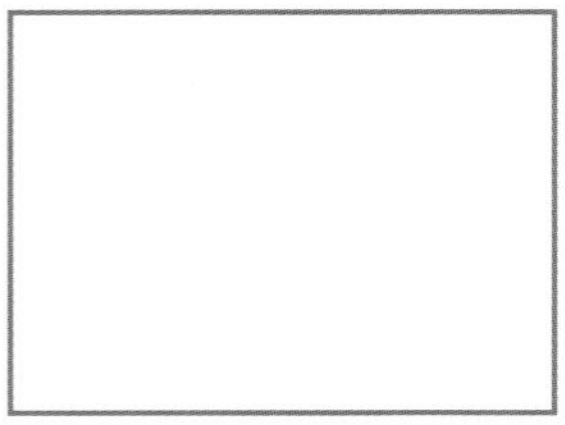

10

11
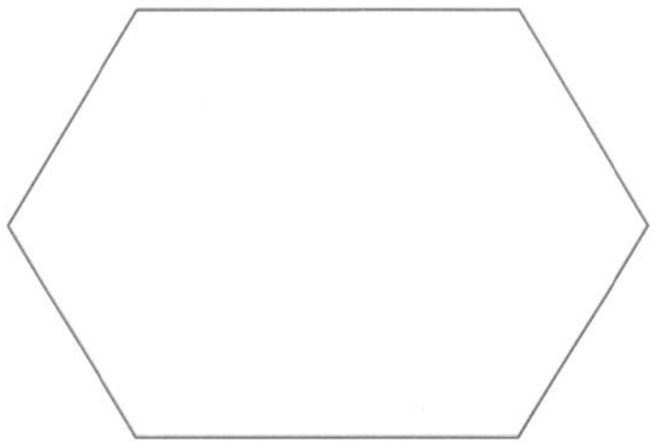

12
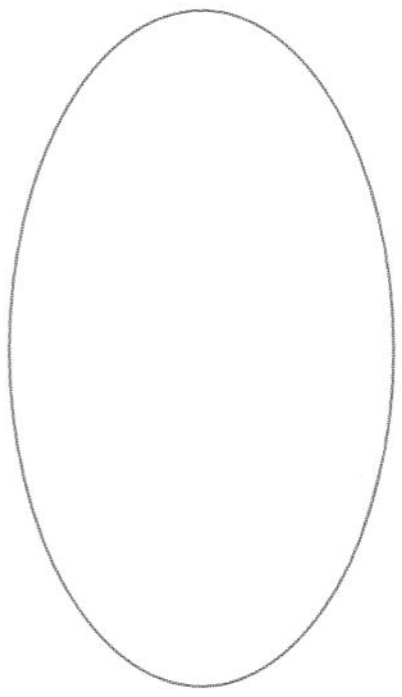

Problem Solving Visual Thinking

13 Find different ways to show fourths.

Notes for Home: Your child showed fourths of whole shapes. *Home Activity*: If you had a bottle of juice, how could you make fourths to share fairly between four people?

Name

Thirds

Learn

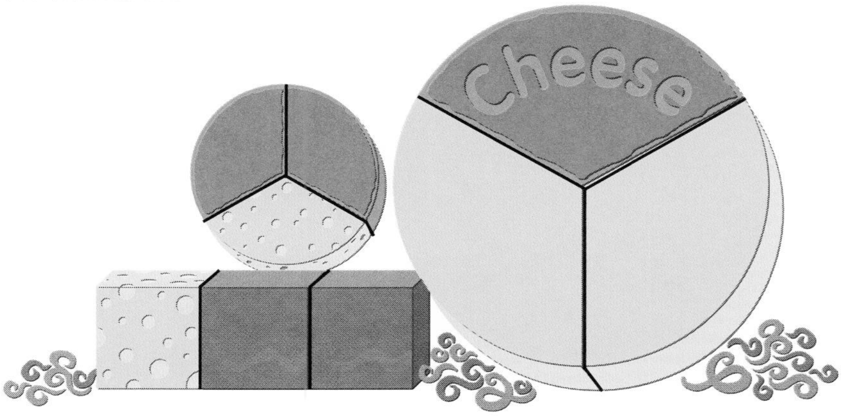

3 equal parts are thirds.

1 out of 3 equal parts is green.

One third is green.

$\frac{1}{3}$ is green.

Check

Circle the shapes that show one third.

1. 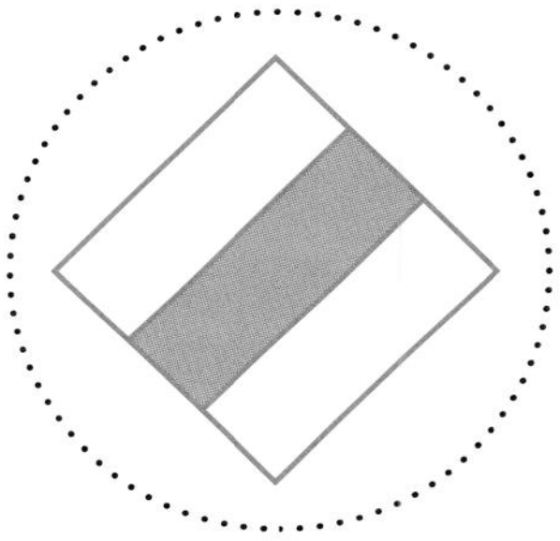
2. 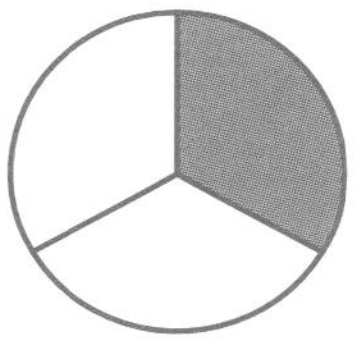
3. 
4. 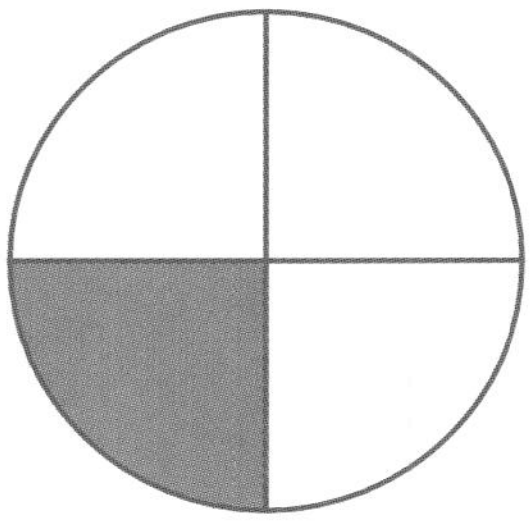
5. 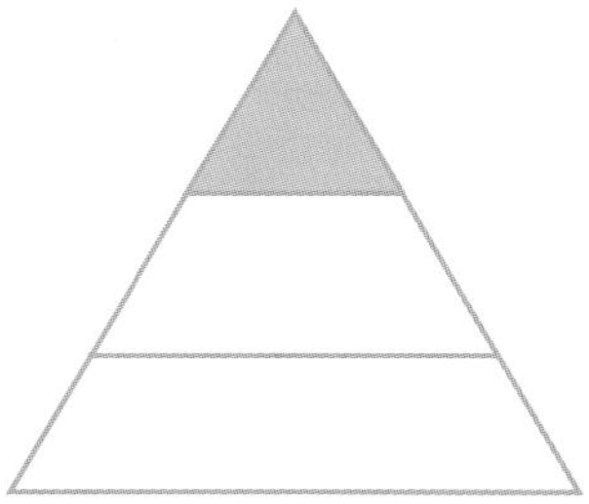
6. 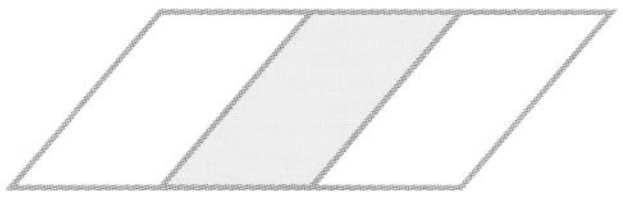

Talk About It These do not show one third. Tell how you know.

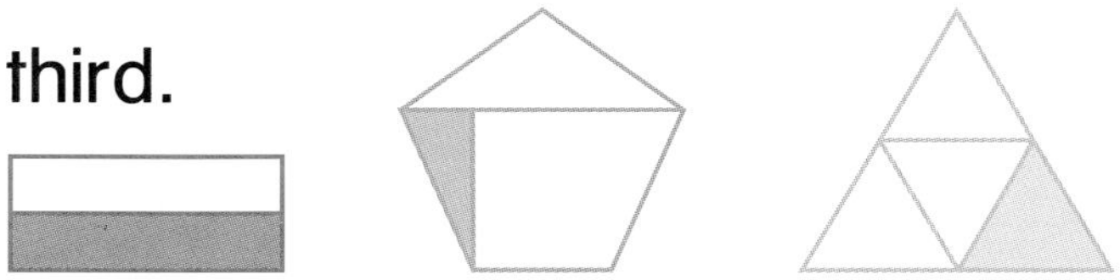

Notes for Home: Your child identified thirds. *Home Activity:* Find things at home that have three equal parts.

Practice

Color to show one third.

7
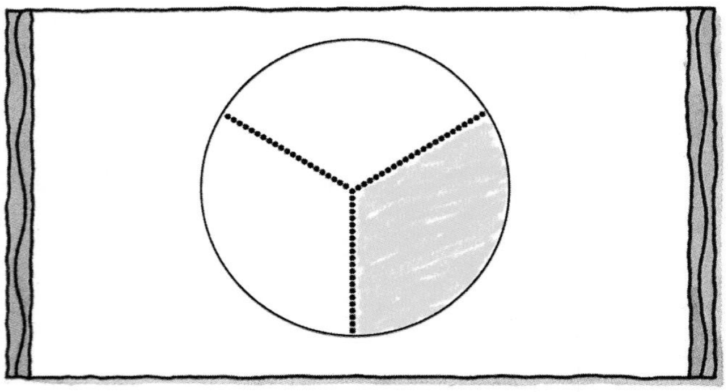

8
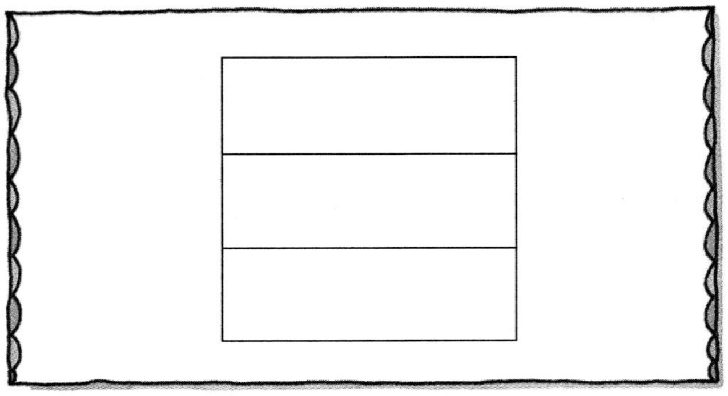

9
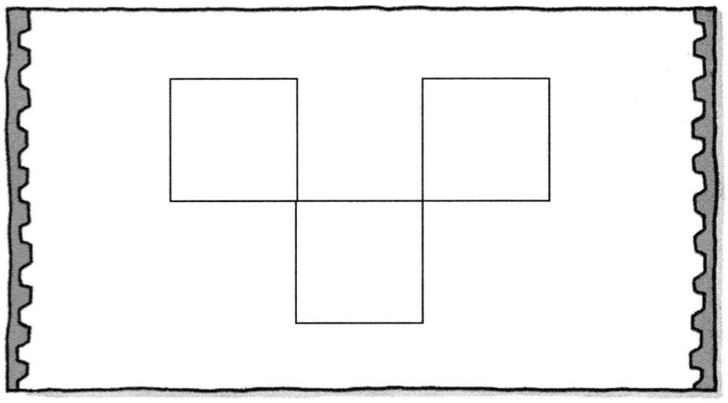

10
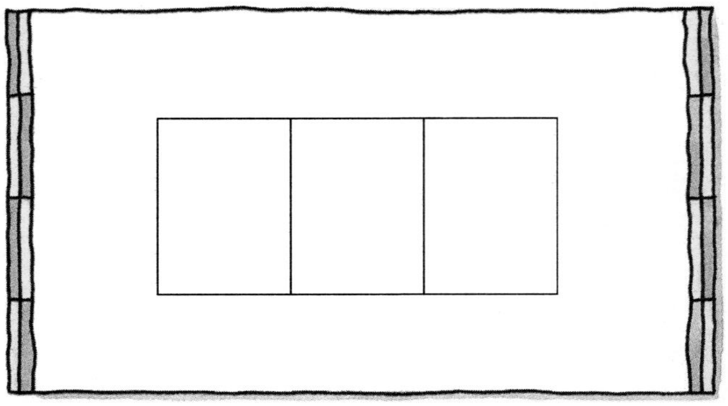

Write your own examples.

11

12

Problem Solving Estimation

13 About how much is gone?
Circle the best estimate.

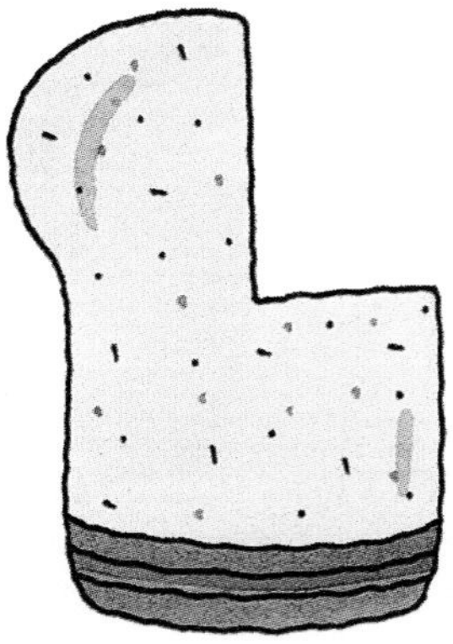

one half

one fourth

one third

Notes for Home: Your child showed thirds of whole shapes. *Home Activity*: Draw several squares on paper. Using one square to show each way, challenge your child to show one half, one fourth, and one third in as many ways as possible.

PRACTICE

Name ________________________________

Find the Fraction

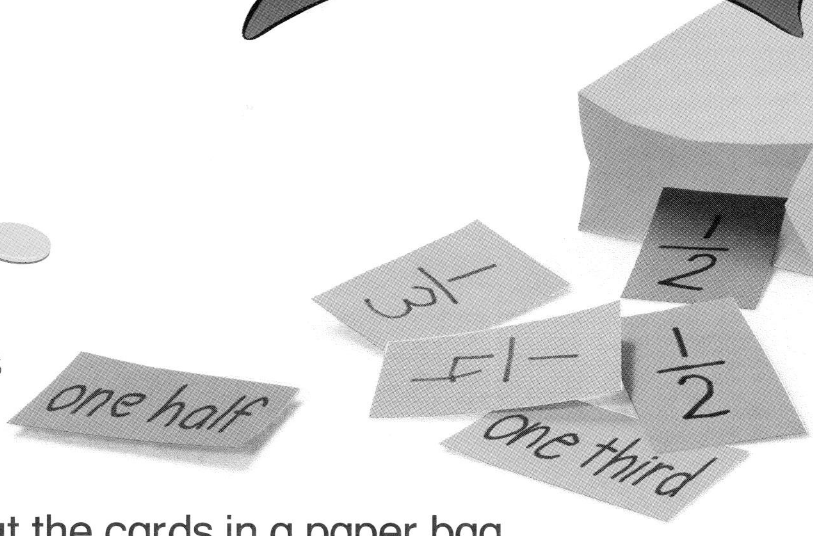

What You Need

16 two-color counters
paper bag
index cards or paper squares

How to Play

1. Make fraction cards. Put the cards in a paper bag.
2. One player uses red counters. One uses yellow.
3. Take turns picking a card.
4. Find a picture that matches the fraction.
5. Cover the picture with your counter.

Notes for Home: Your child played a fraction game to practice matching a fraction to a shape. *Home Activity:* Ask your child to show you how to play the game. Use pennies, buttons, or paper clips for counters. See which player can cover the most pictures.

Name ____________________

STOP and Practice

1 Circle the shape that was traced.

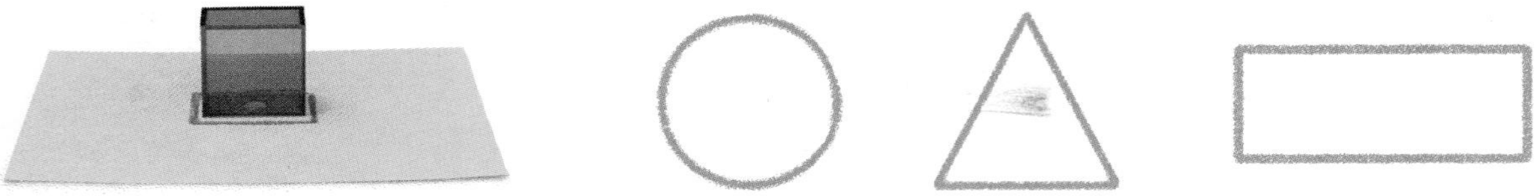

Are these the same size and shape?
Circle *yes* or *no*.

2
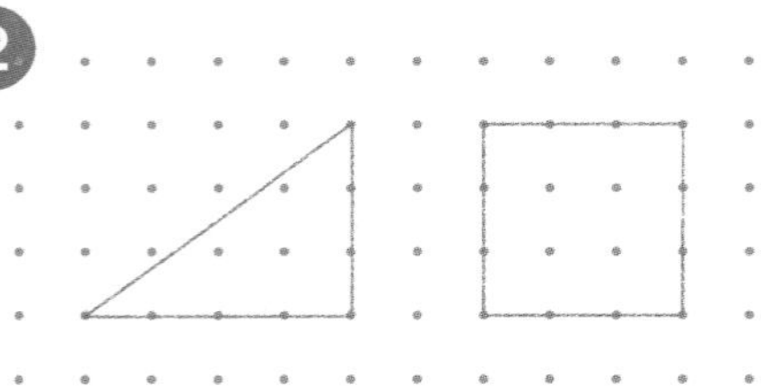

yes
no

3
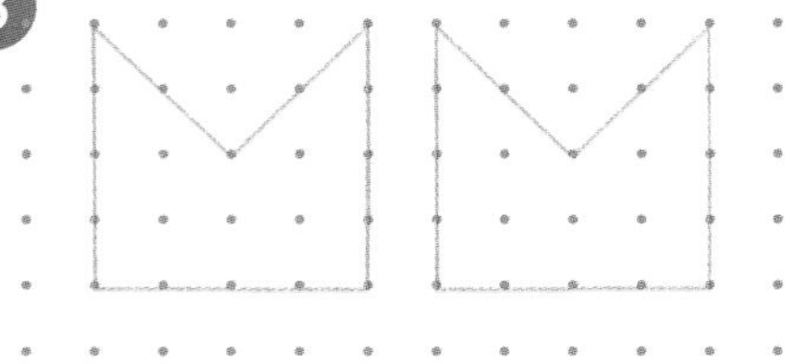

yes
no

What does the shaded part show?
Circle the fraction.

4
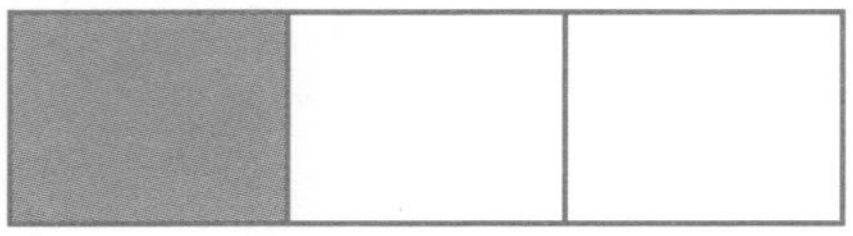

one half   one third

5
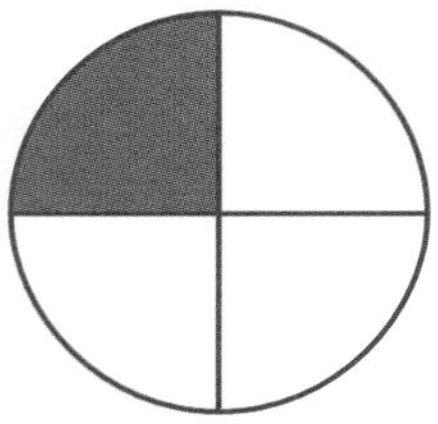

one third   one fourth

Estimation

6 Color part of each one to show about one half full.

Notes for Home: Your child practiced the geometric and fraction concepts from Chapter 5. *Home Activity:* Find things around your home that will make circles if you trace them. How many are cylinders, and how many are other shapes?

PRACTICE

Name

Explore Fractions of a Set

Explore

I see 4 parts.
1 of the 4 parts is green.

1 out of 4 parts is green. One fourth of the set is green.

Use .

Tell how much of the set each color is. Write the fraction.

1 _____ out of _____ parts is pink.

One __________ of the set is pink.

_____ out of _____ parts is purple.

One __________ of the set is purple.

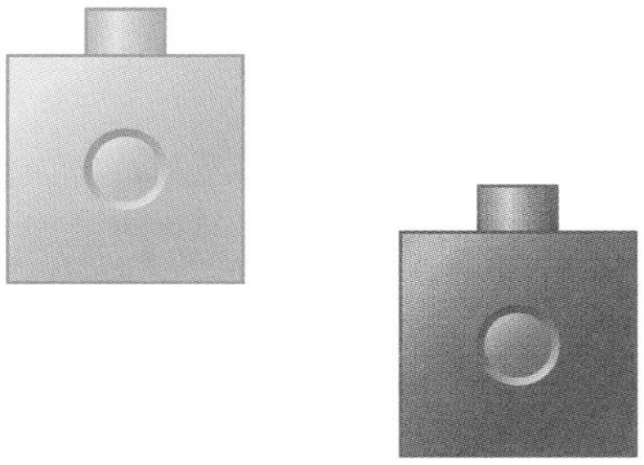

2 _____ out of _____ parts is red.

One __________ of the set is red.

_____ out of _____ parts is black.

One __________ of the set is black.

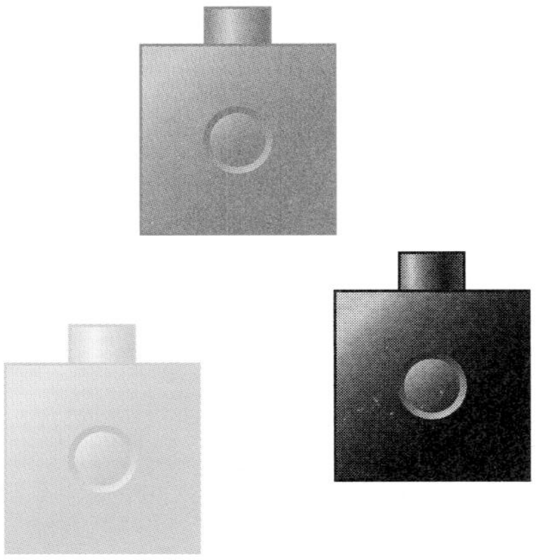

Share

How much of a set with 2 yellow and 2 red is yellow?

Notes for Home: Your child used Snap Cubes to explore finding what part of a set a given color was. *Home Activity:* Show your child two objects such as one spoon and one fork. Ask what part of the set is forks. (one half) Continue with other sets of two objects.

EXPLORE

Connect

This set has 3 blue parts and 3 red parts. 3 out of 6 parts is red.
I put all the blue together. I put all the red together. 1 out of 2 parts is red. One half is red.

Use .

Tell how much of the set each color is.

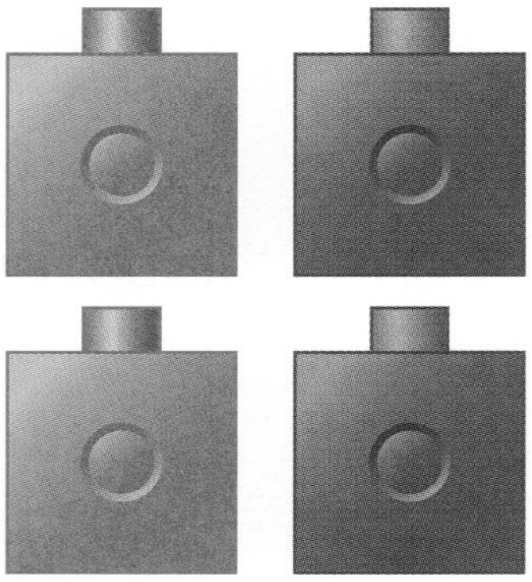

3 _____ out of _____ parts are red.

_____ out of _____ parts are brown.

One _________ of the set is brown.

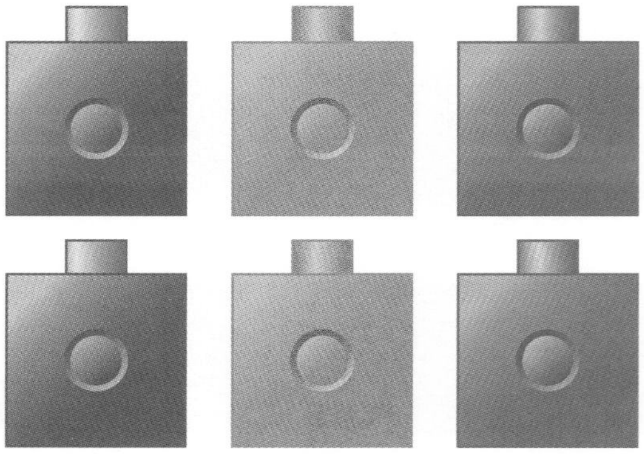

4 _____ out of _____ parts are blue.

_____ out of _____ parts are orange.

One _________ of the set is blue.

Problem Solving Visual Thinking

Show 6 .

5 Tell how much of the set each color is.

_____ out of _____ parts ______________________.

_____ out of _____ parts ______________________.

One _________ of the set ______________________.

Notes for Home: Your child used Snap Cubes to find fractions of sets. *Home Activity:* Ask your child to find sets of two or more objects and tell what fraction of the set one part is.

EXPLORE

Name

Probability

Learn

From which table could you be certain to pick a green plate?
From which table would it be impossible to pick a green plate?

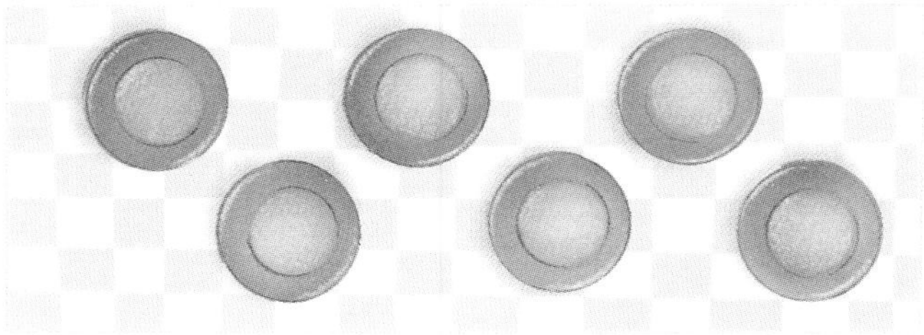

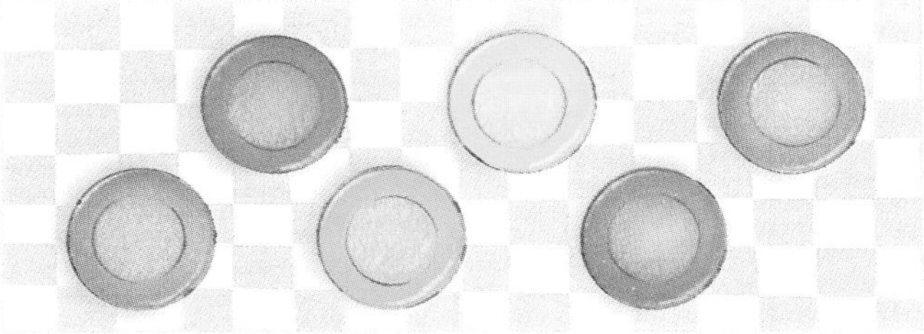

Table A | Table B

You are certain to get a green plate from Table A.
It is impossible to get a green plate from Table B.

Check

Circle the answer.

1. Pick a green grape.

certain
impossible

2. Pick an apple.

certain
impossible

3. Pick a fork.

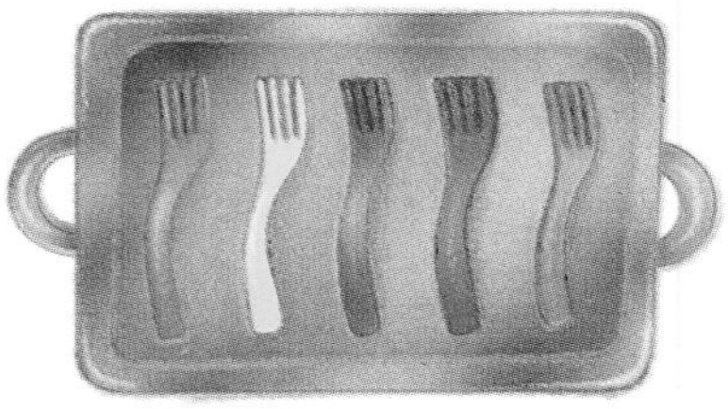

certain
impossible

4. Pick a baseball.

certain
impossible

Talk About It From which table is it impossible to get a red plate?

Notes for Home: Your child used logical reasoning to decide if something was certain or impossible to happen in a given situation. *Home Activity:* Set up a group of toys and ask your child questions about them to which your child can answer certain or impossible.

Practice

Write.

A B C

5 From which bag is it impossible to get a yellow cube? ________

6 From which bag is it certain to get a red cube? ________

7 What color would be impossible to pick from Bag C? ________

8 Draw 5 Snap Cubes in the bag so it is impossible to get a blue one.

9 Draw 4 Snap Cubes in the bag so you are certain to get a blue one.

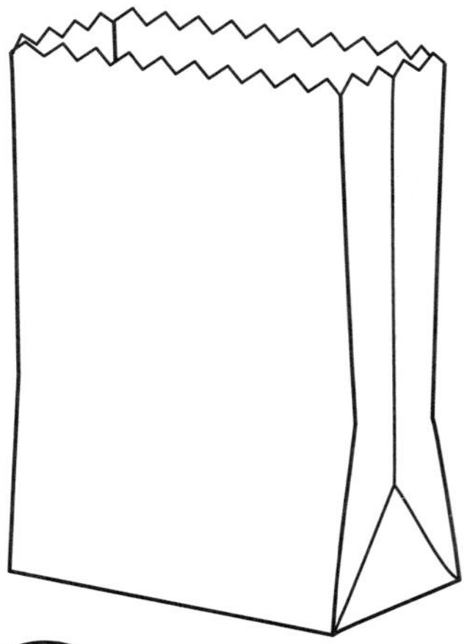

PRACTICE

Problem Solving Visual Thinking

Solve.

10 Draw 6 Snap Cubes in the bag so it is possible to get a red, yellow, or green cube.

11 What color would be impossible to pick from your bag? ________

12 Can you be certain of getting a red cube from your bag? Explain.

Notes for Home: Your child drew pictures to show if getting a particular color of cubes was certain or impossible. *Home Activity:* Ask you child to set up a group of buttons in which getting a particular color would be certain. Then have your child create a group in which getting a color would be impossible.

Name

Problem Solving: Use Data from a Picture

Learn

PROBLEM SOLVING GUIDE

Understand • Plan • Solve • Look Back

Check

Answer the riddles.

1. I show thirds. One third is green. Which am I?

   C

2. I show halves. I am in a red basket. Which am I?

   ______

3. I show fourths. I am on a blue plate. Which am I?

   ______

4. I show fourths. My plate is square. Which am I?

   ______

Talk About It Make up your own riddle.

Notes for Home: Your child used information from a picture to answer riddles. *Home Activity:* Make up riddles about shapes and fractions around your home and neighborhood.

Practice

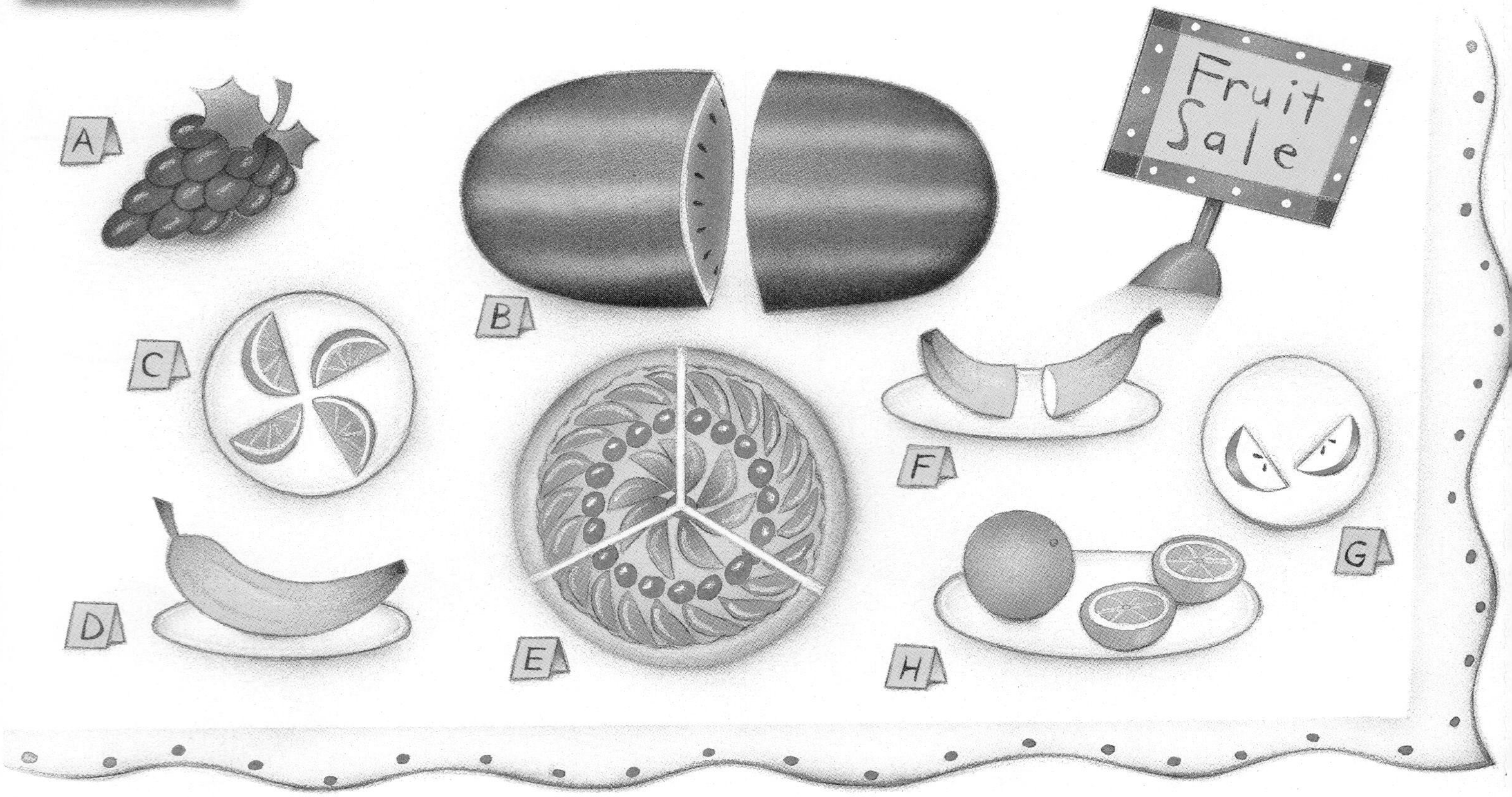

Answer the riddles.

5 I show fourths. I am orange. Which am I?

______

6 I show halves. I am yellow Which am I?

______

7 I show thirds. I am round. Which am I?

______

8 I show halves. I am green on the outside. Which am I?

______

Mental Math

9 The boys are going to eat the  .

Brian has one half of the  . Jerry has one half of the  .

Are there any  left for Phil? Why or why not?

Notes for Home: Your child used a picture to answer more riddles about fractions. *Home Activity:* Cut equal length strips of paper that are the same size. Fold them into halves, thirds, and fourths. Color one half, one third, and one fourth. Compare the fractions. Which is more?

For additional practice, see Skills Practice Bank, page 530, Set 3.

Name

Mixed Practice

Lessons 7–13

Concepts and Skills

Draw a line to show 2 fair shares.

1 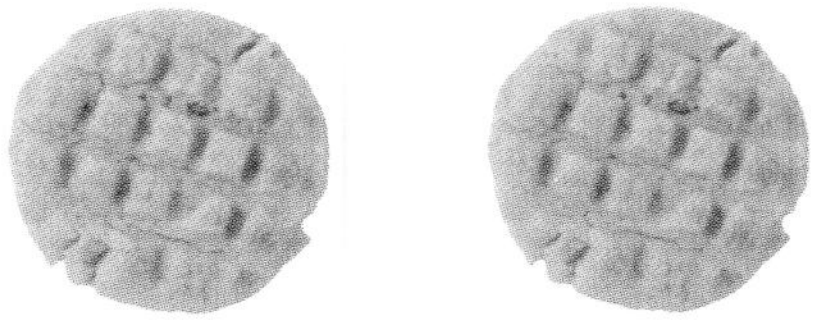

2 

Color to show the fraction.

3 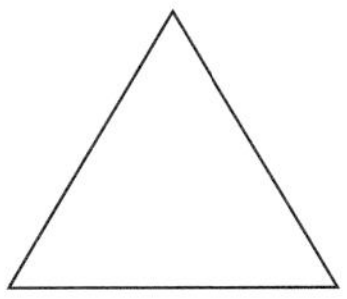

one half $\frac{1}{2}$

4 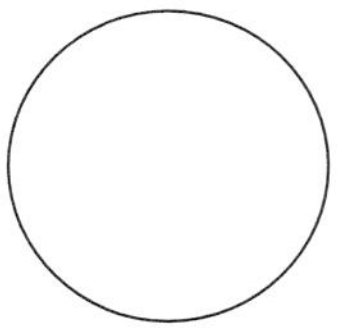

one fourth $\frac{1}{4}$

5 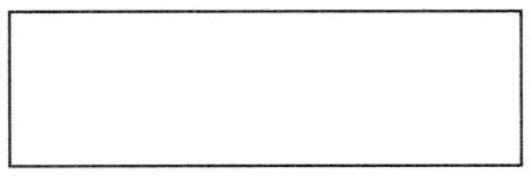

one third $\frac{1}{3}$

Circle the answer.

6 Pick a banana.

certain

impossible

7 Pick a spoon.

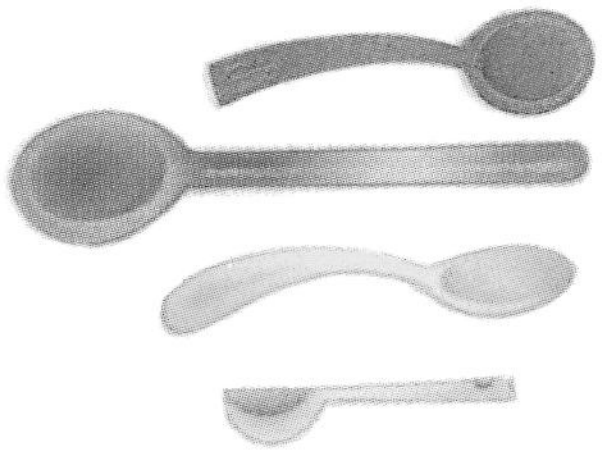

certain

impossible

Problem Solving

8 Look at the fruit. Circle the correct answer.

I show fourths.
Which fruit am I?

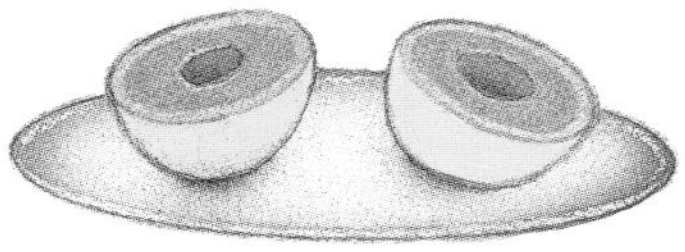

Journal

9 Make a game in which you use a spinner.

Notes for Home: Your child practiced fraction and probability concepts. *Home Activity:* Play a game that uses a spinner. Is the spinner fair?

MIXED PRACTICE

Name ______________________________

Cumulative Review

Chapters 1–5

Concepts and Skills

1 Add.

$$\begin{array}{r} 5 \\ +\,3 \\ \hline \end{array} \qquad \begin{array}{r} 4 \\ +\,5 \\ \hline \end{array} \qquad \begin{array}{r} 5 \\ +\,7 \\ \hline \end{array}$$

2 Subtract.

$$\begin{array}{r} 9 \\ -\,5 \\ \hline \end{array} \qquad \begin{array}{r} 7 \\ -\,5 \\ \hline \end{array} \qquad \begin{array}{r} 6 \\ -\,5 \\ \hline \end{array}$$

Problem Solving

Solve. Write a number sentence.

3 Marcel has 5 
He eats 2.
How many are left?

____ − ____ = ____

4 There are 9 .
3 drive away.
How many  are left?

____ − ____ = ____

Test Prep

Fill in the ○ for the correct answer.
Add or subtract.

5 $9 + 1 =$ ____

○ 1 ○ 8 ○ 9 ○ 10

6 $10 - 2 =$ ____

○ 3 ○ 8 ○ 9 ○ 12

7 $6 - 2 =$ ____

○ 4 ○ 3 ○ 5 ○ 8

8 $7 + 3 =$ ____

○ 4 ○ 10 ○ 9 ○ 11

Notes for Home: Your child reviewed the concepts taught in Chapters 1–5. *Home Activity*: Ask your child to tell a number story for 6 − 2.

Name ______________________________

Chapter 5 Review

Vocabulary

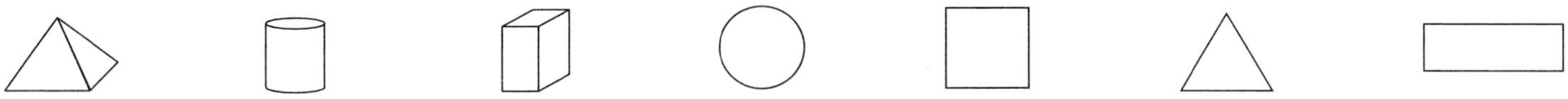

1. Circle the solid that can roll.
2. Color the square blue.
3. Put an X on the shape with three sides.
4. Color one half of the circle green.

Concepts and Skills

5. Tell how much of the set is red.

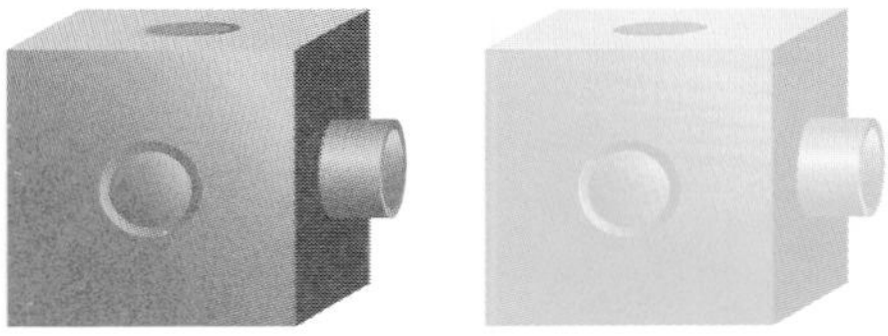

_____ out of _____ parts is red.

6. Circle the answer.
Pick an orange.

certain

impossible

Problem Solving

7. Look at the picture.
Complete the table to tell how many.

	Green	Orange	Purple

Notes for Home: Your child reviewed vocabulary and concepts taught in Chapter 5. *Home Activity*: Ask your child to sort cans or boxes of food by type. Together make a table to show this.

CHAPTER TEST

Name

Chapter 5 Test

1 Circle the solid that can stack.

2 Draw the fold line.

3 Make the same size and shape.

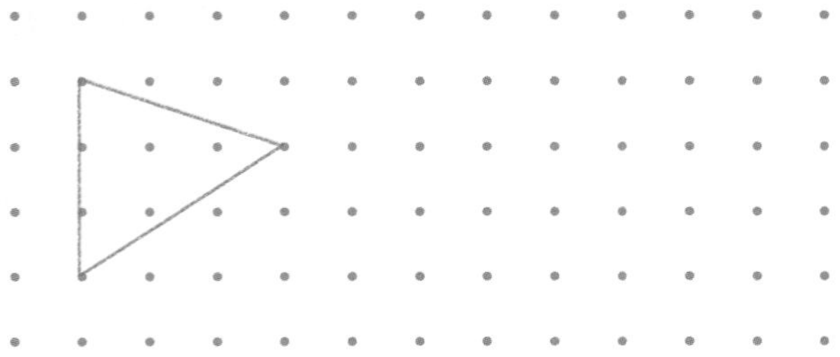

4 Pick an apple.
Circle the answer.

certain

impossible

5 How much of the set is red?

_____ out of _____ parts is red.

6 Circle the shape that shows one fourth.

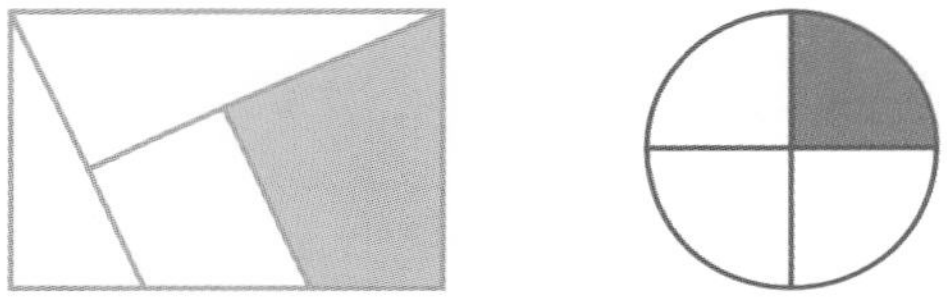

7 Make 2 fair shares.

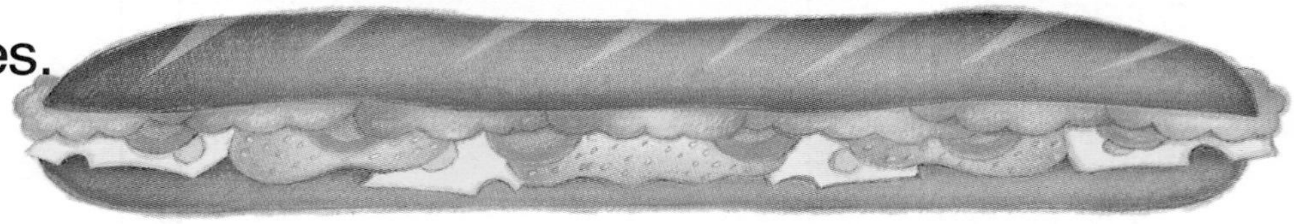

8 Look at the picture. Complete the table to tell how many.

	red	blue	yellow
circle			
square			

Notes for Home: Your child was assessed on Chapter 5 concepts, skills, and problem solving. *Home Activity*: Ask your child to talk about what he or she learned about shapes and fractions in this chapter.

Name _____

Performance Assessment
Chapter 5

What You Need

paper

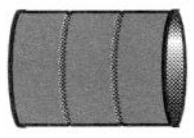

 and

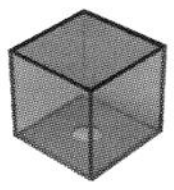

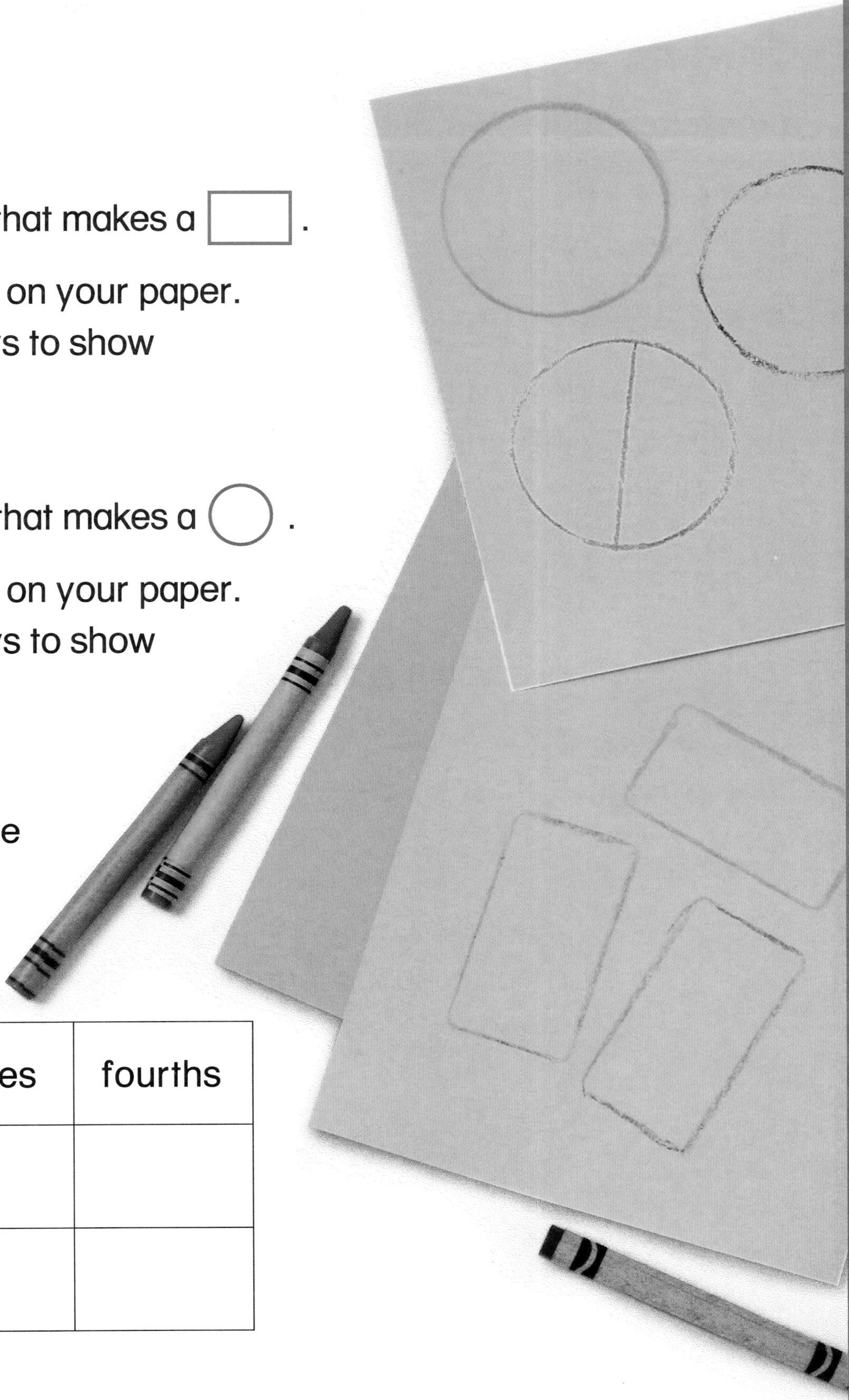

1 Choose the solid that makes a ☐ .

Trace some ☐ on your paper.
Find different ways to show
- 2 equal parts.
- 4 equal parts.

2 Choose the solid that makes a ◯ .

Trace some ◯ on your paper.
Find different ways to show
- 2 equal parts.
- 4 equal parts.

3 Complete the table
to tell how many
ways you made.

	halves	fourths
▭		
◯		

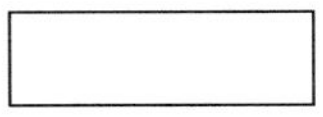

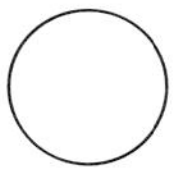

Notes for Home: Your child completed an activity that tested his or her understanding of solids, shapes, and fractions. *Home Activity:* Look for squares and rectangles. Tell how you could make 2 equal parts.

Name ______________________

Explore with a COMPUTER

Shifting Shapes

Computer Skills You Will Need

1. Draw shapes with 3 sides.
   Draw 5 different ones.
   Fill each one with a different color.

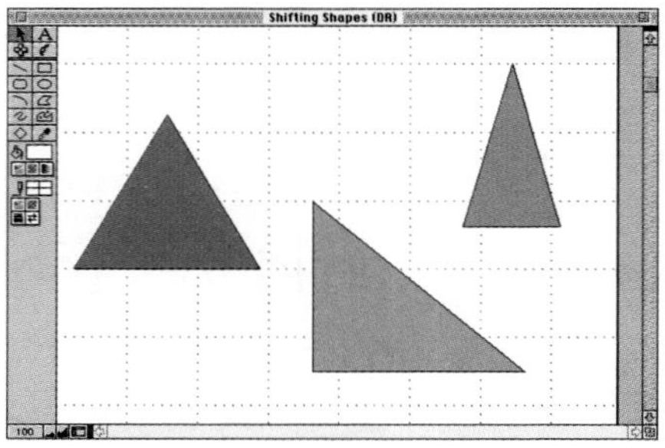

2. Draw shapes with 4 sides.
   Draw 5 different ones.
   Fill each one with a different color.

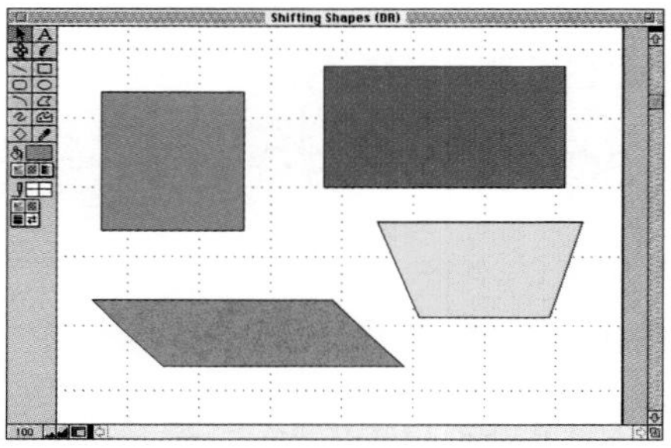

3. Print your shapes. Cut them out.
   Paste 3 or more shapes together. Put them here.

Tech Talk Explain how you drew a shape.

Visit our Web site. **www.parent.mathsurf.com**

Heads or Tails?

Does a penny have an equal chance of landing on heads or tails? What do you think?

Find out by tossing a penny 20 times. Color one box for each flip.

How many times did the penny land on heads?

____

How many times did the penny land on tails?

____

If you flip the penny 20 times again, what do you think will happen? Why?

15	15
14	14
13	13
12	12
11	11
10	10
9	9
8	8
7	7
6	6
5	5
4	4
3	3
2	2
1	1
Heads	**Tails**

Fold down

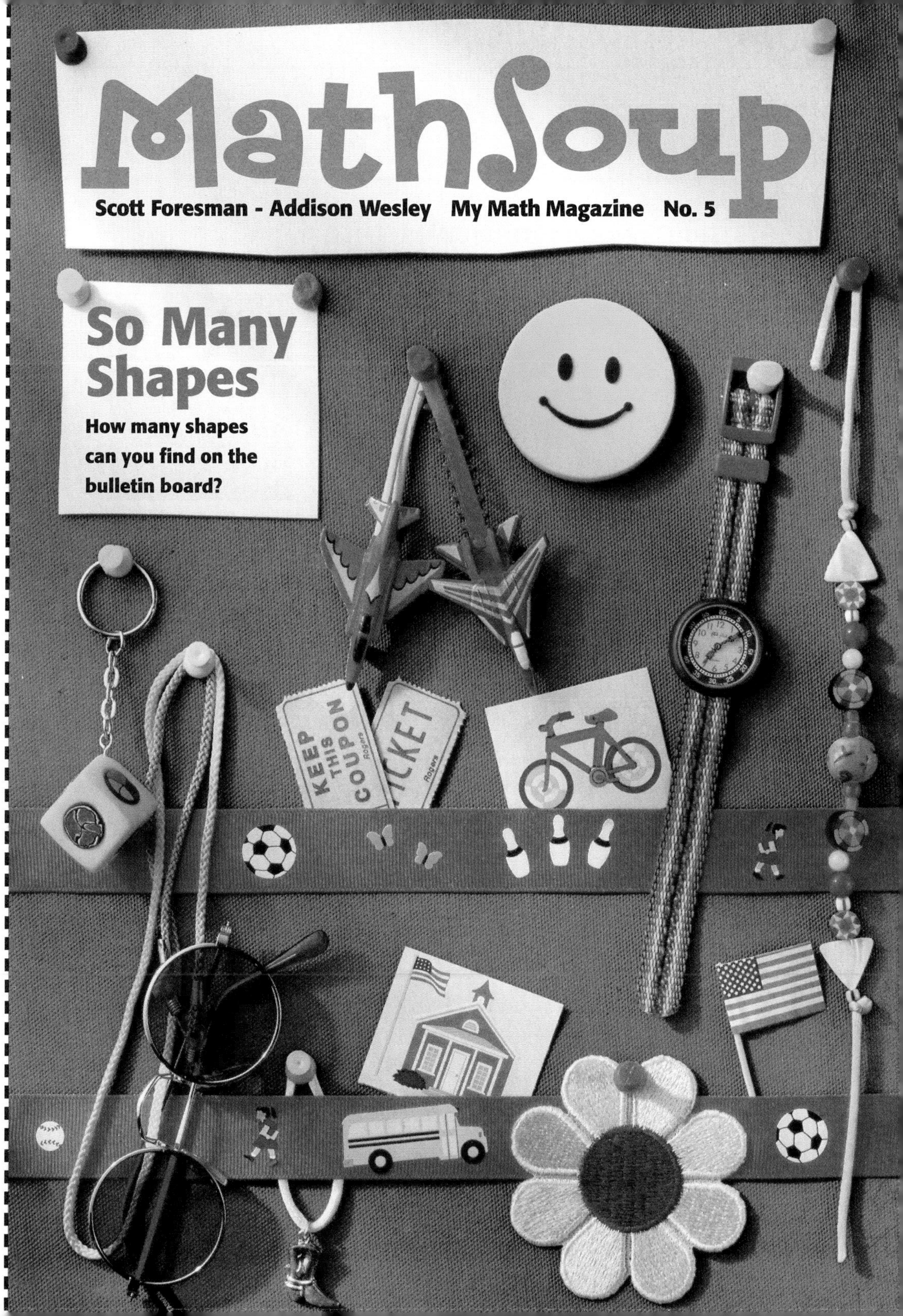

MathSoup
Scott Foresman - Addison Wesley My Math Magazine No. 5
So Many Shapes
How many shapes can you find on the bulletin board?
KEEP THIS COUPON
TICKET

Terrific Triangles

Find the triangles in each picture.

Notes for Home: Your child observed triangle shapes in pictures of buildings. *Home Activity:* Ask your child to look for triangle shapes in buildings in your neighborhood.

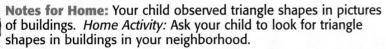

Cut It Out!

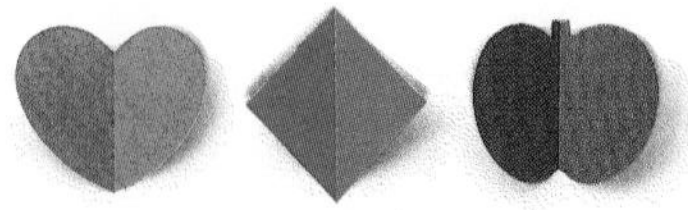

Think of a simple shape you can cut out.

1 Fold a sheet of paper. Draw half of your shape on one side.

2 Cut out your shape. Cut through both parts of the paper

3 Unfold your shape!

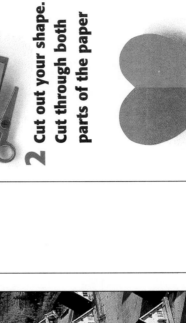

4 Make more shapes. Hang them on a string.

Color a Quilt

This quilt pattern is called "Hole in the Barn Door".

Why do you think it has this name? Color the pattern to find out.

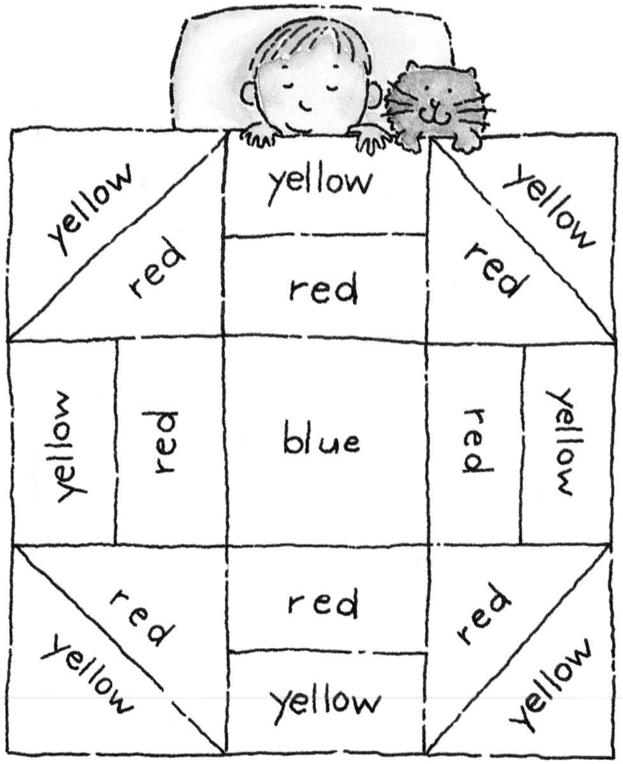

Draw a line in the pattern to make two matching parts.

How can you be sure the parts match?

Notes for Home: Your child colored a pattern and then identified a line of symmetry. *Home Activity:* Ask your child to find another way to divide the pattern into two matching parts.

The Last Straw

What You Need

6 straws, all the same size

4 clay balls

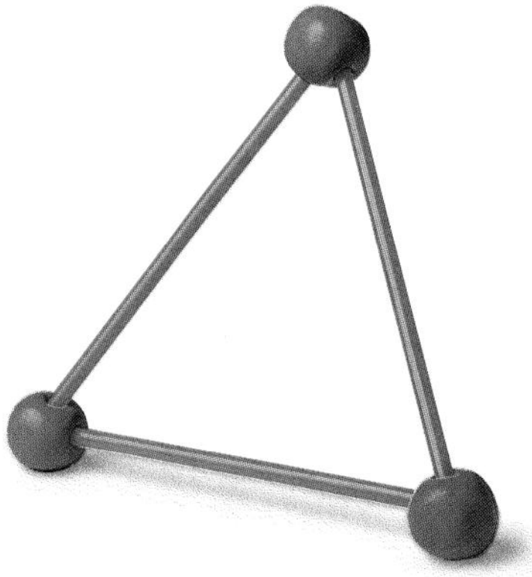

1 **Use 3 straws and 3 clay balls to make a triangle.**

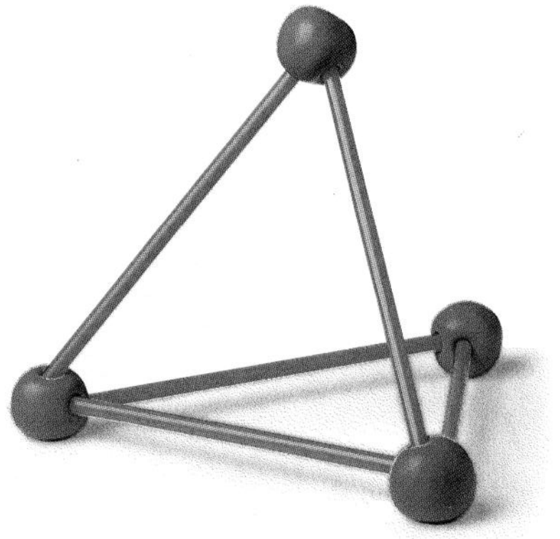

2 **Add 2 more straws. You will need 1 more clay ball.**

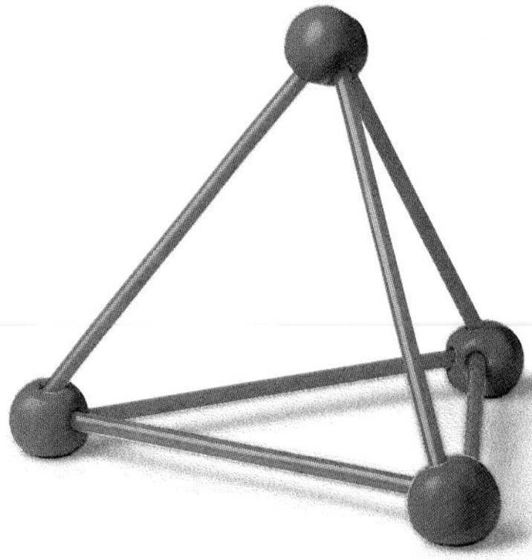

3 **Add the last straw!**

How many triangles do you count?

Cat and Mouse

Tangrams are puzzles that were first made in China. You can make a tangram by tracing this picture. Then cut out each shape.

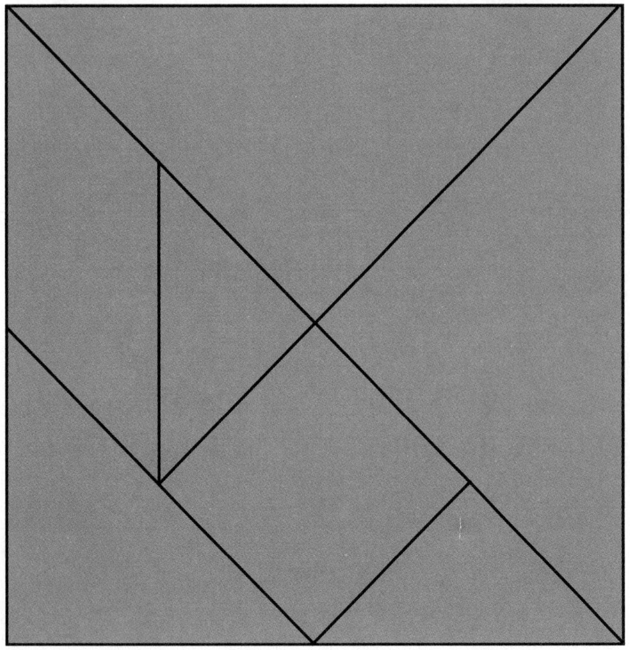

Look at the cut out pieces.

How many triangles are there? _____

How many 4-sided shapes? _____

How many shapes in all? _____

Use your tangram to make a cat picture.
Here are some you can try.

Why are cats so great?
Because they are "purrrfect."
I'm outta here!

What other pictures can you make with your tangram pieces?

Notes for Home: Your child identified shapes in a tangram and used the shapes to create designs. *Home Activity:* Ask your child to use the tangram pieces to make a shape.

CHAPTER 6

More Fact Strategies

Creeping Critters
Stripes and spots! Make math stories with the matching critters.

Notes for Home: Your child told math stories about the animals on the page.
Home Activity: Ask your child to tell you a math story about the animals.

Math at Home

Dear Family,
Our class is starting Chapter 6. We will be learning more ways to add and subtract numbers to 12. Doing the activities on this page will help me practice adding and subtracting.

Double Up

Use small objects such as buttons, shells, or beads to make a group of 1 to 6 objects. Make a group and ask your child to make a matching group. Together, find the total number for both groups.

Three-Sided Math

Make flash cards from paper triangles. In each corner, write one of the three numbers of an addition fact. Cover the greatest number and have your child tell an addition sentence. Cover one of the lesser numbers, and ask for a subtraction sentence.

Community Connection

What creepy crawlers and critters can you and your child count in your neighborhood? Keep a tally of what you find.

Visit our Web site. www.parent.mathsurf.com

Name _____

Add with Doubles

Learn •

These pictures show doubles. They can help us add.

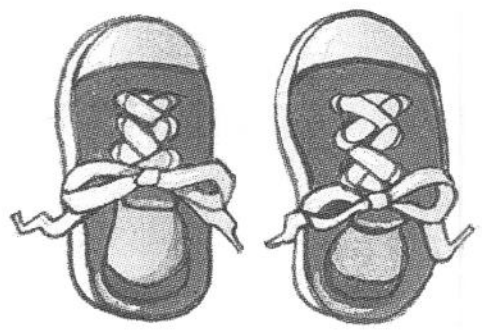

1 + 1 = 2

2 + 2 = 4

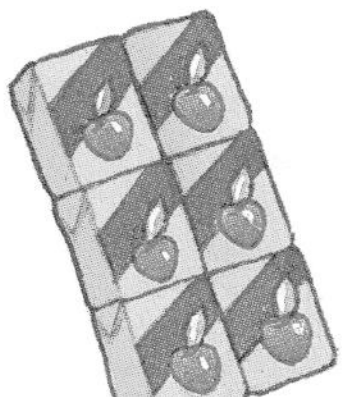

3 + 3 = 6

4 + 4 = 8

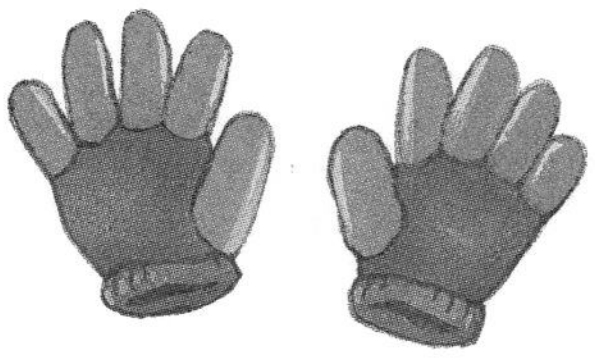

5 + 5 = 10

6 + 6 = 12

Check •

Write the sum.

1. 4 + 4 = _8_ 3 + 3 = ___ 2 + 2 = ___

2. 5 + 5 = ___ 6 + 6 = ___ 1 + 1 = ___

3.
```
  5      6      1      4      0      3      2
+ 5    + 6    + 1    + 4    + 0    + 3    + 2
```

Talk About It What can you find in your classroom or at home that has doubles?

Notes for Home: Your child learned about facts in which both parts are the same number.
Home Activity: Encourage your child to find doubles around home, for example, the two rows of 6 in an egg carton or the two rows of eyelets on shoes with laces.

Practice

PRACTICE

Write the sum. Use the doubles to help.

4. $3 + 3 = \underline{6}$ $\quad 6 + 6 = \underline{\quad}$ $\quad 5 + 5 = \underline{\quad}$

5. $4 + 4$ $\quad 2 + 2$ $\quad 1 + 1$ $\quad 3 + 3$ $\quad 5 + 5$ $\quad 6 + 6$ $\quad 0 + 0$

Mixed Practice Write the sum. Circle the doubles.

6. $3 + 3$ $\quad 5 + 3$ $\quad 4 + 4$ $\quad 7 + 2$ $\quad 6 + 6$ $\quad 9 + 0$ $\quad 1 + 7$

7. $2 + 2$ $\quad 2 + 5$ $\quad 1 + 8$ $\quad 5 + 5$ $\quad 4 + 3$ $\quad 3 + 8$ $\quad 9 + 2$

Problem Solving Critical Thinking

8. Can you use doubles to make 9? Explain.

Notes for Home: Your child practiced addition facts to 12. *Home Activity:* Ask your child to find the doubles in a set of dominoes. Ask, "What is the sum of the two sides?"

For additional practice, see Skills Practice Bank, page 531, Set 1.

Name ____________________

Explore Adding Doubles Plus One

Explore

Show cubes.

Use 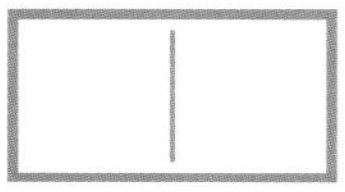.

Make the double.

How many? 4

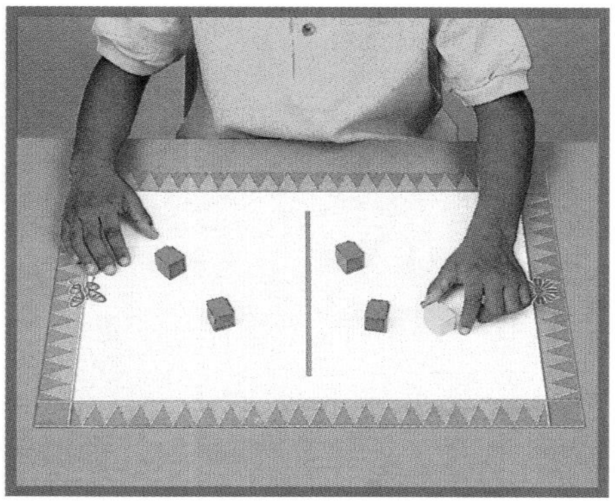

Add 1 more.

How many? 5

Show these cubes.	Make the double. Write how many.	Add 1 more. Write how many.
1 	2	____
2 	____	____
3 	____	____
4 	____	____
What comes next? 5	____	____

EXPLORE

Share

What patterns do you see?

Notes for Home: Your child explored adding one more to a double (such as 2 + 2) and finding how many in all. *Home Activity:* Ask your child to find something at home that comes in doubles, such as the legs on a table. Ask your child to tell how many, add one more, and tell the sum.

Connect

Use a doubles fact to add other facts.

$3 + 4 = 7$

Write the doubles fact that helps.
Add.

6. $\begin{array}{r} 2 \\ +\ 3 \\ \hline 5 \end{array}$ $\quad \begin{array}{r} 2 \\ +\ 2 \\ \hline 4 \end{array}$

7. $\begin{array}{r} 4 \\ +\ 5 \\ \hline \end{array}$ $\quad \begin{array}{r} \square \\ +\ \square \\ \hline \square \end{array}$

8. $\begin{array}{r} 5 \\ +\ 6 \\ \hline \end{array}$ $\quad \begin{array}{r} \square \\ +\ \square \\ \hline \square \end{array}$

Add.

9. $4 + 3 =$ ____ $\quad 4 + 4 =$ ____ $\quad 3 + 2 =$ ____

10. $\begin{array}{r} 6 \\ +\ 5 \\ \hline \end{array}$ $\quad \begin{array}{r} 2 \\ +\ 2 \\ \hline \end{array}$ $\quad \begin{array}{r} 5 \\ +\ 4 \\ \hline \end{array}$ $\quad \begin{array}{r} 3 \\ +\ 3 \\ \hline \end{array}$ $\quad \begin{array}{r} 6 \\ +\ 6 \\ \hline \end{array}$ $\quad \begin{array}{r} 1 \\ +\ 2 \\ \hline \end{array}$ $\quad \begin{array}{r} 5 \\ +\ 5 \\ \hline \end{array}$

Tell a Math Story

11. Make up a math story that uses doubles.
Retell the story, using doubles plus one.

Notes for Home: Your child learned that facts like 3 + 4 = 7 are 1 more than a doubles fact (3 + 3 = 6). *Home Activity:* Say a doubles fact, such as 4 + 4 = 8, and ask your child to name a fact that is 1 more (4 + 5 = 9 or 5 + 4 = 9).

EXPLORE

Name

Add with Doubles Plus One

Learn

Double	Double Plus One	Turnaround Fact
$4 + 4 = 8$	$4 + 5 = 9$	$5 + 4 = 9$

If I know this fact,
then I know this one too.

Check

Complete the number sentence.

1

$3 + 3 = 6$ $3 + 4 =$ ___ $4 + 3 =$ ___

2

$5 + 5 =$ ___ ___ + ___ = ___ ___ + ___ = ___

3

$$\begin{array}{r} 2 \\ +\ 2 \\ \hline \end{array}$$

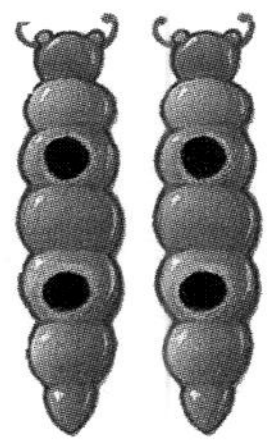

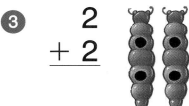

$$\begin{array}{r} 2 \\ +\ 3 \\ \hline \end{array}$$

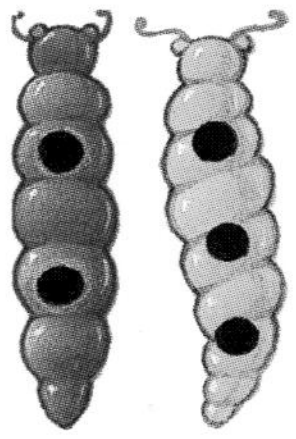

$$\begin{array}{r} 3 \\ +\ 2 \\ \hline \end{array}$$

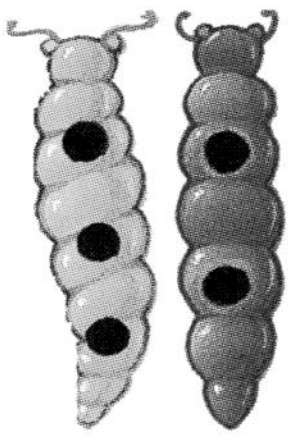

Talk About It How are the sums in each problem alike? How are they different?

Notes for Home: Your child used doubles facts (such as $4 + 4 = 8$) to find sums for other facts (such as $5 + 4 = 9$). *Home Activity:* Ask your child to put 10 objects into two equal groups and say the doubles fact ($5 + 5 = 10$). Add 1 object. Ask your child to say two addition facts ($5 + 6 = 11$ and $6 + 5 = 11$).

Practice

Add.

4. 1 + 1 = 2   1 + 2 = ____   2 + 1 = ____

5. 4 + 4 = ____   4 + 5 = ____   5 + 4 = ____

6.

5	5	6
+ 5	+ 6	+ 5

7.

3	3	4
+ 3	+ 4	+ 3

8.

6	2	1	5	4	3	0
+ 6	+ 2	+ 1	+ 5	+ 4	+ 3	+ 0

9.

4	6	2	5	3	1	0
+ 3	+ 5	+ 1	+ 4	+ 2	+ 6	+ 1

PRACTICE

Problem Solving Critical Thinking

10. Billy Bee threw 3 darts.
His total score was 11.
Circle the 3 numbers he scored.

Notes for Home: Your child practiced using doubles plus one. *Home Activity:* Have your child find 3 numbers on the dart board that equal 7 when added (3 + 3 + 1, 2 + 2 + 3).

Name

Use Doubles to Subtract

Learn

You can use a doubles fact to help you subtract.

$\begin{array}{r} 6 \\ +\ 6 \\ \hline 12 \end{array}$ $\begin{array}{r} 12 \\ -\ 6 \\ \hline 6 \end{array}$

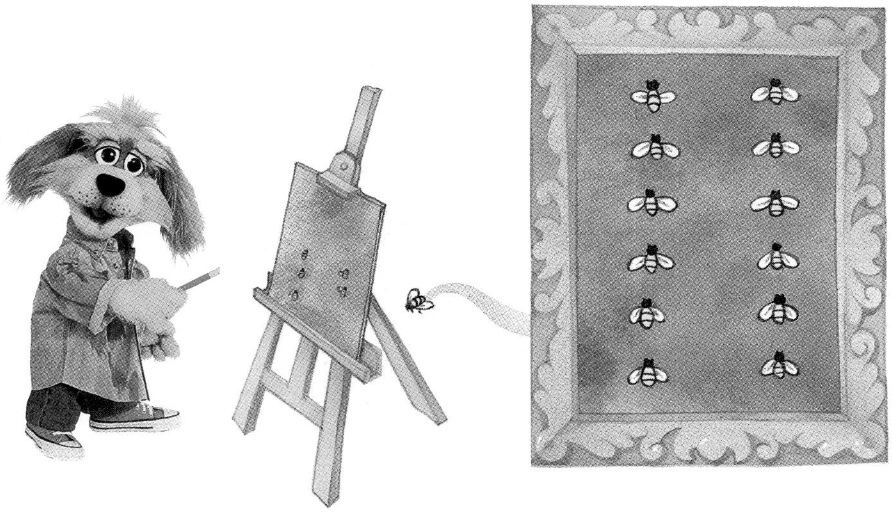

Check

Add or subtract.

1. $\begin{array}{r} 5 \\ +\ 5 \\ \hline 10 \end{array}$ 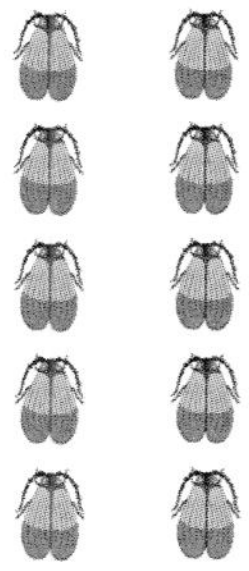 $\begin{array}{r} 10 \\ -\ 5 \\ \hline \end{array}$

2. $\begin{array}{r} 4 \\ +\ 4 \\ \hline \end{array}$ 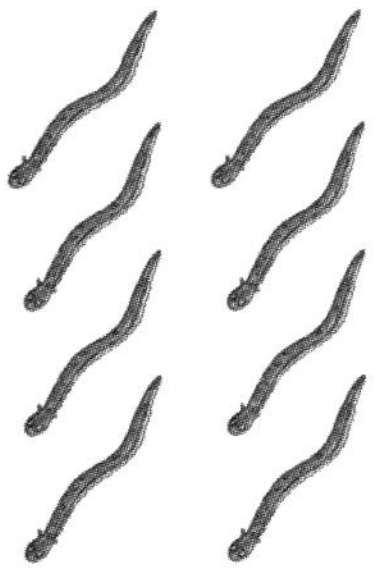 $\begin{array}{r} 8 \\ -\ 4 \\ \hline \end{array}$

3. $\begin{array}{r} 3 \\ +\ 3 \\ \hline \end{array}$  $\begin{array}{r} 6 \\ -\ 3 \\ \hline \end{array}$

4. $\begin{array}{r} 2 \\ +\ 2 \\ \hline \end{array}$  $\begin{array}{r} 4 \\ -\ 2 \\ \hline \end{array}$

5. $\begin{array}{r} 1 \\ +\ 1 \\ \hline \end{array}$ 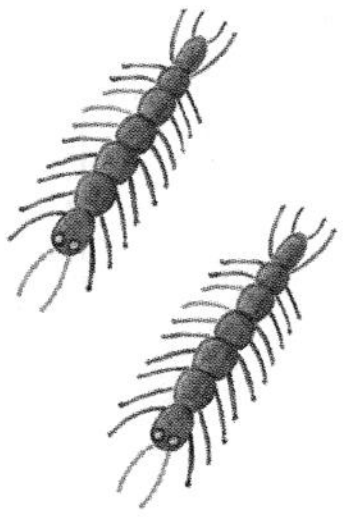 $\begin{array}{r} 2 \\ -\ 1 \\ \hline \end{array}$

6. $\begin{array}{r} 6 \\ +\ 6 \\ \hline \end{array}$ 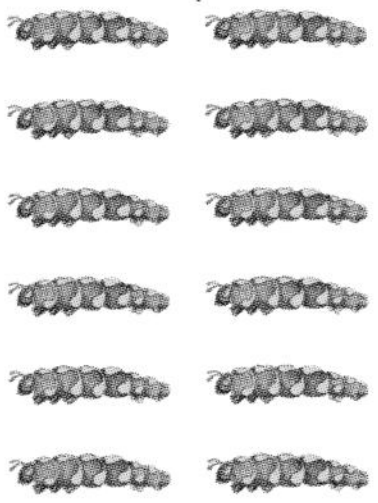 $\begin{array}{r} 12 \\ -\ 6 \\ \hline \end{array}$

Talk About It Explain how you can use doubles to subtract $8 - 4$.

Notes for Home: Your child learned about subtraction facts in which two parts are the same number, such as $10 - 5 = 5$ and $8 - 4 = 4$. *Home Activity:* Say the addition doubles (for example, $5 + 5 = 10$), and have your child give the related subtraction fact ($10 - 5 = 5$).

Practice

Add or subtract.

7. $8 - 4 = \underline{4}$
   $4 + 4 = \_\_\_$

8. $12 - 6 = \_\_\_$
   $6 + 6 = \_\_\_$

9. $4 - 2 = \_\_\_$
   $2 + 2 = \_\_\_$

10. $6 - 3 = \_\_\_$
    $3 + 3 = \_\_\_$

PRACTICE

Subtract. Write the addition facts that help.

11. $10 - 5 = \boxed{5}$ $\quad \boxed{5} + \boxed{5} = \boxed{10}$

12. $8 - 4 = \boxed{}$ $\quad \boxed{} + \boxed{} = \boxed{}$

13. $4 - 2 = \boxed{}$ $\quad \boxed{} + \boxed{} = \boxed{}$

14. $2 - 1 = \_\_\_$
    $\_\_\_ + \_\_\_ = \_\_\_$

15. $12 - 6 = \_\_\_$
    $\_\_\_ + \_\_\_ = \_\_\_$

Tell a Math Story

16. Make up a math story using $10 - 5$.
    Draw a picture for your story.

Notes for Home: Your child practiced using addition and subtraction to find answers. *Home Activity:* Ask your child to say a subtraction fact for things found around your home that come in doubles, for example, 12 eggs minus 6 eggs is 6 eggs.

Name ______________________________

Reading for Math

Compare and Contrast

Look at the pictures. Read the story.

See how spiders and ladybugs are alike and different.

Spider

A spider has 8 legs. It has 2 feelers that look like legs. A spider spins a sticky web. When a fly gets stuck in the web, the spider runs out and wraps up the fly. Later the spider eats the fly.

Ladybug

A ladybug has 6 legs. It has brightly-colored wing cases. To fly, it lifts its 2 hard wings and spreads its 2 softer wings. A ladybug eats tiny insects it finds on plants.

Use tally marks to complete the chart. Write how many.

This | is a tally mark. It means 1.

These tally marks mean 5. 卌

Number of Legs

Bug	Tally	Total
Spider	卌 |||	8
Ladybug		____

1. How many legs does a spider have? ____

2. How many legs does a ladybug have? ____

3. Which has fewer legs? ______________

Talk About It How are spiders and ladybugs alike? How are they different?

Notes for Home: Your child learned that tally marks stand for a number, and compared and contrasted information from a chart. *Home Activity:* Ask your child to draw pictures of a spider and an insect and say a math sentence about the number of legs each has.

Caterpillar

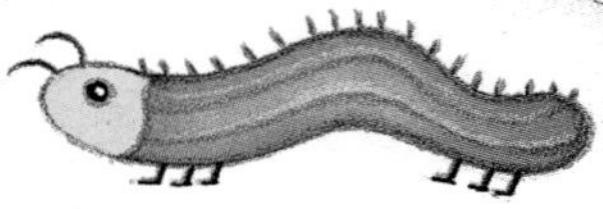

A caterpillar may look as though it has many legs, but it has only 6 true legs. A caterpillar has no wings. It will get its wings when its body changes into a butterfly or a moth.

Atlas Moth

The Atlas moth is one of the biggest moths in the world. It has 4 wings. The wings can be 12 inches across. The Atlas moth has 6 legs.

Count the wings.
Make a tally mark for each wing.
Write how many.

Number of Wings

Insect	Tally	Totals
Caterpillar		0
Moth		

4. Which has wings? ______________________

5. Which has no wings? ______________________

6. How are the caterpillar and the moth different?

____

7. How are they the same? ______________________

Journal

Choose an insect or spider to write about.
What words help you tell how it looks? Use the words in a story.

Notes for Home: Your child completed a chart to compare a caterpillar and a moth.
Home Activity: Ask your child, "How can you tell the difference between a caterpillar and a moth?" (Possible answer: A caterpillar cannot fly. A moth can.)

Name

Problem Solving: Collect and Use Data

Learn

PROBLEM SOLVING GUIDE

Understand • Plan • Solve • Look Back

Your class must choose an insect to study. Which one will you vote for? Use tally marks.

| means 1. 𝍸 means 5.

Check

Tallies can help me count. 5, 10, 11, 12

1. Take a vote.
   Make a class tally. Write the totals.

	Tally	Total
Bee		
Fly		
Ant		

Use the chart to solve.

2. How many voted for flies? ______

3. Which insect got the fewest votes? ______

4. Do any insects have more than 5 votes? Which ones? ______

   ______

5. Which insect do most of the children want to study? How do you know? ______

   ______

Talk About It What other questions can you ask about the chart?

Notes for Home: Your child made tally marks in a chart to record their classmates' responses to a question. *Home Activity:* Ask your child to make a tally of the number of objects in a drawer, such as spoons and forks.

PROBLEM SOLVING

Practice

Mrs. Lee's class went for a walk outside.
Here is what they saw.
Write each total.

Critters	Tally	Total
Butterflies	𝍷𝍷	2
Worms	𝍸 𝍷𝍷𝍷	____
Spiders	𝍸 𝍸	____
Ladybugs	𝍷𝍷𝍷𝍷	____
Bees	𝍸 𝍷	____

Write your own questions.
Use the chart to write 3 questions.
Trade papers. Answer each other's questions.

6 ____

____

7 ____

____

8 ____

____

Patterns

9 Complete the pattern.
Draw the spots. Write the numbers.

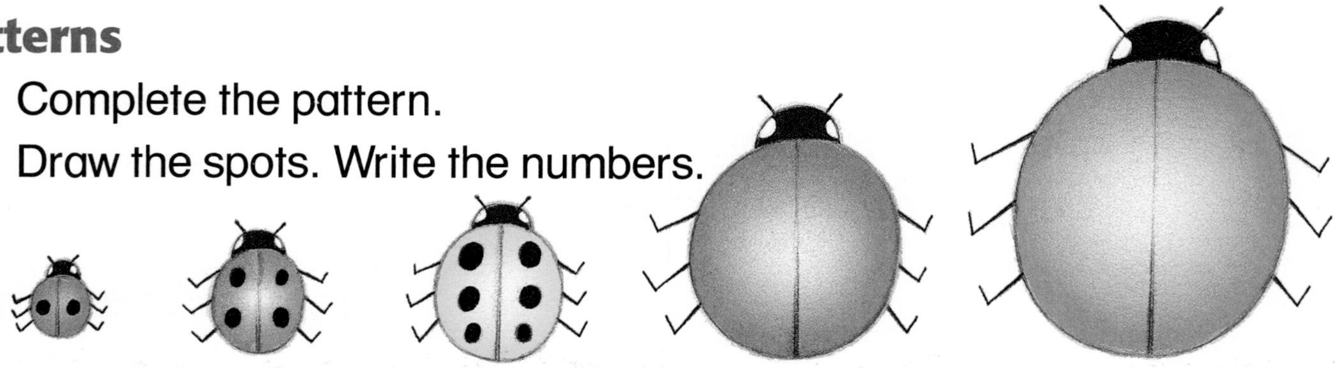

____ ____ ____ ____ ____

Notes for Home: Your child used a tally chart to answer questions. *Home Activity:* Ask your child to make a tally chart for something found at home, such as different canned goods or kinds of socks. Then ask, "Which do we have the fewest of?" "Which do we have the most of?"

Name ____________________

Mixed Practice

Lessons 1–5

Concepts and Skills

Add. Use doubles when you can.

1 $4 + 4$ $4 + 5$ $3 + 3$ $3 + 4$ $5 + 5$ $5 + 6$ $6 + 6$

2 $2 + 2 =$ ____ $2 + 3 =$ ____ $0 + 0 =$ ____

Subtract.

3 $10 - 5$ $8 - 4$ $12 - 6$ $6 - 3$ $2 - 1$ $4 - 2$ $0 - 0$

Problem Solving

Write the totals.

Use the chart to solve.

4 How many chose snails? ____

5 Which one did the most children choose?

____

Critters We Like

Animal	Tally	Total
	𝍸 III	
	𝍸 𝍸	
	𝍸	

Journal

6 Draw a picture to show a double.
Write an addition and a subtraction sentence for the picture.

Notes for Home: Your child practiced adding and subtracting through 12. *Home Activity:* Encourage your child to circle all the problems on this page that use doubles to add or subtract, such as 4 + 4 and 6 – 3, and then write and solve three more doubles problems.

For additional practice, see Basic Facts Review, page 541, Set 3.

Name ________________________________

Cumulative Review

Chapters 1–6

Concepts and Skills

Add or subract.

1	$8 + 3$	$11 - 2$	$8 + 1$	$9 - 1$	$3 - 1$	$4 + 3$	$2 + 5$
2	$2 + 7$	$8 - 2$	$6 - 1$	$6 + 2$	$7 - 2$	$3 + 9$	$4 - 2$

Problem Solving

Write a number sentence. Solve.

3. There are 3 red bugs.
There are 4 green bugs.
How many bugs are there?

______________ bugs

4. 10 ants are walking.
5 ants go into a hole.
How many ants are left?

______________ ants

Test Prep

Fill in the ○ for the correct answer.

Choose the fraction for the shaded part shown.

5. 

$\frac{1}{2}$ ○ $\frac{1}{3}$ ○ $\frac{1}{4}$ ○

6. 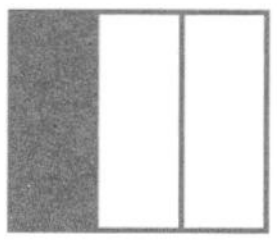

$\frac{1}{2}$ ○ $\frac{1}{3}$ ○ $\frac{1}{4}$ ○

7. 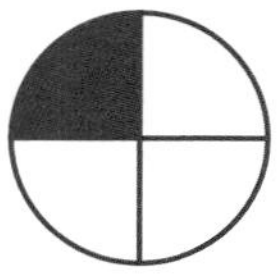

$\frac{1}{2}$ ○ $\frac{1}{3}$ ○ $\frac{1}{4}$ ○

Notes for Home: Your child reviewed adding 1, 2, and 3, subtracting 1 and 2, and identifying fractions. *Home Activity:* Have your child practice addition and subtraction facts in different funny voices, such as a high voice or an animal voice. For example, ask, "How would a parrot say, 11 − 2 = 9?"

Name

Relate Addition and Subtraction

Learn

$$\begin{array}{r} 4 \\ +\ 3 \\ \hline 7 \end{array} \qquad \begin{array}{r} 7 \\ -\ 3 \\ \hline 4 \end{array}$$

These facts are related. They use the same numbers.

Check

Tell an addition story and a subtraction story about the picture.
Find each answer. You can use .

1 $\begin{array}{r} 4 \\ +\ 2 \\ \hline 6 \end{array}$ 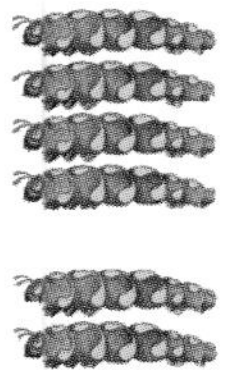 $\begin{array}{r} 6 \\ -\ 2 \\ \hline \end{array}$

2 $\begin{array}{r} 1 \\ +\ 6 \\ \hline \end{array}$ 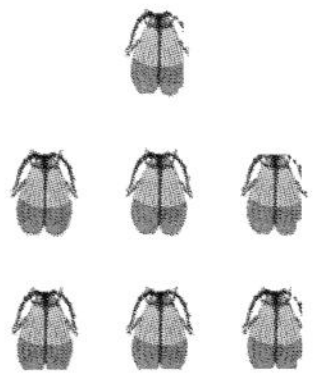 $\begin{array}{r} 7 \\ -\ 6 \\ \hline \end{array}$

3 $\begin{array}{r} 2 \\ +\ 3 \\ \hline \end{array}$  $\begin{array}{r} 5 \\ -\ 3 \\ \hline \end{array}$

4 $\begin{array}{r} 2 \\ +\ 6 \\ \hline \end{array}$ 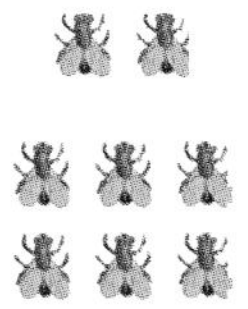 $\begin{array}{r} 8 \\ -\ 6 \\ \hline \end{array}$

5 $\begin{array}{r} 8 \\ +\ 2 \\ \hline \end{array}$ 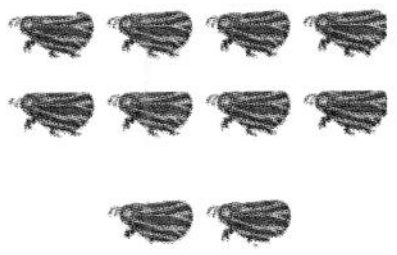 $\begin{array}{r} 10 \\ -\ 2 \\ \hline \end{array}$

6 $\begin{array}{r} 4 \\ +\ 5 \\ \hline \end{array}$ 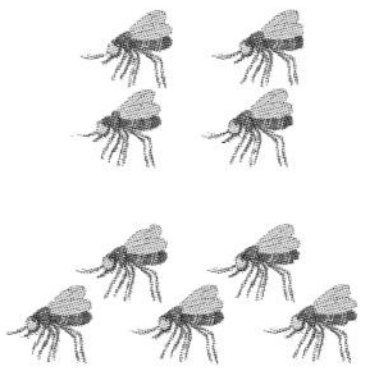 $\begin{array}{r} 9 \\ -\ 5 \\ \hline \end{array}$

Talk About It How are the pairs of facts alike? How are they different?

Notes for Home: Your child used addition facts to help solve subtraction facts. *Home Activity:* Ask your child to explain how knowing 4 + 5 = 9 can be used to solve 9 – 4 and 9 – 5. (Possible answer: Since 4 + 5 = 9, I can subtract either 4 or 5 from 9 and get the other number for the answer.

Practice

Add or subtract. You can use .

7. $\begin{array}{r} 6 \\ +\ 5 \\ \hline \end{array}$  $\begin{array}{r} 11 \\ -\ 5 \\ \hline \end{array}$

8. $\begin{array}{r} 5 \\ +\ 4 \\ \hline \end{array}$ 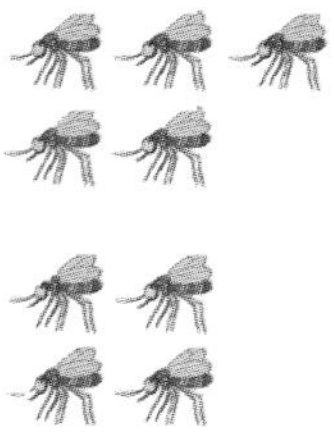 $\begin{array}{r} 9 \\ -\ 4 \\ \hline \end{array}$

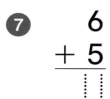

9. $\begin{array}{r} 5 \\ +\ 1 \\ \hline \end{array}$ $\begin{array}{r} 6 \\ -\ 1 \\ \hline \end{array}$

10. $\begin{array}{r} 3 \\ +\ 5 \\ \hline \end{array}$ $\begin{array}{r} 8 \\ -\ 5 \\ \hline \end{array}$

11. $\begin{array}{r} 1 \\ +\ 3 \\ \hline \end{array}$ $\begin{array}{r} 4 \\ -\ 3 \\ \hline \end{array}$

12. $\begin{array}{r} 2 \\ +\ 7 \\ \hline \end{array}$ $\begin{array}{r} 9 \\ -\ 7 \\ \hline \end{array}$

13. $\begin{array}{r} 3 \\ +\ 8 \\ \hline \end{array}$ $\begin{array}{r} 11 \\ -\ 8 \\ \hline \end{array}$

14. $\begin{array}{r} 7 \\ +\ 3 \\ \hline \end{array}$ $\begin{array}{r} 10 \\ -\ 3 \\ \hline \end{array}$

15. $\begin{array}{r} 2 \\ +\ 8 \\ \hline \end{array}$ $\begin{array}{r} 10 \\ -\ 8 \\ \hline \end{array}$

16. $\begin{array}{r} 7 \\ +\ 1 \\ \hline \end{array}$ $\begin{array}{r} 8 \\ -\ 1 \\ \hline \end{array}$

17. $\begin{array}{r} 5 \\ +\ 7 \\ \hline \end{array}$ $\begin{array}{r} 12 \\ -\ 7 \\ \hline \end{array}$

PRACTICE

Problem Solving

Solve.

18. Paca caught 3 fireflies. Then she caught 6 more. How many fireflies did Paca catch?

_____ fireflies

19. Paca had 9 fireflies. She let 6 go. How many fireflies does Paca have?

_____ fireflies

Notes for Home: Your child practiced using addition facts to help solve subtraction facts. *Home Activity:* Ask your child to tell you some ways to add or subtract to get 6 as an answer. (Possible answers: 3 + 3 = 6, 2 + 4 = 6, 1 + 5 = 6, 12 − 6 = 6, 8 − 2 = 6, 10 − 4 = 6).

Name _____

Learn •

Addition

$5 + 2 = 7$
$2 + 5 = 7$

Subtraction

$7 - 2 = 5$
$7 - 5 = 2$

These 4 facts are called a **fact family**. How are the facts related?

Check •

Complete the fact family.

You can use .

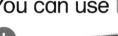

1

$2 + \underline{3} = \underline{}$
$3 + \underline{2} = \underline{}$

$5 - \underline{3} = \underline{}$
$5 - \underline{2} = \underline{}$

2

$3 + \underline{} = \underline{}$
$6 + \underline{} = \underline{}$

$9 - \underline{} = \underline{}$
$9 - \underline{} = \underline{}$

Talk About It Why are these called fact families?

Notes for Home: Your child learned about number relationships in addition and subtraction.
Home Activity: Have your child move groups of objects, such as beads or coins, to demonstrate the four-way relationship of numbers, as in $2 + 6 = 8$, $6 + 2 = 8$, $8 - 2 = 6$, and $8 - 6 = 2$.

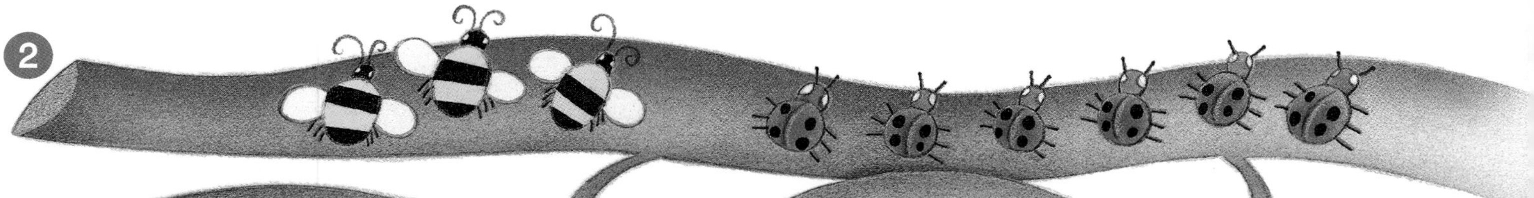

Practice

Complete the fact family.

You can use ▢.

3

2 + 6 = ____   8 − 6 = ____

____ + ____ = ____   ____ − ____ = ____

4

4 + ____ = ____   ____ − ____ = ____

____ + ____ = ____   ____ − ____ = ____

Write your own fact family. Draw a picture to go with it.

5

____ + ____ = ____   ____ − ____ = ____

____ + ____ = ____   ____ − ____ = ____

Problem Solving Critical Thinking

6 There are 8 black ants.
6 red ants come.

How many black ants are there? ____

Notes for Home: Your child practiced writing number sentences to show the number relationships in addition and subtraction. *Home Activity:* Ask your child to use counters, such as 7 paper clips or buttons, to show the four related number sentences 4 + 3, 3 + 4, 7 – 3, and 7 – 4.

PRACTICE

For additional practice, see Skills Practice Bank, page 531, Set 2.

Name

Think Addition to Subtract

Learn

See.
9
− 7
Think.
7
+ 2
9
Write.
9
− 7
2
Sometimes when I subtract, I think about an addition fact I know.

Check

Use addition to help you subtract.

1

$$\begin{array}{r} 6 \\ -\ 4 \\ \hline \boxed{2} \end{array} \qquad \begin{array}{r} 4 \\ +\ \boxed{2} \\ \hline 6 \end{array}$$

2

$$\begin{array}{r} 9 \\ -\ 5 \\ \hline \boxed{} \end{array} \qquad \begin{array}{r} 5 \\ +\ \boxed{} \\ \hline 9 \end{array}$$

3

$$\begin{array}{r} 11 \\ -\ 6 \\ \hline \boxed{} \end{array} \qquad \begin{array}{r} 6 \\ +\ \boxed{} \\ \hline 11 \end{array}$$

4

$$\begin{array}{r} 7 \\ -\ 4 \\ \hline \boxed{} \end{array} \qquad \begin{array}{r} 4 \\ +\ \boxed{} \\ \hline 7 \end{array}$$

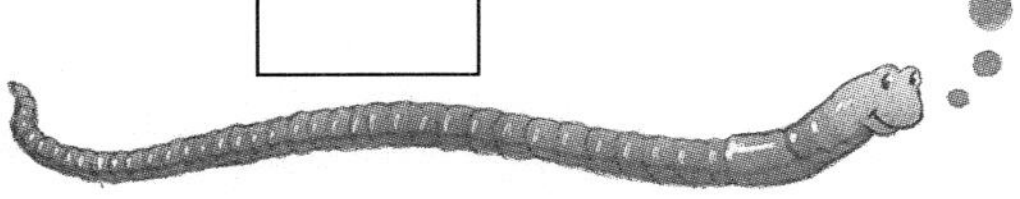

Talk About It How can you use addition to help you subtract?

Notes for Home: Your child used addition facts to help solve subtraction facts. *Home Activity:* Ask your child to tell you the addition fact that can help solve 7 – 5 (5 + 2 = 7).

Practice

Use addition to help you subtract.

5.

$$\begin{array}{r} 12 \\ -\ 7 \\ \hline \boxed{5} \end{array}$$

$$\begin{array}{r} 7 \\ +\ \square \\ \hline 12 \end{array}$$

6.

$$\begin{array}{r} 11 \\ -\ 9 \\ \hline \square \end{array}$$

$$\begin{array}{r} 9 \\ +\ \square \\ \hline 11 \end{array}$$

Mixed Practice Add or subtract.
Draw lines to match related facts.

7.

$$\begin{array}{r} 4 \\ +\ 5 \\ \hline 9 \end{array} \qquad \begin{array}{r} 5 \\ +\ 7 \\ \hline \end{array} \qquad \begin{array}{r} 3 \\ +\ 5 \\ \hline \end{array}$$

$$\begin{array}{r} 8 \\ -\ 5 \\ \hline \end{array} \qquad \begin{array}{r} 12 \\ -\ 5 \\ \hline \end{array} \qquad \begin{array}{r} 9 \\ -\ 4 \\ \hline \end{array}$$

8.

$$\begin{array}{r} 3 \\ +\ 8 \\ \hline \end{array} \qquad \begin{array}{r} 5 \\ +\ 1 \\ \hline \end{array} \qquad \begin{array}{r} 6 \\ +\ 3 \\ \hline \end{array}$$

$$\begin{array}{r} 6 \\ -\ 1 \\ \hline \end{array} \qquad \begin{array}{r} 9 \\ -\ 3 \\ \hline \end{array} \qquad \begin{array}{r} 11 \\ -\ 8 \\ \hline \end{array}$$

Problem Solving Critical Thinking

Solve the riddle.

9. First double me.
Then subtract 1.
You will get 5.
What number am I? _____

Write your own riddle.

10. ______________________________

____

____

Notes for Home: Your child practiced using addition to check subtraction. *Home Activity:* Write a subtraction sentence such as 10 – 7 = ? Ask your child to write the answer, then write an addition fact that can help check the subtraction (10 − 7 = 3; 7 + 3 = 10).

Name ______________________________

Practice Game

Snake Race

Players 2

What You Need

Number cube with numbers 1–6

2 crayons, one color for each player

How to Play

1. With a partner, take turns rolling the cube.
2. Use the number that comes up to complete a number sentence.
3. The player that completes the most parts wins.

10 − 9 = ___	___ + 7 = 11	11 − 8 = ___
___ + 9 = 11	12 − 6 = ___	9 + ___ = 10
10 − 8 = ___	5 + ___ = 11	10 − 5 = ___
___ + 9 = 12	12 − 8 = ___	___ + 7 = 12

Notes for Home: Your child played a game that involved adding and subtracting sums to 12. *Home Activity:* Ask your child to make up a similar game board with incomplete number sentences on another sheet of paper. Then play the game together.

Name ______________________________

STOP and Practice

Add.

1	4	3	9	6	0	7	4
	+ 3	+ 3	+ 2	+ 6	+ 8	+ 2	+ 4

Subtract.

2	12	9	10	11	8	12	11
	− 7	− 9	− 7	− 6	− 4	− 6	− 3

Add or subtract.

3 $11 - 9 =$ ____ $9 - 4 =$ ____ $10 - 1 =$ ____

4	5	3	5	6	8	4	2
	+ 5	+ 9	+ 4	+ 5	+ 2	+ 4	+ 7
5	11	9	7	7	9	12	8
	− 3	− 6	− 4	− 0	− 6	− 3	− 8

Number Riddles

Write the number that answers each riddle.

6 Subtract me from 10.
You will get 8.

Who am I? ____

7 First double me.
Then subtract 3.
You will get 5.

Who am I? ____

PRACTICE

Notes for Home: Your child practiced adding and subtracting sums to 12. *Home Activity:* Ask your child to point to an addition fact and then tell you a related subtraction fact.

Name ______________________________

Fact Families for 10

Learn

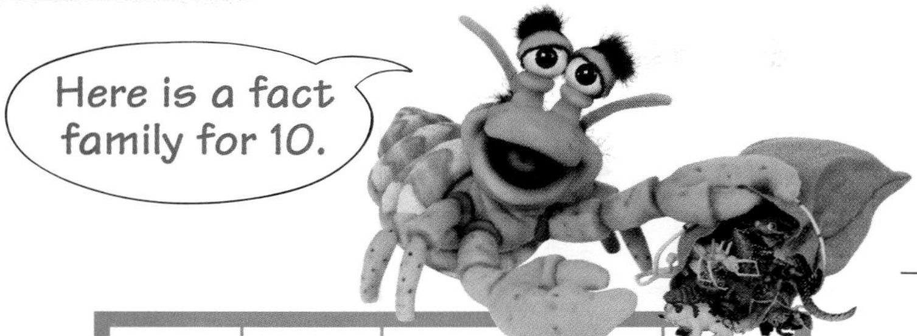
Here is a fact family for 10.

9 + 1 = 10

1 + 9 = 10

10 − 1 = 9

10 − 9 = 1

Check

Complete the fact family for 10.

1

7 + ____ = ____

3 + ____ = ____

10 − ____ = ____

10 − ____ = ____

2

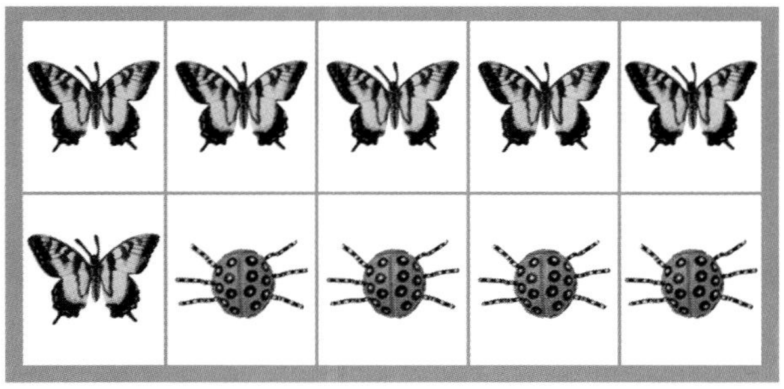

6 + ____ = ____

____ + ____ = ____

____ − ____ = ____

____ − ____ = ____

Talk About It How can you show a fact family for 10 on your fingers?

Notes for Home: Your child wrote number sentences for 10. *Home Activity:* Group pennies to show fact families for 10.

PRACTICE

Practice

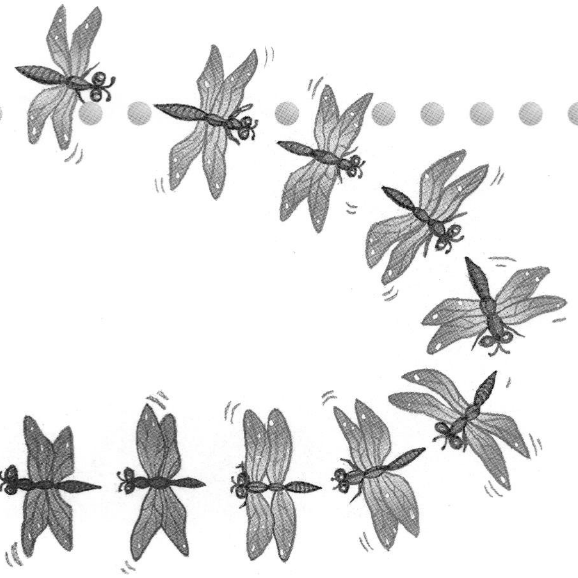

Complete the fact family for 10.

3

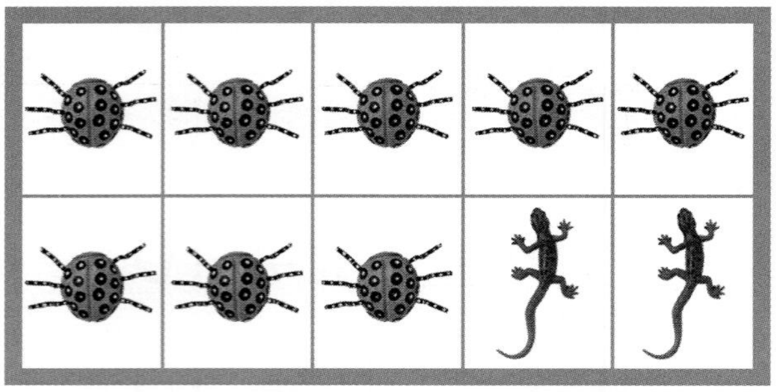

8 + ____ = ____   ____ − ____ = ____

____ + ____ = ____   ____ − ____ = ____

Mixed Practice Add or subtract.
Draw lines to match related facts.

4

1 + 9	3 + 6	6 + 4
10 − 6	10 − 9	9 − 3

5

3 + 7	5 + 5	5 + 3
10 − 7	8 − 5	10 − 5

Problem Solving Visual Thinking

6 There are 10  in all.
How many are in the log?

____ lizards

Notes for Home: Your child practiced addition and subtraction with 10. *Home Activity:* Show your child 10 small objects, such as buttons. Cover some of them. Have your child say an addition and a subtraction sentence to tell about the objects.

Name ______________________________

Problem Solving: Guess and Check

Learn

PROBLEM SOLVING GUIDE

Understand • Plan • Solve • Look Back

How many bees are in the hive?

Use counters.

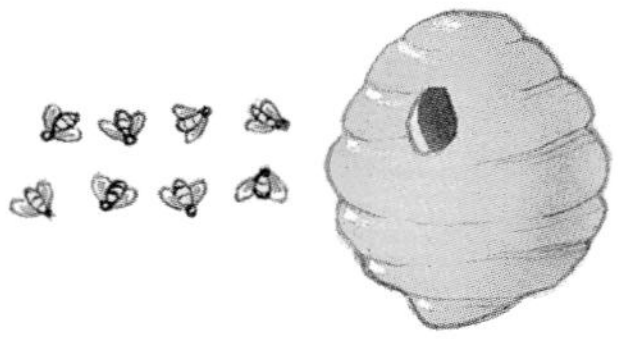

15 bees in all

	Guess	Check	
	Try 8	8 + 8 = 16	Too high
	Try 7	8 + 7 = 15	That's it!

Check

Use counters.

Guess. Then check to find the answer.

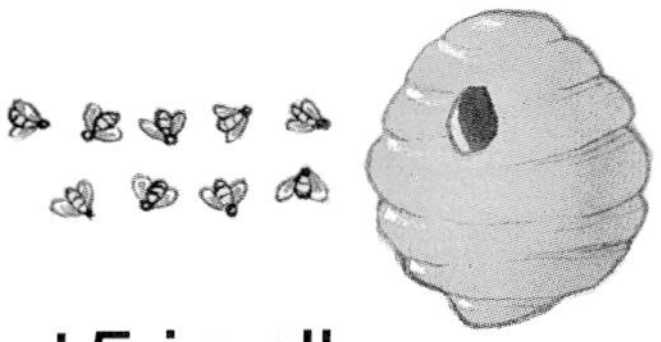

15 in all

1. Try ____ 9 + ____ = ____
   Try ____ 9 + ____ = ____

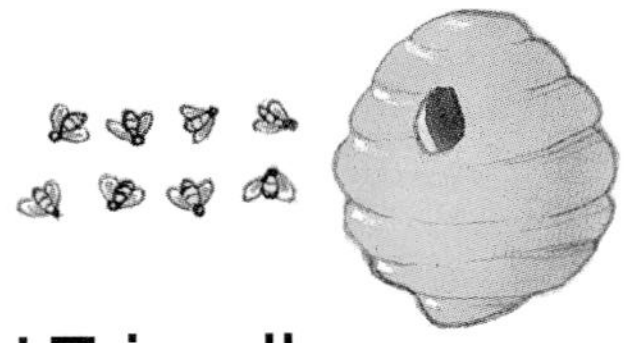

17 in all

2. Try ____ 8 + ____ = ____
   Try ____ 8 + ____ = ____

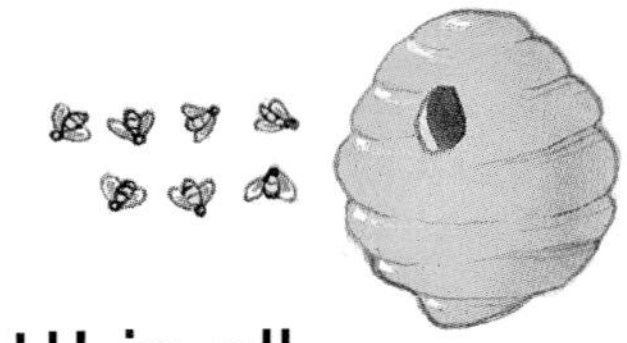

14 in all

3. Try ____ 7 + ____ = ____
   Try ____ 7 + ____ = ____

Talk About It What else can you use to help check to see if your guess is right?

Notes for Home: Your child used the Guess and Check strategy to solve addition and subtraction problems. *Home Activity:* Think of a number between 1 and 12. Ask your child to guess your number. Give the clues "too high" or "too low" until your child correctly guesses the number.

Practice

Use  .

Guess. Then check to find the answer.

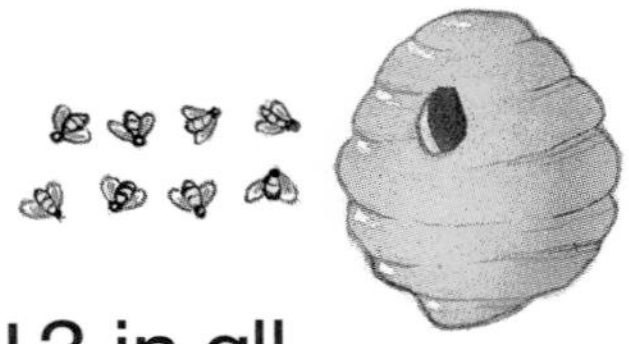

13 in all

4 Try ____ 8 + ____ = ____

Try ____ 8 + ____ = ____

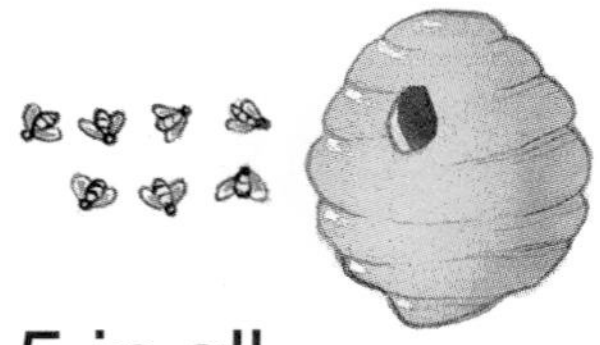

15 in all

5 Try ____ 7 + ____ = ____

Try ____ 7 + ____ = ____

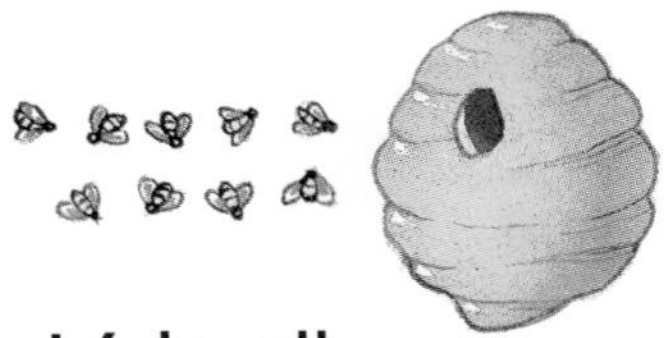

16 in all

6 Try ____ 9 + ____ = ____

Try ____ 9 + ____ = ____

Mental Math

7 Help Lucy Ladybug find her lost spots.
Circle spots that are even numbers less than 15.

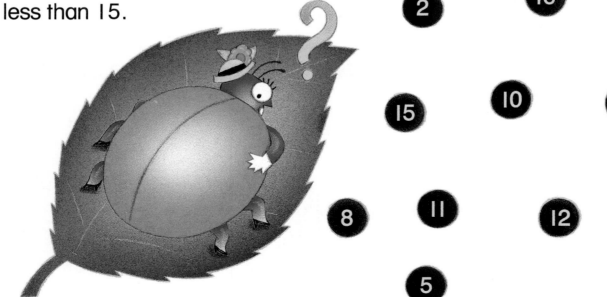

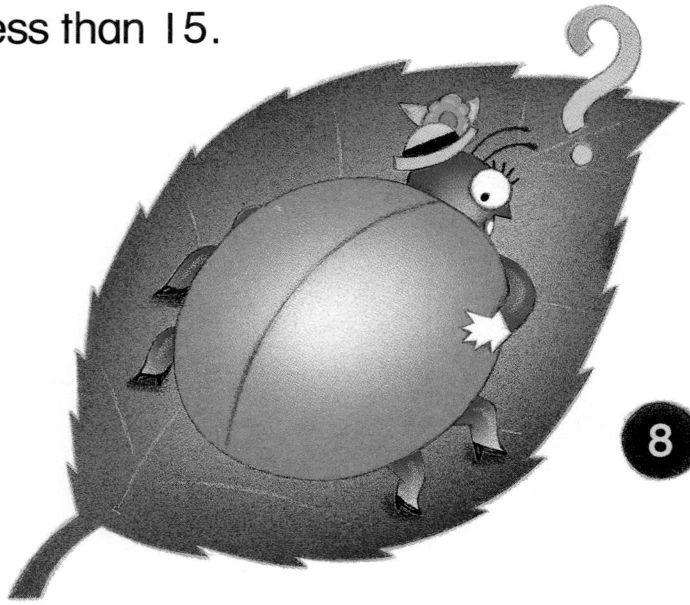

2 16

15 10 7

8 11 12

5

Notes for Home: Your child solved addition and subtraction problems by using the Guess and Check strategy. *Home Activity:* Ask your child to find the spots with odd numbers in the Mental Math activity (7, 11, 15, 5).

For additional practice, see Skills Practice Bank, page 531, Set 3.

Name ______________________________

Mixed Practice

Lessons 6–10

Concepts and Skills

Use ▢. Complete the fact family.

❶ 2 + ____ = ____ ____ − ____ = ____

____ + ____ = ____ ____ − ____ = ____

Add or subtract.

❷	3 + 6	9 − 6	5 + 6	11 − 6	3 + 8	11 − 8	5 + 5
❸	4 + 4	8 − 4	4 + 3	7 − 4	5 + 7	12 − 7	12 − 6

Problem Solving

❹ Guess. Then check to find the answer. You can use ⬭ ⬭.

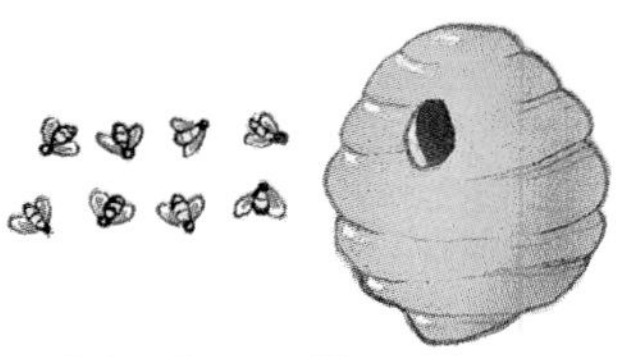

15 in all

Try ____ 8 + ____ = ____

Try ____ 8 + ____ = ____

Journal

❺ Take some ▢ in two colors. Draw a picture of the cubes.
Write the fact family.

Notes for Home: Your child practiced addition and subtraction facts through 12 and problem solving. *Home Activity:* Ask your child to circle one addition and one subtraction problem on this page and draw pictures to show each problem.

For additional practice, see Basic Facts Review, page 541, Set 4.

Name ______________________________

Cumulative Review

Chapters 1–6

Concepts and Skills

Add or subtract.

1

8	5	4	4	5	8	6
− 0	+ 6	− 4	+ 2	+ 5	− 5	+ 6
___	___	___	___	___	___	___

2

0	12	7	3	4	10	9
+ 2	− 5	+ 0	+ 5	− 0	− 5	− 5
___	___	___	___	___	___	___

3 $12 - 3 =$ ____ $7 + 3 =$ ____ $11 - 9 =$ ____

Problem Solving

Write a number sentence.

4 There are 6 frogs.
3 more frogs come.
How many are there now?

________________ frogs

5 Tori saw 5 ladybugs.
4 flew away.
How many are left?

________________ ladybugs

Test Prep

Fill in the ○ for the correct answer.

6 Which shows a circle and square?

○ ○ ○ ○

Notes for Home: Your child reviewed addition and subtraction, writing a number sentence, and identifying shapes. *Home Activity:* Ask your child to tell you a math story for a doubles plus one fact, such as 3+4.

Name ______________________

Chapter 6 Review

Vocabulary

Add. Use doubles when you can.

1

5	5	4	4	3	3	6
+ 5	+ 6	+ 4	+ 5	+ 3	+ 4	+ 6

2 Complete the fact family.

$6 + 3 =$ ____ $9 - 3 =$ ____

$3 + 6 =$ ____ $9 - 6 =$ ____

Concepts and Skills

Use addition to help you subtract.

3

10	8
− 8	+ 2

4

12	6
− 6	+ 6

5

12	9
− 3	+ 3

Problem Solving

Use the chart.

6 How many did Dana see? ____

7 Who saw the most? ________

8 How many did Dana and Eli see together? ____

Fireflies We Saw

Child	Tally	Total
Dana	卌	5
Chen	|||	3
Eli	卌 ||	7

9 Write a number sentence to show something about the graph. ________________

Notes for Home: Your child reviewed addition and subtraction facts, and solving problems by using data. *Home Activity:* Ask your child to make up addition and subtraction facts about the information on the graph.

CHAPTER REVIEW

Name ______________________________

Chapter 6 Test

Add.

1
$$\begin{array}{r}5\\+\,5\\\hline\end{array}\qquad\begin{array}{r}4\\+\,3\\\hline\end{array}\qquad\begin{array}{r}6\\+\,4\\\hline\end{array}$$

Subtract.

2
$$\begin{array}{r}12\\-\,6\\\hline\end{array}\qquad\begin{array}{r}10\\-\,9\\\hline\end{array}\qquad\begin{array}{r}11\\-\,2\\\hline\end{array}$$

3 Complete the fact family.

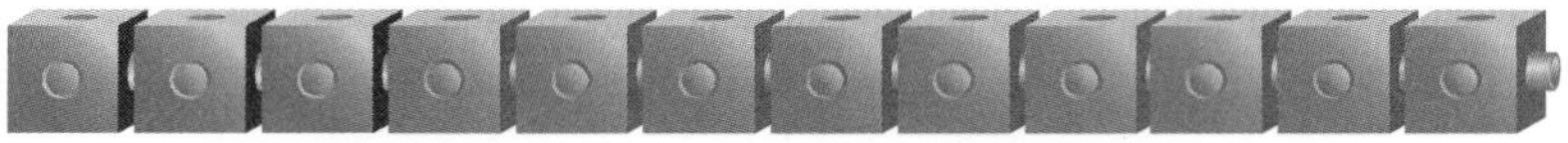

3 + 9 = ____ ____ − ____ = ____

____ + ____ = ____ ____ − ____ = ____

Use the chart to solve.

4 Count the tally marks.
Write the totals.

5 How many like crickets?

____

6 How many children chose butterflies and ladybugs?
Write the number sentence. ______________________

Insects We Like

Insect	Tally	Total
Butterflies	卌 ||	
Crickets	卌 |||	
Ladybugs	||||	

7 Guess. Then check to find the answer.
You can use .

15 in all

Try ____ 7 + ____ = ____

Try ____ 7 + ____ = ____

Notes for Home: Your child was assessed on adding and subtracting with doubles and doubles plus 1, fact families, using data, and the Guess and Check strategy. *Home Activity:* Ask your child to tell a creepy crawler math story.

Name ____

Performance Assessment

Chapter 6

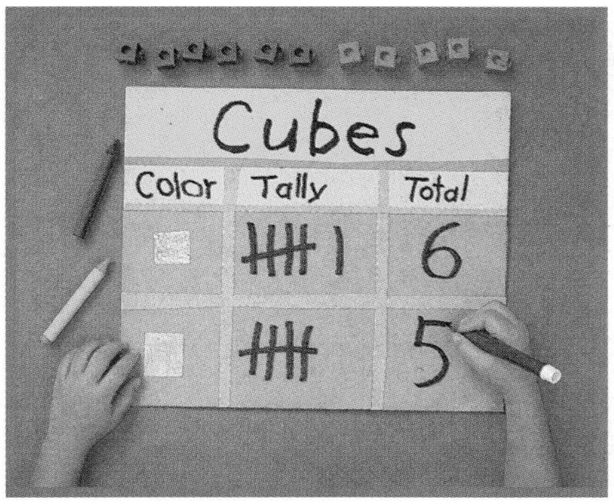

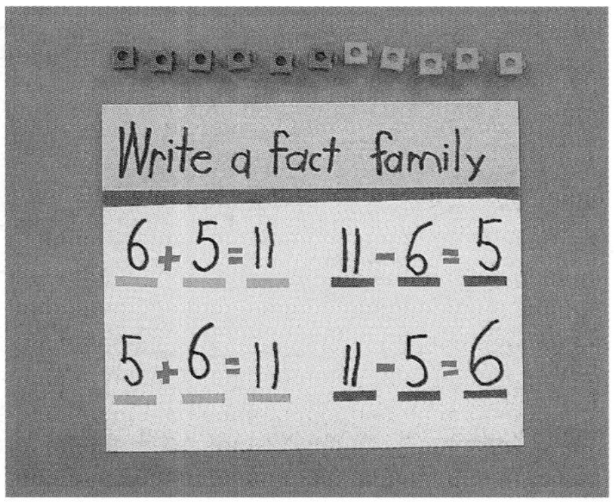

Use two colors of [cube].

Color	Tally	Total

1. Use 6 [cube] or fewer of each color. Make a tally to show how many. Make a train. Write a fact family.

____ + ____ = ____ ____ − ____ = ____

____ + ____ = ____ ____ − ____ = ____

2. Repeat the activity. Use a different number of [cube]. Write the fact family.

____ + ____ = ____ ____ − ____ = ____

____ + ____ = ____ ____ − ____ = ____

Problem Solving Critical Thinking

3. Tell a fact family that has only two number sentences. Why does it have only two number sentences?

Notes for Home: Your child did an activity to assess understanding of related addition and subtraction facts. *Home Activity:* Ask your child to count the number of letters in two names. (J-u-d-y (4) K-i-m (3)), and use the numbers in number sentences (for example, 4 + 3 = 7, 4 − 3 = 1).

Name _____

Number Crunching Snakes

Keys You Will Use | ON/C | + | − | = |

Use a 🖩 to add and subtract.

Write the missing numbers.

1

7 [+] [2] [=] [] [+] [0] [=] [] [+] [3] [=] []

2

1 [1] [−] [4] [=] [] [−] [1] [=] [] [−] [6] [=] []

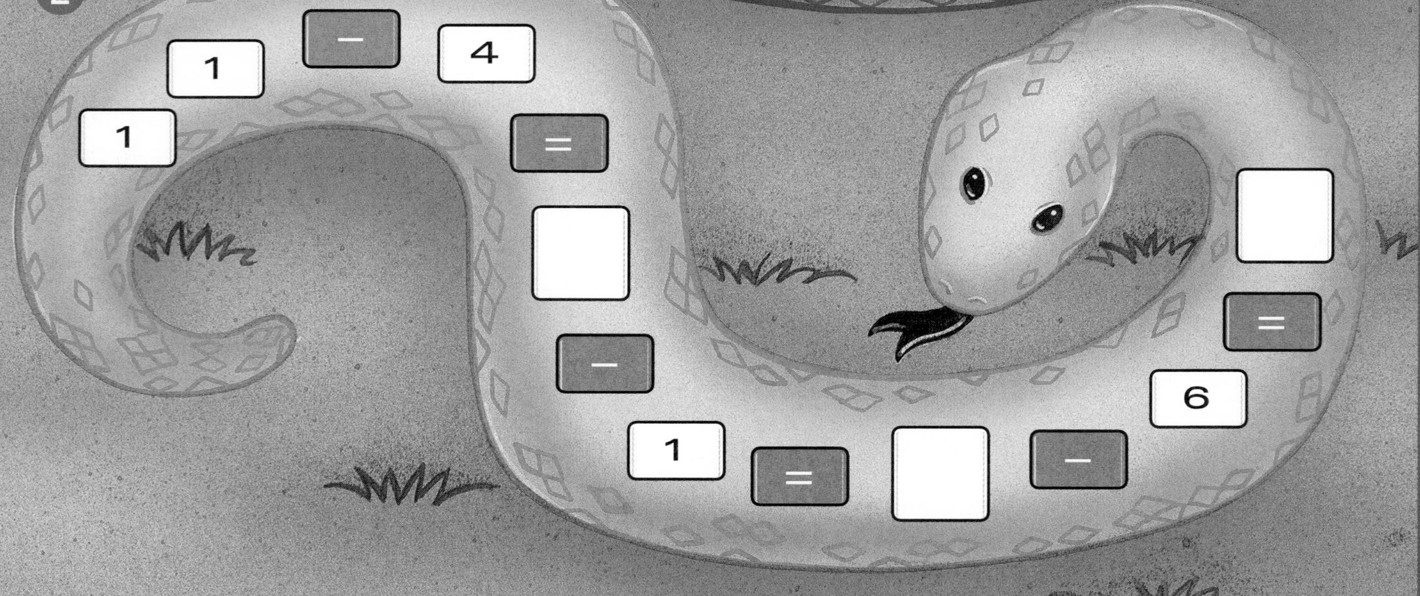

Tech Talk Press [−] in place of [+] in the first problem.
Is the answer different? Why?

☐ ☐ **Visit our Web site.** www.parent.mathsurf.com

© Scott Foresman Addison Wesley

Bug Hunt

Where do bugs live?
You can go on a bug hunt.
Here are some places bugs hide.

Watch for flying insects.
Look under bark.
Turn over rocks.
Look at flowers.
Look carefully at a pond.

Make a chart to show the bugs you find.

Bug	Tally	Total

Fold down

MathSoup

Scott Foresman - Addison Wesley My Math Magazine No. 6

Creeping Critters!

Some creep.
Some fly.
Which insect would you be? Why?

Half Buggy

Hold a mirror along the dotted line to see the rest of each bug.

Draw the missing part to complete the picture.

Notes for Home: Your child observed symmetry in the world of nature. *Home Activity:* Have your child cut out and paste half of a magazine picture on a piece of paper and then draw to complete the picture.

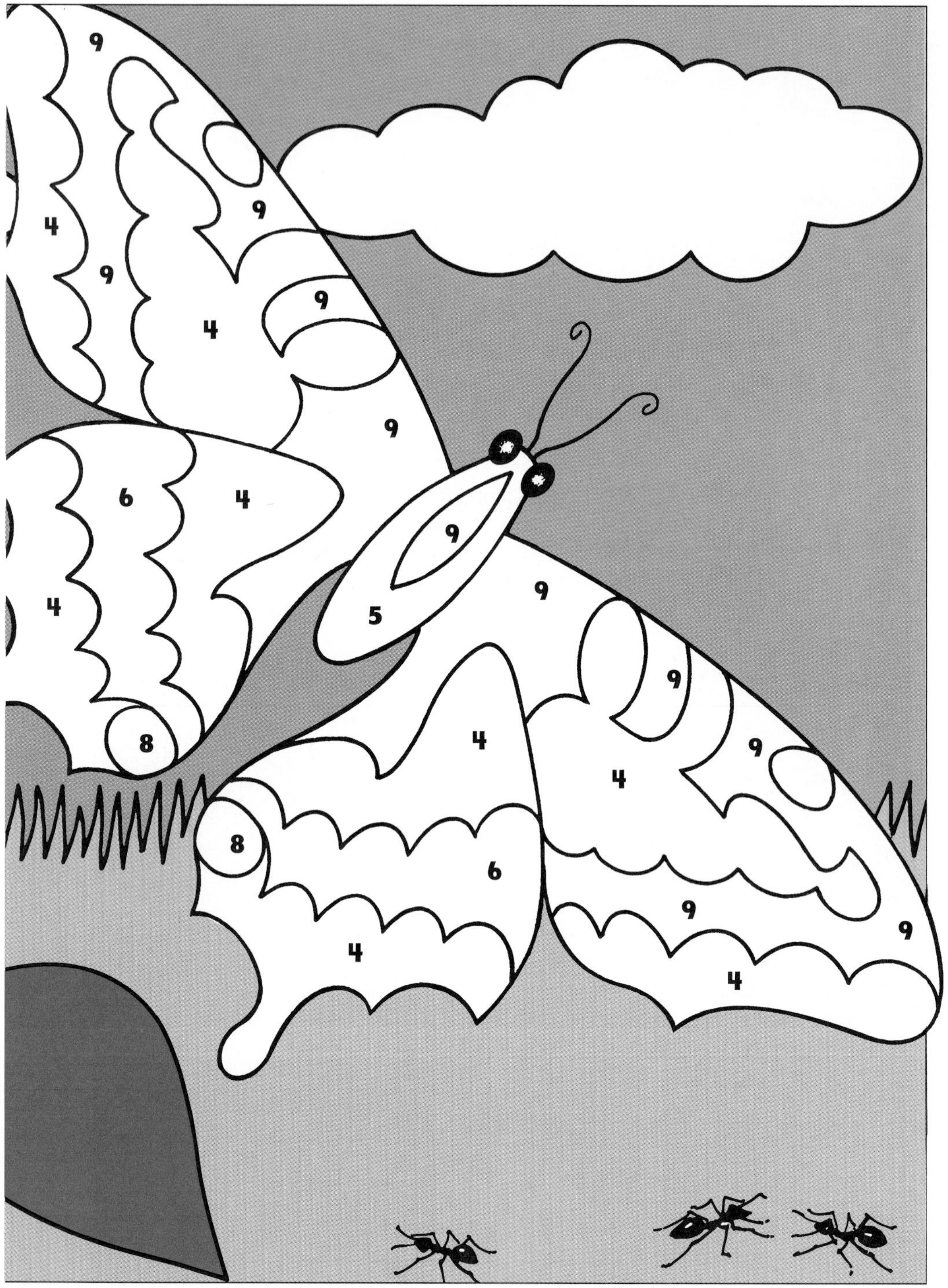

Critters to Color

Insects can be beautiful.
Find each sum or difference.
Use the code to make them colorful.

6 + 3 = black
3 + 1 = yellow
10 – 2 = red
5 + 1 = blue
8 – 1 = green
4 + 1 = brown

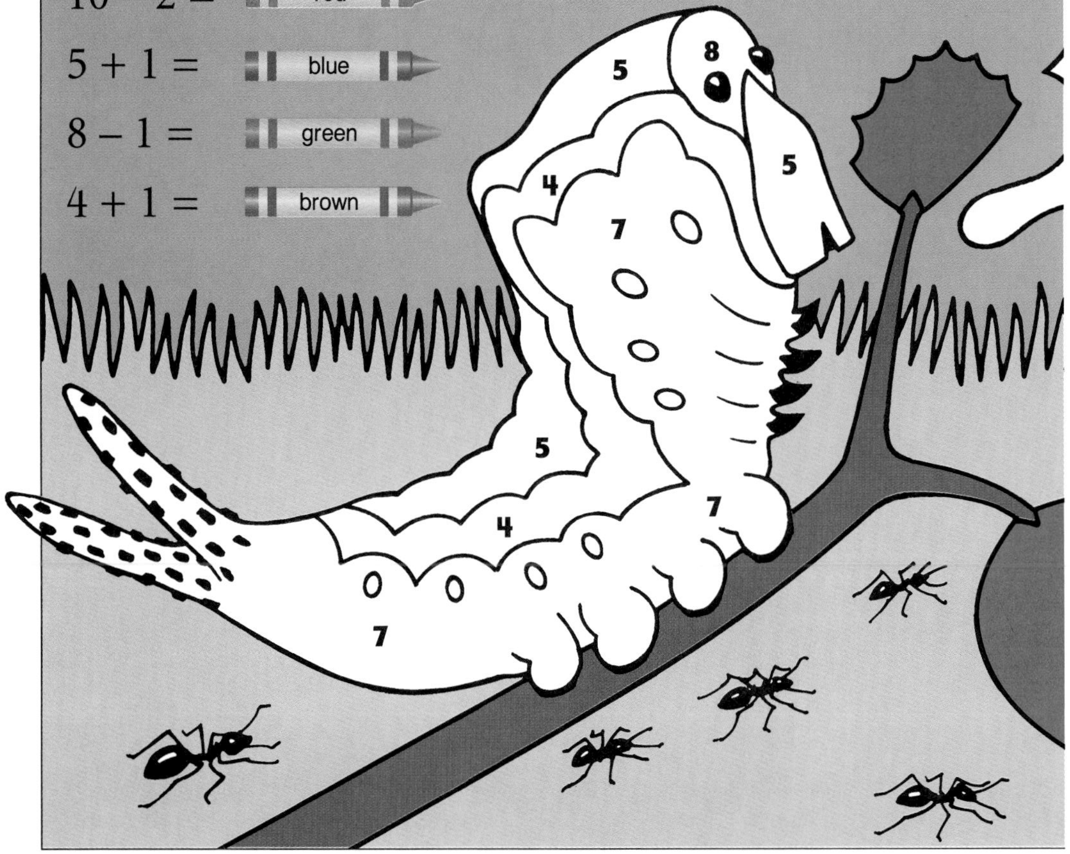

Notes for Home: Your child used knowledge of math facts to color the picture. *Home Activity:* Ask your child to write other math problems that have a sum of 10.

Beekeeper Kid

Here's a look at a busy beekeeper and his bees.

I help my friend take care of his honey bees. Bees live in these white boxes called hives. We wear special suits when we work with bees. I bet you know why.

The bees make honey in the hives. First they build cells with 6 sides. Then they fill the cells with eggs, honey, or pollen.

Notes for Home: Your child learned about bees. *Home Activity:* Together with your child look for numbers in nature, for example, count the petals on a flower, circles in a spider web, or seeds in an apple.

Bee-Bop Hop

What You Need

2 number cubes and 6 counters

How to Play

1 Put a counter on each bee.

2 Roll the number cubes. Add. The sum tells which bee moves one space.

3 Play until one bee reaches the hive.

4 Discuss which bees are more likely to win.

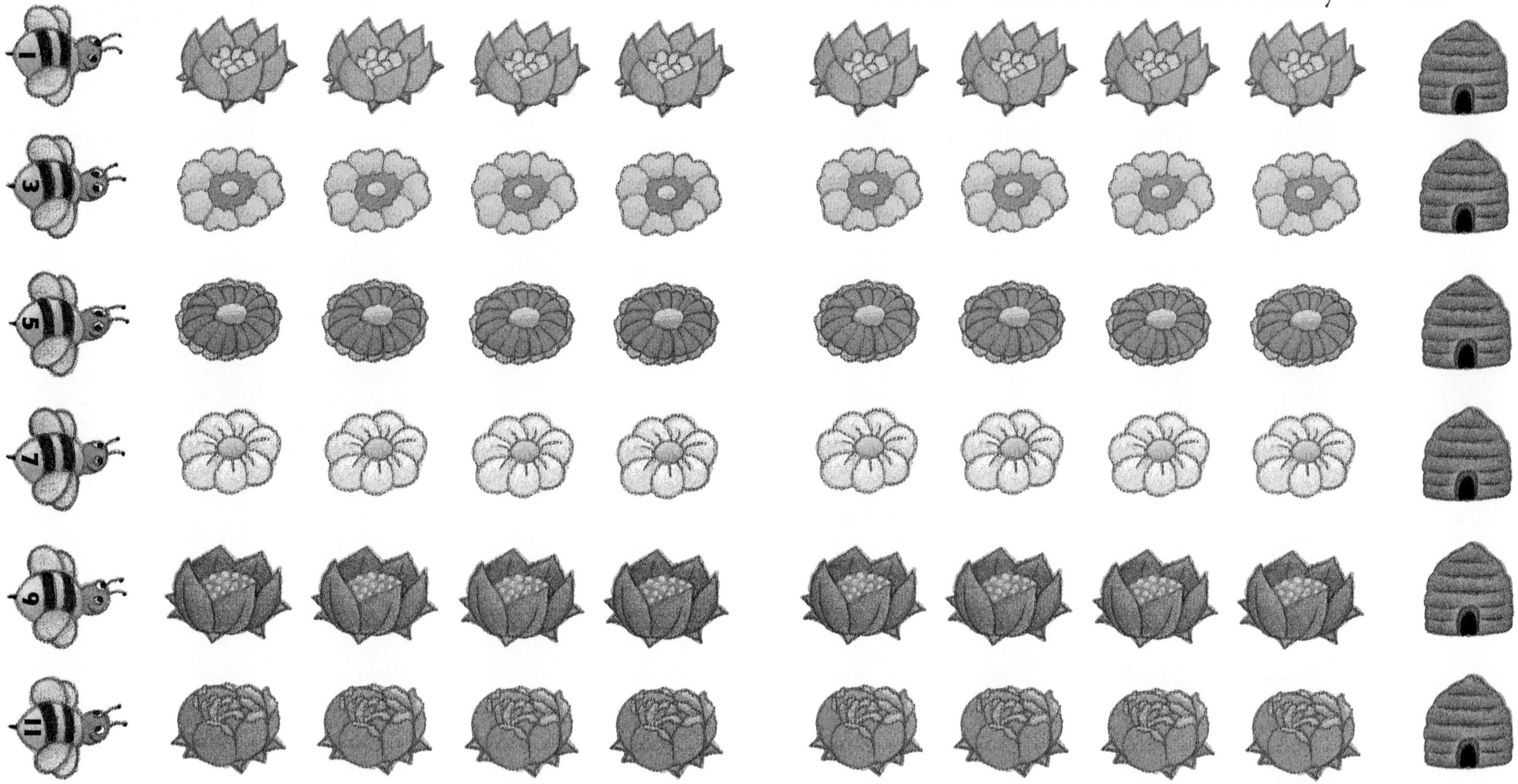

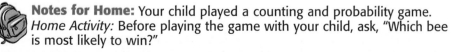

Notes for Home: Your child played a counting and probability game.
Home Activity: Before playing the game with your child, ask, "Which bee is most likely to win?"

CHAPTER

7 Numbers to 60 and Counting Patterns

Collections

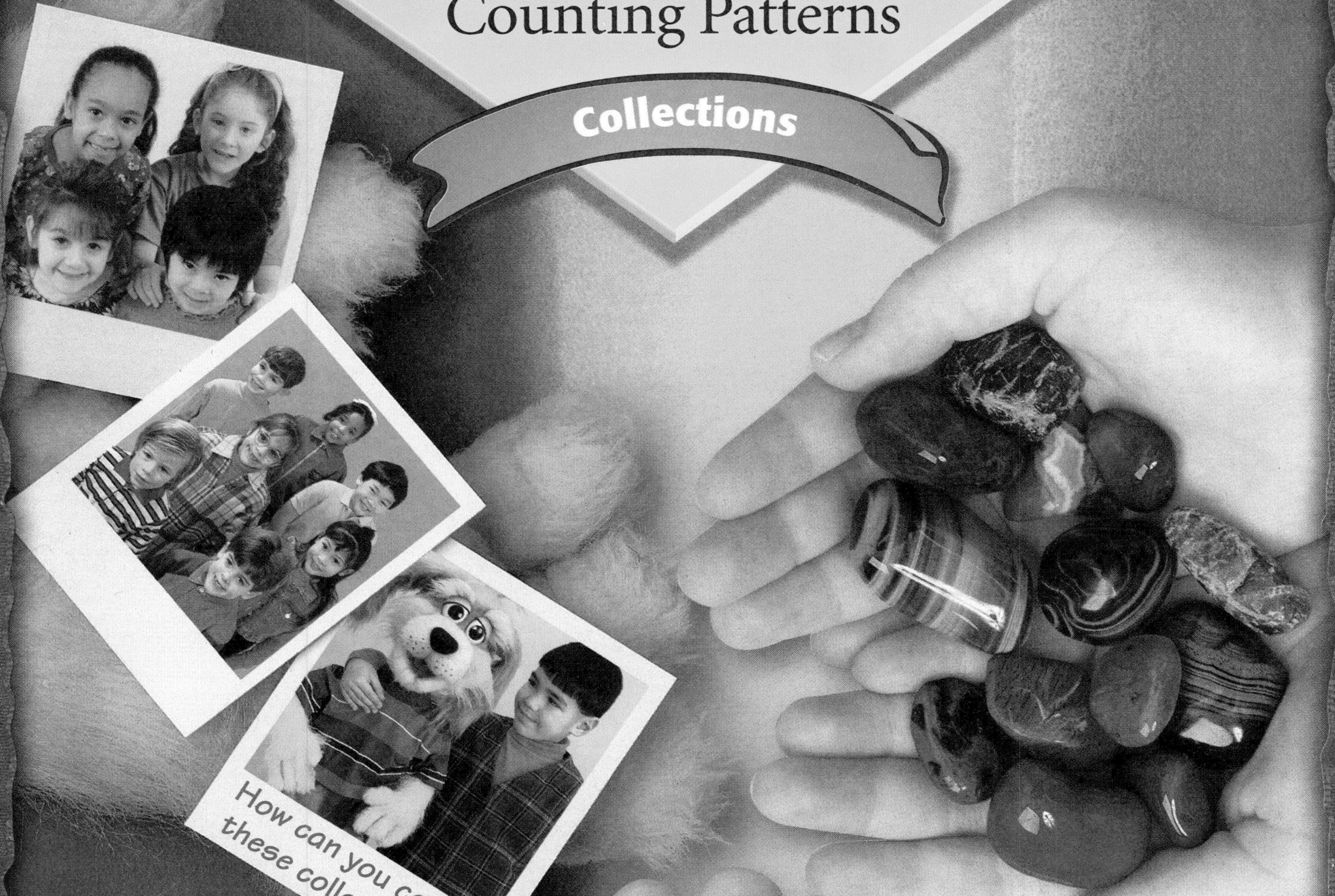
How can you count these collections?

Notes for Home: Your child looked at collections of objects and thought about ways the objects could be counted. *Home Activity:* Ask your child to tell you some ways to count the objects.

Math at Home

Dear Family,
In Chapter 7 we will learn about numbers to 60. We will estimate, write numbers, put them in order, and count by 2s, 5s, and 10s. Here are some activities we can do together.

Page Count

When you read a book together, show your child a page number. Ask what page comes before and after. Turn to another page and try it again.

Put a Collection into Groups

Ask your child to take out pennies, small toys, or other objects. Help your child arrange them into groups of 2, 5, or 10. Then count by 2s, 5s, or 10s to find out how many there are.

Community Connection

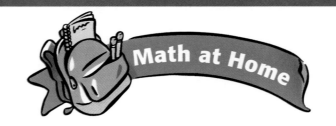

Have your child ask family, friends, or neighbors about their favorite collections. What do they collect? How do they count and organize their collections?

Visit our Web site. **www.parent.mathsurf.com**

Name

Numbers to 19

Learn

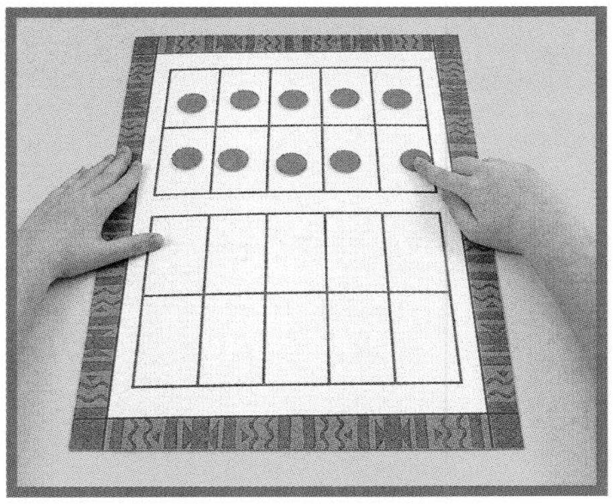

Show 10.

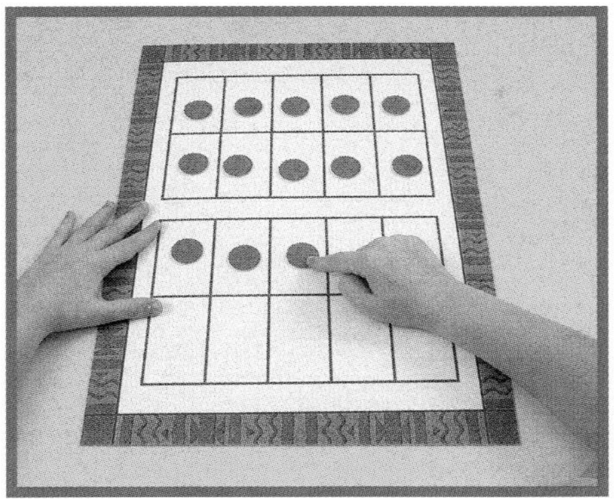

Show 3 more.

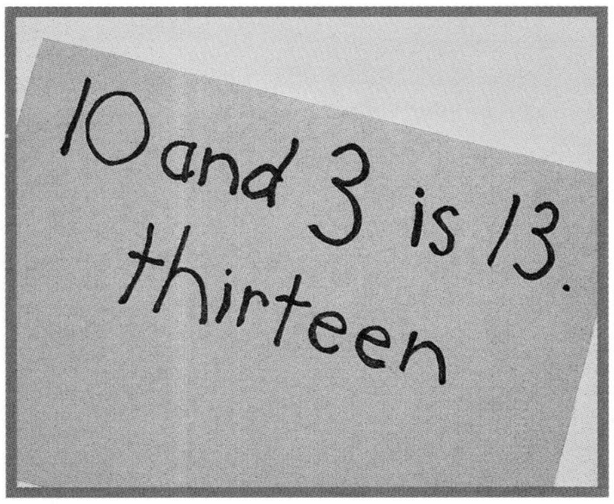

Write the numbers.

Check

Use 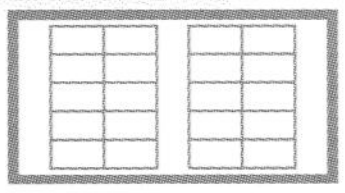 and .
Write the numbers.

1. 10 and 3 is 13. thirteen
2. 10 and 4 is ____. fourteen
3. 10 and 5 is ____. fifteen
4. 10 and 6 is ____. sixteen
5. 10 and 7 is ____. seventeen
6. 10 and 8 is ____. eighteen
7. 10 and 9 is ____. nineteen

Talk About It What number do you have when two ten frames are filled?

Notes for Home: Your child made and wrote numbers to 19. *Home Activity:* Look for these numbers in books, newspapers, and magazines.

Practice

Write the numbers.

8. 14 fourteen

10 and 4 is 14.

9. 12 twelve

10 and ____ is ____.

10. 19 nineteen

10 and ____ is ____.

11. 15 fifteen

10 and ____ is ____.

12. 11 eleven

10 and ____ is ____.

13. 17 seventeen

10 and ____ is ____.

14. 16 sixteen

10 and ____ is ____.

15. 13 thirteen

10 and ____ is ____.

PRACTICE

Problem Solving

16. These are Diane's dolls.
Tell how you found how many she has.

Notes for Home: Your child wrote numbers 11–19 as 10 and ones. *Home Activity:* Practice reading the number words with your child.

Name ______________________________

Tens

Learn

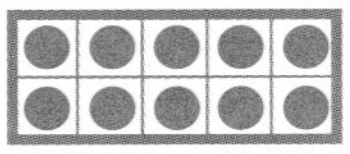

1 ten ten 10

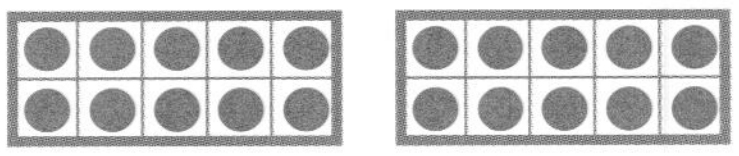

2 tens twenty 20

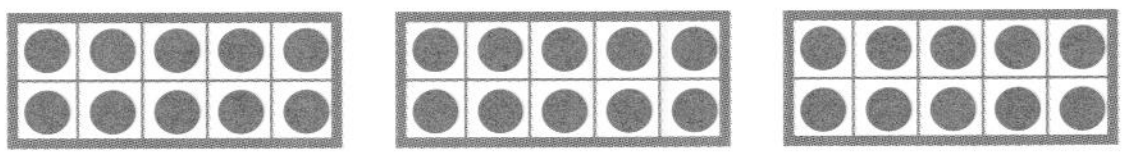

3 tens thirty 30

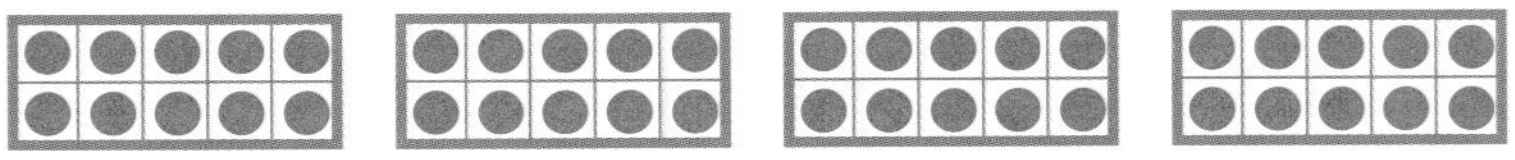

4 tens forty 40

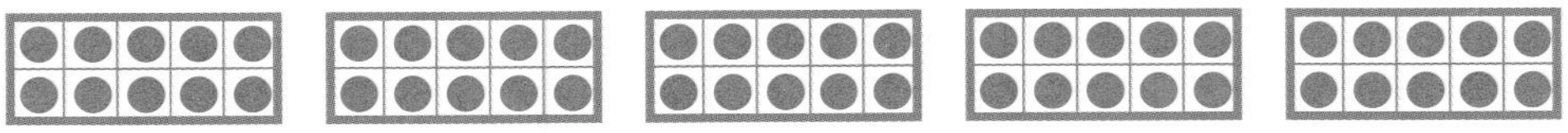

5 tens fifty 50

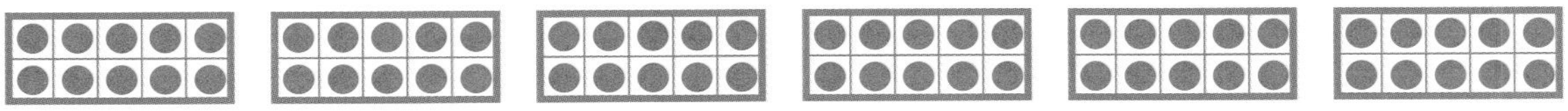

6 tens sixty 60

Check

Write the number.

1. 10 and 0 is 10.
2. 10 and 10 is ______.
3. 20 and 10 is ______.
4. 30 and 10 is ______.

Talk About It How many tens are in 60?
How do you know?

Notes for Home: Your child wrote numbers for groups of ten. *Home Activity:* Practice reading the number words with your child.

Practice

Write the number.

5. 10 and 10 is 20.
6. 50 and 10 is ____.
7. 40 and 10 is ____.
8. 10 and 10 is ____.
9. 30 and 10 is ____.
10. 20 and 10 is ____.

Each  has 10 . How many in all?

11.  ____
12.  ____
13.  ____
14.  ____

Problem Solving

15. This is one page in Ky's photo album.
How many photos are on 4 pages?

____ photos

Notes for Home: Your child counted groups of ten. *Home Activity:* Ask your child to tell where he or she has seen or used numbers like these.

For additional practice, see Skills Practice Bank, page 532, Set 1.

Name ____________________

Numbers to 60

Learn

I circle groups of 10 to help me count.

2 tens and 6 extra is 26.

Check

Circle groups of 10. Write the numbers.

1 

3 tens and 2 extra is ____.

2 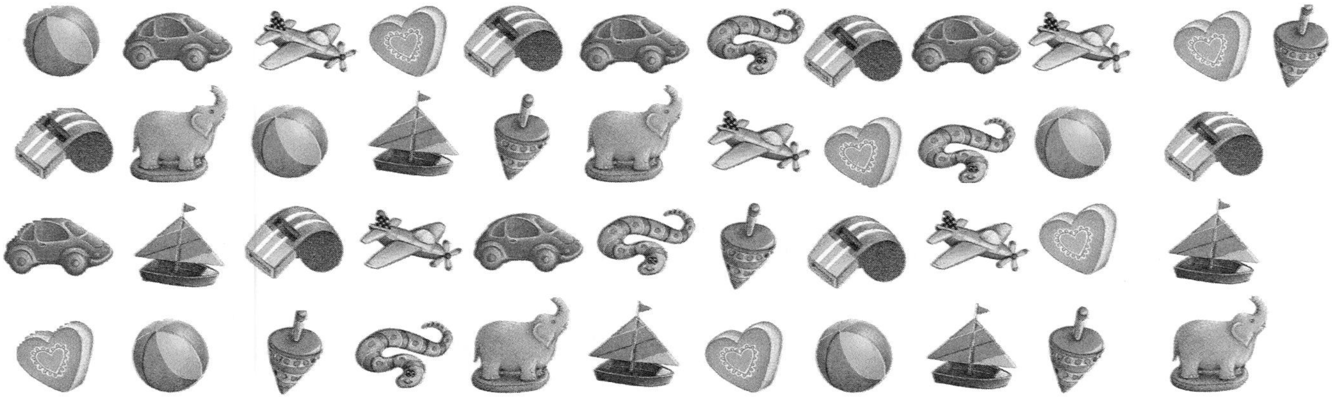

____ tens and ____ extra is ____.

Talk About It Why is it helpful to make groups of 10 when you have a large group of things?

Notes for Home: Your child circled groups of ten to help count large groups of things.
Home Activity: Using a lot of small things, ask your child to make groups of ten and tell how many in all.

Practice

Circle groups of 10. Write the numbers.

3 

_____ tens and _____ extra is _____.

PRACTICE

Write your own problem.

4 Draw a lot of things.
Circle groups of 10.
Write the numbers.

_____ tens and _____ extra is _____.

Estimation

5 About how many are in Jar 2?
Circle the number.

10 30 60

6 Why do you think so?

Notes for Home: Your child put things into groups of ten and wrote the number.
Home Activity: Have your child count eating utensils by putting them in groups of ten.

Name ______________________

Practice Game

Tens Trains

Players 2 or 3

What You Need

2 number cubes 

Snap Cubes 

How to Play

1. Roll the number cubes.
2. Put that many Snap Cubes together to make a train.
3. Take turns until each player has 5 trains.
4. Snap the 5 trains together.
5. Break the train into tens and extras.
6. Tell how many.
7. The player with more wins.

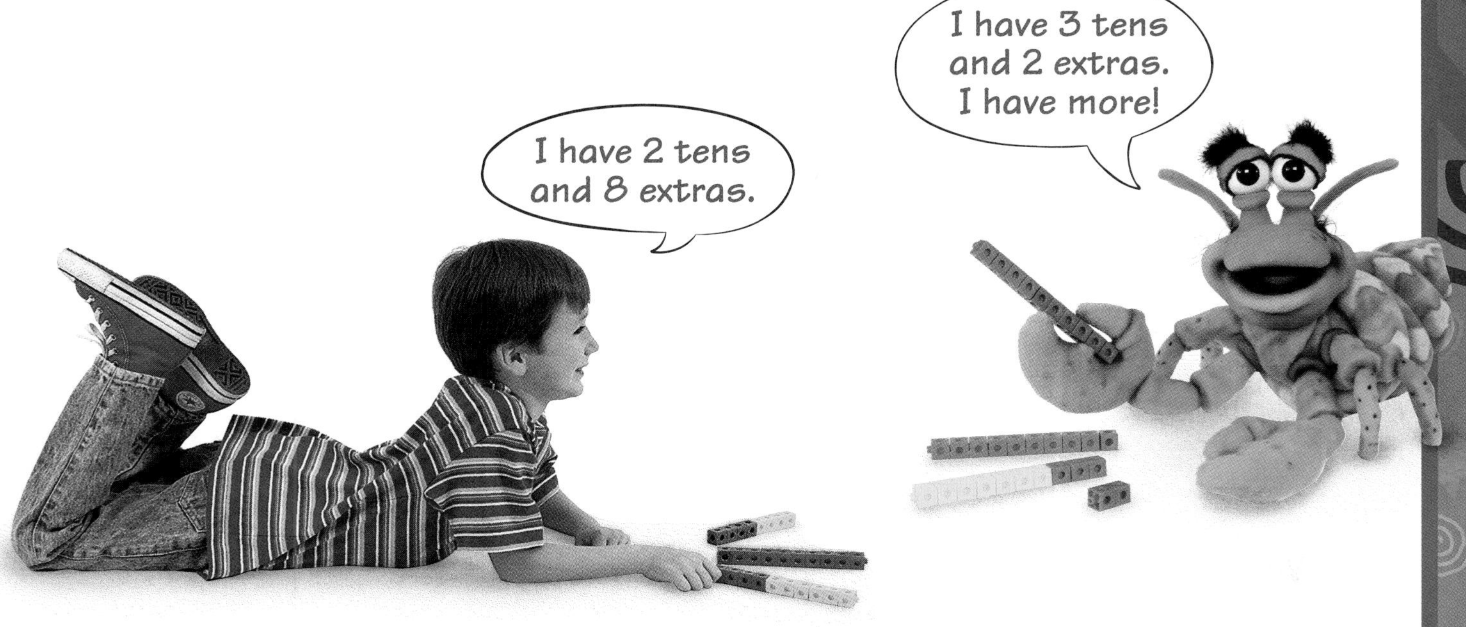

I have 3 tens and 2 extras. I have more!
I have 2 tens and 8 extras.

PRACTICE

Notes for Home: Your child put objects into groups of tens and extras. *Home Activity:* Play the game with your child. Instead of making trains with cubes, objects such as pennies can be grouped. A deck of cards can replace number cubes.

Name ______________________

STOP and Practice

Write the numbers.

1 

_____ and _____ is _____.

2 

_____ and _____ is _____.

3 

_____ and _____ is _____.

4 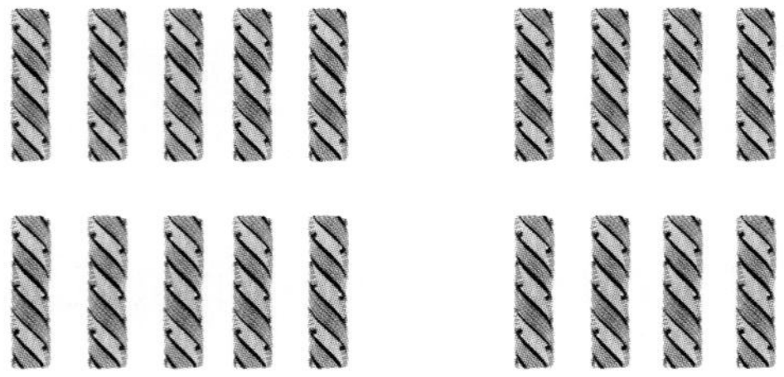

_____ and _____ is _____.

Write the number.

5 20 and 10 is _____.

6 40 and 10 is _____.

Circle groups of 10. Write the numbers.

7 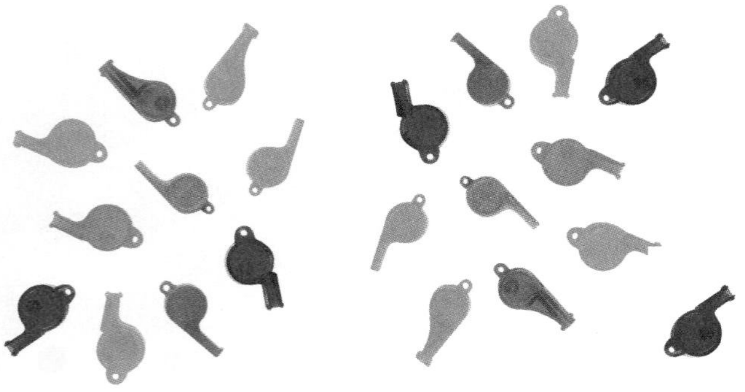

____ tens and ____ extra is ____.

8 

____ tens and ____ extra is ____.

Notes for Home: Your child practiced identifying groups of 10 and counting and writing numbers.
Home Activity: Ask your child to tell you the words for 2 tens, 3 tens, 5 tens, and 6 tens.
(twenty, thirty, fifty, sixty)

PRACTICE

Name ______________________________

Explore Estimation

Explore

I think I have more than 10.
Let me count and see.

Show a handful of counters. Do not count.
Circle to tell if there are more or fewer than 10.
Let your partner count them.

1. **more** **fewer** How many? _____

2. **more** **fewer** How many? _____

3. **more** **fewer** How many? _____

Tell if there are more or fewer than 20.

4. **more** **fewer** How many? _____

Share

What makes a good estimate?

Notes for Home: Your child explored the concept of estimation by telling if an amount of counters was more or fewer than 10. *Home Activity:* Ask your child to estimate how many are in a group of things you have at home, for example, plates in a cupboard or spoons in a drawer.

Connect

Before I count, I can estimate. There are about 20 masks.

Take a lot of counters. Do not count yet.
Estimate how many there are.
Let your partner count how many.

	Estimate.	Draw. Circle tens.	How many in all?
5			
6			
7			

EXPLORE

Journal

8 Write about a collection of things.
Who has it? About how many things are in the collection?

Notes for Home: Your child worked with another child to estimate an amount and to check how good the estimate was. *Home Activity:* At the library, ask your child to count 10 books on a shelf, then help your child to estimate how many are on the whole shelf.

Name ______________________________

Estimation

Learn

I have about 20 buttons.

I count 23 buttons. Yes, you made a good estimate.

Check

Estimate how many. Circle the number.

1

about 20 30 40

2

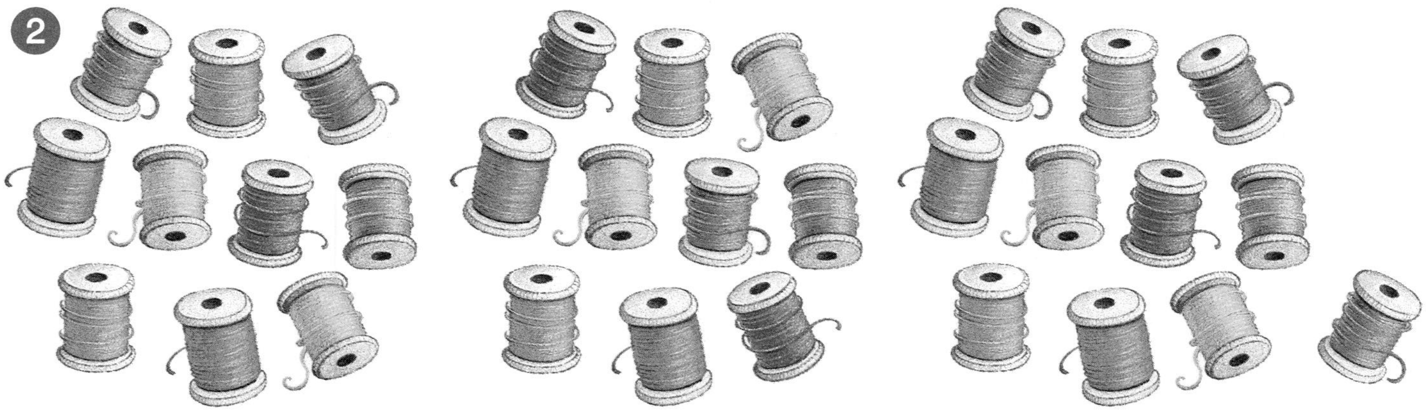

about 10 30 50

Talk About It Herman says he has about 50 shells. Jake counts 51 shells. Did Herman make a good estimate? How do you know?

Notes for Home: Your child estimated about how many things are pictured. *Home Activity:* Ask your child how to estimate the number of words in the Talk About It section on this page (20–30).

Practice

Estimate how many. Circle the number.

3 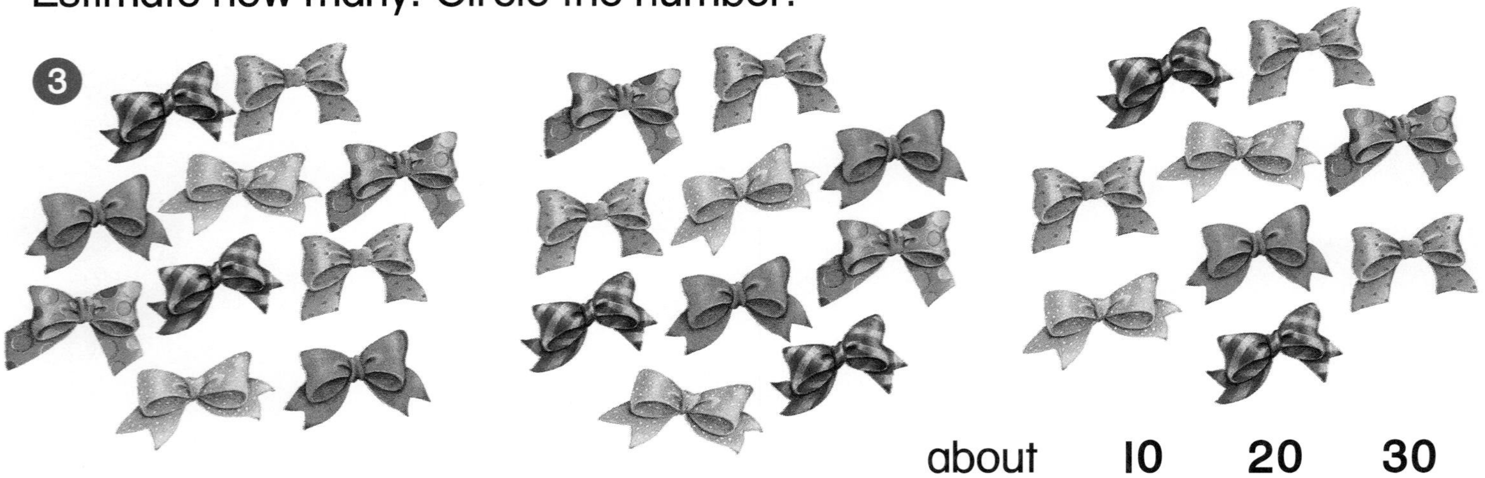

about 10 20 30

4 

about 10 20 40

Write your own problem.

5 Draw some things.
Ask a friend to estimate
how many.

Mental Math

Solve.

6 Annie has 20 buttons in the blue box.
She has 10 buttons in the green box.
How many buttons are in both boxes? ____

Notes for Home: Your child practiced estimating numbers of objects. *Home Activity:* Ask your child to estimate the number of dishes on one shelf.

Name

Problem Solving: Use Data from a Graph

Learn

PROBLEM SOLVING GUIDE

Understand • Plan • Solve • Look Back

Who has the most stickers?

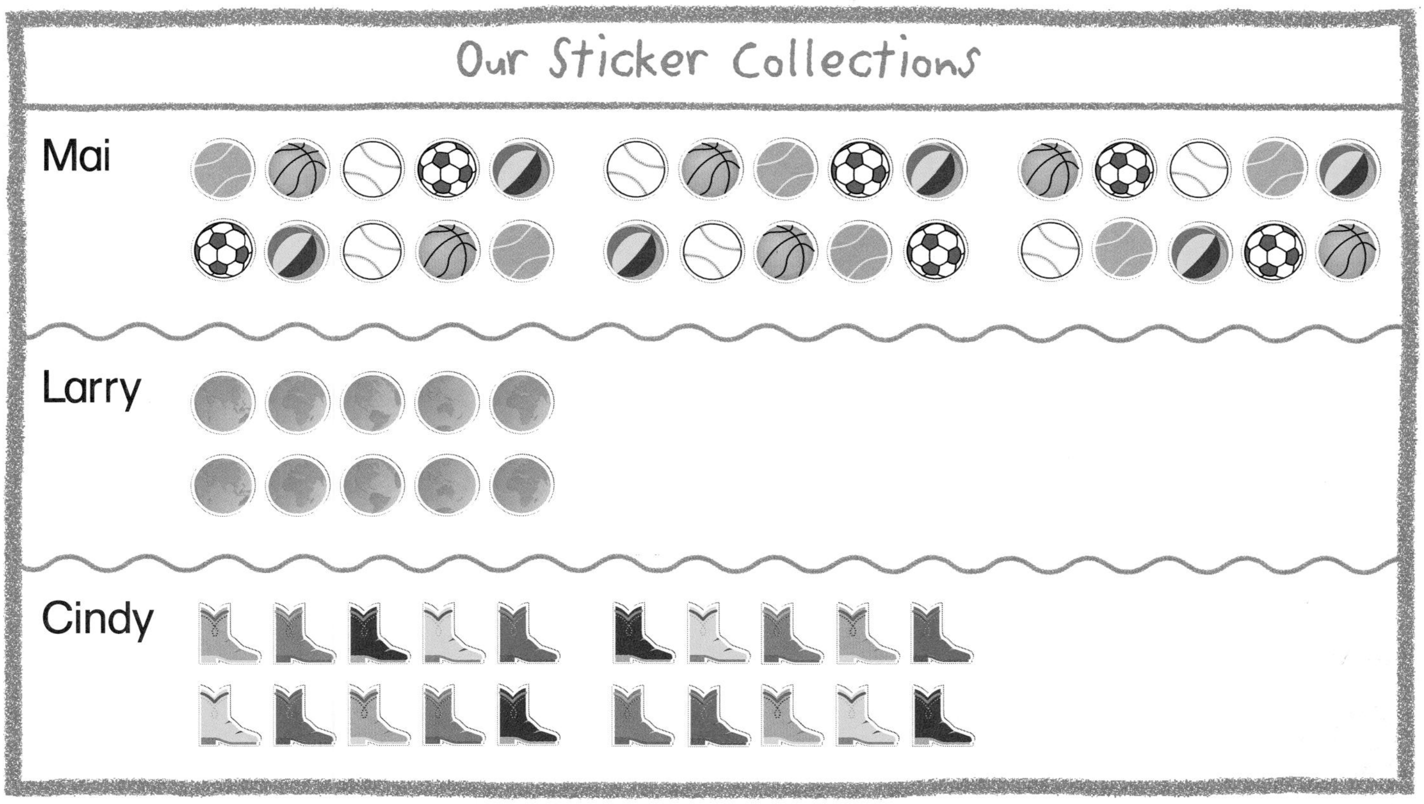

Mai has the most stickers.

Check

Read the graph.

1. Who has 10 more than Larry? ____________

2. How many more does Mai have than Cindy? ____________

3. Do Larry and Cindy together have as many as Mai? ____________

4. How many more does Larry need to have 30? ____________

Talk About It How does the graph help you answer the questions?

Notes for Home: Your child used a graph to answer questions. *Home Activity:* Ask your child to tell how many stickers each person has. (Mai has 30, Larry has 10, Cindy has 20.)

Practice

This graph shows how many stamps the children have made.

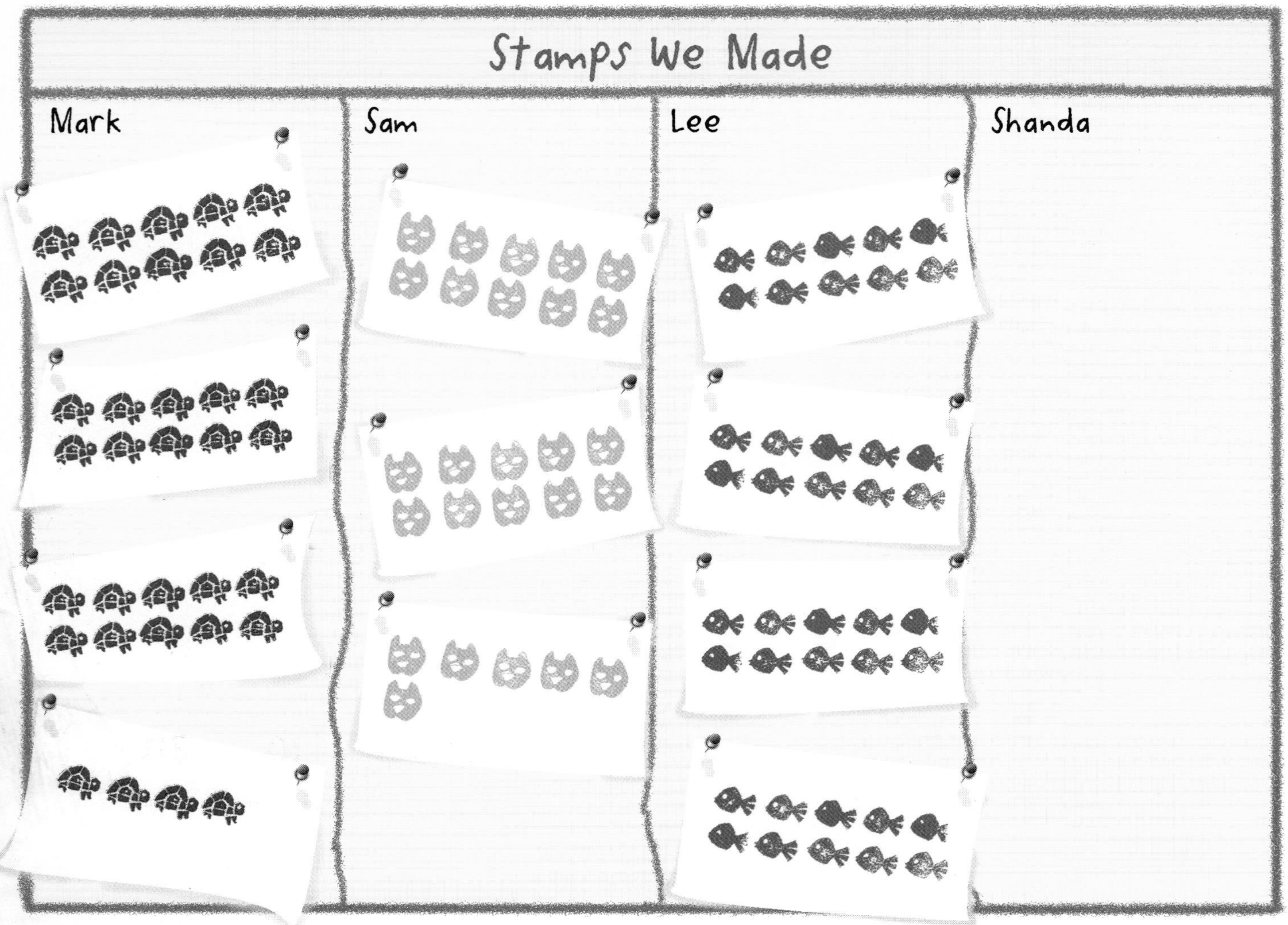

Read the graph.

5. Shanda has 20 stamps. Complete the graph to show this.

6. Who has more stamps than Sam? ______________________

7. How many more stamps does Lee have than Mark? __________

8. How many more stamps does Sam need to have 30? __________

Tell a Math Story

9. Make up your own math story about stamps.
   Tell it to a friend.

Notes for Home: Your child practiced using a graph to find information. *Home Activity:* Encourage your child to make groups of 10 objects, such as pennies, and find how many in all.

For additional practice, see Skills Practice Bank, page 532, Set 2.

Name

Mixed Practice

Lessons 1–6

Concepts and Skills

Write the number.

1. 10 and 4 is _____.
2. 10 and 7 is _____.
3. 30 and 10 is _____.
4. 50 and 10 is _____.

5. Estimate how many. Circle the number.

about **10** **30** **50**

Problem Solving

Read the graph.

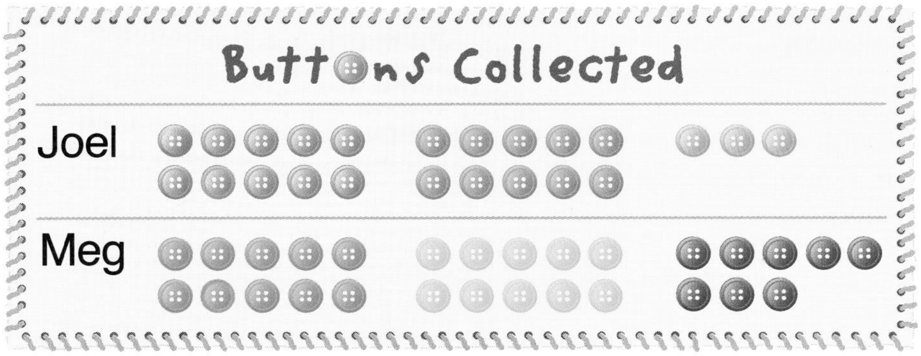

6. How many buttons does Joel have? _____

Journal

7. What are your favorite things to count by tens? Why?

Notes for Home: Your child practiced counting groups of numbers to 60. *Home Activity:* Talk with your child about things that come in 60, such as 60 minutes in one hour and 60 seconds in one minute.

Name ______________________________

Cumulative Review

Chapters 1–7

Concepts and Skills

1. Circle the one that comes next in this pattern.

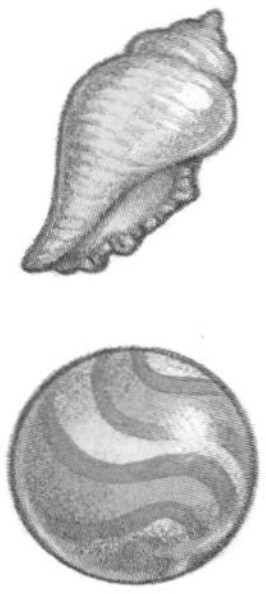

Problem Solving

Write the number sentence.

2. I had 6 marbles.
I got 3 more.
How many do I have now?

____ + ____ = ____

3. Joe had 8 hats.
He lost 3.
How many does he have now?

____ − ____ = ____

Test Prep

Fill in the ○ for the correct answer.

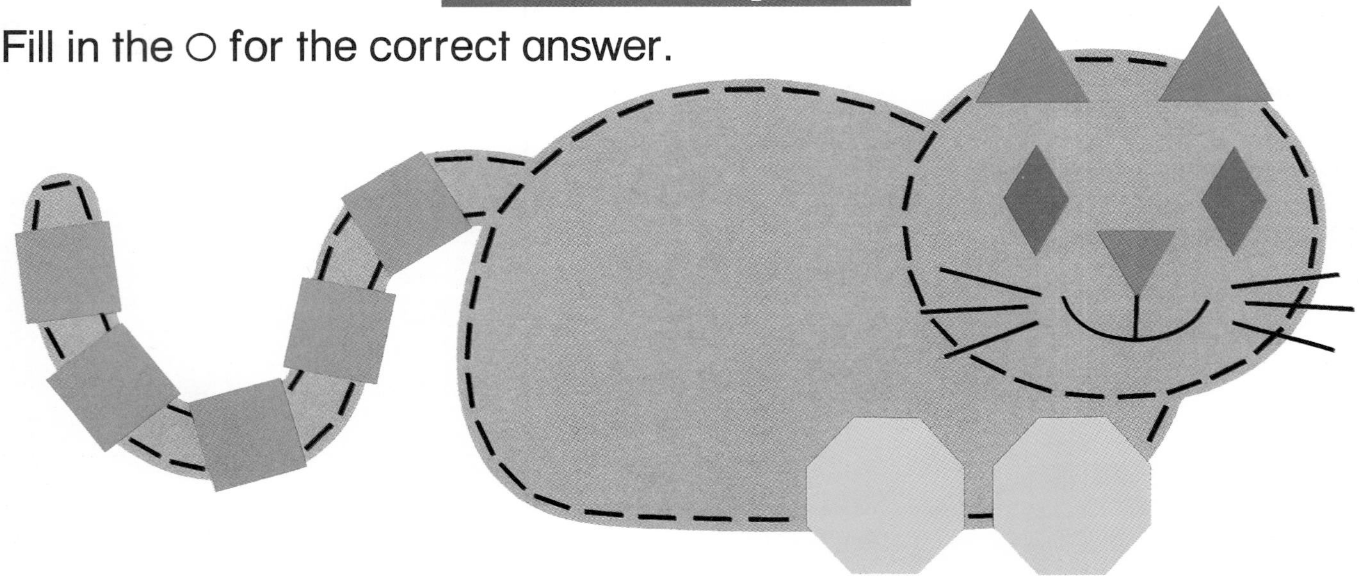

4. How many  ?

3 ○ 4 ○ 5 ○ 6 ○

5. How many  ?

2 ○ 3 ○ 4 ○ 5 ○

Notes for Home: Your child reviewed continuing a pattern, writing number sentences, and counting. *Home Activity:* Ask your child to tell you how to count and record all the shapes in Test Prep. (5 orange squares, 2 yellow shapes with 8 sides, 3 green triangles, 2 blue shapes with 4 sides)

Name

Count by 2s and 10s

Learn

2, 4, 6.
3 children
have 6 legs.

Check

1 How many legs?
Record on the chart.

Children	Legs
1	2
2	____
3	____
4	____
5	____
6	____

2 How many fingers?
Record on the chart.

Children	Fingers
1	____
2	____
3	____
4	____
5	____
6	____

Talk About It What patterns do you see?

Notes for Home: Your child counted by 2s and 10s, and then talked about the counting patterns.
Home Activity: Ask your child to make stacks of 2 pennies and show you how to count by 2s to find the total. Repeat with stacks of 10 pennies.

Practice

3. How many toes? Count by 10s.

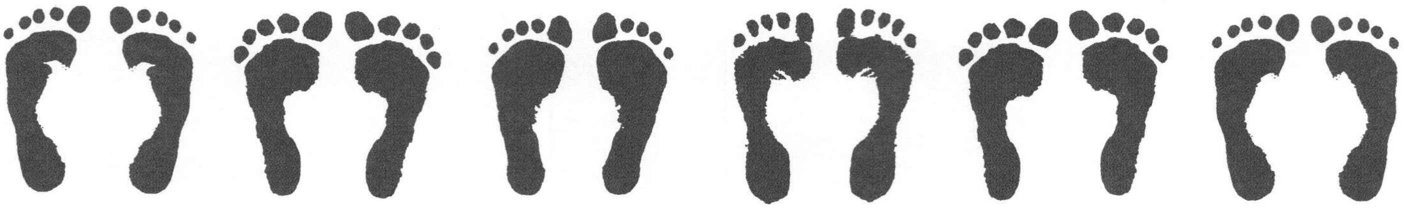

10 ____ ____ ____ ____ 60

4. Count by 2s. You can use a .

Press	Display
	0.
+ 2 =	2.
+ 2 =	
+ 2 =	

Press	Display
+ 2 =	8.
+ 2 =	
+ 2 =	
+ 2 =	

Problem Solving Patterns

Use a . Press the buttons shown below.

5. Count by 10s.

+ 1 0 = = =.

6. Count by 2s.

+ 2 = = =.

7. What happens each time you press = ?

Notes for Home: Your child counted by 2s and 10s. *Home Activity:* Ask your child to count how many legs and fingers in your family.

Name

Count by 2s, 5s, and 10s

Learn

Check

1. Use . Make stacks of 5.
Complete the table.

Stacks	1	2	3	4	5	6
Counters	5					

2. How many fingers? Count by 5s.

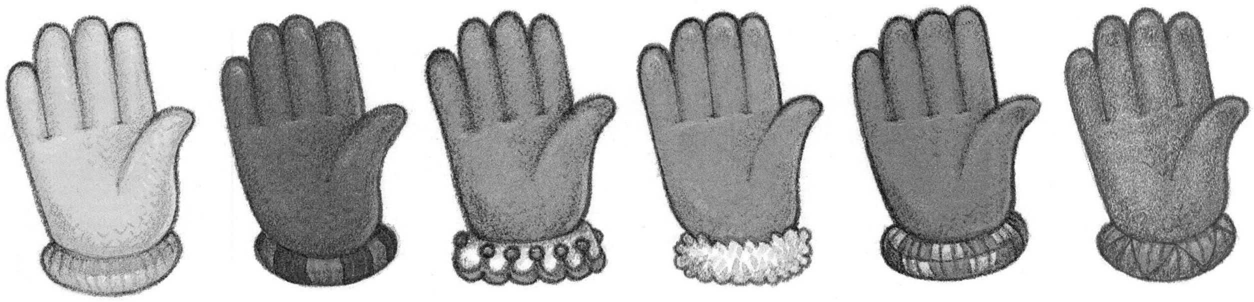

5 ____ ____ ____ ____ 30

Talk About It What pattern do you see?

Notes for Home: Your child used stacks of 5 counters and counted by 5s. *Home Activity:* Ask your child to tell you about number patterns in the table. (The numbers increase by 5. They alternately end in 5 or 0.)

Practice

Count by 5s.

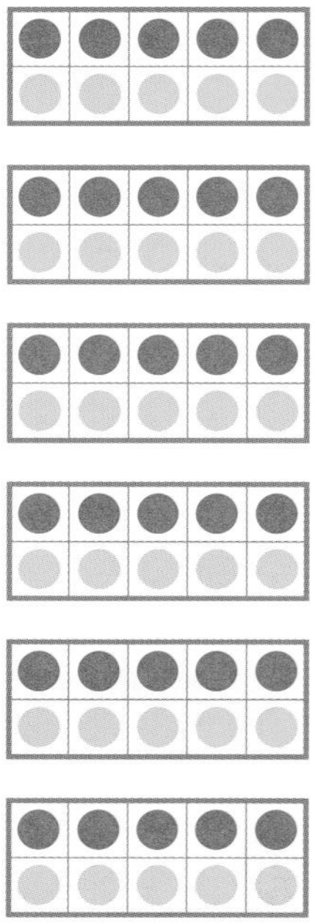

3. 5, 10, 15, ____, ____, ____, ____, 40

4. 20, 25, ____, ____, ____, ____, 50

5. 25, 30, ____, ____, ____, ____, 55, ____

Count by 2s.

6. 2, 4, 6, ____, ____, ____, ____, 16

7. 26, 28, ____, ____, 34, ____, ____, ____, 42

8. 34, 36, ____, ____, ____, ____, 46, ____

Count by 10s.

9. 10, ____, ____, ____, ____, ____

PRACTICE

Write your own counting pattern.

10. ____, ____, ____, ____, ____, ____, ____

Problem Solving Visual Thinking

11. Look at the picture.
Count by 2s.
How many feet
are jumping rope?

____ feet

Notes for Home: Your child practiced counting by 2s, 5s, and 10s. *Home Activity:* Name an even number between 2 and 10 and ask your child to count by 2s from that number.

For additional practice, see Skills Practice Bank, page 532, Set 3.

Name

Ordinals

Learn

first	second	third	fourth	fifth	sixth	seventh	eighth	ninth	tenth
1st	2nd	3rd	4th	5th	6th	7th	8th	9th	10th

Check

Look at the way the animals are facing.

1. Color the fish.

first orange | sixth red | ninth green
fourth purple | seventh yellow | tenth blue

2. Color the birds.

second green | fifth blue | eighth purple
third red | 6th yellow | 9th orange

Talk About It When do you want to be first? When do you want to be last?

Notes for Home: Your child used number words *first* through *tenth* to identify position.
Home Activity: Ask your child to look at the line of birds and point to the second, sixth, and ninth in line.

Practice

❸ Color the floors.

- 1st orange
- second blue
- third green
- fourth yellow
- 5th red
- sixth purple

❹ Color the dolls.

- 2nd red
- 3rd yellow
- 5th blue
- 6th green

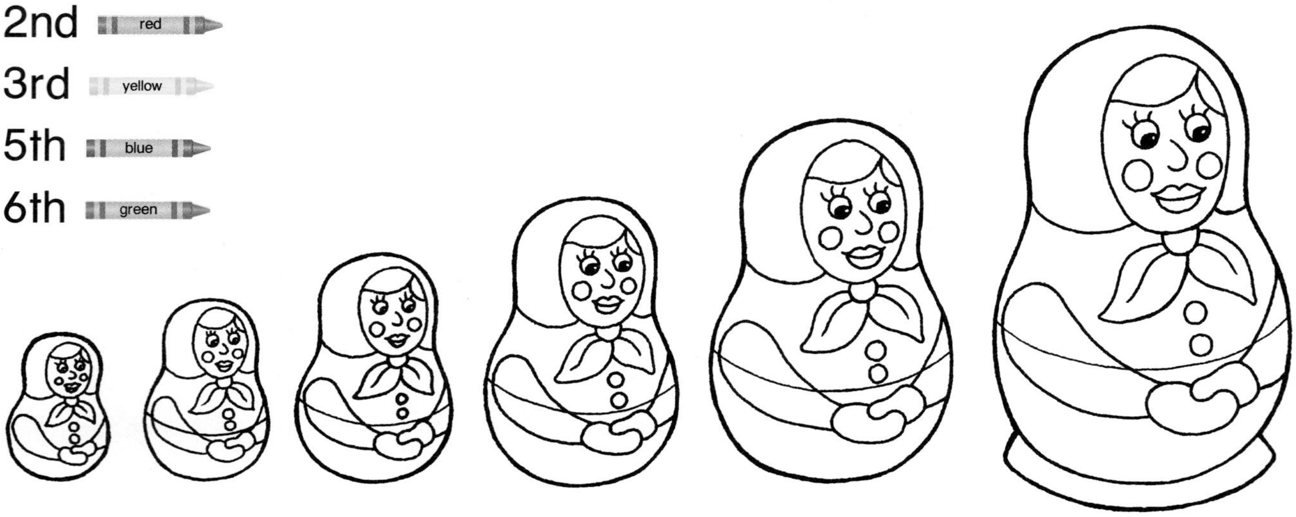

1st

Problem Solving Visual Thinking

❺ How many toys are in the tunnel?

Write how many. ______

fifth fourth first

Notes for Home: Your child practiced number words from *first* through *tenth* to identify position. *Home Activity:* Ask your child to arrange 4 or 5 toys in a line and show you the first, second, third, fourth, and fifth.

Name ______________________

Use Graphic Aids

A chart can help you find data.
Special words help you talk about charts.
Rows go across. Columns go down.

Continue the pattern on each chart.

1 

How many rows? _____

How many columns? _____

I drew this diagonal line. Now you draw one!

2 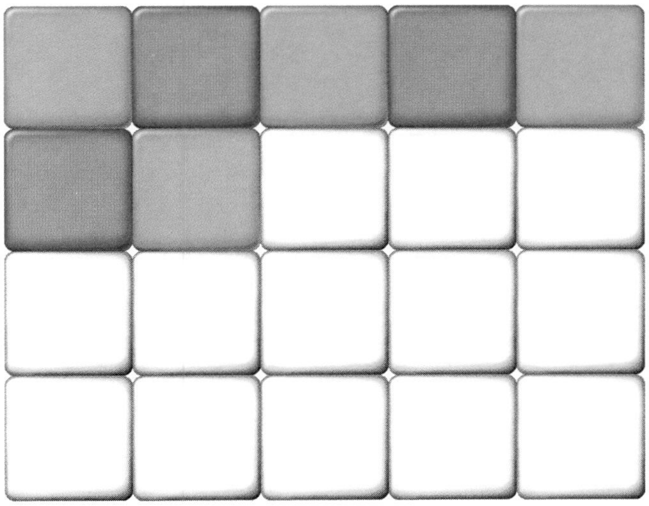

How many rows? _____

How many columns? _____

Talk About It Tell about the patterns in the charts.

Notes for Home: Your child learned about patterns in a chart. *Home Activity:* Ask your child to find rows, columns, and diagonals on a calendar.

3 Make a pattern on the chart.
You can use colors, shapes, or numbers.

Write About It

4 Tell about the colors, shapes, or numbers in your pattern.

____

5 What patterns can you see?

rows _______________________________________

columns ____________________________________

diagonals ___________________________________

Notes for Home: Your child used a chart to make a pattern. *Home Activity:* Ask your child to make a pattern on a calendar using objects such as coins.

Name

Problem Solving: Look for a Pattern

Learn

PROBLEM SOLVING GUIDE

Understand • Plan • Solve • Look Back

What is the pattern on this chart?

1	2	3	4	5	6	7	8	9	10
11	12	13	14	15	16	17	18	19	20

I made this pattern counting by 2s.

Check

Color each chart to continue the pattern.

Start with 2. Count by 2s.

1.

1	2	3	4	5	6	7	8	9	10
11	12	13	14	15	16	17	18	19	20
21	22	23	24	25	26	27	28	29	30

2.

1	2	3	4	5	6	7
8	9	10	11	12	13	14
15	16	17	18	19	20	21
22	23	24	25	26	27	28
29	30	31				

Talk About It How are the patterns the same? How are they different?

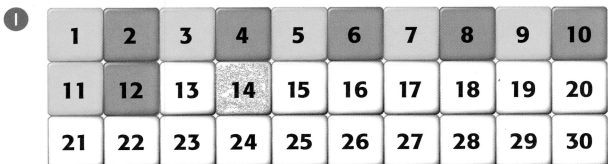

Notes for Home: Your child counted by 2s to make patterns. *Home Activity:* Ask your child to count by 2s. Challenge your child to count past 30.

PROBLEM SOLVING

Practice

Color the charts to continue the pattern.

3. Start with 1. Count by 5s.

1	2	3	4	5	6	7	8	9	10
11	12	13	14	15	16	17	18	19	20
21	22	23	24	25	26	27	28	29	30

4. Start with 3. Count by 3s.

1	2	3	4	5	6	7	8	9	10
11	12	13	14	15	16	17	18	19	20
21	22	23	24	25	26	27	28	29	30
31	32	33	34	35	36	37	38	39	40
41	42	43	44	45	46	47	48	49	50

PROBLEM SOLVING

Write About It

5. Write about one of the patterns. You can use the words in the list.

odd	pattern
even	diagonal
row	chart
column	count

____

____

____

____

Notes for Home: Your child continued making patterns in a chart. *Home Activity:* Ask your child which numbers would be colored if each chart had another row. (35, 40; 51, 54, 57, 60)

Name ______________________________

Mixed Practice

Lessons 7–10

Concepts and Skills

1. Count by 2s. 2, 4, 6, ____, ____, ____, ____, ____

2. Count by 2s. 24, 26, 28, ____, ____, ____, ____, ____

3. Count by 5s. 5, 10, 15, 20, ____, ____, ____, ____

4. Count by 10s. 10, 20, ____, ____, ____, ____

5. Color the cars.

second 

3rd 

sixth 

1st

Problem Solving

6. Color to continue the pattern. Count by 3s.

1	2	3	4	5	6	7	8	9	10
11	12	13	14	15	16	17	18	19	20
21	22	23	24	25	26	27	28	29	30
31	32	33	34	35	36	37	38	39	40

Journal

7. Write about a time when you might want to count by 2s, 5s, or 10s.

Notes for Home: Your child practiced counting by 2s, 5s, or 10s, matching numbers to positions in line and continuing a pattern. *Home Activity*: Ask your child to count aloud by 5s beginning at 15.

Cumulative Review
Chapters 1–7

Concepts and Skills

Count on to add.

1 6 + 2 = ___ 3 + 1 = ___ 5 + 3 = ___

2

10	2	6	1	2	3	5
+ 1	+ 8	+ 3	+ 9	+ 7	+ 7	+ 1

3 Draw more .
Write the sum.

5 + 4 = ___

4 Use the ⊞.
Write the difference.

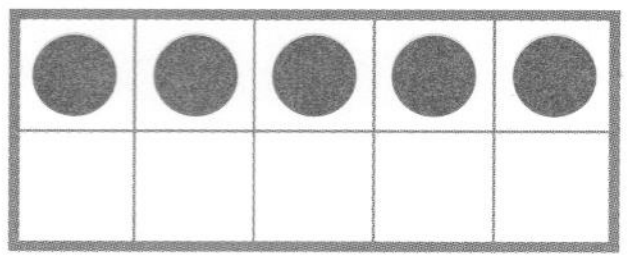

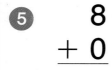

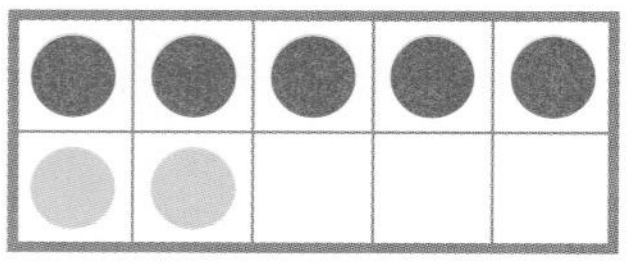

7 − 5 = ___

Test Prep

Fill in the ○ for the correct answer.
Add or subtract.

5

 8
+ 0

 6 7 8 9
 ○ ○ ○ ○

6 12 − 12 = ___

 0 1 2 3
 ○ ○ ○ ○

Notes for Home: Your child reviewed basic addition and subtraction facts. *Home Activity:* Ask your child to explain how to use the ten frame to solve Problem 4.

CUMULATIVE REVIEW

Name

Chapter 7 Review

Vocabulary

1. Color the turtles. 2nd second (green) 5th fifth (red)

1st

2. Estimate how many. Circle groups of ten. Write the numbers. About **20** **40** **60**

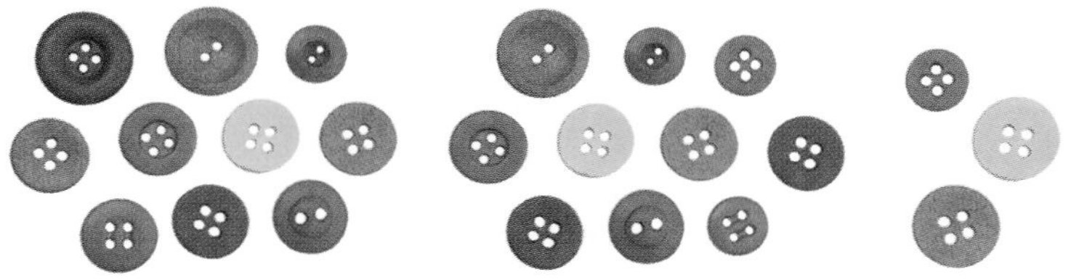

_____ tens and _____ extra is _____.

Concepts and Skills

3. Count by 5s. 5, 10, 15, _____, _____, _____, _____

4. Count by 10s. 10, 20, 30, _____, _____, _____

Problem Solving

Read the graph.

5. How many stickers does Rajeev have? _____

6. How many more stickers does Pam need to have the same number as Rajeev? _____

Notes for Home: Your child reviewed the vocabulary, concepts, skills, and problem solving taught in Chapter 7. *Home Activity:* Put about 30 pennies or other objects in a pile. Ask your child to take a handful, estimate how many, make groups of 10, and then tell how many.

Name ______________________________

Chapter 7 Test

1 Estimate how many.
About **10** **30** **50**

Circle groups of 10.
Write the numbers.

_____ tens and _____ extra is _____.

2 Count by 2s. 2, 4, 6, _____, _____, _____, _____, 16

3 Count by 5s. 5, 10, 15, _____, _____, _____, _____, 40

Read the graph.

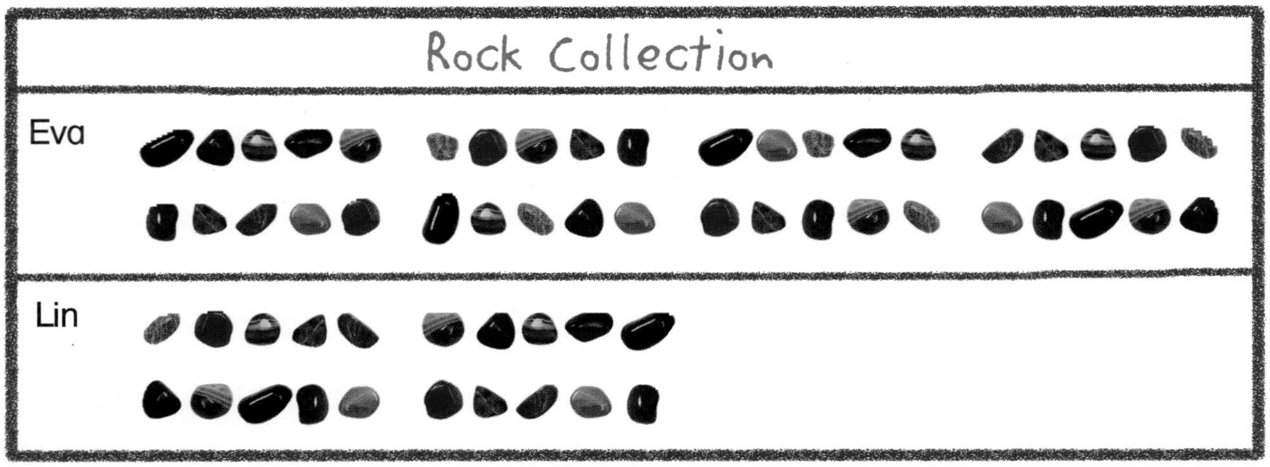

4 How many rocks does Eva have? _____

5 How many more does Eva have than Lin? _____

6 Color.

first 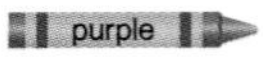

third 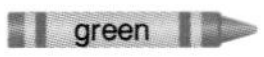

1st

Notes for Home: Your child was assessed on Chapter 7 concepts, skills, and problem solving.
Home Activity: In Problem 5, ask your child how many more rocks Eva needs to have 50 (10).

CHAPTER TEST

Name

Performance Assessment

Chapter 7

1. Try to scoop out 40 counters.
   Use any way you know to find how many you have.

   I have _____.

2. Try for 20 counters.

   I have _____.

3. Try for 60 counters.

   I have _____.

Problem Solving Critical Thinking

4. Which way did you count?
   Why did you choose that way?
   Choose another way to count.
   Did you get the same number?

Notes for Home: Your child did an activity that assessed Chapter 7 skills and concepts.
Home Activity: Ask your child to tell how the counters were counted in Problem 3.

PERFORMANCE ASSESSMENT

Name ______________________________

Explore with a CALCULATOR

Skipping Stones

Keys You Will Use [ON/C] [+] [=]

You can use your calculator to count by any number.

Count by 5s. Press [+] [5] [=].

Press [=] again and again. Write what you see.

5	10					

Use your calculator to find what Suni collects.

1. Count by 4s. Press [+] [4] [=].

   Press [=] again and again. Write what you see.

4						

2. Count by 25s. Press [+] [2] [5] [=].

25			

CODE	
5	R
8	K
24	C
50	S
75	O

What does Suni collect? Use the code.
Write the number in each color. Write the letters.

5				
R	___	___	___	___

Tech Talk How would you use a calculator to count by 9s?

Visit our Web site. www.parent.mathsurf.com

Trash Tally

Collect some things that can be recycled.
What can you collect the most of in two days?
Make a tally to show how many you collect.

Paper

Plastic

Cardboard

Fold down

MathSoup

Scott Foresman - Addison Wesley My Math Magazine No. 7

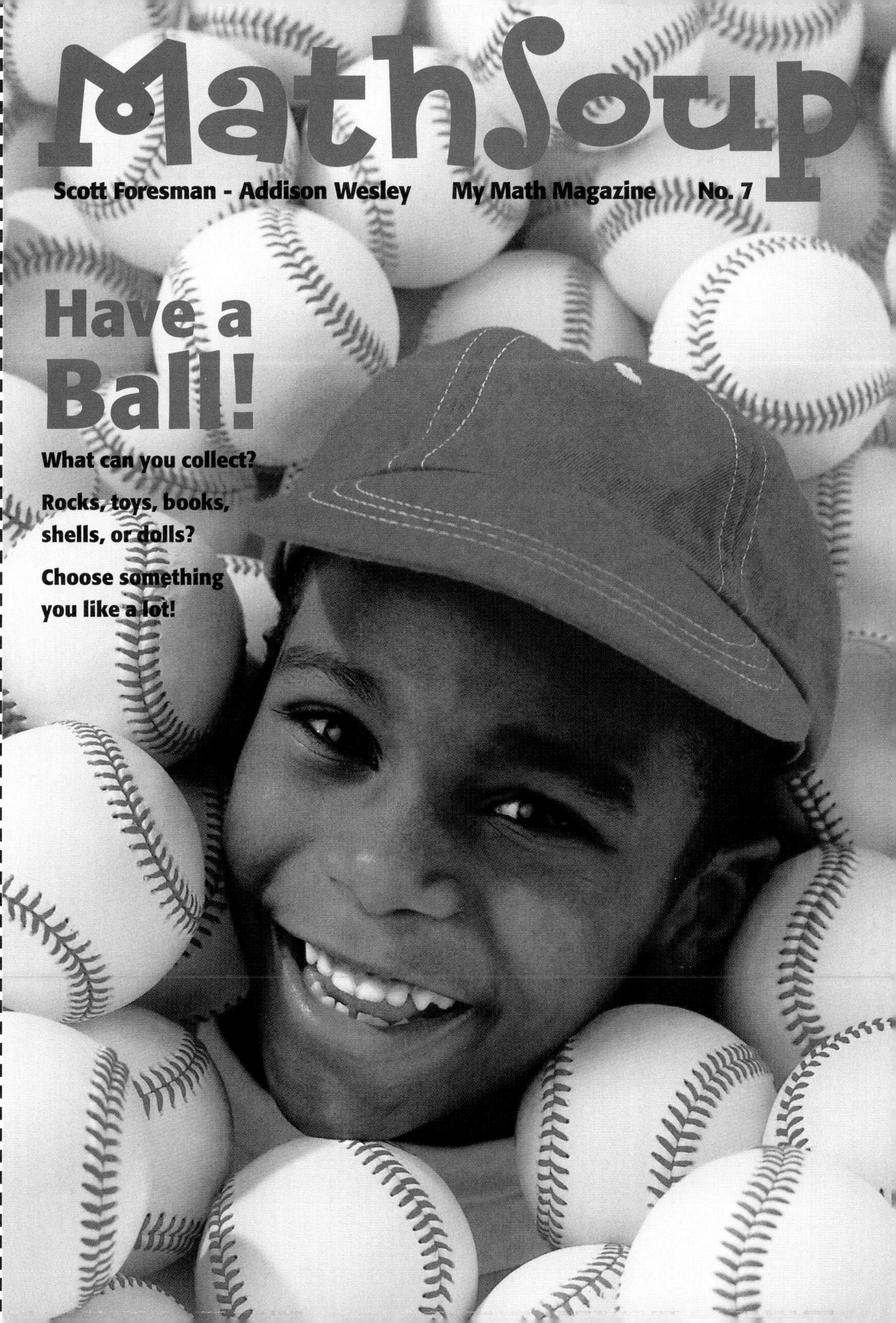

Have a Ball!

What can you collect?

Rocks, toys, books, shells, or dolls?

Choose something you like a lot!

A Ballpark Figure

How many baseballs can you count?
Before you count them, estimate!

There are about ______ baseballs.

Circle groups of 10 baseballs.

Write the number. ______ baseballs

Notes for Home: Your child estimated and counted groups of objects.
Home Activity: Ask your child to help you count and sort socks. Help your child count by 2s to find out how many socks altogether.

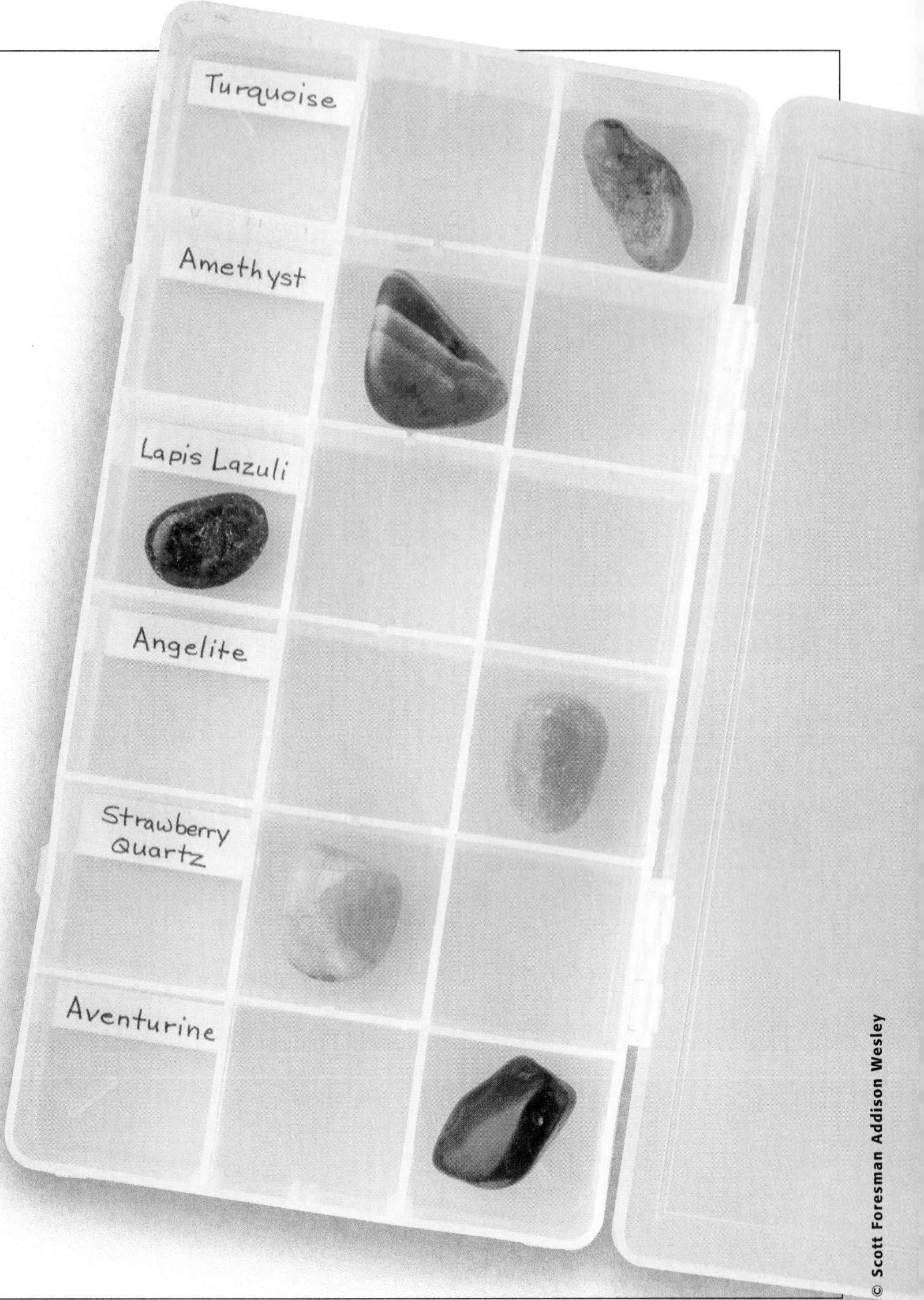

***Rock hound is a name for a person who collects rocks as a hobby.**

Be A Rock Hound*

Pretend the rocks in the Rock Case are your rock collection.
Each rock has a box in the Rock Case.
Draw and color more rocks.

Count your rocks.

I collected ______ . 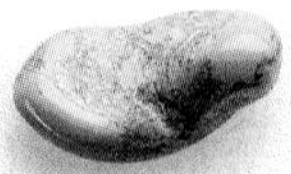

I collected ______ . 

I collected ______ . 

I collected ______ . 

I collected ______ . 

I collected ______ . 

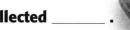

I have ______ rocks in my collection.

Meet a Real Rock Hound

Colin Phillips is a 6 year old rock hound who lives in Bellaire, Texas. He made a rock museum in his house.

Make Your Own Sports Card

Draw yourself playing a sport.
Give yourself a number.

Sport: ______________

Player: ______________

Number: ______________

Age: ______________

Games won: ______________

Notes for Home: Your child drew and colored rocks to practice counting and sorting. *Home Activity:* Help your child gather, sort, and count a collection of rocks or other items.

Start →

Lose a Turn

Lose a Turn

Lose a Turn

Lose a Turn

Go Collecting!

What You Need

Make a spinner with a pencil and a paper clip.

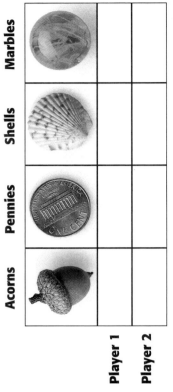

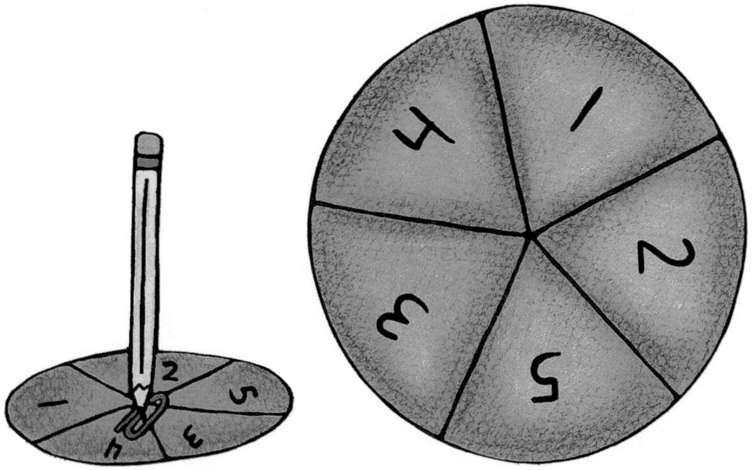

How to Play

1 Both players put the markers on Start.

2 Each player takes turn spinning the spinner and moving the marker that many spaces.

3 When a marker lands on an object, the player makes a check in the chart for that object.

4 The first player to make a check for each object wins.

	Acorns	Pennies	Shells	Marbles
Player 1				
Player 2				

Notes for Home: Your child played a game to practice counting. *Home Activity:* Play the game with your child. For each spin, let players move in either direction.

CHAPTER 8

Place Value

Notes for Home: Your child looked for groups of tens and ones in the picture and then counted to find how many in all. *Home Activity:* Ask your child to show you a group with tens and ones and to find how many in all.

Math at Home

Our class is beginning Chapter 8. We will learn about numbers up to 100. We will learn to read and write these numbers and find numbers that come before and after. Here are some activities we can do together.

Dime Time

Give a pile of up to 9 dimes and 9 pennies to players. Each player counts the dimes and pennies by 10s and 1s then tells the amount. Together decide who has more and who has less.

Number Detective

Provide paper, pencil, and a clipboard, if possible, and ask your child to look around at home for numbers between 10 and 99. Each time a number is found, ask your child to write it and then draw a picture showing where it is.

Community Connection

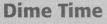

Notice house and building numbers in your neighborhood. Find the patterns in how the numbers change as you go down the street.

Visit our Web Site. www.parent.mathsurf.com

Name

Explore Tens and Ones

Explore

Use [cube] and [ten-frame]. Take a lot of [cube].

Use the [ten-frame] to help make trains of 10 [cube]. Color and record how many tens and ones.

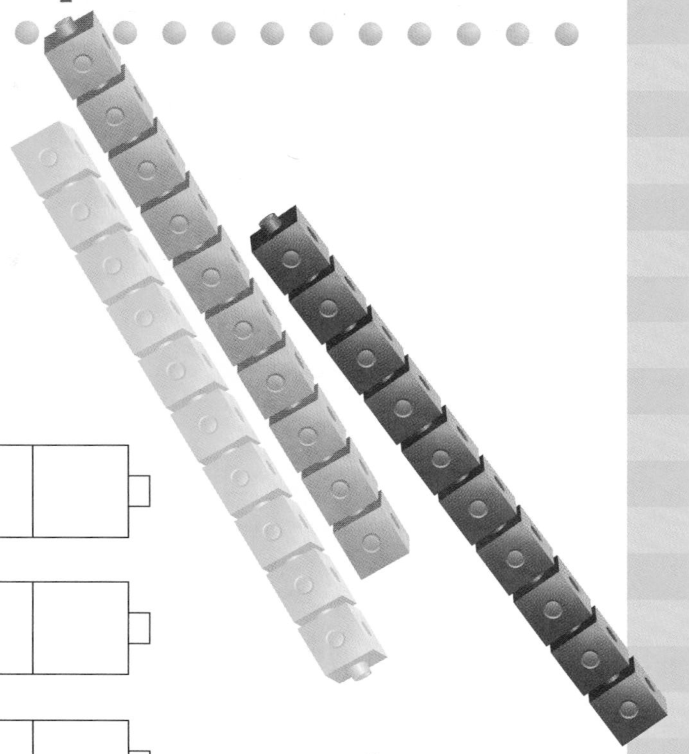

3 tens

4 ones

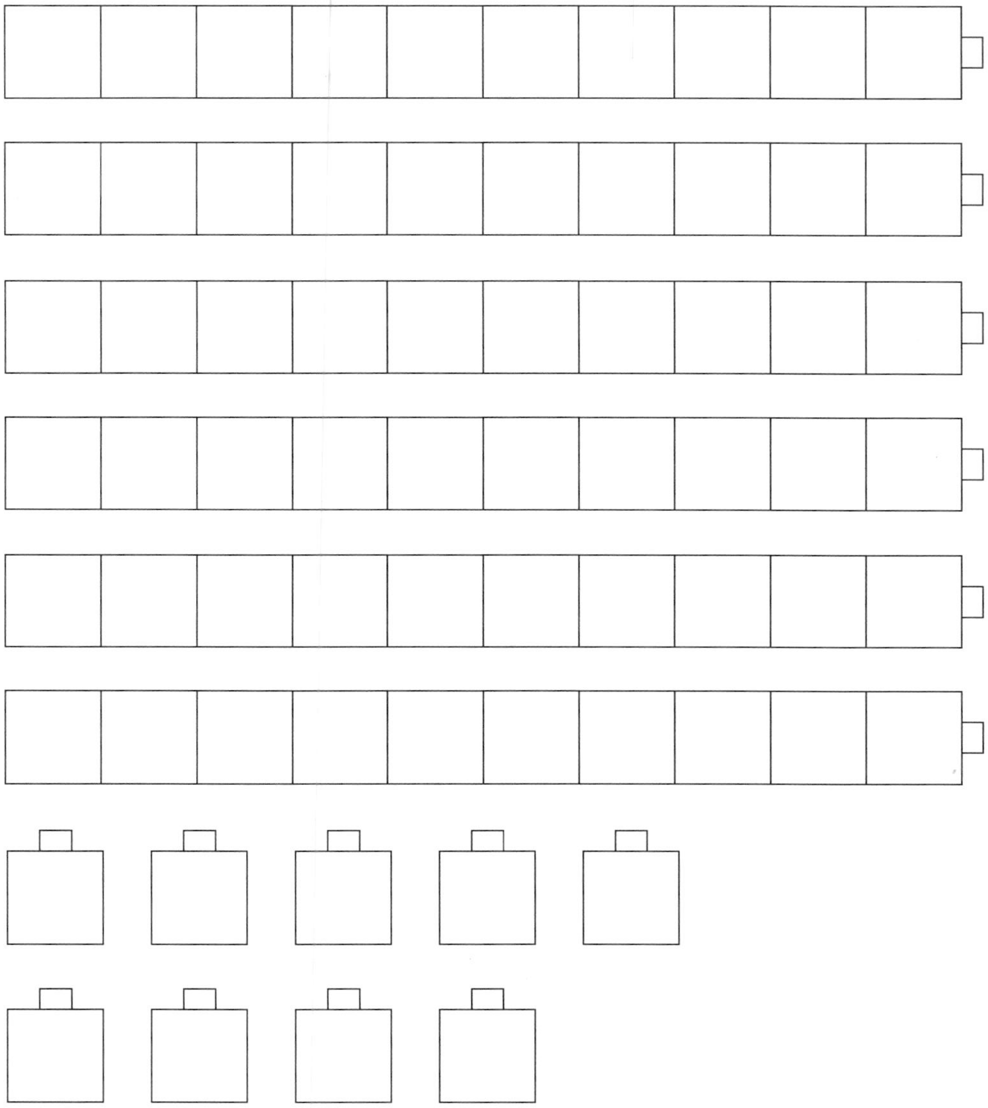

tens	ones

Share

What is the highest number of ones you could have left over?

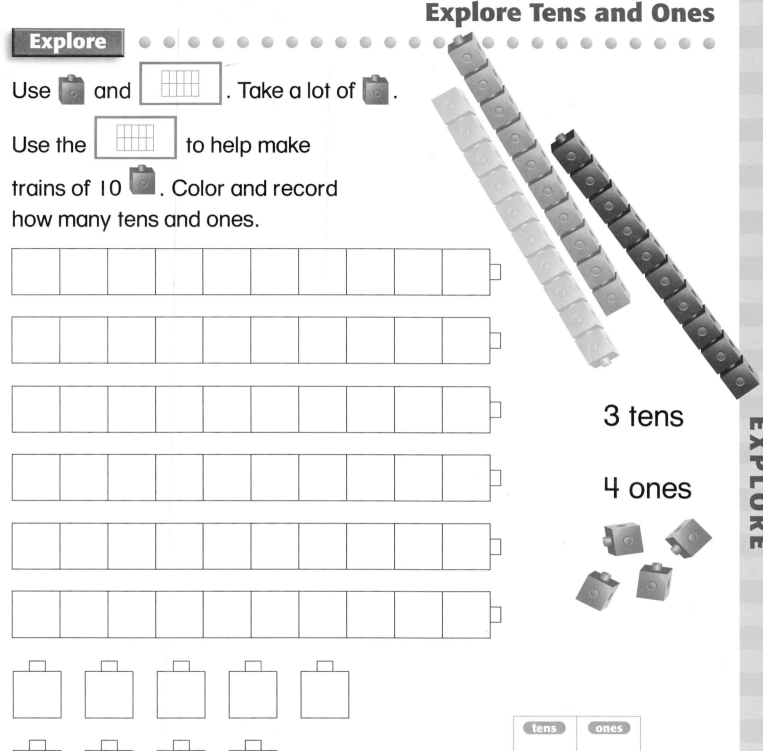

Notes for Home: Your child explored larger numbers using groups of tens and ones. *Home Activity:* Use cards with the numbers 0–9. Each player picks three cards. Use the numbers from your cards to make a two-digit number. Discard the extra card. The player who makes the largest number wins.

Connect

Use  and 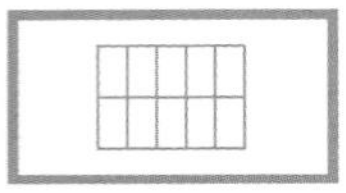. Take a lot of .

Use the 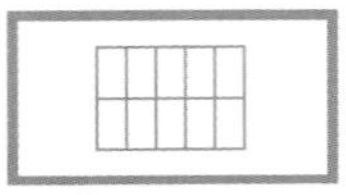 to make trains of 10 .
Record tens and ones.

1

tens	ones

2

tens	ones

3

tens	ones

4

tens	ones

5

tens	ones

6

tens	ones

7

tens	ones

8

tens	ones

9

tens	ones

EXPLORE

Journal

10 Write a list of things that have more than 20 pieces or parts. Write how many tens and ones.

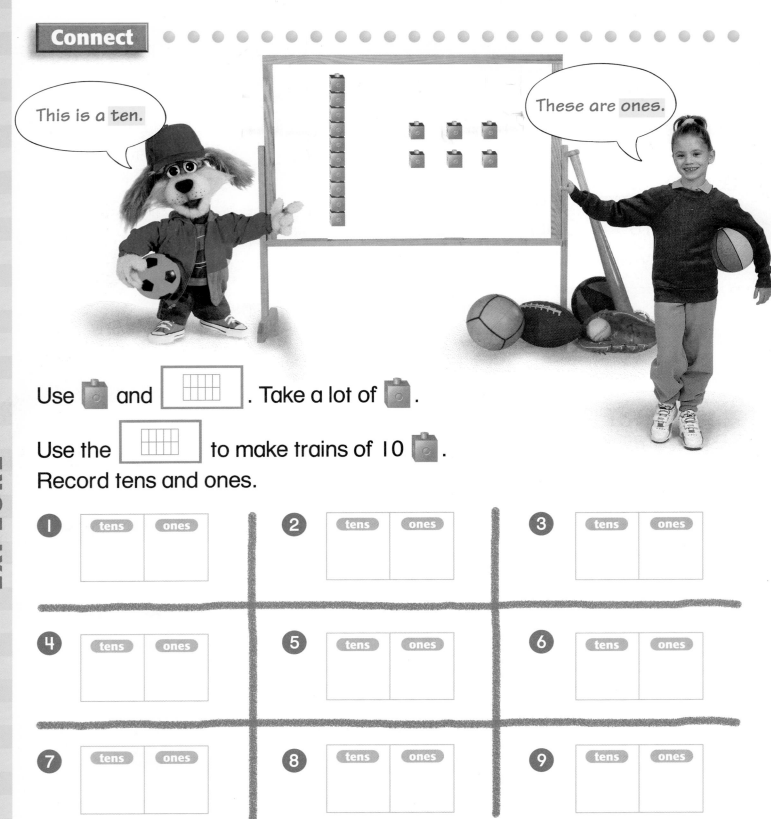

Notes for Home: Your child made groups of tens and ones and then recorded the number of each. *Home Activity:* Make a group of 20–60 small objects (macaroni, dried beans, or paper clips, for example) and help your child make groups of tens and ones and then count how many.

Name

Tens and Ones to 60

Learn

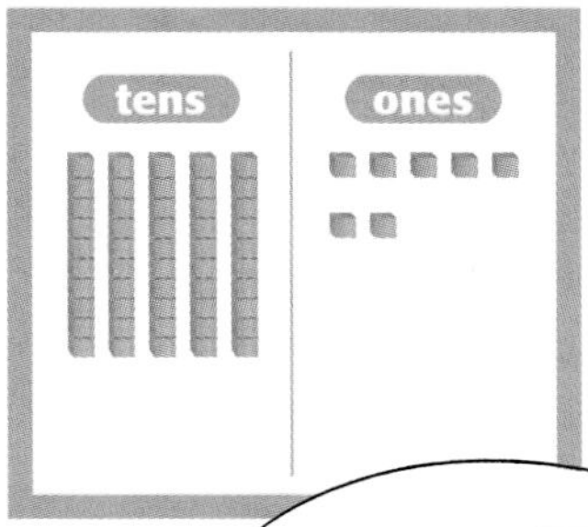

tens	ones
5	7

Check

Use 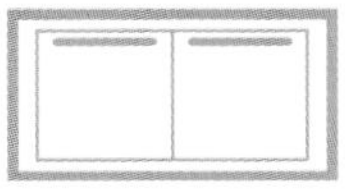 and 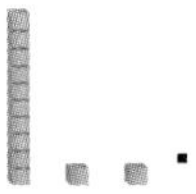.

Count how many tens and ones. Write the number.

1

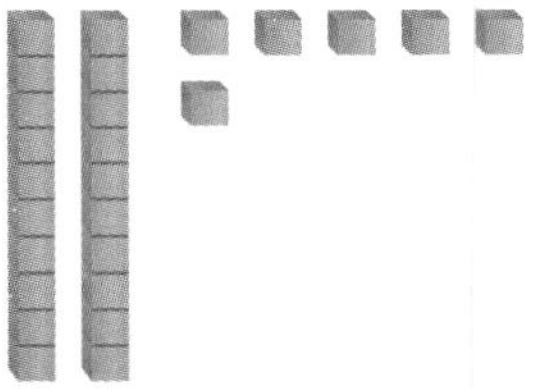

tens	ones
2	6

26

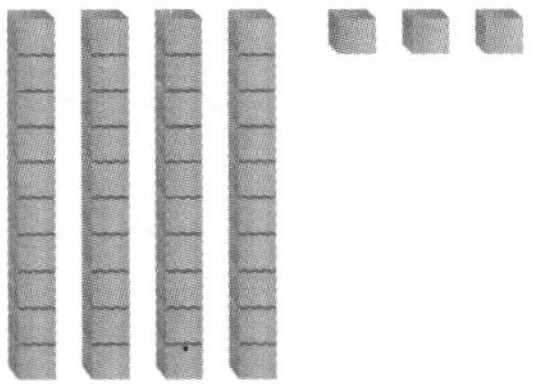

tens	ones

____

2

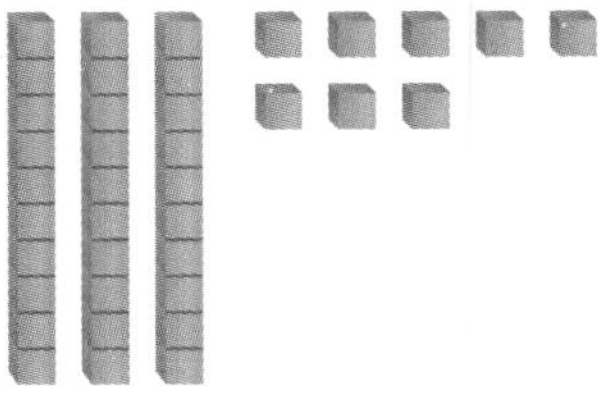

tens	ones

____

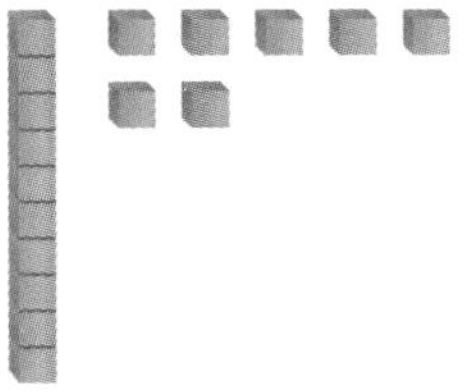

tens	ones

____

Talk About It What does the 0 mean in the number 40?

Notes for Home: Your child modeled a number to 60 and then wrote the number.
Home Activity: Use beans or paper clips to model numbers to 60. Put the groups of ten into the cups of a muffin tin or egg carton.

Practice

Use [workmat] and [tens and ones blocks].

Count how many tens and ones. Write the number.

3 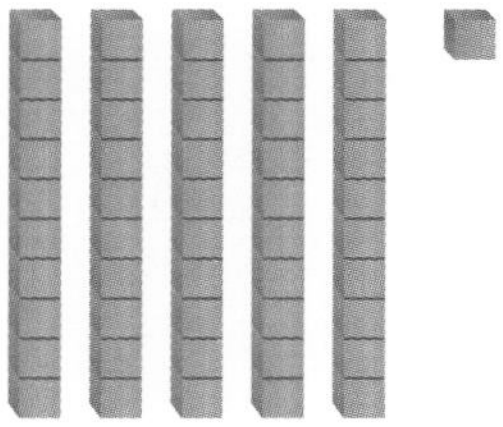

tens	ones
5	1

______

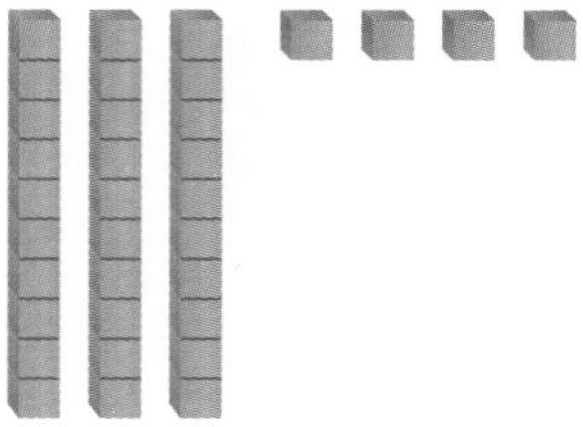

tens	ones

______

4 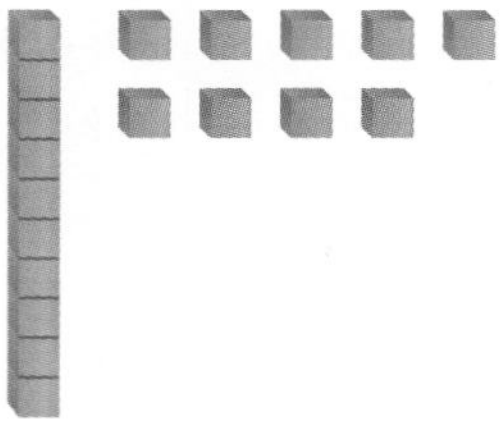

tens	ones

______

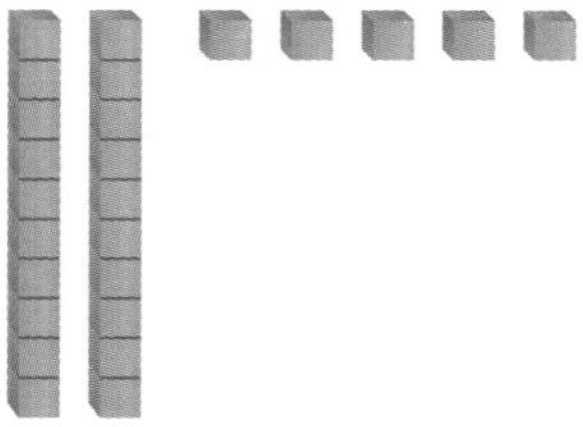

tens	ones

______

Write your own examples. Show with [tens and ones blocks].

5

tens	ones

______

6

tens	ones

______

PRACTICE

Problem Solving

7 Solve.

Ida has 32 baseball cards.

She buys 10 more.

How many does she have now?

______ baseball cards

Notes for Home: Your child modeled tens and ones and then wrote the number. *Home Activity:* Ask your child to find page numbers in books, newspapers, or magazines and then tell how many tens and ones each number has.

Name

Numbers More than Ten

Learn

70	seven tens	seventy
80	eight tens	eighty
90	nine tens	ninety
100	ten tens	one hundred

Check

Count how many tens and ones. Write the number.

1

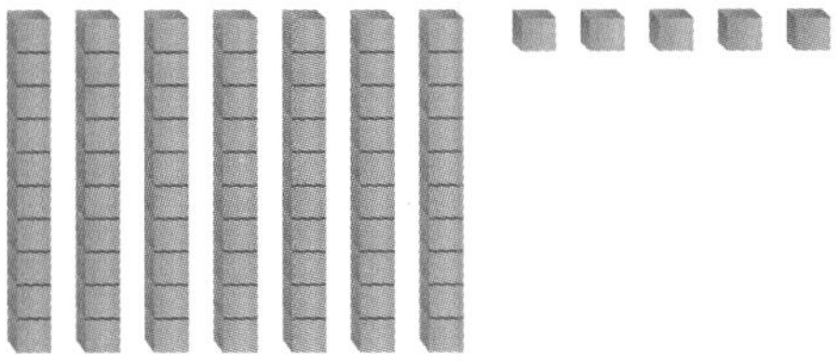

tens	ones
7	5

75

2

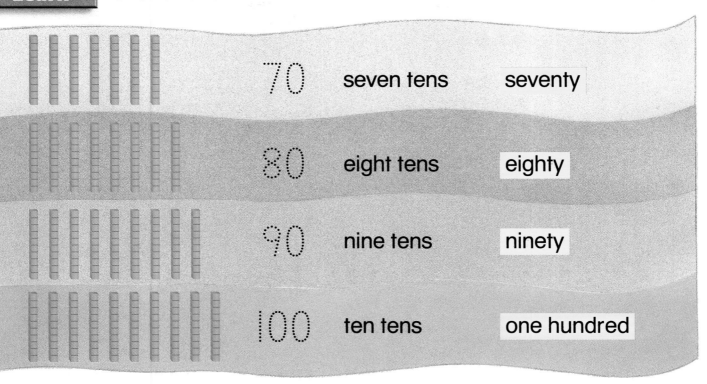

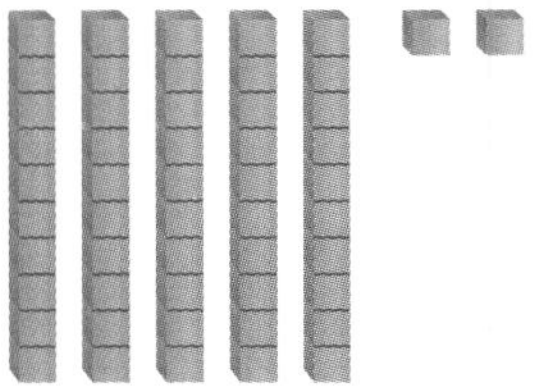

tens	ones

____

Talk About It How can you use the tens and ones blocks to show the number 50?

Notes for Home: Your child counted tens and ones to learn more about place value.
Home Activity: Use small objects, such as buttons, to show numbers up to 100. Count and make groups of ten. Put the groups of ten into small cups.

Practice

How many tens and ones? Write the number.

3 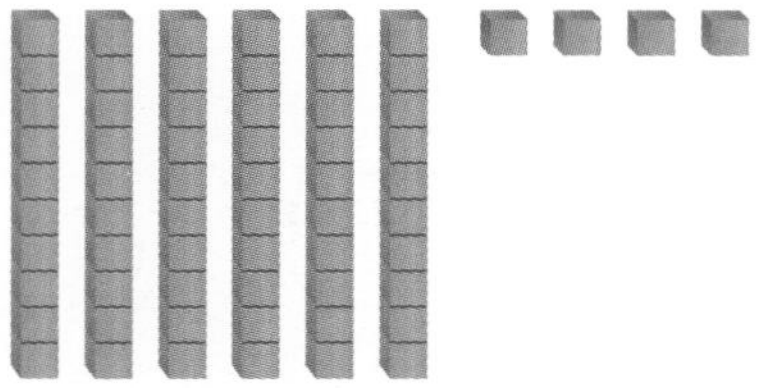

tens	ones
6	4

______

4 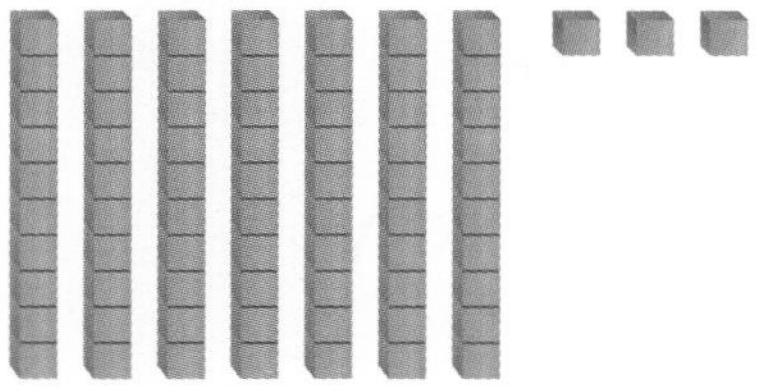

tens	ones

______

5 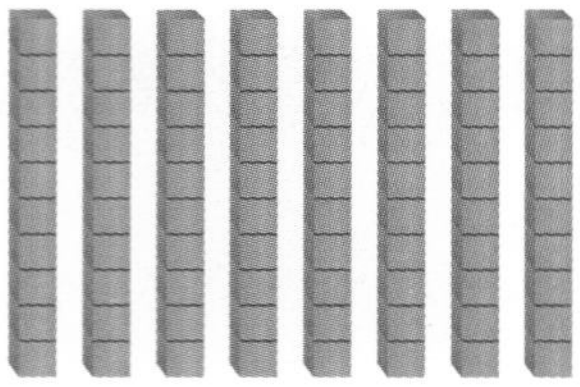

tens	ones

______

6 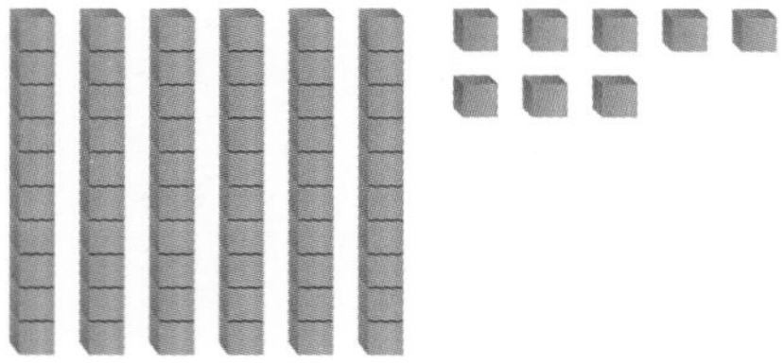

tens	ones

______

7 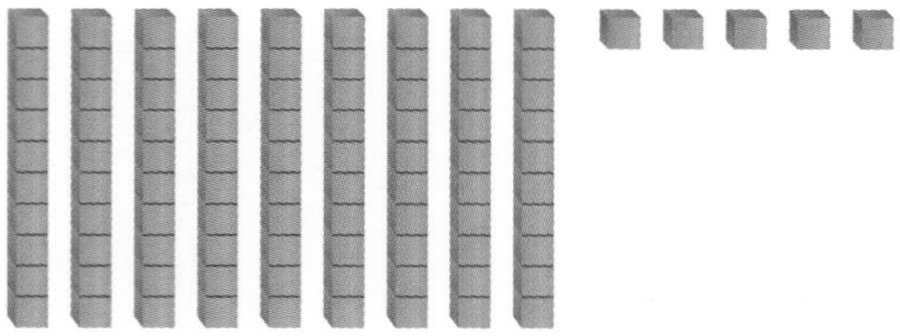

tens	ones

______

PRACTICE

Problem Solving Critical Thinking

8 What are some ways you can show 100 using 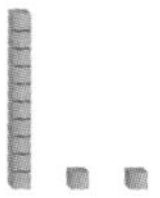 ?

Notes for Home: Your child counted tens and ones and wrote numbers up to 99.
Home Activity: Play a question game: One player picks a number from 1 to 100. The other players may ask up to ten yes or no questions about the number. Then they try to guess the number.

For additional practice, see Skills Practice Bank, page 533, Set 1.

Name

Estimation

Learn

I estimate there are about 30 balls on the mat.

Here are 10 balls.
Use this picture to help you estimate.

Check

Circle groups of 10.
Estimate. Circle about how many.

Count.
Write the number.

1

tens	ones
3	8

About 20 (40) 60

38

2

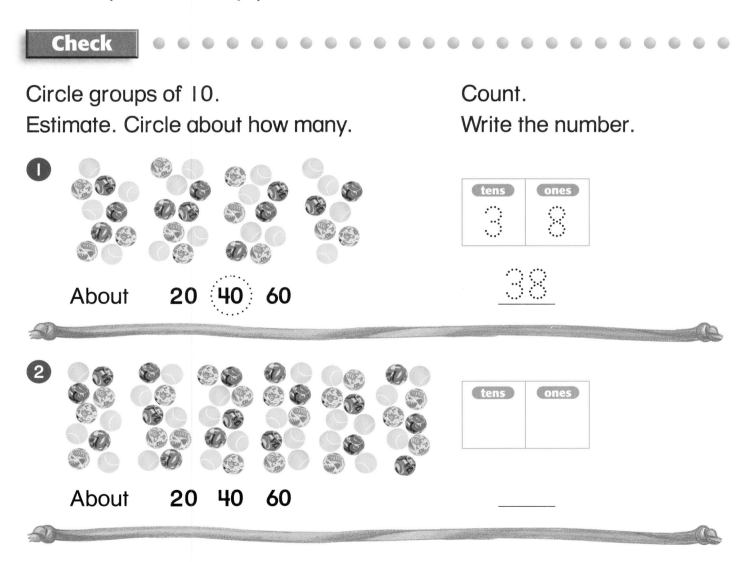

tens	ones

About 20 40 60

_____

Talk About It How did you estimate about how many?

Notes for Home: Your child estimated the number of objects in a large group by looking for groups of ten. *Home Activity:* When shopping, ask your child to estimate how many items are found on a shelf.

Practice

Circle groups of 10.
Estimate. Circle about how many.

Count.
Write the number.

3

tens	ones
5	3

About 50 70 90

_____

4

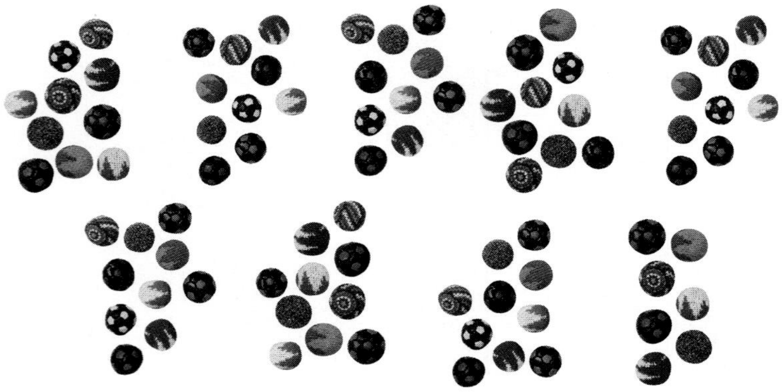

tens	ones

About 50 70 90

_____

Problem Solving Visual Thinking

5 About how many balls are in Al's jar? Circle your estimate. Talk about it with a friend.

Fewer than 20

More than 20

Notes for Home: Your child estimated the number of objects in a large group by looking for groups of 10.
Home Activity: Find numbers from 1 to 100 around the house. How are the numbers used?

PRACTICE

Name

10 Ones Make 1 Ten

Learn

tens
ones
I'll add 1 more.
Now you can exchange 10 ones for 1 ten!

Check

Use tens and ones blocks and a workmat.
Show this many.

Add 1 more.
Can you exchange 10 ones for 1 ten?
Circle yes or no.

Write how many tens and ones.

1 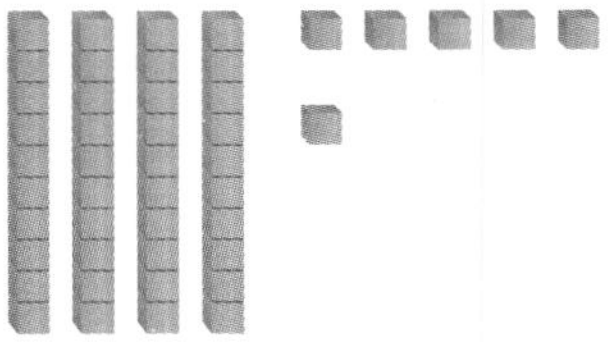

yes

no

tens	ones
4	7

2 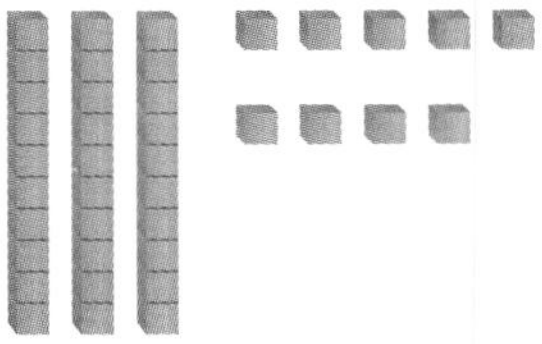

yes

no

tens	ones

3 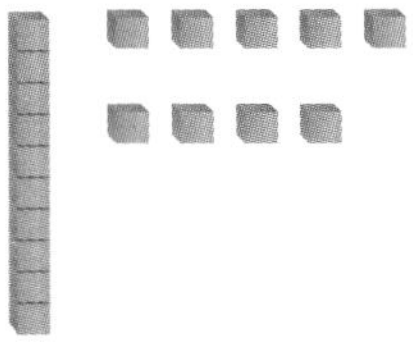

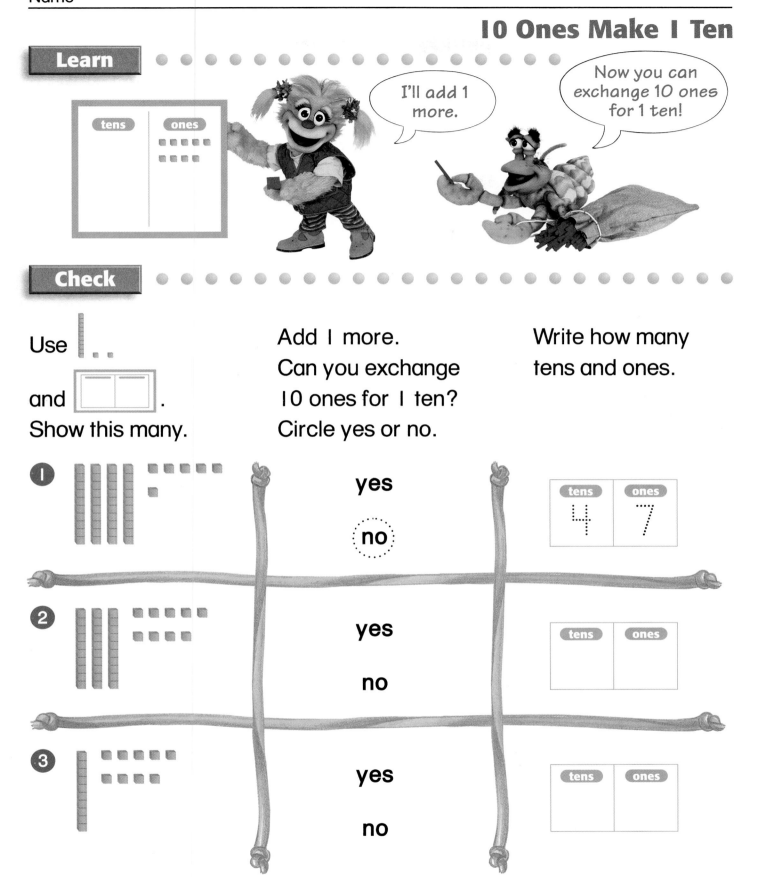

yes

no

tens	ones

Talk About It How do you know when to exchange ones for a ten?

Notes for Home: Your child used tens and ones to help decide when to exchange10 ones for 1 ten.
Home Activity: Look for things that come packaged in groups of ten, such as cookies, gum, and so on.

Practice

Use [tens rod and ones cubes] and [tens and ones mat]. Show this many.

Add 2 more. Can you exchange 10 ones for 1 ten? Circle yes or no.

Write how many tens and ones.

4 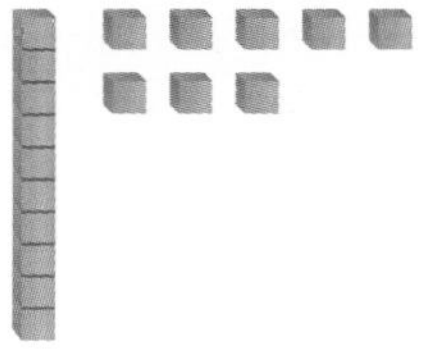

yes

no

tens	ones
2	0

5 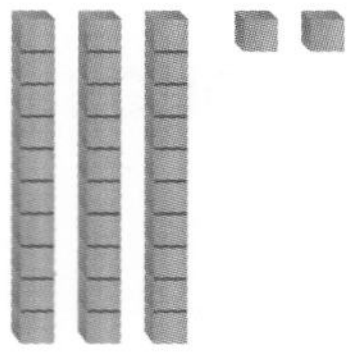

yes

no

tens	ones

6 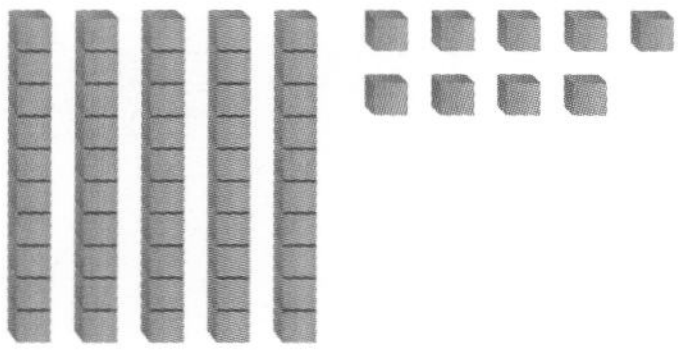

yes

no

tens	ones

7 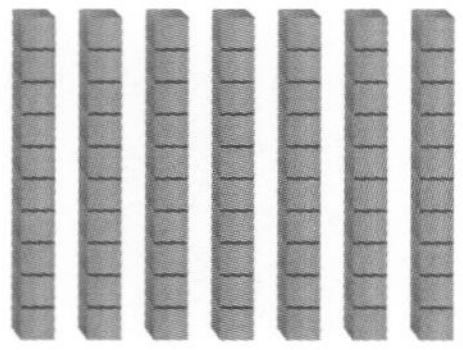

yes

no

tens	ones

Problem Solving **Estimation**

8 Guy has these blocks.
He needs 100. About how many more does he need?

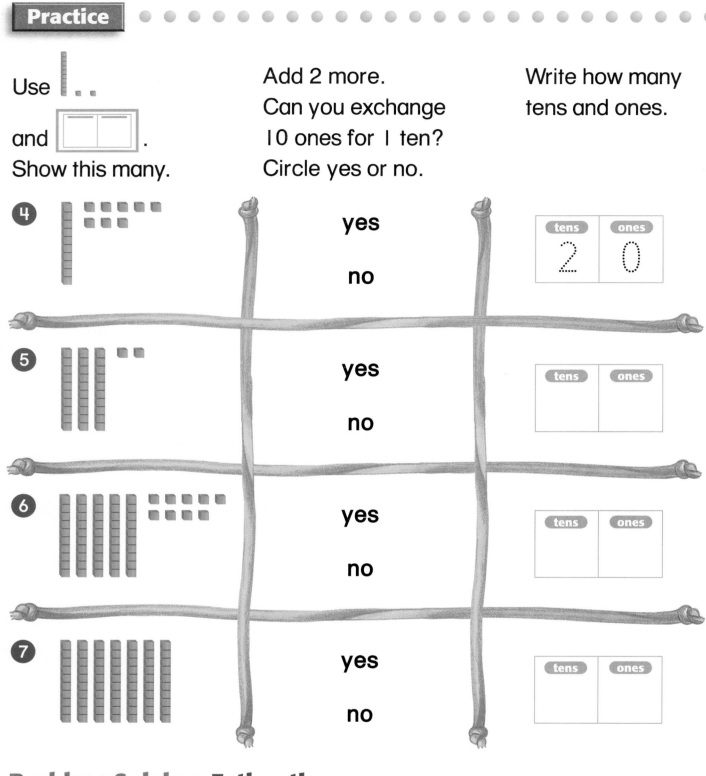

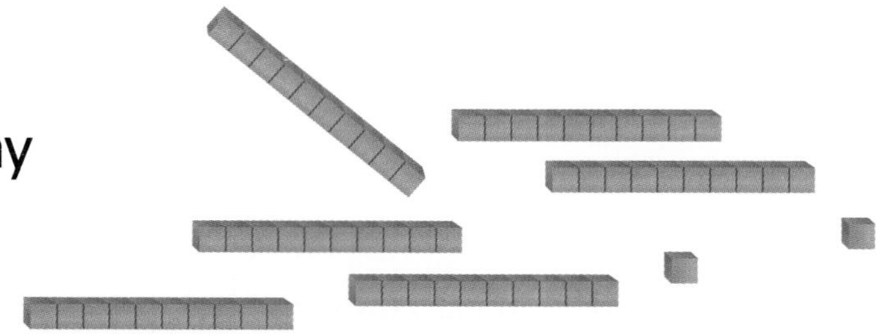

____

Notes for Home: Your child practiced exchanging 10 ones for 1 ten. *Home Activity:* Use dimes and pennies to show more than one way to make 23¢ (2 dimes, 3 pennies; 1 dime, 13 pennies).

Name ________________________________

Practice Game

Drop and Count

Players 2

What You Need

Tens and ones

1 penny

Workmat 2

How to Play

1. Drop a penny on the target.
2. Put that many tens and ones on your workmat.
3. Repeat 1 and 2.
4. Write how many tens and ones.
   Exchange 10 ones for 1 ten if you need to.

PRACTICE

Player 1

Turn 1		Turn 2		Turn 3	
tens	ones	tens	ones	tens	ones

Player 2

Turn 1		Turn 2		Turn 3	
tens	ones	tens	ones	tens	ones

Notes for Home: Your child played a game to practice exchanging 10 ones for 1 ten and writing two-digit numbers. *Home Activity:* Play the game with your child.

Name ______________________________

STOP and Practice

Count how many tens and ones. Write the number.

1

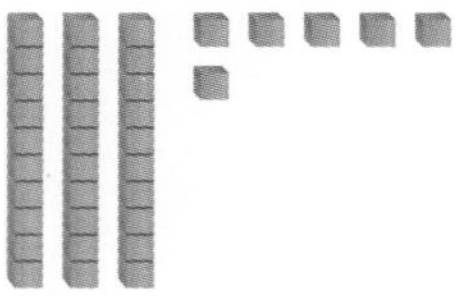

tens	ones

______

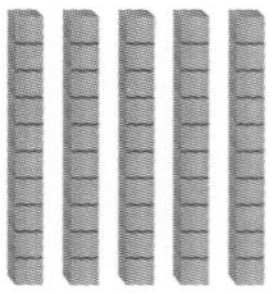

tens	ones

______

2

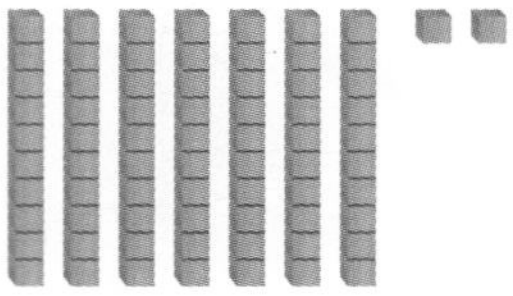

tens	ones

______

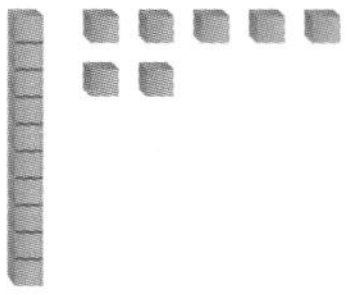

tens	ones

______

3

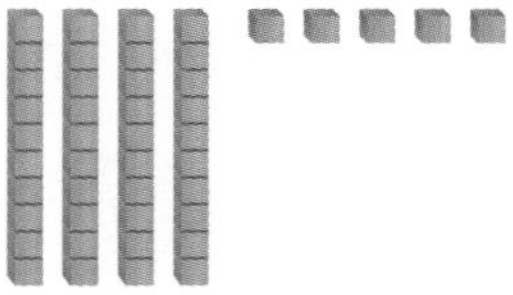

tens	ones

______

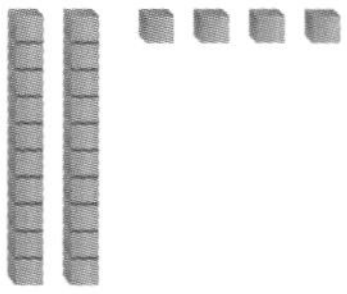

tens	ones

______

Problem Solving

4 Finish the poem.

The Lions had 19 runs.
They thought that was great.
They got 9 more runs.

Now they have _____.

Notes for Home: Your child practiced writing two-digit numbers. *Home Activity:* Ask your child to tell what blocks would be needed to show the number 65 (6 tens and 5 ones).

PRACTICE

Name ______________________________

Problem Solving: Use Objects

Learn

PROBLEM SOLVING GUIDE

Understand • Plan • Solve • Look Back

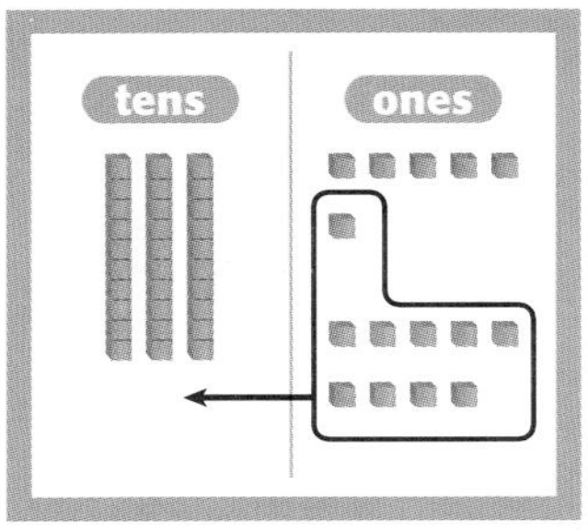

The Comets scored 26 points in the first half.
They scored 19 points in the second half.

How many total points did they score? 45 points

Check

Use 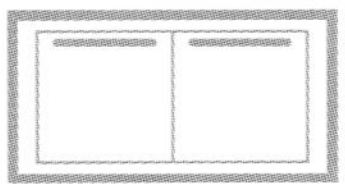 and 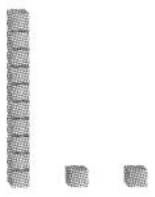. Exchange 10 ones for 1 ten if you need to.

1. The Comets scored these points in Game Two. How many points did they score?

Points for Game Two 36

2. The games are over. Write the points the Comets scored in both games.

Game One: ______

Game Two: ______

What is the total? _____ points

Talk About It The Stars played the Comets in Game One. The Stars scored 51. Who won the game? How do you know?

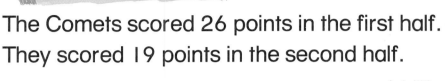

Notes for Home: Your child used tens and ones to solve problems. *Home Activity:* Ask your child to draw a picture or make a collage that shows a favorite number. Help your child think of as many different ways as possible to show the number.

Practice

Use [tens/ones mat] and [tens and ones blocks].
Exchange 10 ones for 1 ten if you need to.

3. The Lions scored these points in a game.
What is their final score?

tens	ones

Final score: _____ points

4. The Tigers scored these points in the game.
What is their final score?

Final score: _____ points

5. Look at the teams' scores.
Circle the team that won the game. **Lions** **Tigers**

Tell a Math Story

6. There are 20 seconds left in this game.
Tell a math story about how the game ends.
Who will score next?
How many points will each team score?

Notes for Home: Your child practiced solving problems using tens and ones. *Home Activity:* Write your favorite teams' scores: for example, Cats, 50; Lions, 45. Ask your child to draw a picture that shows each number with tens and ones. Which number is higher? Which team won?

Name ______________________________

Mixed Practice

Lessons 1–6

Concepts and Skills

1 Estimate how many.
Circle groups of 10.

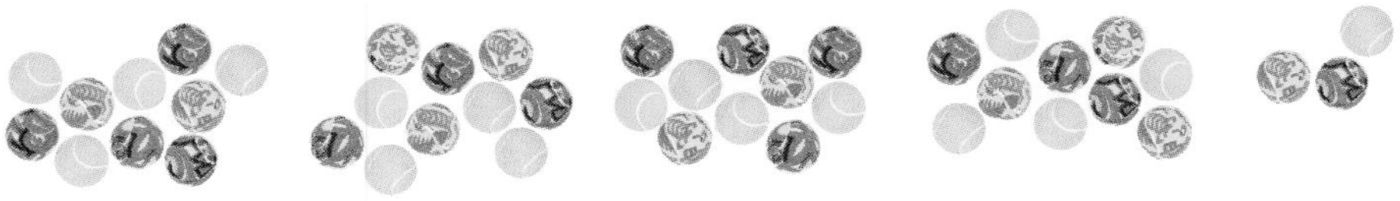

About **20** **40** **60**

Count.
Write the number.

tens	ones

______

2 Count how many.

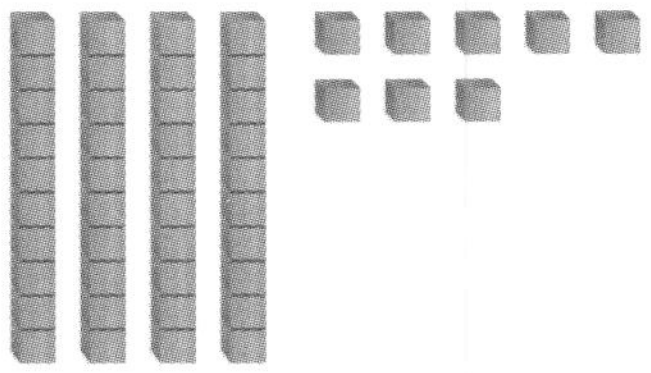

Add 2 more. Do you need to exchange?
Circle yes or no.

yes **no**

Write how many tens and ones.

tens	ones

Problem Solving

Use 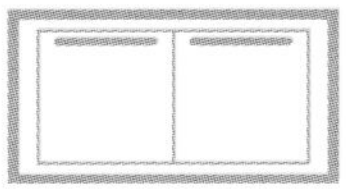 and 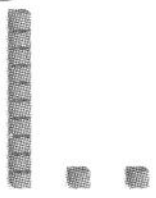. Exchange 10 ones for 1 ten if you need to.

3 What is the All Stars final score?

Final Score: ______ points

4 In which half did the All Stars score more points?

____

Journal

5 Draw a picture that shows 3 tens and 4 ones.
Write the number.

Notes for Home: Your child practiced estimating, counting numbers to 99, and problem solving. *Home Activity:* With your child, look for numbers on the front page of a newspaper. How are the numbers used (for example, date, page, addresses, number of people)?

Name ________________________________

Cumulative Review

Chapters 1–8

Concepts and Skills

Complete the fact family.

1. $6 + 4 = $ ____
   $4 + 6 = $ ____
   $10 - 4 = $ ____
   $10 - 6 = $ ____

2. $5 + 3 = $ ____
   $3 + 5 = $ ____
   $8 - 3 = $ ____
   $8 - 5 = $ ____

Problem Solving

Write a number sentence.

3. 9 children played ball.
   6 went home.
   How many play ball now?

   ____

4. Jamie scored 8 points
   Taylor scored 3 points.
   How many points did they score together?

   ____

Test Prep

Fill in the ○ for the correct answer.

Do the parts match when you fold on the line?

5. 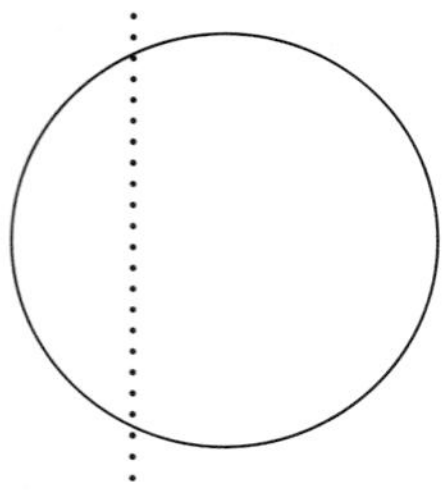

   yes ○ no ○

6. 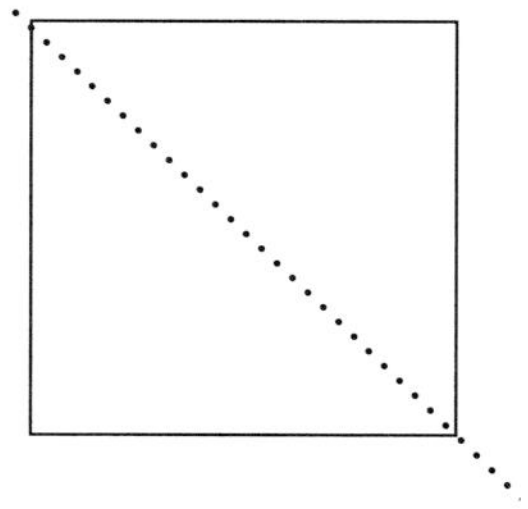

   yes ○ no ○

7. 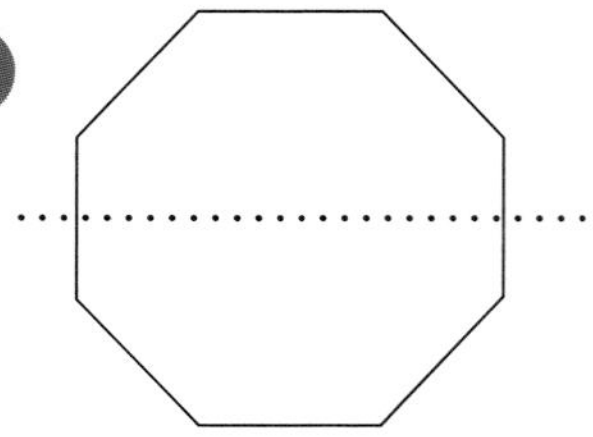

   yes ○ no ○

Notes for Home: Your child reviewed fact families, problem solving, and finding shapes with parts that match. *Home Activity:* Look for numbers in the sports section of a newspaper. How are these numbers used (for example, scores, batting averages, innings, quarters)?

CUMULATIVE REVIEW

Name ______________________________

Compare Numbers

Learn

8 tens 7 ones 7 tens 8 ones

Check

Use 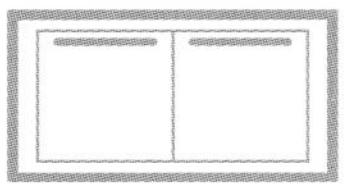 and 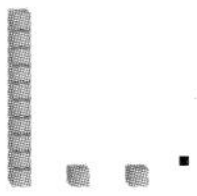.

Write the tens and ones. Circle the number that is greater.

1. 56 __5__ tens __6__ ones
   (61) __6__ tens __1__ one

2. 74 _____ tens _____ ones
   89 _____ tens _____ ones

3. 31 _____ tens _____ one
   19 _____ ten _____ ones

4. 77 _____ tens _____ ones
   59 _____ tens _____ ones

Talk About It

These numbers each have 6 tens.
Which number is less?
How do you know?

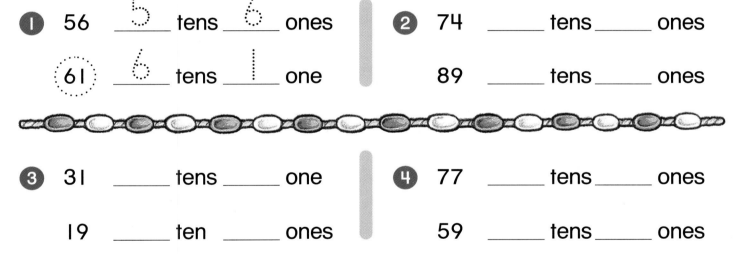

Notes for Home: Your child compared two numbers to tell which is greater. *Home Activity:* Look at numbers while at the library with your child. How are they used? How does it help to know how to compare numbers (When things are listed numerically, you can find them more easily)?

Practice

Use [workmat] and [tens and ones blocks].

Write the tens and ones. Circle the number that is less.

5. 46 __4__ tens __6__ ones
   (39) __3__ tens __9__ one

6. 91 _____ tens _____ ones
   29 _____ tens _____ ones

7. 67 _____ tens _____ ones
   80 _____ tens _____ one

8. 58 _____ tens _____ ones
   72 _____ tens _____ ones

9. 41 _____ tens _____ one
   14 _____ ten _____ ones

10. 64 _____ tens _____ ones
    93 _____ tens _____ ones

PRACTICE

Write your own numbers. Circle the number that is more.

11. _____ _____ tens _____ ones
    _____ _____ tens _____ ones

12. _____ _____ tens _____ ones
    _____ _____ tens _____ ones

Problem Solving Visual Thinking

13. Circle the one that is more.

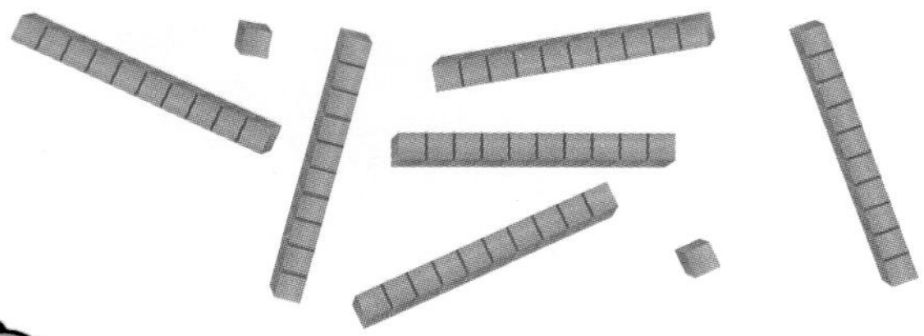

Notes for Home: Your child compared two numbers to tell which is less. *Home Activity:* Look for numbers while at the grocery store. How are they used (for example, to label aisles and to show cost)?

Name

Order Numbers to 100

Learn

Check

1. Write the missing numbers.

1	2	3	4					9	
	12				16				20
				25				29	
		33							40
41							48		
			54						
	62				66				
		73						79	
81						87			
				95					100

Talk About It Tell about 87. Use before, after, and between.

Notes for Home: Your child wrote the numbers 1 to 100 in order on a hundred chart. *Home Activity:* Ask your child to color the boxes that have a number that ends in 0. Talk about the pattern that you see (one column, the last, is colored. The numbers are 10 apart.)

Practice

Write the number that comes after.

2 64 65
3 26 ____
4 52 ____
5 49 ____
6 61 ____
7 75 ____

Write the number that comes before.

8 ____ 72
9 ____ 36
10 ____ 54
11 ____ 98
12 ____ 41
13 ____ 59

Write the numbers that come between .

14 27, ____, ____, 30
15 78, ____, ____, 81
16 57, ____, ____, 60
17 83, 84, ____, ____, 87

Problem Solving Critical Thinking

18 Jo picked three of these cards.
They were even numbers between 58 and 65.
Circle the cards she picked.

Notes for Home: Your child learned about numbers that come before, after, and between.
Home Activity: With your child take turns choosing a number between 1 and 100. Give clues about the number using more than, less than, before, after, and between.

For additional practice, see Skills Practice Bank, page 533, Set 2.

ALGEBRA READINESS

Name ______________________________

Patterns on the 100 Chart

Learn

1	2	3	4	5	6	7	8	9	10
11	12	13	14	15	16	17	18	19	20
21	22	23	24	25	26	27	28	29	30
31	32	33	34	35	36	37	38	39	40
41	42	43	44	45	46	47	48	49	50
51	52	53	54	55	56	57	58	59	60
61	62	63	64	65	66	67	68	69	70
71	72	73	74	75	76	77	78	79	80
81	82	83	84	85	86	87	88	89	90
91	92	93	94	95	96	97	98	99	100

I am coloring a pattern on my 100 chart. What is the next number in my pattern?

25

Check

Color the pattern.

1. Use red.
Begin at 20. Add 5 at a time.

2. Use orange.
Begin at 8. Add 10 at a time.

3. Use blue.
Begin at 52. Add 10 at a time.
Where do you stop? _____

4. Use yellow.
Begin at 34. Add 10 at a time.
Where do you stop? _____

Talk About It What pattern do the even numbers make?

Notes for Home: Your child colored number patterns on a hundred chart. *Home Activity:* Ask your child to find numbers on the chart, such as birthdays, ages of family members, familiar addresses, number of brothers and sisters, or number of children in the class.

Practice

Write the missing numbers.

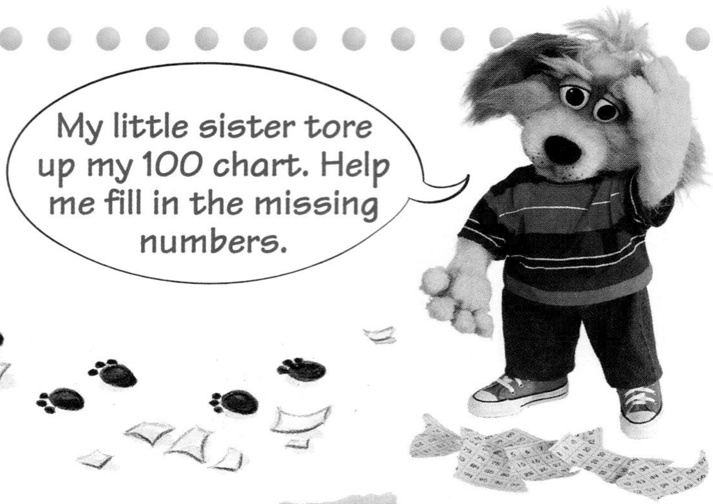

My little sister tore up my 100 chart. Help me fill in the missing numbers.

5

21	22	23
	32	33

6

	88		
	98	99	

7

	48	49	
57		59	

8

	74	75
83		

9

35	36		
	46		

10

8	9	
	19	

11

	55		57
64	65	66	67

Problem Solving Patterns

12 What comes next?
Circle the next shape in the pattern.

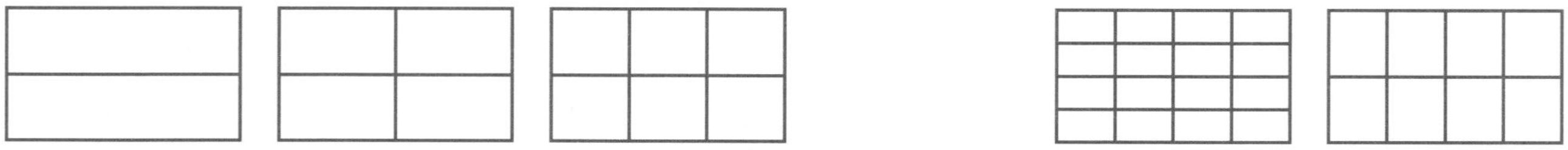

Notes for Home: Your child used the patterns in a hundred chart to help find missing numbers. *Home Activity:* Find patterns on old calendars with your child. Count by twos, threes, fours, or fives and color the boxes. Are the patterns the same as the ones on the hundred chart?

PRACTICE

Name ______________________

Reading for Math

Classify

1. What kinds of things are in the blue ring?

____

2. What other things can you put in the blue ring?

____

3. What kinds of things are in the red ring?

____

4. What other things can you put in the red ring?

____

Talk About It What can you put in both rings?

Notes for Home: Your child learned to read a diagram. *Home Activity:* With your child, look around your home to find things that have been sorted. How are they sorted? Why did someone sort them?

5 What kind of things are in the yellow ring?

____

6 What kind of things are in the green ring?

____

7 What kind of things are inside both rings?

____

Journal

8 Draw your own rings. Sort some toys you have.
Write about the way you sorted.
What things belong in both rings?

Notes for Home: Your child practiced reading a diagram. *Home Activity:* Use toys or other objects you have at home. With your child, think of different ways to sort them. You can use string to make the circles for your own diagram.

Name

Problem Solving: Collect and Use Data

Learn

PROBLEM SOLVING GUIDE

Understand • Plan • Solve • Look Back

Check

1. Put your name where it belongs.
Ask 4 friends to put their names in.

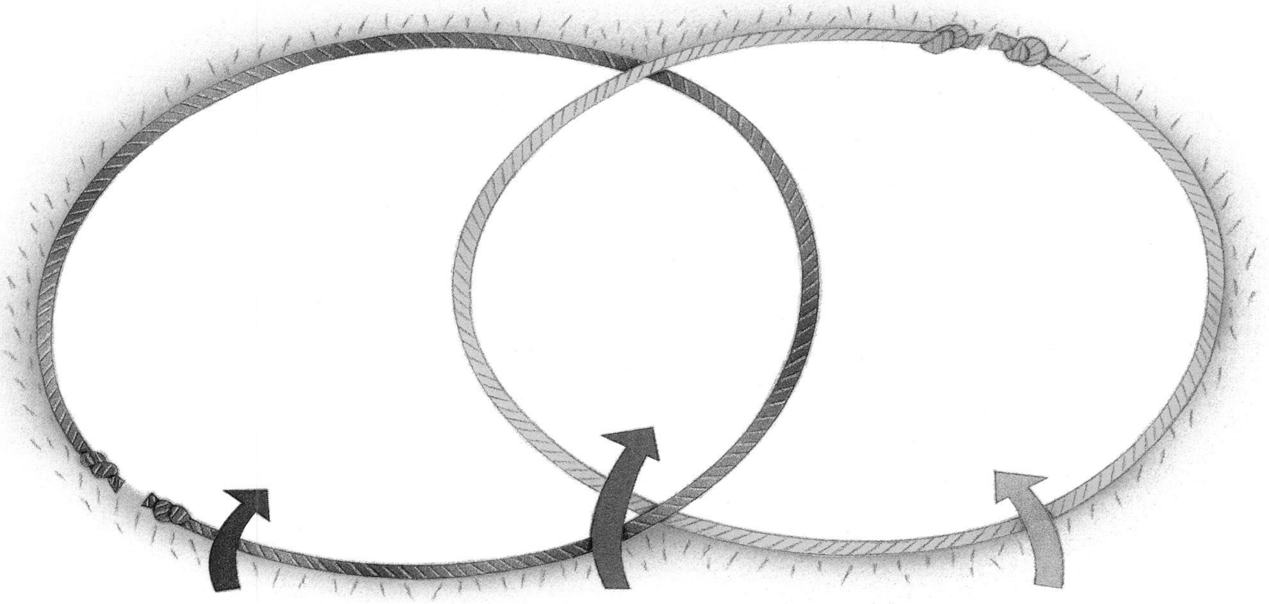

Likes to swim   Likes both   Likes to play soccer

Talk About It How many names are in your yellow ring? How many in your blue ring?

Notes for Home: Your child collected data and displayed it on a diagram. *Home Activity:* Make a diagram to show things your family likes, such as types of weather, sports, games, or foods.

Practice

2 Put your name where it belongs.
Ask 6 friends to put their names in.

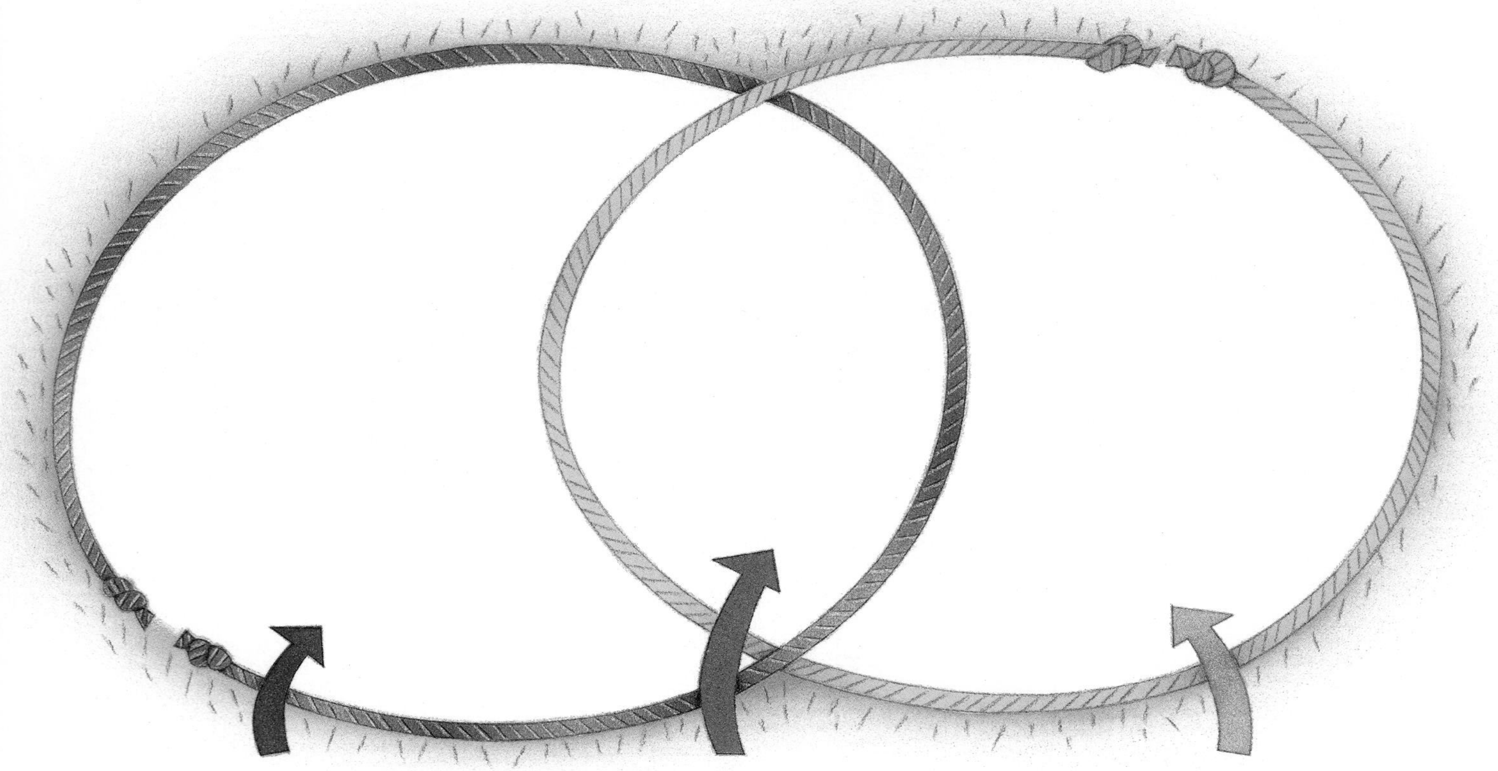

Plays on a team　　Likes to do both　　Likes to watch sports

Write About It

3 Which children put their names in the blue ring?

____

4 What can you tell about a child whose name

belongs in both rings? ______________________________

____

____

Notes for Home: Your child made a diagram and answered questions about it. *Home Activity:* Make a diagram to show places you and your child have been, hobbies, or what you had for dinner.

For additional practice, see Skills Practice Bank, page 533, Set 3.

Name ______________________________

Mixed Practice

Lessons 7–10

Concepts and Skills

1 Write the missing numbers.

31	32						38		40
				45	46				
51		53							60

Write the missing numbers.

2 37, 38, ____

3 ____, 60, 61

4 22, ____, 24

5 ____, 81, 82,

6 77, ____, 79

7 90, 91, ____

Problem Solving

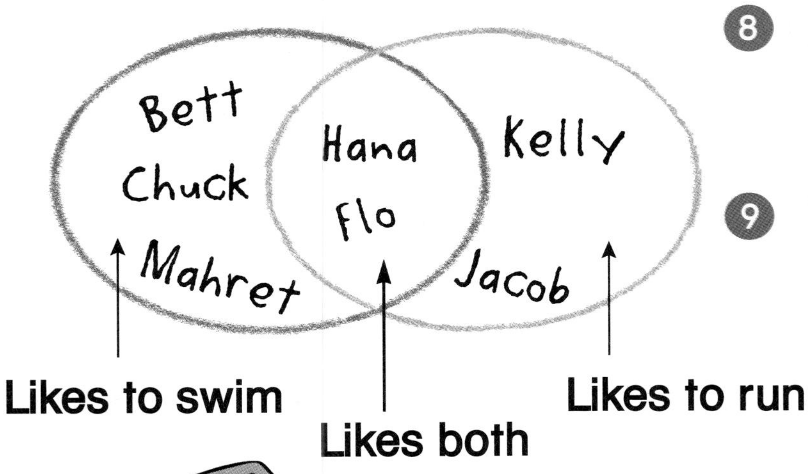

8 How many of the children like to swim? ____

9 Which children like to swim and run? ____________

Journal

10 Which is greater, 47 or 51? How do you know?

Notes for Home: Your child practiced using numbers to 99 and reading a diagram to solve problems. *Home Activity:* Find some things in your neighborhood that are in sets of 20–50. Can you find anything that comes in a group of more than 50? More than 100?

Name ______________________________

Cumulative Review

Chapters 1–8

Concepts and Skills

Subtract.

1. $\begin{array}{r} 3 \\ +\ 8 \\ \hline \end{array}$ $\begin{array}{r} 11 \\ -\ 8 \\ \hline \end{array}$

2. $\begin{array}{r} 5 \\ +\ 4 \\ \hline \end{array}$ $\begin{array}{r} 9 \\ -\ 4 \\ \hline \end{array}$

3. $\begin{array}{r} 4 \\ -\ 3 \\ \hline \end{array}$ $\begin{array}{r} 1 \\ +\ 3 \\ \hline \end{array}$

4. 1 + 8 = ____
   9 − 8 = ____

5. 0 + 8 = ____
   8 − 8 − ____

6. 3 + 4 = ____
   7 − 4 = ____

Problem Solving

7. Circle the shape that shows one half.

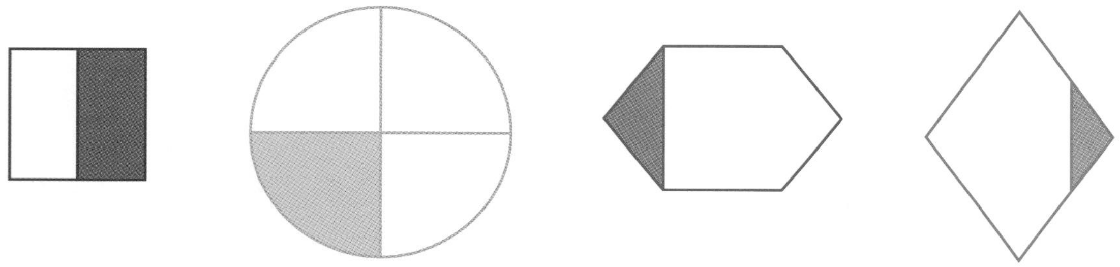

Test Prep

Fill in the ○ for the correct answer.
What number comes next?

8. 2, 4, 6, 8, ____

   ○ 9 ○ 10 ○ 11 ○ 12

9. 5, 10, 15, 20, ____

   ○ 21 ○ 22 ○ 25 ○ 30

Notes for Home: Your child reviewed basic addition and subtraction facts, problem solving, and skip counting. *Home Activity:* Ask your child to call out the numbers on a license plate. Have your child add or subtract the first two numbers.

Name ______________________________

Chapter 8 Review

Vocabulary

Write the tens and ones. Circle the number that is less.

1. 46 _____ tens _____ ones
   90 _____ tens _____ ones

2. 32 _____ tens _____ ones
   18 _____ ten _____ ones

Write the tens and ones. Circle the number that is greater.

3. 50 _____ tens _____ ones
   28 _____ tens _____ ones

4. 52 _____ tens _____ ones
   64 _____ tens _____ ones

Concepts and Skills

Count how many tens and ones. Write the number.

5. 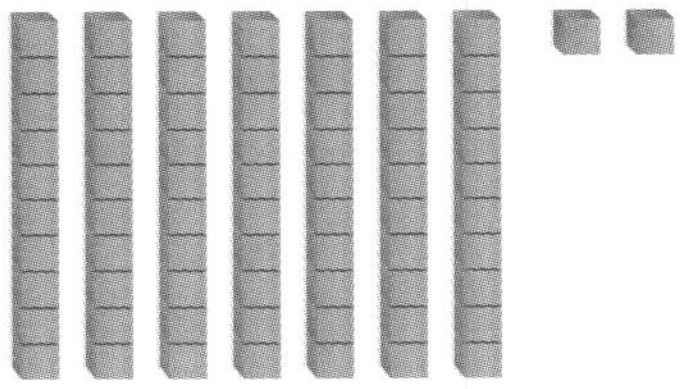

tens	ones

_____

Problem Solving

Use 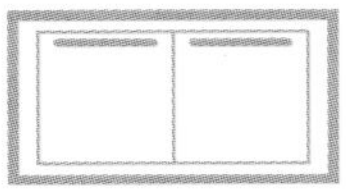 and 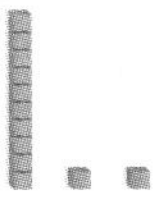. Exchange 10 ones for 1 ten if you need to.

6. The Kits scored these points in a game.
   What is the final score?

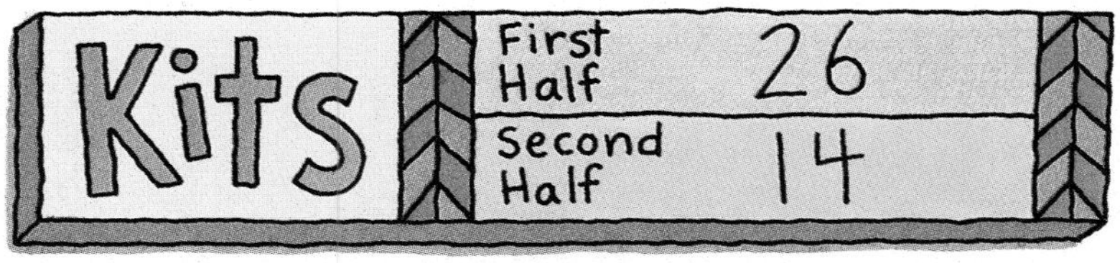

tens	ones

Final score _____ points

Notes for Home: Your child reviewed vocabulary, numbers to 100, and problem solving. *Home Activity:* Use an old calendar or a hundred chart to keep track of numbers you see in your neighborhood. When your child finds a number, color in the box on the chart or circle the number on the calendar.

Name

Chapter 8 Test

You can use 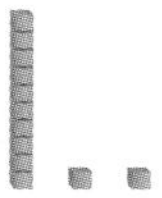 .

1 Count how many.

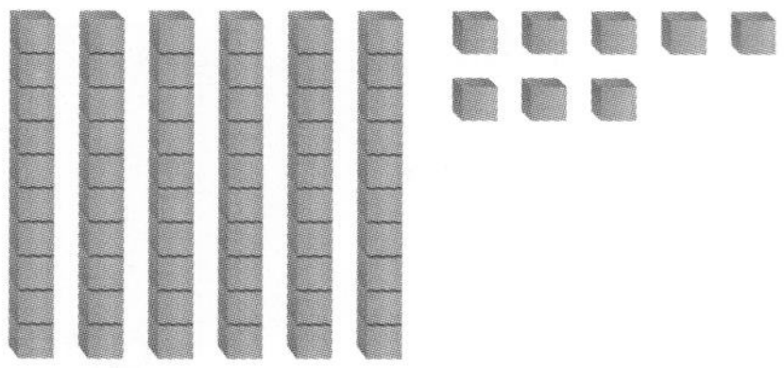

Add 2 more.
Do you need to exchange?

yes

no

Write how many tens and ones.

tens	ones

2 Estimate how many. Make groups of 10.

10

30

50

3 Write the missing numbers.

	63			66
72			75	

Write the numbers that come before, after, and between.

4 _____, 86, _____

5 68, _____, _____, 71

Answer the questions.

6 How many play soccer? _____

7 Who plays soccer and t-ball?

____

____

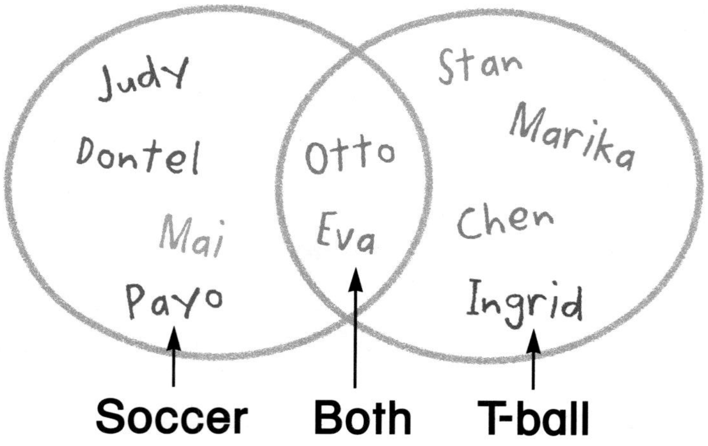

Notes for Home: Your child was assessed on the concepts, skills, and problem solving taught in Chapter 8. *Home Activity:* Draw some numbers with your child using objects instead of numbers. Use happy faces to show how many tens, and bow ties to show how many ones.

Name ____

Performance Assessment

Chapter 8

Choose a number.

46 **68** **79** **87**

Use 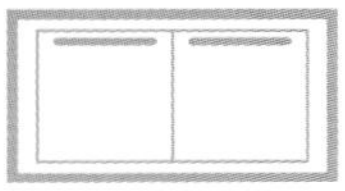 and 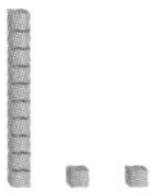 to show the number.
Add one or two each time.
Complete the chart.

Write your number. ______

		Number added	New number
1	Add one or two. Circle. Write the number.	1 2	______
2	Add one or two. Circle. Write the number.	1 2	______
3	Add one or two. Circle. Write the number.	1 2	______
4	Add one or two. Circle. Write the number.	1 2	______
5	Add one or two. Circle. Write the number.	1 2	______

Problem Solving Critical Thinking

6. Write a number that is greater than your final number. ______

7. Write a number that is less than your final number. ______

Notes for Home: Your child did an activity that assessed understanding of number concepts for numbers to 100. *Home Activity:* Ask your child to write down a number from 1–100 and then circle the ones and mark an X on the tens.

Name ______________________

Explore with a CALCULATOR

Count On by 10

Keys You Will Use [ON/C] [+] [−] [=]

1. Enter an odd number between 20 and 50. Write it. ______
   Press [+] [1] [0]. Write the display. ______
   Press [=]. Write the display. ______
   Press [=]. Write the display. ______

2. Enter an odd number between 50 and 90. Write it. ______
   Press [−] [1] [0]. Write the display. ______
   Press [=]. Write the display. ______
   Press [=]. Write the display. ______

3. What number would you need to enter if you pressed [+] [1] [0] [=] [=] and the display reads 53? ______

4. What number would you need to enter if you pressed [−] [1] [0] [=] [=] and the display reads 47? ______

Tech Talk What calculator steps did you use to find the answers for the last question?

Visit our Web site. www.parent.mathsurf.com

Number Hunt

Get the sports section of your local newspaper. Better make sure everyone has read it first. Now go on a number hunt. Circle every number you can find on one page.

Whoops…don't forget the numbers that are written as words, too.

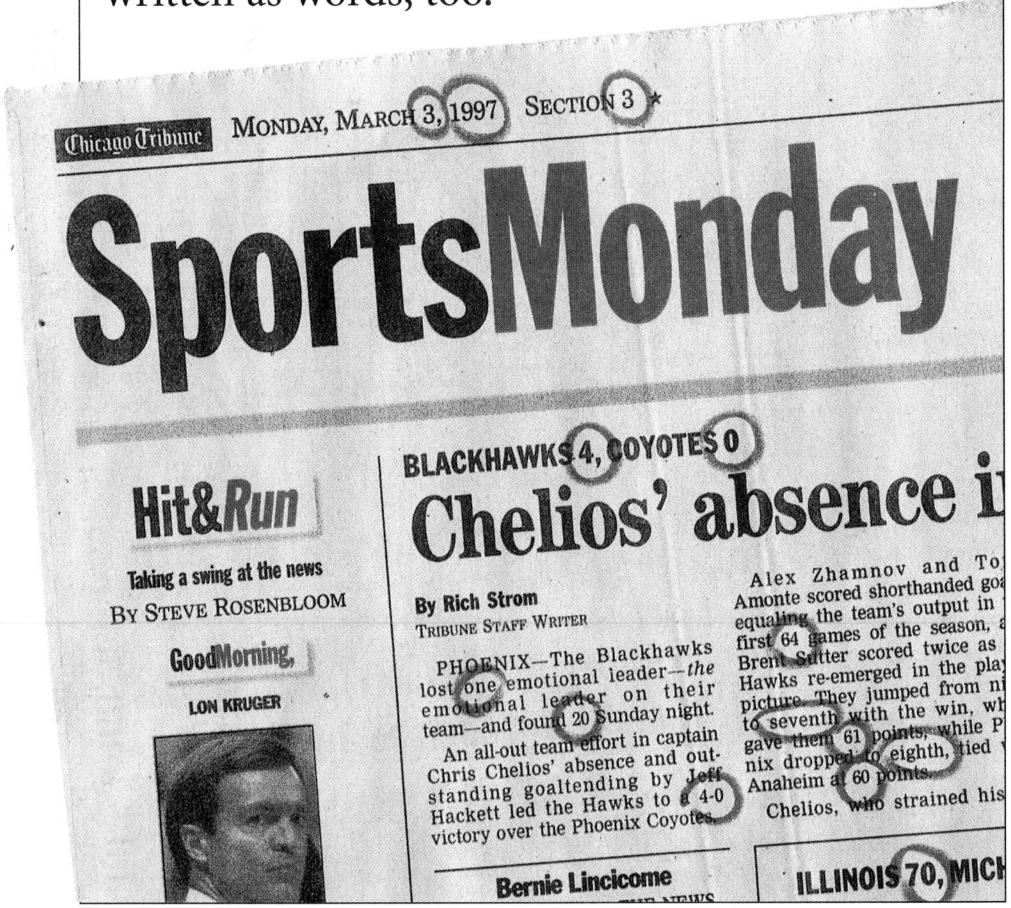
Chicago Tribune MONDAY, MARCH 3, 1997 SECTION 3 *

SportsMonday

Hit&Run

Taking a swing at the news

BY STEVE ROSENBLOOM

GoodMorning,

LON KRUGER

BLACKHAWKS 4, COYOTES 0

Chelios' absence i

By Rich Strom

TRIBUNE STAFF WRITER

PHOENIX—The Blackhawks lost one emotional leader—*the* emotional leader on their team—and found 20 Sunday night.

An all-out team effort in captain Chris Chelios' absence and outstanding goaltending by Jeff Hackett led the Hawks to a 4-0 victory over the Phoenix Coyotes.

Alex Zhamnov and To Amonte scored shorthanded go equaling the team's output in first 64 games of the season, Brent Sutter scored twice as Hawks re-emerged in the pla picture. They jumped from n to seventh with the win, wh gave them 61 points, while P nix dropped to eighth, tied Anaheim at 60 points.

Chelios, who strained his

Bernie Lincicome

ILLINOIS 70, MICH

Fold down

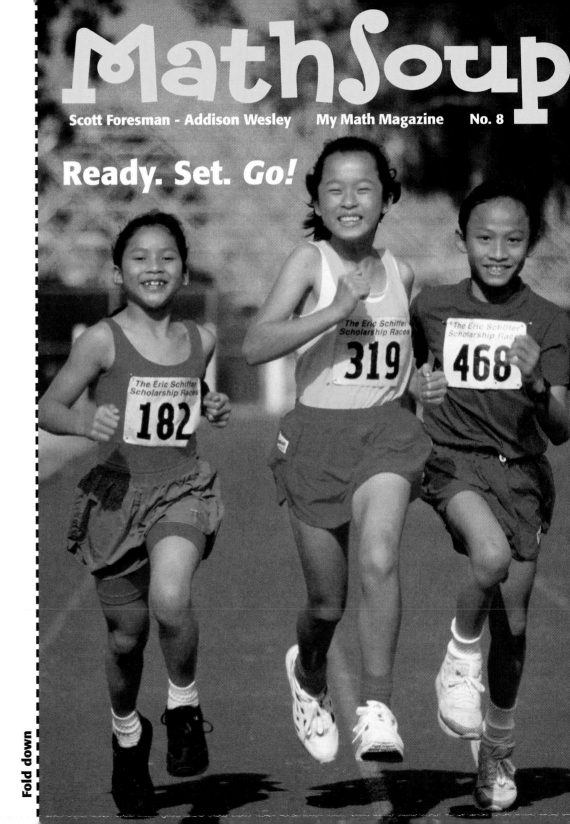

MathSoup

Scott Foresman - Addison Wesley My Math Magazine No. 8

Ready. Set. *Go!*

Break the Record

Is there something you like to do a lot?
Make your own record book.
Can you beat your own "world" record?
Here are a few ideas to get your book started.

How long can you hula-hoop?

How far can you kick a ball?

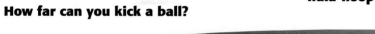

What You Need

A soft ball for each player, and a bowling pin made from a two-liter soda bottle filled with sand. Four to six players works best.

How to Play

1 Make a starting line. Then set your soda-bottle pin 20 to 30 feet from the starting line.
2 Roll the ball toward the pin. Try to get the ball as close to the pin as you can.
3 Players can knock another player's ball out of the way. After everyone has bowled, the player whose ball is the closest to the pin is the winner.

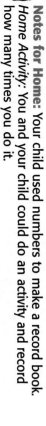

Notes for Home: Your child used numbers to make a record book. *Home Activity:* You and your child could do an activity and record how many times you do it.

Let's Mazate!

Mazate (mah-ZAH-tay) is a bowling game played in Guatemala. You can play it at home!

Notes for Home: Your child played a Central American bowling game. *Home Activity:* When playing games at home, ask your child to keep score.

How many times can you jump rope?

Ready, Set, Goal

How to Play

1 Use strips of masking tape to lay out a game board like this on a desk or table top.

2 Label as shown.

3 Flick a paper clip with your finger from the edge of the table. If you land inside 10, you score 10. Take turns shooting. Keep track of your score. Try to score 100.

Notes for Home: Your child played a game that practices adding tens. *Home Activity:* With your child, look at games you play to see how numbers are used.

CHAPTER

9

Money

Notes for Home: Your child compared prices in this picture to see which items could be purchased for 75¢. *Home Activity:* Ask your child to tell you which items in the picture could be purchased with 75¢.

Math at Home

Dear Family,
Our class is starting Chapter 9. We will learn about money. We will count and make groups of pennies, nickels, dimes, and quarters. Here are some activities we can do together.

10¢ Store

Make a 10¢ store with your child. Gather items and pretend to sell them to each other for 10¢ or less. Have available 1 dime, 2 nickels, and 10 pennies.

Making Cents

Help your child look for coupons or ads in the newspaper. When you find items for less than 99¢, take turns using pennies, nickels, and dimes to show the amount. You can also compare items to see which costs more or less.

Community Connection

When doing errands with your child, point out coin-operated machines such as newspaper vending machines and public telephones. Identify the coins needed to operate them.

Visit our Web site. www.parent.mathsurf.com

Name

Nickels and Pennies

Learn

I penny
I ¢
I cent

I nickel
5¢
5 cents

I can show 5¢ with 5 pennies or with 1 nickel.

or

Check

Count. Write the amount. You can use .

1  5 ¢

2  ____ ¢

3  ____ ¢

4  ____ ¢

5  ____ ¢

Talk About It You have I nickel and 2 pennies.
Which coin do you count first? Why?

Notes for Home: Your child counted groups including a nickel and pennies and learned that 5 pennies and 1 nickel have the same value. *Home Activity:* Using a nickel and pennies, have your child find their total value. Repeat using a different amount.

Practice

Circle the coins you need.

6

7

8

9

10

PRACTICE

Problem Solving Patterns

11 Is there enough money to buy the flower?
Count the nickels by 5s.
Circle Yes or No.

5 ¢ 10 ¢ 15 ¢ ____ ¢ ____ ¢

Yes

No

Notes for Home: Your child practiced counting groups of nickels and pennies. *Home Activity:* Using coins, ask your child to show you two ways to make 8¢ (a nickel and 3 pennies or 8 pennies).

Name ______________________________

Dimes and Pennies

Learn

1 dime
10¢
10 cents

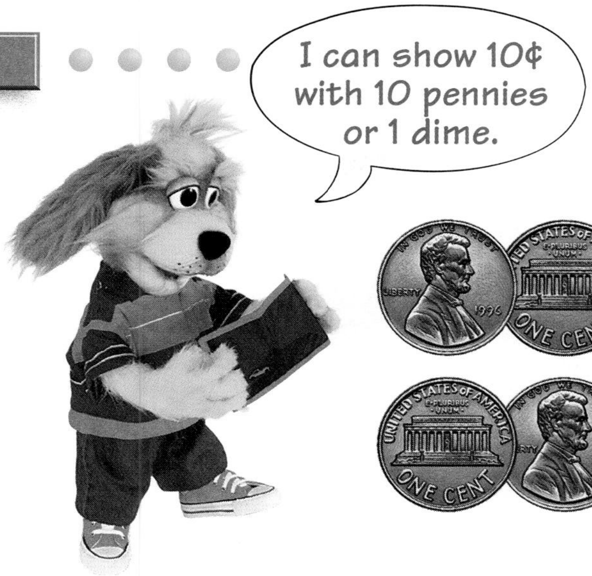

I can show 10¢ with 10 pennies or 1 dime.

or

Check

Count. Write the amount. You can use  .

1

10 ¢

2

_____ ¢

3

_____ ¢

Talk About It What coins do these drawings show?

Notes for Home: Your child counted groups including a dime and pennies and learned that 10 pennies and 1 dime have the same value. *Home Activity:* Using a dime and pennies, have your child find the value of the coins. Repeat using a different amount.

Practice

Circle the coins you need.

4

5

6

7

8

PRACTICE

Problem Solving Critical Thinking

9 Ryan has 1 coin.
June has 2 coins.
Each has 10¢.
What coins do they have?
Draw their coins.

Notes for Home: Your child practiced counting groups of dimes and pennies. *Home Activity:* Using coins, ask your child to show you two ways to make 11¢ (a dime and a penny or 11 pennies).

Name ______________________________

Dimes, Nickels, and Pennies

Learn

Count by 10s. Count by ones.

10 20 30 31 32 33

33 ¢

Count by 5s. Count by ones.

5 10 15 16 17

17 ¢

Check

Use . Count by 10s or 5s and ones. Write the amount.

1

10, 20, 30, 40, 41, 42 — 42 ¢

2

____, ____, ____, ____, ____, ____ — ____ ¢

Talk About It Is a big coin worth more than a smaller coin? Is a small coin worth less than a bigger coin?

Notes for Home: Your child counted dimes and pennies and nickels and pennies. *Home Activity:* Have your child find the value of a group of dimes and pennies. Repeat using nickels and pennies.

Practice

Count. Write the amount.

3 

33 ¢

10, 20, ____, ____, ____, ____

4 

____ ¢

____, ____, ____, ____, ____, ____

5 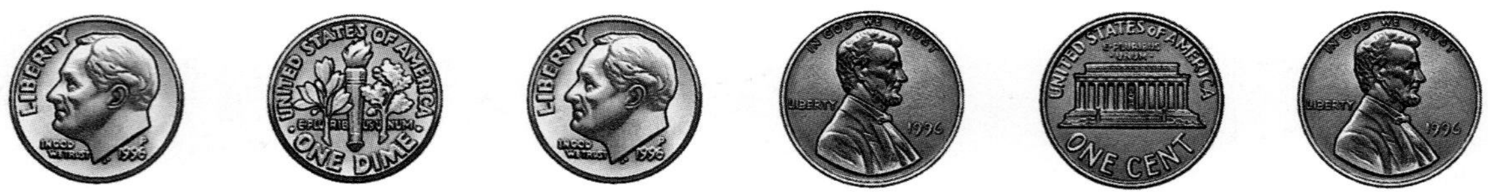

____ ¢

____, ____, ____, ____, ____, ____

PRACTICE

Problem Solving Critical Thinking

6 Which bank has more coins? Circle it.
Which has more money? Draw a box around it.
Write each amount.

____ ¢

____ ¢

Notes for Home: Your child counted groups of coins by 10s, 5s, and ones. *Home Activity:* Look at the Problem Solving activity. Ask your child to explain how the bank with fewer coins could have more money (A dime is worth 10¢. 3 pennies and 1 nickel are worth only 8¢.).

For additional practice, see Skills Practice Bank, page 534, Set 1.

Name ____________________

Count Mixed Coins

Learn

Count by 10s, 5s, and ones. Start with the coin of greatest value.

10, 20, 25, 30, 31 — 31 ¢

Check

Count. Write the amount. You can use .

1. 

10, 15, 16, 17 — 17 ¢

2. 

____, ____, ____, ____ — ____ ¢

3. 

____, ____, ____, ____, ____ — ____ ¢

Talk About It Count some coins by starting with pennies instead of dimes. Is it harder or easier?

Notes for Home: Your child learned to count groups of dimes, nickels, and pennies by counting by 10s, 5s, and ones. *Home Activity:* Ask your child to show you how to count a group of dimes, nickels, and pennies.

Practice

Circle the coins you need.

4 

5 

6 

7 

PRACTICE

Mental Math

8 Kofi bought a toy. It cost more than 5 nickels but less than 3 dimes. Circle the toy Kofi bought.

Notes for Home: Your child decided which coins are needed to buy an item. *Home Activity:* Ask your child to show you the coins needed to buy the toys at the bottom of the page (for example, 2 dimes, 1 nickel, and 4 pennies is 29¢).

Name ______________________________

Spin and Exchange

Players 2 to 4

What You Need

10 pennies each

4 nickels each

paper clip

pencil

How to Play

1. Put all coins in one pile.
2. Take turns spinning.
3. Take that many pennies.
4. Exchange for a nickel when you have 5 pennies.
5. The winner is the first player with 4 nickels.

Play Again with Dimes

Use the rules for Spin and Exchange.
Each player will need 10 pennies and 3 dimes.
The winner is the first player with 3 dimes.

Notes for Home: Your child played a game to practice exchanging pennies for nickels and dimes.
Home Activity: Play Spin and Exchange with your child.

Name ______________________

STOP and Practice

Count the money. Write the amount.

1

_____ ¢

2

_____ ¢

3

_____ ¢

4

_____ ¢

5

_____ ¢

Write your own.

6 How much could this cost?
Write a price between 10¢ and 50¢.
Draw the coins.

_____ ¢

Notes for Home: Your child practiced counting groups of dimes, nickels, and pennies. *Home Activity:* Ask your child to show you how to count by 10s, 5s, and ones when counting groups of dimes, nickels, and pennies.

PRACTICE

Name ______________________________

Problem Solving: Use Data from a Picture

Learn

PROBLEM SOLVING GUIDE

Understand • Plan • Solve • Look Back

Check

Count the money. Write the amount.
Circle the toys each child can buy.

1 Kira has

36 ¢

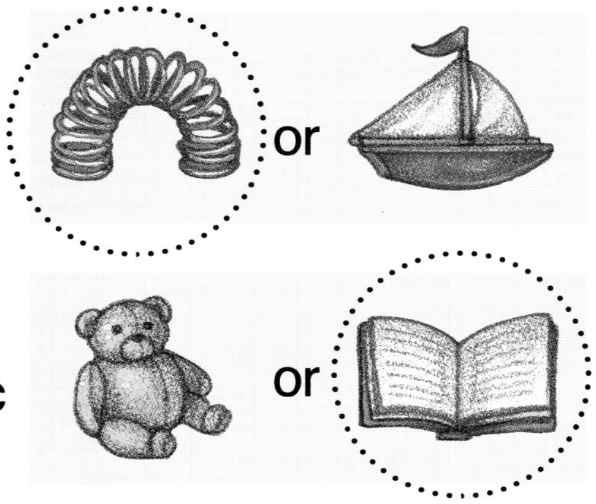

2 Pedro has

______ ¢

Talk About It How did you know which toys the children could buy?

Notes for Home: Your child solved problems by finding which of two items shown in a picture could be bought with a group of coins. *Home Activity:* Show 45¢. Ask your child to tell which item or items in the picture he or she could buy (any of the items except the stuffed bear).

Practice

Use the picture. Count the money.
Write the amount. Circle the toy you can buy.

3. You have

26 ¢

4. You have

_____ ¢

Write About It

5. Choose one thing to buy from Lee's store. Circle it. Draw the coins you can use.

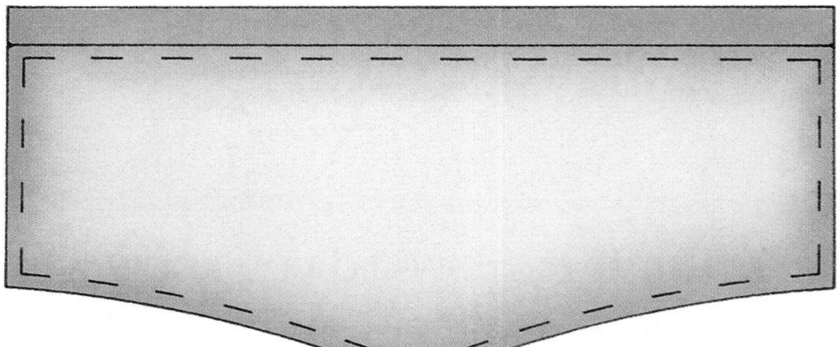

Notes for Home: Your child practiced solving problems using information in a picture. *Home Activity:* Label small objects such as a pencil or a juice box with amounts under 50¢. Provide dimes, nickels, and pennies and ask your child to show the coins needed to buy each item.

For additional practice, see Skills Practice Bank, page 534, Set 2.

Name

Mixed Practice

Lessons 1–5

Concepts and Skills

Count the money. Write the amount.

1 

_____ ¢

_____, _____, _____, _____, _____

2 

_____ ¢

_____, _____, _____, _____, _____, _____, _____

Problem Solving

3 Count your money. Write the amount.

_____ ¢

4 Circle what you can buy.

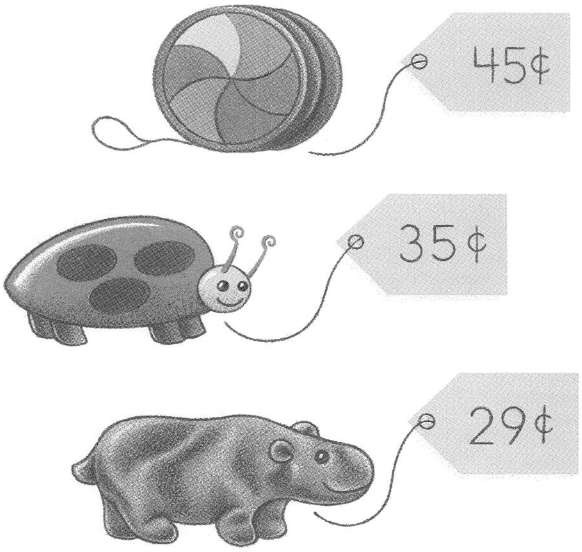

Journal

5 Pretend you have a store. What would you sell?
How much money would it cost?

Notes for Home: Your child practiced counting groups of dimes, nickels, and pennies.
Home Activity: Show a group of coins such as 2 dimes, 1 nickel, and 4 pennies and ask your child to show how to count the coins.

MIXED PRACTICE

Name ______________________________

Cumulative Review

Chapters 1–9

Concepts and Skills

Write the numbers.

1 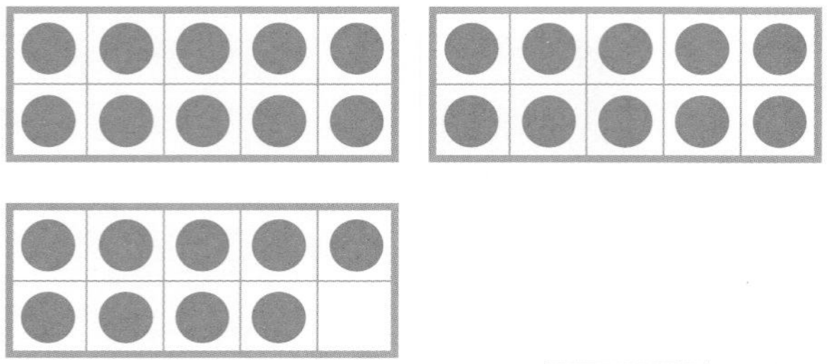 ______

2 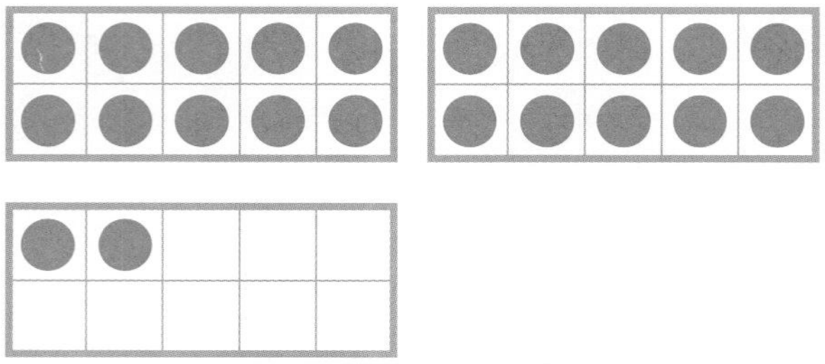 ______

Add or subtract.

3

$$\begin{array}{r} 3 \\ +\ 7 \\ \hline \end{array} \quad \begin{array}{r} 11 \\ -\ 8 \\ \hline \end{array} \quad \begin{array}{r} 12 \\ -\ 5 \\ \hline \end{array} \quad \begin{array}{r} 5 \\ +\ 4 \\ \hline \end{array} \quad \begin{array}{r} 3 \\ +\ 8 \\ \hline \end{array} \quad \begin{array}{r} 6 \\ +\ 4 \\ \hline \end{array} \quad \begin{array}{r} 12 \\ -\ 9 \\ \hline \end{array}$$

Problem Solving

Complete the number sentence.

4 Mr. Wood bought 6 red apples.
He bought 6 yellow apples.
How many apples did he buy?

_____ + _____ = _____

5 Susan bought 10 cherries.
She ate 5.
How many cherries are left?

_____ − _____ = _____

Test Prep

Fill in the ○ for the correct answer.

6 Which number is greater than 75?

42 ○ 23 ○ 78 ○ 50 ○

7 Which number is less than 46?

45 ○ 48 ○ 51 ○ 60 ○

Notes for Home: Your child reviewed counting to 50, using addition and subtraction, and comparing numbers. *Home Activity:* Open a book to a page less than 100. Ask your child to name a number that is greater than or less than that number.

Name

Explore Quarters

Explore

1 quarter
25¢
25 cents

Use .
Find 3 ways to show 25¢.
Draw the coins.

1

2

3

Share

Do you think there are more ways
to show 25¢? Explain.

Notes for Home: Your child learned that a quarter has the value of 25¢ and that this amount can be made with several groups of coins. *Home Activity:* Ask your child to use coins to show you some ways to make 25¢.

EXPLORE

Connect

10, 20, 25

25 ¢

Here are two ways to show 25¢

Circle the coins that show 25¢.

4

5

6

Problem Solving

7 You have 5 coins in your pocket.
The coins are worth 25¢.
Draw the coins you have.

Notes for Home: Your child practiced counting groups of coins that make 25¢. *Home Activity:* Ask your child to show you 25¢ using 4 coins (1 dime and 3 nickels).

Name ______________________________

Quarters, Dimes, Nickels, and Pennies

Learn

Start with 25¢. Then count on.

25, 35, 40, 41

41 ¢

Check

Count the money. Write the amount.

You can use .

1 

25, 35, 45, 55, 65

65 ¢

2 

25, 30, 35, ____, ____

____ ¢

3 

____, ____, ____, ____

____ ¢

Talk About It What pattern do you see in Problem 1?

Notes for Home: Your child counted groups of quarters, dimes, nickels, and pennies.
Home Activity: Have your child find the value of a group of quarters, dimes, nickels, and pennies.

Practice

Count the money. Write the amount.

4 

60 ¢

25, 35, 45, 50, 55, 60

5 

_____ ¢

_____, _____, _____, _____, _____

6 

_____ ¢

_____, _____, _____ _____, _____

PRACTICE

Problem Solving Critical Thinking

You have 25¢. Write what you can buy.

ring	yoyo	horn	ball	charm
10¢	15¢	20¢	5¢	5¢

7 _______________ and _______________ or

8 _______________ and _______________ and _______________.

Notes for Home: Your child counted mixed groups of coins. *Home Activity:* Ask your child which toys he or she could buy with 15¢ (yoyo; ring and ball; ring and charm).

For additional practice, see Skills Practice Bank, page 534, Set 3.

Name ______________________________

Reading for Math

Read a Table

Erica earns money doing jobs.

How Erica Earns Money			
Feed cat	2	1	
Water plants		3	5

Use .

How much money did Erica earn for each job?

Read across each row to find out.

Feed cat

1. How many dimes? _____
2. How many nickels? _____
3. How many pennies? _____
4. How much in all? _____ ¢

Water plants

5. How many dimes? _____
6. How many nickels? _____
7. How many pennies? _____
8. How much in all? _____ ¢

Talk About It Think of a job you can do. How much would it cost to do?

Notes for Home: Your child leaned how to read a table. *Home Activity:* Help your child make a table that shows ways to earn money.

Justin went shopping at a yard sale.

What Justin Bought			
Book		2	10
Hat	3	1	

Use  .

How much money did Justin spend for each thing at the yard sale? Read across the rows to find out.

Book

9. How many dimes? ______
10. How many nickels? ______
11. How many pennies? ______
12. How much did the book cost? ______¢

Hat

13. How many dimes? ______
14. How many nickels? ______
15. How many pennies? ______
16. How much did the hat cost? ______¢

Notes for Home: Your child read a table to answer questions. *Home Activity:* Add numbers to the dime and penny sections in the table above. Have your child read the table to find the new cost of the book and puzzle.

Name

Problem Solving: Make a List

Learn

PROBLEM SOLVING GUIDE

Understand • Plan • Solve • Look Back

Walk the dog
Earn 15¢
1
1
3
Yesterday I earned a dime and a nickel.
Today I earned 3 nickels. I made a list.

Check

1 Use  to find some ways to show 15¢. Make a list.

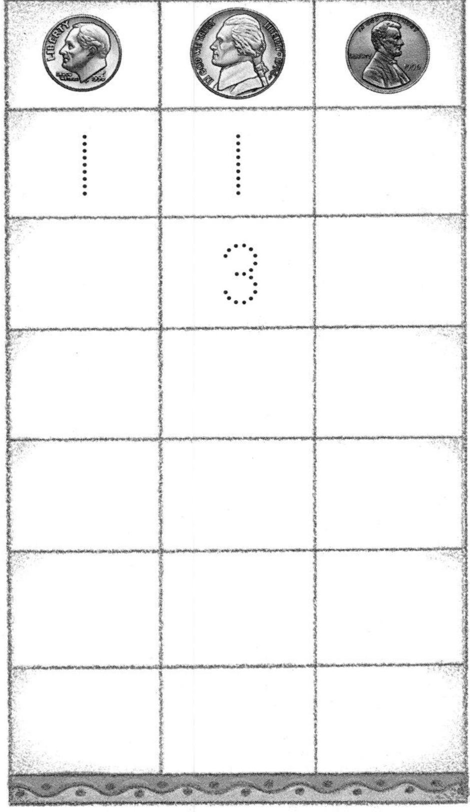

1	1	
	3	

Talk About It How do you know if you found all of the ways to show 15¢?

Notes for Home: Your child made a list of ways to show 15¢. *Home Activity:* Ask your child to show you 15¢ using the fewest and the most number of coins possible (fewest: dime and nickel; most: 15 pennies).

PROBLEM SOLVING

Practice

Pat earns 20¢ for washing the dishes.
What coins might Pat get?

2 Use  to find some ways to show 20¢.
Make a list.

2		

Journal

3 What can you buy for 15¢ or 20¢?

Notes for Home: Your child made a list of ways to show 20¢. *Home Activity:* Ask your child to show you 20¢ using the fewest and the most number of coins possible (fewest: 2 dimes; most: 20 pennies).

Name ________________________________

Mixed Practice

Lessons 6–8

Concepts and Skills

1 Circle the coins that show 25¢.

2 Count the money. Write the amount.

_____ ¢

_____, _____, _____, _____, _____, _____

Problem Solving

3 Christina and J. P. sold lemonade for 10¢ a glass.
Find ways to make 10¢.
Make a list.

Journal

4 Would you rather have a handful of pennies or a handful of quarters? Why?

Notes for Home: Your child practiced counting groups of coins, and solving a problem by making a list. *Home Activity:* Ask your child to show you several ways to show 25¢ (such as, 1 quarter, 2 dimes and 1 nickel; 5 nickels, 25 pennies, and so on).

Name ______________________________

Cumulative Review

Chapters 1–9

Concepts and Skills

Add or subtract.

1 $\begin{array}{r} 11 \\ -\ 2 \\ \hline \end{array}$ $\begin{array}{r} 8 \\ +\ 2 \\ \hline \end{array}$ $\begin{array}{r} 5 \\ +\ 7 \\ \hline \end{array}$ $\begin{array}{r} 10 \\ -\ 9 \\ \hline \end{array}$ $\begin{array}{r} 12 \\ -\ 3 \\ \hline \end{array}$ $\begin{array}{r} 5 \\ +\ 6 \\ \hline \end{array}$ $\begin{array}{r} 6 \\ +\ 6 \\ \hline \end{array}$

2 $6 + 2 =$ ____ $9 - 7 =$ ____ $4 + 6 =$ ____

Problem Solving

Read the graph.

3 How many pennies does Tony have? ____

4 How many more pennies does Misha need to have 30? ____

Test Prep

Fill in the ○ for the correct answer.

Which number sentence is not part of the fact family?

5

○ $2 + 4 = 6$

○ $6 - 3 = 3$

○ $6 - 4 = 2$

○ $4 + 2 = 6$

6

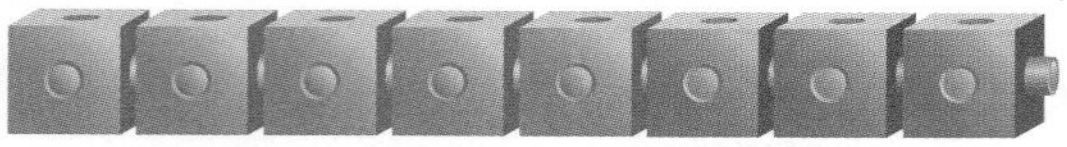

○ $5 + 3 = 8$

○ $8 - 3 = 5$

○ $5 + 4 = 9$

○ $8 - 5 = 3$

Notes for Home: Your child reviewed addition and subtraction facts, reading a graph, and finding facts in a fact family. *Home Activity:* Ask your child how many dimes Misha would have if he exchanged his pennies for dimes (2 dimes).

Name ______________________________

Chapter 9 Review

Vocabulary

1 Draw a line to match.

5¢	25¢	1¢	10¢
nickel	quarter	penny	dime

Concepts and Skills

Count the money. Write the amount.

2

_____ ¢

3

_____ ¢

Problem Solving

4 Write the amount.
Circle what you can buy.

You have _____ ¢.

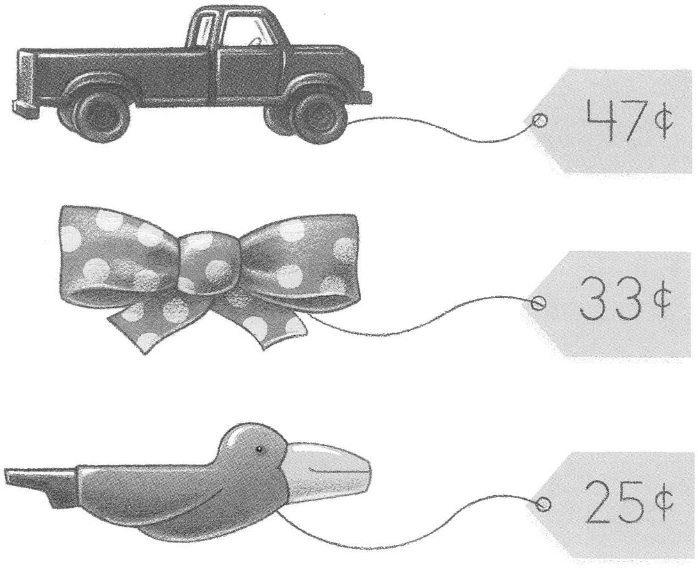

Notes for Home: Children reviewed the vocabulary, concepts, skills, and problem solving taught in Chapter 9. *Home Activity:* Ask your child to pick a handful of coins and count them aloud to find the total.

Name

Chapter 9 Test

Count the money. Write the amount.

1. 

_____ ¢

2. 

_____ ¢

3. Count your money.

Write the amount. _____ ¢

Circle what you can buy.

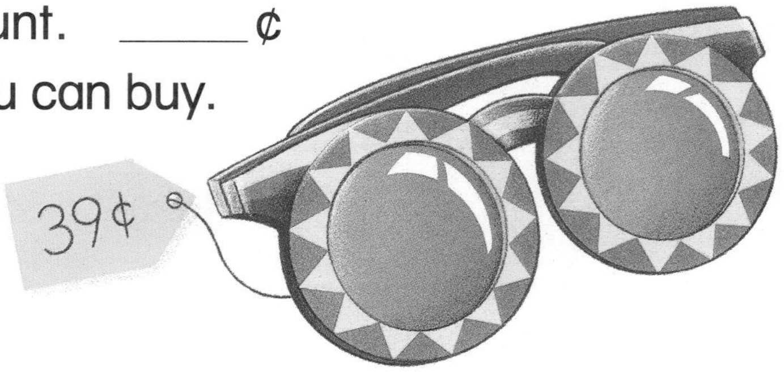

4. Find 4 ways to show 25¢.
Make a list.

Notes for Home: Your child was assessed on counting groups of coins and on problem solving. *Home Activity:* Ask your child how to show 47¢ in several ways, such as 1 quarter, 2 dimes, and 2 pennies.

Name

Performance Assessment

Chapter 9

Put these coins in a bag.
1 quarter, 4 dimes, 4 nickels, 4 pennies.

Take 5 coins from the bag. Draw them.	Write the amount.	Draw what you can buy.
1	____¢	
2	____¢	
3	____¢	

Problem Solving Critical Thinking

4 Which things could you buy from the School Store with 3 dimes? How do you know?

Notes for Home: Your child did an activity that assessed Chapter 9 skills and concepts.
Home Activity: Ask your child to use coins and show the amount for each item in the School Store.

Name ______________________________

Explore with a CALCULATOR

Count the Money

Keys You Will Use [ON/C] [+] [=]

Use your  to add.
Find out how much each friend has.

					Total
Mario	1	2	1	1	
Peg	0	3	2	1	
Bert	1	2	2	3	
Alma	0	5	1	7	

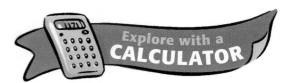

Use the chart to solve.

1. Who has 41¢? ______________
2. Who has 10¢ more than Peg? ______________
3. Who has 7¢ less than Bert? ______________
4. How much does Alma need to have 75¢? ______________

Tech Talk What 2 numbers can you press to show 2 dimes? [ ] [ ]

Visit our Web site. www.parent.mathsurf.com

Flip Your Lid

Can you make pennies float?

What You Need

a small plastic lid, a tub of water, and lots of pennies

What You Do

1 Float the lid in the tub of water.

2 Place pennies, one at a time, on the lid.

How many pennies can you float before the lid sinks? Try a larger lid. Can you float more or fewer pennies now?

Fold down

MathSoup

Scott Foresman - Addison Wesley My Math Magazine No. 9

Welcome to Penny Lane

On which side of Penny Lane would you like to live? Why?

So Many Pennies

People save pennies for many reasons.
What would you do with lots of pennies?

Over 100 years ago, the Statue of Liberty had no place to stand. School children sent their pennies and dimes to help pay for a pedestal so Lady Liberty could stand in New York Harbor.

This is our 3rd president, Thomas Jefferson.

This building was his home in Virginia.

This is our 32nd president, Franklin D. Roosevelt.

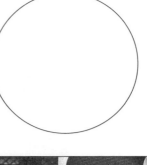

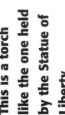

This is a torch like the one held by the Statue of Liberty.

Make your own coin.

Whose picture will you put on your coin?

How much will your coin be worth?

Notes for Home: Your child read about children's pennies that contributed to large projects. *Home Activity:* Encourage your child to collect pennies and then use them for themselves or a charitable donation.

Coin Stories

Take a close look at a penny, nickel, and dime. What do you see?

This is our 16th president, Abraham Lincoln.

This building is the Lincoln Memorial. Can you see the statue of Lincoln inside?

Children gave more than 300,000 pennies to help build this park in Evanston, Illinois. So what do you call a park like this? Penny Park, of course.

A statue in Philadelphia, Pennsylvania is made of pennies! Schoolchildren there collected 80,000 pennies to make a statue of Benjamin Franklin, who once said, "A penny saved is a penny earned."

Notes for Home: Your child learned about the designs on U. S. coins. *Home Activity:* Have your child do a rubbing of a coin by placing a piece of lightweight paper over a coin and lightly rubbing with a blunt pencil.

One Cent Ruler

Count the number of pennies lined up along the bottom of this page. How many are there?

We can say that this page is about

_____ pennies long.

About how many pennies would it take to cover this entire page?

What else can you measure with pennies?

About how long is a pencil?

About how long is a book?

About how long is your hand?

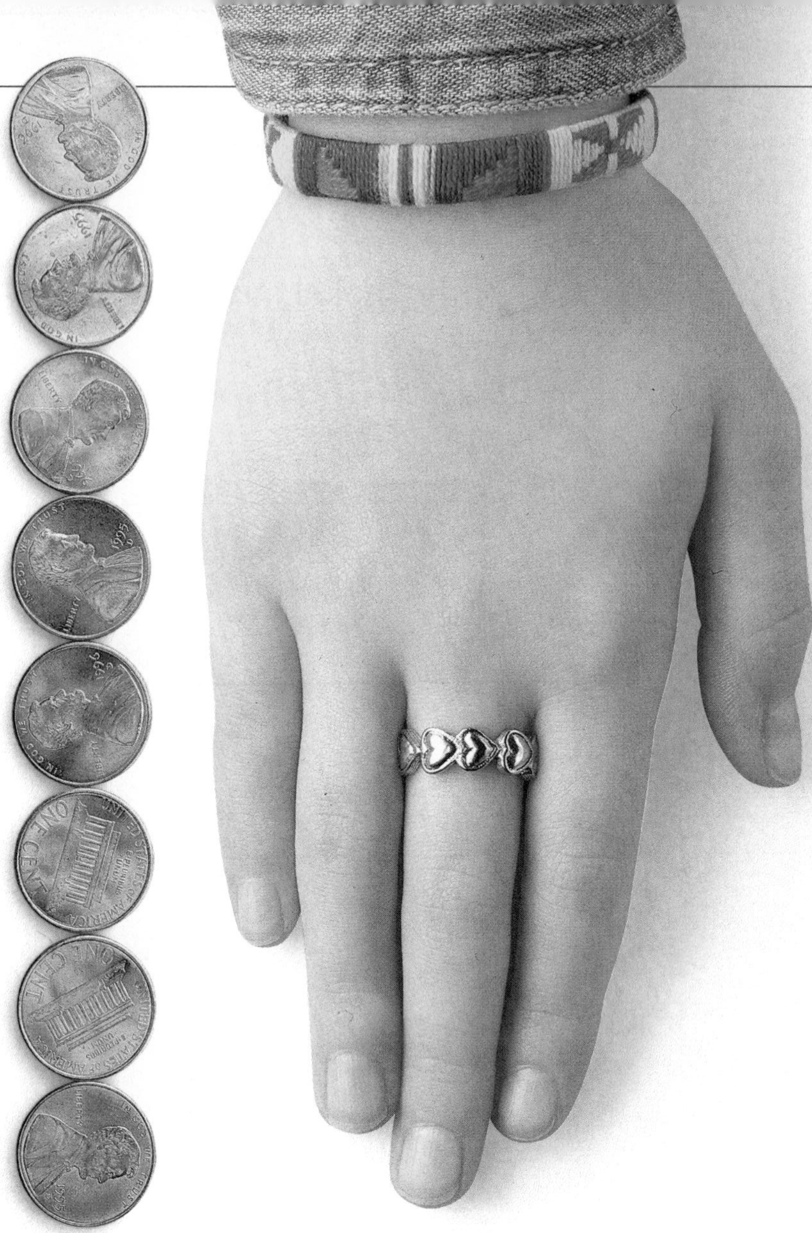

Notes for Home: Your child used a penny as a nonstandard unit of length. *Home Activity:* Ask your child to find something at home that is the length of one penny, one nickel, or one dime.

CHAPTER
10
Telling Time

Timekeepers
FINISH
30
4
16
April
MONDAY
What time is it when the clock strikes 13? Time to fix the clock.

Notes for Home: Your child discussed different daily activities and the times they occur. *Home Activity:* As daily routines, such as waking up, eating dinner, and bedtime occur, have your child pause to read a clock and tell you the time.

Dear Family,
Our class is beginning Chapter 10. We will learn how to tell time to the hour and to the half hour. We will learn how to use a calendar. Here are some activities we can do at home.

Red-Letter Days

Look at the calendar together and find the day's date. Then find and mark the dates for birthdays, holidays, and special family events. Talk about how many days, weeks, or months from now until the special days.

Tick Tock. Where's the Clock?

Go on a clock hunt. Challenge your child to find and count all the clocks in your home. Some examples might be wall clocks, wristwatches, and clocks on microwave ovens, videotape recorders, computers, radios, and telephone answering machines.

Community Connection

With your child, look for the hours of operation for places such as the library or a store. When at home, your child can draw clock faces to show the opening and closing times.

Visit our Web site. www.parent.mathsurf.com

Name

Explore Time

Explore

Which is your favorite time of day?

morning **afternoon** **night**

1 Draw something you do during that time.

Share

Tell about your picture. Use words that tell about time.

Notes for Home: Your child explored connecting the events of the day with the time of day.
Home Activity: Help your child write down the time he or she goes to bed to the nearest hour each night for one week. Ask, "Was it about the same time each night?"

My alarm clock wakes me up.

Connect

A clock shows time. Where can you see a clock?
Here are places you could see a clock.

❷ Draw a clock you could see in each place.

at school

at home

on a person

outside

in a car

Talk About It

❸ Choose a place that has a clock.
Tell why a clock is useful there.

EXPLORE

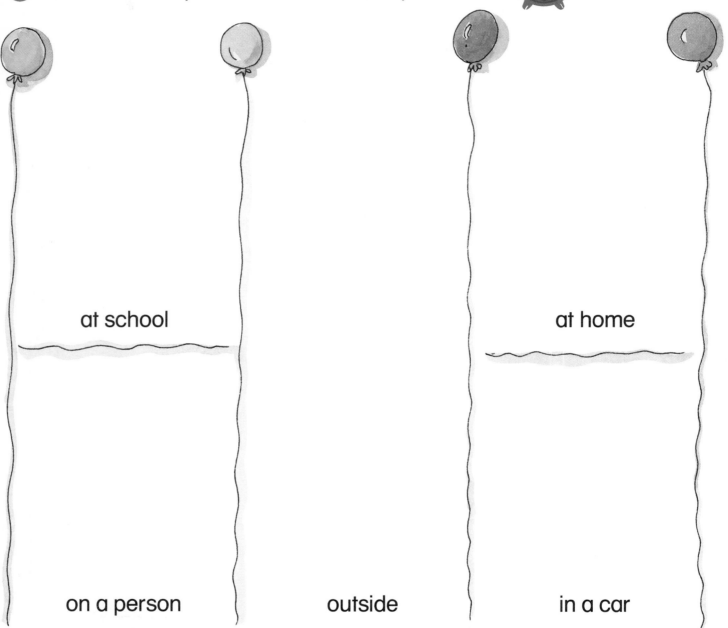

Notes for Home: Your child talked about and drew pictures of clocks. *Home Activity:* Ask your child to find examples of things around home that measure or show amounts of time, such as an egg timer, kitchen timer, clock, and calendar.

Name

Clocks

Learn

A clock has numbers and hands.
It is 3 o'clock.

The short hand is called the hour hand. It is pointing to 3.
The long hand is called the minute hand. It is pointing to 12.

Check

1 Complete the clock.
Write the numbers.
Draw the hands to show 3 o'clock.

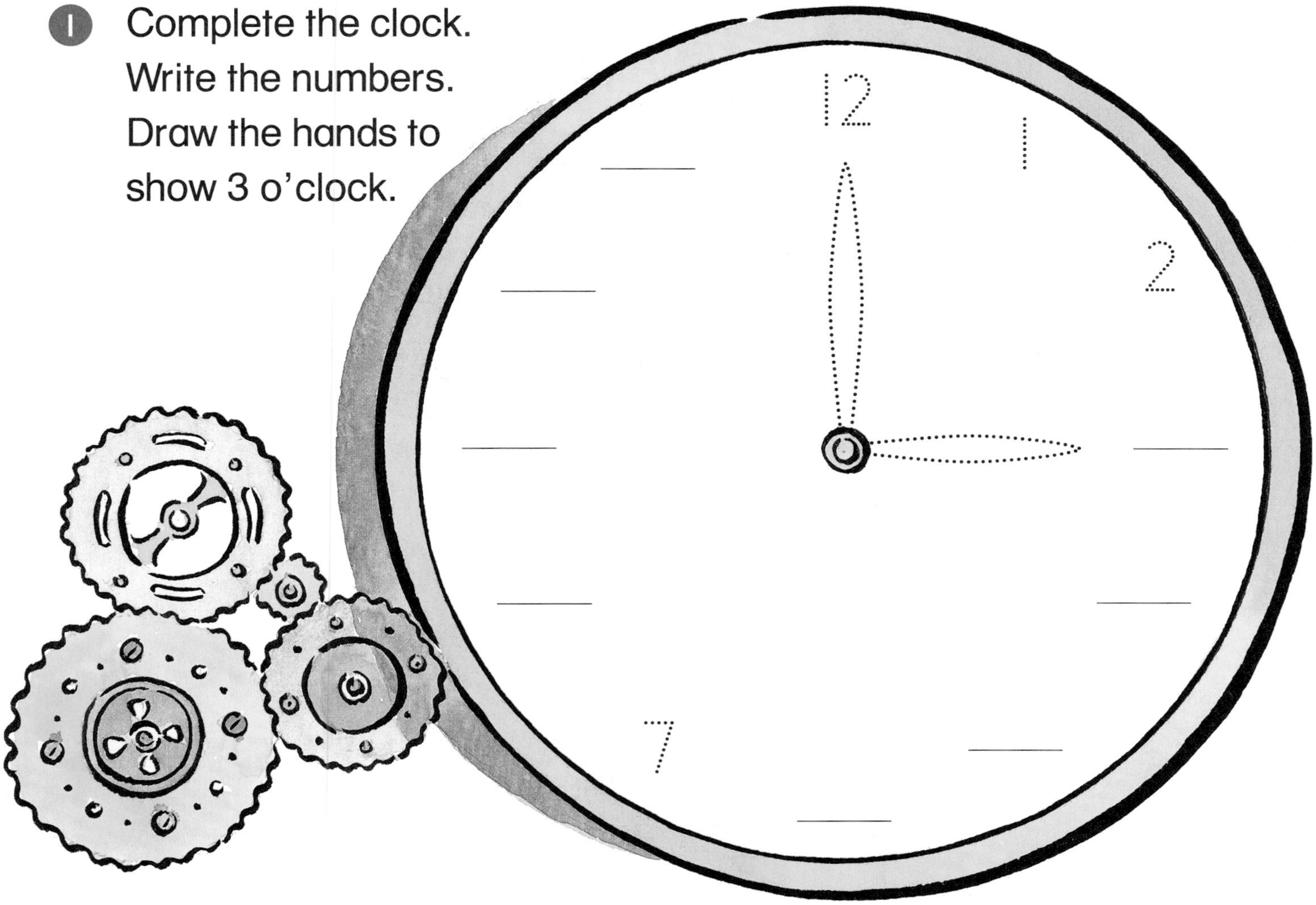

Talk About It When do you need to know the time?

Notes for Home: Your child learned to read a clock that shows time to the hour. *Home Activity:* Show your child a wristwatch or clock that has hands but few or no numbers on the face. Talk about how you know what time it is when all the numbers are not there.

Practice

Write the time.

2 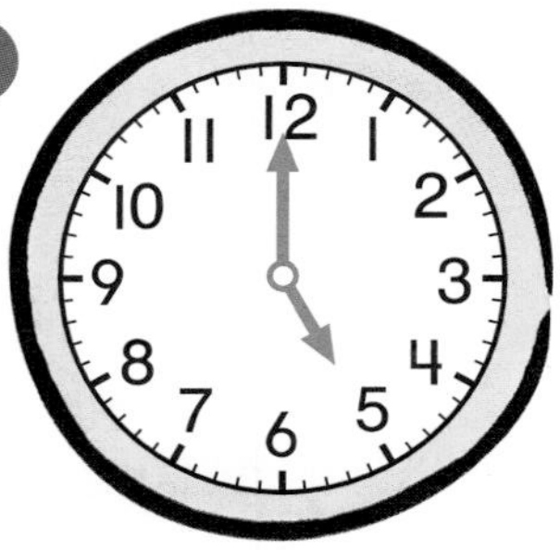

5 o'clock

3 

____ o'clock

4 

____ o'clock

5 

____ o'clock

6 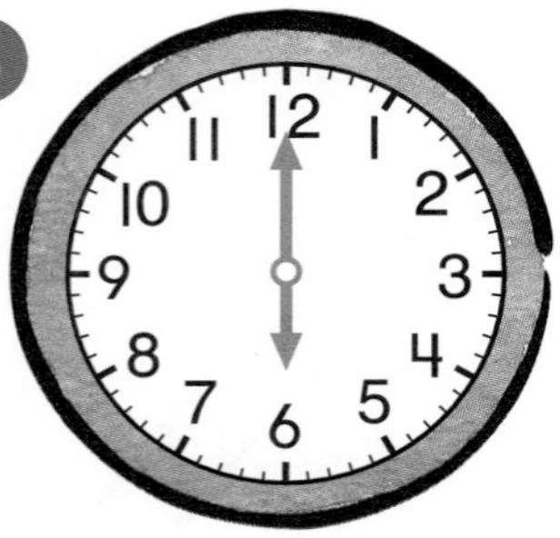

____ o'clock

7 

____ o'clock

8 

____ o'clock

9 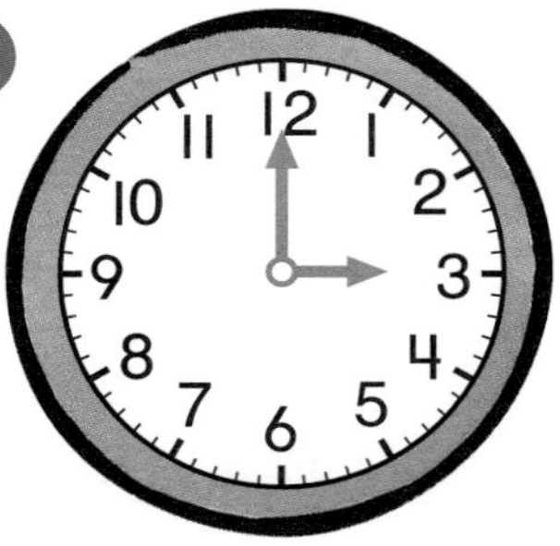

____ o'clock

PRACTICE

Problem Solving **Visual Thinking**

Write the time.

10 

____ o'clock

11 

____ o'clock

12 

____ o'clock

Notes for Home: Your child practiced reading a clock and writing the time to the hour. *Home Activity:* Use time in your directions or conversations with your child, for example, "It's 8:00. Time to leave for school."

Name ______________________________

Write Time to the Hour

Learn

7:00

It is 7 o'clock

I get up at 7:00.
What time do
you get up?

Check

Write the time.

1. 

   9:00

2. 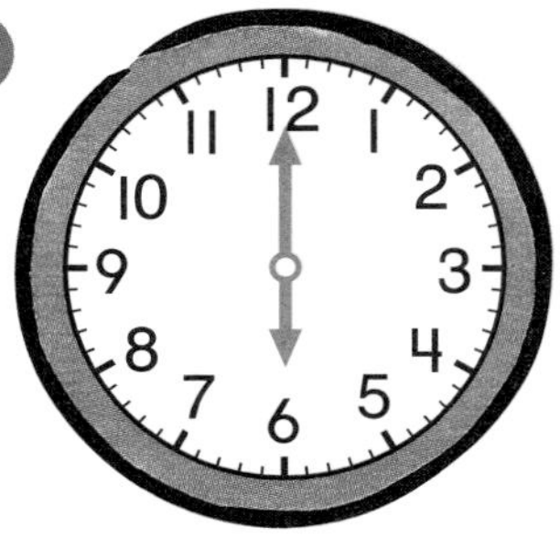

   ___ : ___

3. 

   ___ : ___

4. 

   ___ : ___

5. 

   ___ : ___

6. 

   ___ : ___

7. 

   ___ : ___

8. 

   ___ : ___

Talk About It Start at 1:00. Say each hour that comes next.

Notes for Home: Your child learned to read and write time to the hour. *Home Activity:* Ask your child to make a list of a day's activities and next to each activity write the time that it begins to the nearest hour.

Practice

Match the clocks that show the same time.

9

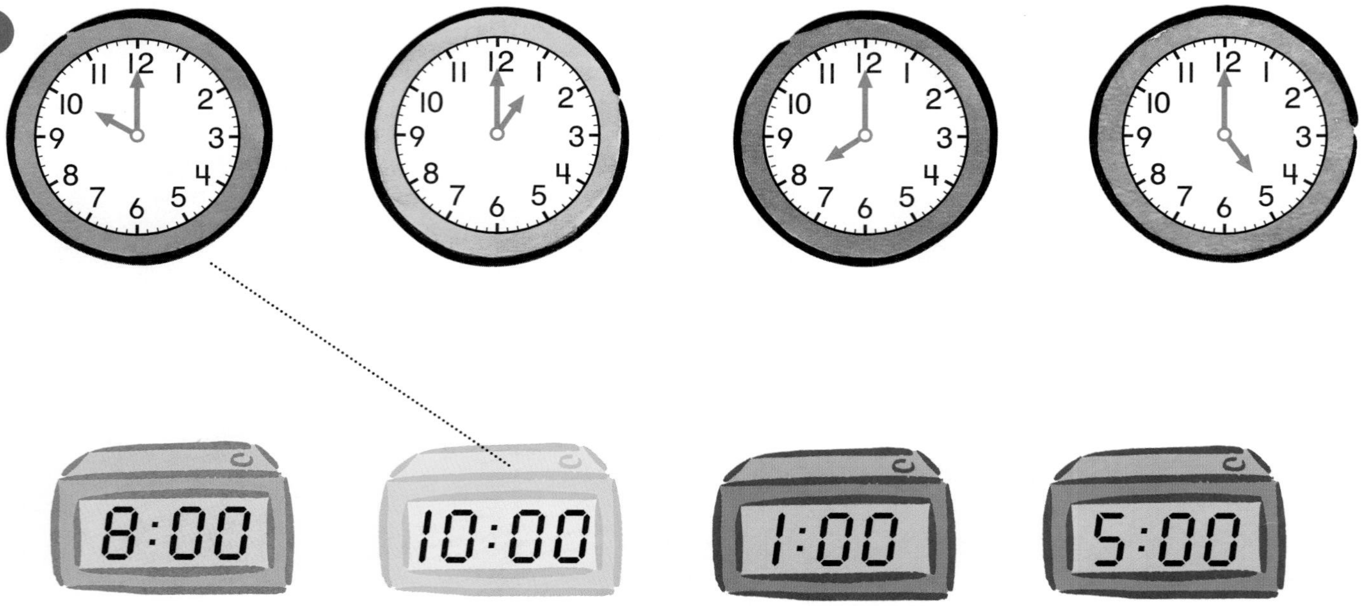

Write the time.

10

___:___

11

___:___

12

___:___

13

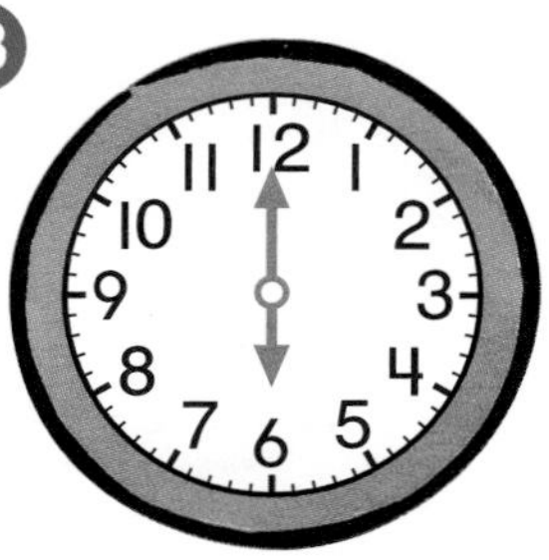

___:___

PRACTICE

Write About It

14 Write a message.
Put a time in your message.

____

____

____

Notes for Home: Your child practiced reading and writing time to the hour. *Home Activity:* Ask your child to draw a picture of something that begins on an hour, such as dinner at 6:00 or watching a favorite television cartoon at 4:00. Help your child label the picture with the time.

Name

Write Time to the Half Hour

Learn

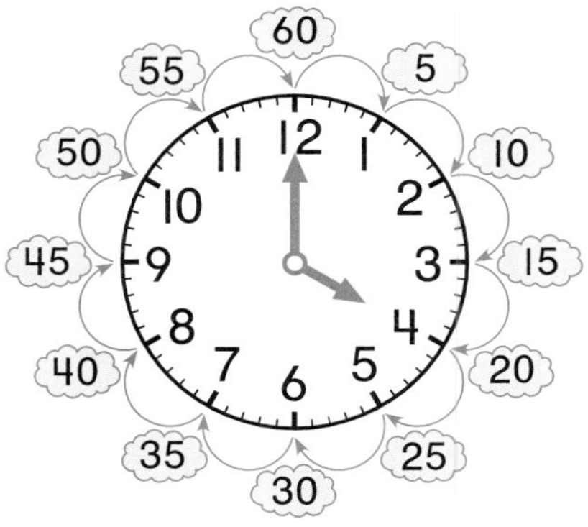

I see the minute hand is halfway around the clock.

I see the hour hand is halfway between 4 and 5.

There are 60 minutes in one hour.

There are 30 minutes in a half hour.

Check

Complete the note. Add the time.

1

Remember: Soccer
game at 5:30

Write the time.

2

___:___

3

___:___

4

___:___

5

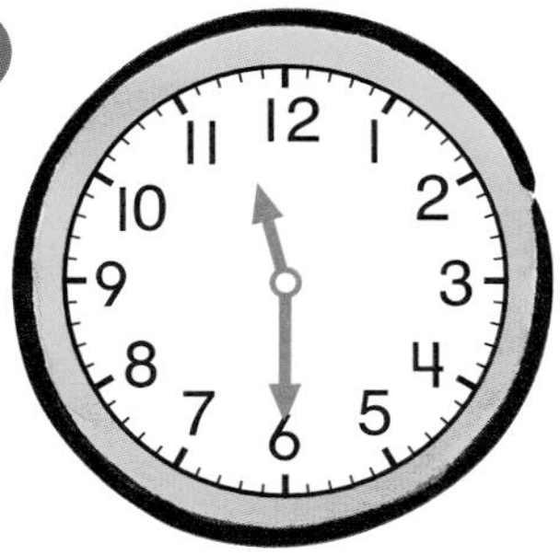

___:___

Talk About It What do you do that begins on the half hour?

Notes for Home: Your child learned to read and write time to the half hour. *Home Activity:* Talk with your child about things that begin or end on the half hour, such as the school day, music lessons, or television shows.

Practice

Write the time.

6

7

8

9

10

11

12

13

PRACTICE

Problem Solving Visual Thinking

14 Complete the TV schedule.

News

Nature

Comedy

Sports

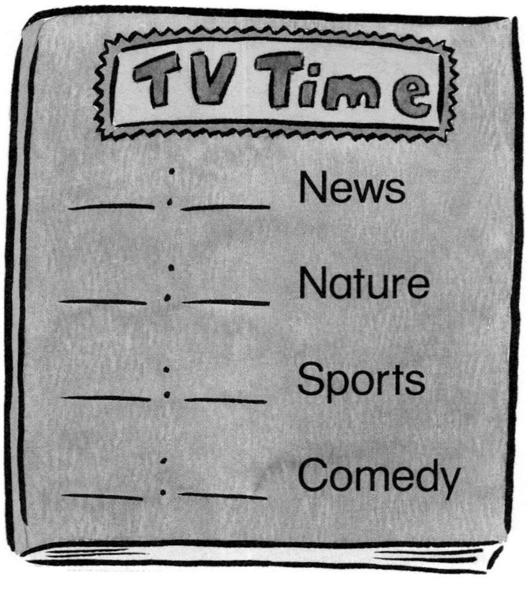

Notes for Home: Your child practiced reading and writing time to the half hour. *Home Activity:* Help your child write a schedule for one evening, for example: dinner 6:00, homework 6:30, television 7:30, bedtime 8:00. Help your child use a clock to follow the schedule.

For additional practice, see Skills Practice Bank, page 535, Set 1.

Name ______________________

Tell Time

Learn

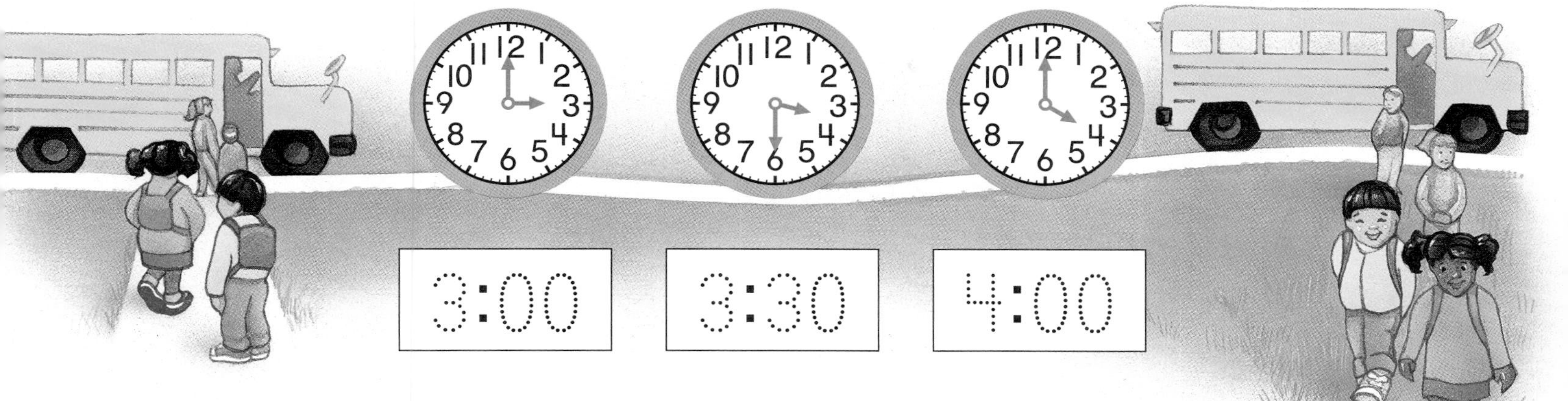

The children get on the bus at 3:00.
They get off at 4:00. The bus ride takes 1 hour.

Check

Write the times.

1

2

Talk About It How long did each activity last?

Notes for Home: Your child wrote times to show how long an activity lasted. *Home Activity:* Have your child write the times when an activity begins and when it ends. Ask, "How long did your activity last?"

Practice

3

4

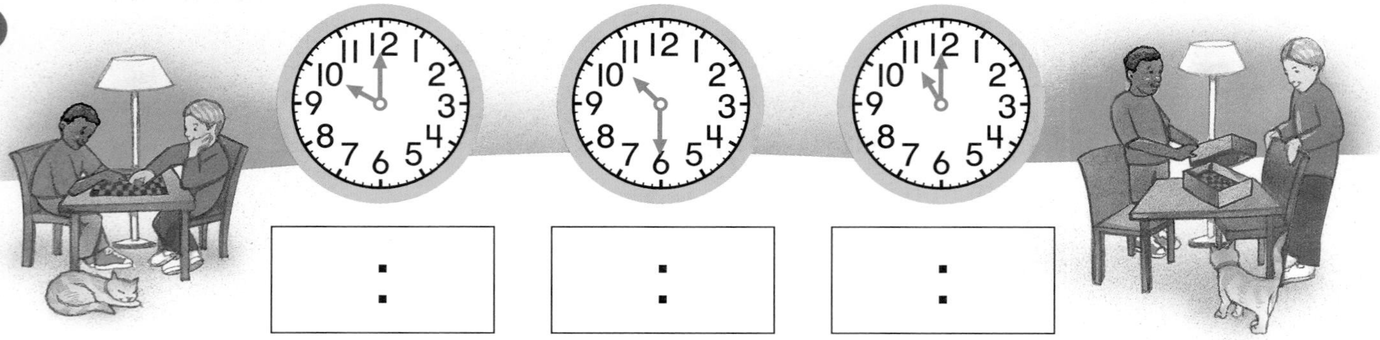

PRACTICE

Write your own time problem.

5 Draw pictures. Write the times.

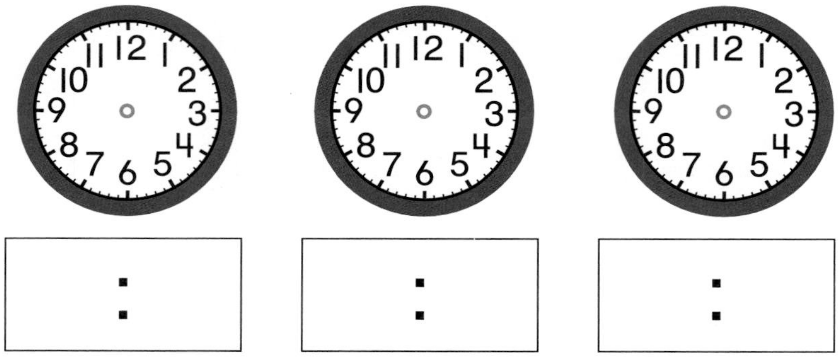

Problem Solving

Solve.

6 Dinner starts at 6:00.
It takes 1 hour.
What time does dinner end?

___ : ___

7 Soccer practice begins at 4:30.
It ends at 5:30.
How long does it take?

____

Notes for Home: Your child practiced writing time to the hour and half hour. *Home Activity:* Time an activity you and your child do together, for example, washing dishes or taking a walk.

Name ______________________________

Practice Game

Tick Tock Time

What You Need

10 two-color counters 

clock 

How to Play

1. Choose red or yellow for your color.
2. Take turns placing a counter in one of the squares below.
3. Show the time on your clock.
4. Act out something you do at that time of day.
5. Have other players guess what you are doing.

9:00	5:30	8:00	7:30	12:00
3:00	1:30	2:00	10:30	4:00

PRACTICE

Notes for Home: Your child played a game to practice telling time. *Home Activity:* Ask your child to make a clock face using a paper plate and construction paper hands. Use a paper fastener through the center to hold the moveable hands in place.

Name ______________________________

STOP and Practice

Circle the time the clock shows.

1 

12:00 11:00

2 

7:00 5:00

3 

3:30 6:00

4 

6:00 12:00

Write the time.

5 

___ : ___

6 

___ : ___

7 

___ : ___

8 

___ : ___

9 

___ : ___

10 

___ : ___

11 

___ : ___

12 

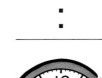

___ : ___

13 Write your favorite time. ___ : ___
Draw what you do at that time.

Notes for Home: Your child practiced reading and writing times to the hour and half hour.
Home Activity: Set a timer or an alarm clock to ring on the half hour and have your child tell the time when it goes off.

PRACTICE

Name

Problem Solving: Logical Reasoning

Learn

PROBLEM SOLVING GUIDE

Understand • Plan • Solve • Look Back

I wake up at 7:00.
Tom wakes up first.
Dad wakes up after me.
Who wakes up second?

I know Tom is first.
I know Dad is last. I
know there are 3 people.
I must be second.

Check

Solve.

1. Mary leaves before Denis.
Denis leaves at 8:00.
Mom leaves after Denis.
Who leaves last?
Mom ________

2. Aponi came at 9:00.
Sheila came at 9:30.
Marcos came before Aponi.
Who came last?
____

3. The show started at 3:00.
Alice came at 2:30.
Victor came at 3:30.
Who came late?
____

4. Devin is the youngest.
Barb is older than Tim.
Barb is younger than Evelyn.
Who is the oldest?
____

Talk About It What is something you did today?
At what time did you do it?

Notes for Home: Your child solved problems by thinking logically. *Home Activity:* Ask your child to tell the order in which family members come home each day.

PROBLEM SOLVING

Practice

Solve.

5. Kate is last in the line.
Zan is in front of Kate.
Albert is in front of Zan.
Who is first in line?

____

6. Tomas eats dinner at 5:30.
Olga eats dinner at 5:00.
Kevin eats dinner at 6:00.
Who eats dinner first?

____

7. Pete gets home at 4:00.
He walks the dog with his dad.
Pete's dad gets home at 5:00.
What time might Pete walk the dog?

____

8. Clare is first in line.
David is in front of Goro.
Lois is right after Clare.
List the children in order.

____

Critical Thinking

9. Choose and write the time that goes with each picture.

3:00 2:30 2:00

___ : ___

___ : ___

___ : ___

Notes for Home: Your child practiced solving problems. *Home Activity:* Look at a television schedule with your child and talk about the times that favorite shows are shown.

For additional practice, see Skills Practice Bank, page 535, Set 2.

Name ______________________________

Mixed Practice

Lessons 1–6

Concepts and Skills

Write the time.

1. 

_____ o'clock

2. 

_____ o'clock

3. 

_____ o'clock

4. 

_____ o'clock

5. 

[:]

6. 

[:]

7. 

[:]

8. 

[:]

9. 

[:]

10. 

[:]

11. 

[:]

12. 

[:]

Problem Solving

Solve.

13. Ramon has a piano lesson at 3:30.
Sara has a lesson at 4:30.
Oren has a lesson after Sara.
Who has the first lesson?

____

Journal

14. Draw something you do at 6:00. Add a clock to your picture.

Notes for Home: Your child practiced telling time to the hour and half hour and solved a problem about time. *Home Activity:* Ask your child to use the time shown on a digital clock to set the hands on a face clock.

Cumulative Review
Chapters 1–10

Concepts and Skills

1 Add or subtract.

$$12 \quad\quad 4 \quad\quad 7 \quad\quad 11 \quad\quad 2 \quad\quad 4 \quad\quad 9$$
$$\underline{-6} \quad \underline{+6} \quad \underline{+5} \quad \underline{-3} \quad \underline{+8} \quad \underline{+4} \quad \underline{-0}$$

Problem Solving

2 Make a picture graph.

Color a picture for each and .

| | 1 | 2 | 3 | 4 | 5 | 6 | 7 | 8 | 9 | 10 |

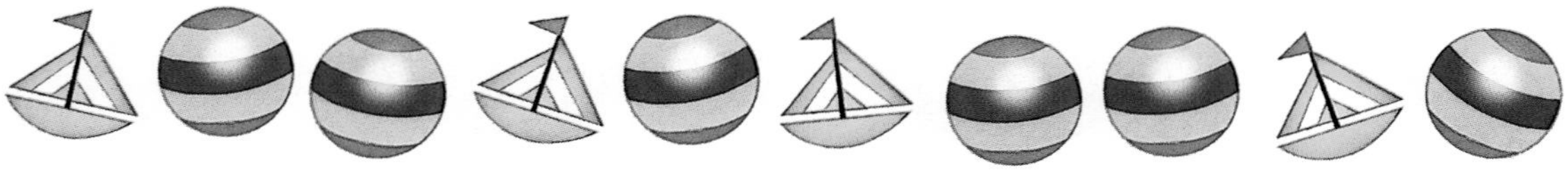

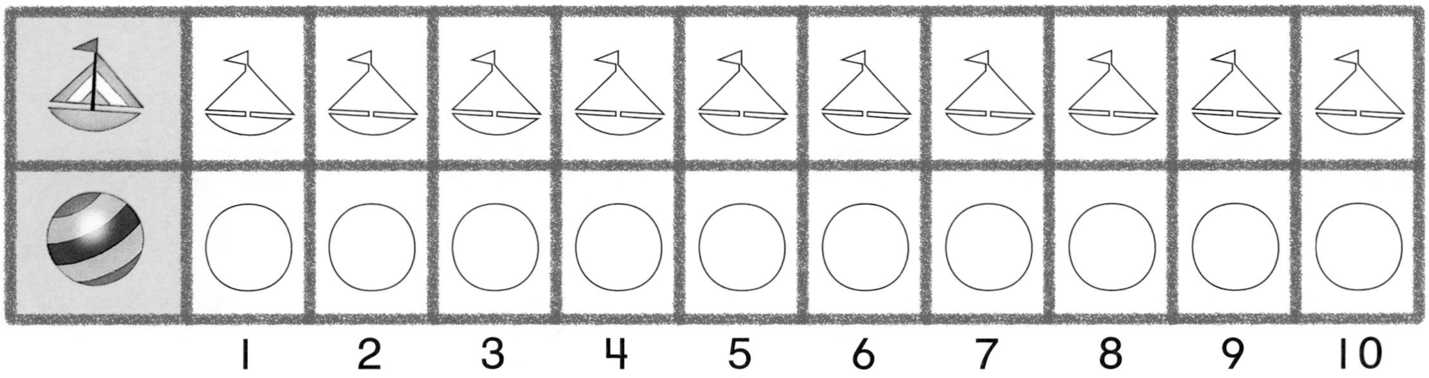

Test Prep

Fill in the ○ for the correct answer.

Choose the number that tells how many.

3

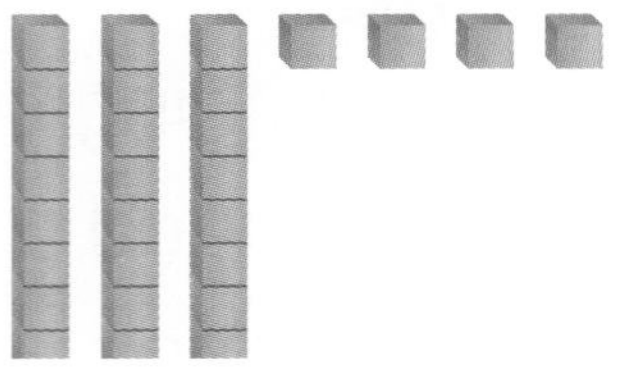

34 ○ 43 ○ 24 ○ 35 ○

4

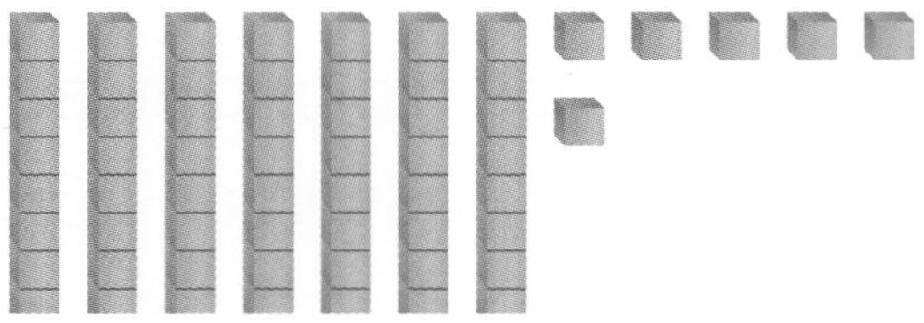

74 ○ 66 ○ 67 ○ 76 ○

Notes for Home: Your child reviewed addition and subtraction, graphing, and tens and ones. *Home Activity:* Ask your child to show you problems 3 and 4 using dimes and pennies (3 dimes and 4 pennies; 7 dimes and 6 pennies).

Name

Order Events

Learn

My photo album is a mess. Write 1st, 2nd, and 3rd to help me put it in order.

Check

Write 1st, 2nd, and 3rd to put the pictures in order.

1

2

Talk About It Choose one of the picture stories. Tell the story.

Notes for Home: Your child put a series of events in order. *Home Activity:* Ask your child to name three things he or she did today and tell them in the order that they were done.

Practice

Write 1st, 2nd, and 3rd to put the pictures in order.

3

4

5 Write 1st, 2nd, and 3rd to put the times in order.

PRACTICE

Problem Solving Critical Thinking

6 Write 1st, 2nd, and 3rd to show the order the girls arrived.

Ana, Beth, and Casey went to a party.

Beth arrived on time.

Casey arrived before Beth.

Ana arrived late.

Ana _____ Beth _____ Casey _____

Notes for Home: Your child reordered events into the correct sequence using 1st, 2nd, and 3rd. *Home Activity:* Ask your child to write or draw pictures to show the events of their day and to write the approximate time next to each event.

Name

Estimate Time

Learn

It takes me about 1 minute to put on my dance shoes. My dance class takes about 1 hour.
about 1 minute
about 1 hour

Check

Circle the time it takes.

1

about 1 minute   about 1 hour

2

about 1 minute   about 1 hour

3

about 1 minute   about 1 hour

4

about 1 minute   about 1 hour

Talk About It Which of the 4 activities above takes the longest time? the shortest time?

Notes for Home: Your child circled the time it takes to do an activity.
Home Activity: Talk with your child about activities you do that take about an hour.

Practice

Circle the time it takes.

5

about 1 minute   about 1 hour

6

about 1 minute   about 1 hour

7

about 1 minute   about 1 hour

8

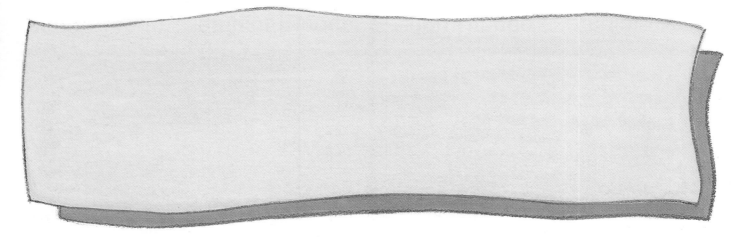

about 1 minute   about 1 hour

9 Draw your own time problem.

Tell a Math Story

10 Tell about something you did.

Tell what time you started and what time you stopped.

Notes for Home: Your child estimated times for familiar activities. *Home Activity:* Do an activity with your child, estimate how long it will take, and then time how long it does take.

Name ______________________________

Calendar

Learn

August						
Sunday	Monday	Tuesday	Wednesday	Thursday	Friday	Saturday
		1	2	3	4	5
6				10		
	14				18	
		22				26
				31		

These are the months of the year.

January
February
March
April
May
June
July
August
September
October
November
December

Complete the calendar.
August is one month.
It is a little more than 4 weeks long.

Check

Use a calendar.

1. What day of the week is August 1? Tuesday
2. What is the first month of the year? ______________
3. What month comes right after August? ______________
4. What was last month? ______________

Talk About It What are some ways you use a calendar?

Notes for Home: Your child read a calendar and identified the days of the week. *Home Activity:* Look at a calendar with your child and ask, "What is the first day of the week and the last day of the week of this month?"

Practice

5 Make a calendar for this month.

Month: ____________________

Sunday	Monday	Tuesday	Wednesday	Thursday	Friday	Saturday

Use your calendar.

6 Today is ____________________.

7 Yesterday was ____________________.

8 Tomorrow will be ____________________.

9 In two more days it will be ____________________.

Problem Solving Patterns

10 On what day of the week will next month start? ____________________

Notes for Home: Your child completed a calendar for the current month. *Home Activity:* Point to upcoming events on a calendar and ask your child to tell you the month, date, and day of the week for each event.

For additional practice, see Skills Practice Bank, page 536, Set 3.

Name ______________________________

Reading for Math

Main Idea and Supporting Details

The main idea tells what a story is all about.
Details tell more about the main idea.

1. Write details to complete the chart.
Cross out the details you don't need.

Erin's Day at Horse Park

Erin had fun at Horse Park.
She is 6 years old.
At 2:00 Erin rode a horse named Ted.
She brushed Ted.
She gave him apples.

Main Idea		
Erin had fun at Horse Park.		
Detail	Detail	Detail

Talk About It Can you make this story into a math problem? How?

Notes for Home: Your child wrote the details of a story. *Home Activity:* Ask your child to tell a story involving time. Help your child determine the main idea and the details in that story.

2 Circle the sentence that tells the main idea.
Draw what Ben builds.
Cross out the details you don't need to draw your picture.

Ben's Clock Tower

It was Saturday morning.
Ben built a tower of blocks.
First, he put a large red block on the bottom.
He put a blue block on top of the red block.
He put a small yellow block on top of the blue block.
He put an old clock on top.

Journal

3 Write a story about something you might build.

Notes for Home: Your child prepared for a problem solving lesson by using a main idea and supporting details to draw a picture. *Home Activity:* Ask your child to use details to describe an object in your home.

Name

Problem Solving: Too Much Information

Learn

PROBLEM SOLVING GUIDE

Understand • Plan • Solve • Look Back

I don't need to know how many books to solve this problem.

~~Henry bought 3 books.~~

He read for 1 hour.

He played outside for 2 hours.

For how many hours did Henry read and play? 3 hours

Check

Cross out the information you do not need.

Solve.

1. Max draws 4 pictures on Saturday.
   He draws 5 pictures on Sunday.
   He gives 2 pictures to his teacher.
   How many pictures does he draw? _____ pictures

2. Hannah walks for 8 minutes.
   She meets 3 friends.
   They walk for 4 more minutes to school.
   How long does it take Hannah to walk to school? _____ minutes

3. Today is Monday.
   In 2 more days it will be Ken's birthday.
   Ken will be 7 years old.
   On what day is Ken's birthday? ____________

Talk About It How do you know what to cross out?

Notes for Home: Your child learned to identify and disregard unnecessary information in a problem. *Home Activity:* Ask your child to tell the information that is not needed to solve this problem: We will shop at 4:00. We need to buy 5 apples and 6 bananas. How many pieces of fruit do we need?

Practice

Cross out the information you do not need. Solve.

4. On Sunday, Park goes to Grandma's.
He stays at Grandma's for 3 hours.
Grandma visits Park three days later.
On which day does Grandma visit Park? ______________

5. Vita needs 12 hats for her party.
Her party is on Tuesday.
She has 9 hats.
How many more hats does Vita need? _____ hats

6. Kara leaves for a trip on Monday.
Her family will drive 3 hours.
After a rest stop, they will drive 4 more hours.
How long will Kara's family drive? _____ hours

7. January, March, May, July, August,
October, and December have 31 days.
April, June, September, and November
have 30 days.
How many months have 31 days? _____ months

Visual Thinking

What time does each clock show? Write the time.

8. 

___:___

9. 

___:___

10. 

___:___

Notes for Home: Your child practiced solving problems that give too much information.
Home Activity: Share with your child times when you don't use all the information, such as checking a recipe to see what ingredients you do not need to buy.

Name ______________________________

Mixed Practice

Lessons 7–10

Concepts and Skills

Write 1st, 2nd, and 3rd to put the pictures in order.

1. 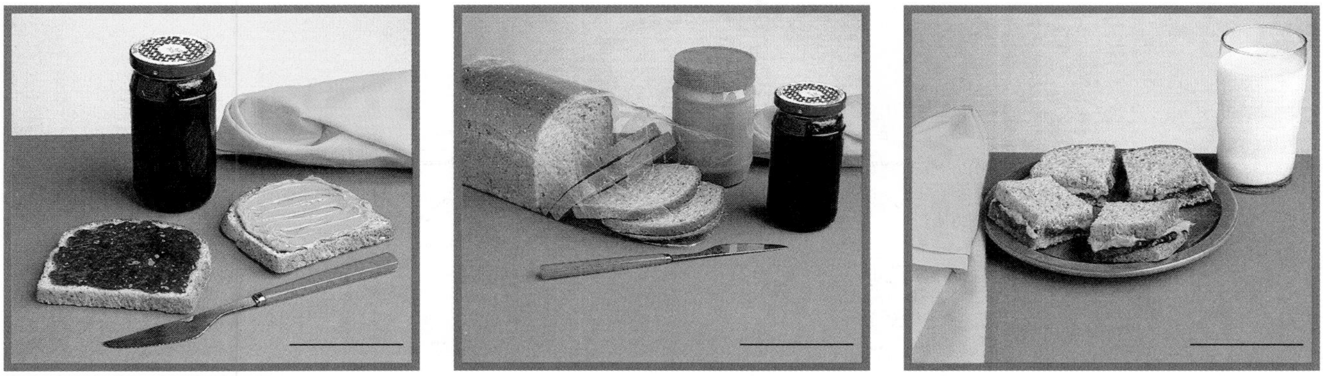

Use the calendar to answer the question.

2.

May		
Sunday	Monday	Tuesday
1	2	3
8	9	10

Circle the correct day.

May 2	**Monday**	**Tuesday**
May 8	**Sunday**	**Monday**

MIXED PRACTICE

Problem Solving

Cross out what you do not need. Solve.

3. Tea goes to the library at 3:00.
She gets 3 animal books.
She gets 5 books for her sister.
How many books did she get? ______ books

Journal

4. Write about something you do that takes more time than it takes to eat an apple.

Notes for Home: Your child practiced ordering events, reading a calendar, and solving problems.
Home Activity: Ask your child to look at the calendar and tell you the date of the first Friday this month.

Name ____________________

Cumulative Review

Chapters 1–10

Concepts and Skills

Circle the shape that belongs.

1 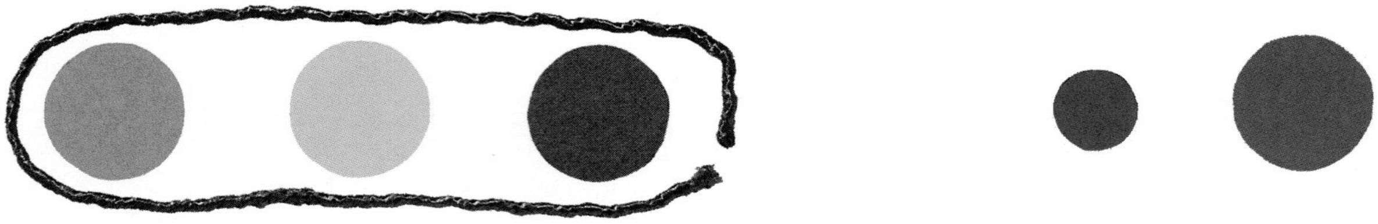

Problem Solving

2 Count your money.
Circle what you can buy.

Write the amount. _____ ¢

Test Prep

Fill in the ○ for the correct answer. Add.

3 $8 + 3 =$ ____

9 ○ 10 ○ 11 ○ 12 ○

4 $3 + 8 =$ ____

12 ○ 11 ○ 10 ○ 9 ○

5 $4 + 5 =$ ____

9 ○ 10 ○ 11 ○ 12 ○

6 $5 + 4 =$ ____

12 ○ 11 ○ 10 ○ 9 ○

Notes for Home: Your child reviewed sorting, using money, and addition. *Home Activity:* Ask your child how much more money is needed to buy the 39¢ balloon in Problem 2 (8¢ more).

Name

Chapter 10 Review

Stay Sharp

Vocabulary

1. Circle the days of the week.
2. Underline the months of the year.

Sunday	January	Friday	March	April	Monday
May	Tuesday	July	October	Saturday	June

3. Match.

60 minutes	30 minutes	8 o'clock
half hour	8:00	hour

Concepts and Skills

Write the time.

4. 

_____ o'clock

5. 

[:]

6. 

[:]

7. 

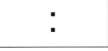

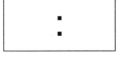

[:]

Problem Solving

Cross out the information you do not need. Solve.

8. The baseball game started at 1:00.
One team had 5 runs.
The other team had 6 runs.
How many runs did both teams make? _____ runs

Notes for Home: Your child reviewed telling time to the hour and half hour, and solving problems. *Home Activity:* Draw a clock face and ask your child to draw the hands to show 3:00. Repeat for other times.

CHAPTER TEST

Name ____________________

Chapter 10 Test

1 Write the times.

[:] [:] [:]

2 Circle about how long the mowing takes. **1 minute** **1 hour**

3 Solve.
Abuela goes to bed at 8:00.
Juanita goes to bed first.
Papa goes to bed after Abuela.
Who goes to bed second?

____

4 Cross out the information you do not need. Solve.
Today is Saturday.
Bev's birthday will be in 2 days
She will be 8 years old.
What day is her birthday?

____

5 Write 1st, 2nd, and 3rd to put the pictures in order.

______

______

______

6 Circle the correct day.

June 2 **Sunday** **Monday**

June 10 **Monday** **Tuesday**

June		
Sunday	Monday	Tuesday
1	2	3
8	9	10

Notes for Home: Your child was assessed on telling time to the hour and half hour, logical reasoning, estimating time, ordering events, and reading a calendar. *Home Activity:* Ask your child to read the days of the week on the calendar and identify the weekdays and the weekend days.

Name ______________________________

Performance Assessment

Chapter 10

Help Scott plan his day.
Draw the hands on the clock or write the time.
Write 1st, 2nd, 3rd, 4th, 5th, and 6th to show the order.

___ : ___

Go to school. _____

9:00

School begins. _____

7:00

Wake up. _____

___ : ___

Eat lunch. _____

6:00

Eat dinner. _____

___ : ___

Play after school. _____

Problem Solving Critical Thinking

What did Scott do before lunch?
What did he do after lunch?

Notes for Home: Your child completed an activity that tested understanding of telling time to the hour and half hour. *Home Activity:* Help your child begin a chart to record activities done at a certain hour, such as 7:00 each evening for a week.

Name ______________________________

What Month Is Your Birthday?

Computer Skills You Will Need

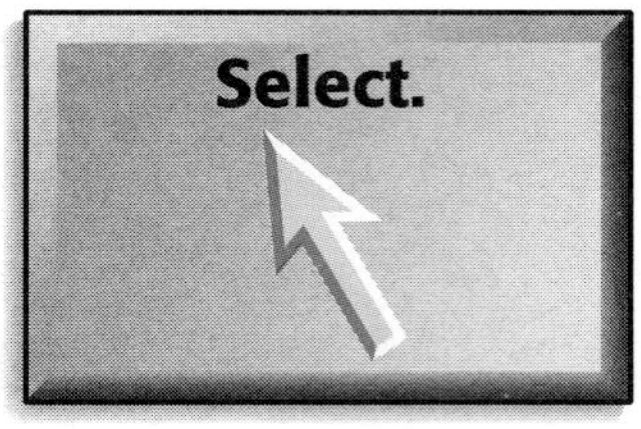

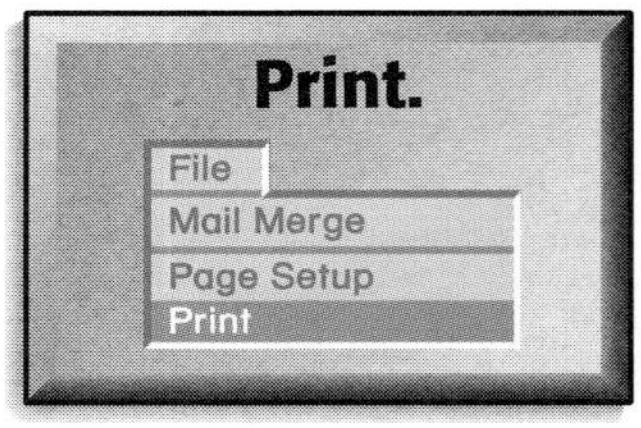

Use your drawing program to make a calendar for the month of your birthday.

1. Draw a large rectangle.
2. Draw 6 lines from top to bottom.
3. Draw 6 or 7 lines from side to side. Print out the calendar.
4. Write the month. Write the days of the week.
5. Fill in the dates.
6. Decorate your calendar.

I know the days of the week: Sunday, Monday, Tuesday, Wednesday, Thursday, Friday, and Saturday.

I know the months of the year: January, February, March, April, May, June, July, August, September, October, November, and December.

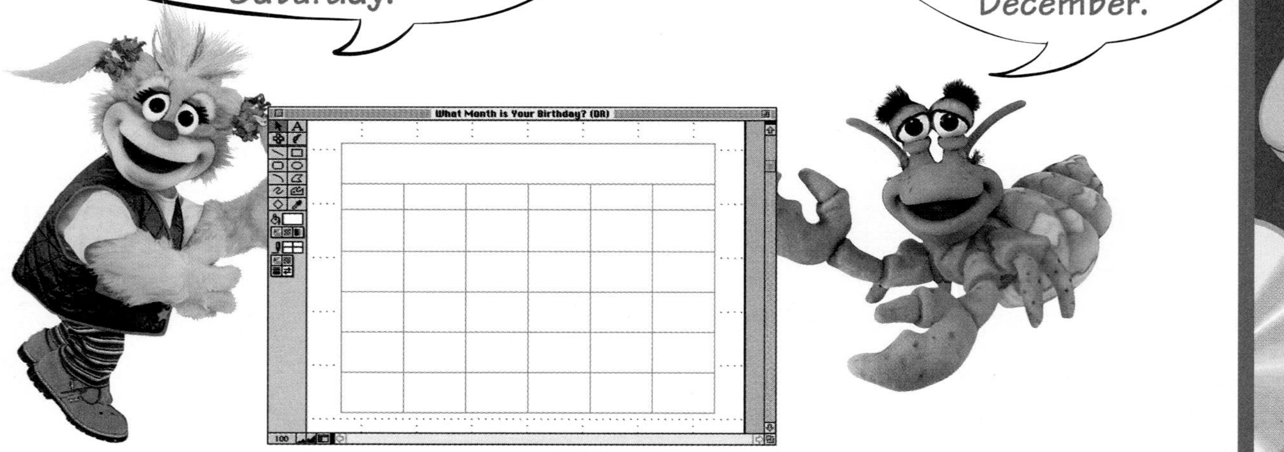

Tech Talk How could you use a computer to make a graph?

Visit our Web site. **www.parent.mathsurf.com**

Time Tracker

How much time do you spend reading, eating, and so on?

Color in one box for each hour you spend doing each activity.

How I Spend My Day

HOURS					
10					
9					
8					
7					
6					
5					
4					
3					
2					
1					
	Reading	Watching TV	Eating	Riding in a car	Sleeping

Fold down

MathSoup

Scott Foresman - Addison Wesley My Math Magazine No. 10

Right on Time!

What is a question you can ask all day and always get a different answer?

What time is it?

Crazy Clocks

Clocks come in lots of shapes and sizes.
Some even run backward!
Can you tell what time it is on these clocks?

The hour hand and minute hand are on separate clocks.

Turn this clock to put the 12 on top.

Notes for Home: Your child read the time on unusual clock faces.
Home Activity: With your child look at clocks in your home and talk about how they are similar and different.

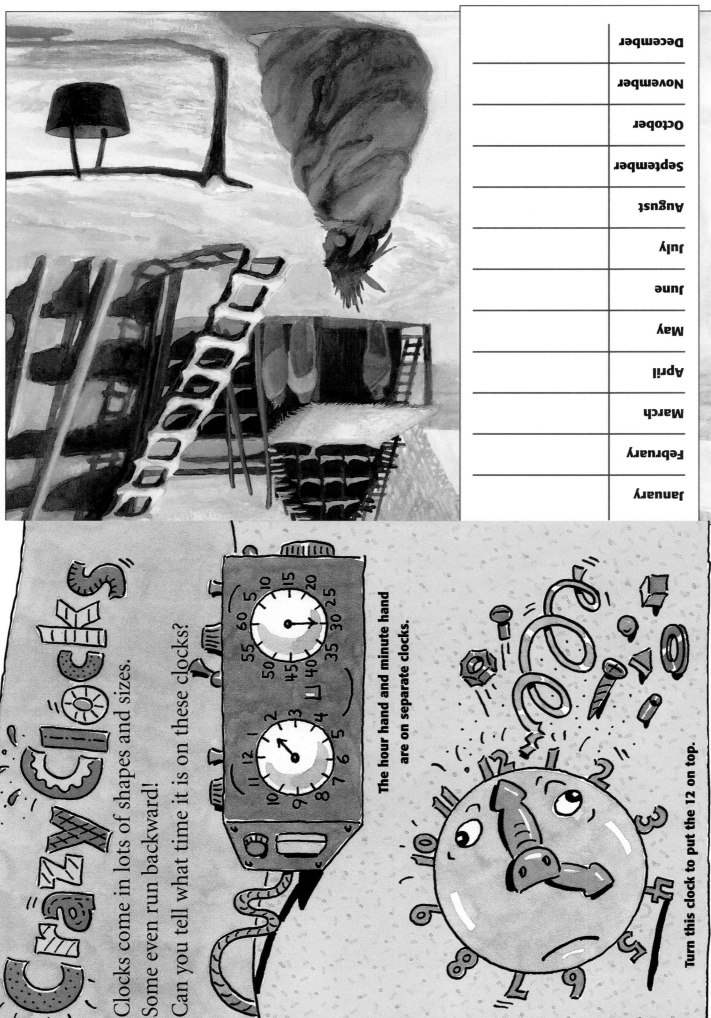

January	
February	
March	
April	
May	
June	
July	
August	
September	
October	
November	
December	

Home Activity: Ask your child to draw pictures for some of the names they gave the months.

Many Moons

Long ago, the Native Americans called Iroquois watched the moon. From what they saw, they made their own calendar. A moon is about the same length as a month. Each moon had a name that told something about that time of year.

First moon – Nis-ko-wok-neh, which means the moon of snow and blizzards.

Fifth moon – Wen-taa-kwo, which means the flowers.

Ninth moon – Ke-to-ok-neh, which means the harvest.

My Own Moons

Make up a new name for each of the 12 months to tell about that time of year.

Months of the Year	My name for this month

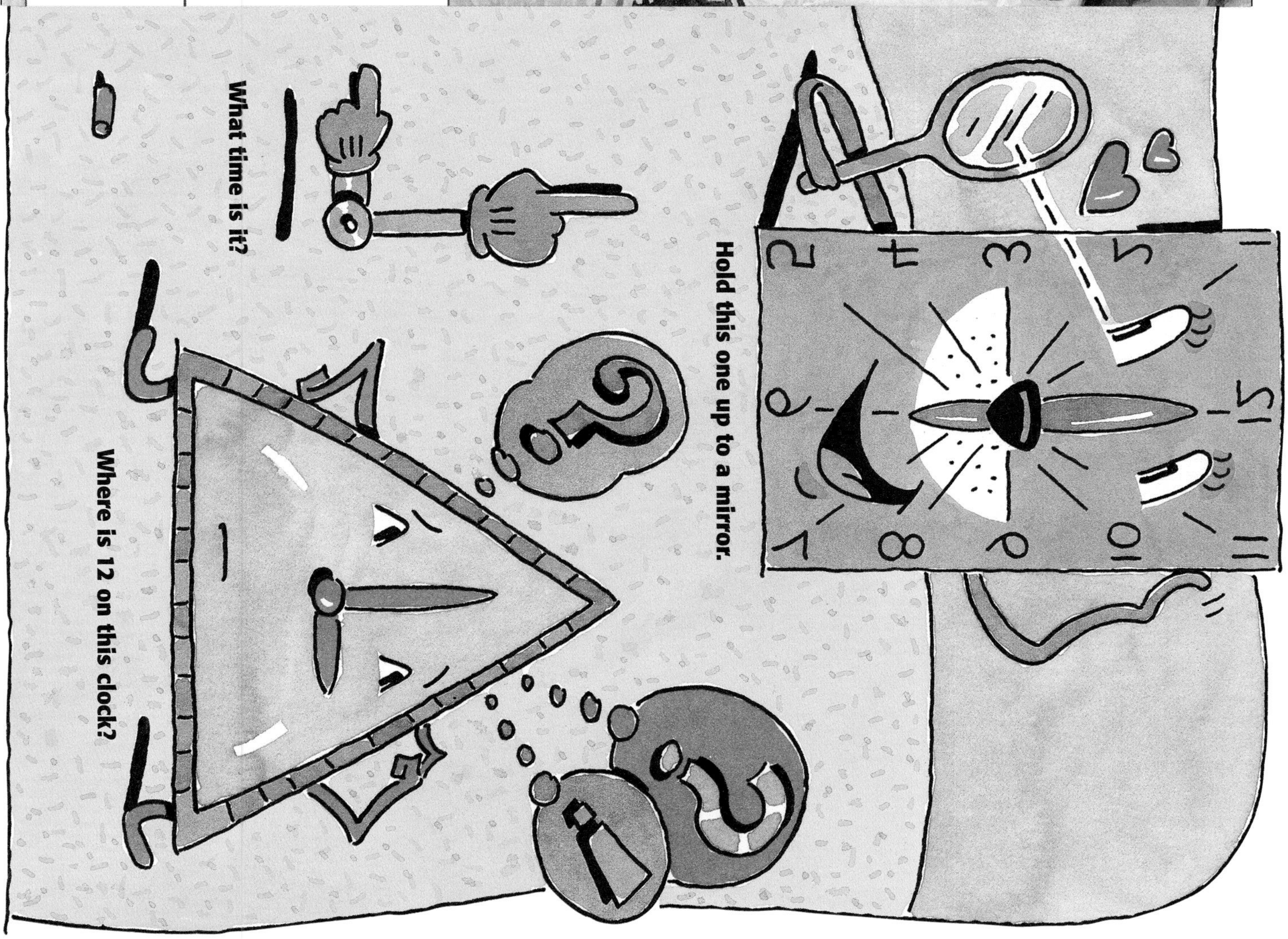

Notes for Home: Your child learned about a Native American calendar and then renamed the months to show something about that time of year.

Funday

If you could plan the best day ever, what would you do?

Plan a Funday. Write the times that you would do each activity.

What things would you do every Funday?

Notes for Home: Your child used favorite activities to create a schedule. *Home Activity:* Talk to your child about when you could plan to do one of these activities.

CHAPTER 11

Measurement

In the Garden

Notes for Home: Your child discussed ways to measure some things in the picture. *Home Activity:* Ask your child to suggest ways some things at home might be measured, such as how to measure the water or flour that gets added to a cake or muffin batter.

Math at Home

Dear Family,
Our class is beginning Chapter 11. We will learn how to measure length, weight, capacity, and temperature and learn to choose which measurement tool to use. Here are some activities we can do at home.

Cook Some Math

Bake some cookies together or whip up a special fruit drink using a favorite recipe. Have your child measure the ingredients, comparing the sizes of the bowls and measuring cups you use.

A Long and Short Treasure Hunt

Attach 6 paper clips to make a chain. Go on a treasure hunt together looking for objects that are close to the length of the chain. Find five objects longer than the chain and five shorter than the chain.

Community Connection

On your next trip to the grocery store, weigh any fruits and vegetables you buy. Before placing an item on the scale, encourage your child to guess the weight, then weigh the items.

Visit our Web site. www.parent.mathsurf.com

Name ______________________________

Explore Measuring with Nonstandard Units

Explore

How tall are you? How tall is your partner?

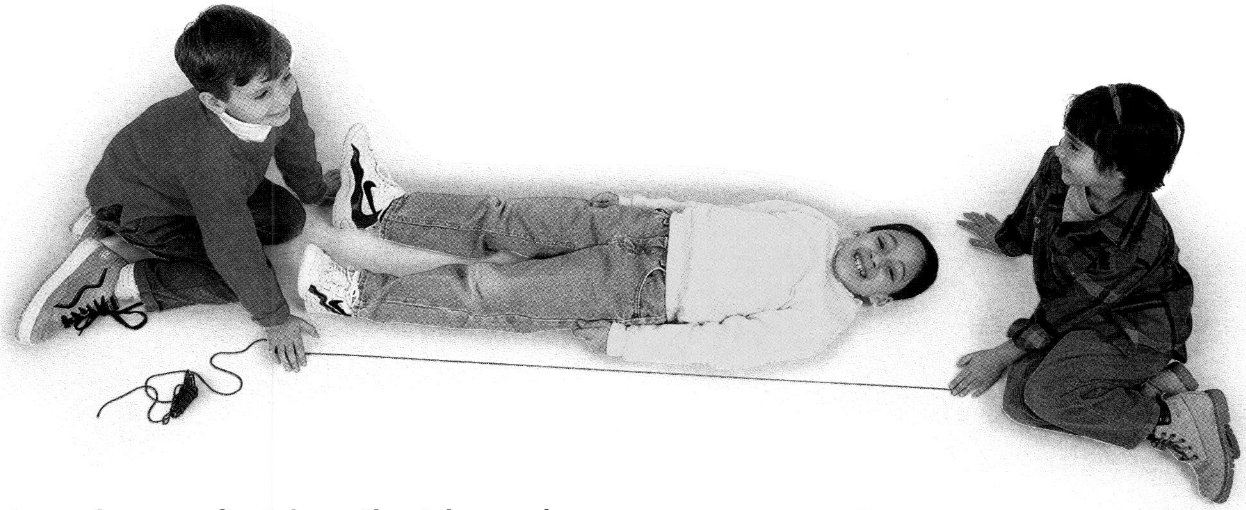

Cut a piece of string that is as long as your partner.
Your partner does the same for you.
Measure the length of each piece of string in different ways.

	Use to Measure Length	The Length of Your String	The Length of Your Partner's String
1	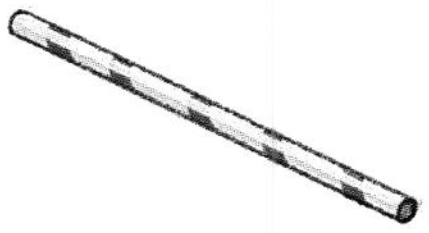	about ______ 	about ______ 
2	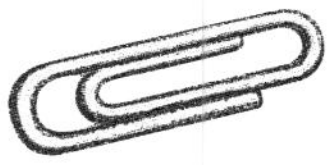	about ______ 	about ______ 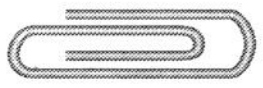
3		about ______ 	about ______ 

Share

Who is taller? How do you know?

Notes for Home: Your child explored measuring length using straws, paper clips, and Snap Cubes.
Home Activity: Ask your child to measure the length of an arm using small objects, such as paper clips or buttons, placed end to end.

Connect

How wide is your chair?

Estimate. Then use straws to measure.

An estimate is what I think it will measure.
This chair is about 2 straws wide.

How wide?

Use.	Estimate.	Measure.
4 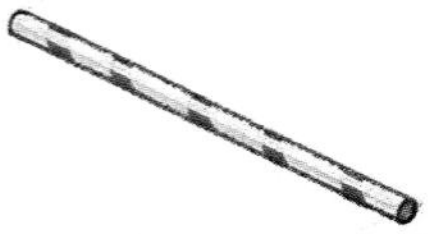	about ____ straws	about ____ straws
5 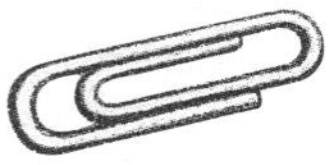	about ____ paper clips	about ____ paper clips

How tall?

Use.	Estimate.	Measure.
6 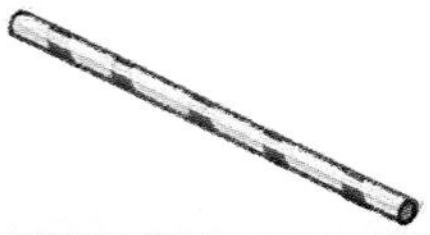	about ____ straws	about ____ straws
7 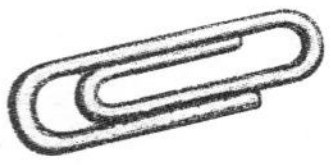	about ____ paper clips	about ____ paper clips

Talk About It Did you use more straws or more paper clips?
Why do you think that happened?

Notes for Home: Your child estimated and measured length using straws and paper clips. *Home Activity:* Ask your child to show you how to measure something around the house (such as the length of a tabletop) using objects such as pennies, spoons, or unsharpened pencils placed end to end.

Name

Estimate, Measure, and Compare Lengths

Learn

Does the desk look taller than 10 cubes?

(yes) no

I am using a train of 10 Snap Cubes to estimate.

Check

Make a train of 10 cubes. Use it to estimate.

Find the object. Measure with cubes.	Does it look longer than 10 cubes?	About how many cubes long?
1 	yes (no)	about 8 cubes
2 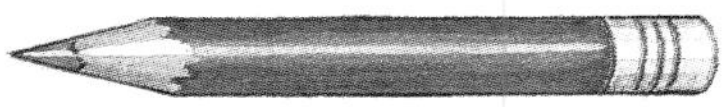	yes no	about _____ cubes
3 	yes no	about _____ cubes

Talk About It Which object is the shortest? Which object is the longest? How do you know?

Notes for Home: Your child used Snap Cubes to measure the length of things in the classroom. *Home Activity:* Ask your child to measure the length of a shoe or a comb with small objects, such as paper clips laid end to end. Ask your child to first estimate if the object looks longer than 10 paper clips.

Practice

Make a train of 5. Use it to estimate the length.

Find the object. Measure with .	Does it look longer than 5 ?		How many long?
4 	yes	no	about ______
5 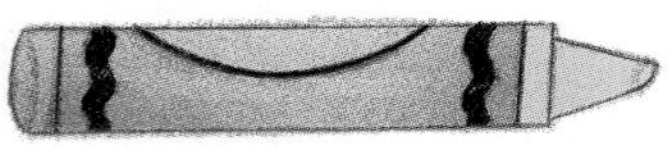	yes	no	about ______
6 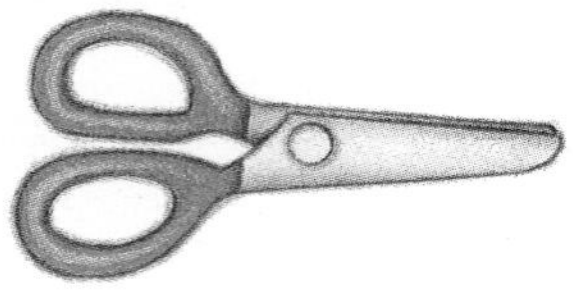	yes	no	about ______

Write your own.

7 Choose an object.
Draw it.
Estimate its length.
Measure its length.

Problem Solving Estimation

Circle the best answer.

8 Art is about 57 tall.
About how tall is Abbie?

Abbie is about 50 60 70 80 tall.

Notes for Home: Your child practiced using Snap Cubes to measure lengths of classroom objects. *Home Activity:* Give your child an object such as a crayon. Ask your child to think of some things that are longer than 5 crayons and shorter than 5 crayons. Measure with the crayon to check.

Name ____

Estimate and Measure with Inches

Learn

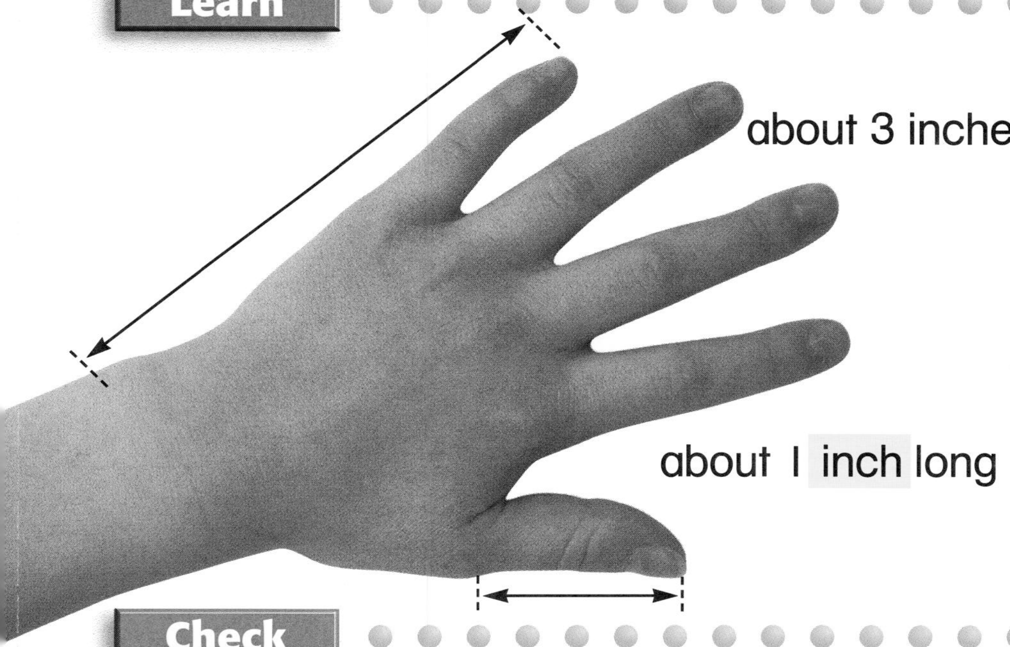

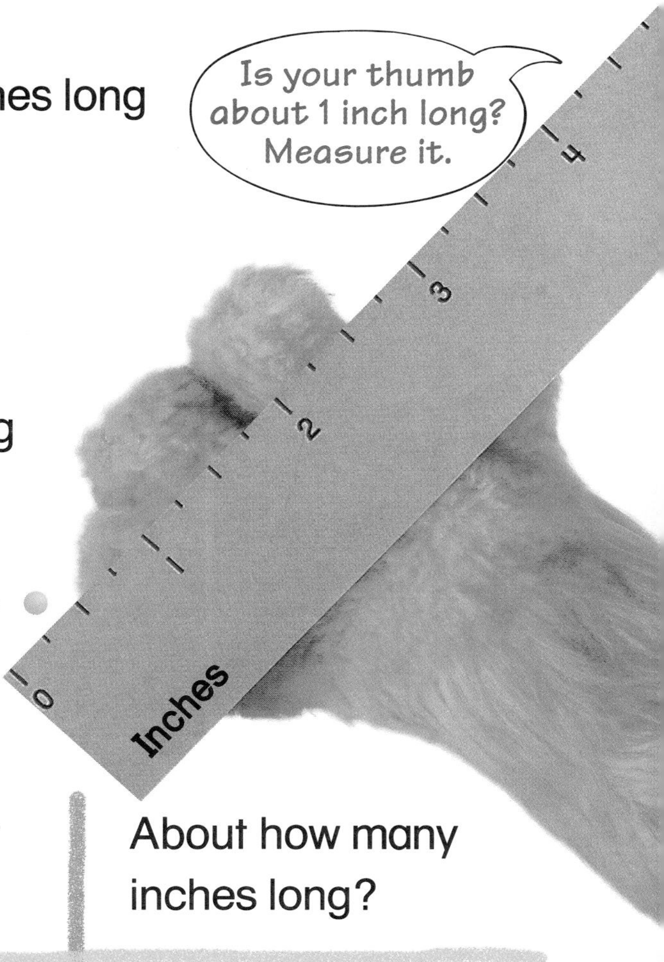

Check

Estimate. Measure with your  .

Find the object.	Does it look longer than 3 inches?	About how many inches long?
1 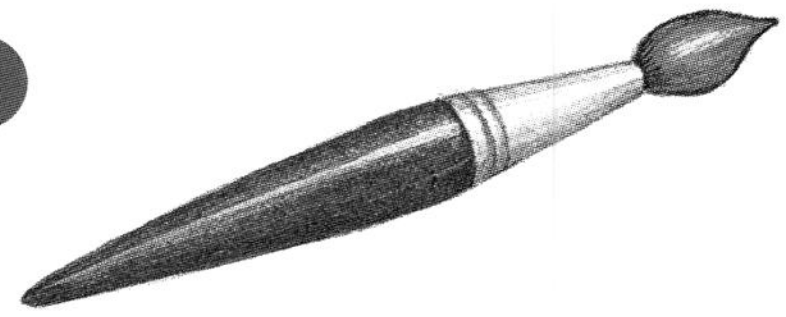	(yes) no	8 inches
2 	yes no	____ inches

Talk About It How is measuring length with inches like measuring length with cubes? How is it different?

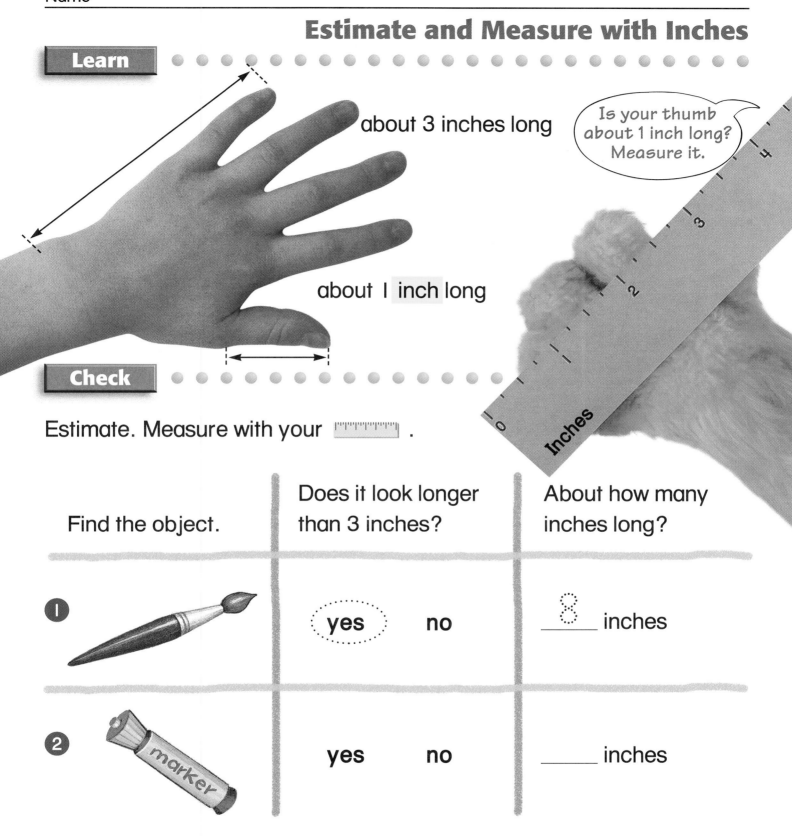

Notes for Home: Your child learned to measure length with an inch ruler. *Home Activity:* Ask your child to use an inch ruler and measure to find objects around the house that are longer and shorter than 3 inches.

Practice

About how long? Estimate. Measure. Use your ruler.

3
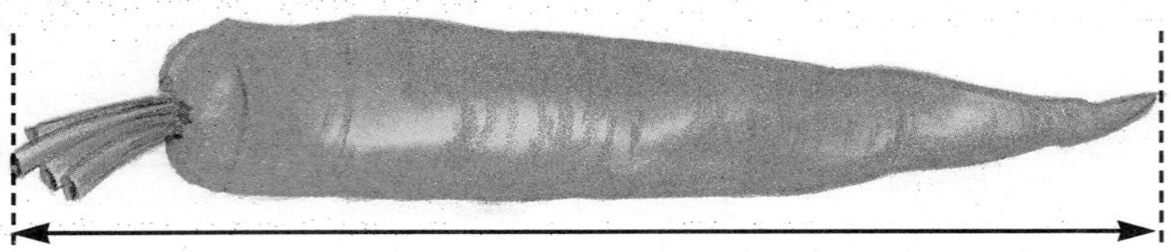

Estimate. ______ inches

Measure. ______ inches

4
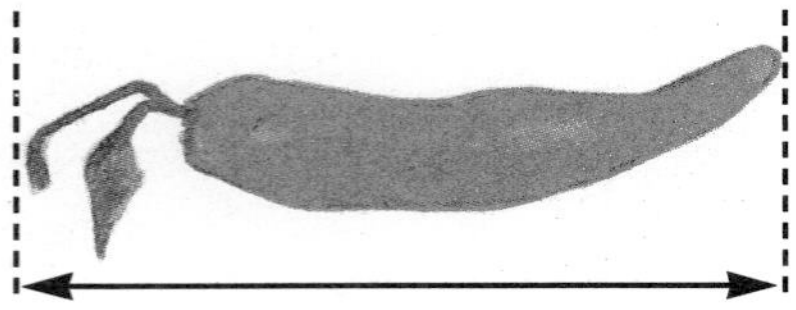

Estimate. ______ inches

Measure. ______ inches

5
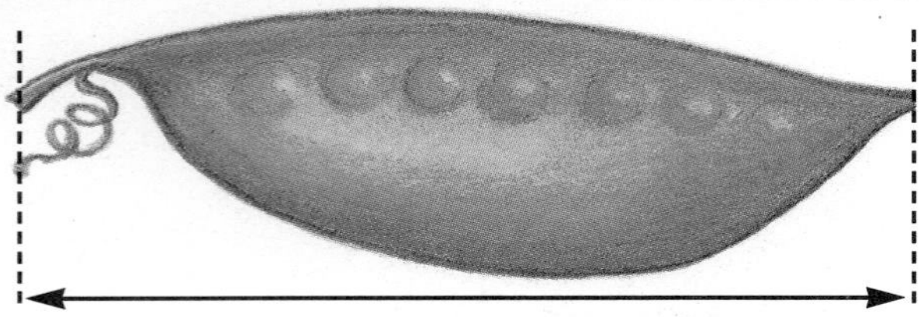

Estimate. ______ inches

Measure. ______ inches

Start at the dot.

6 Draw a line that is about 5 inches long.

●

7 Draw another line.
Make it longer than 5 inches and shorter than 7 inches.

●

Problem Solving Visual Thinking

8 Circle the best answer.
Andre is fixing a hole in the fence.
Which piece of wood will fit best?

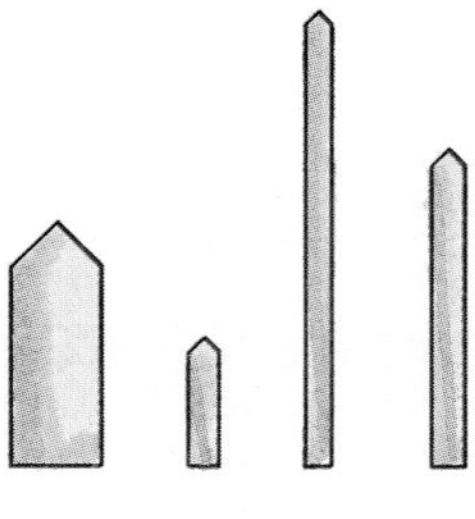

Notes for Home: Your child practiced estimating and measuring lengths of objects on the page with an inch ruler. *Home Activity:* Have your child use a ruler or the length of a small paper clip as an inch measure. Then ask your child to estimate and measure the length of several objects in inches.

For additional practice, see Skills Practice Bank, page 537, Set 1.

Name ______________________________

Compare to One Foot

Learn

These things are about 1 foot long.

Check

Find things you think are about 1 foot long.
Measure with your 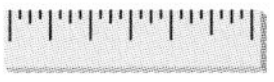 .
Draw a picture in the correct space below.

1

Shorter than 1 foot	About 1 foot	Longer than 1 foot

Talk About It What did you find that is about 1 foot long?

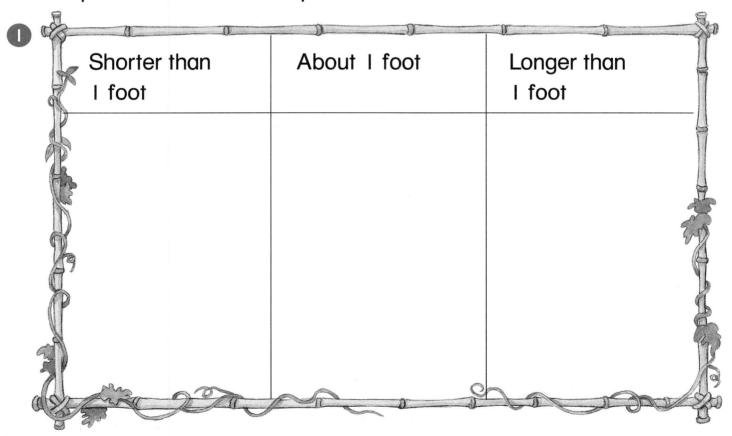

Notes for Home: Your child compared the lengths of objects to 1 foot. *Home Activity:* Ask your child to find objects in your home that are about 1 foot long.

Practice

How long would each object be? Circle the best answer.

2 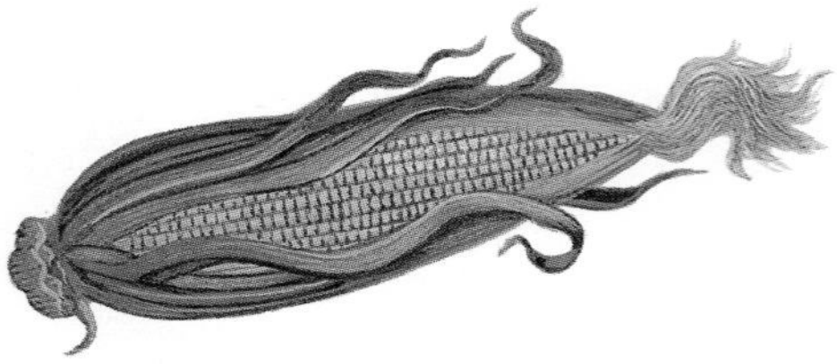

shorter than 1 foot

about 1 foot

longer than 1 foot

3 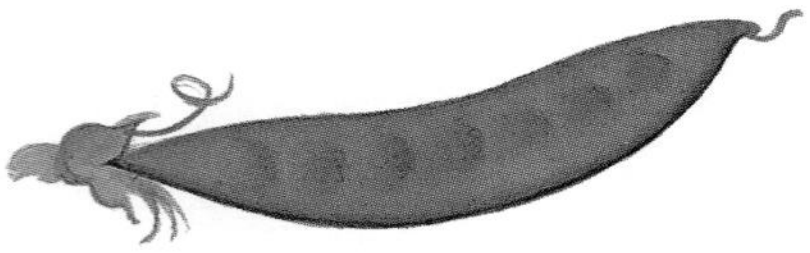

shorter than 1 foot

about 1 foot

longer than 1 foot

4 

shorter than 1 foot

about 1 foot

longer than 1 foot

5 

shorter than 1 foot

about 1 foot

longer than 1 foot

6 

shorter than 1 foot

about 1 foot

longer than 1 foot

7 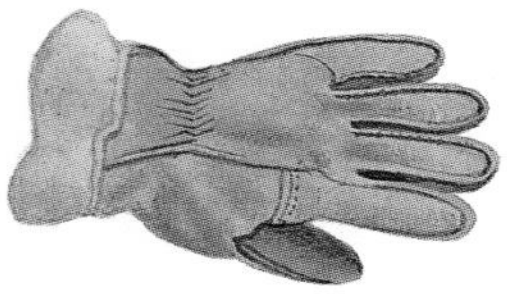

shorter than 1 foot

about 1 foot

longer than 1 foot

Problem Solving

8 Erna grew a very big cucumber in her garden. It was more than 1 foot long! She measured it and found it was about 1 foot and 3 inches long. About how many inches long was it? ______ inches

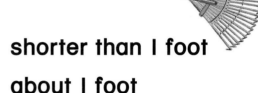

Notes for Home: Your child practiced identifying whether an object is about 1 foot long, shorter than 1 foot, or longer than 1 foot. *Home Activity:* Ask your child to find objects in your home that are longer than 1 foot and shorter than 1 foot.

PRACTICE

Name ______________________

Inchworm Foot Race

What You Need

inch ruler for each player

12 one-inch squares for each player

pencil and paper clip

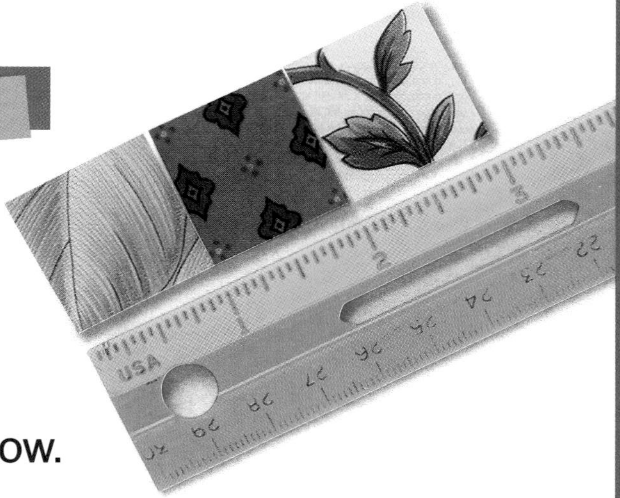

How to Play

1. Play with 2 to 4 friends.
2. Take turns spinning the spinner below.
3. Measure the length of the worm the spinner points to.
4. Place that many inch squares along your ruler.
5. The first player to make 1 foot wins.

PRACTICE

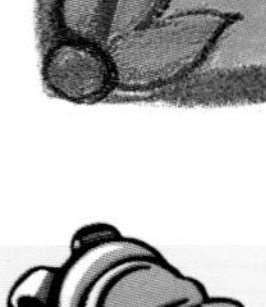

Notes for Home: Your child played a game to practice measuring length in inches. *Home Activity:* Ask your child to show you how to play the game. Use an inch ruler to make the 12 one-inch paper squares.

Name ____________________

STOP and Practice

Measure the length. Use [ruler].

1 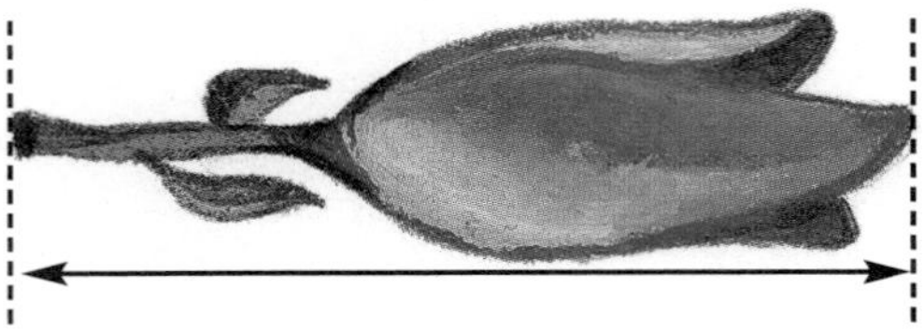

about _____ inches

2 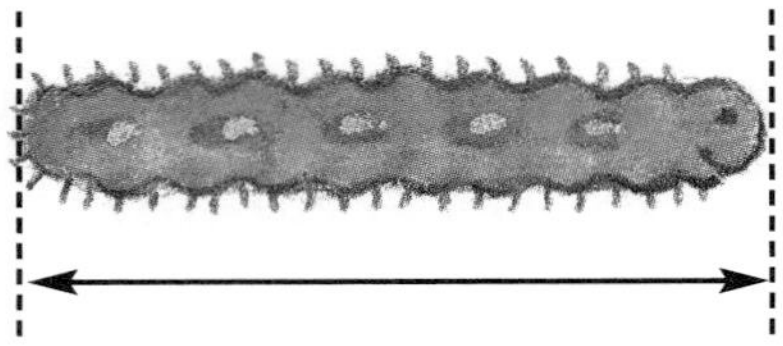

about _____ inches

3 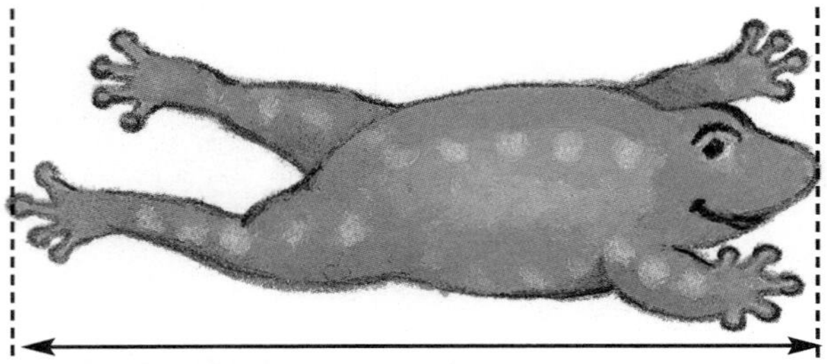

about _____ inches

4 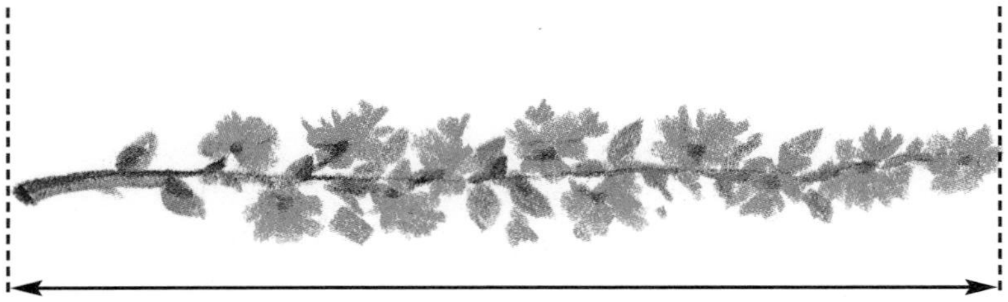

about _____ inches

5 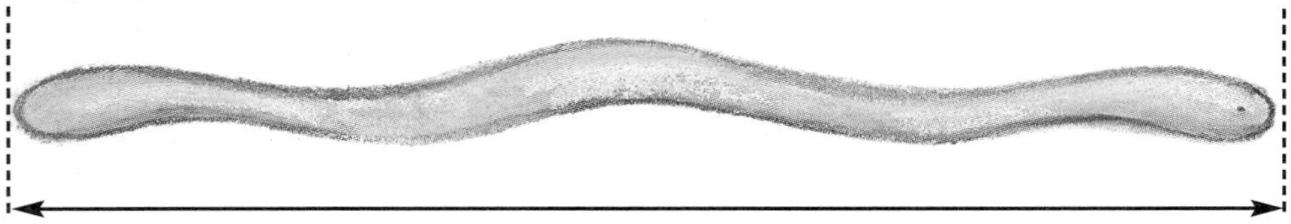

about _____ inches

6 Circle the object that would be longer than one foot.

Notes for Home: Your child practiced measuring length in inches. *Home Activity:* Ask your child to find two things in your home that are about 1 foot. Check by measuring their lengths.

PRACTICE

Name

Estimate and Measure with Centimeters

Learn

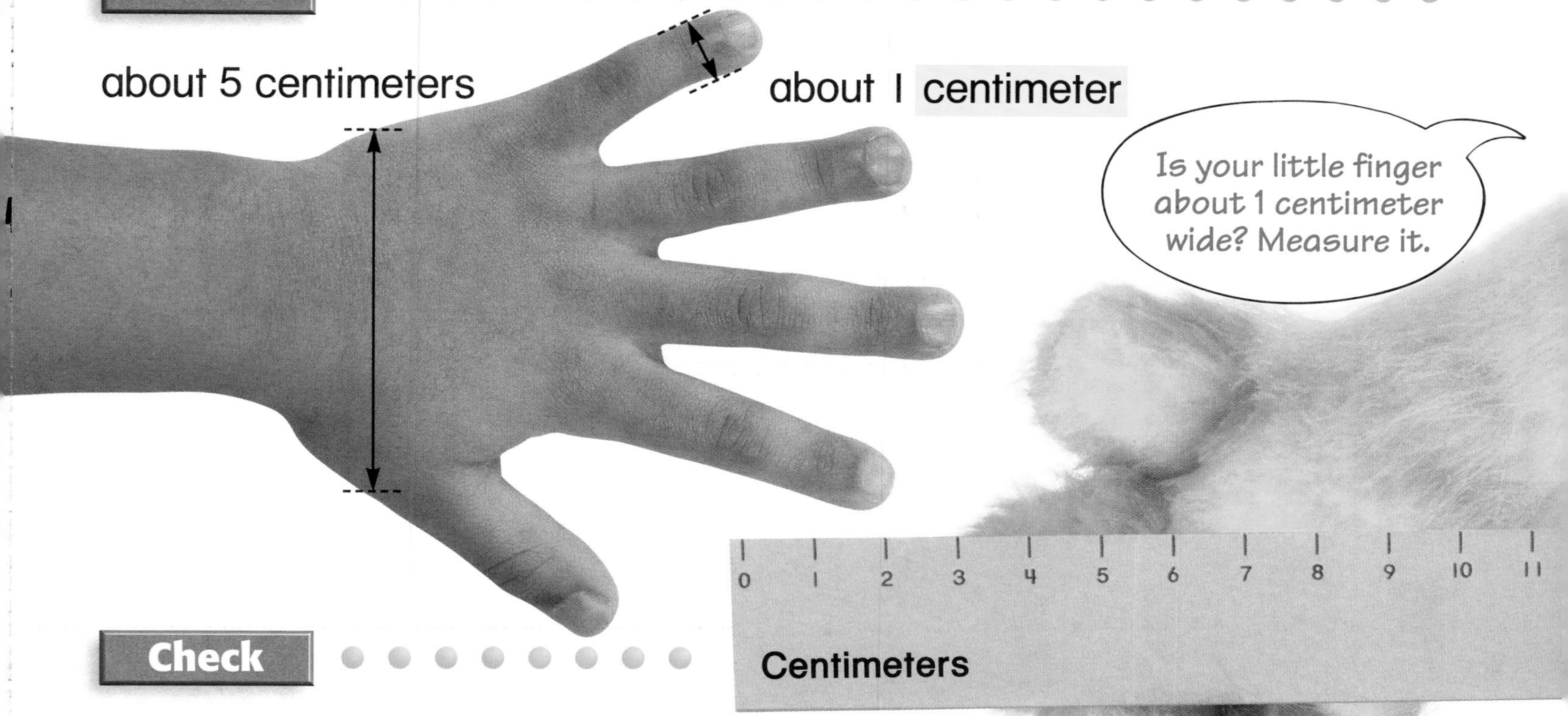

Check

Estimate. Measure with your 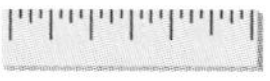 .

Find the object.	Does it look longer than 10 centimeters?	About how many centimeters long?
1 	yes no	____ centimeters
2 	yes no	____ centimeters

Talk About It How is measuring with centimeters like measuring with inches? How is it different?

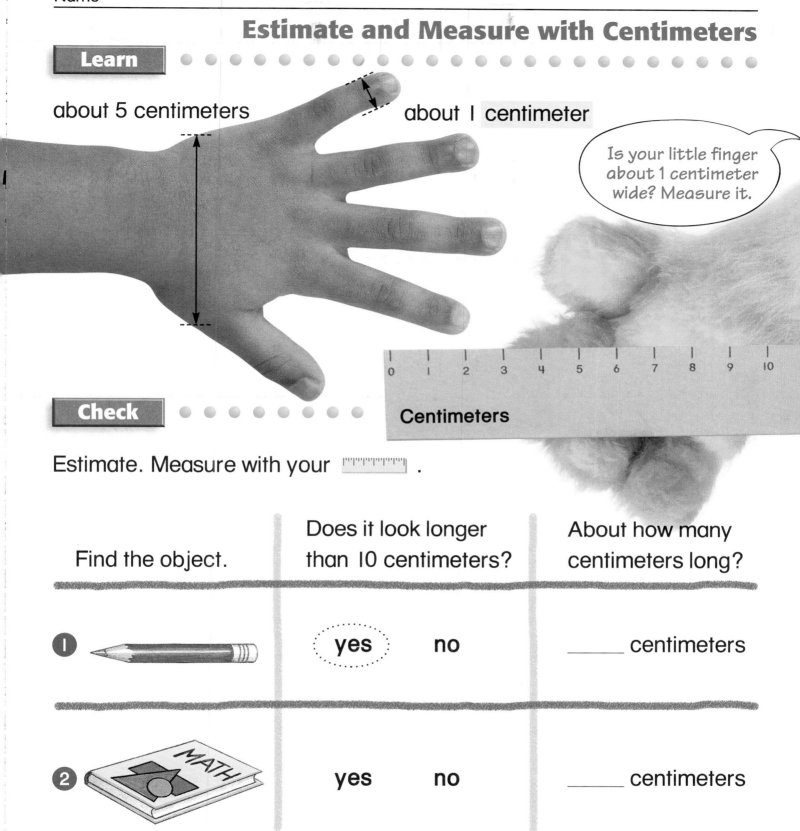

Notes for Home: Your child learned to measure length with a centimeter ruler. *Home Activity:* Ask your child to use a centimeter ruler or the width of a little finger as a centimeter measure. Have your child find objects around the house that are longer and shorter than 10 centimeters.

Practice

About how long? Estimate. Measure. Use your ruler.

3 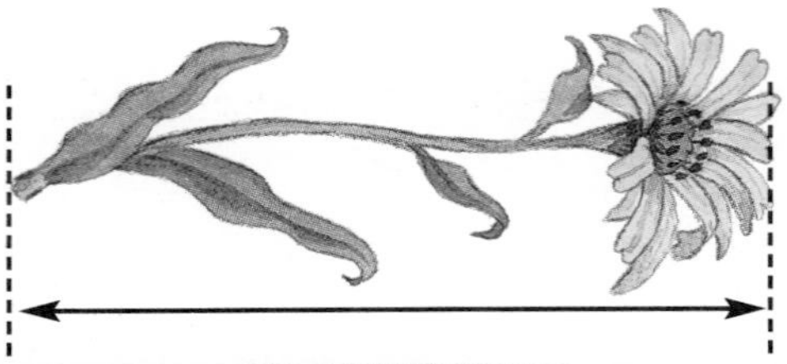

Estimate. _____ centimeters

Measure. _____ centimeters

4 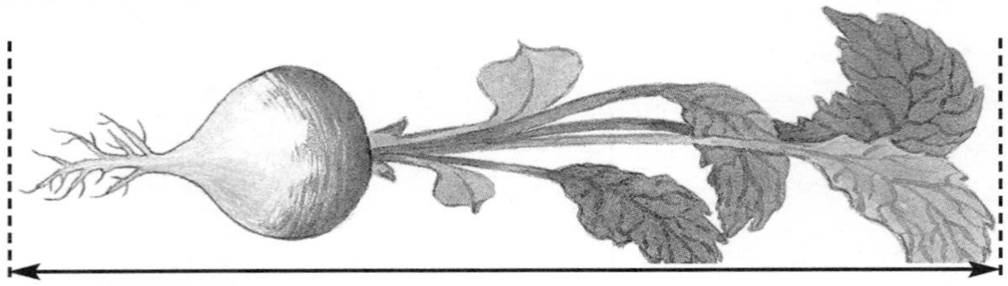

Estimate. _____ centimeters

Measure. _____ centimeters

5 

Estimate. _____ centimeters

Measure. _____ centimeters

Start at the dot.

6 Draw a line that is about 7 centimeters long.

●

7 Draw another line.
Make it longer than 8 centimeters
and shorter than 12 centimeters.

●

Problem Solving Critical Thinking

8 Solve.
Suki is shorter than Dee.
Ron is taller than Jasper.
Jasper is taller than Dee.

Who is the tallest? __________

Notes for Home: Your child practiced estimating and measuring lengths of objects with a centimeter ruler. *Home Activity:* Ask your child to estimate and then measure the length of these objects in centimeters: a crayon, pencil, an envelope, and a stamp.

Name

Problem Solving: Group Decision Making

Learn

PROBLEM SOLVING GUIDE
Understand • Plan • Solve • Look Back

Check

Work with a group. Write the answers.

1. Think of 3 things your group can measure around.
Put a check next to the one your group will measure.

____

____

____

Talk About It How did your group decide what to measure?

Notes for Home: Your child worked with a group to choose a measurement project.
Home Activity: Ask your child to show you how to use a string and a ruler to measure the distance around a bucket or wastebasket.

Practice

Work with your group. Write the answers.

2. Your group has only string and a ruler. Talk about how you can use these to measure your object. Draw what you will do.

3. Estimate. How big around does the group think your object is?

____

4. Measure. How big around is it?

____

5. Talk it over. Was string a good thing to use? Why or why not?

____

Journal

6. Write about your group.
How did you work together?
What did each member of the group do?
What went well? What problems did you have?

Notes for Home: Your child worked with a group to choose tools and carry out a measurement project. *Home Activity:* Work with your child to measure the distance around some large things in your home, such as a box, a bed, or a room.

Name

Mixed Practice

Lessons 1–6

Concepts and Skills

Use the rulers to measure length. Write the answer.

1. 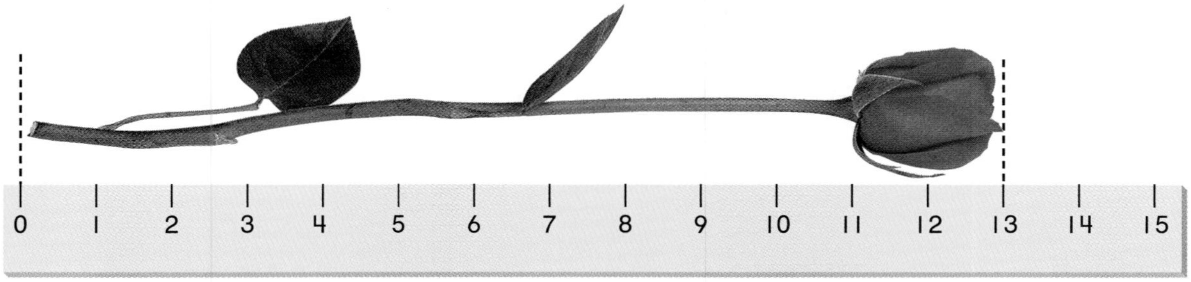

about _____ centimeters

2. 

about _____ inches

How long would a rake be? Circle the best answer.

3. 

shorter than 1 foot

about 1 foot long

longer than 1 foot

Problem Solving

4. John needs to know how wide his garden is. Would it be easier to measure it with inches or feet?

_____

Journal

5. What is something you would measure with inches? Draw a picture of it. Estimate how long it is.

MIXED PRACTICE

Notes for Home: Your child practiced working with centimeters, inches, and feet. *Home Activity:* Ask your child to find something in your home that you would measure the length of in feet. Measure it together.

Name ______________________________

Cumulative Review

Chapters 1–11

Concepts and Skills

1 Add or subtract.

11	5	12	10	9	6	11
− 8	+ 7	− 12	− 6	+ 3	− 4	− 6

2 Circle the best estimate.

about

10 20 40

Test Prep

Fill in the ○ for the correct answer.
Read the graph.

3 How many berries does Don have?

35 ○ 25 ○ 18 ○

4 How many more berries does Rosa have than Don?

5 ○ 7 ○ 10 ○

Notes for Home: Your child reviewed addition and subtraction, estimation, and graphing. *Home Activity:* Have your child estimate how many objects are in a group of objects such as buttons or pennies.

Name

Explore Weight

Explore

The  and  weigh about the same.

The bar is level.
We weigh the same.

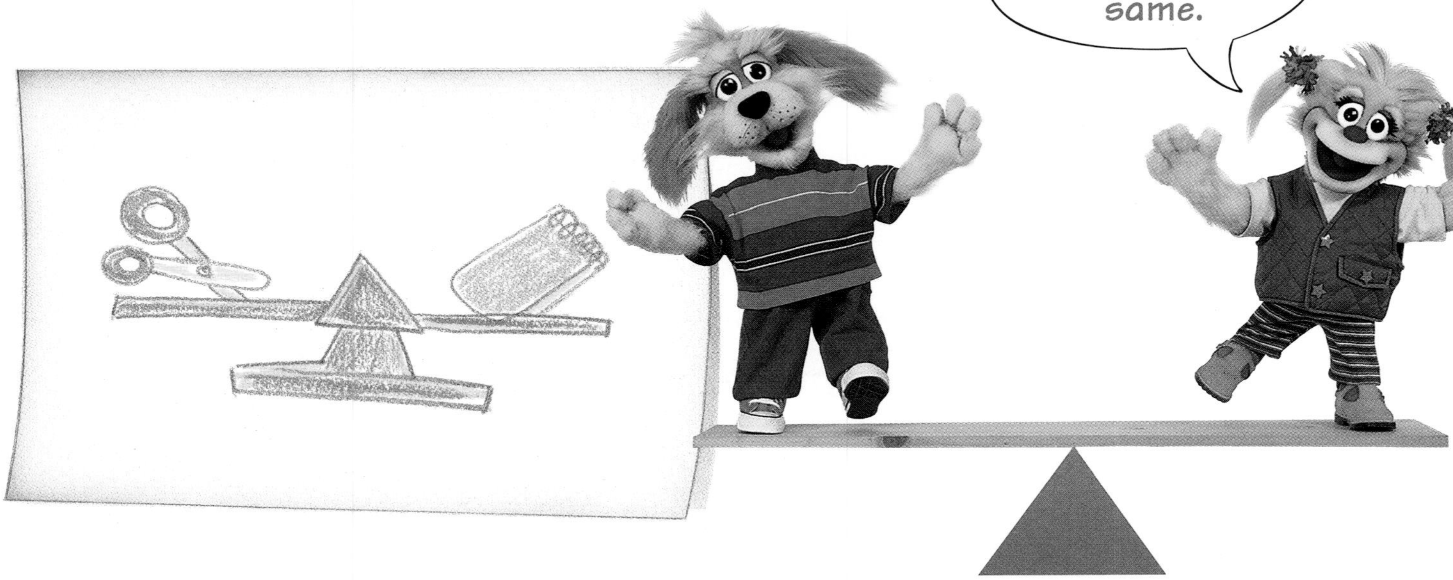

Find things that weigh about the same. Draw.

1

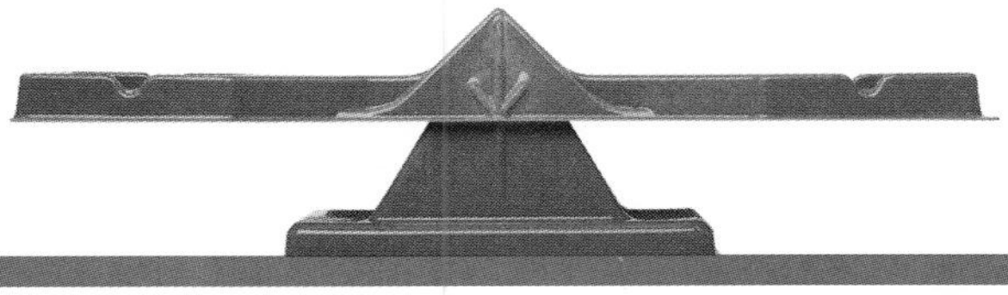

2

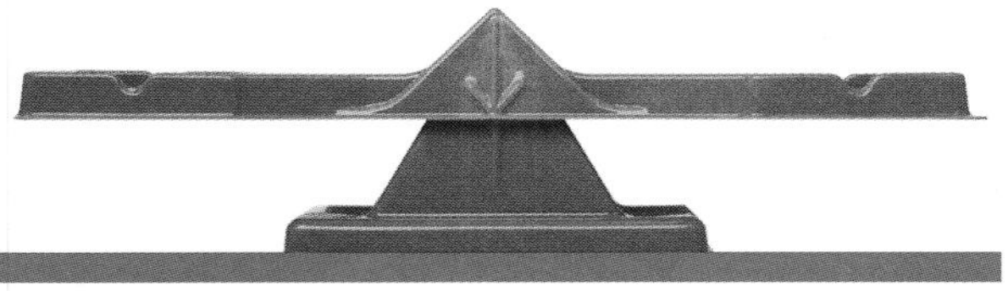

3

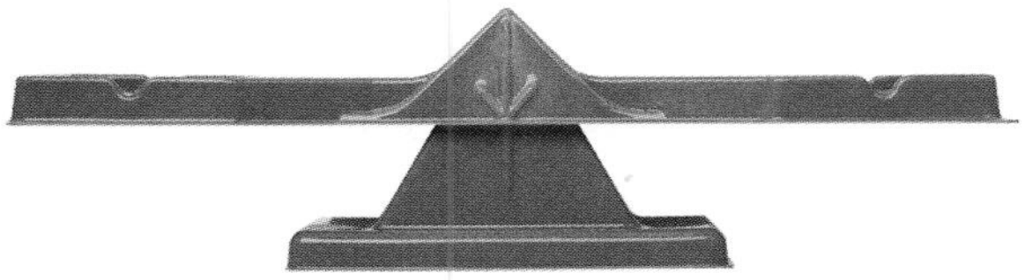

4

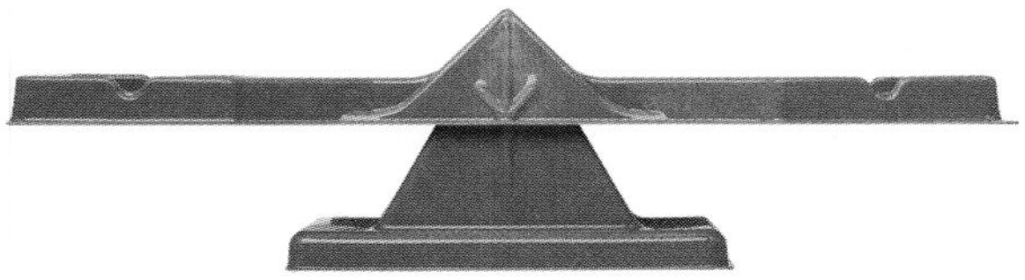

Share

What objects did you find that did not weigh the same?
How did you know?

Notes for Home: Your child explored things that weigh about the same. *Home Activity:* Ask your child to find two objects at home that weigh about the same, holding one object in each hand to feel the weight.

EXPLORE

Connect

The paper weighs less. The bone weighs more.
The apple weighs about the same as the orange.
less
more
same
same

Compare these weights. Write **more, less,** or **same.**

5

_______ _______

6

_______ _______

7

_______ _______

8

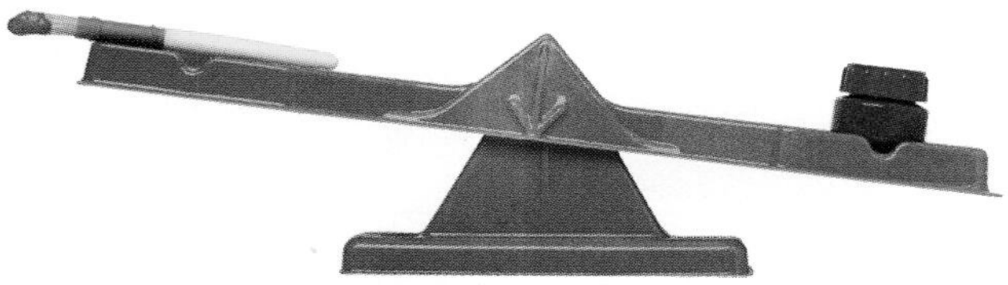

_______ _______

Talk About It What are some other ways you can use to find out how much something weighs?

Notes for Home: Your child compared the weights of objects. *Home Activity:* Ask your child to hold two objects and tell which one weighs more.

Name

Compare to One Pound

Learn

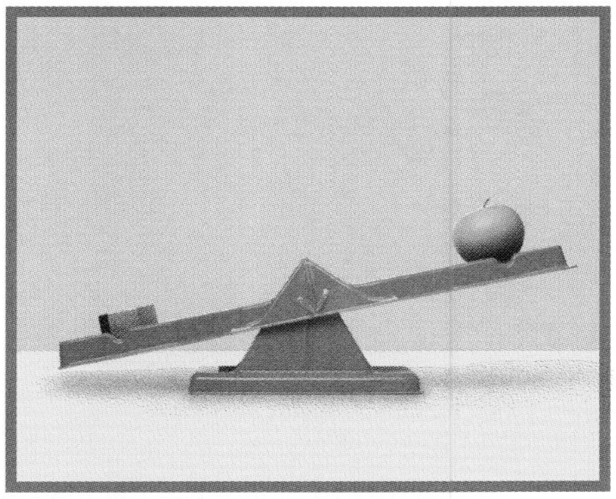

lighter than 1 pound

about 1 pound

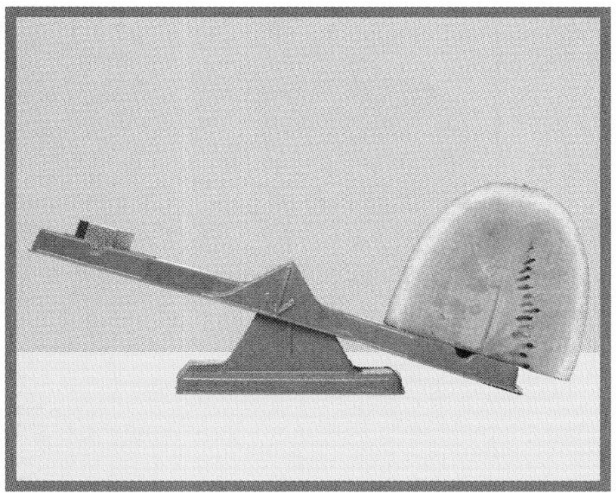

heavier than 1 pound

Check

Find things in your classroom.
Weigh them on your  .
Draw a picture in the correct space below.

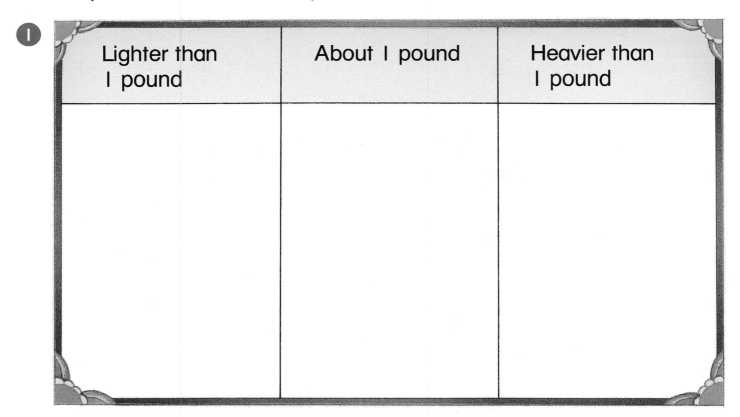

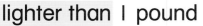

1

Lighter than 1 pound	About 1 pound	Heavier than 1 pound

Talk About It What did you find that weighs about 1 pound?

Notes for Home: Your child used a balance scale to find things that weigh about one pound.
Home Activity: Find packaged food items that weigh about one pound. Help your child read the labels to find out how much they weigh. Compare them to the weight of other items.

Practice

How heavy would each object be? Circle the best answer.

2

lighter than 1 pound
about 1 pound
heavier than 1 pound

3

lighter than 1 pound
about 1 pound
heavier than 1 pound

4

lighter than 1 pound
about 1 pound
heavier than 1 pound

5

lighter than 1 pound
about 1 pound
heavier than 1 pound

PRACTICE

Mental Math

Count by tens to solve.

6 Carlo is buying a melon.
It costs 10¢ a pound.
The melon weighs 6 pounds.
How much will it cost?

______¢

Notes for Home: Your child compared the weights of objects to one pound. *Home Activity:* While at the grocery store, help your child weigh fruits and vegetables. Find some that weigh about one pound.

Name

Compare to One Kilogram

Learn

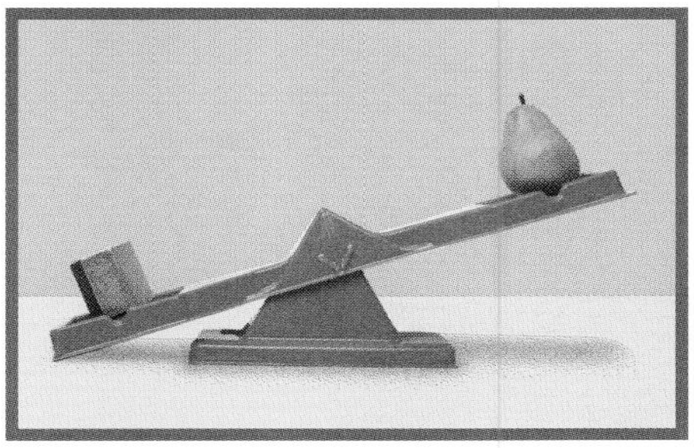

lighter than 1 kilogram

about 1 kilogram

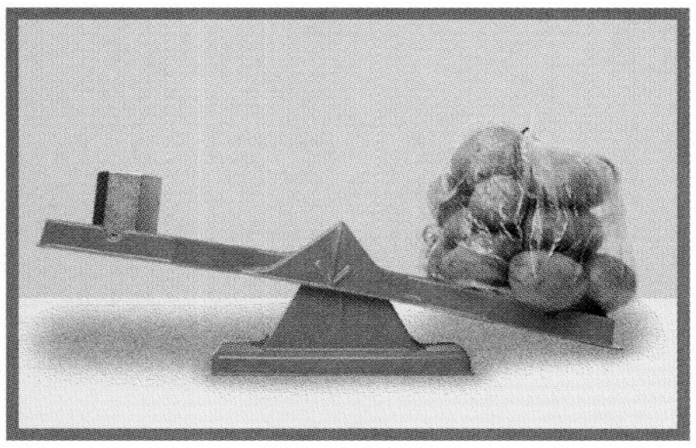

heavier than 1 kilogram

Check

Find things in your classroom. Use the  to measure.
Draw a picture in the correct space below.

1

Lighter than 1 kilogram	About 1 kilogram	Heavier than 1 kilogram

Talk About It What did you find that measures about 1 kilogram?

Notes for Home: Your child used a balance scale to find things that are about as heavy as one kilogram. *Home Activity:* Ask your child to make a list of things in your home or neighborhood that are heavier than one kilogram.

Practice

How heavy would each object be? Circle the best answer.

2

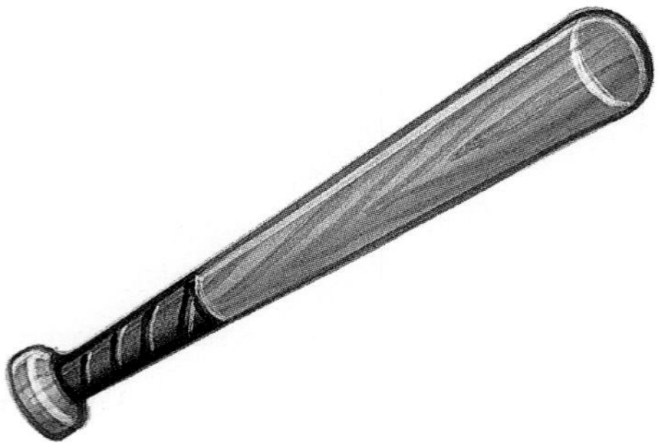

lighter than 1 kilogram

about 1 kilogram

heavier than 1 kilogram

3

lighter than 1 kilogram

about 1 kilogram

heavier than 1 kilogram

4

lighter than 1 kilogram

about 1 kilogram

heavier than 1 kilogram

5

lighter than 1 kilogram

about 1 kilogram

heavier than 1 kilogram

Problem Solving Critical Thinking

6 Is a kilogram of bricks heavier than a kilogram of feathers? Explain.

Notes for Home: Your child estimated whether things are heavier or lighter than one kilogram. *Home Activity:* Ask your child to make a list of things in your home or neighborhood that are lighter than one kilogram.

PRACTICE

Name

Compare Cups, Pints, and Quarts

Learn

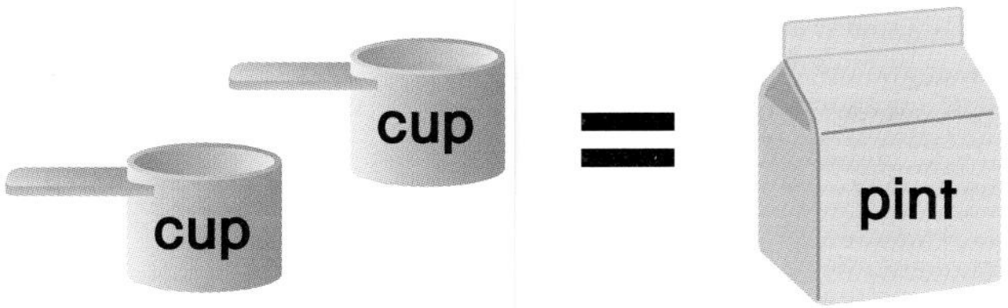

2 cups are the same as 1 pint.

2 pints are the same as 1 quart.

I think that means 4 cups is the same as 1 quart. Whew, I'm thirsty!

Check

Use 4 containers. Fill each container with water.
Circle the words that tell how much each container holds.

1. Container A holds:

   less than 1 cup
   about 1 cup
   more than 1 cup

2. Container B holds:

   less than 1 pint
   about 1 pint
   more than 1 pint

3. Container C holds:

   less than 1 quart
   about 1 quart
   more than 1 quart

4. Container D holds:

   less than 1 cup
   about 1 cup
   more than 1 cup

Talk About It Which container holds the most?
How do you know?

Notes for Home: Your child used cups, pints, and quarts to fill various containers. *Home Activity:* Ask your child to find some containers in your house that hold about 1 cup, 1 pint, and 1 quart.

Practice

Circle the things that could hold less than 1 cup.

Mark an X on the things that could hold more than 1 cup.

5

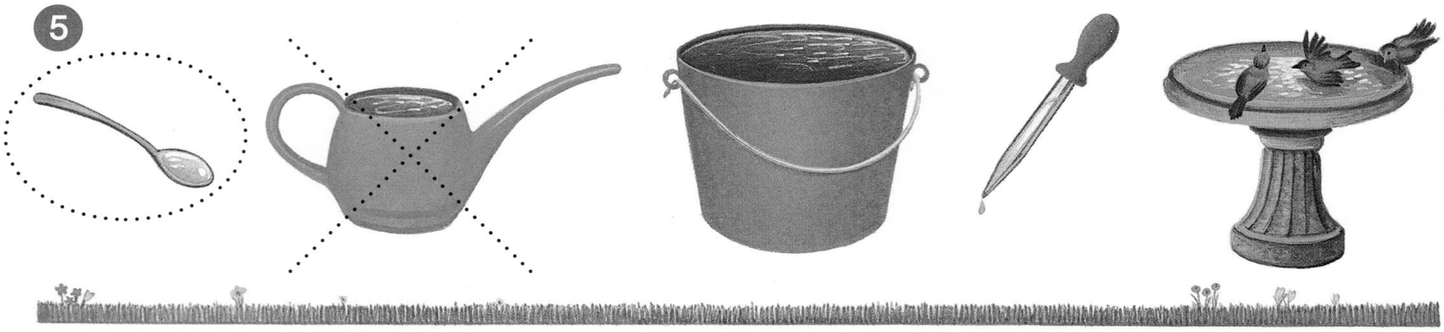

Circle the things that could hold less than 1 pint.

Mark an X on the things that could hold more than 1 pint.

6

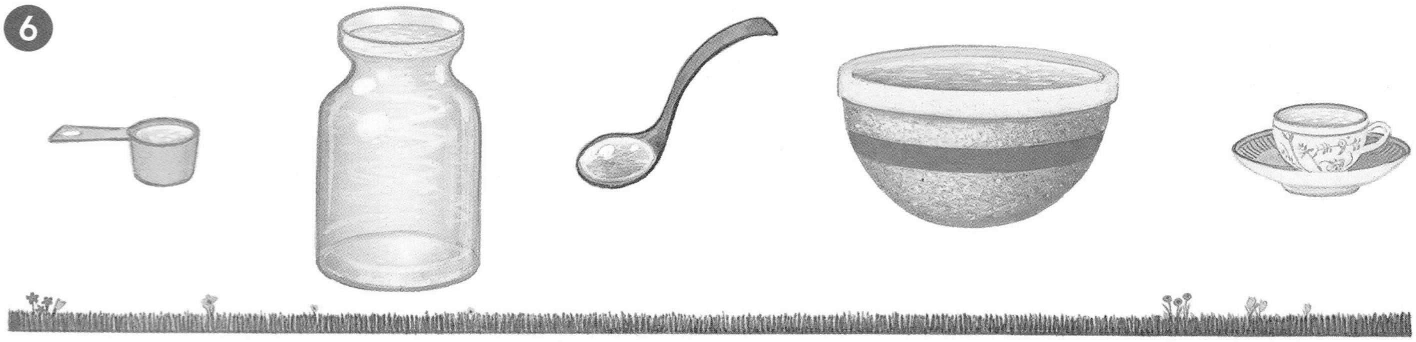

Circle the things that could hold less than 1 quart.

Mark an X on the things that could hold more than 1 quart.

7

Tell a Math Story

8 Tell how to make your favorite recipe.
Tell what you need to make it and how much.

Notes for Home: Your child identified containers that hold more or less than 1 cup, 1 pint, and 1 quart. *Home Activity:* Show your child some containers from your kitchen and ask if they hold more or less than a cup. Repeat for pint and quart. Use a measuring cup to check.

PRACTICE

Name

Compare to One Liter

Learn

Less than 1 liter	1 liter	More than 1 liter
	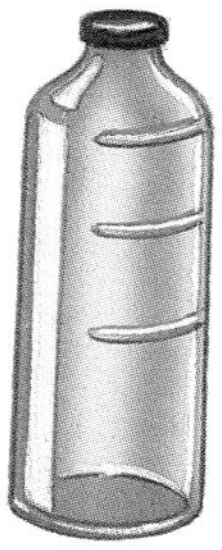	

Check

Use 4 containers. Fill each one with water.
Circle the words that tell how much each container holds.

1. Container A holds:

   less than 1 liter
   about 1 liter
   more than 1 liter

2. Container B holds:

   less than 1 liter
   about 1 liter
   more than 1 liter

3. Container C holds:

   less than 1 liter
   about 1 liter
   more than 1 liter

4. Container D holds:

   less than 1 liter
   about 1 liter
   more than 1 liter

Talk About It Which containers hold more than 1 liter? How do you know?

Notes for Home: Your child used a liter container to compare the capacity of different containers to one liter. *Home Activity:* Ask your child to find a container in your home that holds about one liter. Use a liter soda or water bottle to check.

Practice

Check how much each container could hold.

	Container	Less than 1 liter	About 1 liter	More than 1 liter
5	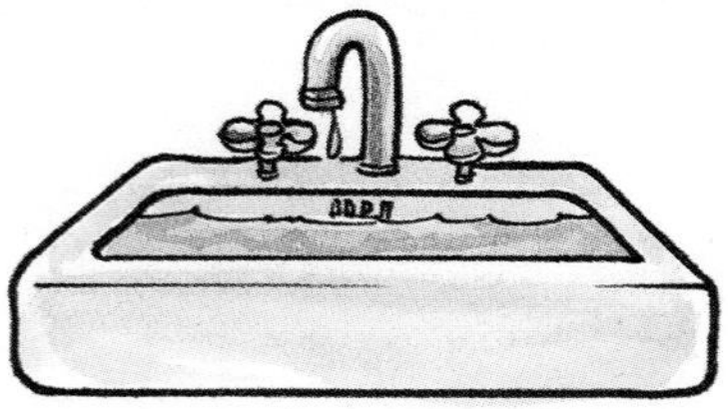			✓
6				
7				
8				
9				

PRACTICE

Mental Math

10 Helga went to the store. She got 4 bottles of juice. Each bottle held 2 liters. How many liters of juice did she buy?

Notes for Home: Your child checked whether various containers hold more or less than 1 liter. *Home Activity:* Ask your child to explore the capacity of containers while helping to wash the dishes.

Name

Use a Thermometer

Learn

A **thermometer** measures the **temperature.**

Check

Draw a line from the thermometer to the correct picture.

1
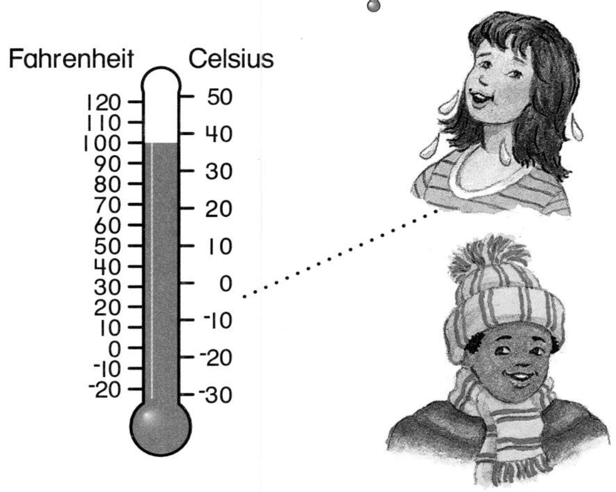

2
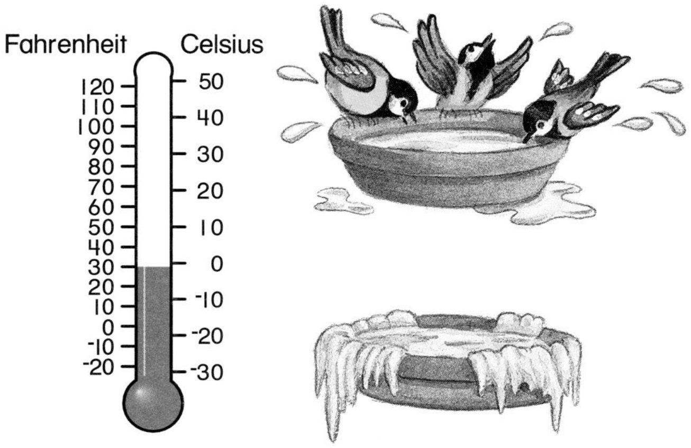

3
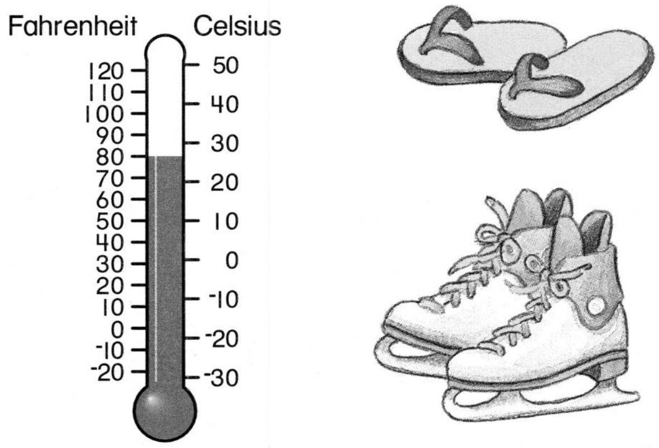

4
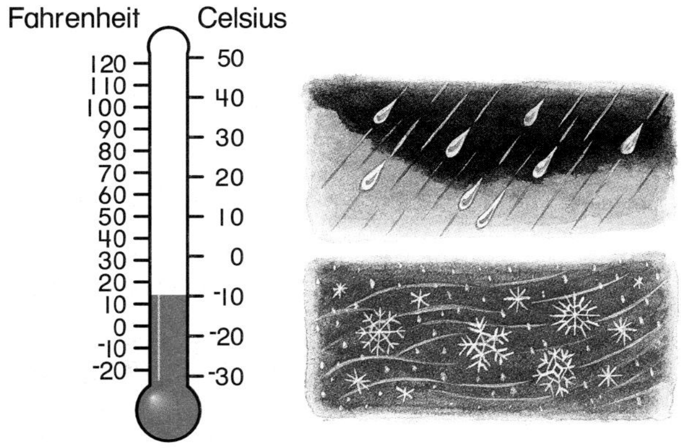

Talk About It If you looked at a thermometer outside today, what would the temperature be? How do you know?

Notes for Home: Your child matched a thermometer reading to a corresponding picture. *Home Activity:* Help your child measure and record temperatures around the house, for example, the temperature of hot coffee, milk, ice cream, and so on.

Practice

Look at the thermometer.
Draw a picture to show how it looks outside.

5

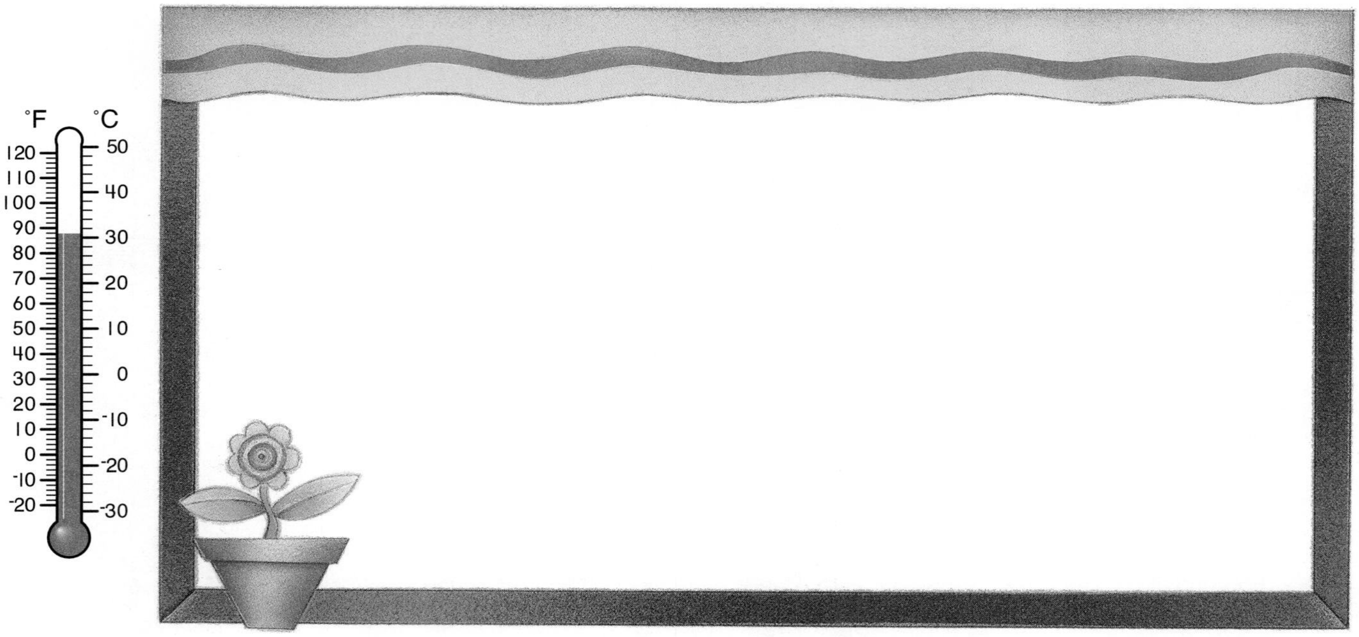

6

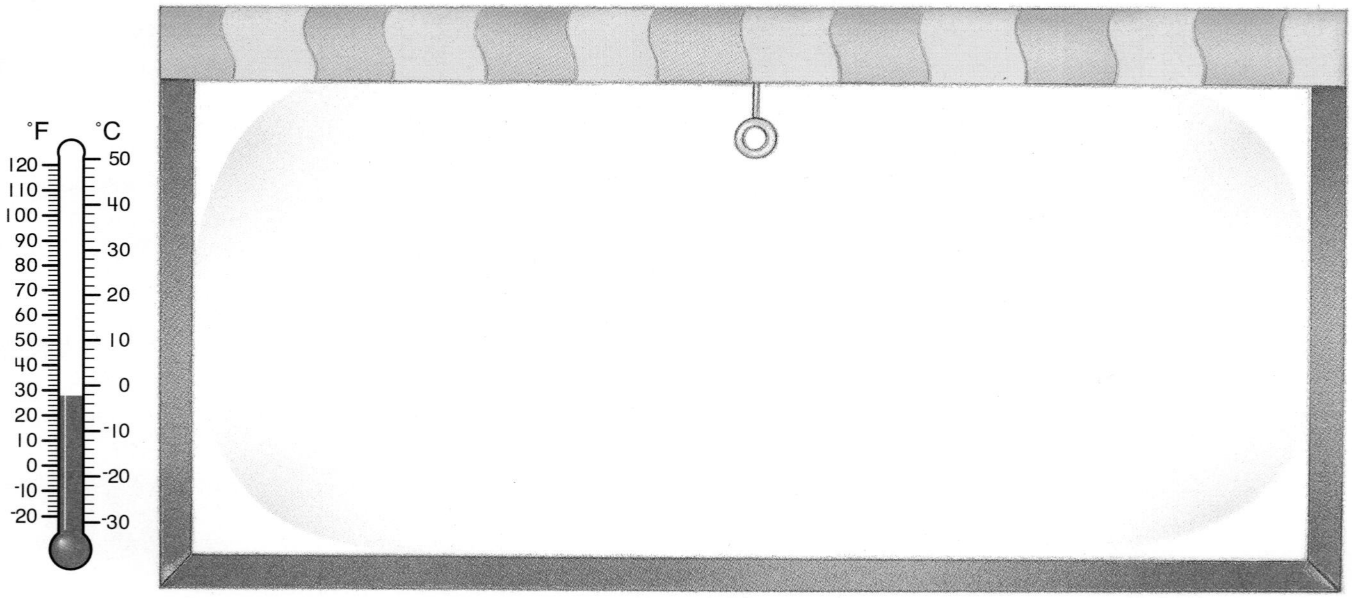

PRACTICE

Journal

7 Write about some things you like to do outside when it is very hot. Write about some things you like to do outside when it is very cold.

Notes for Home: Your child drew pictures to show understanding of the temperature shown on a thermometer. *Home Activity:* Help your child record the temperature at different times of the day, at the same time on different days, or in different places around your home.

Name ______________________

Reading for Math

Technical Words

Sometimes stories have special math words.

Bear's Plant

Bear had a plant in his garden.
He wanted to know how tall it was.
Bear brought his balance
scale outside.
He started to pull up the plant.
Just then Elephant came by.
"Stop!" said Elephant.
"I have what you need to measure
how tall your plant is."

Circle the word or words that answer the question.

1. What was Bear trying to use to measure how tall the plant was?

   ruler   balance scale

2. What do you think Elephant will use to measure the plant?

   ruler   balance scale

Talk About It Name three things you can measure with a ruler. Name three things you might measure with a balance scale.

Notes for Home: Your child used words for tools that measure length, width, and weight and listened to a silly story about a bear who didn't know which tool to use. *Home Activity:* Choose something at your home to measure and let your child tell you the best tool to use.

Bear Cooks

Bear wanted to make pancakes.
He got out the milk.
Would his mixing bowl hold
a pint of milk?
He put a ruler inside the bowl.
Just then Elephant came by.
"Stop!" said Elephant.
"I have what you need to
measure how much the
bowl holds."

Circle the word or words that answer the question.

3. What did Bear try to use to measure the milk?

   measuring cup **ruler**

4. What do you think Elephant will tell Bear to use?

   measuring cup **scale**

Journal

5. Bear and Elephant make 20 pancakes.
   They want to know if the pancakes
   weigh as much as an orange.
   How can they find out?

Notes for Home: Your child used words for tools that tell how much something weighs and how much something holds. *Home Activity:* Have your child help you measure one cup of something the next time the need arises.

Name

Problem Solving: Logical Reasoning

Learn

PROBLEM SOLVING GUIDE

Understand • Plan • Solve • Look Back

I want to find out how tall my plant is. What tool should I use?

Check

Circle the best tool to use.

1. How much water does it hold?

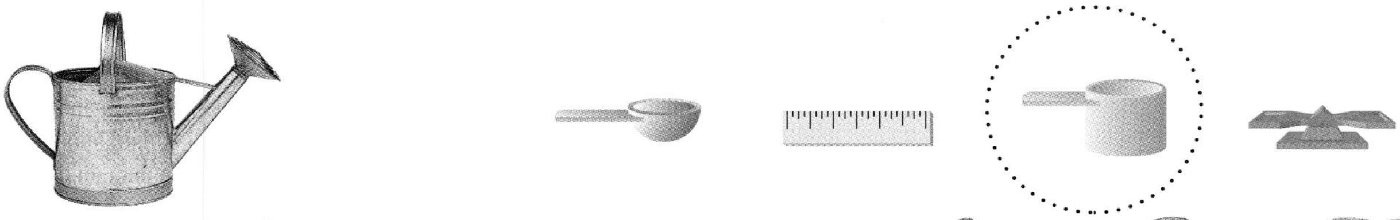

2. How heavy is it?

3. How long is it?

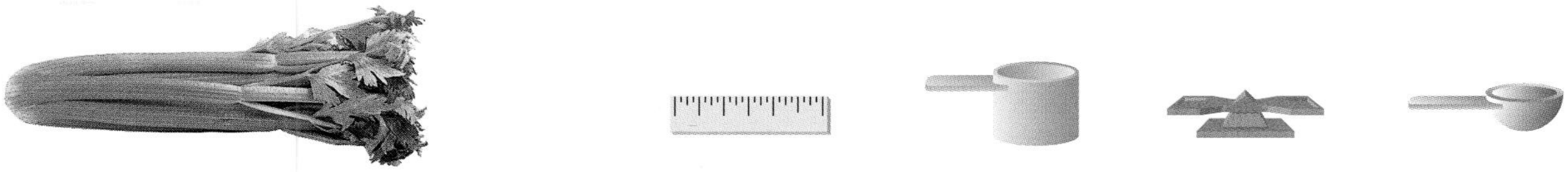

Talk About It How could you use a spoon to find out how much water a cup holds?

Notes for Home: Your child learned to choose the appropriate tool to measure an object. *Home Activity:* Ask your child to name the measurement tool that might be used to measure the width of a doorway or the length of a rug (ruler, yardstick, tape measure).

PROBLEM SOLVING

Practice

Circle the best tool to use.

4 How heavy is it?

5 How cold is it?.

6 How much water does it hold?

7 How long is it?

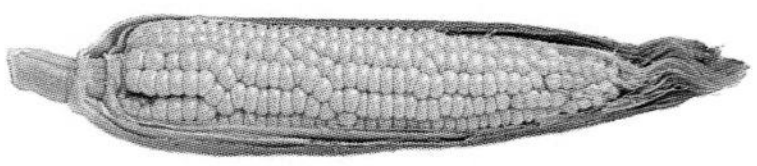

Tell a Math Story

8 Bob has a garden. Tell a story about this garden. Use 2 of these things in your story.

Notes for Home: Your child practiced choosing tools to measure length, weight, and capacity. *Home Activity:* Ask your child to find objects in your home to measure such as a desk, a book, and a thermos. Ask your child to help you measure length, weight and/or capacity for appropriate items.

For additional practice, see Skills Practice Bank, page 537, Set 2

Name

Mixed Practice

Lessons 7–13

Concepts and Skills

Circle the words that tell about the object.

1. The fruit measures

less than 1 kilogram.

about 1 kilogram.

more than 1 kilogram.

2. The cherries weigh

less than 1 pound.

about 1 pound.

more than 1 pound.

3. The bottle holds

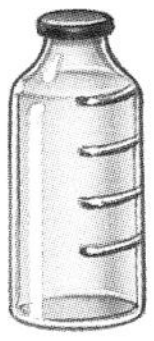

less than 1 liter.

about 1 liter.

more than 1 liter.

4. The spoon holds

less than 1 cup.

about 1 cup.

more than 1 cup.

Problem Solving

Circle the best tool to use.

5. How high is a fence?

Journal

6. Record the length and weight of a toy.

Notes for Home: Your child practiced estimating weight and capacity measures. *Home Activity:* Ask your child to tell you why you might measure a table with a ruler (to find out how long, wide, or tall it is).

MIXED PRACTICE

Name ______________________________

Cumulative Review

Chapter 1–11

Concepts and Skills

Add.

1. 5 + 5 = ____   5 + 6 = ____   6 + 5 = ____

2. 4 + 4 = ____   4 + 5 = ____   5 + 4 = ____

Problem Solving

Write a number sentence.

3. Marcy grew 13 tomatoes.
She ate 4.
How many were left?

____

4. Tanya picked 4 red flowers.
She picked 7 yellow flowers.
How many flowers did she pick?

____

Test Prep

Fill in the ○ for the correct answer.
What time does the clock show?

5. 

○ 2:30
○ 3:00
○ 3:30

6. 

○ 4:00
○ 5:00
○ 6:00

7. 

○ 11:30
○ 12:30
○ 6:00

8. 

○ 9:30
○ 10:00
○ 10:30

Notes for Home: Your child reviewed addition, writing number sentences, and telling time.
Home Activity: Ask your child to tell you an addition and subtraction story for 5 + 8 and 13 – 8.

Name ______________________________

Chapter 11 Review

Vocabulary

Use a ruler to measure.

1

about _____ centimeters

2

about _____ inches

Concepts and Skills

Circle the words that tell about the object.

3

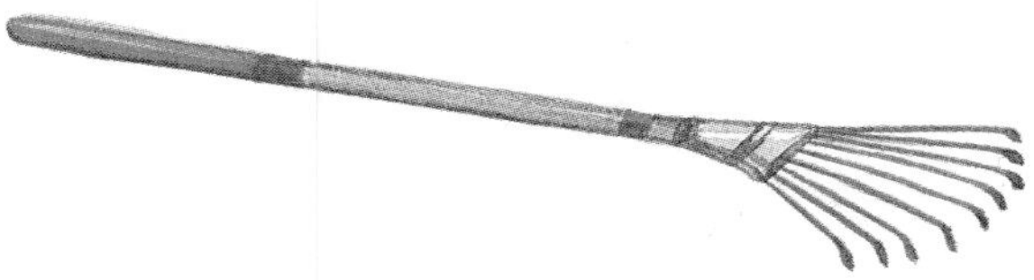

shorter than 1 foot
about 1 foot
longer than 1 foot

4

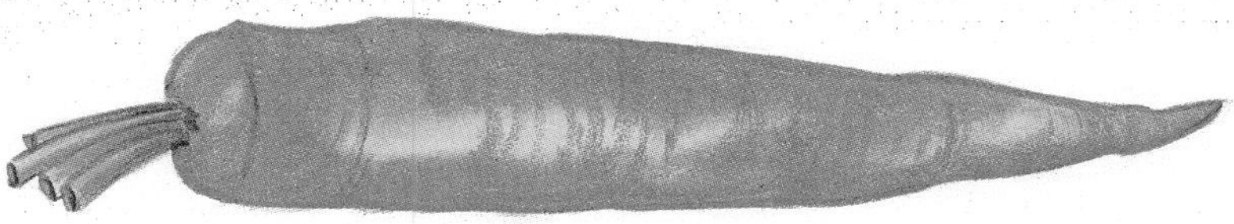

lighter than 1 kilogram
about 1 kilogram
heavier than 1 kilogram

5

less than 1 liter
about 1 liter
more than 1 liter

Problem Solving

6 How heavy is a pumpkin?
Circle the best tool to use.

Notes for Home: Your child reviewed the vocabulary, concepts, skills, and problem solving taught in Chapter 11. *Home Activity:* With your child measure the length, weight, and how much a bowl or other container holds.

Name

Chapter 11 Test

Concepts and Skills

Circle the best answer.

1 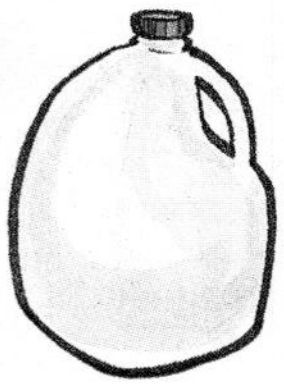 less than 1 cup / about 1 cup / more than 1 cup

2  less than 1 liter / about 1 liter / more than 1 liter

3 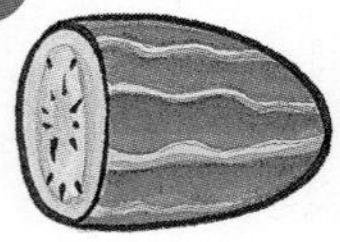 lighter than 1 kilogram / about 1 kilogram / heavier than 1 kilogram

4  lighter than 1 pound / about 1 pound / heavier than 1 pound

5 This page is about 1 _____ long   inch   foot

Measure. Tell about how many inches.

6 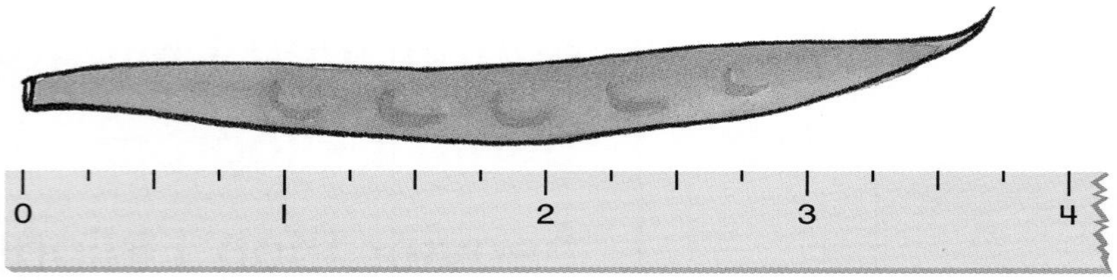

_____ inches

7 Circle the best tool to use. How heavy is a  ?

8 Draw a line from the  to the correct picture.

Notes for Home: Your child was assessed on Chapter 11 concepts, skills, and problem solving.
Home Activity: Ask your child to measure different objects in your home with a ruler.

CHAPTER TEST

Name ______________________________

Performance Assessment

Chapter 11

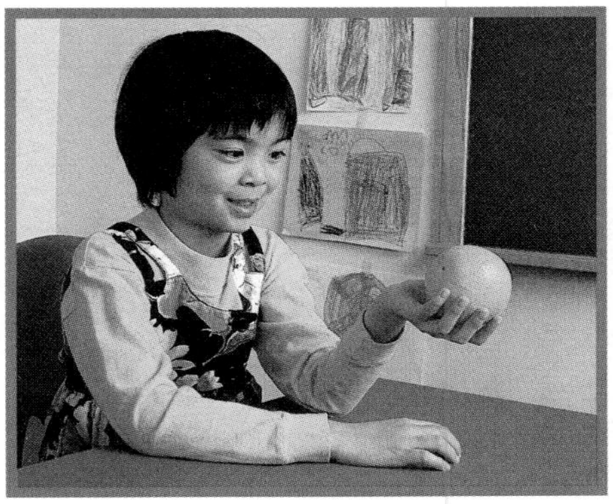

Find an object. Choose what to measure.

Decide which tool to use.

Measure. Record.

	Object to Find	What to Measure	Tool to Use	Record
1		Length How much it holds Weight		
2		Length How much it holds Weight		
3		Length How much it holds Weight		

Problem Solving Critical Thinking

4 How can you tell if 2 glasses hold the same amount?

Notes for Home: Your child did activities that assessed Chapter 11 skills, concepts, and problem solving. *Home Activity:* Ask your child to tell how he or she might measure some objects in your kitchen such as how heavy a roast is, how long a wooden spoon is, or how much soup is in a can.

Name ______________________________

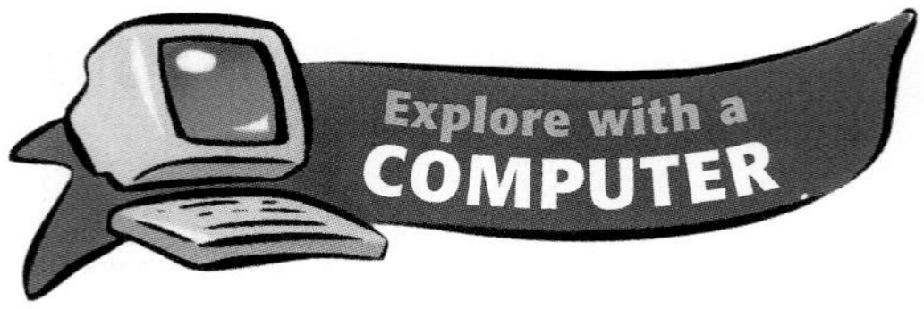
Explore with a
COMPUTER

How Does It Measure Up?

Computer Skills You Will Need

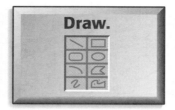

Use a mouse.
Draw.
Select.
Print.
File
Mail Merge
Page Setup
Print

Calculator Keys You Will Use ON/C + =

1. Draw a shape with 3 sides.
2. Draw a shape with 4 sides.
3. Print your shapes.
4. Use a ruler to measure each side.

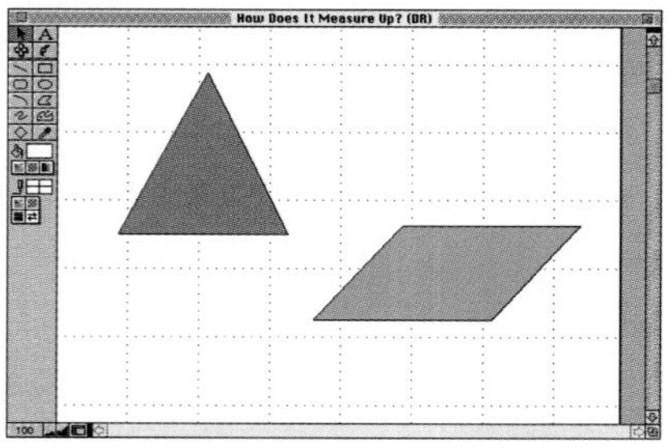

5. Complete the table. Use your calculator to find the totals.

3 sides	
Side	Measure
1	
2	
3	
Total	

Use ON/C to **clear** the first total.

4 sides	
Side	Measure
1	
2	
3	
4	
Total	

Tech Talk What would happen if you did not clear the first total?

Visit our Web site. **www.parent.mathsurf.com**

Math at Home

Potato Power

What You Need

a sweet potato, a jar, water, and toothpicks

What You Do

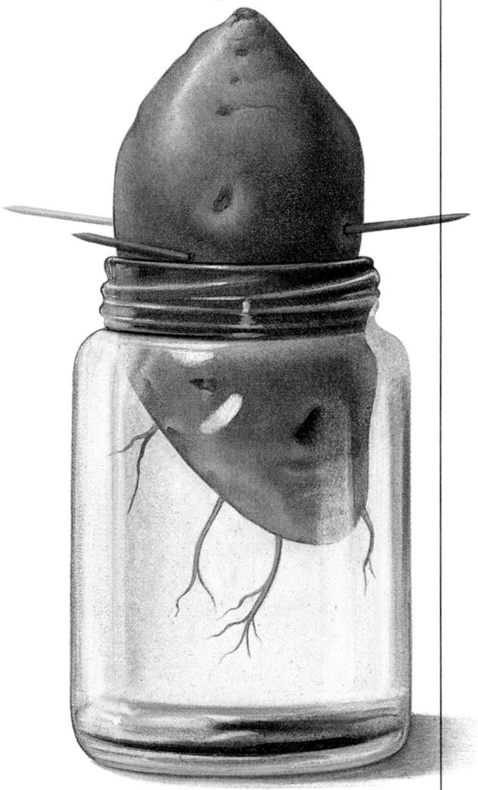

1. **Stick toothpicks into a sweet potato to hold it half in and half out of a jar. Use an old, firm, plump sweet potato that has begun to sprout.**
2. **Put the fatter end up.**
3. **Pour in only enough water to just touch the thinner end.**
4. **Set your potato in a cool, dark place for ten days. Then bring your potato into a warm, light place. Keep it watered and watch it grow!**

Your Potato's Diary

How long is my stem?

1 week	2 weeks
3 weeks	4 weeks

Fold down

A Green Thumb?

If you have a green thumb, it means you are good at making things grow.
These kids have green thumbs.
They live in the city and grow vegetables in a city garden.

Notes for Home: Your child read about a garden in the city and planned a garden. *Home Activity:* With your child, look for gardens in places like window boxes, backyards, and neighborhood garden plots.

What will you make?
Wrapping paper?
Birthday cards?
Note paper?

Potato Printing

A potato can be baked, fried, or mashed.
A potato can also be stamped!

What You Need

a potato, a plastic knife, paint, and paper

What You Do

1 Have a grownup help you cut a potato in half.
2 Have the grown up help you cut designs into both sides of the potato.
3 Dip the potato into paint and stamp, stamp, stamp a pattern on paper.

Hint: To change colors, rinse your potato with water first.

Notes for Home: Your child made a potato stamp and used it to design a pattern. *Home Activity:* Help your child make a potato stamp at home to decorate writing paper and then write a letter to a relative or friend.

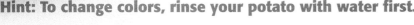

Room to Grow

Pretend this is a garden.
Plant carrots, beans, and tomatoes.
Draw the plants one inch apart.

Key

carrot ◢ bean ⬬ tomato ●

Which is Bigger?

Is one gardener taller than the other?
Is the center of one flower larger than the other?
Is one garden hose longer than the other?
Guess. Then measure to see if they are the same size or different.

Notes for Home: Your child measured the optical illusions above. *Home Activity:* Have your child draw a flower optical illusion by tracing a coin for identical circles and drawing different-sized petals around each circle.

CHAPTER

12

Facts and Strategies to 18

Notes for Home: Your child talked about ways to join two groups to find how many in all.
Home Activity: Ask your child to tell an addition or subtraction story about the picture.

Math at Home

Dear Family,

We are starting Chapter 12. We will learn about adding and subtracting numbers to 18. Here are some activities we can do together.

Duck Pond

Put 12–15 small objects, such as beans, in a cup. Spill them onto a small piece of paper, or "pond," so that only part of them land on the paper. Make up math stories. If 8 land on and 6 land off the paper, a story might be, "14 ducks were in the pond. 6 ducks flew away. (14 – 6 = 8) 8 ducks are left."

Seeing Double

Put 7 pieces of fruit, cereal, or other snacks on the table. Ask your child to double it. Together, say an addition fact about the snack:

$7 + 7 = 14$.

Then eat half of the snack and say a subtraction fact:

$14 - 7 = 7$.

Community Connection

When you do errands or go for a walk with your child, add the number of legs in the group. For instance, if two people go for a walk with a dog, add $2 + 2 + 4$ (8).

Visit our Web site. www.parent.mathsurf.com

Name ______________________________

Add Doubles to 18

Learn

These pictures show doubles.

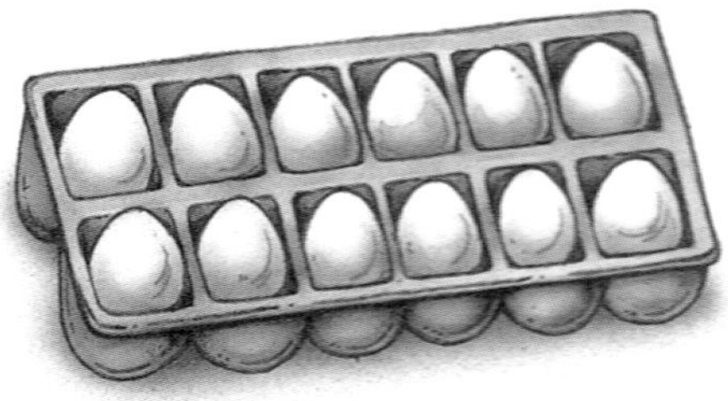

$6 + 6 = 12$

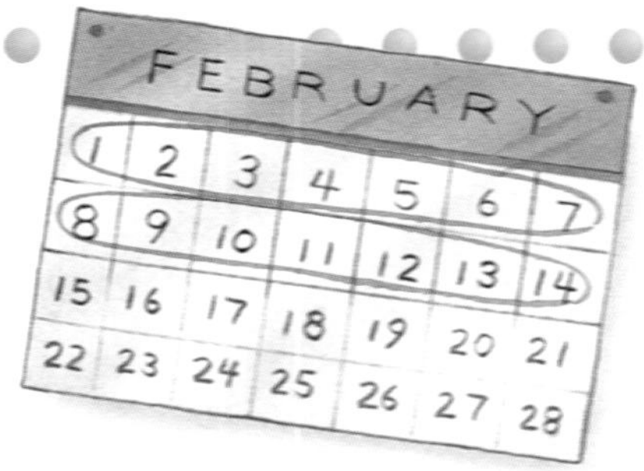

$7 + 7 = 14$

$8 + 8 = 16$

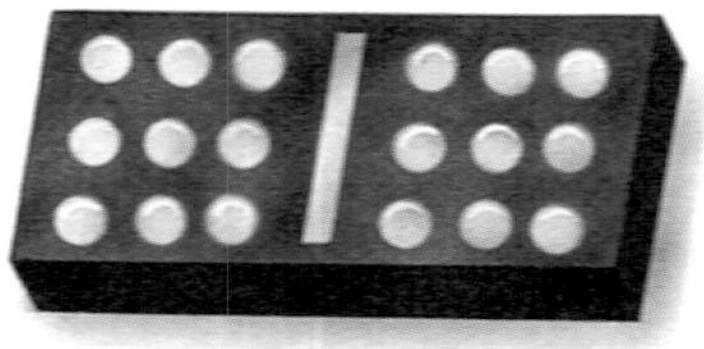

$9 + 9 = 18$

Check

Write the sum.

1. $6 + 6 =$ 12 $4 + 4 =$ ____ $7 + 7 =$ ____
2. $3 + 3 =$ ____ $8 + 8 =$ ____ $1 + 1 =$ ____
3. $9 + 9 =$ ____ $2 + 2 =$ ____ $5 + 5 =$ ____
4. $\begin{array}{r} 8 \\ +8 \\ \hline \end{array}$ $\begin{array}{r} 6 \\ +6 \\ \hline \end{array}$ $\begin{array}{r} 0 \\ +0 \\ \hline \end{array}$ $\begin{array}{r} 7 \\ +7 \\ \hline \end{array}$ $\begin{array}{r} 3 \\ +3 \\ \hline \end{array}$ $\begin{array}{r} 9 \\ +9 \\ \hline \end{array}$ $\begin{array}{r} 2 \\ +2 \\ \hline \end{array}$

Talk About It Which one is not a doubles fact? Tell why.

$5 + 5 = 10$ $9 + 8 = 17$

Notes for Home: Your child added doubles such as 6 + 6, 7 + 7, 8 + 8, and 9 + 9.
Home Activity: Ask your child to find something in your home that shows double 6, 7, 8, or 9.

Practice

PRACTICE

Write the sum.

5 7 + 7 = 14   6 + 6 = ____   9 + 9 = ____

6 8 + 8 = ____   5 + 5 = ____   4 + 4 = ____

Mixed Practice Write the sum. Circle the doubles.

7

5	7	9	7	8	3	3
+ 6	+ 7	+ 2	+ 5	+ 8	+ 3	+ 4
11						

8

5	7	6	1	4	9	6
+ 5	+ 3	+ 6	+ 9	+ 4	+ 9	+ 5

Problem Solving Visual Thinking

9 Mrs. Lopez took her dog for a walk.
They walked to the park.
Then they walked back home.
How far did they walk?

____ blocks

Notes for Home: Your child practiced doubles facts such as 6 + 6, 7 + 7, 8 + 8, and 9 + 9.
Home Activity: Say a doubles sum (14). Have your child tell the doubles fact that goes with it (7 + 7).

Name ______________________________

Add Doubles Plus One

Learn

$6 + 6 =$ 12　　$6 + 7 =$ 13　　$7 + 6 =$ 13

Check

Write the number sentence.

1

___ + ___ = 14

___ + ___ = ___

___ + ___ = ___

2

___ + ___ = ___

___ + ___ = ___

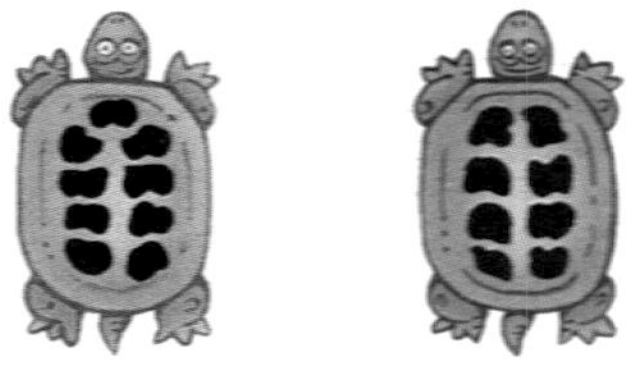

___ + ___ = ___

Talk About It How can knowing $8 + 8$ help you find the sum for $8 + 9$?

Notes for Home: Your child used doubles facts such as $8 + 8 = 16$ to learn other facts such as $8 + 9 = 17$. *Home Activity:* Show two groups of 8 pennies and ask how many in all (16). Then add one more penny and ask how many now (17).

Practice

PRACTICE

Write the sum.

3	$8 + 8 = 16$	$8 + 9$	$9 + 8$	4	$3 + 3$	$3 + 4$	$4 + 3$
5	$7 + 7$	$7 + 8$	$8 + 7$	6	$6 + 6$	$6 + 7$	$7 + 6$

7. $4 + 4 =$ ____ $9 + 9 =$ ____ $5 + 4 =$ ____

8. $8 + 7 =$ ____ $3 + 4 =$ ____ $3 + 3 =$ ____

9. $9 + 8 =$ ____ $4 + 5 =$ ____ $8 + 9 =$ ____

Problem Solving

Solve. Write the number sentence.

10. Carmen saw 6 red fish.
She saw 7 yellow fish.
How many fish did Carmen see?

____ + ____ = ____

____ fish

11. Jeff saw 8 turtles on a log.
He saw 7 turtles in the water.
How many turtles did Jeff see?

____ + ____ = ____

____ turtles

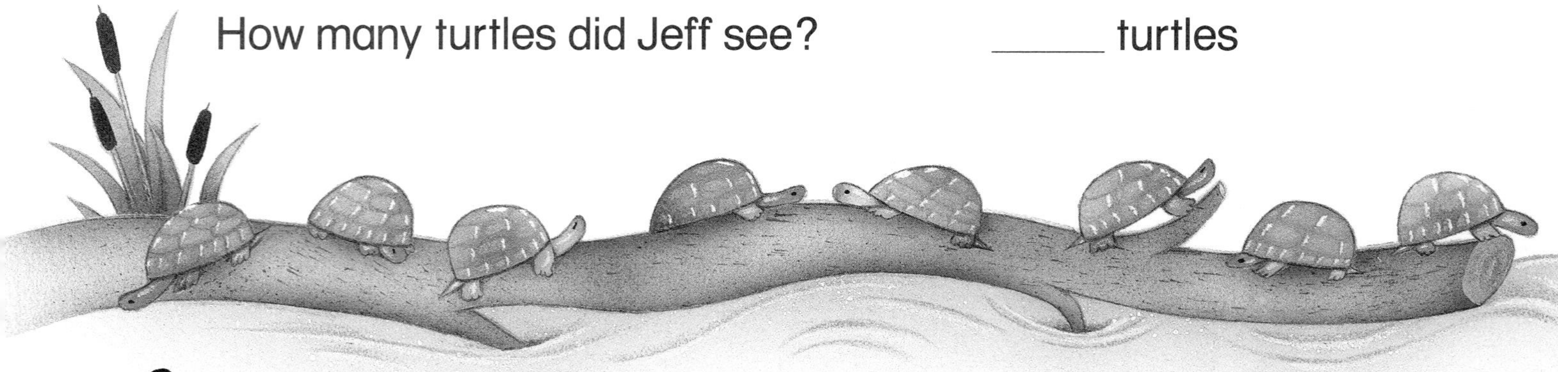

Notes for Home: Your child practiced using a doubles fact, such as 6 + 6 = 12, to solve other facts. *Home Activity:* Draw groups of dots to show 7 + 7. Ask your child to write a fact for the picture (7 + 7 = 14), draw one more dot, then write a new fact (7 + 8 = 15 or 8 + 7 = 15).

For additional practice, see Skills Practice Bank, page 538, Set 1.

Name ______________________________

Add 3 Numbers

Learn

Add the doubles.

$$\begin{array}{r} 4 \\ 3 \\ +\ 4 \\ \hline 11 \end{array}$$

4 + 4 = 8

8 + 3 = 11

Add in order.

$$\begin{array}{r} 3 \\ 4 \\ +\ 8 \\ \hline 15 \end{array}$$

3 + 4 = 7

7 + 8 = 15

Make a 10.

$$\begin{array}{r} 5 \\ 6 \\ +\ 4 \\ \hline 15 \end{array}$$

6 + 4 = 10

10 + 5 = 15

It is easy for me to add 6 + 4 first.

Check

Write the sum. Circle the numbers you add first.

1

$$\begin{array}{r} 2 \\ 5 \\ +\ 2 \\ \hline 9 \end{array} \quad \begin{array}{r} 4 \\ 9 \\ +\ 1 \\ \hline \end{array} \quad \begin{array}{r} 2 \\ 3 \\ +\ 3 \\ \hline \end{array} \quad \begin{array}{r} 2 \\ 2 \\ +\ 6 \\ \hline \end{array} \quad \begin{array}{r} 1 \\ 5 \\ +\ 2 \\ \hline \end{array} \quad \begin{array}{r} 6 \\ 3 \\ +\ 7 \\ \hline \end{array} \quad \begin{array}{r} 3 \\ 8 \\ +\ 1 \\ \hline \end{array}$$

2

$$\begin{array}{r} 6 \\ 3 \\ +\ 4 \\ \hline \end{array} \quad \begin{array}{r} 3 \\ 4 \\ +\ 3 \\ \hline \end{array} \quad \begin{array}{r} 4 \\ 2 \\ +\ 5 \\ \hline \end{array} \quad \begin{array}{r} 5 \\ 5 \\ +\ 3 \\ \hline \end{array} \quad \begin{array}{r} 2 \\ 5 \\ +\ 4 \\ \hline \end{array} \quad \begin{array}{r} 3 \\ 4 \\ +\ 4 \\ \hline \end{array} \quad \begin{array}{r} 8 \\ 8 \\ +\ 2 \\ \hline \end{array}$$

Talk About It Choose one problem. Tell how you added.

Notes for Home: Your child learned strategies for adding three numbers. *Home Activity:* Write the numbers 1, 5, and 4 on separate pieces of paper. Ask your child to place the numbers in the order in which they will be added.

Practice

Use a paper clip and pencil. Spin.
Write the number in the box. Add.

3

4	5	☐
4	3	7
+ ☐ 2	+ ☐	+ 3
10		

4

5	1	6	☐
2	☐	☐	6
+ ☐	+ 9	+ 6	+ 4

5

4	3	☐	8	0	2
☐	1	4	2	☐	☐
+ 2	+ ☐	+ 4	+ ☐	+ 5	+ 2

Mental Math

6 Katie caught 3 fish.
She added the numbers
on the fish.
Her total score was 13.
Circle the 3 fish she caught.

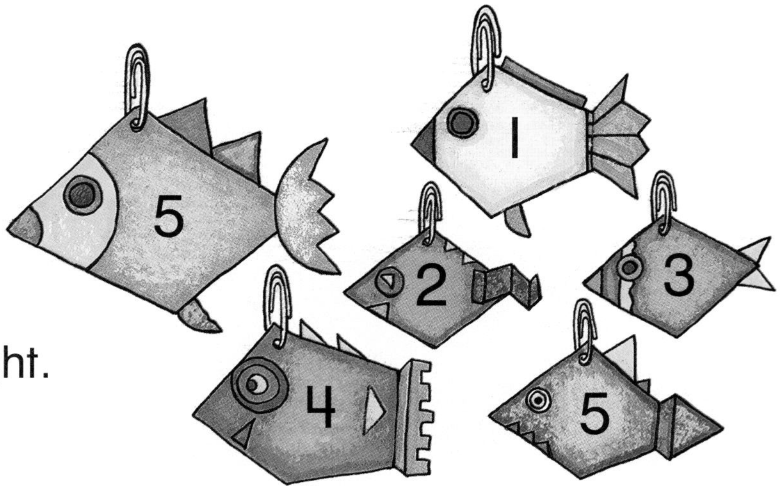

Notes for Home: Your child practiced adding three numbers. *Home Activity:* Ask your child to find three numbers that have a sum of 10 (sample answer: 3 + 2 + 5).

Name ______________________________

Practice Game

Rolling Along

What You Need

3 number cubes

16 two-color counters

How to Play

1. Play with a friend.
2. Take turns tossing all the cubes.
3. Add the 3 numbers.
4. Put a counter on the sum.
5. If the number is already covered you lose your turn.
6. The player with the most counters wins.

3	4	5	6
7	8	9	10
11	12	13	14
15	16	17	18

4 + 5 + 2 = 11.
I'll put my counter on 11.

Notes for Home: Your child practiced adding 3 numbers. *Home Activity:* Play the game with your child. Use objects such as coins or buttons for counters. A deck of cards can replace number cubes.

PRACTICE

Name ______________________________

STOP and Practice

Add.

1	1	3	2	6	1	4
	8	7	1	6	7	6
	+ 7	+ 4	+ 9	+ 3	+ 9	+ 5

2	1	7	8	3	4	6
	9	7	8	3	2	2
	+ 7	+ 3	+ 2	+ 4	+ 9	+ 8

3	7	9	6	7	8	8
	+ 8	+ 9	+ 7	+ 7	+ 9	+ 8

PRACTICE

Number Puzzle

Use these numbers: 1, 2, 3, 4, 5, 6.

4 Write one in each ◯ so that the sum of each side is 12.

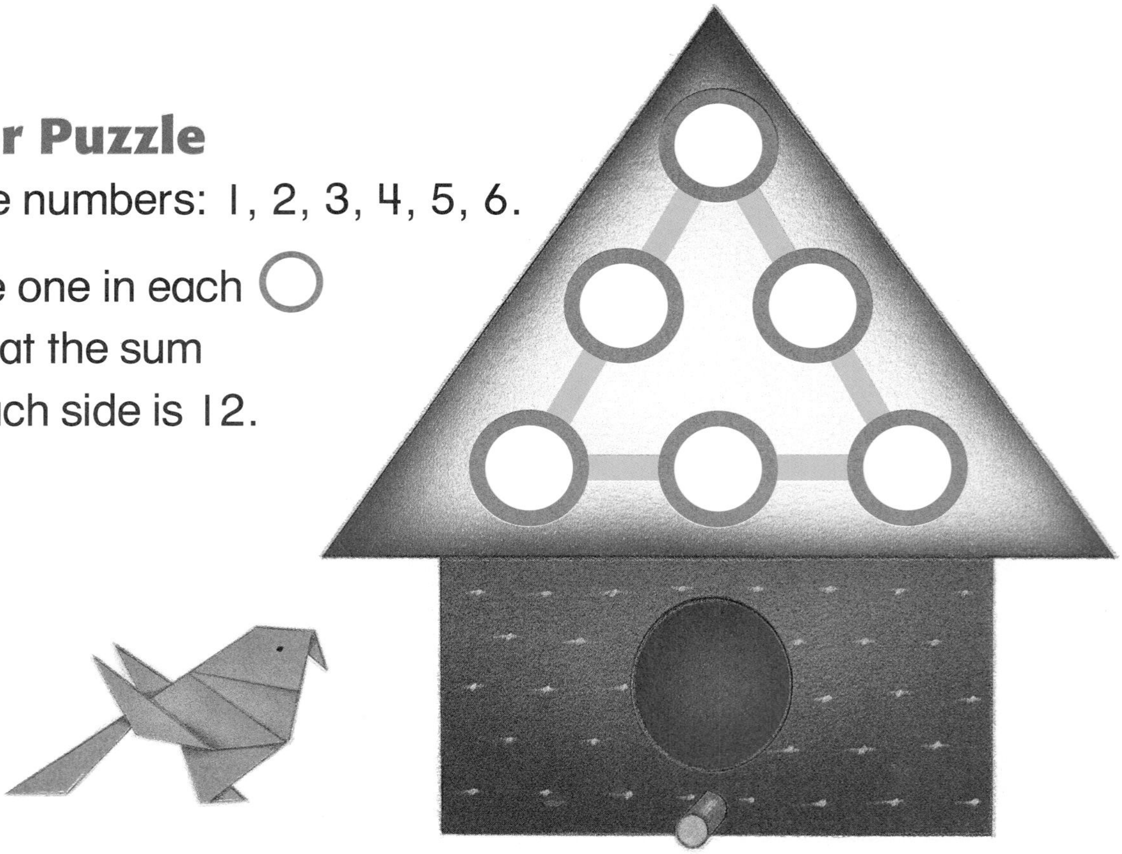

Notes for Home: Your child practiced adding three numbers. *Home Activity:* Have your child do the puzzle using the numbers 0, 1, 2, 3, 4, 5 with a sum of 9 on each side. (The answer: clockwise starting at the top, the numbers should be 5, 0, 4, 2, 3, 1.)

Name ____________________

Explore Making 10 to Add 7, 8, or 9

Explore

Choose a number. Complete the number sentence.	Draw more counters.	Complete the number sentence.
1 [4] [5] 7 + 4 = ____	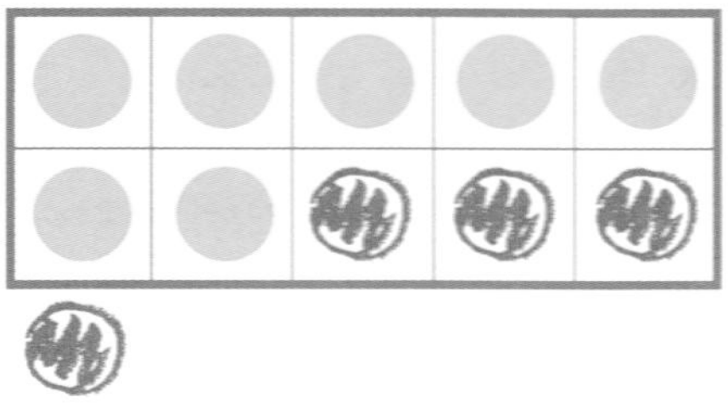	10 + 1 = ____
2 [3] [4] [5] [6] 8 + ____ = ____	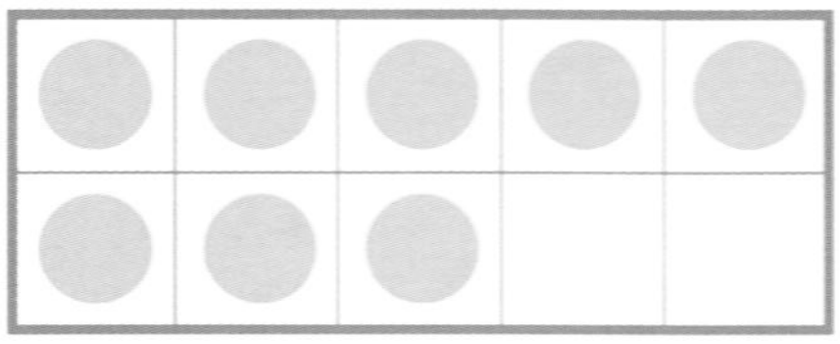	10 + ____ = ____
3 [2] [3] [4] [5] [6] [7] 9 + ____ = ____	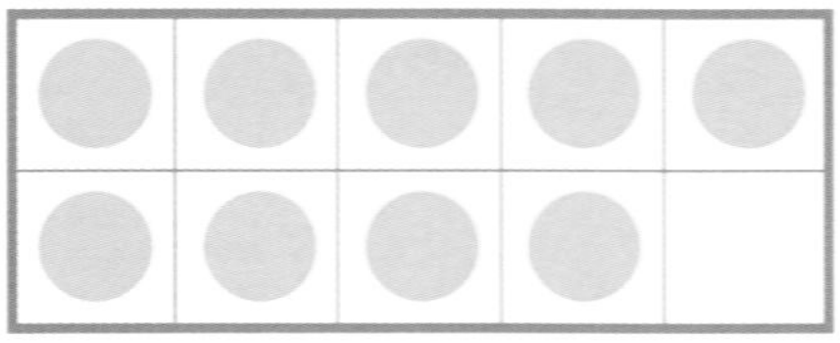	10 + ____ = ____
4 [3] [4] [5] [6] 8 + ____ = ____	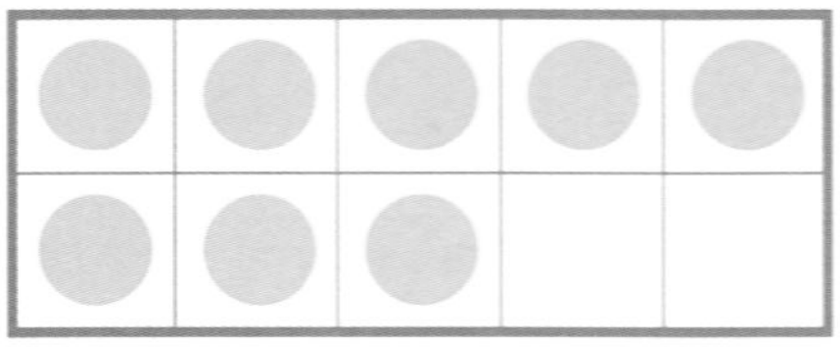	10 + ____ = ____

Share

How does the ten frame help you see the answer?

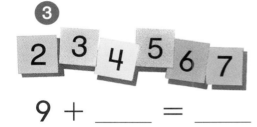

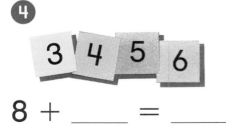

Notes for Home: Your child explored making a 10 to add 7, 8, or 9. *Home Activity:* Use objects such as pennies. Ask your child to show you 8 + 5 and 10 + 3 and tell you how they are the same.

Connect

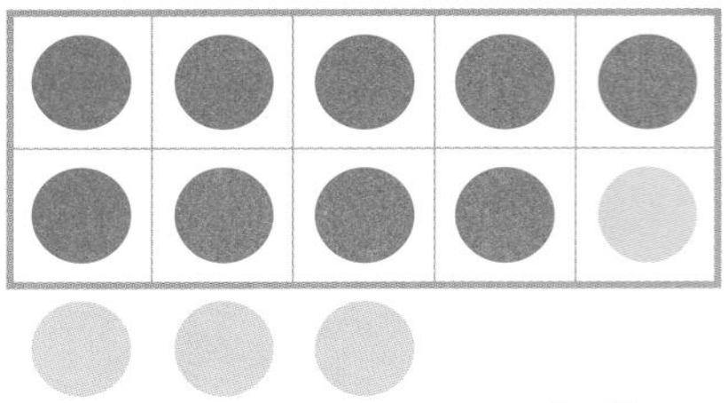

$9 + 4 =$ 13

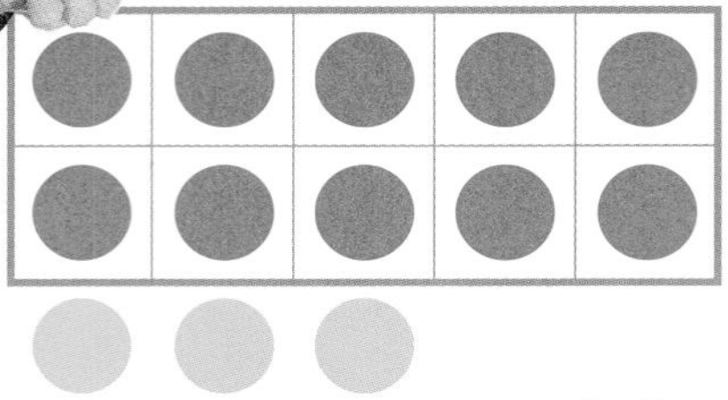

$10 + 3 =$ 13

Use counters and workmat.
Write the sum. Match.

5

7	8	9	7	6	8	5
+ 5	+ 6	+ 7	+ 8	+ 7	+ 9	+ 6
12						

6

10	10	10	10	10	10	10
+ 6	+ 3	+ 2	+ 7	+ 4	+ 1	+ 5
		12				

Problem Solving

7 Fido had 8 bones.
He found 5 more.
How many bones
does he have now?

_____ bones

How many bones will not fit in the box?

_____ bones

Notes for Home: Your child matched facts such as $7 + 5 = 12$ and $10 + 2 = 12$. *Home Activity:* Ask your child how many bones Fido would have if he found 7 more (15), or 8 more (16).

EXPLORE

Name ______________________________

Make 10 When Adding 7, 8, or 9

Learn

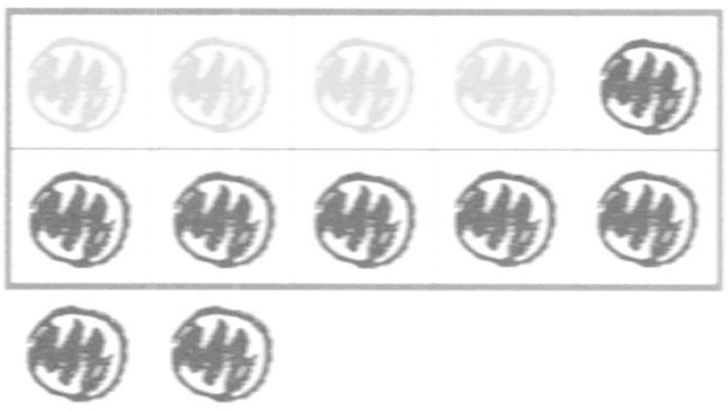

$4 + 8 = \underline{12}$ $10 + 2 = \underline{12}$

Check

Draw ● ● to show the number sentence. Add.

1

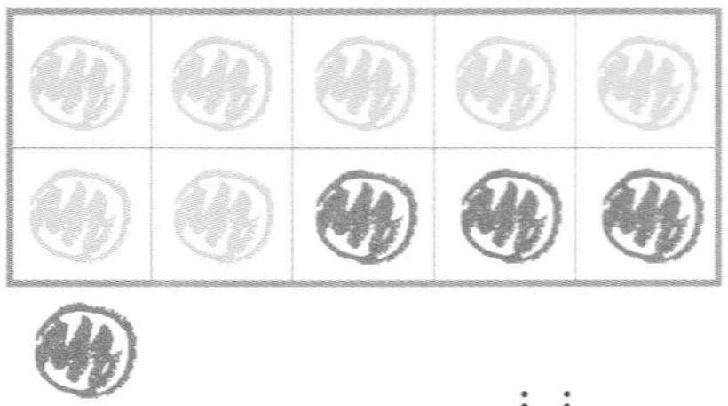

$7 + 4 = \underline{11}$

$10 + \underline{1} = \underline{11}$

2

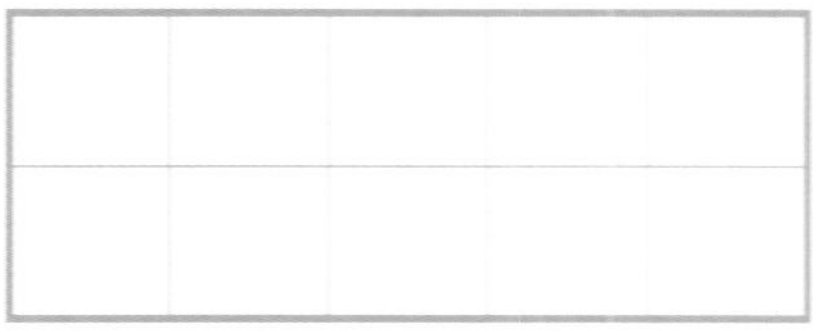

$9 + 3 = \_\_\_\_$

$10 + \_\_\_\_ = \_\_\_\_$

3

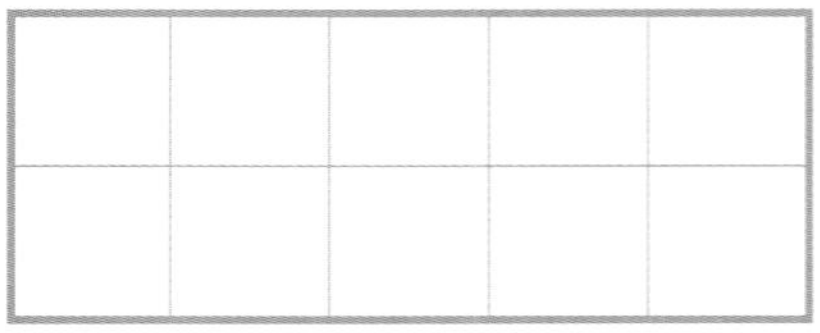

$8 + 6 = \_\_\_\_$

$10 + \_\_\_\_ = \_\_\_\_$

4

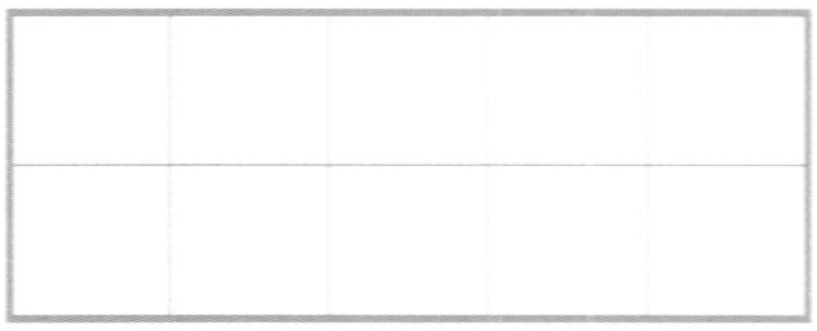

$7 + 5 = \_\_\_\_$

$10 + \_\_\_\_ = \_\_\_\_$

Talk About It Is it easier for you to add 8 + 4 or 10 + 2. Why?

Notes for Home: Your child added 7, 8, or 9 to another number by first making 10. *Home Activity:* Make groups of 7, 8, or 9 objects, such as pennies. First, ask your child to make 10, then tell the sum.

Practice

Draw counters to show the number sentence. Add.

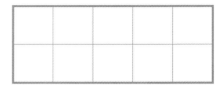

5

$9 + 5 = 14$

$10 + \_\_\_ = \_\_\_$

6

$8 + 3 = \_\_\_$

$10 + \_\_\_ = \_\_\_$

Add. You can use counters and a ten-frame.

7

6	8	7	4	8	3	7
+ 4	+ 5	+ 4	+ 9	+ 6	+ 8	+ 5

8

8	6	9	6	9	2	4
+ 4	+ 9	+ 3	+ 8	+ 7	+ 9	+ 7

PRACTICE

Problem Solving Visual Thinking

9 Mrs. Mouse is fixing dinner for 12 friends. How many more berries, nuts, and seeds does Mrs. Mouse need to have 12 of each?

____ more berries

____ more nuts

____ more seeds

Notes for Home: Your child practiced adding 7, 8, or 9 to another number by making a 10 first. *Home Activity:* Ask your child how many more berries, nuts, and seeds Mrs. Mouse would need to have 13 of each (4 more berries; 5 more nuts; 6 more seeds).

Name _____

Problem Solving: Choose a Strategy

PROBLEM SOLVING GUIDE
Understand ● Plan ● Solve ● Look Back

16 horses are in the barn.

7 are in the field.

How many horses are on the farm?

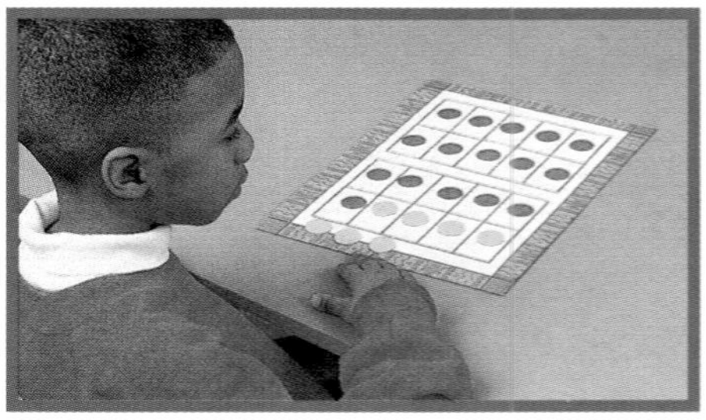

Use Objects

How would you solve the problem?

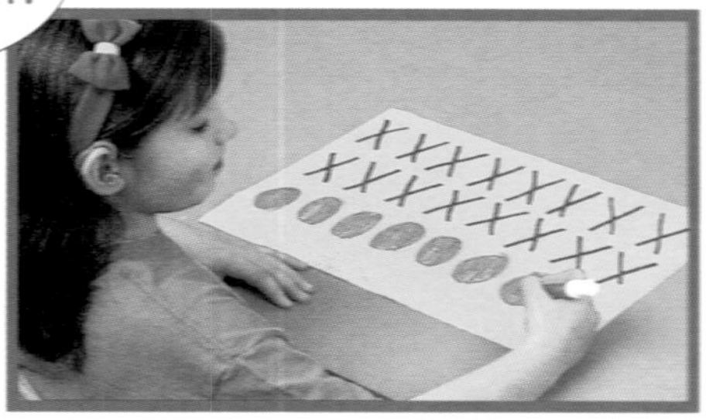

Draw a Picture

There are __23__ horses.

Check ●

Solve. Use and ▦ or draw a picture.

1 Michelle fed 5 brown chickens.

She fed 19 white chickens.

How many chickens did Michelle feed?

_____ chickens

~~~~~~

2 23 cows were in the field.

6 went into the barn.

Now how many cows are in the field?

_____ cows

~~~~~~

Talk About It How did you solve each problem?

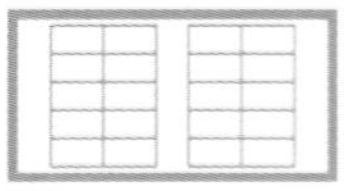

 Notes for Home: Your child solved problems by drawing a picture or using objects. *Home Activity:* Tell a problem such as, "We have 12 teaspoons and 9 soup spoons. How many spoons do we have?" Ask your child to use objects such as pennies or to draw a picture to solve the problem.

PROBLEM SOLVING

Practice

Solve. Use  and 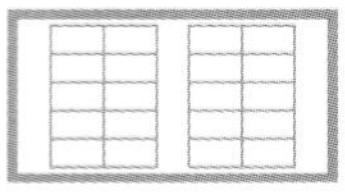 or draw a picture.

3. Mel saw 12 ducks in the pond.
He saw 9 ducks in the grass.
How many ducks did Mel see?

_____ ducks

4. 17 sheep were asleep.
11 of them woke up.
How many sheep are still asleep?

_____ sheep

5. Jordan counted all the pigs.
9 pigs were eating.
5 were sleeping. 8 were playing in the mud.
How many pigs did Jordan count?

_____ pigs

Tell a Math Story

6. Tell a math story about the picture.

Notes for Home: Your child practiced solving problems by drawing a picture or using objects.
Home Activity: Ask your child to make up a math story for 9 + 8, then solve the problem.

For additional practice, see Skills Practice Bank, page 538, Set 2.

Name ______________________________

Mixed Practice

Lessons 1–6

Concepts and Skills

Write the sum. Circle the doubles.

1

7	8	9	6	7	8	4
+ 6	+ 8	+ 4	+ 9	+ 7	+ 5	+ 7

2

9	9	6	9	7	6	8
+ 8	+ 5	+ 8	+ 9	+ 9	+ 6	+ 7

Add.

3

1	3	3	4	4	5	5
9	5	3	6	3	5	3
+ 5	+ 8	+ 7	+ 8	+ 2	+ 4	+ 2

MIXED PRACTICE

Problem Solving

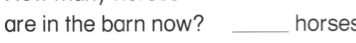

Solve. Use  and 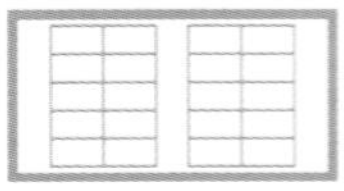 or draw a picture.

4 17 horses were in the barn.
13 ran to the field.
How many horses
are in the barn now? ______ horses

Journal

5 Draw a picture to show a doubles fact. Write the fact.

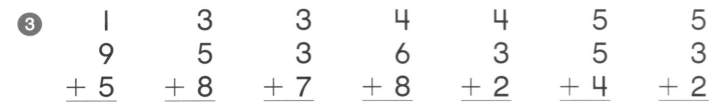

Notes for Home: Your child practiced adding two and three numbers and solving problems by drawing a picture or using objects. *Home Activity:* Ask your child how 8 + 8 = 16 could be used to find the answer for 8 + 9 (Since 9 is 1 more than 8, the sum will be 1 more than 16, 17.).

For additional practice, see Basic Facts Review, page 542, Set 5.

Name ______________________

Cumulative Review

Chapters 1–12

Concepts and Skills

Add or subtract.

1. 4 + 5 = ____ 7 + 3 = ____ 3 + 8 = ____

9 − 4 = ____ 10 − 3 = ____ 11 − 8 = ____

Problem Solving

Count these shapes. Record the shapes in the table.

2.

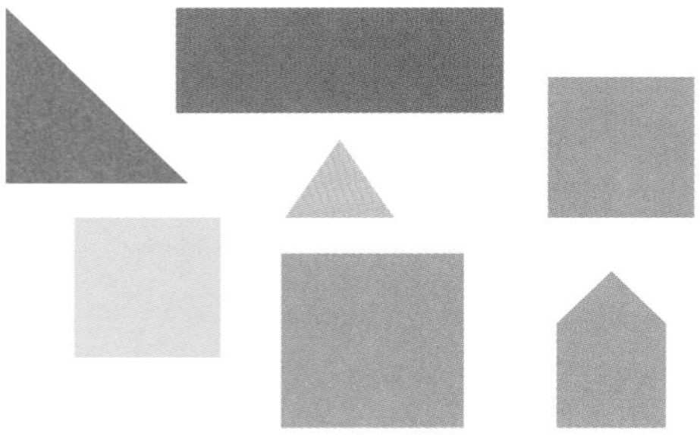

	3 sides	4 sides	5 sides
Number of Shapes			

Test Prep

Fill in the ○ for the correct answer.

Count the money.

3.

21¢ ○ 35¢ ○ 36¢ ○ 50¢ ○

4.

28¢ ○ 40¢ ○ 45¢ ○ 50¢ ○

Notes for Home: Your child reviewed addition and subtraction, making a table, and counting money. *Home Activity:* Show a group of coins up to 50¢ and ask your child to count and tell how much in all.

CUMULATIVE REVIEW

Relate Addition and Subtraction

Learn •

Addition can help you subtract.

I know that
9 + 3 = 12,
so I also know that
12 − 9 = 3.

9 + 3 = __12__ 12 − 9 = __3__

Check •

Add. Use the addition fact to help you subtract.
You can use .

❶ 7 + 4 = __11__ 5 + 8 = ___ 7 + 8 = ___

 11 − 7 = ___ 13 − 8 = ___ 15 − 8 = ___

❷ 12 + 0 = ___ 9 + 5 = ___ 6 + 5 = ___

 12 − 0 = ___ 14 − 9 = ___ 11 − 6 = ___

❸ 5 12 ❹ 6 13 ❺ 7 16
 + 7 − 5 + 7 − 6 + 9 − 7

Talk About It How do you use addition to help you subtract?

Notes for Home: Your child used an addition fact such as 7 + 4 = 11 to solve a related subtraction fact such as 11 − 7 = 4. *Home Activity:* Ask your child to tell how to use an addition fact to solve a subtraction fact.

Practice

Add. Use the addition fact to help you subtract.

You can use counters.

6. $\begin{array}{r} 8 \\ +\ 3 \\ \hline \end{array}$ $\begin{array}{r} 11 \\ -\ 8 \\ \hline \end{array}$

7. $\begin{array}{r} 8 \\ +\ 4 \\ \hline \end{array}$ $\begin{array}{r} 12 \\ -\ 4 \\ \hline \end{array}$

8. $\begin{array}{r} 9 \\ +\ 4 \\ \hline \end{array}$ $\begin{array}{r} 13 \\ -\ 9 \\ \hline \end{array}$

9. $\begin{array}{r} 6 \\ +\ 9 \\ \hline \end{array}$ $\begin{array}{r} 15 \\ -\ 9 \\ \hline \end{array}$

10. $\begin{array}{r} 8 \\ +\ 6 \\ \hline \end{array}$ $\begin{array}{r} 14 \\ -\ 6 \\ \hline \end{array}$

11. $\begin{array}{r} 8 \\ +\ 8 \\ \hline \end{array}$ $\begin{array}{r} 16 \\ -\ 8 \\ \hline \end{array}$

Add or subtract.

Draw a line to match an addition with a subtraction fact.

12. $5 + 7 =$ ____ $13 - 7 =$ ____

13. $7 + 6 =$ ____ $12 - 7 =$ ____

14. $6 + 8 =$ ____ $14 - 6 =$ ____

PRACTICE

Write About It

15. Complete the number sentences.
Draw or write a story to go with them.

$9 + 8 =$ ____

$17 - 8 =$ ____

Notes for Home: Your child practiced using an addition fact such as $8 + 4 = 12$ to solve a related subtraction fact such as $12 - 8 = 4$. *Home Activity:* Ask your child to name a subtraction fact that uses the same numbers as $9 + 3 = 12$ ($12 - 9 = 3$ or $12 - 3 = 9$).

Name ____________________

Use Doubles to Subtract

Learn

Check

Add or subtract.

1. $\begin{array}{r} 7 \\ +\ 7 \\ \hline 14 \end{array}$ $\quad$ $\begin{array}{r} 14 \\ -\ 7 \\ \hline 7 \end{array}$

2. $\begin{array}{r} 9 \\ +\ 9 \\ \hline \end{array}$ $\quad$ $\begin{array}{r} 18 \\ -\ 9 \\ \hline \end{array}$

3. $\begin{array}{r} 8 \\ +\ 8 \\ \hline \end{array}$ $\quad$ $\begin{array}{r} 16 \\ -\ 8 \\ \hline \end{array}$

4. $4 + 4 =$ ____ $\quad$ $5 + 5 =$ ____ $\quad$ $3 + 3 =$ ____

   $8 - 4 =$ ____ $\quad$ $10 - 5 =$ ____ $\quad$ $6 - 3 =$ ____

Subtract. Write the addition fact that helps.

5. $\begin{array}{r} 12 \\ -\ 6 \\ \hline \end{array}$ $\quad$ $\begin{array}{r} \square \\ +\ \square \\ \hline \square \end{array}$

6. $\begin{array}{r} 18 \\ -\ 9 \\ \hline \end{array}$ $\quad$ $\begin{array}{r} \square \\ +\ \square \\ \hline \square \end{array}$

7. $\begin{array}{r} 16 \\ -\ 8 \\ \hline \end{array}$ $\quad$ $\begin{array}{r} \square \\ +\ \square \\ \hline \square \end{array}$

Talk About It What addition fact can help you find $10 - 5$?

Notes for Home: Your child used an addition double such as 7 + 7 = 14 to solve a related subtraction fact such as 14 – 7 = 7. *Home Activity:* Name an addition double such as 8 + 8 = 16. Ask your child to tell a subtraction fact that uses the same numbers (16 – 8 = 8).

Add or subtract.

8 $9 + 9 =$ _18_ $4 + 4 =$ ___ $7 + 7 =$ ___

 $18 - 9 =$ ___ $8 - 4 =$ ___ $14 - 7 =$ ___

9 $8 + 8 =$ ___ $3 + 3 =$ ___ $6 + 6 =$ ___

 $16 - 8 =$ ___ $6 - 3 =$ ___ $12 - 6 =$ ___

Subtract. Write the addition fact that helps.

10
$$\begin{array}{r} 14 \\ -\ 7 \\ \hline \end{array} \quad + \quad \boxed{7} \atop \boxed{7} \atop \overline{\boxed{14}}$$

11
$$\begin{array}{r} 10 \\ -\ 5 \\ \hline \end{array} \quad + \quad \boxed{} \atop \boxed{} \atop \overline{\boxed{}}$$

12
$$\begin{array}{r} 16 \\ -\ 8 \\ \hline \end{array} \quad + \quad \boxed{} \atop \boxed{} \atop \overline{\boxed{}}$$

Problem Solving Patterns

13 Write the missing numbers on the machine.
Tell what the machine does.

If I put the number 3 in, the number 6 comes out.

In	Out		In	Out
1	2		6	
2	4		7	
3	6		8	
4			9	
5				

Notes for Home: Your child practiced using an addition double such as 5 + 5 to solve a related subtraction fact such as 10 − 5. *Home Activity:* Ask your child to use pennies to add 9 + 9 and find the sum, then say a subtraction fact that uses the same numbers (18 − 9 = 9).

Name

Subtraction Facts for 13 and 14

Learn

See.

13
− 8
?

Remember, addition can help you subtract.

Think.

8
+ 5
13

Write.

13
− 8
5

Check

Subtract. Write the addition fact that helps.

1
13
− 7
☐

7
+ ☐
13

2
14
− 5
☐

5
+ ☐
14

3
14
− 8
☐

8
+ ☐
14

4
13
− 9
☐

9
+ ☐
13

Talk About It How are these two facts alike? How are they different?

$9 + 5 = 14$
$14 - 5 = 9$

Notes for Home: Your child used an addition fact such as 8 + 5 = 13 to help solve a related subtraction fact, such as 13 − 8 = 5. *Home Activity:* Arrange small objects, such as buttons, into two groups. Ask your child to tell a related addition and subtraction fact.

Practice

Subtract. Write the addition fact that helps.

5

$$\begin{array}{r} 13 \\ -\ 4 \\ \hline \boxed{9} \end{array} \qquad \begin{array}{r} 4 \\ +\ \boxed{9} \\ \hline 13 \end{array}$$

6

$$\begin{array}{r} 14 \\ -\ 6 \\ \hline \boxed{} \end{array} \qquad \begin{array}{r} 6 \\ +\ \boxed{} \\ \hline 14 \end{array}$$

7

$$\begin{array}{r} 13 \\ -\ 6 \\ \hline \boxed{} \end{array} \qquad \begin{array}{r} 6 \\ +\ \boxed{} \\ \hline 13 \end{array} \qquad \begin{array}{r} 13 \\ -\ 8 \\ \hline \boxed{} \end{array} \qquad \begin{array}{r} 8 \\ +\ \boxed{} \\ \hline 13 \end{array} \qquad \begin{array}{r} 14 \\ -\ 9 \\ \hline \boxed{} \end{array} \qquad \begin{array}{r} 9 \\ +\ \boxed{} \\ \hline 14 \end{array}$$

PRACTICE

Subtract.

8 $14 - 8 =$ ____ $13 - 9 =$ ____ $13 - 6 =$ ____

9 $13 - 5 =$ ____ $14 - 0 =$ ____ $14 - 5 =$ ____

Tell a Math Story

10 Use these numbers: 4, 9, 13.
Write an addition and a subtraction fact.

____ + ____ = ____ ____ − ____ = ____

11 Use each fact to tell a math story.

Notes for Home: Your child practiced subtracting from 13 and 14. *Home Activity:* Read the subtraction facts on this page. Let your child give the answer for each.

Name ______________________________

Subtraction Facts for 15 to 18

Learn

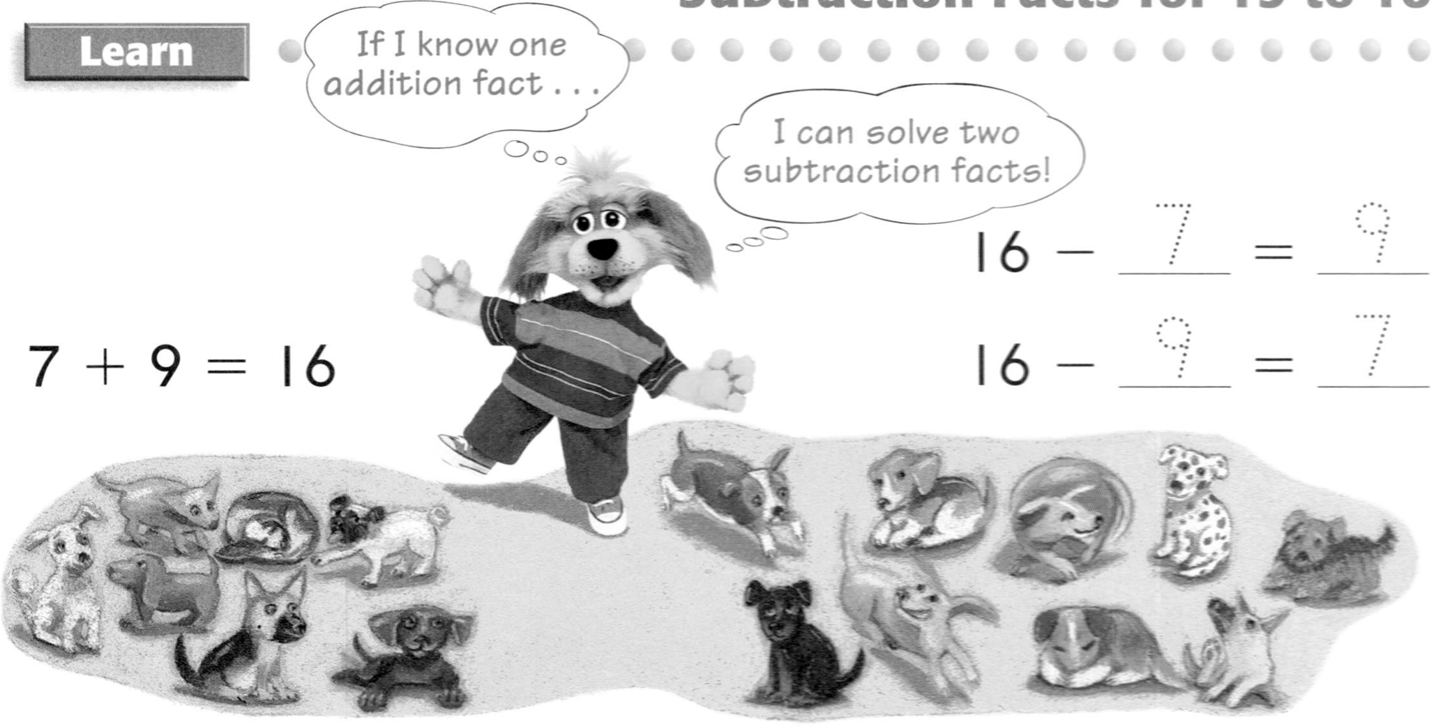

$7 + 9 = 16$

$16 - \underline{7} = \underline{9}$

$16 - \underline{9} = \underline{7}$

Check

Complete the addition fact. Write the subtraction facts.

You can use  .

1

$\underline{9} + \underline{6} = \underline{15}$

$15 - \underline{6} = \underline{9}$

$15 - \underline{9} = \underline{6}$

2

$8 + 9 = \_\_\_\_$

$17 - \_\_\_\_ = \_\_\_\_$

$17 - \_\_\_\_ = \_\_\_\_$

3

$7 + 8 = \_\_\_\_$

$15 - \_\_\_\_ = \_\_\_\_$

$15 - \_\_\_\_ = \_\_\_\_$

Talk About It What addition fact can help you subtract 15 − 8 and 15 − 7? Why?

Notes for Home: Your child solved subtraction facts by thinking of the related addition fact.
Home Activity: Ask your child to name two subtraction facts that use the same numbers as 9 + 6 = 15 (15 − 9 = 6, 15 − 6 = 9).

Practice

Complete the addition fact.
Write the subtraction facts.
You can use .

4

$15 - \_\_\_ = 7$

$8 + 7 = 15$ $\quad 15 - \_\_\_ = 8$

Mixed Practice Subtract.

5	17 − 8	16 − 8	13 − 9	16 − 7	15 − 6	17 − 9	18 − 0
6	15 − 9	18 − 9	11 − 4	15 − 8	14 − 7	13 − 4	15 − 7
7	13 − 6	16 − 0	14 − 5	13 − 7	11 − 9	14 − 8	13 − 5

PRACTICE

Problem Solving Critical Thinking

8 Circle two toys you can buy with these coins.

How much money will you have left? _____ ¢

Notes for Home: Your child practiced subtraction facts such as 15 − 7 = 8 and 15 − 8 = 7.
Home Activity: Write the numbers 7, 8, and 9 on pieces of paper. Ask your child to choose two pieces, add the numbers, then write two subtraction sentences related to the addition.

For additional practice, see Skills Practice Bank, page 538, Set 3.

Name ______________________________

Fact Families

Learn

These four facts are a fact family.

This fact family uses the numbers 6, 9, and 15.

$9 + 6 =$ 15 $\quad 15 - 6 =$ 9

$6 + 9 =$ 15 $\quad 15 - 9 =$ 6

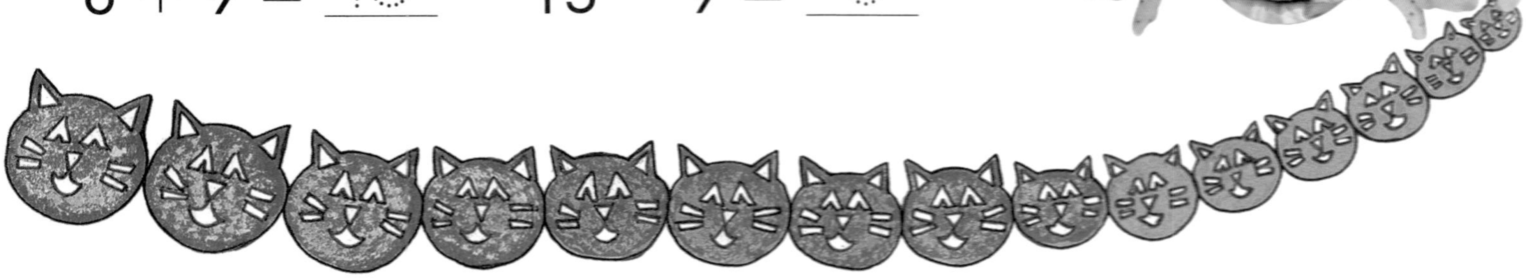

Check

Complete the fact family. You can use counters.

1. $8 + 6 =$ 14 $\quad 14 - 6 =$ ____
   $6 + 8 =$ ____ $\quad 14 - 8 =$ ____

2. $9 + 8 =$ ____ $\quad 17 - 8 =$ ____
   $8 + 9 =$ ____ $\quad 17 - 9 =$ ____

3. $9 + 7 =$ ____ $\quad 16 - 7 =$ ____
   $7 + 9 =$ ____ $\quad 16 - 9 =$ ____

Talk About It How many facts do most fact families have?

Notes for Home: Your child added and subtracted using fact families. *Home Activity:* Give your child 13 objects, such as pennies. Have your child show or say four different number sentences using 8, 5, and 13 (8 + 5 = 13, 5 + 8 = 13, 13 – 5 = 8, 13 – 8 = 5).

Practice

Complete the fact family.

You can use  .

4. $7 + 4 =$ ____ $11 - 4 =$ ____

   $4 + 7 =$ ____ $11 - 7 =$ ____

5. $7 + 6 =$ ____ $13 - 6 =$ ____

   $6 + 7 =$ ____ $13 - 7 =$ ____

6. $9 + 5 =$ ____ $14 - 5 =$ ____

   $5 + 9 =$ ____ $14 - 9 =$ ____

7. **Write your own** fact family.

   ____ + ____ = ____ ____ − ____ = ____

   ____ + ____ = ____ ____ − ____ = ____

Problem Solving Critical Thinking

8. Most fact families have four facts.
   This fact family has only two facts. Why?
   $7 + 7 = 14$ $14 - 7 = 7$

9. Which other fact families have only two facts?

   ____

   ____

Notes for Home: Your child practiced addition and subtraction using fact families.
Home Activity: Have your child show or say four different number sentences for 8, 9, and 17 ($8 + 9 = 17$, $9 + 8 = 17$, $17 - 9 = 8$, $17 - 8 = 9$).

Name ______________________________

Reading for Math

Main Idea

The main idea is what a story is about.

Read the math story.

Tammy has fish for pets.
She keeps the fish in a big tank.
There are 9 blue fish.
There are 4 orange fish.
Tammy feeds her fish every day.

1. Circle the sentence in the story that tells the main idea.
2. Circle the best title for the story.

Fish Tanks

Tammy's Pets

How to Feed Fish

3. How many fish does Tammy have?
   Write a number sentence to show how many.

   ____

Notes for Home: Your child read a story and identified the main idea. *Home Activity:* Read a simple story to your child. Ask what the story is about.

Read the math story.

Mark had too many hamsters.
He had 11 in all.
His mom said, "Sell some."
Mark sold 7 hamsters to the pet store.
He kept the rest.

4. Circle the sentence in the story that tells the main idea.
5. Circle the best title for the story.

Mark's Pet Hamster

Hamster

Too Many Hamsters

6. How many hamsters does Mark have left?
Write a number sentence to show how many.

____

Problem Solving Critical Thinking

Solve.

7. How many more hamsters does Mark need to sell if he wants only 1 hamster?

____

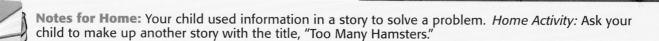

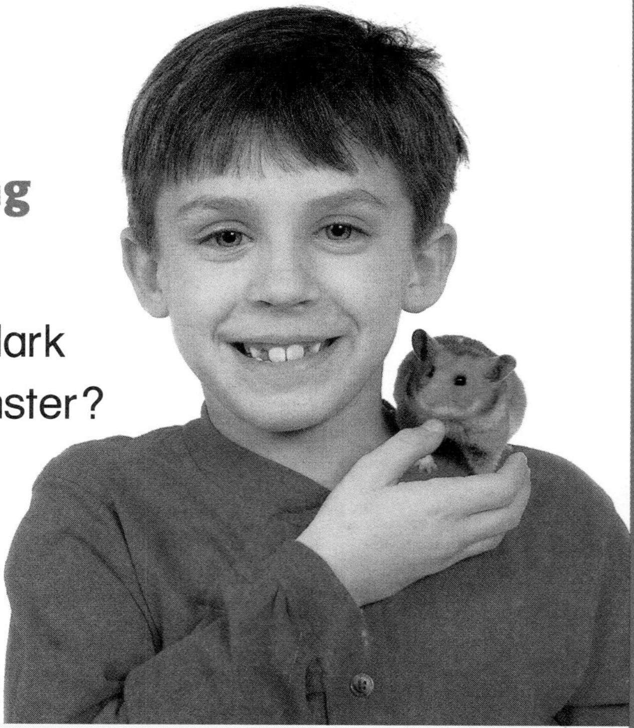

Notes for Home: Your child used information in a story to solve a problem. *Home Activity:* Ask your child to make up another story with the title, "Too Many Hamsters."

Name ______________________________

Problem Solving: Choose an Operation

Learn

PROBLEM SOLVING GUIDE
Understand • Plan • Solve • Look Back

There are 9 kittens sleeping.
5 wake up.
How many kittens are still asleep?

add **(subtract)**

9 (−) 5 = 4

4 kittens are asleep.

Check

To take groups away, subtract.
Need to put groups together? Add.

Circle add or subtract.
Complete the number sentence.
Solve.

1. Last year Setta had 8 puppies. This year she had 9. How many puppies did Setta have? **add** **subtract**

   Setta had _____ puppies.

   _____ (+) _____ = _____

2. Marcus had 14 dog treats. He gave 5 to Sparky. How many does he have left? **add** **subtract**

   Marcus has _____ dog treats.

   _____ ( ) _____ = _____

Talk About It How do you know when to add or subtract?

Notes for Home: Your child decided whether to add or subtract, then wrote a number sentence to solve a problem. *Home Activity:* Ask your child to make up a math story for the number sentence $9 + 8 = 17$.

PROBLEM SOLVING

Practice

Circle add or subtract.
Complete the number sentence. Solve.

3. There are 15 hamsters. **add** **subtract**
A man buys 6.
How many are left?

There are 9 hamsters left. 15 ◯ ____ = ____

4. 6 dogs run in the park. **add** **subtract**
Then 8 more come.
Now how many are in the park?

There are ____ dogs in the park. ____ ◯ ____ = ____

5. Marian sees 13 fish in the tank. **add** **subtract**
7 swim behind a big rock.
Now how many fish can she see?

She sees ____ fish. ____ ◯ ____ = ____

Tell a Math Story

6. Use the picture to tell a math story.
Write a number sentence
to go with your story.

____

Notes for Home: Your child practiced solving problems by deciding whether to add or subtract. *Home Activity:* Tell a simple story problem such as "9 fish are in the tank. 6 more fish are added. How many fish are in the tank now?" Have your child tell whether to add or subtract (add; 15 fish in all).

Name ____________________

Mixed Practice

Lessons 7–12

Concepts and Skills

Add or subtract.

1	$7 + 9$	$16 - 9$	2	$15 - 7$	$15 - 8$	3	$4 + 8$	$12 - 8$

Subtract.

4	$13 - 7$	$18 - 9$	$14 - 9$	$14 - 7$	$17 - 8$	$13 - 5$	$16 - 7$

Problem Solving

Circle add or subtract.

Complete the number sentence. Solve.

5. P. T. had 14 guppies.
He gave 6 away.
Now how many guppies
does he have?

add subtract

____ ◯ ____ = ____

He has ____ guppies.

Journal

6. Write a math story about 14 animals.
Write a number sentence for your story.

Notes for Home: Your child practiced addition and subtraction facts to 18, and choosing addition or subtraction to solve a problem. *Home Activity:* Ask your child how 7 + 9 = 16 could be used to help answer 16 – 9 and 16 – 7.

For additional practice, see Basic Facts Review, page 543, Set 6.

Name ______________________________

Cumulative Review

Chapters 1–12

Concepts and Skills

Add.

1	3	5	1	1	4	5	7
	3	0	6	2	4	3	2
	+ 1	+ 3	+ 1	+ 4	+ 3	+ 1	+ 2

Problem Solving

2. Count the money. _____ ¢
3. Circle what you can buy.

Test Prep

Fill in the ○ for the correct answer.

4. Use the ruler to measure.

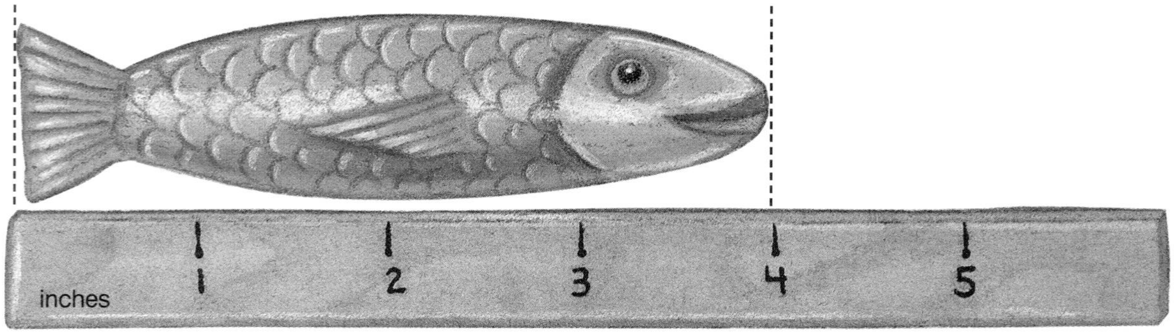

2 inches ○ 3 inches ○ 4 inches ○

Notes for Home: Your child reviewed adding three numbers, counting money, and measurement.
Home Activity: Ask your child to find a household object and measure its length in inches or centimeters.

Name ______________________________

Chapter 12 Review

Vocabulary

Write the sum. Circle the doubles.

1					3	2	3
	7	7	8	9	4	5	3
	+ 7	+ 8	+ 8	+ 8	+ 2	+ 1	+ 1

Concepts and Skills

Add or subtract.

2	15	6	11	13	14	17	8
	− 9	+ 7	− 7	− 8	− 5	− 8	+ 6

Complete the fact family.

3 $8 + 4 =$ ____ $12 - 4 =$ ____

$4 + 8 =$ ____ $12 - 8 =$ ____

Problem Solving

4 Circle add or subtract.
Complete the number sentence.

Spot had 9 bones.
He found 6 more.
How many bones
does he have now?

add **subtract**

____ ◯ ____ = ____

Notes for Home: Your child reviewed Chapter 12 vocabulary, concepts, skills, and problem solving. *Home Activity:* Ask your child how many bones Spot would have if he found 7 more instead of 6 more (16).

Name ______________________________

Chapter 12 Test

Add.

1

				3	8	6
6	8	8	7	4	9	6
+ 7	+ 8	+ 9	+ 7	+ 7	+ 1	+ 3

Add or subtract.

2

4	12	13	7	15	15	9
+ 8	− 8	− 7	+ 6	− 6	− 9	+ 6

3 $16 - 8 =$ ____ $14 - 7 =$ ____ $18 - 9 =$ ____

Complete the fact family.

4 $8 + 6 =$ ____ $14 - 6 =$ ____

$6 + 8 =$ ____ $14 - 8 =$ ____

5 Solve. Draw a picture or use objects.
Complete the number sentence.

Janelle had 14 goldfish.
She gave away 6.
How many does she have now?

____ ◯ ____ = ____

Notes for Home: Your child was assessed on Chapter 12 concepts, skills, and problem solving.
Home Activity: Ask your child to tell a math story using animals.

Name ______________________

Performance Assessment

Chapter 12

Show What You Know

Pick one number.

Write it in every box on the page. 13 14 15

1. Write facts for your number.

___ + ___ = ☐   ☐ − ___ = ___

___ + ___ = ☐   ☐ − ___ = ___

___ + ___ = ☐   ☐ − ___ = ___

___ + ___ = ☐   ☐ − ___ = ___

2. Find two ways to make your number by adding 3 numbers.

___ + ___ + ___ = ☐   ___ + ___ + ___ = ☐

Problem Solving Critical Thinking

3. How are these facts alike?
How are they different?

$8 + 9 = 17$

$4 + 4 + 9 = 17$

$8 + 5 + 4 = 17$

Notes for Home: Your child did an activity which tested Chapter 12 concepts, skills, and problem solving. *Home Activity:* Ask your child to find one or two more facts for the number he or she chose.

Name ____________________________

Explore with a CALCULATOR

Know Your Signs!

Keys You Will Use ON/C + −

Use your calculator to add or subtract.

Write + or − in each □.

1. 9 [−] 3 [+] 8 = 14
   9 [+] 3 [−] 8 = 4

2. 17 □ 9 □ 8 = 16
   17 □ 9 □ 8 = 0

3. 16 □ 7 □ 6 = 15
   16 □ 7 □ 6 = 3

4. 7 □ 2 □ 8 = 17
   7 □ 2 □ 8 = 13

5. 8 □ 7 □ 9 = 6
   8 □ 7 □ 9 = 10

6. 18 □ 9 □ 7 = 2
   18 □ 9 □ 7 = 16

7. 15 □ 8 □ 6 = 13
   15 □ 8 □ 6 = 1

8. 7 □ 3 □ 4 = 8
   7 □ 3 □ 4 = 14

Tech Talk What do you notice about each problem?

Visit our Web site. **www.parent.mathsurf.com**

Thumbprint Pals

Did you know that experts can tell people apart by their fingerprints? That's because no two people have the same fingerprints!

Try this at home! Use your fingers to create your own one-of-a kind animals.

1 **Roll your finger or thumb over an ink pad.**

2 **Make some prints on a piece of paper.**

3 **Fill in eyes, legs, tails, and ears with markers or crayons.**

Fold down

MathSoup

Scott Foresman - Addison Wesley My Math Magazine No. 12

Does Your Pet Look Like You?

Did you know that every dog has its own nose print? That's how experts tell dogs apart.

Great and Small

This shrew is one of the smallest animals on earth.
It is so small it can sleep in a teaspoon.
It weighs as much as a ping-pong ball!

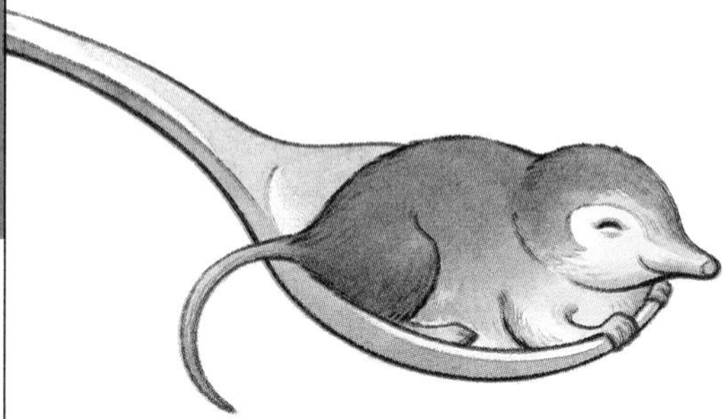

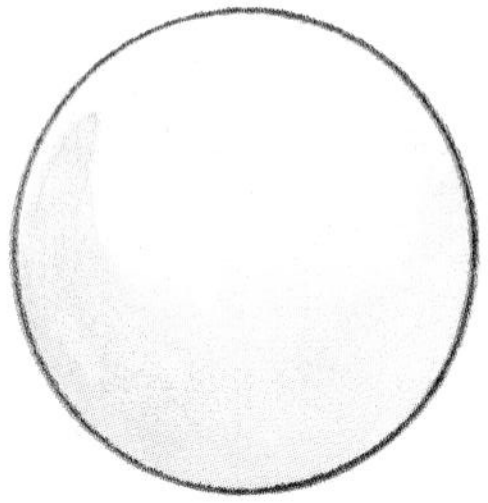

Make a drawing to show about how much each animal weighs.

The heaviest deer weighs about as much as a small car.

How to Play

1 Roll the 3 number cubes. Add the numbers.

2 Does the number match a number on the farm? If so, move one of your bean animals to that place.

3 The first player to put all their animals to bed wins.

Notes for Home: Your child compared the weights of animals to people and everyday objects. *Home Activity:* Ask your child to hold two things such as a dinner plate and a saucer, and tell which weighs more.

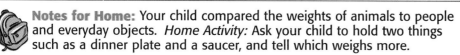

Say Goodnight

It's nighttime for the farm animals. Play this game to put them to bed.

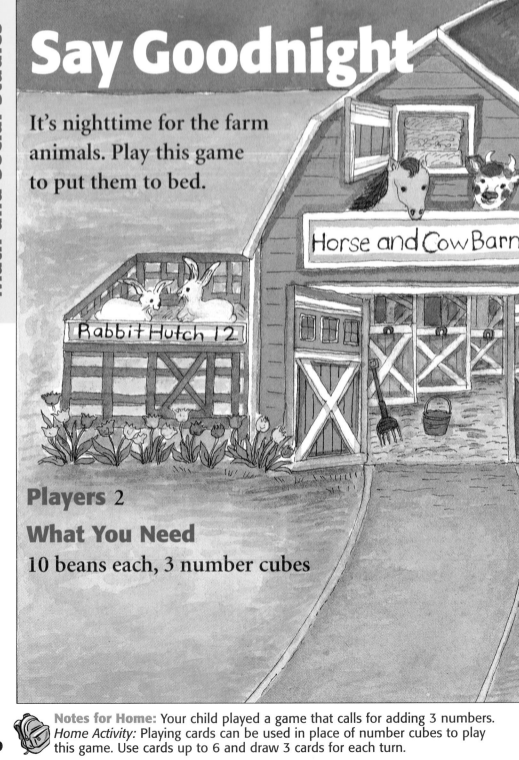

Players 2

What You Need

10 beans each, 3 number cubes

The heaviest bird weighs about as much as 3 grown-ups.

The heaviest dog weighs about as much as 4 first graders.

The lightest bird weighs about the same as a dime.

Notes for Home: Your child played a game that calls for adding 3 numbers. *Home Activity:* Playing cards can be used in place of number cubes to play this game. Use cards up to 6 and draw 3 cards for each turn.

Whose Pet Is That?

Some people think pets and their owners look alike. What do you think?

Draw a line to match each pet with its owner.

Notes for Home: Your child matched similar pictures and completed a math crossword puzzle. *Home Activity:* Occasionally, encourage your child to write the words for numbers when making lists or writing messages.

Scratching Post Crossword

Write a number for each clue.

ten	**twelve**	**fourteen**	**sixteen**	**eighteen**
eleven	**thirteen**	**fifteen**	**seventeen**	**nineteen**

1 Six and six and six again
2 Six and zero. Then add a ten.
3 Double six and add one more.
4 Double seven. Then subtract four.

CHAPTER

13

Two-Digit Addition and Subtraction

Here Comes Summer!

Notes for Home: Your child looked at the picture and thought about ways to add to find how many fireworks displays there are in all. *Home Activity:* Talk to your child about ways you use addition in your home or work.

Math at Home

Dear Family,
In Chapter 13 we will use tens and ones as models to show how we add and subtract two-digit numbers. Here are some activities we can do together.

Stocking the Pantry

Place several packages and cans of food on the table. Write a price tag for each item, using amounts such as 20¢, 30¢, and 35¢. Pretend with your child that you can spend up to 90¢. Decide together which items you would buy.

Double-Digit Drop

To play this game, draw a circle with numbers on a large sheet of paper like the one shown. With your child, drop two pennies or buttons on the circle and then add the numbers. The player with the highest score wins the round.

Community Connection

Look for opportunities to use 2-digit numbers while traveling in a car or bus. For example, point out speed limit and mileage signs. Talk about numbers on billboards.

Visit our Web site. **www.parent.mathsurf.com**

Name ______________________________

Explore Adding Tens

Explore

Put 9 ▪ in a bag. Put 9 ▮ in a bag.

Choose some tens and some ones. Write your first number.

Choose only tens. Write your second number.

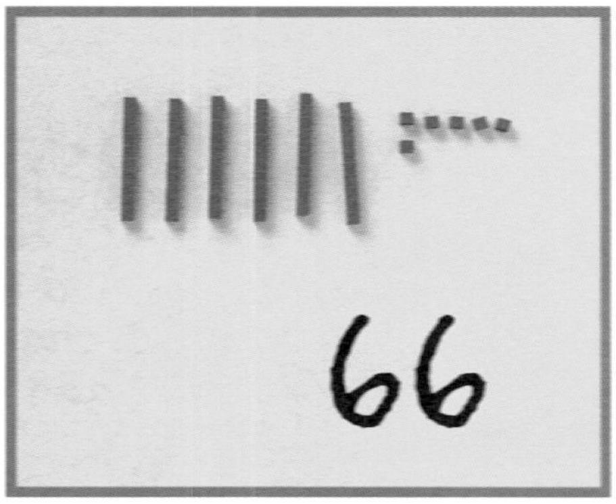

Put them together. Write the sum.

	My first number	My second number	The sum
1	______	______	______
2	______	______	______
3	______	______	______
4	______	______	______

Share

Talk about the ways you can find the sums.

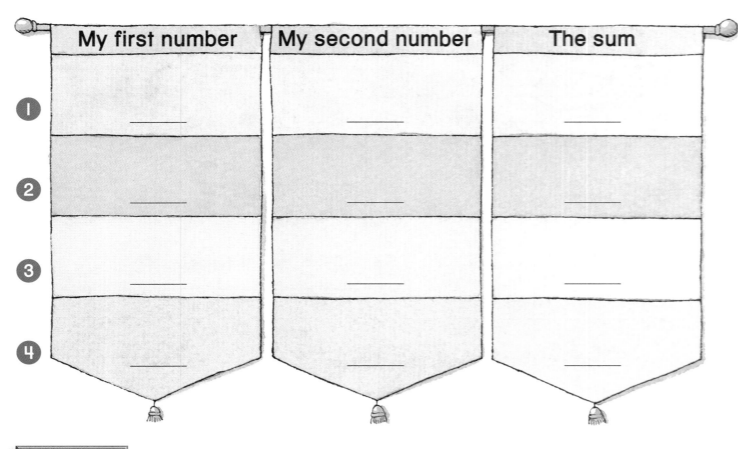

Notes for Home: Your child used tens and ones to explore addition. *Home Activity:* Say a number between 1 and 89, have your child add 10, and tell you the answer.

Connect

22 and 2 tens more is 42.

Use or to add tens to these numbers.

Use a 100 chart to add tens.

1	2	3	4	5	6	7	8	9	10
11	12	13	14	15	16	17	18	19	20
21	22	23	24	25	26	27	28	29	30
31	32	33	34	35	36	37	38	39	40
41	42	43	44	45	46	47	48	49	50
51	52	53	54	55	56	57	58	59	60
61	62	63	64	65	66	67	68	69	70
71	72	73	74	75	76	77	78	79	80
81	82	83	84	85	86	87	88	89	90
91	92	93	94	95	96	97	98	99	100

	Find	Add	Sum
5	15	1 ten	25
6	21	2 tens	_____
7	33	3 tens	_____
8	56	2 tens	_____
9	68	3 tens	_____
10	77	1 ten	_____
11	42	4 tens	_____

Problem Solving Critical Thinking

12. If you put a dime into a bank every day, how many cents would you have in 1 week? _____ cents

13. How many days would it take you to save 90 cents? _____ days

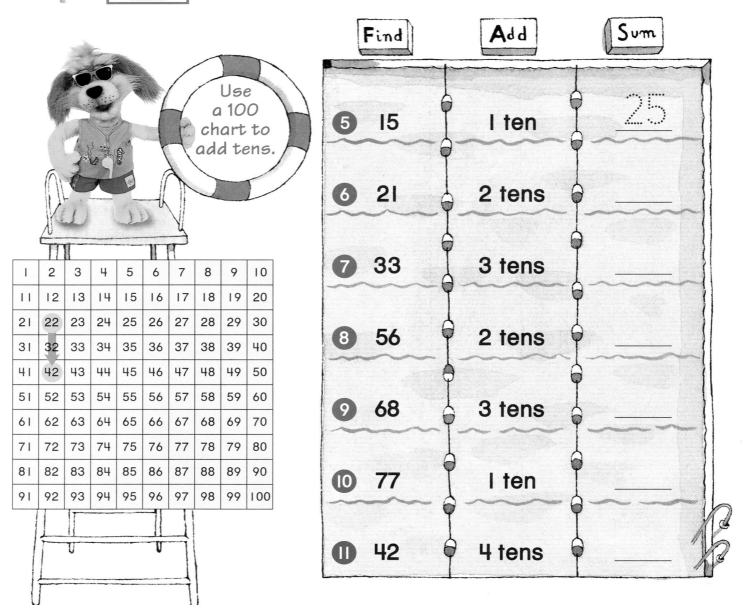

Notes for Home: Your child continued to explore adding tens using a 100 chart. *Home Activity:* Ask your child to add 10 to numbers with 0 in them. Ask, "What pattern do you see?" (All will end in 0.)

EXPLORE

Name ______________________________

Add Tens

Learn

What was the final score?

Add.

38 + 20

	tens	ones
	3	8
+	2	0
	5	8

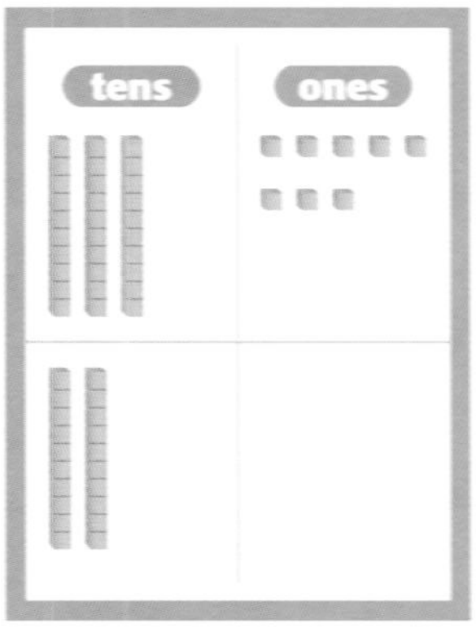

Check

Add. Use workmat and tens and ones blocks.

1

	tens	ones
	4	6
+	1	0
	5	6

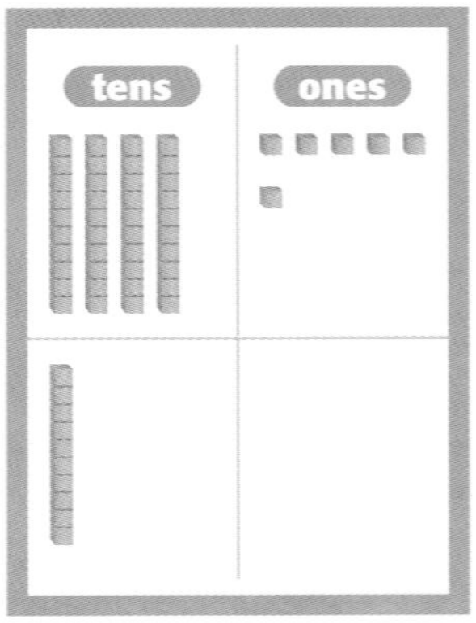

2

	tens	ones
	5	5
+	3	0

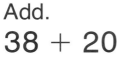

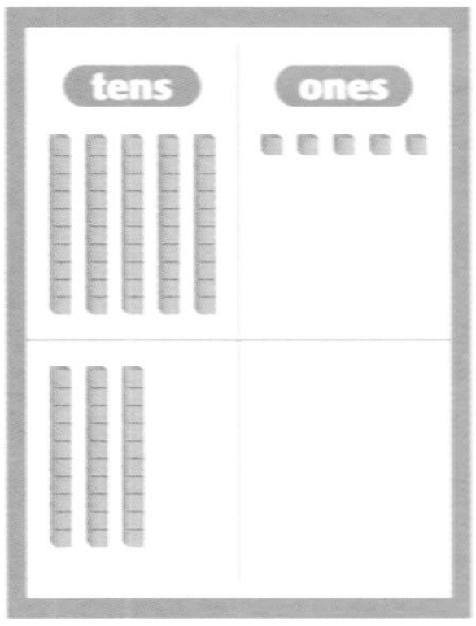

3

	tens	ones
	3	0
+	1	3

	tens	ones
	1	7
+	4	0

	tens	ones
	2	0
+	2	2

	tens	ones
	1	6
+	4	0

Talk About It How would you use tens and ones blocks to show an addition problem with the sum of 77?

Notes for Home: Your child added tens to a two-digit number. *Home Activity:* Ask your child to count to 100 by tens (10, 20, 30, 40, 50, 60, 70, 80, 90, 100).

Add. Use and ▮...

4

tens	ones
3	8
+ 2	0
5	8

tens	ones
1	0
+ 3	6

tens	ones
2	2
+ 1	0

tens	ones
3	0
+ 6	8

5

34	65	20	30	53	46
+ 10	+ 30	+ 14	+ 22	+ 30	+ 40

6

30	48	70	31	50	75
+ 37	+ 10	+ 19	+ 10	+ 25	+ 20

7

58	20	27	20	30	60
+ 40	+ 19	+ 40	+ 29	+ 31	+ 10

Problem Solving Patterns

8 Marco uses a 🖩 to find the

total for these 2 sets of cards.

He presses these keys once:

3	7	+	1	0

He presses | = | three times.

He sees 47, 57, then 67.

What pattern did Marco use to add?

Marco's cards
37 bird cards
3 sets of 10 cat cards

Notes for Home: Your child practiced adding two-digit numbers and tens. *Home Activity:* Ask your child to count backwards from 100 by tens (100, 90, 80, 70, 60, 50, 40, 30, 20, 10).

Name ______________________________

Add Tens and Ones

Learn

Betty brought 31 cups. Shawn brought 25 cups.
How many cups are there in all?
Add.
31 + 25

	tens	ones
	3	1
+	2	5
	5	6

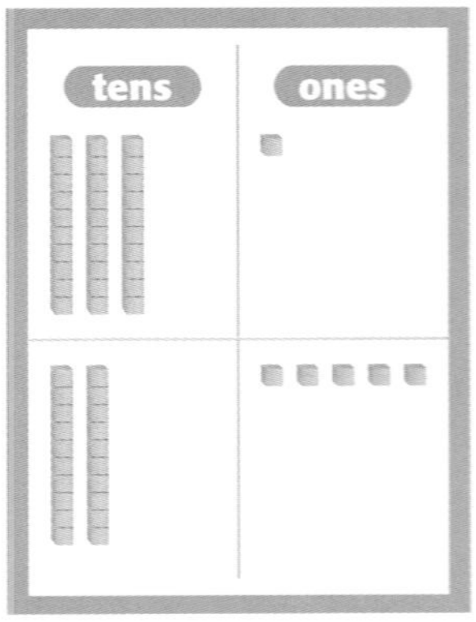

Check

Add. Use 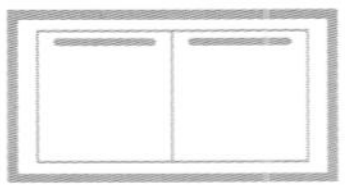 and 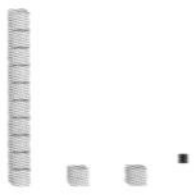.

1

	tens	ones
	4	2
+		6
	4	8

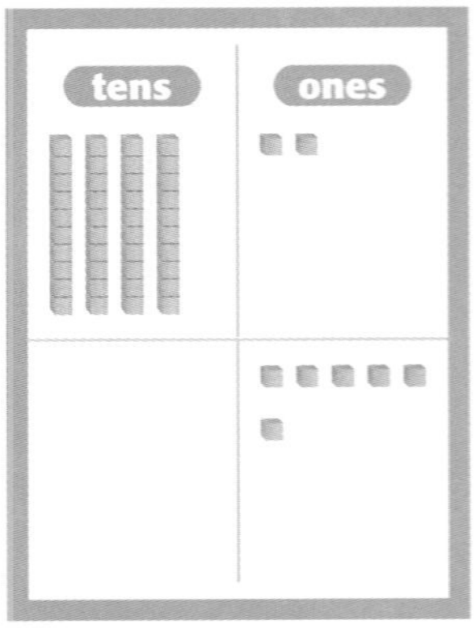

2

	tens	ones
	2	3
+	2	4

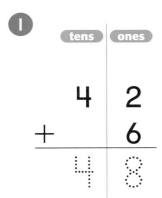

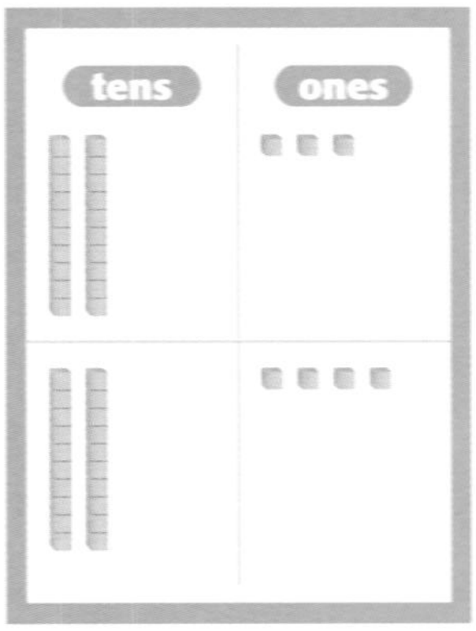

3

	tens	ones
	1	3
+	3	2

	tens	ones
	1	6
+	2	1

	tens	ones
	3	0
+		6

	tens	ones
	7	2
+	1	2

Talk About It How many ways can you show a sum of 9?

Notes for Home: Your child learned to add numbers like 43 + 15. *Home Activity:* Find the scores for a baseball game in the newspaper and ask your child to find the total points scored by both teams.

Add. Use ☐☐ and |...

4

tens	ones
3	5
+ 3	3
6	8

tens	ones
1	1
+ 3	2

tens	ones
1	6
+ 2	2

tens	ones
3	6
+ 2	2

5

21　　45　　61　　16　　17　　53
+ 32　+ 23　+ 17　+ 31　+ 12　+ 46

6

14　　27　　42　　73　　31　　41
+ 21　+ 41　+ 17　+ 14　+ 15　+ 11

7

81　　14　　20　　43　　30　　26
+ 3　+ 12　+ 5　+ 34　+ 16　+ 63

Problem Solving Critical Thinking

8 Use ☐☐ and |... to find 4 ways to get the sum of 49.

tens	ones
☐	☐
+ 2	2
4	9

tens	ones
☐	☐
+ 3	1
4	9

tens	ones
☐	☐
+ 1	3
4	9

tens	ones
☐	☐
+ 4	2
4	9

Notes for Home: Your child practiced adding numbers like 36 + 12. *Home Activity:* Give the price of two items in the kitchen, such as a juice box at 35¢ and an apple at 30¢. Ask your child to find the price of both items and show the cost with coins.

　For additional practice, see Skills Practice Bank, page 539, Set 1.

Name

Regroup with Addition

Learn

Use 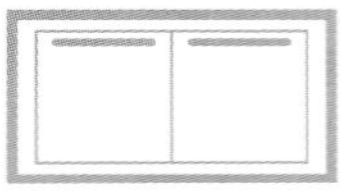 and 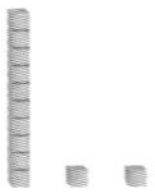 to show 37 + 6.

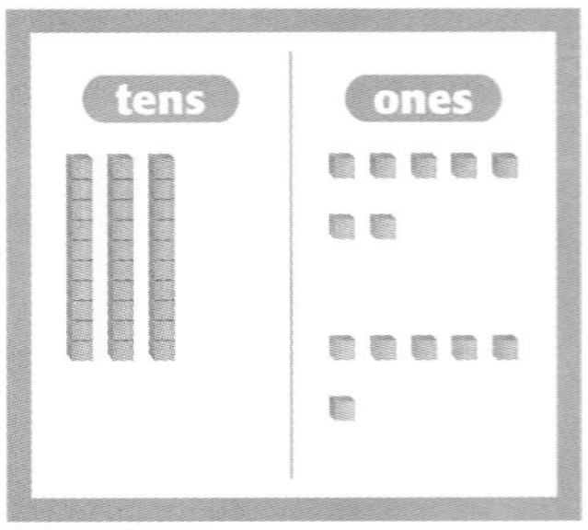

There are more than 9 ones. Regroup.

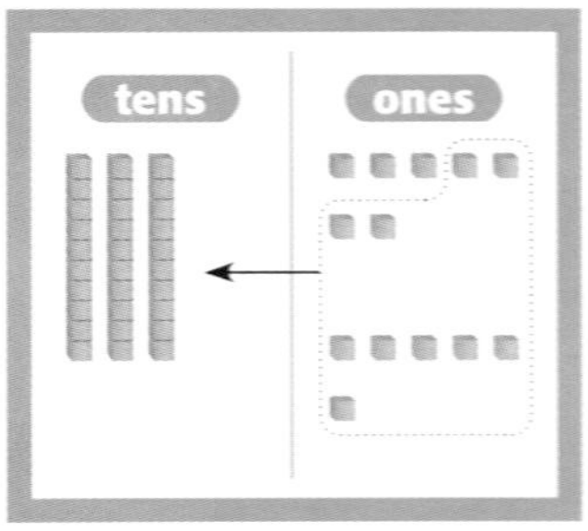

Exchange 10 ones for 1 ten.

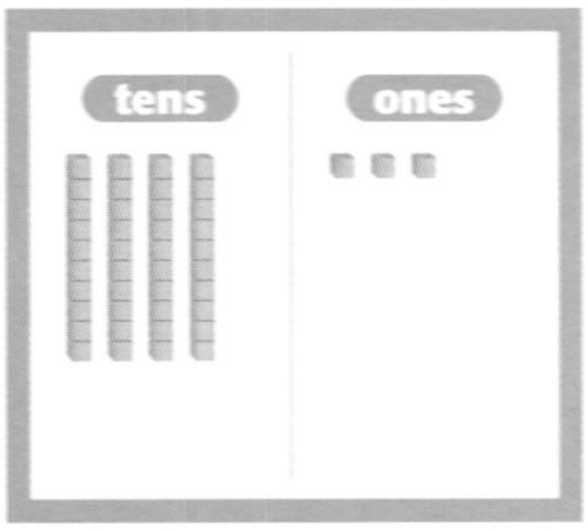

Now there are 4 tens and 3 ones.

Check

Use 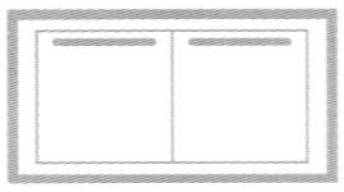 and 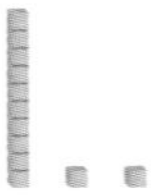.

	Show this many.	Add this many.	Do you need to regroup?	Solve.
1	25	8	(yes) no	25 + 8 = 33
2	17	4	yes no	17 + 4 = ____
3	43	3	yes no	43 + 3 = ____
4	35	7	yes no	35 + 7 = ____

Talk About It How do you know when to regroup ones to make a ten?

Notes for Home: Your child worked with tens and ones to find sums for number sentences like 37 + 9. *Home Activity:* Using dimes and pennies ask your child to show 15¢. Then add 1 penny at a time to reach 23¢. Exchange 10 pennies for a dime when you reach 20¢.

Practice

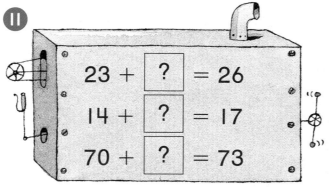

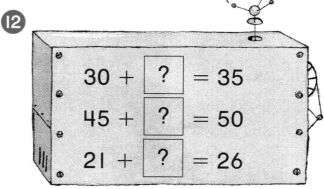

Sometimes you don't need to regroup.
Think before you add.

Use [place-value mat] and [tens and ones blocks].

	Show this many.	Add this many.	Do you need to regroup?	Solve.
5	15	2	yes (no)	$15 + 2 =$ 17
6	34	8	yes no	$34 + 8 =$ ____
7	63	5	yes no	$63 + 5 =$ ____
8	27	4	yes no	$27 + 4 =$ ____
9	32	6	yes no	$32 + 6 =$ ____
10	48	5	yes no	$48 + 5 =$ ____

Mental Math

What's My Rule? What number does each machine add?

11

$23 + \boxed{?} = 26$

$14 + \boxed{?} = 17$

$70 + \boxed{?} = 73$

This machine adds ____.

12

$30 + \boxed{?} = 35$

$45 + \boxed{?} = 50$

$21 + \boxed{?} = 26$

This machine adds ____.

Notes for Home: Your child practiced combining tens and ones to find sums for number sentences like 28 + 6. *Home Activity:* Show 25¢ in dimes and pennies. Add one more penny and ask for the total. Continue adding 1 penny at a time until you reach 38¢. When you can, exchange 10 pennies for a dime.

Name ____________________

Reading for Math

Retell the Story

T. J. wrote about his summer vacation.

Last summer my family and I went fishing. I caught 13 fish from the dock. My two sisters each caught 6 fish from the boat. Then, guess what! We cooked the fish and had a picnic lunch.

Draw four pictures to show the story.

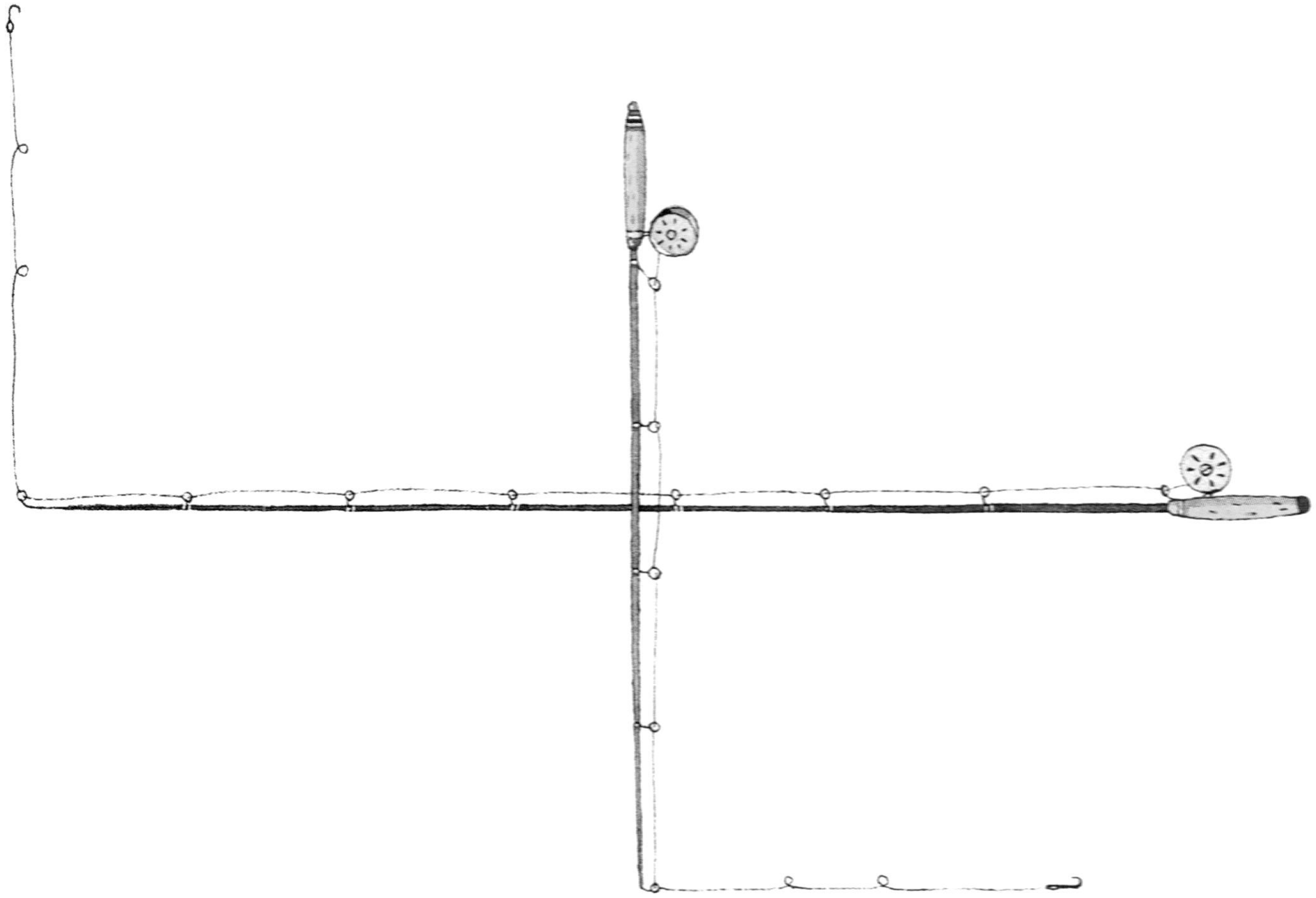

Talk About It Use your pictures to tell the story to a friend. What could you add to your pictures to make the story easier to tell?

Notes for Home: Your child drew pictures to show a story, then retold the story from pictures. This skill helps prepare your child for an upcoming problem solving lesson. *Home Activity:* Ask your child to tell you a story about the pictures he or she drew.

Nina wrote about her summer vacation.

I had a lemonade business.
First, I made a stand.
Then each day I made lemonade.
One hot day I sold 34 cups.
Another day I sold 22 cups.
I bought 3 new books with the money.

Draw four pictures to show the story.

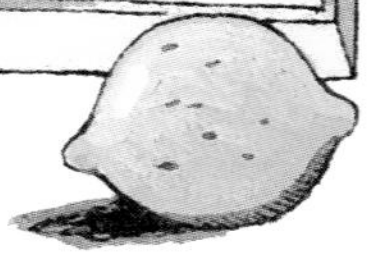

Use your pictures to tell the story to a friend.

Journal

Write or tell your own story about something you did.
Draw four pictures to show your story.

Notes for Home: Your child practiced drawing pictures to show a story and retelling it.
Home Activity: Read a story aloud and ask your child to draw pictures to show the story. Then take turns retelling the story using the pictures.

Name ______________________________

Problem Solving: Use Objects

Learn

PROBLEM SOLVING GUIDE

Understand • Plan • Solve • Look Back

31 children are on the Ferris wheel.
8 more children get on.
How many children are there now?

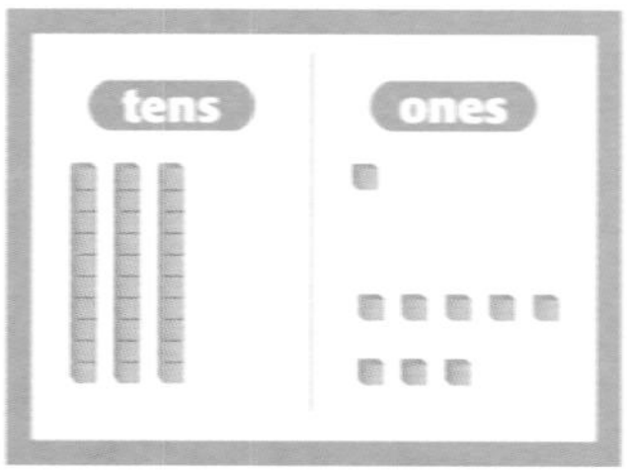

31 + 8 = 39 children

Check

Use 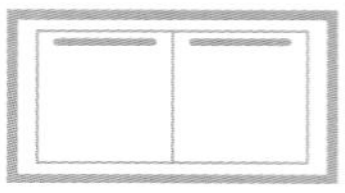 and 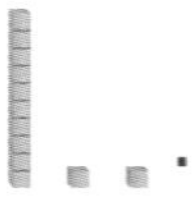.
Write the number sentence. Solve.

1. 23 children went down the giant slide. Then 6 more children went down. How many children went down the slide?

   ______________________ children

2. May sold 32 boxes of popcorn. Nick sold 13 boxes. How many boxes of popcorn did both children sell?

   ______________________ boxes

3. At the ring toss, 19 girls won prizes. 22 boys won prizes there too. How many won at the ring toss?

   ______________________ prizes

Talk About It What other ways can you solve these problems?

Notes for Home: Your child solved problems by adding two numbers such as 24 + 5.
Home Activity: Read this problem aloud. "I bought a box of 12 donuts and a box of 6 donuts. How many donuts did I buy?" Help your child solve the problem. (18 donuts)

PROBLEM SOLVING

Practice

Use [workmat] and [tens and ones blocks].

Write the number sentence. Solve.

4 The stand has 30 bags of popcorn.
Jan fills 25 more bags with popcorn.
How many bags are there now? 30 + 25 = 55 bags

5 24 children ride the bumper cars.
Then 6 more children get on.
How many children are on the cars? ______________ children

6 Zal takes 25 tickets for the horse ride.
Then he takes 20 more tickets.
How many tickets does he take in all? ______________ tickets

7 30 children are at the puppet show.
8 more children come.
How many children are at
the show now? ______________ children

Visual Thinking

Solve.

8 23 children are on the ride.
How many are in the tunnel?

_____ children

Notes for Home: Your child practiced solving problems involving addition. *Home Activity:* Ask your child to make up a problem using the numbers 34 and 20.

Name ______________________________

Mixed Practice

Lessons 1–5

Concepts and Skills

Use 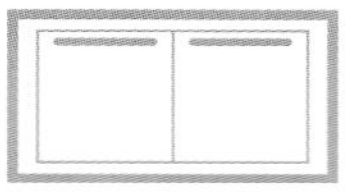 and 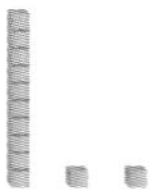. Add.

1

31	30	18	53	50	60
+ 10	+ 47	+ 20	+ 40	+ 28	+ 15

2 13 + 24 = ____ 42 + 17 = ____ 65 + 21 = ____

Circle yes or no to tell if you need to regroup. Solve.

3 49 + 3 = ____ yes no

4 31 + 7 = ____ yes no

5 23 + 6 = ____ yes no

6 18 + 2 = ____ yes no

Problem Solving

Use 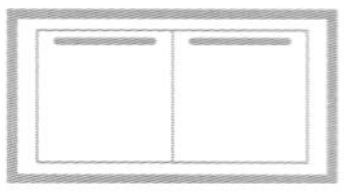 and 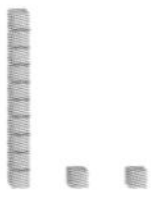. Write the number sentence. Solve.

7 32 girls go to camp.
41 boys go to camp.
How many children go to camp?

____________ children

8 A camp store has 62 t-shirts.
They get 30 more.
Now how many t-shirts does the store have?

____________ t-shirts

Journal

9 Use 30 and 25 to write an addition math story.

Notes for Home: Your child practiced the concepts, skills, and problem solving taught in lessons 1–5.
Home Activity: Ask your child to explain how to add 23 + 14 (37).

Name ________________________________

Cumulative Review

Chapters 1–13

Stay Sharp

Concepts and Skills

How many tens and ones?

1. 80 _____ tens _____ ones
2. 54 _____ tens _____ ones
3. 38 _____ tens _____ ones
4. 12 _____ ten _____ ones
5. 67 _____ tens _____ ones
6. 79 _____ tens _____ ones
7. 92 _____ tens _____ ones
8. 26 _____ tens _____ ones

Problem Solving

Write a number sentence.

9. Maria found 17 worms.
8 got away.
How many worms are left?

_______________ worms

10. Roger caught 5 fish.
Then he caught 8 more.
How many fish did he catch?

_______________ fish

Test Prep

Fill in the ○ for the correct answer.

Add.

11. $6 + 2 + 4$
○ 11 ○ 12 ○ 13 ○ 14

12. $7 + 1 + 5$
○ 13 ○ 14 ○ 15 ○ 16

13. $5 + 6 + 1$
○ 12 ○ 13 ○ 14 ○ 15

14. $3 + 9 + 3$
○ 14 ○ 15 ○ 16 ○ 17

Notes for Home: Your child reviewed place value concepts, problem solving, and addition skills. *Home Activity:* Give your child a number. Ask how many tens and how many ones are in the number.

Subtract Tens

 Learn •

Subtract.

58 − 20

tens	ones
5	8
− 2	0
3	8

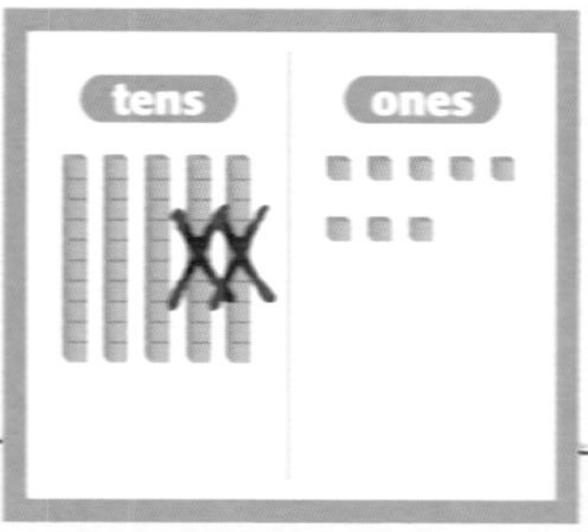

To subtract 20, take away 2 tens.

tens	ones

Check •

Use ☐ and |·· . Subtract.

1

tens	ones
4	5
− 3	0
1	5

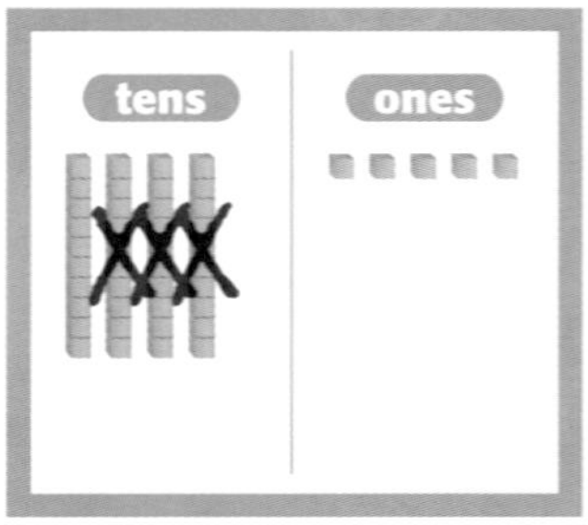

tens	ones

2

tens	ones
1	9
− 1	0

tens	ones

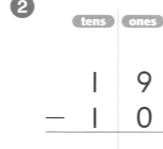

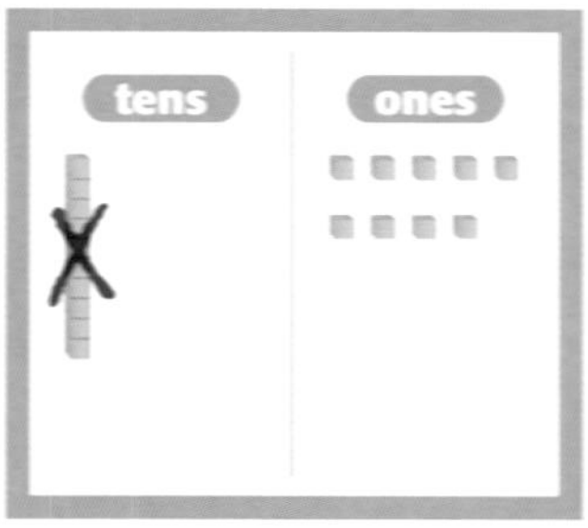

3

tens	ones
5	4
− 1	0

tens	ones
3	3
− 2	0

tens	ones
2	7
− 1	0

tens	ones
9	8
− 4	0

Talk About It Tell how you would use |·· to find 37 − 20.

 Notes for Home: Your child learned to subtract tens from a two-digit number. *Home Activity:* Ask your child to show you how to subtract 25 − 10 using dimes and pennies, then write the answer.

Practice

Subtract.

Use [place-value mat] and [tens and ones blocks].

4

tens	ones
2	2
− 1	0
1	2

tens	ones
3	7
− 2	0

tens	ones
4	4
− 4	0

tens	ones
5	3
− 3	0

5

$$\begin{array}{r} 42 \\ -\ 10 \\ \hline \end{array} \quad \begin{array}{r} 63 \\ -\ 30 \\ \hline \end{array} \quad \begin{array}{r} 47 \\ -\ 20 \\ \hline \end{array} \quad \begin{array}{r} 78 \\ -\ 20 \\ \hline \end{array} \quad \begin{array}{r} 95 \\ -\ 10 \\ \hline \end{array} \quad \begin{array}{r} 62 \\ -\ 20 \\ \hline \end{array}$$

6

$$\begin{array}{r} 88 \\ -\ 40 \\ \hline \end{array} \quad \begin{array}{r} 73 \\ -\ 50 \\ \hline \end{array} \quad \begin{array}{r} 49 \\ -\ 30 \\ \hline \end{array} \quad \begin{array}{r} 79 \\ -\ 60 \\ \hline \end{array} \quad \begin{array}{r} 85 \\ -\ 80 \\ \hline \end{array} \quad \begin{array}{r} 82 \\ -\ 60 \\ \hline \end{array}$$

PRACTICE

Problem Solving

Write your own problem.

7 Write a problem about the baseball game in the picture. Tell if you add or subtract. Write a number sentence. Solve.

____

____

____

Notes for Home: Your child practiced subtracting tens from a two-digit number. *Home Activity:* Using dimes and pennies, ask your child to show you how to use subtraction to do some of the problems on the page.

Name

Subtract Tens and Ones

Learn

Subtract.

37 − 24

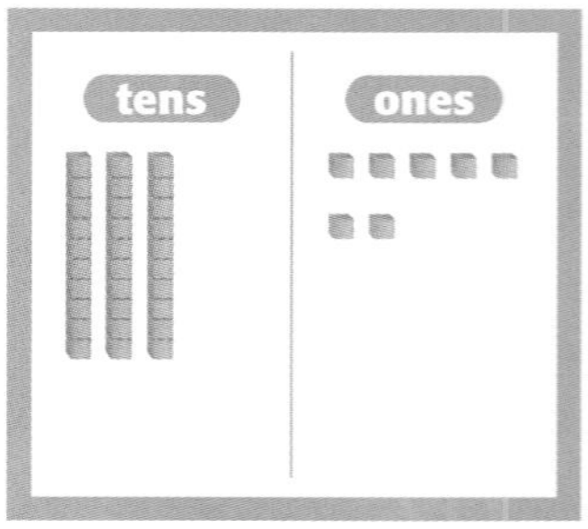

Take away 4 ones.
Take away 2 tens.
1 ten and 3 ones are left.

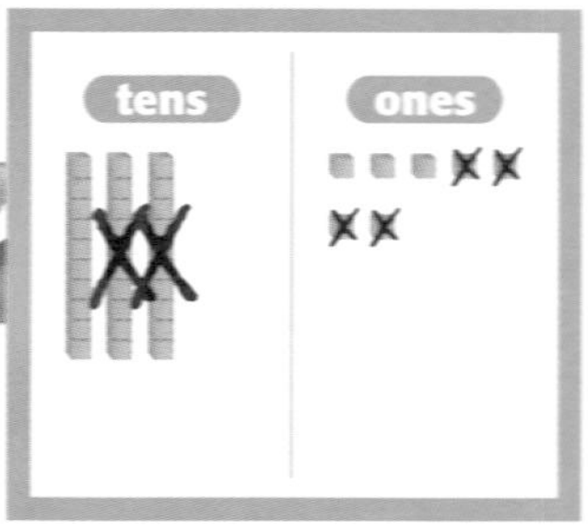

tens	ones
3	7
− 2	4
1	3

Check

Use [place-value mat] and [tens and ones blocks]. Subtract.

Cross off the ones and tens you take away.

1

tens	ones
2	7
− 1	3
1	4

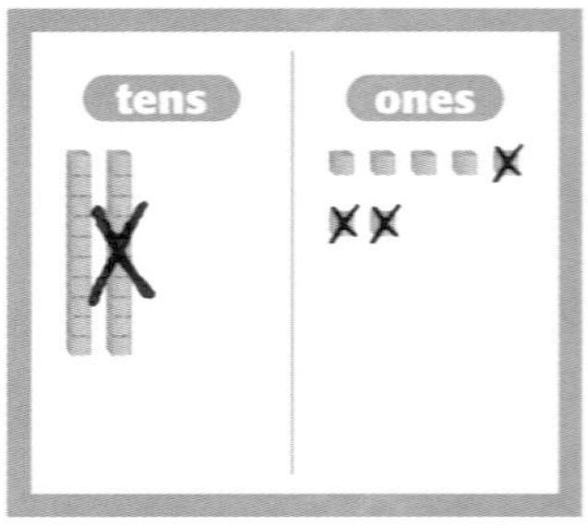

2

tens	ones
4	5
− 2	1

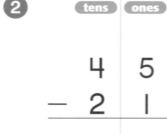

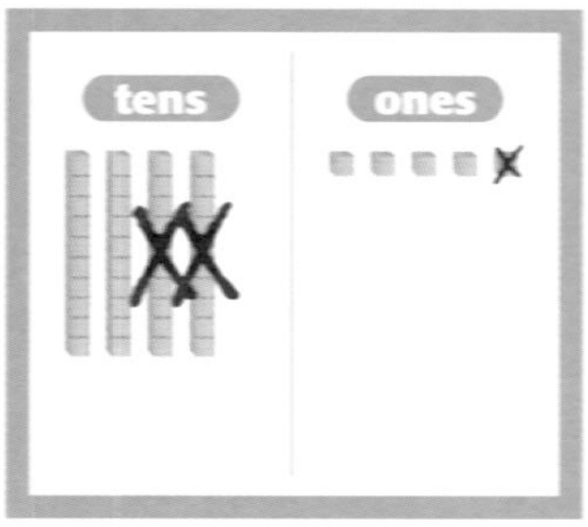

3

tens	ones
5	8
− 2	2

tens	ones
3	9
− 1	6

tens	ones
4	4
− 2	1

tens	ones
9	1
− 4	0

Talk About It When do you use subtraction?

Notes for Home: Your child used tens and ones to learn how to subtract. *Home Activity:* Talk with your child about times when you use subtraction around the home or at work.

Use and ▌⋮ . Subtract.

4

tens	ones
5	7
− 1	6
4	1

tens	ones
3	8
− 1	2

tens	ones
7	6
−	4

tens	ones
5	2
− 1	2

5

$$56 \qquad 37 \qquad 65 \qquad 48 \qquad 87 \qquad 79$$
$$-31 \qquad -17 \qquad -21 \qquad -41 \qquad -22 \qquad -\ 7$$

Mixed Practice Add or subtract.

6

$$74 \qquad 45 \qquad 78 \qquad 93 \qquad 69 \qquad 53$$
$$-30 \qquad -\ 4 \qquad -14 \qquad -20 \qquad -13 \qquad -21$$

7

$$41 \qquad 86 \qquad 30 \qquad 61 \qquad 53 \qquad 44$$
$$+17 \qquad +11 \qquad +25 \qquad +32 \qquad +12 \qquad +45$$

Problem Solving

Solve.

8 My friend has these marbles.
He gives me 15.
How many does he have left?

_____ marbles

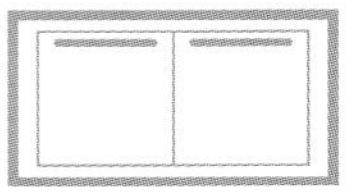

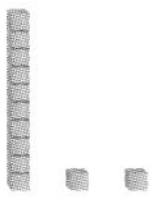

 Notes for Home: Your child practiced subtraction problems like 34 − 22. *Home Activity:* Show 34¢ in dimes and pennies. Tell your child that you want to buy a drink for 22¢. Ask your child to show you how much will be left. (12¢)

For additional practice, see Skills Practice Bank, page 539, Set 2.

Name ____________________

Regroup with Subtraction

Learn

Use 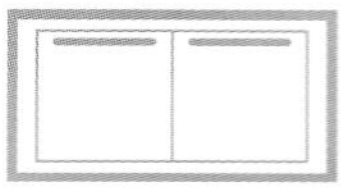 and 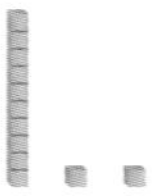 to show 42 − 5.

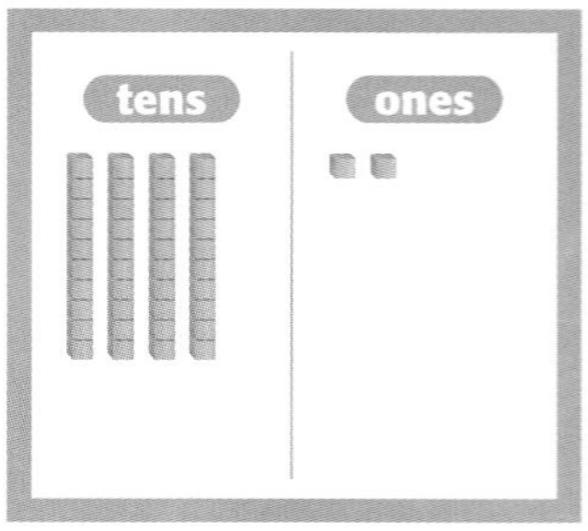

You cannot take 5 ones away.

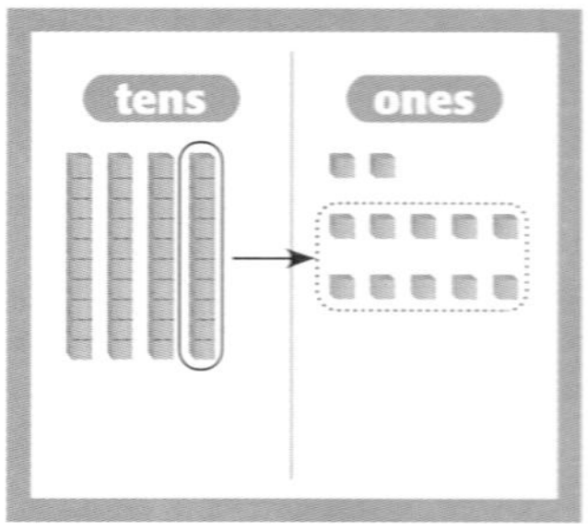

Regroup. Exchange 1 ten for 10 ones.

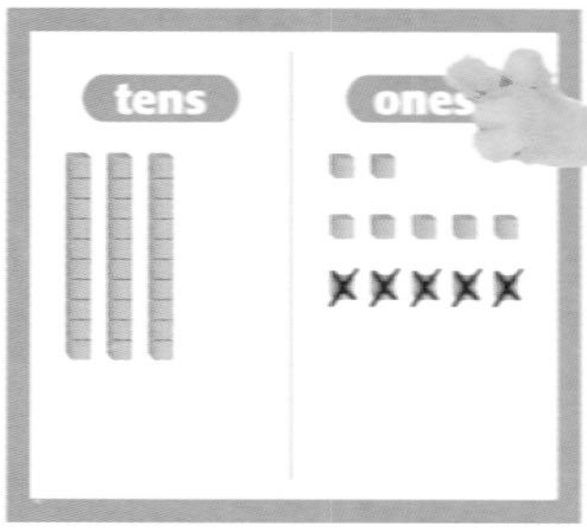

Now take away 5 ones. There are 3 tens and 7 ones left.

Check

Use 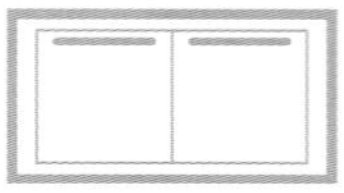 and 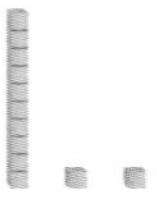.

	Show this many.	Subtract this many.	Do you need to regroup?	Solve.
1	34	8	yes (circled) no	34 − 8 = 26
2	35	4	yes no	35 − 4 = ____
3	42	9	yes no	42 − 9 = ____
4	62	5	yes no	62 − 5 = ____

Talk About It How do you know when to exchange a ten to make 10 ones?

Notes for Home: Your child worked with tens and ones to find differences for number sentences like 32 – 9. *Home Activity:* Using dimes and pennies ask your child to take a penny away from 15¢. Continue the process. Help your child exchange 1 dime for 10 pennies when only the dime is left.

Practice

Use 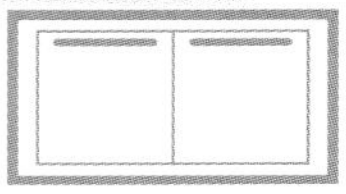 and 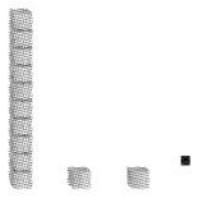.

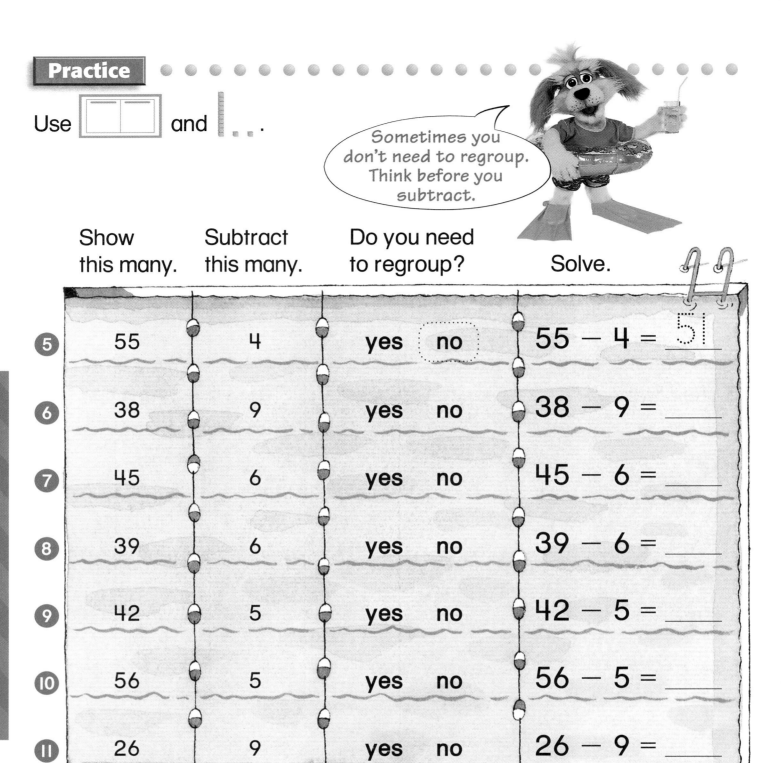

	Show this many.	Subtract this many.	Do you need to regroup?	Solve.
5	55	4	yes no	55 − 4 = 51
6	38	9	yes no	38 − 9 = ____
7	45	6	yes no	45 − 6 = ____
8	39	6	yes no	39 − 6 = ____
9	42	5	yes no	42 − 5 = ____
10	56	5	yes no	56 − 5 = ____
11	26	9	yes no	26 − 9 = ____

PRACTICE

Problem Solving

Write a number sentence. Solve.

12. Liz has 25 ride tickets.
She uses 6 for the fun house.
How many tickets does Liz have left? ________________ tickets

Notes for Home: Your child practiced working with tens and ones to find differences for number sentences like 23 – 7. *Home Activity:* Using dimes and pennies ask your child to take a penny away from 25¢. Continue taking a penny away. Help your child exchange 1 dime for 10 pennies when appropriate.

Name _____

Target 99

Players 2

What You Need

Workmat ☐☐ for each player

Tens and ones

Number cube

How to Play

1. Roll the number cube.

2. Choose. Take as many ones or tens as the number rolled.

3. Put your into the correct column of ☐☐ .

 When you get ten ones, you must regroup them for a ten.

4. If you go over 99, take ones or tens away.

5. Roll the cube seven times.
 The player who is closest to 99 wins.

 Notes for Home: Your child played a game to practice addition and subtraction.
Home Activity: Ask your child to explain how to play the game and then play it together.

Name ______________________

STOP and Practice

You can use 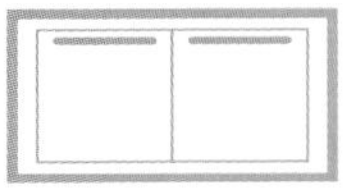 and 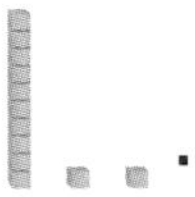.

Add.

1	27	10	75	50	12	40
	+ 40	+ 39	+ 20	+ 18	+ 30	+ 20
2	13	44	63	26	11	49
	+ 25	+ 21	+ 16	+ 23	+ 14	+ 50

Subtract.

3	56	37	95	67	48	21
	− 50	− 10	− 40	− 20	− 30	− 20
4	34	46	57	25	68	19
	− 13	− 21	− 46	− 5	− 38	− 8

Logical Reasoning

Solve.

5 I had 8 dimes.
I gave 1 dime to my sister.
I spent 3 dimes for a cone.
How many dimes do I have left?

Notes for Home: Your child practiced addition and subtraction skills. *Home Activity:* Help your child create a riddle similar to the one on this page.

PRACTICE

Name

Problem Solving: Choose an Operation

Learn

PROBLEM SOLVING GUIDE

Understand • Plan • Solve • Look Back

Leroy goes to the Fourth of July parade.
He has 76¢.
He spends 45¢ on a flag for his bike.
How much money does he have left?

add **subtract** 76 ¢ (−) 45 ¢ = 31 ¢

Check

Circle add or subtract.
Write a number sentence. Solve.

1. Amy buys a red, white, and blue hat for 60¢.
   She also buys a baton for 29¢.
   How much money does she spend?

   add **subtract** ____ ◯ ____ = ____

2. Brenda has 29¢.
   She spends 5¢ for a whistle.
   How much does she have left?

   add **subtract** ____ ◯ ____ = ____

Talk About It Tell an addition story using 25¢ and 14¢.
Tell a subtraction story using the same amounts of money.

Notes for Home: Your child solved problems after deciding if they could be solved by adding or subtracting. *Home Activity:* When shopping, find two items that cost less than 50¢. Help your child find the total cost for both items.

Practice

Circle add or subtract.
Write a number sentence.

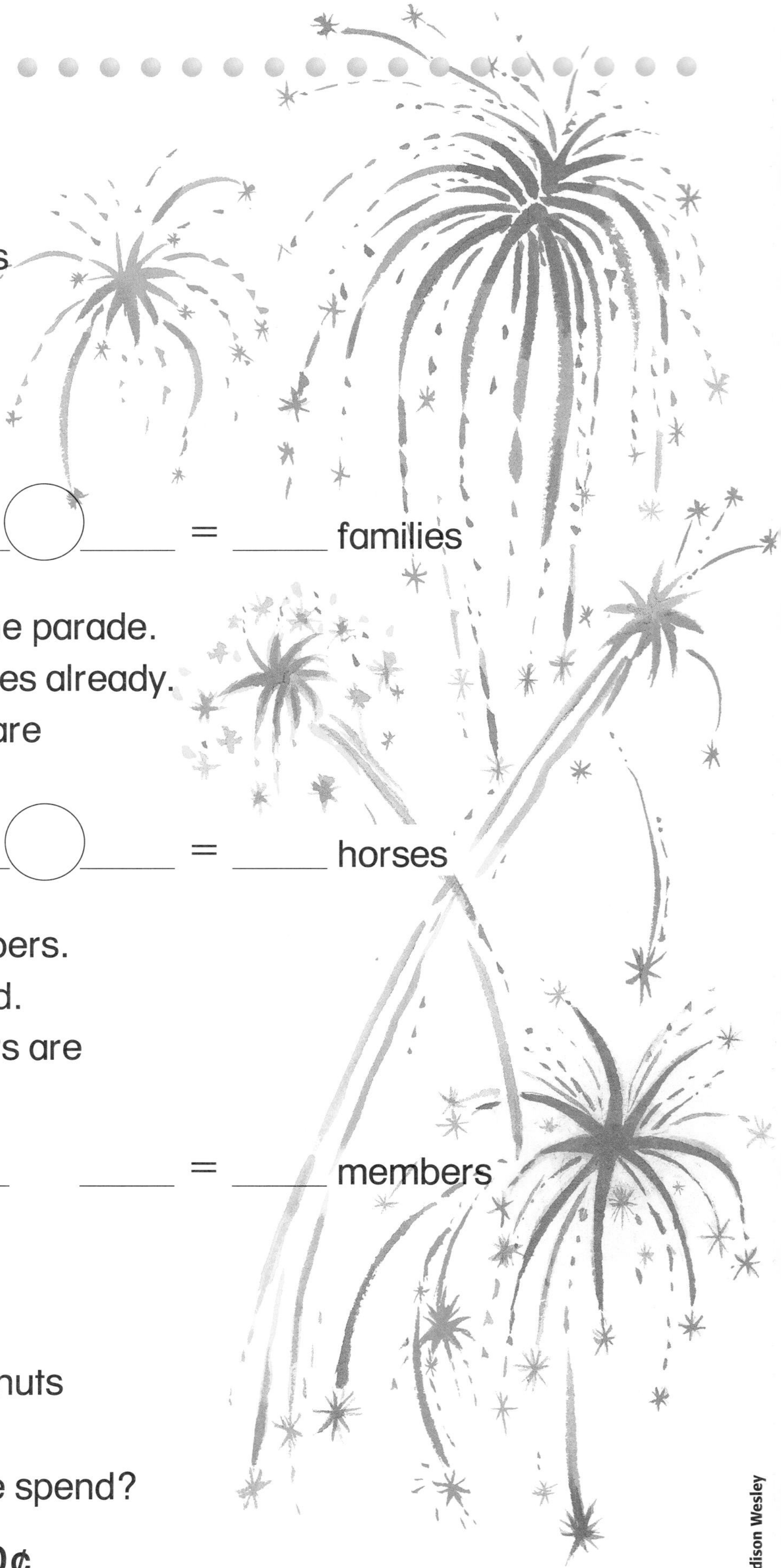

3. Louis counted 55 families at the fireworks show. 14 more families came. How many families watched the show?

add **subtract** ____ ◯ ____ = ____ families

4. There are 79 horses in the parade. Tyeesa has seen 45 horses already. How many more horses are to come?

add **subtract** ____ ◯ ____ = ____ horses

5. There are 40 band members. 8 drummers join the band. How many band members are there in all?

add **subtract** ____ ____ = ____ members

Estimation

6. Circle the best estimate.
Juan spends 29¢ on peanuts and 42¢ on juice.
About how much does he spend?

10¢ **50¢** **70¢**

Notes for Home: Your child continued solving problems involving addition or subtraction.
Home Activity: When shopping, find an item that costs 99¢ or less. Help your child find the difference of the item and 99¢.

For additional practice, see Skills Practice Bank, page 539, Set 3.

Name ______________________________

Mixed Practice

Lessons 6–9

Concepts and Skills

Use 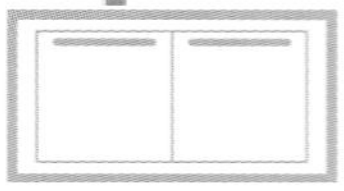 and 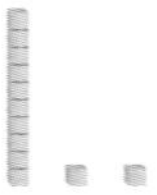. Subtract.

1	$45 - 20$	$63 - 30$	$71 - 50$	$32 - 10$	$86 - 40$	$24 - 20$
2	$67 - 26$	$49 - 15$	$96 - 35$	$26 - 16$	$75 - 71$	$32 - 20$

Circle yes or no to tell if you need to regroup. Solve.

3. $64 - 3 =$ ____ yes no
4. $58 - 8 =$ ____ yes no
5. $31 - 2 =$ ____ yes no
6. $19 - 7 =$ ____ yes no
7. $56 - 5 =$ ____ yes no
8. $20 - 1 =$ ____ yes no

Problem Solving

Circle add or subtract. Write a number sentence.

9. Wendy has 59¢.
She spends 34¢.
How much does she have left now?

add subtract

____ ◯ ____ = ____

Journal

10. Write a number story for 37¢ − 5¢.

Notes for Home: Your child practiced the concepts, skills, and problem solving taught in lessons 6–9.
Home Activity: Ask your child to create an addition and subtraction story using the numbers 45 and 23.

Name ______________________

Cumulative Review

Chapters 1–13

Concepts and Skills

Use the ruler to measure. Write the length.

1 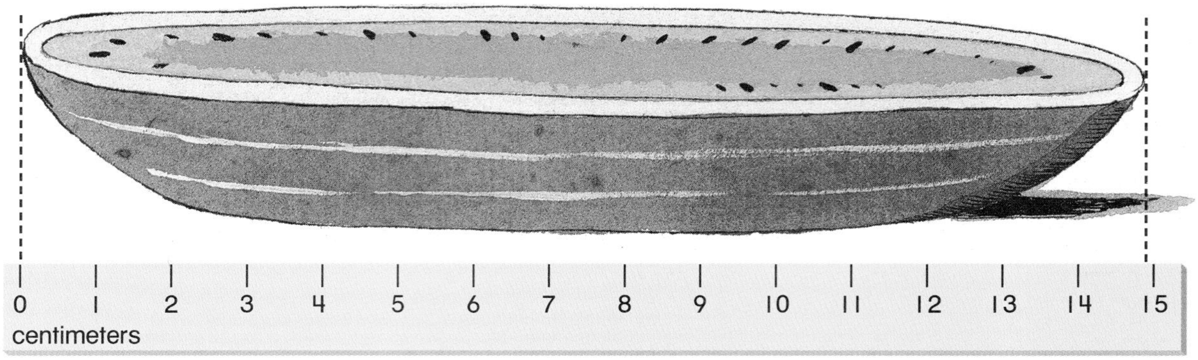

about _____ centimeters

Add.

2 $70 + 10 =$ ___ $60 + 30 =$ ___ $40 + 50 =$ ___

Problem Solving

Solve.

3 Tina found 16 shells. She gave away 8. How many does she have now?

_____ shells

4 Mr. Ling had 15 balloons. 6 of them popped. How many are left?

_____ balloons

Test Prep

Fill in the ○ for the correct answer.

Subtract.

5 $17 - 9$ ○6 ○7 ○8 ○9

6 $14 - 6$ ○5 ○6 ○7 ○8

7 $18 - 9$ ○7 ○8 ○9 ○10

Notes for Home: Your child reviewed measurement, subtraction facts, and problem solving. *Home Activity:* Ask your child to write subtraction facts for 12 ($12 - 3 = 9$, $12 - 4 = 8$, and so on). Practice these facts with your child.

Name ______________________________

Chapter 13 Review

Vocabulary

Circle yes or no to tell if you need to regroup. Solve.

1. $34 + 3 =$ ____ yes no
2. $28 + 3 =$ ____ yes no
3. $40 + 2 =$ ____ yes no
4. $56 - 5 =$ ____ yes no
5. $89 - 7 =$ ____ yes no
6. $70 - 2 =$ ____ yes no

Concepts and Skills

Use 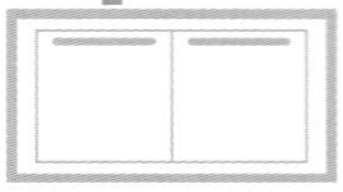 and . Add or subtract.

7.

62	15	40	33	13	20
+ 20	+ 43	+ 21	+ 51	+ 62	+ 50

8.

85	74	63	47	56	30
− 60	− 34	− 20	− 13	− 35	− 20

Problem Solving

Circle add or subtract. Write a number sentence.

9. Adam has 22¢.
He earns 50¢ watering flowers.
How much money does Adam have now?

add **subtract**

____

10. It is 65 miles to the camp.
The Bush family has gone 42 miles.
How many more miles do they need to go?

add **subtract**

______________________ miles

Notes for Home: Your child reviewed the vocabulary, concepts, skills, and problem solving taught in Chapter 13. *Home Activity:* Talk with your child about ways to earn money.

Name ______________________________

Chapter 13 Test

Add or subtract.

You can use 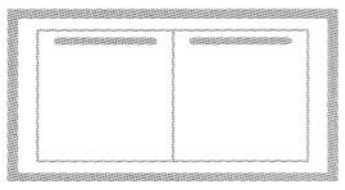 and 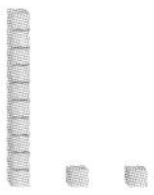.

1

53	71	24	70	31	40
+ 16	+ 20	+ 32	+ 15	+ 46	+ 36

2

47	68	83	75	38	54
− 41	− 25	− 20	− 61	− 12	− 33

Circle yes or no to tell if you need to regroup.
Solve.

3 48 + 3 = _____ **yes no**

4 50 + 8 = _____ **yes no**

5 35 − 5 = _____ **yes no**

6 20 − 2 = _____ **yes no**

Use objects. Circle add or subtract.
Write a number sentence. Solve.

7 April has 87¢ to spend. She buys a pool pass for 25¢. How much money does April have now?

add **subtract**

____

8 Keri found 37 cans and 41 bottles to recycle. How many things did Keri find to recycle?

add **subtract**

______________________ things

Notes for Home: Your child was assessed on the concepts, skills, and problem solving taught in Chapter 13. *Home Activity:* Talk with your child about something he or she would like to buy.

CHAPTER TEST

Name ______________________

Performance Assessment

Chapter 13

What You Need

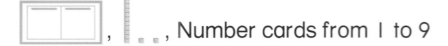

, , Number cards from 1 to 9

1. Use to make a number.
Then pick a number card.
Add that many ones to your number.
Regroup if you need to.
Write the number sentence. ______________________

2. Use to make another number.
Then pick a number card.
Subtract that many ones from your number.
Regroup if you need to.
Write the number sentence. ______________________

3. Use to make a number.
Then pick a number card.
Add. Write the number sentence. ______________________

4. Use the sum for 3.
Pick another number card.
Subtract. Write the number sentence. ______________________

Problem Solving Critical Thinking

5. When do you exchange 10 for a ? Tell why.

Notes for Home: Your child did an activity to assess understanding of the concepts of addition and subtraction of two-digit numbers. *Home Activity:* Ask your child to show you how this activity is done.

Name _____

It's All Wet!

Keys You Will Use

Use your to solve the riddle:

Where does it shower without clouds?

1. `5` `8` `–` `7` `=` | 5̱1̱ | B

2. `4` `2` `+` `3` `5` `=` | ☐ | B

3. `1` `2` `+` `4` `9` `=` | ☐ | T

4. `2` `9` `–` `1` `3` `=` | ☐ | T

5. `3` `1` `+` `1` `9` `=` | ☐ | H

6. `7` `5` `–` `5` `2` `=` | ☐ | U

7. `6` `9` `+` `2` `1` `=` | ☐ | A

Write the letter for each answer.

B̲ ___ ___ ___ ___ ___ ___
51 90 16 50 61 23 77

Tech Talk Is there another way to make 90 on your ? Show it.

🖵⇄🖳 **Visit our Web site.** www.parent.mathsurf.com

Vacation Days

How long is your school vacation?
Use a calendar to find out.

1 Count the days off from school in each of your vacation months.

________ ________ ________

Add up the numbers. Do you have more or less than 100 vacation days?

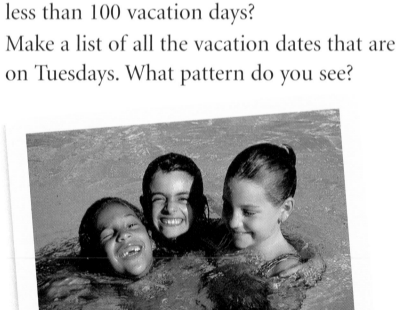

2 Make a list of all the vacation dates that are on Tuesdays. What pattern do you see?

Fold down

Summertime!

How deep is the pool?
What other math ideas do you see in the picture?

A Ferry Good Time

Nell and her Grandfather are taking a ferry ride.

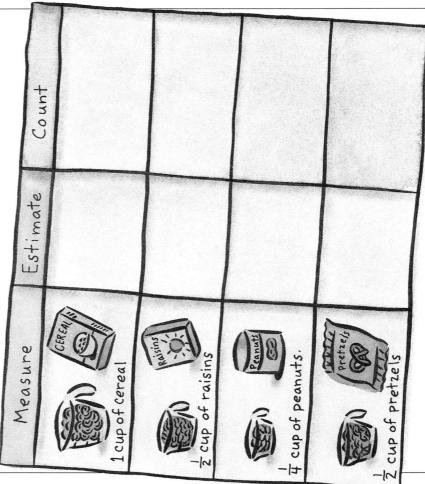

What did one car say to the others?
Wheel be seeing you!

Notes for Home: Your child solved problems involving addition and subtraction. *Home Activity:* When you are going places with your child, talk about how long the outings will take.

Crunch! Crunch!

Fresh air and exercise make a hiker hungry.

Let's make trail mix.

First, measure each ingredient.

Next, estimate and then count the number of pieces in each amount.

Measure	Estimate	Count
1 cup of cereal		
$\frac{1}{2}$ cup of raisins		
$\frac{1}{4}$ cup of peanuts.		
$\frac{1}{2}$ cup of pretzels		

Notes for Home: Your child estimated amounts in a recipe and made a healthy snack. *Home Activity:* Try this recipe at home with other ingredients, such as cut-up dates, other cereals, or small crackers.

Help the Hikers

Help these hikers cross the bridges, only one hiker to a bridge.
Add the weight of each hiker and the weight of each hiker's pack.
Each hiker must weigh less than the limit on the bridge.
Draw a line from the hiker to the hiker's bridge.

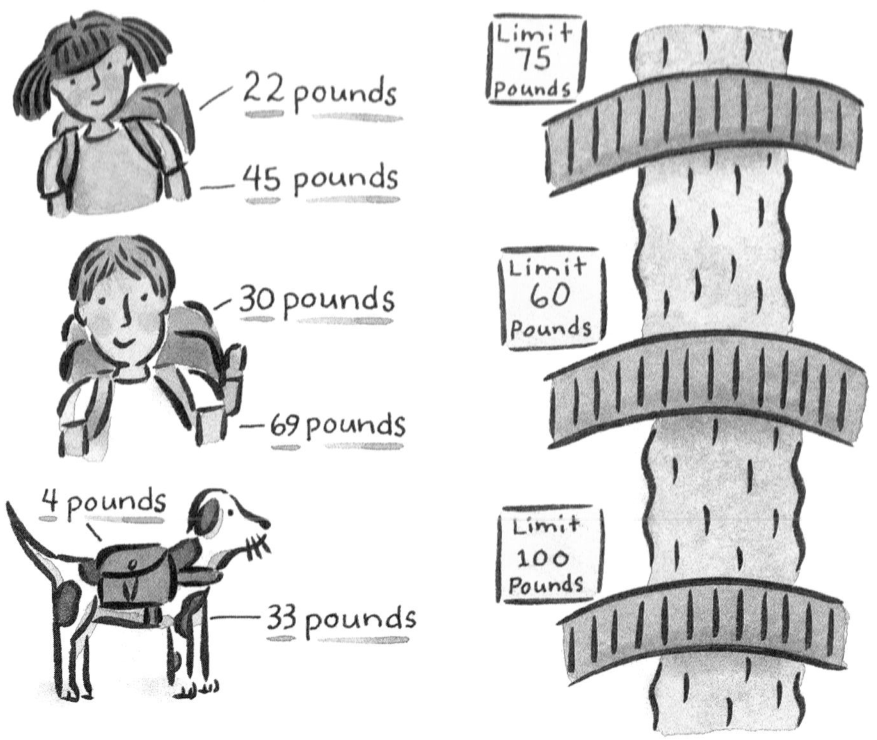

Notes for Home: Your child added two-digit numbers to solve a problem. *Home Activity:* Ask your child to stand on a bathroom scale and hold a variety of objects to find the combined weight.

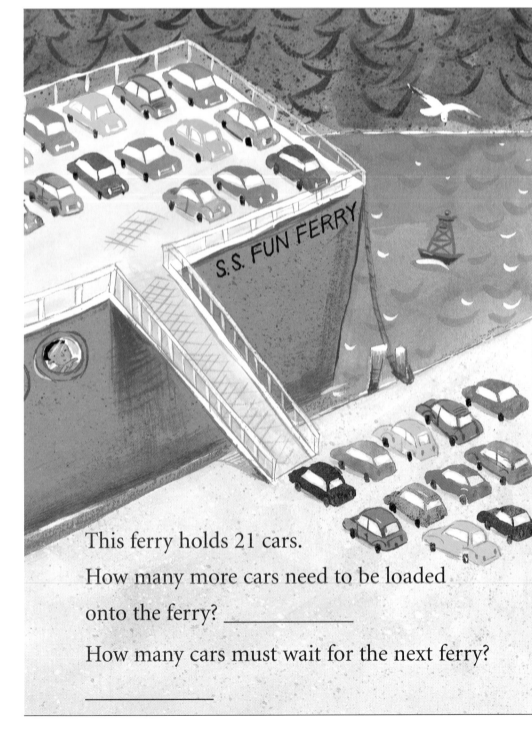

This ferry holds 21 cars.
How many more cars need to be loaded onto the ferry? ____________
How many cars must wait for the next ferry?

____

Seen at the Beach

Philip took pictures of things he saw at the beach.
Can you match his pictures with the real thing?

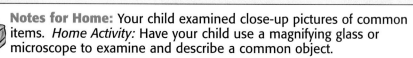

+LIFEGUARD
What does a clam say when it answers the phone?
Shello!

Notes for Home: Your child examined close-up pictures of common items. *Home Activity:* Have your child use a magnifying glass or microscope to examine and describe a common object.

Name ______________________________

Skills Practice Bank

Chapter 1

Set 1 For use after page 12.

Write how many.

1 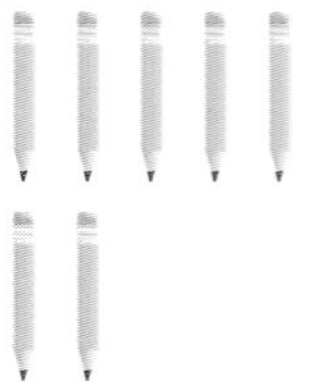 ____

2 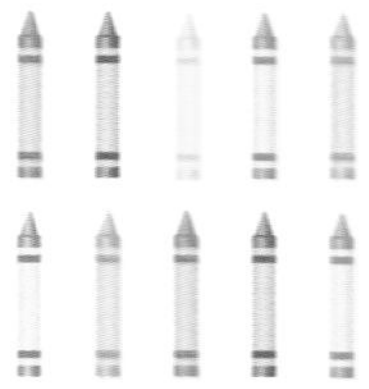 ____

3  ____

Set 2 For use after page 24.

Circle the number.

1 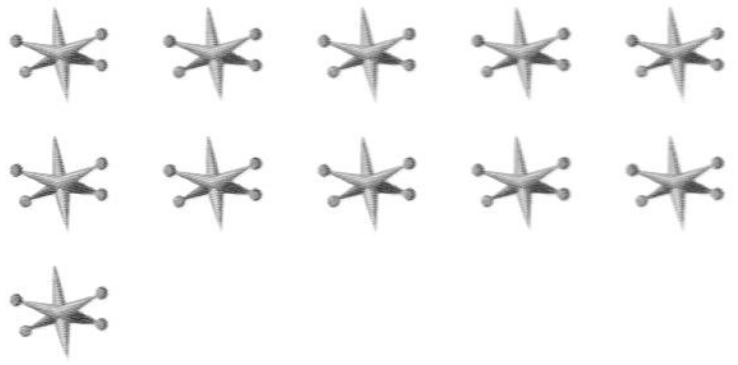

10 11 12

2 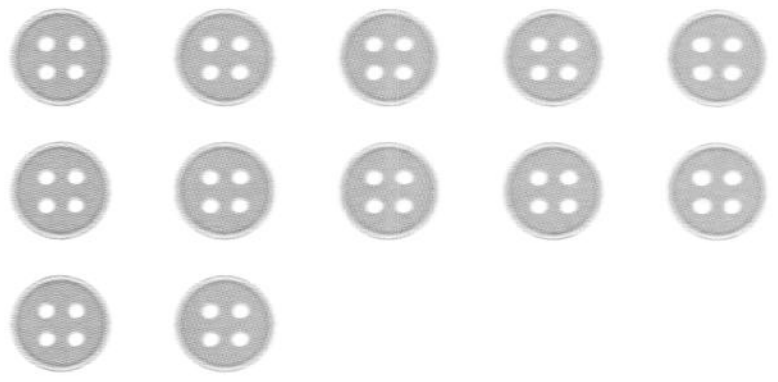

10 11 12

3 

10 11 12

4 

10 11 12

Set 3 For use after page 38.

Make a graph.

Color one box for each.

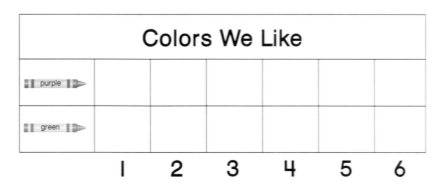

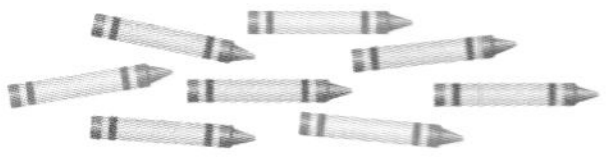

Colors We Like						
purple						
green						
	1	2	3	4	5	6

Name ______________________________

Skills Practice Bank

Chapter 2

Set 1 For use after page 56.

Show ways to make 8. Write the numbers.

1 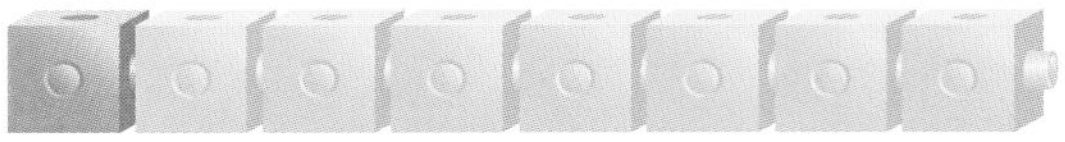

_____ and _____ is _____.

2 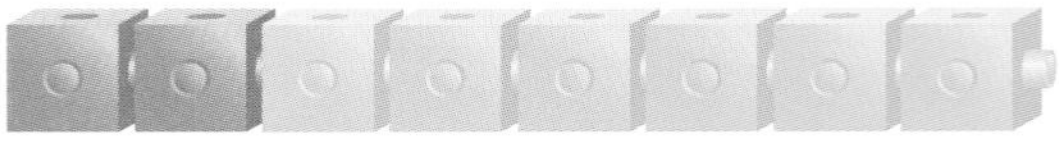

_____ and _____ is _____.

3 

_____ and _____ is _____.

4 

_____ and _____ is _____.

Set 2 For use after page 62.

How many ways can you put

3  into 2 ?

_____ ways

		In All

Set 3 For use after page 74.

How many things are under the ?

1 9 in all

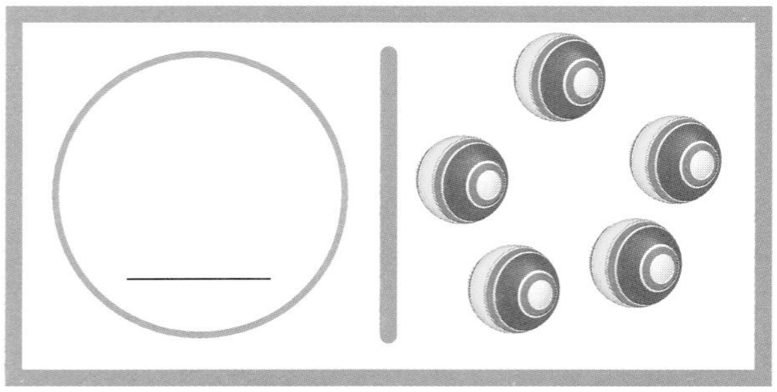

2 10 in all

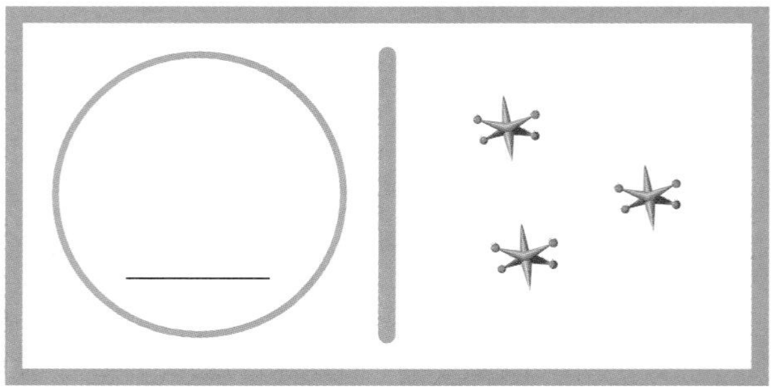

Name ______________________________

Skills Practice Bank

Chapter 3

Set 1 For use after page 100.

Use  to add.

1	3	6	4	0	9	2	3
	+ 3	+ 1	+ 2	+ 5	+ 3	+ 8	+ 5
2	1	2	3	8	4	4	9
	+ 9	+ 6	+ 2	+ 1	+ 6	+ 7	+ 0

Set 2 For use after page 114.

Use  to subtract.

1	4	3	5	6	7	6	8
	− 1	− 2	− 2	− 3	− 2	− 5	− 3
2	9	6	9	10	8	10	12
	− 7	− 1	− 1	− 7	− 7	− 5	− 3

Set 3 For use after page 120.

Circle add or subtract. Complete the number sentence.

1. 12  are in the box. **add** **subtract**

   5  jump out.

   How many are in the box now? 12 ◯ 5 = ____ 

Name ______________________________

Skills Practice Bank

Chapter 4

Set 1 For use after page 138.

Think of the greater number. Count on to add.

1 $3 + 8 =$ ____ $3 + 9 =$ ____ $7 + 2 =$ ____

$8 + 3 =$ ____ $9 + 3 =$ ____ $2 + 7 =$ ____

Set 2 For use after page 156.

Subtract.

1 $10 - 10 =$ ____ $10 - 0 =$ ____ $10 - 2 =$ ____

2

11	7	12	10	7	8	5
− 2	− 7	− 0	− 5	− 2	− 0	− 2

Set 3 For use after page 162.

You can use  and . Write a number sentence.

1 Mom washed 8 .

We ate 8 .

How many were left?

____

2 Dad ate 6 .

He ate 5 more 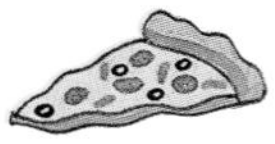.

How many did he eat?

____

3 Mrs. Lott had 5 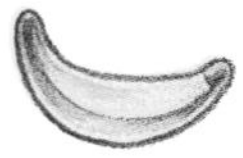.

Mr. Wick had 4 .

How many did they have?

____

4 Bob had 9 .

He ate 0.

How many are left?

____

SKILLS PRACTICE BANK

Name

Skills Practice Bank

Chapter 5

Set 1 For use after page 182.

Copy. Make one the same size and shape.

1 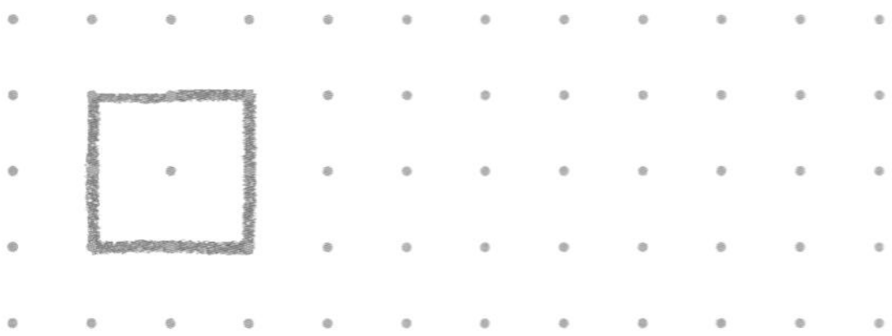

2 

3 

4 

Circle the ones that are the same size and shape.

5

Set 2 For use after page 192.

Draw lines to show fair shares.

1 

2 

3 

4 

Name

Skills Practice Bank

Chapter 5 cont.

Set 3 For use after page 206.

Answer the riddles.

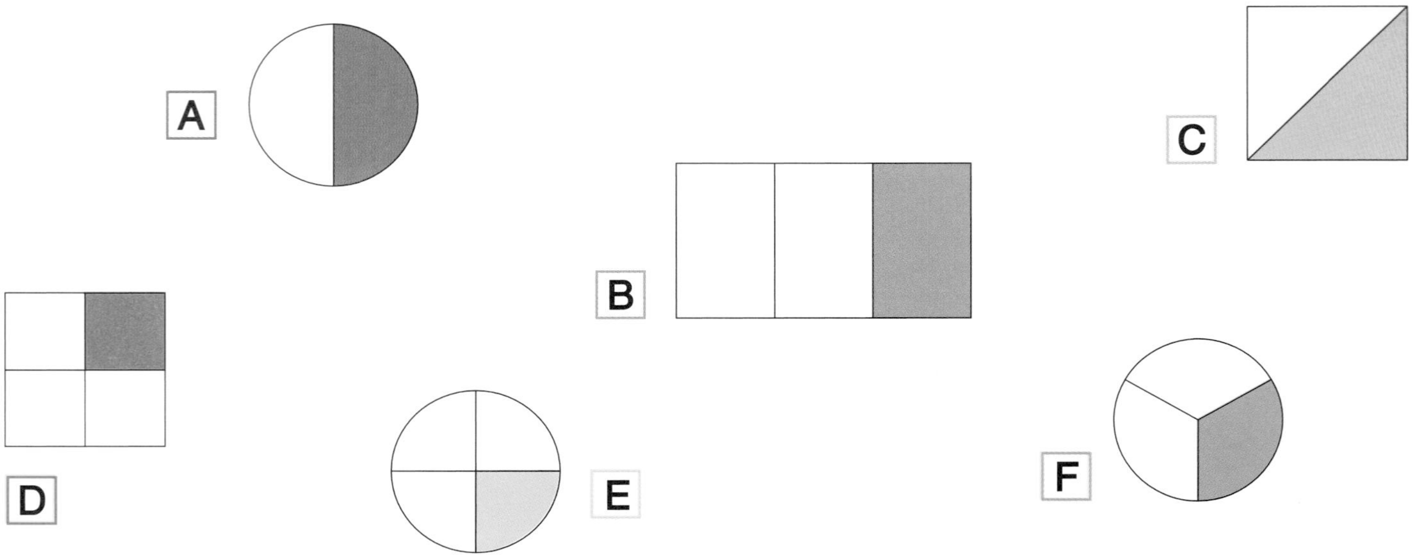

1. I show thirds. I am round. Which am I?

2. I show fourths. I am a square. Which am I?

3. I show halves. I am square. Which am I?

4. I show thirds. I am long. Which am I?

5. I show fourths. I am round. Which am I?

6. I show halves. I am round. Which am I?

Name ______

Skills Practice Bank
Chapter 6

Set 1 For use after page 220.

Write the sum. Circle the doubles.

1	6 + 6	4 + 3	9 + 2	0 + 0	1 + 7	5 + 3	5 + 5
2	2 + 7	4 + 4	8 + 3	7 + 3	3 + 6	3 + 3	9 + 0

Set 2 For use after page 236.

Complete the fact families.

1 

3 + ____ = ____

6 + ____ = ____

9 − ____ = ____

9 − ____ = ____

2 

4 + ____ = ____

2 + ____ = ____

6 − ____ = ____

6 − ____ = ____

Set 3 For use after page 244.

Guess. Then check. You can use .

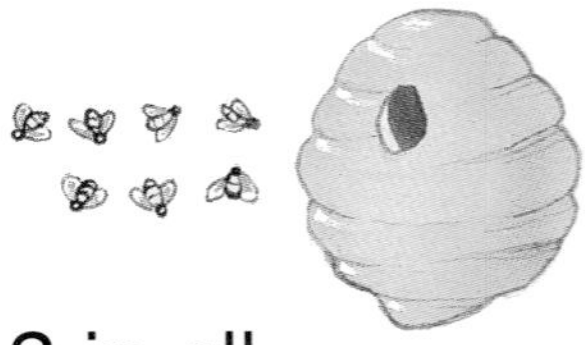

13 in all

1 Try ____ 7 + ____ = ____

Try ____ 7 + ____ = ____

Name ______________________________

Skills Practice Bank

Chapter 7

Set 1 For use after page 260.

Complete the number sentence.

1. 30 and 10 is ____.
2. 10 and 10 is ____.
3. 40 and 10 is ____.
4. 20 and 10 is ____.
5. 50 and 10 is ____.
6. 0 and 10 is ____.

Set 2 For use after page 270.

Read the graph.

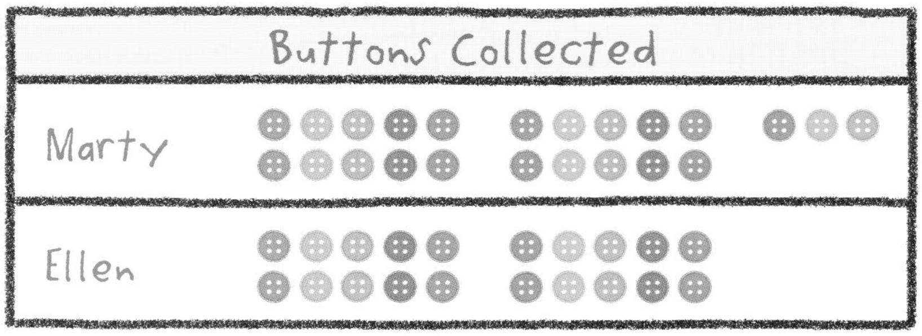

1. How many buttons does Marty have? ____
2. How many more buttons does Marty have than Ellen? ____

Set 3 For use after page 276.

1. Count by 2s. 2, 4, 6, ____, ____, ____, ____, ____
2. Count by 5s. 5, 10, 15, ____, ____, ____, ____, ____
3. Count by 10s. 10, 20, ____, ____, ____
4. Count by 2s. 24, 26, 28, ____, ____, ____, ____

SKILLS PRACTICE BANK

Name ____________________

Skills Practice Bank

Chapter 8

Set 1 For use after page 300.

How many tens and ones? Write the number.

1. 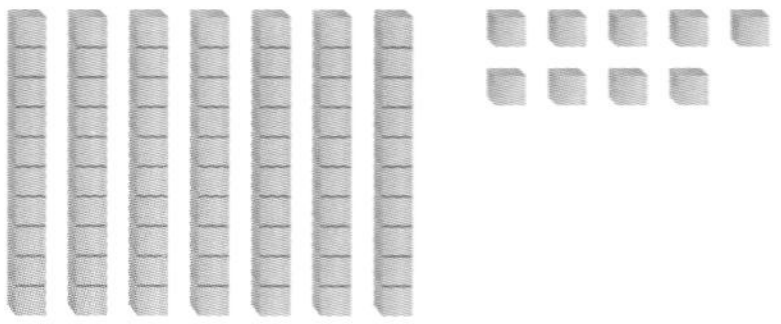

tens	ones

______

2. 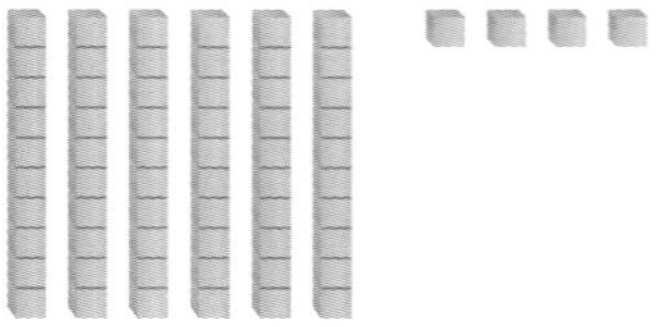

tens	ones

______

Set 2 For use after page 314.

Write the number that comes after.

1. 65 ______
2. 27 ______
3. 76 ______
4. 98 ______
5. 80 ______
6. 54 ______

Write the number that comes before.

7. ______ 64
8. ______ 41
9. ______ 78
10. ______ 94
11. ______ 80
12. ______ 59

Set 3 For use after page 320.

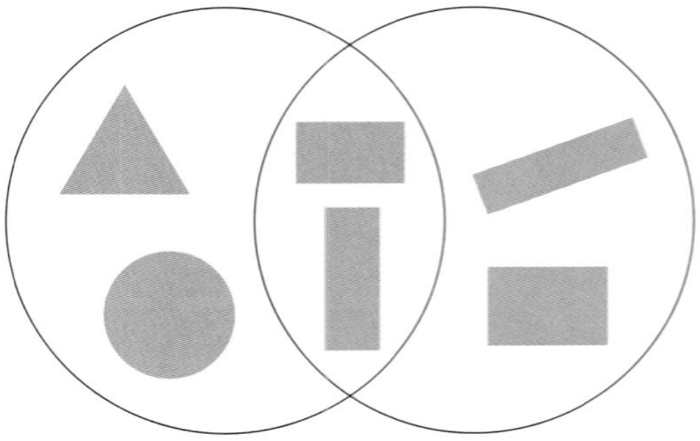

1. How many shapes are green?

______

2. What shapes belong in both circles? ______

Name ________________________________

Skills Practice Bank

Chapter 9

Set 1 For use after page 338.

Count. Write the amount.

1  ______¢

______, ______, ______, ______, ______, ______

2  ______¢

______, ______, ______, ______, ______, ______

Set 2 For use after page 344.

Count. Write the amount. Circle what you can buy.

1 You have

______¢

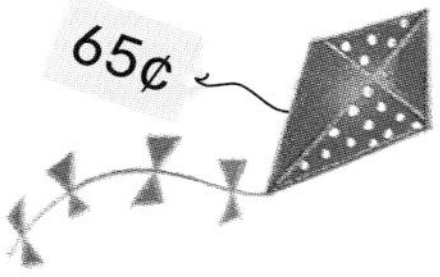

or

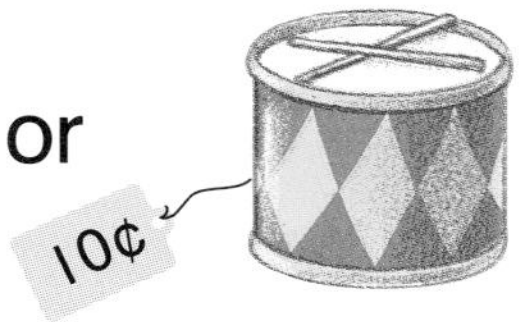

or

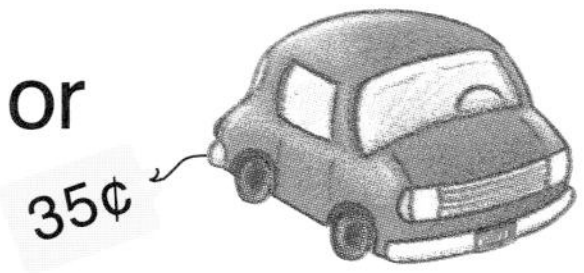

Set 3 For use after page 350.

Count. Write the amount.

1  ______¢

______, ______, ______

2  ______¢

______, ______, ______

SKILLS PRACTICE BANK

Name ______

Skills Practice Bank

Chapter 10

Set 1 For use after page 374

Write the time.

1. 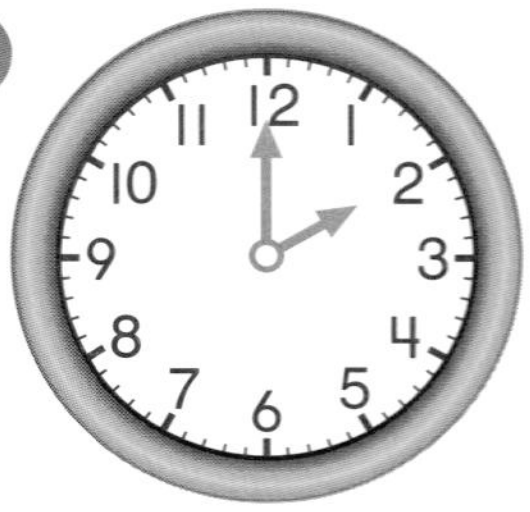
   ____ o'clock
2. 
   ____ o'clock
3. 
   ____ o'clock
4. 
   ____ o'clock
5. 
   [:]
6. 
   [:]
7. 
   [:]
8. 
   [:]
9. 
   [:]
10. 
   [:]
11. 
   [:]
12. 
   [:]

Set 2 For use after page 380.

Solve.

1. Nikki eats at 12:30.
   Luke eats at 12:00.
   Mom eats at 1:00.
   Who eats first?
   ______

2. Nolan came at 3:00.
   Yuli came at 3:30.
   Jake came before Nolan.
   Who came last?
   ______

Name

Skills Practice Bank

Chapter 10 cont.

Set 3 For use after page 388.

1. Complete the calendar.

June						
Sunday	Monday	Tuesday	Wednesday	Thursday	Friday	Saturday
		1	2		4	
6						
		15				
				24		
	28					

Use the calendar. Answer the questions.

It is June 20.

2. What day of the week is it? __________

3. What is the date in 2 days? __________

4. On what day did May end? __________

5. On what day will July begin? __________

SKILLS PRACTICE BANK

Name

Skills Practice Bank

Chapter 11

Set 1 For use after page 410.

About how long? Estimate. Measure. Use your  .

1. 

Estimate. ______ inches

Measure. ______ inches

2. 

Estimate. ______ inches

Measure. ______ inches

3. 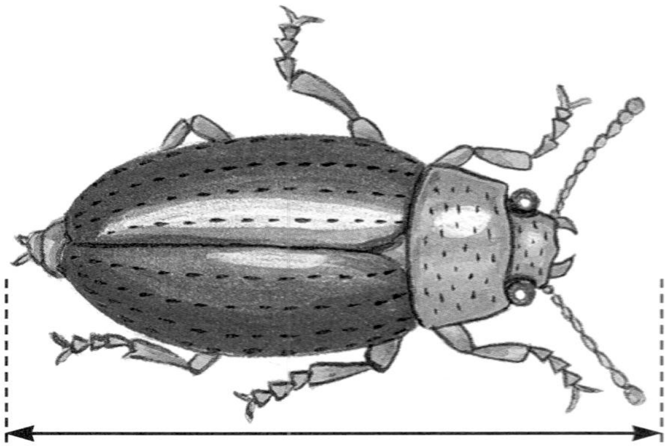

Estimate. ______ inches

Measure. ______ inches

Set 2 For use after page 436.

Circle the best tool to use.

1. How heavy is it?  

2. How cold is it?  

3. How much does it hold?  

4. How long is it?  

SKILLS PRACTICE BANK

Name ______________________________

Skills Practice Bank

Chapter 12

Set 1 For use after page 452.

Write the sum.

1. $\begin{array}{r} 8 \\ +\ 8 \\ \hline \end{array}$ $\quad$ $\begin{array}{r} 8 \\ +\ 9 \\ \hline \end{array}$ $\quad$ $\begin{array}{r} 9 \\ +\ 8 \\ \hline \end{array}$

2. $\begin{array}{r} 6 \\ +\ 6 \\ \hline \end{array}$ $\quad$ $\begin{array}{r} 6 \\ +\ 7 \\ \hline \end{array}$ $\quad$ $\begin{array}{r} 7 \\ +\ 6 \\ \hline \end{array}$

3. $7 + 8 =$ ____ $\quad$ $6 + 5 =$ ____ $\quad$ $9 + 9 =$ ____

Set 2 For use after page 462.

Solve. Use  or draw a picture.

1. 17 frogs were in the box.
   11 hopped out.
   How many frogs are in the box now?

   _____ frogs

Set 3 For use after page 472.

Subtract.

1. $\begin{array}{r} 13 \\ -\ 4 \\ \hline \end{array}$ $\quad$ $\begin{array}{r} 15 \\ -\ 7 \\ \hline \end{array}$ $\quad$ $\begin{array}{r} 18 \\ -\ 9 \\ \hline \end{array}$ $\quad$ $\begin{array}{r} 15 \\ -\ 9 \\ \hline \end{array}$ $\quad$ $\begin{array}{r} 16 \\ -\ 7 \\ \hline \end{array}$ $\quad$ $\begin{array}{r} 15 \\ -\ 6 \\ \hline \end{array}$ $\quad$ $\begin{array}{r} 17 \\ -\ 9 \\ \hline \end{array}$

2. $\begin{array}{r} 14 \\ -\ 8 \\ \hline \end{array}$ $\quad$ $\begin{array}{r} 13 \\ -\ 5 \\ \hline \end{array}$ $\quad$ $\begin{array}{r} 18 \\ -\ 0 \\ \hline \end{array}$ $\quad$ $\begin{array}{r} 15 \\ -\ 8 \\ \hline \end{array}$ $\quad$ $\begin{array}{r} 16 \\ -\ 9 \\ \hline \end{array}$ $\quad$ $\begin{array}{r} 17 \\ -\ 8 \\ \hline \end{array}$ $\quad$ $\begin{array}{r} 13 \\ -\ 13 \\ \hline \end{array}$

Skills Practice Bank
Chapter 13

Set 1 For use after page 496.

Add. Use and [] [] .

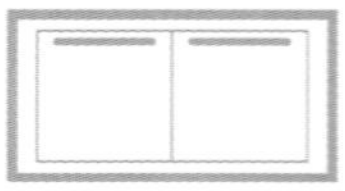

1

31	26	41	82	50	61
+ 15	+ 63	+ 55	+ 16	+ 40	+ 18

2

14	73	30	36	81	27
+ 21	+ 14	+ 16	+ 22	+ 5	+ 41

Set 2 For use after page 508.

Subtract. Use ⬤ ⬤ and [] [] .

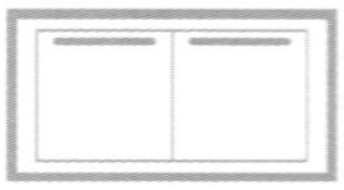

1

40	37	76	56	86	30
− 20	− 12	− 5	− 32	− 11	− 20

2

74	53	44	96	83	67
− 30	− 12	− 23	− 45	− 70	− 35

Set 3 For use after page 514.

Circle add or subtract. Write a number sentence.

1 65 people came to see the play.

34 people came to eat dinner.

How many people came in all?

Main Street
School Fair
Dinner 5:00
Play 6:00

add **subtract** _____ people

Name ____________________

Basic Facts Review

Set 1 For use after page 147.

Add.

1	1	2	3	1	2	3	1
	+ 2	+ 3	+ 4	+ 5	+ 6	+ 7	+ 8
2	2	3	1	2	3	1	2
	+ 9	+ 0	+ 3	+ 4	+ 5	+ 6	+ 7
3	3	1	2	3	1	2	3
	+ 8	+ 9	+ 0	+ 9	+ 7	+ 5	+ 3

4 1 + 4 = ____ 2 + 8 = ____ 6 + 3 = ____

Set 2 For use after page 163.

Subtract.

1	9	8	7	6	5	4	3
	− 1	− 2	− 0	− 5	− 1	− 2	− 0
2	5	7	6	1	7	8	2
	− 5	− 1	− 2	− 0	− 5	− 1	− 2
3	4	8	5	6	0	9	3
	− 0	− 5	− 2	− 1	− 0	− 5	− 2

4 9 − 2 = ____ 4 − 1 = ____ 7 − 2 = ____

Name ____________________

Set 3 For use after page 231.

Add or subtract.

1

1	6	9	6	4	5	1
+ 2	− 3	− 1	+ 6	− 2	+ 6	+ 1

2

6	5	2	5	4	4	2
− 2	+ 5	+ 1	− 2	+ 5	− 1	+ 3

3

2	12	3	10	3	8	4
+ 2	− 6	+ 4	− 5	+ 3	− 4	+ 4

4 $9 - 2 =$ ____ $3 + 8 =$ ____ $1 + 7 =$ ____

Set 4 For use after page 245.

Add or subtract.

1

5	10	5	11	9	10	4
+ 5	− 5	+ 6	− 6	+ 1	− 9	+ 6

2

8	12	12	7	10	10	12
+ 4	− 8	− 4	+ 3	− 3	− 7	− 6

3

2	10	10	3	6	10	10
+ 8	− 2	− 8	+ 7	+ 4	− 6	− 4

4 $11 - 5 =$ ____ $7 + 4 =$ ____ $11 - 7 =$ ____

BASIC FACTS REVIEW

Name ______________________________

Set 5 For use after page 463.

Add.

1	9 + 7	8 + 5	7 + 3	6 + 1	6 + 8	5 + 4	6 + 0
2	3 + 3	7 + 2	8 + 4	6 + 9	0 + 4	5 + 5	4 + 4
3	8 + 3	7 + 1	2 + 2	6 + 6	4 + 7	2 + 7	3 + 5
4	9 + 5	6 + 4	8 + 2	0 + 5	1 + 1	2 + 6	3 + 9
5	7 + 8	9 + 9	6 + 5	5 + 9	7 + 7	4 + 9	2 + 5
6	2 + 9	8 + 7	9 + 8	9 + 6	5 + 8	7 + 4	8 + 8
7	8 + 6	7 + 5	5 + 6	7 + 6	3 + 6	5 + 7	2 + 3

8 $6 + 7 =$ _____ $9 + 7 =$ _____ $7 + 0 =$ _____

9 $2 + 8 =$ _____ $3 + 4 =$ _____ $8 + 9 =$ _____

Name ______________________________

Set 6 For use after page 479.

Subtract.

1	15 − 9	14 − 7	10 − 3	9 − 6	11 − 8	7 − 7	16 − 7
2	8 − 5	12 − 3	17 − 8	13 − 9	9 − 7	10 − 5	18 − 9
3	16 − 8	11 − 4	14 − 6	9 − 9	15 − 7	12 − 5	10 − 8
4	8 − 4	13 − 5	17 − 9	15 − 6	16 − 9	10 − 7	11 − 3
5	14 − 9	10 − 2	15 − 8	11 − 5	13 − 7	9 − 5	12 − 4
6	10 − 1	14 − 8	11 − 9	10 − 6	8 − 7	13 − 4	9 − 8
7	12 − 8	10 − 9	11 − 7	13 − 6	14 − 5	12 − 7	11 − 6

8. 11 − 2 = ____   12 − 9 = ____   13 − 8 = ____

9. 12 − 6 = ____   10 − 4 = ____   8 − 8 = ____

Picture Glossary

after

1, 2, 3, 4, 5

4 comes **after** 3.

bar graph

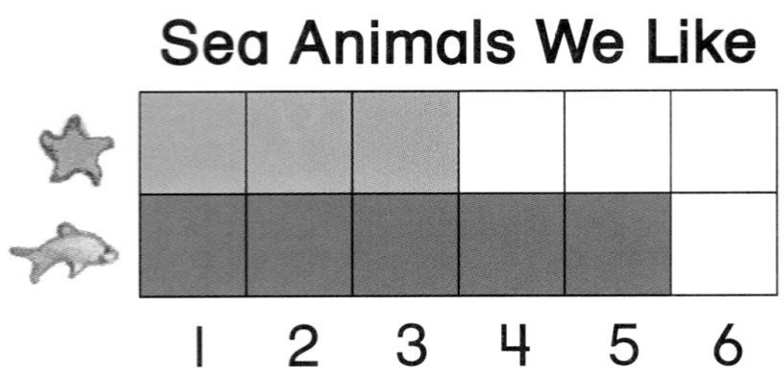

before

1, 2, 3, 4, 5

2 comes **before** 3.

between

1, 2, 3, 4, 5

3 comes **between** 2 and 4.

cent (¢)

A penny is 1¢.

centimeter

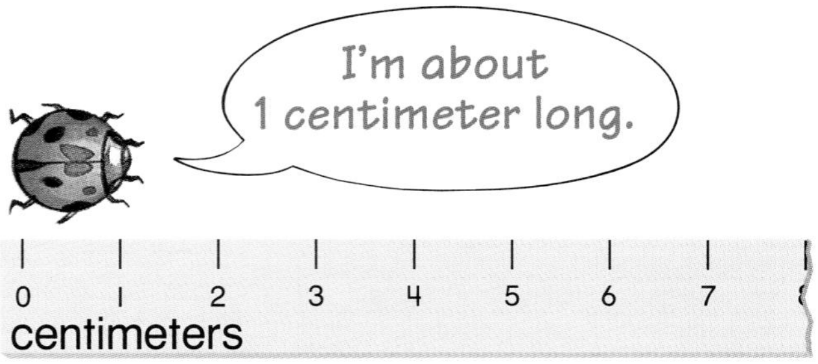

circle

cone

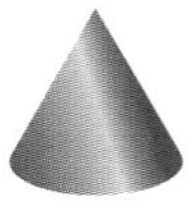

count back

3, **2**

$3 - 1 = 2$

count on

3, **4**

$3 + 1 = 4$

cube

cup

cylinder

difference

$7 - 1 = 6$

$$\begin{array}{r} 7 \\ -\ 1 \\ \hline 6 \end{array}$$

↑ **difference** ↑

dime

10¢

doubles $4 + 4 = 8$

$8 - 4 = 4$

doubles + 1

$7 + 7 = 14$, so $7 + 8 = 15$.

equal sign (=)

$2 + 3 = 5$

even

2, 4, 6, 8, and 10 are **even** numbers.

fact family

$2 + 4 = 6$ $6 - 4 = 2$

$4 + 2 = 6$ $6 - 2 = 4$

foot

fraction

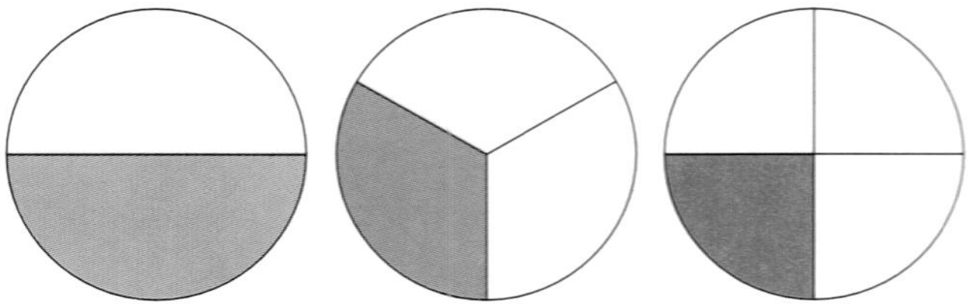

one half $\frac{1}{2}$ one third $\frac{1}{3}$ one fourth $\frac{1}{4}$

greater than

6 is **greater than** 4.

half hour

heavier

hour

hour hand

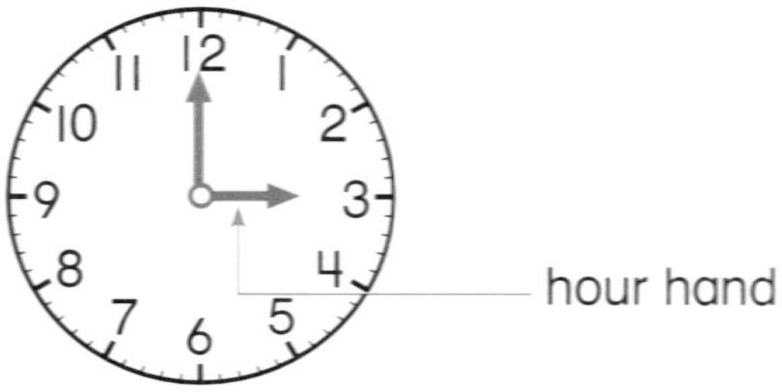

inch

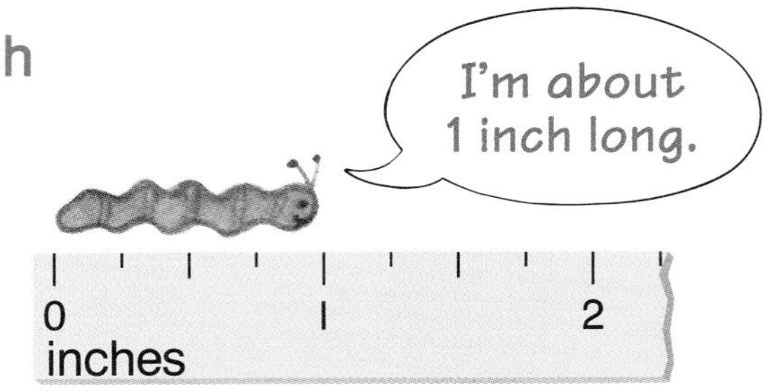

kilogram

The brick is about as heavy as 1 **kilogram.**

less than

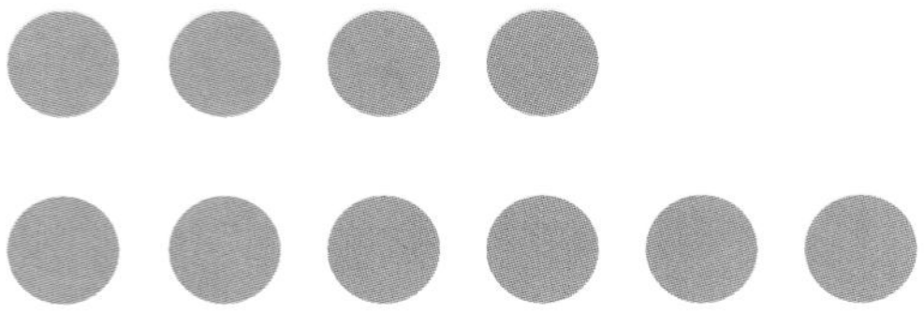

4 is **less than 6**.

line of symmetry

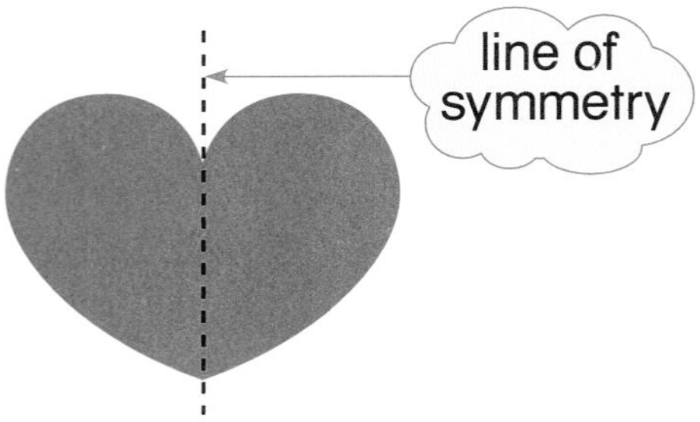

liter

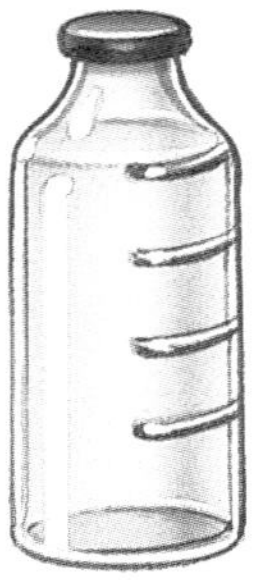

minute hand

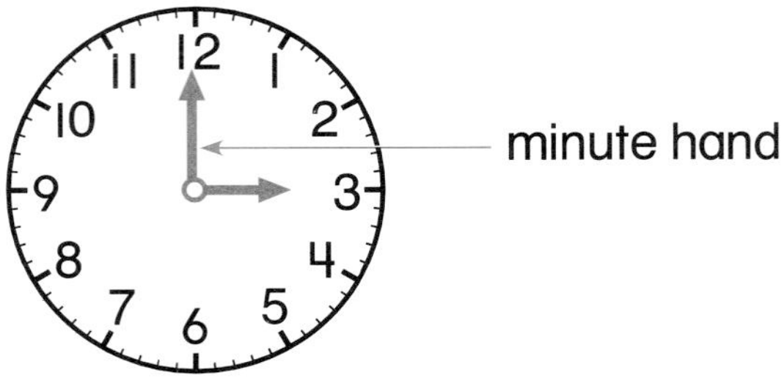

nickel

5¢

number line

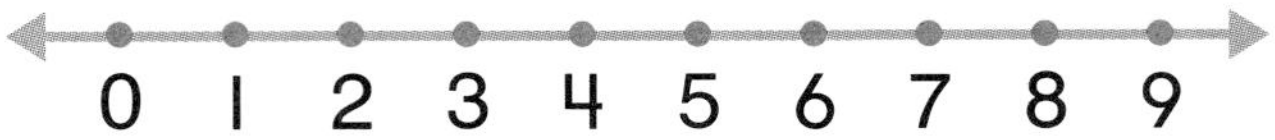

number sentence

$1 + 4 = 5$

$6 - 2 = 4$

odd

1, 3, 5, 7, and 9 are **odd** numbers.

ones

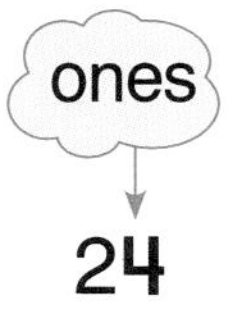

penny

1¢

pictograph

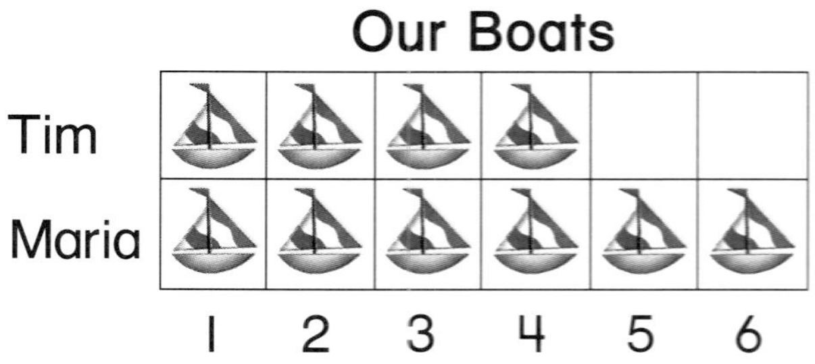

pint

pound

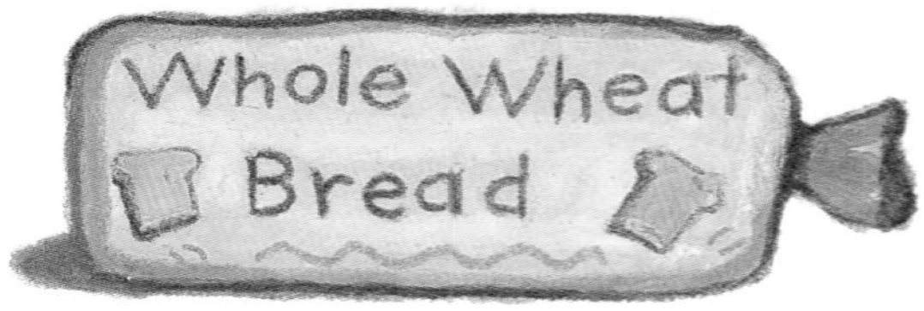

The bread weighs about 1 **pound.**

quart

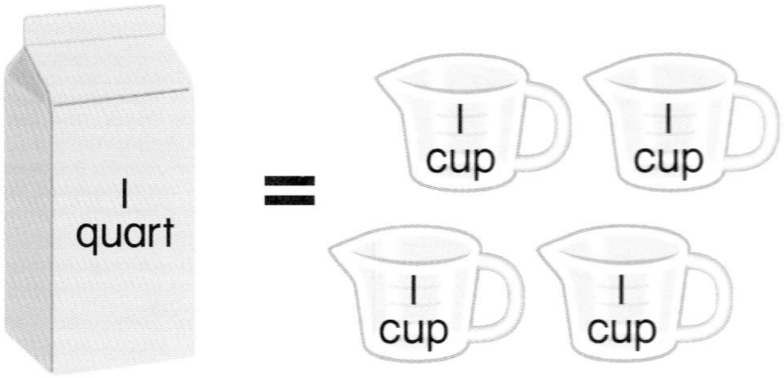

quarter

25¢ 

rectangle

rectangular prism

sphere

square

sum

$2 + 3 = 5$

$$\begin{array}{r} 2 \\ +\ 3 \\ \hline 5 \end{array}$$

sum

tally marks

tens

tens

24

triangle

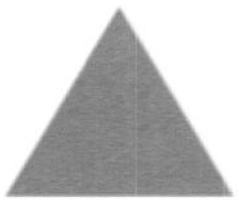

turnaround fact

$3 + 4 = 7$ $4 + 3 = 7$

Credits

Illustration

Barbee, Pat 173, 178, 200, 403

Becker, Pamela 3, 4, 5, 6, 7, 10, 15, 16, 19, 20, 21, 22, 23, 24, 41, 32, 136, 151, 152, 154, 158, 219, 223, 224, 225, 226, 229, 233, 237, 242, 243, 369, 368, 384, 396

Belcher, Cynthia 237, 238, 453, 459

Cable, Annette 90, 93, 110, 115, 117, 118, 261, 262, 267, 268, 331, 458

Daugavietis, Ruta 13, 14, 15, 25, 27, 29, 53, 54, 72, 191, 202, 305

Dieterichs Morrison, Shelley 365, 367, 368, 370, 371, 372, 373, 374, 375, 376, 378, 379, 380, 381, 382, 385, 387, 388, 392, 393, 394, 395, 396, 397, 398

Dugan, Karen 272, 275, 276, 260, 339, 343, 347, 350, 351, 352, 353, 354, 355, 358

Fauser, Janet 177, 454, 461, 467

Freeman, Nancy 1

Galkin, Simon 293, 407, 409, 411, 416, 431, 436, 439, 459, 469, 470, 477

Griesbach/Martucci 217, 225, 233

Harris, Diane Teske 51, 52, 53, 54, 57, 58, 60, 62, 63, 64, 65, 66, 70, 71, 72, 73, 74, 75, 76, 77, 78, 79, 81, 92, 93, 94, 95, 96, 97, 99, 100, 101, 102, 103, 104, 105, 106, 108, 109, 110, 111, 112, 113, 114, 115, 117, 118, 121, 122, 123, 125, 175, 176, 206, 207, 221, 224, 227, 228, 230, 235, 236, 239, 244, 246, 278, 297, 299, 300, 320, 462, 465, 468, 469, 477

Hein, Joy 58, 63

Kovalik, Terry 449, 450, 451, 457, 459, 460, 461

Laden, Nina 471, 472, 473, 475, 476, 478, 480

Lash-Ruff, Michelle 84, 126, 168, 225, 233, 236, 250

Leonard, Tom 412, 428

Levine, Melinda 403

Peppler, Matthew 217, 221, 222, 223, 224, 225, 227, 228, 229, 230, 231, 232, 233, 234, 236, 237, 238, 241, 242, 243, 244, 245, 246, 247, 248, 249

Matje, Martin 491, 492, 493, 495, 497, 498, 499, 500, 501, 502, 505, 507, 509, 510, 512, 516

Mauterer, Erin 73, 77, 80, 177, 178, 200, 297, 298, 303, 316, 406, 409, 410, 411, 416, 418, 419, 421, 423, 427, 430, 431, 432, 434, 435, 436, 438, 439, 440, 441, 442

Melmon, Deborah Haley 1, 2, 5, 7, 8, 10, 11, 12, 17, 18, 20, 22, 24, 26, 27, 28, 29, 30, 35, 36, 37, 38, 39, 40, 41, 42, 43, 134, 135, 136, 137, 139, 140, 142, 143, 144, 145, 146, 147, 148, 149, 153, 157, 158, 159, 160, 164, 165

Moffatt, Judy 1, 447

Muzick, Terra 98, 99, 116, 122, 334, 336, 338, 340, 344, 348

Ortiz Godfrey, Raymond 19, 61, 63, 71, 72, 74, 180, 181, 182, 184, 187, 188, 189, 190, 193, 194, 195, 196, 197, 198, 199, 200, 201, 202, 203, 204, 207, 208, 209, 210, 211

Parnell, Miles 369, 370, 371, 372, 373, 374, 375, 376, 383, 384, 385, 389, 390, 394

Petrone, Valeria 7, 8, 11, 12, 22, 31

Pinkney, Debbie 61, 62

Polfus, Roberta 331, 333, 334, 335, 336, 337, 338, 339, 340, 341, 342, 343, 344, 345, 346, 348, 349, 350, 355, 356, 357, 358, 359, 360

Roller, Becky 173, 175, 177, 195, 212

Sharp, Paul & Alice 55, 56, 306, 307, 308

Sheperd, Roni 89, 91, 92, 107, 108, 111, 112, 120

Shola, Georgia 89, 293, 299, 317, 318

Steiger, Terry 489, 490, 494, 501, 502, 506, 513, 514

Stuart, Don 137, 138

Tagel, Peggy 264, 266, 267, 268, 272, 277, 278, 285

Temko, Florence 447

Thompson, Emily 80, 81, 82, 180, 184, 185, 193, 198, 199

Valley, Gregg 64, 65, 67, 131, 186, 205, 208, 262, 277, 278, 283, 284, 285, 286, 295, 296, 297, 298, 299, 300, 301, 302, 303, 304, 306, 307, 309, 311, 313, 315, 316, 317, 318, 321, 323, 324, 325

Vargo, Sharon Hawkins 454, 458, 473, 483

Weissman, Bari 260, 261, 262, 266, 267, 475

Wickart, Mark 59, 62, 67, 68, 69, 70, 180, 184, 189, 193, 194, 195, 209, 405, 408, 420, 421, 423, 425, 426, 427, 429, 432, 433, 434, 436, 437, 452, 456, 462, 465, 468, 469, 477

Wolf, Elizabeth 53, 59, 192, 199, 314, 319, 413, 414, 417, 424

Math Soup Illustration

Chapter 1
Dietrichs, Shelly 6
Kock, Carl 4
Meisel, Paul 1, 3

Chapter 2
Berry, Holly 2
Mattews, Scott 5
Pillo, Cary 6

Chapter 3
Harris, Teske 1, 4

Chapter 4
Davick, Linda 6, 8

Chapter 5
Oversat, Laura 5, 6

Chapter 6
McIntyre, Larry 4, 8
Poedke, C. K. 6

Chapter 9
Kock, Carl 1

Chapter 10
Kock, Carl 2
Lyon, Tammie Speer 4
Sanarsky, Susan 8
Ward, Michael 6

Chapter 11
Martucci, Stanley 8
Pillo, Cary 3, 4

Chapter 12
Berret, Lisa 4
Oversat, Laura 8
Snyder, Jackie 2, 3
VanRynbach, Iris 6

Chapter 13
Blatsutta, Mary Lynn 6, 7
Cravath, Lynn 2
Oversat, Laura 1
Wescott, Nadine 4

Photography

Unless otherwise acknowledged, all photos are the property of Scott Foresman - Addison Wesley. Math Soup photography created expressly for Scott Foresman - Addison Wesley by Fritz Geiger and Michael Walker.

Cover Mark Hamblin/Oxford Scientific Films/ANIMALS ANIMALS

Daniel Putterman/Stock Boston 96
David Young-Wolff/PhotoEdit 145

Math Soup Photography

Chapter 2
Scott Halleran 1, 2

Chapter 4
Jade Albert 1
Courtesy of Wellman, Inc./Photo: Nando Buco 7

Chapter 5
Superstock 2(l)
Bob Torrez/Tony Stone Images 2(tc)
Rob Crandall/Stock Boston 2(tr)
Paul Mozell/Stock Boston 2(cr)
Mark Segal/Tony Stone Images 2(br)

Chapter 6
Stephan Dalton/ANIMALS ANIMALS 1 (Bee, Row 1 l)
Superstock 1(Beetle, Row 1 r)
Superstock 1(Bee, Row 2 l)
Stephan Dalton/ANIMALS ANIMALS 1(Bee, Row 2 r)
Superstock 1(Spotted June bug & Spider, Row 3 l & r)
Superstock 1(Bee, Row 4 l)
Superstock 1(Harlequin Cabbage Bug, Row 4 c)
Superstock 1(Spotted June Bug, Row 5 r)
Superstock 2(tl & br)
Lynda Richardson 3(t)
M. A. Chappell/ANIMALS ANIMALS 3(b)

Chapter 7
Phillips Family 6

Chapter 8
Lawrence Migdale 1

Chapter 9
Superstock 2–3(t)
Charles Fryer 2(b)
Office of the City Representative, Philadelphia 3(b)
Chicago Historical Society 4
Franklin D. Roosevelt Library 5(b)

Chapter 10
Amanda Clement/Image Bank 1

Chapter 11
Les Morsillo 1
Jonathan Nourok/PhotoEdit 2(tl)
The Library of the New York Botanical Garden, Bronx, N.Y./Photo: Muriel Weinerman 2(tr)
David Young-Wolff/PhotoEdit 2(b)

Chapter 12
Jade Albert 1

Chapter 13
Kathy Ferguson/PhotoEdit 8

Workmat 1

Workmat 2

tens	ones

Workmat 3

Workmat 4

1	2	3	4	5	6	7	8	9	10
11	12	13	14	15	16	17	18	19	20
21	22	23	24	25	26	27	28	29	30
31	32	33	34	35	36	37	38	39	40
41	42	43	44	45	46	47	48	49	50
51	52	53	54	55	56	57	58	59	60
61	62	63	64	65	66	67	68	69	70
71	72	73	74	75	76	77	78	79	80
81	82	83	84	85	86	87	88	89	90
91	92	93	94	95	96	97	98	99	100